ETHICAL THEORY
AND SOCIAL ISSUES

DAVID THEO
GOLDBERG

School of Justice Studies
Arizona State University

ETHICAL THEORY

AND

SOCIAL ISSUES

HISTORICAL

TEXTS AND

CONTEMPORARY

READINGS

Second Edition

Vice President, Publisher	Ted Buchholz
Senior Acquisitions Editor	David Tatom
Senior Project Editor	Charles J. Dierker
Production Manager	Melinda Esco
Art Director	Garry Harman

ISBN: 0-15-501501-X

Library of Congress Catalog Card Number: 94-72773

Address for Editorial Correspondence: Harcourt Brace College Publishers, 301 Commerce Street, Suite 3700, Fort Worth, TX 76102.

Address for Orders: Harcourt Brace & Company, 6277 Sea Harbor Drive, Orlando, FL 32887-6777. 1-800-782-4479, or 1-800-433-0001 (in Florida).

Printed in the United States of America
5 6 7 8 9 0 1 2 3 4   090   9 8 7 6 5 4 3 2 1

For Alena

and for the future of Gabriel Dylan

Student curiosity about ethics is often prompted by an interest in discussing pressing social issues. Instructors tend to rely on several pedagogical methods. One places emphasis on the traditional philosophical concerns surrounding ethical theory. Another tackles the contemporary social issues that form the focus of student concern. Those employing a methodological mix usually proceed in either of two ways: They may begin by presenting ethical theories in their historical setting and then turn to discuss contemporary issues; or they may tease out the underlying theoretical considerations from a direct discussion of the social issues.

Textbooks available for ethics courses reflect these methodological dispositions. Some include only chronologically ordered selections from the history of ethics. These usually open with Plato and close, perhaps, with Rawls. Other textbooks include only articles about contemporary social problems. Recently, a few textbooks have sought to combine theoretical and applied readings. They tend, however, to cover only those theories or traditions that in one way or another are currently fashionable. Finally, there are those books that are structured thematically, rather than historically or topically. These tend, by contrast, to restrict the material on contemporary social problems.

Ethical Theory and Social Issues includes ethical theory and contemporary applications within the covers of a single book. It strives to provide instructors and students with a wide range of selections covering the history of ethical theory and analysis of contemporary moral and legal issues. And because it illustrates, as far as is feasible, the relevance of ethical theory to an understanding of the social issues covered, it has two primary aims. The first is to provide a clear picture of the historical development of ethical theory in the "Western" philosophical tradition; the second is to provide a firm theoretical foundation on the basis of which contemporary moral problems may be addressed. Instructors preferring to concentrate exclusively on historical material may encourage students to pursue the contemporary material on their own. Correspondingly, instructors concentrating primarily on applied ethics will be able to refer students back to the underlying theoretical arguments.

This second edition has been restyled and divided into three parts. Part One includes substantial and chronologically ordered selections from the work of the best known and most widely used of theorists from the historical tradition. Part Two includes three chapters covering readings on contemporary liberalism, communitarianism, and feminism. Part Three covers seven topics of current moral relevance: citizenship, affirmative action, censorship and hate speech, AIDS, abortion, euthanasia, and punishment and the death penalty. Similarly, the contemporary social topics that form the focus of Part Three have been updated. Thus, a chapter on citizenship now frames Part Three, and new chapters have been added on hate speech and AIDS. Where relevant, each of the chapters in Part Three includes extracts from majority and dissenting opinions in major Supreme Court cases. Finally, the book offers a brief glossary at the back.

In choosing readings for the second edition, I have been guided by the desire to provide readers with a wide range of selections to reflect the interplay of theory and application and to provide an even mixture of familiar and challenging material. I have restricted the section introductions to allow for greater scope in the selections. In any introduction to texts of this sort, the choice is between (some mixture of) the philosophical or social context of the issues covered in the selections, a survey of the arguments selected, and critical discussion of the arguments. Presentation of arguments is logically prior to their criticism. Thus I have provided some background context and a summary of the central points of the arguments. These should be taken as guides for readers, whose task becomes the philosophical one of reconstructing the argumentation. Discussion of criticisms is limited to those that are considered central to interpretation and understanding. I also have noted the relationship between theory and social applications wherever this can be done in a concise manner.

Bibliographies that follow each section offer some guidance for further reading and research. I have added suggestions for discussion. These questions are not intended as traditional study guides for the selections. Rather, their aim is to encourage thinking about the connections between theory and application: how theoretical considerations might determine social decisions, or be challenged by them, and what theoretical considerations underlie an established decision. These questions are suggestions for class discussion, for conversations students might pursue, or for philosophy club topics.

I take pleasure in extending my gratitude to the many colleagues and friends whose thoughtful comments, criticisms, kind advice, and encouragement were of great benefit in revising the book. Correspondence with Professors Hugo Bedau, Nadine Strossen, Richard Mohr, Stanley Fish, and Bill Lawson led to improvements in the chapters in which their articles appear. Colleagues and students at Arizona State University who have used the first edition offered keen and critical accounts of its strengths and weaknesses. Many conversations with Pat Lauderdale, my colleague and friend, have prompted revisions large and small. The publisher's reviewers took time out from very busy schedules to offer thoughtful and insightful comments. I would like to thank James Muyskens of the University of Kansas, Jan Boxill of the University of North Carolina, Alan Mabe of the University of Florida, and especially Michael Fischer of the University of California, Riverside, whose efforts were especially helpful. The book would not have been completed but for the incredible energies of my assistant, Barbara Lammi, who overlooked no detail and pursued every task with characteristic humor. I wish also to thank my editor at Harcourt Brace, David Tatom, and his supportive editorial assistant, Leanne Winkler, for so smoothly producing the second edition. Alena and Gabriel remain my primary sources of inspiration. As before, gratitude is no substitute for responsibility in the case of error, which remains entirely mine.

■ NOTE TO STUDENTS

The bibliographies at the end of each part are intended as guides to further readings or research. The lists are alphabetically ordered.

TABLE OF CONTENTS

Over the past few years Dr. Jack Kevorkian, a Michigan physician, directly or indirectly has assisted several suicides by people suffering painful and debilitating terminal illnesses. To some he is a moral hero practicing the physician's imperative to alleviate suffering where all other means have failed. To others he is "Doctor Death," deeply implicated in the morally questionable practice of aiding, if not enabling, the ending of innocent lives. Which, then, is he, moral saint or immoral monster? Clearly he cannot be both, though of course he might be neither. Did he thus perform permissible acts, if not those required of him as his moral duty? Or is he to be blamed for having done something morally reprehensible, and so impermissible? Doctors have a duty, as human beings and especially in their professional capacity, to diminish suffering whenever they can; but they also have a duty to respect life. How, indeed, can such issues be settled, if they can be settled at all?

A priest, passionately engaged in the antiabortion movement, marched through the streets of Buffalo holding up for all to see a fetus aborted at a relatively advanced stage of pregnancy. His aim, of course, was to make the antiabortion point to those present, and via the media to the nation at large, that abortion is the taking of innocent human life and as such amounts to murder. His supporters praised his courage. His critics, not all proabortionists, were outraged at what they considered a callous act. They charged that he was "using" the fetus unethically to make a political point. Who was right here, supporters or critics? Do the ends, provided they are good ones, justify the means? Again, how do we decide these questions, if they can be decided objectively at all?

On campuses across the country college communities are especially sensitive to the values of free expression. They urge that censorship should find a home least of all in those institutions devoted to the pursuit of knowledge and learning. This principled commitment to free expression, however, has enabled some people to engage in derogatory expression directed at some students on the basis of their race or gender. Recently, universities have responded to such highly publicized incidents with equally publicized speech codes, principles designed to discourage, if not straightforwardly delimit, harassing speech on campus. Critics have cried censorship, arguing that these are unjust limitations on the right to free speech. Proponents have responded that in environments where racism and sexism persist, codes are necessary to promote equal opportunity and freedom from harms following from such derogatory speech. Are campus speech codes, then, morally permissible means of restricting harm and facilitating equal opportunities, or are they undue limitations on free speech? Indeed, should free speech entitle bigots to express their bigotry even at the expense of those depicted in derogatory fashion?

These examples depict moral dilemmas of various sorts. We face a moral dilemma when social circumstances—circumstances that we may have taken part in making or causing to occur—enable us to fulfill one moral duty, meet one obligation, live up to one responsibility, or invoke one right only by violating another. Here apparently convincing reasons can be given for choices that mutually exclude each other: choosing to do one act or pursue one (seemingly required) option excludes the possibility of doing or pursuing the other. Yet, at least on the face of it, both seem morally compelling. If Dr. Kevorkian (or any other doctor, as he would have it) leaves the ailing person to die of natural causes, then that doctor fails in his duty to reduce suffering (assuming that no painkilling drug will help); and if the doctor causes death, he or she fails to respect life. So choosing either alternative seems to imply doing something that is from one point of view right, and from another wrong. Similarly, an unqualified right to free speech licenses bigotry; but restricting bigoted speech places limitations on what many take to be a basic right, no matter the consequences.

Moral dilemmas are the central concern of this book. How do we recognize and resolve them? In addressing this question, we necessarily face other, perhaps prior questions: How can we make moral judgments at all? How do—or should—such judgments affect what we do? And how do we judge persons who follow, or fail to follow, such judgments?

Resolving dilemmas and answering questions of these sorts require ethical analysis of the relevant facts, concepts, and theoretical principles, and how they inform action. Persons confronted by ethical dilemmas need to make judgments about what they are required, or at least permitted, to do in the circumstances at hand. Of course, the questions "How ought I to act here?" or "What am I required or permitted to do?" are not posed only for moral dilemmas: they may be asked of a wide variety of circumstances faced by human beings. Practical deliberation or reasoning, if properly done, is supposed to tell us what we are required or permitted to do. Theoretical reasoning about ethics involves formulating the principles, rules, and reasons that underlie and support moral judgments and choices in particular circumstances. Practical reasoning should inform the doctor whether or not he ought to facilitate a dying patient's request to die, the priest whether or not his provocative act was the wrong one, a university administrator whether "hate speech" ought to be permitted or restricted, resisted by counterspeech or censored. Theoretical analysis reveals the principles by which the proper practical judgments in these matters can be reached.

In keeping with this distinction between theory and practical application, Part I of this book covers the major historical contributions to ethical theory. Part II covers contemporary ethical theory. Part III illustrates the application of various and often competing principles elaborated in Parts I and II by establishing what it is right to do in the case of numerous and pressing social issues like those represented in the previous examples.

Moral Concepts   Ethical judgments loom large in our lives, and especially in our relations with others. We often judge some belief, rule, or act to be good or right or proper or just; and we sometimes wonder whether someone has the right to act in a specific way. These judgments may be made about acts that are done or intended, about hypothetical or institutional rules, or about possible or actual beliefs. One might ask, "Was I right to break my appointment without notice?" or "Should I keep the book or CD or jacket I borrowed?" We may be taught that it is *good* to be kind or that it is *just* to help the homeless, that these are the things we *ought* or have an *obligation* to do. We tend to think that we have a *duty* to care for the elderly or someone dying of AIDS, or a duty not to steal. Like George Washington, we might believe that *it is right* never to lie, but that *we have a right* to express ourselves freely. More general judgments are made about character, whether a person or action is *virtuous* in some respect or another. In renting an apartment or applying for a job, one is likely to be asked for character references: "What kind of person is he?" or "Can she be trusted with sensitive information?" At a moral level even more general than this, we make judgments about the *justice* of some institution or society. We argue over how social goods like health care should be allocated, about the principles of distributing or redistributing wealth, about the rights a society ought to extend to its members or the duties it should command.

Ethics and Morality   At this point you may be wondering about the use of the terms *ethics* and *morality*. These terms have different roots, and correspondingly different popular usages. The word *ethics* derives from the classical Greek terms *ethos* and *ta ethika; morality,* by contrast, stems from the Latin term *mores*. To the ancient Greeks, *ethos* meant personal character, and *ta ethika* signified investigation into the nature of the virtuous life or the right way to live. In Latin, *mores* means social habits or customs. These distinctions in meaning are sometimes reflected in contemporary popular usage. We might refer to someone's "personal ethics" or character, while "morality" is often used in discussions about social conventions and custom. However, contemporary philosophers generally take the terms to be synonymous. So we use the terms here interchangeably to denote philosophical inquiry into the problems of and judgments about acceptable human conduct and character.

Descriptive Ethics   The inquiry into the nature of morality can be approached in different ways. One way is simply *to describe* how some person, members of a culture, or society address the sorts of moral issues raised previously, what customs they have, and how they are accustomed to behave. This is called *descriptive ethics,* and it is largely a concern of cultural anthropologists, sociologists, and historians. The philosopher's focus upon ethics differs from this. The fundamental philosophical concerns have to do not with how people and cultures in fact behave, but with how we *ought* to treat and be treated by others, what kind of life we should live, and what sort of society we should strive to institute.

Metaethics   Two kinds of questions can be asked about ethical judgments. First, we can ask for the *meanings* of the moral terms employed, and for the appropriate *method* for addressing moral questions. The major moral terms include *good* and *bad* (or *evil*), *right* and *wrong, propriety* and *impropriety, duties* and *rights, obligations* and *claims,* and *justice* and *injustice*. Here we are concerned to understand the use of these terms, their logical form, and the "objects" to which they refer. What, in short, are the logical and conceptual differences between ethical language and other forms of linguistic expression? And regarding moral method, we can ask how we should address moral questions and dilemmas if we are to resolve them. This analysis of moral language and method is called *metaethics.*

Normative Ethics   Second, we can ask a different kind of question concerning whether acts, principles, or rules are (morally) right or wrong, what characteristics make a person virtuous or vicious, and what reasons can be given for these judgments. This inquiry into the norms or principles of justifiable behavior and the values they embody is called *normative ethics*. It is on the basis of these norms, principles, and values that conduct is judged permissible or impermissible. A fundamental mark of moral justification is the claim that social beliefs, principles, policies, and conduct not be arbitrary. Citing reasons to support moral beliefs, principles, policies, and conduct is required as a test of their nonarbitrariness and justifiability. If Dr. Kevorkian's assisted suicides are to meet this moral test, he should be able to offer reasons in their support that would persuade any reasonable person. Of course, simply citing reasons to support some belief or bit of behavior is not sufficient grounds to make it moral. The reasons must be relevant, and they must impartially convince any reasonable person who has no vested interest in the matter at hand.

Thus anyone concerned with the grounds of ethical analysis must be careful to distinguish among the three kinds of undertakings we have identified here. The question "Do members of some society believe that capital punishment or hate speech is wrong?" is one posed by descriptive ethics. "What does it mean for members of that society to say that capital punishment or hate speech is wrong?" is a metaethical question. Questions of normative ethics are more direct: "Is capital punishment or hate speech right or abortion wrong, and what are the grounds for believing so?"

The primary concern of this book is with normative ethical issues: in general, what kinds of acts are right or permissible, what kind of life is good, and what sort of society just? Social justice is interpreted widely to include not only inquiry into the principles of distributive justice but also the permissibility of such practices as affirmative action, censorship, abortion, euthanasia, and capital punishment, and the range of morally appropriate responses to the AIDS crisis. We focus, in particular, upon the reasoned grounds offered to justify the answers to these questions, and we do it in the context of what conceptions of citizenship are justifiable. Clearly, normative concerns touch upon descriptive and metaethical considerations, and these are incorporated wherever relevant.

Explanation and Justification   One way the difference between descriptive and normative (or evaluative) ethics manifests concerns the distinction between the explanation of behavior and its justification. Explanation of some bit of behavior involves factual investigation and analysis of what gave rise to it, what caused it to come about, perhaps what function it was intended to serve. Justification involves evaluating the adequacy of reasons supporting the propriety or permissibility of the belief, act, or rule at issue. Generally, a belief or an act may be justified in terms of a rule or principle, and these in turn are justified in terms of a moral theory or system of principles. One of the primary aims of a normative moral theory, then, is to establish in a principled way how we ought or ought not to act.

Necessary and Sufficient Conditions   Explanations for things or events, as well as their justifications, most often involve specifying conceptually the conditions necessary or sufficient for bringing them about. A *necessary condition* for the existence or occurrence of something is that precondition without which that thing could not occur or exist. If the thing exists or event occurs, the necessary condition for it must exist or occur. For example, persons will now be diagnosed as having AIDS if they have tested HIV positive and have a T-cell blood count of less than 200. Thus, two individual conditions are necessary before one is diagnosed with AIDS: that one be HIV positive and that one's T-cell count fall below 200. Together, both count as sufficient conditions for the occurrence of AIDS. That is, if these conditions occur together in a person, they are enough to warrant the diagnosis. A sufficient condition for the occurrence or existence of something, then, means that the thing or event must exist or occur if the precondition(s) do. Clearly, the same condition can count as both a necessary and sufficient condition for an event or thing's existence.

Explanations of things will involve spelling out those conditions necessary and sufficient for bringing them about and then observing whether such conditions pertain in the circumstances at hand. So, too, with spelling out not just why things did occur, but why they are justified in occurring or why we think it a good thing that they occurred. The difference between explanations and justifications, then, have to do with the fact that the necessary and sufficient conditions relevant to explanations will be spelled out largely (if not exclusively) in terms of facts, while those employed in justifications will involve value judgments. An explanation of why a college introduces a hate speech code concerns the commitment of the college to resist racist expression on campus; a justification of the code's introduction involves the judgments that racism is an evil that ought to be resisted, and that a code is an effective and permissible means of such resistance.

Fact and Value   Thus the distinctions between description and explanation, on one hand, and evaluation and justification, on the other, rest upon the underlying distinction between fact and value. A fact is an event, occurrence, or act that has taken place; a value is that quality of a thing or act that makes it worthy or desirable. Facts concern the way things actually are; evaluations are judgments about how things *ideally* are or ought to be. *If* abortion causes pain to the fetus, then there must be some physical evidence, and we should be able to explain it physiologically. Yet even if the fetus suffers some pain, this alone does not justify a principle that abortions ought not to be permitted. Some convincing reasons or adequate argument must be provided showing that the pain in cases of this kind is unwarranted, unacceptable, or impermissible. And this can only be done by appealing to some more general moral principle, ideal, or value, such as "It is wrong to cause harm to the innocent." Whether *this* principle, or the value it embodies, is sufficient to justify the impermissibility of abortion will depend upon whether there are any relevant exceptions to it; that is, whether it can be overridden by any competing principle and whether a fetus is in the relevant sense innocent.

Relativism   One popular form that ethical justification often assumes is relativism. A number of related claims are basic to the theory of relativism: Ethical values and principles are taken to vary from one society, generation, or individual to another; the values of one society, generation, or individual have no privileged claim to truth; and moral truth or objectivity is restricted to the shared values of the society or generation. Two views are expressed here. *Cultural relativism* holds that an act, rule, or practice that is *thought* wrong by one culture may be *thought* right by another, whereas *ethical relativism* holds that an act, rule, or practice that *is* right for one society, culture, or individual may actually *be* wrong for another. Where a basic ethical value of one society or individual conflicts with that of another, ethical relativism insists that no principled way of judging between them exists, for there are no universal, transcultural, or absolute moral values. The values of each society or individual are considered to be equally acceptable. *Right* or *good* or *valuable* acquire content only relative to some society or individual.

Clearly, different societies have different practices and correspondingly different values: it may be thought permissible, in the Netherlands, say, for a doctor to inject a terminally ill patient with a lethal dose of morphine, but the practice may be impermissible in another country, such as the United States. One normative implication of this is that members of one society should not object to practices of those in another. This perspective has some appeal, for it seems to undermine social chauvinism or the condemnation of other societies just because they are different. Nevertheless, we are prevented by the same token from asking whether there is a right way to act that is independent of culture, and we are restricted in criticizing other societies for practices, such as racial discrimination, that we find genuinely abhorrent.

Simple forms of cultural relativism face a basic theoretical objection. Because an act may be right relative to the values or ideals of one society or culture and wrong according to those of another, the relativist appears committed to the apparent contradiction that the same act is both right and wrong. A relativist may counter that the values according to which the act is thought right differ from those in terms of which it is wrong: the doctor's lethal injection may be considered permissible in the Netherlands in terms of the value of ending unnecessary suffering, but it may be impermissible in the United States in virtue of taking an innocent life. An act may be deemed right in terms of value *V1* in one society or culture, but wrong in terms of *V2* in the other. Though different, *V1* and *V2* need not be contradictory values. So the relativist seems not to be committed to a contraction. Yet an inconsistency may arise elsewhere: in claiming that it is wrong to object to practices of a society different from one's own, the relativist is forced to use a notion of "wrong" that is no longer relative but transcultural. It is for reasons of these kinds that philosophers have tended to reject the simpler forms of relativism as justification for ethical principles. (Nevertheless, Richard Rorty in Chapter 5 and Alasdair MacIntyre and Michael Walzer in Chapter 6 offer sophisticated defenses of ethical relativism that escape these shortcomings.)

Moral Conflict   So, a basic concern of ethical analysis in its practical applications is to clarify the nature of moral disagreements or conflicts, with the goal of resolving them. Moral conflicts may be a function, as we have seen, of disagreements concerning *facts* or *concepts or values*. Where the conflict is factual, ethical analysis may be able to resolve the problem by uncovering and encouraging agreement on all the relevant facts. For example, proponents of capital punishment often appeal to the claimed fact that the death penalty deters violent crime. If the evidence shows that the rate of violent crime is either unchanged or increases when the death penalty is in place, then appeal to its deterrent effect can no longer serve as justification for capital punishment and proponents would have to claim some other justification or renounce their support.

Sometimes moral conflict turns on underlying or hidden conceptual disagreement. Resolution may then depend upon establishing agreement about the meanings of relevant concepts in use. Conflict concerning the permissibility of abortion often involves the concept of a person. There may be agreement on the principle that one ought never to harm an innocent person, but disagreement over whether the fetus is a person (and not simply a human being in the physical or genetic sense). No factual evidence will resolve this issue, and calling the fetus a baby simply assumes what has to be established by argument. Conceptual clarification is required. Similarly, parties may agree that people have a basic right to free speech, while disagreeing as to whether racist expression amounts merely to offensive speech or to harmful deed. No appeal to facts will resolve this question; nor do the differences simply reflect ideological divisions. Conceptual clarification will go a long way to illuminating the implications of each position.

Finally, disagreement may concern moral rules, principles, or values. Parties may disagree about norms or principles that ought morally to be endorsed, or they may disagree about the values to be considered primary. For example, some may consider the Offense Principle (that restriction of a person's liberty can be justified to prevent offense to others) sufficiently strong to limit freedom of expression, while others may reject this principle (see Chapter 10). The former may appeal to offensiveness in trying to justify the impermissibility of homosexuality, while the latter will reject the principle in accepting the freedom of homosexuals to express their sexual preference. One attempt to resolve this conflict at the level of institutional principles has been to encourage proponents of the Offense Principle to acknowledge its limits, in light of the more compelling principle of Respect for Persons, that is, that persons are owed respect as autonomous agents (see Chapter 3).

Thus moral philosophers aim to get agreement on the facts, to clarify the definition of relevant concepts, and to analyze justifications offered for underlying values. Should moral disagreement persist, it is likely to concern the basic source of grounds of moral value; for example, whether an act's value is taken to be determined by its consequences (see Chapter 4) or by its intrinsic worth (see Chapter 3).

The complexity of such issues as affirmative action, censorship and hate speech, abortion, capital punishment, or AIDS does not consist simply in the fact that persuasive arguments can be offered for conflicting points of view. These issues are by nature social; they must be resolved, accordingly, at the level of social policy. Social policies, in the form of institutional rules, regulations, and laws, direct individual conduct, and they often clash with individual convictions. It is important, then, to get clear about the theoretical basis and scope of moral judgments and about the application of ethical principles in determining social policy and practice. The application of laws and the underlying legal analysis may lead to different constraints on social action than does moral inquiry.

Law and moral principles do not always coincide. It is unlikely that every law will meet moral constraints; nor should every moral principle or rule be embodied in a law. Laws can be altered or added by legislation; moral obligations and rights are not so easily created or destroyed. Indeed, laws can be critically evaluated and attacked on the basis of moral principles; yet we do not ordinarily criticize a moral principle or value in terms of some given law. So where some law clashes with a moral principle, especially if they constrain us to act in mutually exclusive ways, morality may require that we oppose the law. For example, Rosa Parks rightly and courageously opposed the racist statute in Montgomery, Alabama, that required blacks to occupy only the rear seats in public buses. Opposition to unjust or immoral laws will not always require civil disobedience, though in extreme cases like the one facing Ms. Parks and others it did. In less severe circumstances, opposition can take the form of lobbying or letter-writing, peaceful protests or voting. Discussions of the legal and moral problems in Part III draw at many points and in many ways on the theoretical moral principles developed and discussed in Parts I and II. The general aim is to furnish a forum for readers to construct for themselves reasoned and critical dispositions to moral action for each of the social topics at issue.

FOR FURTHER READING

Appiah, A. *Necessary Questions.* Englewood Cliffs: Prentice-Hall, 1989.

Becker, L. C. and Becker, C. B., eds. *Encyclopaedia of Ethics.* Hamden: Garland, 1992.

———, eds. *A History of Western Ethics.* Hamden: Garland, 1993.

Holmes, R. *Basic Moral Philosophy.* Belmont, Calif.: Wadsworth, 1992.

Hudson, W. D. *Modern Moral Philosophy.* London: Macmillan, 1970.

Krausz, M., and Meiland, J., eds. *Relativism, Cognitive and Moral.* South Bend: University of Notre Dame Press, 1982.

Kupperman, J. *Character*. New York: Oxford University Press, 1991.

Ladd, J., ed. *Ethical Relativism*. Belmont, Calif.: Wadsworth, 1973.

Lyons, D. *Ethics and the Rule of Law*. Cambridge: Cambridge University Press, 1984.

MacIntyre, A. *A Short History of Ethics*. New York: Macmillan, 1966.

Nagel, T. *Equality and Partiality*. New York: Oxford University Press, 1991.

Nielsen, K. *Ethics Without God*. London: Pemberton, 1973.

Norman, R. *The Moral Philosophers*. Oxford: Clarendon Press, 1973.

Olson, G. *The Morality of Self-Interest*. New York: Harcourt, 1965.

Outka, G., and Reeder, J., eds. *Religion and Morality*. New York: Anchor Books, 1973.

Rachels, J. *The Elements of Moral Philosophy*. New York: Random House, 1986.

Raphael, D. D. *Moral Philosophy*. Oxford: Oxford University Press, 1981.

Reiman, J. *Justice and Modern Moral Philosophy*. New Haven: Yale University Press, 1990.

Rescher, N. *Moral Absolutes: An Essay on the Nature and Rationale of Morality*. New York: Lang, 1989.

Scheffler, S. *Human Morality*. New York: Oxford University Press, 1992.

Singer, P. *Practical Ethics,* 2nd ed. New York: Cambridge University Press, 1993.

Singer, P., ed. *A Companion to Ethics*. Oxford: Basil Blackwell, 1991.

Spaemann, R. *Basic Moral Concepts*. New York: Routledge, 1989.

Stoljar, S. *Moral and Legal Reasoning*. New York: Harper & Row, 1980.

Teichman, J., and Evans, K. C. *Philosophy: A Beginner's Guide*. Oxford: Basil Blackwell, 1991.

Toulmin, S. *Reason in Ethics*. Cambridge: Cambridge University Press, 1971.

Williams, B. *Morality: An Introduction*. New York: Harper & Row, 1972.

ETHICAL THEORY:

HISTORICAL TEXTS

INTRODUCTION

Criteria of Evaluation   An act, policy, or institution that is right, good, or just shares some characteristic features or properties with other acts, policies, or institutions that are similarly characterized. Normative ethical theories set out to establish just what these shared features or properties are. In evaluating ethical theories, it is useful to bear in mind the following set of criteria. First, the principles of the theory must be *consistent:* they must be capable of being jointly true. Further, implications to which the theory gives rise must be consistent with every principle of the theory. Second, *the wider the scope* of the theory—that is, the more moral data it is capable of accounting for—the more acceptable it will be. Third, the theory must provide a *decision procedure* for establishing what act is morally permissible or required in any act context. A theory that fails to specify what act is required, or at least a range of permissible acts, will be useless. Fourth, *the fewer the basic moral precepts* of the theory, the better. Of two theories equally wide in scope, the simpler one will be more appealing. Two theories that have great historical and contemporary influence, Kant's deontology (see Chapter 3) and utilitarianism (see Chapter 4), specify one fundamental ethical principle each. Particular rules of behavior in actual act contexts are supposed to be derivable from the basic principle. Finally, the theory must be capable of rendering moral judgments that *conform with* a set of widely held, carefully considered, and reasonable *moral intuitions* about what is right and wrong. A viable theory might challenge some popular moral beliefs. However, no acceptable theory will endorse such acts as murder, such practices as political torture, or such institutions as slavery. There are good reasons for considering such acts, practices, and institutions to be morally unacceptable.

These criteria are unlikely to establish a single prevailing moral theory to the exclusion of all others. Nevertheless, they will reduce the field of viable alternatives to a manageable handful. Moreover, those theories that may be considered viable are unlikely to be flawless. In this respect, moral theories mirror scientific ones: we adopt the best available theory, adapting and revising it in accordance with the test of experience.

Classification of Classical Theories   The ethical theories included in Part I are laid out chronologically. It is possible also to order them thematically, and it may help to give a brief characterization of each thematic category. *Virtue* theories take the basic inquiry of morality to concern the moral *character* of individuals, rather than the rightness or wrongness of *actions*. The fundamental question for virtue theories concerns what sort of person one should be or what sort of character one should develop in order to be virtuous, rather than what sort of action one ought to do. *Natural Law* theories hold that moral principles or laws reflect the nature or rational order of things. For human laws and actions to be moral, they must conform with the natural law. (Note that while Hobbes is included in this category, he imputes a different sense to the concept of a law of nature, and may be interpreted as challenging traditional Natural Law theories.) *Deontological* theories reject the claim that the moral rightness or wrongness of an act is to be defined in terms of its production of goodness or badness. Rather, acts will be right if they are implied or commanded by some binding or overriding moral principle(s) or system of duties. *Social contract* theories take morality to consist in a set of rules establishing how members of a society ought to treat each other. The rules are those that would be (contractually) agreed to by any rational member of the society, if all members accepted them, because these rules would maximize their mutual benefits. *Utilitarian* theories judge the moral worth of actions or rules solely in terms of the goodness or badness of their consequences. Accordingly, an act or rule will be right if it produces greater goodness in general, or perhaps greater goodness for each person affected by it, than any alternative. *Right-based* theories take the basic concept of morality to be rights; that is, freedoms and claims. These theories attempt to derive a general system of rights, goals, and duties from one fundamental right or from a small number of basic rights.

CHAPTER ONE

PLATO AND ARISTOTLE

The "Western" philosophical tradition, sometimes now critically referred to as "Eurocentric," is commonly considered to have begun with the early Greek philosophers in the fifth century B.C. Evidence suggests that the classical Greek thinkers were themselves influenced by earlier non-Greeks, most notably Egyptians. Nevertheless, the kinds of questions posed and the sorts of responses offered to them within the "Western" philosophical tradition—questions about the nature of the universe, of the place and nature of human beings in it, and of proper human conduct and social arrangements—are traced generally to their inception with the Greeks. Among the classical Greek thinkers, the contributions of Socrates, Plato, and Aristotle are deemed seminal.

■ PLATO (427–347 B.C.): THE IDEAL GOOD

Plato and Socrates   Plato developed the philosophical legacy of his teacher, Socrates (c. 470–399 B.C.). In Plato's best known work, *The Republic,* as in his other mature dialogues, the literary figure of Socrates represents Plato's philosophical views. Both Socrates and Plato focused primarily on the question "What is the good or virtuous life?" In *The Republic,* Plato's overriding concern was with the nature of justice. Here, the question of the life most worthy of human pursuit assumes a fundamentally social character. Human beings are social by nature, and the just or right way to live can be defined only in terms of their relations with others.

The Sophists   Plato criticized philosophical and social views commonly expressed in classical Greece, especially those of the Sophists. The Sophists were a loosely related class of professional teachers, representing a variety of subjects, who accepted payment for their instruction. Their primary social importance lay in teaching activities central to Greek political life. These skills included management of family and estate, and rhetoric or the art of persuasion to one's opinion without concern for the truth. Though there is no single set of Sophistic views, it may be possible to establish a common theme in Sophistic thinking about the nature of virtue. The Sophists considered virtue to be *relative* to common opinion about it. Thus it was thought that virtue is not innate, and that it can be taught. Some Sophists appear also to have supported the dictum that "might makes right," that justice is determined by those who have power. In short, the Sophists insisted that morality and justice are a matter not of nature, human or cosmic, but of social convention, custom, and tradition.

Plato's Criticism of the Sophists   Plato's Socrates attacks a version of this view, as represented by the Sophist Thrasymachus, in the opening book of *The Republic,* excerpted here. Thrasymachus defined justice or right as what the stronger parties take to be in their own interests. Socrates shows that this definition of justice involves a contradiction and is accordingly false. Thrasymachus then contends that injustice pays while justice does not, so that doing what is morally wrong must be superior to justice. In response, Socrates demonstrates that because effective injustice necessitates some cooperation, injustice is inevitably self-defeating. Hence, justice must be superior to injustice.

Justice and Reason   In addition to these criticisms of Thrasymachus's views, Socrates argues positively that the proper performance of reason is a necessary condition for all human functions. Persons will be just if their ideas are, and their lives will thus be good. For Plato, reason is fundamental to establishing what ought to be done; it is central to living the good and just life. This is highlighted in the extracts from *The Republic,* Books VI and VII, which concern Plato's views about reality and how we acquire knowledge of it.

Plato held that beliefs or opinions grounded in sense perceptions of physical objects do not amount to knowledge. The proper objects of knowledge are not physical; rather, they are abstract universal Forms. These Forms or Ideas—representing essences of things—exist for Plato in an independent idealized realm. They are real, but do not exist in and are independent of the physical world. Reason, equally universal and immortal, is that faculty of the soul capable of contemplating and knowing these eternally true ideal objects. Nevertheless, human beings need sense perceptions. The senses assist in the development of the soul, which is necessary for rational contemplation or knowledge of these ideal Forms. On Plato's view, sense perceptions of like objects lead us to conceive the ideal or formal properties in virtue of which the perceived objects can be judged alike. Learning, then, is a matter of bringing these Forms from the cavelike darkness of the soul to the light of reason's "eye." The Form represents the Good (in the sense of "best") for each class of object or quality. Thus, Plato holds that the value of objects or qualities is not established contextually or by social convention; rather, value is determined by the degree to which objects or qualities embody the formal properties of constancy, purity, and truth.

To know the Good, for Plato, is ultimately to have complete knowledge; that is, knowledge that is the best, true, and most stable. A knowledgeable person will accordingly do good acts. By contrast, immoral acts imply ignorance; the ignorant person is one who failed to know what was truly or essentially good in the instance at hand. Plato drew the important moral distinction between undertaking the right *act,* thereby acting justly, and being a just or virtuous *person* because one has done the act *for the right reason.* For example, it is right to remove a dangerous weapon from the reach of a person bent on doing harm. Yet if one removes the weapon with the intention of using it oneself to commit some other harm, the act of removal is done for the wrong reason and one would be unjust. Plato thought that because philosophers alone have knowledge of the Good and of justice, they should rule the Republic or ideal state. Philosophers would rule for the good of all classes in the state, and not out of self-concern.

Justice and the State   Elsewhere in *The Republic,* Plato defined a just state as one in which the members of each class do what they are best suited for, for the good of all, and mind their own business: workers produce, soldiers defend, and guardians rule. Members of one class do not impose upon members of other classes their ill-informed *opinions* of how the latter ought to perform their respective functions. As justice individually is the harmony among parts of the soul (the appetitive, the spirited, and the rational), so social justice consists in this special cooperation among classes of the state.

Plato set the standard for moral reasoning. Whatever views one holds about the nature of morality, reasons must be cited to support them if others are to agree or be convinced. If the reasons are poor or overridden by better ones supporting another belief or act, commitment to the former view must be given up. Plato encourages us to think deeply about the relation among our moral beliefs, the acts we undertake, the kinds of persons we are, and the sort of society we live in. Socrates underscores these concerns in his famous remark that "the unexamined life is not worth living."

Plato

THE REPUBLIC

BOOK I

. . . That I learn of others, I replied, is quite true; but that I am ungrateful I wholly deny. Money I have none, and therefore I pay in praise, which is all I have; and how ready I am to praise any one who speaks well you will very soon find out when you answer, for I expect that you will answer well.

Listen, then, [Thrasymachus] said; I proclaim that might is right, justice the interest of the stronger. But why don't you praise me?

Let me first understand you, I replied. Justice, as you say, is the interest of the stronger. Now what, Thrasymachus, is the meaning of this? You cannot mean to say that because Polydamas, the pancratiast, who is stronger than we are, finds the eating of beef for his interest, that this is equally for our interest who are weaker than he is?

That's abominable of you, Socrates; why you are just taking the words in the way which is most damaging to the argument.

Not at all, my good sir, I said; I am trying to understand them; and I wish that you would be a little clearer.

Well, he said, I suppose you know that forms of government differ, there are tyrannies, and there are democracies, and there are aristocracies?

Yes, I know that.

And the government is that which has power in each State?

From *The Republic*, trans. by Benjamin Jowett, *The Dialogues of Plato* (Oxford University Press, 1892).

Certainly.

And the different forms of government make laws democratical, aristocratical, tyrannical, with a view to their several interests; and these laws, which are made by them for their interests, they deliver to their subjects as justice, and punish him who transgresses them as a breaker of the law, and unjust. And that is what I mean when
339 I say that in all States there is the same principle of justice, which is neither more nor less than the interest of the government; and as the government must be supposed to have power, the reasonable conclusion is, that everywhere there is one principle of justice, which is the interest of the stronger.

Now I understand you, I said; and whether you are right or not I will try to learn. But let me first remark, that you have yourself said "interest," although you forbade me to use that word in answer. I do not, however, deny that in your definition the words are added "of the stronger."

A slight addition, that you must allow, he said.

Great or small, never mind that; the simple question is, whether what you are saying is the truth. Now we are both agreed that justice is interest of some sort, but we are not agreed as to the additional words "of the stronger"; and this is the point which I will now examine.

Proceed.

That I will; and first tell me, Do you admit that it is just for subjects to obey their rulers?

I do.

But are the rulers of States absolutely infallible, or are they sometimes liable to err?

To be sure, he replied; they are liable to err.

Then in making their laws they may sometimes make them rightly, but they are not always right?

True.

When they make them rightly, they make them agreeably to their interests; when they are mistaken, contrary to their interests—that is what you would say?

Yes.

And the laws which they make must be obeyed by their subjects—and that is what you call justice?

Doubtless.

Then justice, according to your argument, is not only the interest of the stronger but the reverse?

What are you saying? he asked flurriedly.

I am only saying what you were saying, I believe. But let us consider. Have we not admitted that the rulers may be mistaken about their own interests in what they command, and also that to obey them is justice? Has not that been admitted?

Yes.

Then you must also have acknowledged that justice is not the interest of the stronger, when the rulers who are stronger unintentionally command that which is to their own injury. For if, as you say, justice is the obedience which the subject renders to their commands, then in the case supposed, O thou wisest of men, is there any escape from the conclusion that justice is the injury and not the interest of the stronger, which is imposed on the weaker?

Nothing can be clearer, Socrates, said Polemarchus.

340   Yes, said Cleitophon, interposing, if you are admitted as his witness.

But there is no need of any witness, said Polemarchus, for Thrasymachus himself acknowledges that rulers command what is not for their own interest, and that to obey them is justice.

Yes, Polemarchus—Thrasymachus said that for subjects to do what was commanded by the rulers was just.

Yes, but he also said that justice was the interest of the stronger, and, while admitting both these propositions, he further admitted that the stronger commands what is not for his own interest; whence follows that justice is the injury quite as much as the interest of the stronger.

But, said Cleitophon, he meant by the interest of the stronger what the stronger thought to be for his interest.

That was not the statement, said Polemarchus.

Never mind, I said; let us accept the new statement, if Thrasymachus has changed his opinion.

Tell me then, I said, Thrasymachus, did you mean by justice what the stronger thought to be his interest whether really so or not?

Certainly not, he said.

Do you suppose that I call him who is mistaken the stronger at the time when he is mistaken?

Yes, I said, that I supposed to be your meaning when you admitted that the ruler was not infallible and might be mistaken.

You are a sharper, Socrates, in argument. Pray do you imagine that he who is mistaken about the sick is a physician in that he is mistaken and at the time that he is mistaken? or that he who errs in arithmetic or grammar is an arithmetician or grammarian in that he is mistaken and at the time that he is mistaken? True, we say that the arithmetician or grammarian or physician has made a mistake, but this is only a way of speaking; for the fact is that neither the grammarian nor any other person of skill every makes a mistake in as far as he is what his name implies: they all of them err only when their skill fails them. No craftsman or sage or ruler errs at the time when he is what he is called, though he is commonly said to err; and after this

341   manner I answered you. But the more precise expression, since you will have precision, is that the ruler, as ruler, is unerring, and, being unerring, always commands that which is for his own interest; and the subject is required to execute this: and therefore, as I said at first and now repeat, justice is the interest of the stronger.

. . . Is the physician, in that strict sense of which you are speaking, a healer of the sick or a maker of money? And remember that I am now speaking of the true physician.

A healer of the sick, he replied.

And the pilot—that is to say, the true pilot—is he a captain of sailors or a mere sailor?

A captain of sailors.

The circumstance that he sails in the ship is not to be reckoned; this is an accident only, and has nothing to do with the name pilot, which is significant of his skill and of his authority.

Now I said, each of these has an interest?

Certainly.

And the art has to find and provide for this interest?

Yes, that is the aim of the art.

And the interest of each of the arts is the perfection of each of them; nothing but that?

What do you mean?

I mean what I may illustrate negatively by the example of the body. Suppose you were to ask me whether the body is self-sufficing or has wants, I should reply: Certainly the body has wants; for the body may be ill and require to be cured, and has therefore interests to which the art of medicine ministers; and this is the origin and intention of medicine, as you will acknowledge. Am I not right in saying that?

Quite right, he replied.

342　　But is the art of medicine or any other art faulty or deficient in any quality in the same way that the eye may be deficient in sight or the ear fail of hearing, and, in consequence of this defect, require another art to provide for the interest of seeing and hearing? Has art, I say, any similar liability to fault or defect, and does every art require another supplementary art to provide for its interests, and that another and another without end? Or may the arts be said to look after their own interests? Or have they no need of either—having no faults or defects, they have no need to correct them, either by the exercise of their own art or of any other—that is not required of them for the preservation of their interest; they have only to consider the interest of their subject-matter, for every art remains pure and faultless while remaining true—that is to say, while perfect and unimpaired? Is not all this clear? And I would have you take the words in your precise manner.

Yes, that is clear.

Then medicine does not consider the interest of medicine, but the interest of the body.

True, he said.

Nor does farriery consider the interests of farriery, but the interests of the horse; neither do any other arts care for themselves, for they have no needs, but they care only for that which is the subject of their art?

True, he said.

But surely, I added, the arts are the superiors and rulers of their own subjects: you will admit that, Thrasymachus?

To this he assented with a good deal of reluctance.

Then, I said, no science or art considers or enjoins the interest of the stronger or superior, but only the interest of the subject and weaker? He acquiesced in this after a feint of resistance. Then, I continued, no physician, in as far as he is a physician, considers his own good but the good of the patient; for the true physician is also a ruler having the human body as a subject, and is not a mere money-maker; that has been admitted?

Yes.

And the pilot likewise, in the strict sense of the term, is a ruler of sailors and not a mere sailor?

That has been admitted.

And such a pilot and ruler will provide and prescribe for the interest of the sailor who is under him, and not for his own or the ruler's interest?

He gave a very reluctant "Yes."

Then, I said, Thrasymachus, there is no one in any rule who, in as far as he is a ruler, considers or enjoins that which is for his own interest, but always that which is for the interest of his subject and of his art; to that he looks, and that alone he considers in everything which he says and does.

343   When we had got to this point in the argument, and every one saw that the definition of justice had been completely reversed, Thrasymachus . . . said . . . you further imagine that the rulers of States, who are true rulers, never think of their subjects as sheep, and that they are not studying their own advantage day and night. O, no; and so entirely astray are you in the very rudiments of justice and injustice as not even to know that justice and the just are in reality another's good; that is to say, the interest of the ruler and stronger, and the loss of the subject and servant; whereas the reverse holds in the case of injustice; for the unjust is lord over the truly simple and just: he is the stronger, and his subjects do what is for his benefit, and minister to his happiness, which is very far from being their own. Consider further, most foolish Socrates, that the just is always a loser in comparison with the unjust. First of all in their private dealings: whenever the unjust is the partner of the just the conclusion of the affair always is that the unjust man has more and the just less. Next in their dealings with the State: when there is an income tax the just man will pay more and the unjust less on the same amount of income; and when there is anything to be received the one gains nothing and the other much. Observe also that when they come into office, there is the just man neglecting his affairs and perhaps suffering other losses, but he will not compensate himself out of the public purse because he is just; moreover he is hated by his friends and relations for refusing to serve them in unlawful ways. Now all this is reversed in the case of the unjust man. I am speaking of injustice on a large scale in which the

344   advantage of the unjust is most apparent, and my meaning will be most clearly seen in that highest form of injustice the perpetrator of which is the happiest of men, as the sufferers or those who refuse to do injustice are the most miserable—I mean tyranny, which by fraud and force takes away the property of others, not retail but wholesale; comprehending in one, things sacred as well as profane, private and public; for any one of which acts of wrong, if he were detected perpetrating them singly, he would be punished and incur greater dishonor; for they who are guilty of any of these crimes in single instances are called robbers of temples, and man-stealers and burglars and swindlers and thieves. But when a man has taken away the money of the citizens and made slaves of them, then, instead of these dishonorable names, he is called happy and blessed, not only by the citizens but by all who hear of his having achieved the consummation of injustice. For injustice is censured because the censurers are afraid of suffering, and not from any fear which they have of doing injustice. And thus, as I have shown, Socrates, injustice, when on a sufficient scale, has more strength and freedom and mastery than justice; and, as I said at first,

justice is the interest of the stronger, whereas injustice is a man's own profit and interest.

. . . So far am I from agreeing with Thrasymachus that justice is the interest of the stronger. That, however, is a question which I will not now further discuss; but when Thrasymachus says that the life of the unjust is more advantageous than that of the just, this new statement of his appears to me to be a far more serious matter. Which of us is right, Glaucon? And which sort of life do you deem most advantageous?

The life of the just, he answered.

348   Did you hear all the advantages of the unjust which Thrasymachus was rehearsing?

Yes, I heard him, but I was not convinced by him.

And would you desire to convince him, if we can only find a way, that he is saying what is not true?

Most certainly, he replied.

If, I said, he makes a set speech, and we make another set speech and tell our friend all the good of being just, and he answers and we rejoin, there must be a numbering and measuring of the goods that are claimed on either side, and the end will be that we shall want judges to decide; but if we proceed in our inquiry as we lately did, by a method of mutual agreement, we shall unite the office of judge and advocate in our own persons.

Very good, he said.

And which method do I understand you to prefer? I said.

That which you propose.

Well then, Thrasymachus, I said, suppose that you begin at the beginning and answer me. Your statement is that perfect injustice is more gainful than justice?

Yes, that is my statement, the grounds of which I have also stated.

And you would call one of them virtue and the other vice?

Certainly.

I suppose that you would call justice virtue and injustice vice?

That is a charming notion and so likely, seeing that I affirm injustice to be profitable and justice not.

What else then?

The opposite, he replied.

And would you call justice vice?

No, I would rather say sublime simplicity.

And would you call injustice malignity?

No; I would rather say discretion.

And do the unjust appear to you to be wise and good?

Yes, he said; at any rate this is true of those who are able to be perfectly unjust, and who have the power of subduing States and nations; but I dare say that you imagine me to be talking of cutpurses. Even that, if undetected, has advantages, though they are hardly worth mentioning when compared with the other.

I do not think that I misapprehend your meaning, Thrasymachus, I replied; but still I cannot hear without amazement that you class injustice with wisdom and virtue, and justice with the opposite.

Certainly, that is the way in which I do class them.

Now, I said, you are on more substantial and almost unanswerable ground; for if the injustice which you were maintaining to be profitable had been admitted by you or by other men to be vice and deformity, an answer might have been given to you on received principles; but now I perceive that you will call injustice strong and honorable, and to the unjust you will assign all the qualities which were assigned by us before to the just, seeing that you do not hesitate to place injustice on the side of wisdom and virtue.

That is exactly the truth, he replied.

Now, I said, I see that you are speaking your mind, and therefore I do not shrink from the argument; for I do believe, Thrasymachus, that you are in earnest, and are not amusing yourself at our expense.

What is it to you, he said, whether I am in earnest or not? Your business is to refute the argument.

Very true, I said; and will you be so good as to answer another question—Does the just man try to gain any advantage over the just?

Far otherwise; if he did he would not be the simple amusing creature which he is.

And does he try to gain more than his just share in action?

He does not.

And how would he regard the attempt to gain an advantage over the unjust man or action; would that be considered by him as just or unjust?

He would think that just, and would try to gain the advantage. But he could not.

Whether he could or could not, I said, is not the question. I simply asked whether the just man, while refusing to have more than another just man, would wish and claim to have more than the unjust?

Yes, he would.

And what of the unjust—does he claim more than the just man and more than the just action?

Of course, he said, he claims to have more than all men.

And the unjust man will desire more than the unjust man and action, and will strive to get more than all?

True.

Let us put the matter thus, I said; the just does not desire more than his like but more than his unlike, whereas the unjust desires more than both like and unlike.

Nothing, he said, can be better than that statement.

And the unjust is good and wise, and the just is neither?

Good again, he said.

And is not the unjust like the wise and good and the just unlike them?

Of course, he said, he who is just is like the just, and the unjust is like the unjust. Each of them, I said, is such as his like is? Then now, Thrasymachus, I said, let us try these statements by the analogy of the arts. You would admit that one man is a musician and another not a musician?

Yes.

And the musician is wise, and he who is not a musician is unwise?

Yes.

And in that he is wise he is good, and in that he is unwise he is bad?

Yes.

And you would say the same sort of thing of the physician?

Yes.

And do you think, my excellent friend, that a musician when he adjusts the lyre would desire or claim to be in excess of a musician in the tightening or loosening the strings?

I do not think that he would.

But he would claim to be in excess of the non-musician?

Of course.

350   And what would you say of the physician? In prescribing meats and drinks would he wish to go beyond another physician or beyond the art of medicine?

He would not.

But he would wish to exceed the non-physician?

Yes.

And about knowledge and ignorance in general; see whether you think that any man of intelligence whatsoever would wish to have the choice of saying or doing more than another man of intelligence. Would he not rather say or do the same as his like in the same case?

That I suppose is not to be denied.

And what would you say of the unintelligent? Would he not desire to have more than either intelligent or unintelligent?

That, I suppose, must be as you say.

And the intelligent is wise?

Yes.

Then the wise and good will not desire to gain more than his like, but more than his unlike?

That is evident.

Whereas the bad and ignorant will desire to gain more than both?

Yes.

But were you not saying, Thrasymachus, that the unjust exceeds both his like and unlike?

Yes, I did say that.

And you also said that the just will not exceed his like but his unlike?

Yes, he said.

Then the just is like the wise and good, and the unjust like the evil and ignorant?

That is the inference.

And each of them is such as his like is?

That was admitted.

Then the just has turned out to be wise and good and the unjust evil and ignorant . . .

. . . that the just are clearly wiser and better and abler than the unjust, and that the unjust are incapable of common action—this has been already shown; nay more, when we speak thus confidently of gangs of evil-doers acting together, this is not strictly true, for if they had been perfectly unjust, they would have laid hands upon one another, but there must evidently have been some remnant of justice in them, or they would have injured one another as well as their victims, and then they would have been unable to act together, they were but semi-villainous, for had they been whole villains, wholly unjust, they would have been wholly incapable of action. That, as I believe, is the truth of the matter, and not what you said at first. But whether the just have a better and happier life than the unjust is a further question which we also proposed to consider. I think that they have, and for the reasons which I have given; but still I should like to examine further, for this is no light matter, concerning nothing less than the true rule of life.

Proceed.

I will proceed by asking a question: Would you not think that a horse has some end or use?

I should.

And that would be the end or use of a horse or anything which could not be accomplished, or not so well accomplished, by any other thing?

I do not understand, he said.

Let me explain then. Can you see, except with the eye?

Certainly not.

Or hear, except with the ear?

No.

These then are the uses or ends of these faculties?

They are.

353   But you can cut off a vine-branch with a carving-knife or with a chisel?

Of course.

And yet not so well as with a pruning-hook made for the purpose?

True.

May we not say, then, that this is the use of the pruning-hook?

We may.

Then now I think you will have no difficulty in understanding my meaning when I said that the end or use of anything was that which could not be accomplished, or not so well accomplished, by any other thing?

I understand your meaning, he said, and assent.

And as all things have ends, have they not also excellence? Need I ask again whether the eye has an end.

It has.

And has not the eye an excellence?

Yes.

And the ear has an end and an excellence also?

True.

And the same is true of all other things; they have each of them an end and a special excellence?

That is so.

Well, and can the eyes fulfill their end if they are wanting in their own proper excellence and have a defect instead?

How can they, he said, if they are blind?

You mean to say, if they have lost their proper excellence, which is sight; but I have not arrived at that point yet. I would rather ask the question more generally, and only inquire whether the things which fulfill their ends fulfill them by their own proper excellence, and fail of fulfilling them by their proper defect?

Yes, I assent to that, he replied.

I might say the same of the ears; when deprived of their own proper excellence they cannot fulfill their end?

True.

And the same may be said of all other things?

I agree.

And has not the soul an end which nothing else can fulfill? for example, to provide and command and advise, and the like. Are not these peculiar to the soul and can they rightly be assigned to any other?

To no other.

And is not life to be reckoned among the ends of the soul?

Assuredly, he said.

And has not the soul an excellence also?

Yes.

And can she or can she not fulfill her ends or uses when deprived of that excellence?

She cannot.

Then an evil soul must necessarily be an evil ruler, and a good soul a good ruler?

Yes, that must be as you say.

And we have admitted that justice is the excellence of the soul and injustice the defect of the soul?

That has been admitted.

Then the just soul and the just man will live well, and the unjust man will live ill?

That is involved in your argument.

354 And he who lives well will be blessed and happy, and he who lives ill the reverse of happy?

Certainly.

Then the just is happy, and the unjust miserable?

Granted.

But happiness and not misery is profitable. Then, my blessed Thrasymachus, injustice can never be more profitable than justice.

BOOK VI

. . . You have to imagine, then, that there are two ruling powers, and that one of them is set over the intellectual world, the other over the visible. I do not say heaven, lest you should fancy that I was refining about the name (ὀυρανός, ὁρατός). May I suppose that you have this distinction of the visible and intelligible fixed in your mind?

I have.

Now take a line which has been cut into two unequal parts, and divide each of them again in the same proportion, and suppose the two main divisions to answer, one to the visible and the other to the intelligible, and then compare the subdivisions as to their relative clearness and want of clearness, and you will find that the first section in the sphere of the visible consists of images. And by images I mean, in the first place, shadows, and in the second place, reflections in water and in solid, smooth and polished bodies, and all that sort of thing, as you understand.

510

Yes. I understand.

Imagine now, the other section, of which this is only the resemblance, to include ourselves and the animals, and everything in nature and everything in art.

Very good.

Would you not admit that this latter section has a different degree of truth, and that the copy is to the object which is copied as the sphere of opinion is to the sphere of knowledge?

Most undoubtedly.

Next proceed to consider the manner in which the sphere of the intellectual is to be divided.

In what manner?

As thus: there are two subdivisions, in the lower of which the soul uses the figures given by the former division as images; the inquiry can only be hypothetical, and instead of going upwards to a principle descends to the other end; in the higher of the two, the soul passes out of hypotheses, and goes up to a principle which is above hypotheses, making no use of images as in the former case, but proceeding only in and by the ideas themselves.

I do not quite understand your meaning, he said.

I will try again. I said: for you will understand me better now that I have made these preliminary remarks. You are aware that students of geometry, arithmetic, and the kindred sciences assume the odd and the even and the figures and three kinds of angles and the like in their several branches of science; these are their hypotheses, which everybody is supposed to know, and of which therefore they do not deign to give any account either to themselves or others; but they begin with these, and go on until they arrive at last, and in a consistent manner, at their conclusion?

Yes, he said, I know that.

And do you know also that although they use and reason about the visible forms, they are thinking not of these, but of the ideals which they resemble; not of the figures which they draw, but of the absolute square and the absolute diameter, and so on: and, while using as images these very forms which they draw or make, and which in turn have their shadows and reflections in the water, they are really seeking for the things themselves, which can only be seen with the eye of the mind?

511

That is true.

And of this kind I still spoke as intelligible, although in inquiries of this sort the soul is compelled to use hypotheses; not proceeding to a first principle because unable to ascend above hypotheses, but using as images the objects of which the shadows are resemblances in a still lower sphere, they having in relation to the shadows a higher value and distinctness.

I understand, he said, that you are speaking of geometry and the sister arts.

And when I speak of the other division of the intellectual, you will also understand me to speak of that knowledge which reason herself attains by the power of dialectic, using the hypotheses not as first principles, but only as hypotheses—that is to say, as steps and points of departure into a region which is above hypotheses, in order that she may soar beyond them to the first principle of the whole; and clinging to this and then to that which depends on this, by successive steps she descends again without the aid of any sensible object, beginning and ending in ideas.

I understand you he replied; not perfectly, for the matter of which you speak is too great for that; but, at any rate, I understand you to say that knowledge and being, which the science of dialectic contemplates, are clearer than the notions of the arts, as they are termed, which proceed from hypotheses only: these are also contemplated by the understanding, and not by the senses: yet, because they start from hypotheses and do not ascend to a principle, those who contemplate them appear to you not to exercise the higher reason upon them, although when a first principle is added to them they are cognizable by the higher reason. And the habit which is concerned with geometry and the cognate sciences I suppose that you would term understanding and not reason, as being intermediate between opinion and reason.

You have quite conceived me, I said; and now, corresponding to these four sections, let there be four faculties in the soul—reason answering to the highest, understanding to the second, faith or persuasion to the third, and knowledge of shadows to the last—and let there be a scale of them, and let us suppose that the several faculties have clearness in the same degree that their objects have truth.

I understand, he replied, and give my assent, and will arrange them as you say.

BOOK VII

After this, I said, imagine the enlightenment or ignorance of our nature in a figure: Behold! human beings living in a sort of underground den, which has a mouth open towards the light and reaching all across the den; they have been here from their childhood, and have their legs and necks chained so that they cannot move and I can only see before them; for the chains are arranged in such a manner as to prevent them from turning round their heads. At a distance above and behind them the light of a fire is blazing, and between the fire and the prisoners there is a raised way; and you will see, if you look, a low wall built along the way, like the screen which marionette players have before them, over which they show the puppets.

I see, he said.

And do you see, I said, men passing along the wall carrying vessels, which appear over the wall; also figures of men and animals, made of wood and stone and various materials; and some of the passengers, as you would expect, are talking, and some of them are silent?

That is a strange image, he said, and they are strange prisoners.

Like ourselves, I replied; and they see only their own shadows, or the shadows of one another, which the fire throws on the opposite wall of the cave?

True, he said; how could they see anything but the shadows if they were never allowed to move their heads?

And of the objects which are being carried in like manner they would only see the shadows?

Yes, he said.

And if they were able to talk with one another, would they not suppose that they were naming what was actually before them?

Very true.

And suppose further that the prison had an echo which came from the other side, would they not be sure to fancy that the voice which they heard was that of a passing shadow?

No question, he replied.

There can be no question, I said, that the truth would be to them just nothing but the shadows of the images.

That is certain.

And now look again, and see how they are released and cured of their folly. At first, when any one of them is liberated and compelled suddenly to go up and turn his neck round and walk and look at the light, he will suffer sharp pains; the glare will distress him, and he will be unable to see the realities of which in his former state he had seen the shadows; and then imagine some one saying to him, that what he saw before was an illusion, but that now he is approaching real being and has a truer sight and vision of more real things—what will be his reply? And you may further imagine that his instructor is pointing to the objects as they pass and requiring him to name them,—will he not be in a difficulty? Will he not fancy that the shadows which he formerly saw are truer than the objects which are now shown to him?

Far truer.

And if he is compelled to look at the light, will he not have a pain in his eyes which will make him turn away to take refuge in the object of vision which he can see, and which he will conceive to be clearer than the things which are not being shown to him?

True, he said.

And suppose once more, that he is reluctantly dragged up a steep and rugged ascent, and held fast and forced into the presence of the sun himself, do you not think that he will be pained and irritated, and when he approaches the light he will have his eyes dazzled, and will not be able to see any of the realities which are not affirmed to be the truth?

Not all in a moment, he said.

He will require to get accustomed to the sight of the upper world. And first he will see the shadows best, next the reflections of men and other objects in the water, and then the objects themselves; next he will gaze upon the light of the moon and the stars; and he will see the sky and the stars by night, better than the sun, or the light of the sun, by day?

And at last he will be able to see the sun, and not mere reflections of him in the water, but he will see him as he is in his own proper place, and not in another, and he will contemplate his nature.

Certainly.

And after this he will reason that the sun is he who gives the seasons and the years, and is the guardian of all that is in the visible world, and in a certain way the cause of all things which he and his fellows have been accustomed to behold?

Clearly, he said, he would come to the other first and to this afterwards.

And when he remembered his old habitation, and the wisdom of the den and his fellow-prisoners, do you not suppose that he would felicitate himself on the change, and pity them? . . .

Yes, he said, I think that he would rather suffer anything than live after their manner.

Imagine once more, I said, that such an one coming suddenly out of the sun were to be replaced in his old situation, is he not certain to have his eyes full of darkness?

Very true, he said.

517 And if there were a contest, and he had to compete in measuring the shadows with the prisoners who have never moved out of the den, during the time that his sight is weak, and before his eyes are steady (and the time which would be needed to acquire this new habit of sight might be very considerable), would he not be ridiculous? Men would say of him that up he went and down he comes without his eyes; and that there was no use in even thinking of ascending: and if any one tried to loose another and lead him up to the light, let them only catch the offender in the act, and they would put him to death?

No question, he said.

This allegory, I said, you may now append to the previous argument; the prison is the world of sight, the light of the fire is the sun, the ascent and vision of the things above you may truly regard as the upward progress of the soul into the intellectual world; that is my poor belief, to which, at your desire, I have given expression. Whether I am right or not God only knows; but, whether true or false, my opinion is that in the world of knowledge the idea of good appears last of all, and is seen only with an effort; and, when seen, is also inferred to be the universal author of all things beautiful and right, parent of light and the lord of light in this world, and the source of truth and reason in the other: this is the first great cause which he who would act rationally either in public or private life must behold.

I agree, he said, as far as I am able to understand you.

I should like to have your agreement in another matter, I said. For I would not have you marvel that those who attain to this beatific vision are unwilling to descend to human affairs; but their souls are ever hastening into the upper world in which they desire to dwell; and this is very natural, if our allegory may be trusted.

Certainly, that is quite natural . . .

518   Any one who has common sense will remember that the bewilderments of the eyes are of two kinds, and arise from two causes, either from coming out of the light or from going into the light, which is true of the mind's eye, quite as much as of the bodily eye; and he who remembers this when he sees the soul of any one whose vision is perplexed and weak, will not be too ready to laugh; he will first ask whether that soul has come out of the brighter life, and is unable to see because unaccustomed to the dark, or having turned from darkness to the day is dazzled by excess of light. And then he will count the one happy in his condition and state of being. and he will pity the other; or, if he have a mind to laugh at the soul which comes from below into the light, there will be more reason in this than in the laugh which greets the other from the den.

That, he said, is a very just remark.

But if this is true, then certain professors of education must be mistaken in saying that they can put a knowledge into the soul which was not there before, like giving eyes to the blind.

Yes, that is what they say, he replied.

Whereas, I said, our argument shows that the power is already in the soul; and that as the eye cannot turn from darkness to light without the whole body, so too, when the eye of the soul is turned round, the whole soul must be turned from the world of generation into that of being, and become able to endure the sight of being, and of the brightest and best of being—that is to say, of the good.

Very true.

■ ARISTOTLE (384–323 B.C.): VIRTUES AND PRACTICAL REASONING

Aristotle's Teleology   Like Plato, with whom he studied for many years, Aristotle considered the life of contemplation to be the essential human good. Aristotle's conception of nature, including human nature, is *teleological,* that is, each class or kind of thing has an end (*telos*). To bring this *telos* about is its natural function. A member of the class or kind will be more or less good to the extent that it fulfills the natural function of its kind. The function of hearts, say, is to pump blood. A good heart is one that pumps well; it fulfills its function.

Eudaimonia   Aristotle began and ended his study of ethics (*Nicomachean Ethics,* Books I and X) by inquiring into the nature of the good for human beings. He claimed that the goal of human beings is to live well or happily. (*Eudaimonia,* the term Aristotle used, is probably best translated as "well-being.") It is not uncommon to equate happiness with pleasure. Nevertheless, Aristotle was careful to distinguish between them, arguing that a life of happiness, unlike one of pleasure, will be self-sufficient, complete, and chosen for its own sake (see Book I). Thus pleasure is rejected as the proper *telos* of human acts.

It should be noted that although Aristotle's view of human nature is teleological, his account of how we decide what is right or wrong is not *consequentialist;* that is, he does not consider an act to be moral or immoral on the basis of the pleasurable or painful consequences it effects. (In this, Aristotle's view differs fundamentally from utilitarianism; see Chapter 4).

Reason and the Virtues   Aristotle was concerned to spell out the conditions of a life worth living. Unlike Plato, for whom the most worthy life is strictly contemplative, Aristotle stressed that human life is by nature social and active, and that human virtue or excellence should reflect this. Reason, for Aristotle, has both intellectual and practical states, and so there are intellectual and practical virtues (excellences). The moral or practical virtues are accordingly the conclusions to excellent practical reasoning in existing contexts. For example, generosity is the moral virtue established by excellent practical reasoning in the case of giving or taking property; courage is the virtue in battle. Vices in each context are extremes either of excess or insufficiency (defect). In the case of property, the excessive vice is wastefulness and the defect is stinginess; for battle, they are foolhardiness and cowardice, respectively. For a particular act to be virtuous or vicious, it must be voluntary. A set of criteria for distinguishing between voluntary and involuntary acts is laid out in Book III. Where the moving principle of the act is outside the agent—an act done from imposed force, for example—it will be involuntary. A voluntary act is one for which the determining cause is in the agent, when he or she could have done otherwise. Voluntary acts are praiseworthy or blameworthy; involuntary acts, by contrast, are pardonable. Thus Aristotle articulated distinctions that have since become institutionalized in "Western" conceptions of law.

Practical Reasoning   The moral virtues require right choice. On Aristotle's account, the intellectual virtue of correct practical reasoning effects right choice: its aim is to act well. So correct practical reasoning or deliberation underlies the moral virtues. The virtue of practical deliberation is analyzed in Book VI. Excellence in deliberation involves the right process of reasoning, leading in conclusion to a timely choice of the right act, and with the view to bringing about the right end. Good choice requires that the reasoning be true and that desire follow what reason determines (Aristotle accordingly calls choice either "desiderative reason" or "ratiocinative desire").

Right reason concerns the proper relation between universal and particular premises. *Universal premises* express value judgments about the general class of object under consideration; for example, "Drunk driving is dangerous." *Particular premises* are factual claims about the concrete circumstances in which the agent stands: "A friend offers me a ride home; he is drunk." For Aristotle, practical ethical choices cannot be reduced to a set of universal rules. *Perception* of the agent's particular circumstances is crucial, and this may prompt a revision of the universal rules or laws. The conclusion to the practical reasoning, then, is not a tendency or conviction to act in some way. The reasoning ends in actually bringing about the act; in our example, "I take the keys and drive my friend home" or "I call a cab." Error in deliberation leading to a wrong or vicious act may involve a mistake either in the universal or particular premise of the practical reasoning. My decision to accept a ride home with my drunk friend may follow from a mistaken universal premise, "Drunk driving is not dangerous," or from a false impression of my friend's sober state.

Justice   In contrast to the intellectual virtue of practical deliberation, justice—like courage—is a moral virtue, and injustice a moral vice. In Book V, Aristotle distinguished between two senses of justice (the lawful and the fair) and two senses of injustice (the unlawful and the unfair). The lawful is equivalent to the whole of virtue; the unlawful, to the whole of vice. For Aristotle, the notion of the law is a collection of wise or rational judgments about excellent or virtuous actions in all kinds of circumstances. As a summary of past experience, laws guide choice. Thus to act in terms of the appropriate law in every case is to be completely virtuous. Nevertheless, it should be stressed that good judgment in the actual situation confronting agents involves properly identifying their specific circumstances, and this is a matter of what Aristotle called *perception.*

Justice as fairness, by contrast, is a particular virtue, and the unfair is a particular vice. Aristotle distinguished between two kinds of fairness: distributive and rectificatory. *Distributive* justice involves establishing principles for proportionate equality or fairness in distributing goods among citizens. *Rectificatory* or corrective justice concerns setting right or "equalizing" harms for injuries done, whether these harms are a matter of unfair distributions of goods or of injurious acts. Equality is to be restored either by way of a redistribution of goods or by corrective punishment.

Much of the contemporary moral concern about social problems is tied up with the notion of justice in both of Aristotle's senses. The general questions that are raised for each of the social issues in Part III of this book were part of Aristotle's primary focus: "What is the right action for me to do here, and how do I decide this?" But questions can be asked also about the justice of institutions basic to any social fabric. These include concerns about the principles of just distribution of social resources (see the contributions of John Rawls and Robert Nozick in Chapter 5) and the principles of punishment (see Chapter 14). Aristotle's view represents one way to set about answering both sets of questions. However, his historical importance is perhaps more basic, for he furnished the very terms of the debate.

Aristotle

NICOMACHEAN ETHICS

BOOK I

1   Every art and every inquiry, and similarly every action and pursuit, is thought to aim at some good; and for this reason the good has rightly been declared to be that at which all things aim. But a certain difference is found among ends; some are

From *Ethica Nicomachea*, trans. by W. D. Ross for *The Oxford Translation of Aristotle*, edited by W. D. Ross, vol. 9 (1925). Reprinted by permission of Oxford University Press.

activities, others are products apart from the activities that produce them. Where there are ends apart from the actions, it is the nature of the products to be better than the activities. Now, as there are many actions, arts, and sciences, their ends also are many; the end of the medical art is health, that of shipbuilding a vessel, that of strategy victory, that of economics wealth. But where such arts fall under a single capacity—as bridle-making and the other arts concerned with the equipment of horses fall under the art of riding, and this and every military action under strategy, in the same way other arts fall under yet others—in all of these the ends of the master arts are to be preferred to all the subordinate ends; for it is for the sake of the former that the latter are pursued. It makes no difference whether the activities themselves are the ends of the actions, or something else apart from the activities, as in the case of the sciences just mentioned.

2 If, then, there is some end of the things we do, which we desire for its own sake (everything else being desired for the sake of this), and if we do not choose everything for the sake of something else (for at that rate the process would go on to infinity, so that our desire would be empty and vain), clearly this must be the good and the chief good. Will not the knowledge of it, then, have a great influence on life? Shall we not, like archers who have a mark to aim at, be more likely to hit upon what is right? If so, we must try, in outline at least to determine what it is, and of which of the sciences or capacities it is the object. It would seem to belong to the most authoritative art and that which is most truly the master art. And politics appears to be of this nature: for it is this that ordains which of the sciences should be studied in a state, and which each class of citizens should learn and up to what point they should learn them; and we see even the most highly esteemed of capacities to fall under this, e.g., strategy, economics, rhetoric; now, since politics uses the rest of the sciences, and since, again, it legislates as to what we are to do and what we are to abstain from, the end of this science must include those of the others, so that this end must be the good for man. For even if the end is the same for a single man and for a state, that of the state seems at all events something greater and more complete whether to attain or to preserve; though it is worth while to attain the end merely for one man, it is finer and more godlike to attain it for a nation or for city-states. These, then, are the ends at which our inquiry aims, since it is political science, in one sense of that term. . . .

5 . . . To judge from the lives that men lead, most men, and men of the most vulgar type, seem (not without some ground) to identify the good, or happiness, with pleasure; which is the reason why they love the life of enjoyment. For there are, we may say, three prominent types of life—that just mentioned, the political, and thirdly the contemplative life. Now the mass of mankind are evidently quite slavish in their tastes, preferring a life suitable to beasts, but they get some ground for their view from the fact that many of those in high places share the tastes of Sardanapallus. A consideration of the prominent types of life shows that people of superior refinement and of active disposition identify happiness with honour, for this is, roughly speaking, the end of the political life. But it seems too superficial to what we

are looking for, since it is thought to depend on those who bestow honour rather than on him who receives, it, but the good we divine to be something proper to a man and not easily taken from him. Further, men seem to pursue honour in order that they may be assured of their goodness: at least it is by men of practical wisdom that they seek to be honoured, and among those who know them, and on the ground of their virtue; clearly, then, according to them, at any rate, virtue is better. And perhaps one might even suppose this to be, rather than honour, the end of the political life. But even this appears somewhat incomplete; for possession of virtue seems actually compatible with being asleep, or with lifelong inactivity, and further, with the greatest sufferings and misfortunes: but a man who was living so no one would call happy, unless he were maintaining a thesis at all costs. But enough of this; for the subject has been sufficiently treated even in the current discussions. Third comes the contemplative life, which we shall consider later.

The life of money-making is one undertaken under compulsion, and wealth is evidently not the good we are seeking; for it is merely useful and for the sake of something else. And so one might rather take the aforenamed objects to be ends; for they are loved for themselves. But it is evident that not even these are ends, yet many arguments have been thrown away in support of them. Let us leave this subject, then.

6   We had perhaps better consider the universal good and discuss thoroughly what is meant by it, although such an inquiry is made an uphill one by the fact that the Forms have been introduced by friends of our own. Yet it would perhaps be thought to be better, indeed to be our duty, for the sake of maintaining the truth even to destroy what touches us closely, especially as we are philosophers or lovers of wisdom; for, while both are dear, piety requires us to honour truth above our friends. . . .

. . . Clearly, then, goods must be spoken of in two ways, and some must be good in themselves, the others by reason of these. Let us separate, then, things good in themselves from things useful, and consider whether the former are called good by reference to a single Idea. What sort of goods would one call good in themselves? Is it those that are pursued even when isolated from others, such as intelligence, sight, and certain pleasures and honours? Certainly, if we pursue these also for the sake of something else, yet one would place them among things good in themselves. Or is nothing other than the Idea of good good in itself? In that case the Form will be empty. But if the things we have named are also things good in themselves, the account of the good will have to appear as something identical in them all, as that of whiteness is identical in snow and in white lead. But of honour, wisdom, and pleasure, just in respect of their goodness, the accounts are distinct and diverse. The good, therefore, is not some common element answering to one Idea. . . .

7   Let us again return to the good we are seeking, and ask what it can be. It seems different in different actions and arts; it is different in medicine, in strategy, and in the other arts likewise. What then is the good of each? Surely that for whose sake everything else is done. In medicine this is health, in strategy victory, in architecture a house, in any other sphere something else, and in very action and pursuit the

end; for it is for the sake of this that all men do whatever else they do. Therefore, if there is an end for all that we do, this will be the good achievable by action, and if there are more than one, these will be the goods achievable by action.

So the argument has by a different course reached the same point; but we must try to state this even more clearly. Since there are evidently more than one end, and we choose some of these (e.g., wealth, flutes, and in general instruments) for the sake of something else, clearly not all ends are final ends; but the chief good is evidently something final. Therefore, if there is only one final end, this will be what we are seeking, and if there are more than one, the most final of these will be what we are seeking. Now we call that which is in itself worthy of pursuit more final than that which is worthy of pursuit for the sake of something else, and that which is never desirable for the sake of something else more final than the things that are desirable both in themselves and for the sake of that other thing, and therefore we call final without qualification that which is always desirable in itself and never for the sake of something else.

Now such a thing happiness, above all else, is held to be; for this we choose always for itself and never for the sake of something else, but honour, pleasure, reason, and every virtue we choose indeed for themselves (for if nothing resulted from them we should still choose each of them), but we choose them also for the sake of happiness, judging that by means of them we shall be happy. Happiness, on the other hand, no one chooses for the sake of these, nor, in general, for anything other than itself.

From the point of view of self-sufficiency the same result seems to follow; for the final good is thought to be self-sufficient. Now by self-sufficient we do not mean that which is sufficient for a man by himself, for one who lives a solitary life, but also for parents, children, wife, and in general for his friends and fellow citizens, since man is born for citizenship. But some limit must be set to this; for if we extend our requirement to ancestors and descendants and friends' friends we are in for an infinite series. Let us examine this question, however, on another occasion; the self-sufficient we now define as that which when isolated makes life desirable and lacking in nothing; and such we think happiness to be; and further we think it most desirable of all things, without being counted as one good thing among others—if it were so counted it would clearly be made more desirable by the addition of even the least of goods; for that which is added becomes an excess of goods, and of goods the greater is always more desirable. Happiness, then, is something final and self-sufficient, and is the end of action.

Presumably, however, to say that happiness is the chief good seems a platitude, and a clearer account of what it is is still desired. This might perhaps be given, if we could first ascertain the function of man. For just as for a flute-player, a sculptor, or any artist, and, in general, for all things that have a function or activity, the good and the "well" is thought to reside in the function, so would it seem to be for man, if he has a function. Have the carpenter, then, and the tanner certain functions or activities, and has man none? Is he born without a function? Or as eye, hand, foot, and in general each of the parts evidently has a function, may one lay it down that man similarly has a function apart from all these? What then can this be? Life seems to be common even to plants, but we are seeking what is peculiar to man. Let us exclude, therefore, the life of nutrition and growth. Next there would be a life of perception, but *it* also seems to be common even to the horse, the ox, and every animal. There remains, then, an active life of the element that has a rational principle; of this, one part has such a principle in the sense of being obedient to one, the other in the sense of possessing one and exercising thought. And, as "life of the rational element" also has two meanings, we must state that life in the sense of activity is what we mean; for this seems to be the more proper sense of the term. Now if the function of man is an activity of soul which follows or implies a rational principle, and if we say "a so-and-so" and "a good so-and-so" have a function which is the same in kind, e.g., a lyre-player and a good lyre-player, and so without qualification in all cases, eminence in respect of goodness being added to the name of the function (for the function of a lyre-player is to play the lyre, and that of a good lyre-player is to do so well): if this is the case, [and we state the function of man to be a certain kind of life, and this to be an activity or actions of the soul implying a rational principle, and the function of a good man to be the good and noble performance of these, and if any action is well performed when it is performed in accordance with the appropriate excellence: if this is the case] human good turns out to be activity of soul in accordance with virtue, and if there are more than one virtue, in accordance with the best and most complete.

But we must add "in a complete life." For one swallow does not make a summer, nor does one day; and so too one day, or a short time, does not make a man blessed and happy.

Let this serve as an outline of the good. . . .

8 . . . Another belief which harmonizes with our account is that the happy man lives well and does well; for we have practically defined happiness as a sort of good life and good action. . . .

With those who identify happiness with virtue or some one virtue our account is in harmony; for to virtue belongs virtuous activity. But it makes, perhaps, no small difference whether we place the chief good in possession or in use, in state of mind or in activity. For the state of mind may exist without producing any good result, as in a man who is asleep or in some other way quite inactive, but the activity cannot; for one who has the activity will of necessity be acting, and acting well. And as in the Olympic Games it is not the most beautiful and the strongest that are crowned but those who compete (for it is some of these that are victorious), so those who act win, and rightly win, the noble and good things in life.

Their life is also in itself pleasant. For pleasure is a state of *soul*, and to each man that which he is said to be a lover of is pleasant; e.g., not only is a horse pleasant to the lover of horses, and a spectacle to the lover of sights, but also in the same way just acts are pleasant to the lover of justice and in general virtuous acts to the lover of virtue. Now for most men their pleasures are in conflict with one another because these are not by nature pleasant, but the lovers of what is noble find pleasant the things that are by nature pleasant; and virtuous actions are such, so that these are pleasant for such men as well as in their own nature. Their life, therefore, has no further need of pleasure as a sort of adventitious charm, but has its pleasure in itself. For, besides what we have said, the man who does not rejoice in noble actions is not even good; since no one would call a man just who did not enjoy acting justly, nor any man liberal who did not enjoy liberal actions; and similarly in all other cases. If this is so, virtuous actions must be in themselves pleasant. But they are also *good* and *noble*, and have each of these attributes in the highest degree, since the good man judges well about these attributes; his judgment is such as we have described. Happiness then is the best, noblest, and most pleasant thing in the world, and these attributes are not severed . . . For all these properties belong to the best activities; and these, or one—the best—of these, we identify with happiness.

Yet evidently . . . it needs the external goods as well; for it is impossible, or not easy, to do noble acts without the proper equipment. In many actions we use friends and riches and political power as instruments; and there are some things the lack of which takes the lustre from happiness, as good birth, goodly children, beauty; for the man who is very ugly in appearance or ill-born or solitary and childless is not very likely to be happy, and perhaps a man would be still less likely if he had thoroughly bad children or friends or had lost good children or friends by death.

9   For this reason also the question is asked, whether happiness is to be acquired by learning or by habituation or some other sort of training, or comes in virtue of some divine providence or again by chance. Now if there is *any* gift of the gods to men, it is reasonable that happiness should be god-given, and most surely god-given of all human things inasmuch as it is the best. But this question would perhaps be more appropriate to another inquiry; happiness seems, however, even if it is not god-sent but comes as a result of virtue and some process of learning or training, to be among the most god-like things; for that which is the prize and end of virtue seems to be the best thing in the world, and something god-like and blessed. . . .

The answer to the question we are asking is plain also from the definition of happiness; for it has been said to be a virtuous activity of soul, of a certain kind. Of the remaining goods, some must necessarily pre-exist as conditions of happiness, and others are naturally co-operative and useful as instruments. And this will be found to agree with what we said at the outset; for we stated the end of political science to be the best end, and political science spends most of its pains on making the citizens to be of a certain character, viz. good and capable of noble acts.

It is natural, then, that we call neither ox nor horse nor any other of the animals happy; for none of them is capable of sharing in such activity. For this reason also a boy is not happy; for he is not yet capable of such acts, owing to his age; and boys who are called happy are being congratulated by reason of the hopes we have for them. For there is required, as we said, not only complete virtue but also a complete life, since many changes occur in life, and all manner of chances, and the most prosperous may fall into great misfortunes in old age, as is told of Priam in the Trojan Cycle; and one who has experienced such chances and has ended wretchedly no one calls happy.

Since happiness is an activity of soul in accordance with perfect virtue, we must consider the nature of virtue; for perhaps we shall thus see better the nature of happiness. . . . [C]learly the virtue we must study is human virtue; for the good we were king was human good and the happiness human happiness. By human virtue we mean not that of the body but that of the soul; and happiness also we call an activity of soul. . . .

Of the irrational element one division seems to be widely distributed, and vegetative in its nature, I mean that which causes nutrition and growth; for it is this kind of power of the soul that one must assign to all nurslings and to embryos, and this same power to full-grown creatures; this is more reasonable than to assign some different power to them. Now the excellence of this seems to be common to all species and not specifically human. . . .

There seems to be also another irrational element in the soul—one which in a sense, however, shares in a rational principle. For we praise the rational principle of the continent man and of the incontinent, and the part of their soul that has such a principle, since it urges them aright and towards the best objects; but there is found in them also another element naturally opposed to the rational principle, which fights against and resists that principle. For exactly as paralyzed limbs when we intend to move them to the right turn on the contrary to the left, so is it with the soul; the impulses of incontinent people move in contrary directions. But while in the body we see that which moves astray, in the soul we do not. No doubt, however, we must none the less suppose that in the soul too there is something contrary to the rational principle, resisting and opposing it. In what sense it is distinct from the other elements does not concern us. Now even this seems to have a share in a rational principle . . . at any rate in the continent man it obeys the rational principle—and presumably in the temperate and brave man it is still more obedient; for in him it speaks, on all matters, with the same voice as the rational principle.

Therefore the irrational element also appears to be twofold. For the vegetative element in no way shares in a rational principle, but the appetitive, and in general the desiring element in a sense shares in it, in so far as it listens to and obeys it; this is the sense in which we speak of "taking account" of one's father or one's friends, not that in which we speak of "accounting" for a mathematical property. That the irrational element is in some sense persuaded by a rational principle is indicated also by the giving of advice and by all reproof and exhortation. . . .

Virtue too is distinguished into kinds in accordance with this difference; for we say that some of the virtues are intellectual and others moral, philosophic wisdom and understanding and practical wisdom being intellectual, liberality and temperance moral. For in speaking about a man's character we do not say that he is wise or has understanding but that he is good-tempered or temperate; yet we praise the wise man also with respect to his state of mind; and of states of mind we call those which merit praise virtues.

BOOK II

1   Virtue, then, being of two kinds, intellectual and moral, intellectual virtue in the main owes both its birth and its growth to teaching (for which reason it requires

experience and time), while moral virtue comes about as a result of habit, whence also its name *ethiki* is one that is formed by a slight variation from the word *ethos* (habit). From this it is also plain that none of the moral virtues arises in us by nature; for nothing that exists by nature can form a habit contrary to its nature. . . . Neither by nature, then, nor contrary to nature do the virtues arise in us; rather we are adapted by nature to receive them, and are made perfect by habit.

. . . [T]he virtues we get by first exercising them, as also happens in the case of the arts as well. For the things we have to learn before we can do them, we learn by doing them, e.g., men become builders by building and lyre-players by playing the lyre; so too we become just by doing just acts, temperate by doing temperate acts, brave by doing brave acts.

This is confirmed by what happens in states; for legislators make the citizens good by forming habits in them, and this is the wish of every legislator, and those who do not effect it miss their mark, and it is in this that a good constitution differs from a bad one.

Again, it is from the same causes and by the same means that every virtue is both produced and destroyed, and similarly every art; for it is from playing the lyre that both good and bad lyre-players are produced. And the corresponding statement is true of builders and of all the rest; men will be good or bad builders as a result of building well or badly. For if this were not so, there would have been no need of a teacher, but all men would have been born good or bad at their craft. This, then, is the case with the virtues also; by doing the acts that we do in our transactions with other men we become just or unjust, and by doing the acts that we do in the presence of danger, and being habituated to feel fear or confidence, we become brave or cowardly. The same is true of appetites and feelings of anger; some men become temperate and good-tempered, others self-indulgent and irascible, by behaving in one way or the other in the appropriate circumstances. Thus, in one word, states of character arise out of like activities. This is why the activities we exhibit must be of a certain kind; it is because the states of character correspond to the differences between these. It makes no small difference, then, whether we form habits of one kind or of another from our very youth; it makes a very great difference, or rather *all* the difference.

2   Since, then, the present inquiry does not aim at theoretical knowledge like the others (for we are inquiring not in order to know what virtue is, but in order to become good, since otherwise our inquiry would have been of no use), we must examine the nature of actions, namely how we ought to do them; for these determine also the nature of the states of character that are produced, as we have said. Now, that we must act according to the right rule is a common principle and must be assumed—it will be discussed later, i.e., both what the right rule is, and how 't is related to the other virtues. But this must be agreed upon beforehand, that the hole account of matters of conduct must be given in outline and not precisely. . . .

But though our present account is of this nature we must give what help we First, then, let us consider this, that it is the nature of such things to be ed by defect and excess, as we see in the case of strength and of health (for to gain light on things imperceptible we must use the evidence of sensible things); both excessive and defective exercise destroys the strength, and similarly drink or food which is above or below a certain amount destroys the health, while that which is proportionate both produces and increases and preserves it. So too is it, then, in the case of temperance and courage and the other virtues. For the man who flies from and fears everything and does not stand his ground against anything be-comes a coward, and the man who fears nothing at all but goes to meet every danger becomes rash; and similarly the man who indulges in every pleasure and abstains from none becomes self-indulgent, while the man who shuns every pleasure, as boors do, becomes in a way insensible; temperance and courage, then, are destroyed by excess and defect, and preserved by the mean.

But not only are the sources and causes of their origination and growth the same as those of their destruction, but also the sphere of their actualization will be the same, for this is also true of the things which are more evident to sense, e.g., of strength; it is produced by taking much food and undergoing much exertion, and it is the strong man that will be most able to do these things. So too is it with the virtues; by abstaining from pleasures we become temperate, and it is when we have become so that we are most able to abstain from them; and similarly too in the case of courage; for by being habituated to despise things that are terrible and to stand our ground against them we become brave, and it is when we have become so that we shall be most able to stand our ground against them.

4   The question might be asked, what we mean by saying that we must become just by doing just acts, and temperate by doing temperate acts; for if men do just and temperate acts, they are already just and temperate, exactly as, if they do what is in accordance with the laws of grammar and of music, they are grammarians and musicians.

Again, the case of the arts and that of the virtues are not similar, for the prod-ucts of the arts have their goodness in themselves, so that it is enough that they should have a certain character, but if the acts that are in accordance with the virtues have themselves a certain character it does not follow that they are done justly or temperately. The agent also must be in a certain condition when he does them; in the first place he must have knowledge, secondly he must choose the acts, and choose them for their own sakes, and thirdly his action must proceed from a firm and unchangeable character. These are not reckoned in as conditions of the possession of the arts, except the bare knowledge; but as a condition of the posses-sion of the virtues knowledge has little or no weight, while the other conditions count not for a little but for everything, i.e., the very conditions which result from often doing just and temperate acts.

Actions, then, are called just and temperate when they are such as the just or the temperate man would do; but it is not the man who does these that is just and temperate, but the man who also does them *as* just and temperate men do them. It is well said, then, that it is by doing just acts that the just man is produced, and by doing temperate acts the temperate man; without doing these no one would have even a prospect of becoming good.

But most people do not do these, but take refuge in theory and think they are being philosophers and will become good in this way, behaving somewhat like patients who listen attentively to their doctors, but do none of the things they are ordered to do. As the latter will not be made well in body by such a course of treatment, the former will not be made well in soul by such a course of philosophy.

5   Next we must consider what virtue is. Since things that are found in the soul are of three kinds—passions, faculties, states of character, virtue must be one of these. By passions I mean appetite, anger, fear, confidence, envy, joy, friendly feeling, hatred, longing, emulation, pity, and in general the feelings that are accompanied by pleasure or pain; by faculties the things in virtue of which we are said to be capable of feeling these, e.g., of becoming angry or being pained or feeling pity; by states of character the things in virtue of which we stand well or badly with reference to the passions, e.g., with reference to anger we stand badly if we feel it violently or too weakly, and well if we feel it moderately; and similarly with reference to the other passions.

Now neither the virtues nor the vices are *passions*, because we are not called good or bad on the ground of our passions, but are so called on the ground of our virtues and our vices, and because we are neither praised nor blamed for our passions (for the man who feels fear or anger is not praised, nor is the man who simply feels anger blamed, but the man who feels it in a certain way), but for our virtues and our vices we *are* praised or blamed.

Again, we feel anger and fear without choice, but the virtues are modes of choice or involve choice. Further, in respect of the passions we are said to be moved, but in respect of the virtues and the vices we are said not to be moved but to be disposed in a particular way.

For these reasons also they are not *faculties*; for we are neither called good nor bad, nor praised nor blamed, for the simple capacity of feeling the passions; again, we have the faculties by nature, but we are not made good or bad by nature; we have spoken of this before.

If, then, the virtues are neither passions nor faculties, all that remains is that they should be *states of character*.

Thus we have stated what virtue is in respect of its genus.

6   We must, however, not only describe virtue as a state of character, but also say what sort of state it is. We may remark, then, that every virtue or excellence both brings into good condition the thing of which it is the excellence and makes the work of that thing be done well; e.g., the excellence of the eye makes both the eye and its work good; for it is by the excellence of the eye that we see well. Similarly the excellence of the horse makes a horse both good in itself and good at running nd at carrying its rider and at awaiting the attack of the enemy. Therefore, if this is e in every case, the virtue of man also will be the state of character which makes n good and which makes him do his own work well.

low this is to happen we have stated already, but it will be made plain also by owing consideration of the specific nature of virtue. In everything that is continuous and divisible it is possible to take more, less, or an equal amount, and that either in terms of the thing itself or relatively to us; and the equal is an intermediate between excess and defect. By the intermediate in the object I mean that which is equidistant from each of the extremes, which is one and the same for all men; by the intermediate relatively to us that which is neither too much nor too little—and this is not one, nor the same for all. For instance, if ten is many and two is few, six is the intermediate, taken in terms of the object; for it exceeds and is exceeded by an equal amount; this is intermediate according to arithmetical proportion. But the intermediate relatively to us is not to be taken so; if ten pounds are too much for a particular person to eat and two too little, it does not follow that the trainer will order six pounds; for this also is perhaps too much for the person who is to take it, or too little—too little for Milo, too much for the beginner in athletic exercises. The same is true of running and wrestling. Thus a master of any art avoids excess and defect, but seeks the intermediate and chooses this—the intermediate not in the object but relatively to us.

If it is thus, then, that every art does its work well—by looking to the intermediate and judging its works by this standard (so that we often say of good works of art that it is not possible either to take away or to add anything, implying that excess and defect destroy the goodness of works of art, while the mean preserves it; and good artists, as we say, look to this in their work), and if, further, virtue is more exact and better than any art, as nature also is, then virtue must have the quality of aiming at the intermediate. I mean moral virtue, for it is this that is concerned with passions and actions, and in these there is excess, defect, and the intermediate. For instance, both fear and confidence and appetite and anger and pity and in general pleasure and pain may be felt both too much and too little, and in both cases not well; but to feel them at the right times, with reference to the right objects, towards the right people, with the right motive, and in the right way, is what is both intermediate and best, and this is characteristic of virtue. Similarly with regard to actions also there is excess, defect, and the intermediate. Now virtue is concerned with passions and actions, in which excess is a form of failure, and so is defect, while the intermediate is praised and is a form of success; and being praised and being successful are both characteristics of virtue. Therefore virtue is a kind of mean, since, as we have seen, it aims at what is intermediate.

Again, it is possible to fail in many ways (for evil belongs to the class of the unlimited, as the Pythagoreans conjectured, and good to that of the limited), while to succeed is possible only in one way (for which reason also one is easy and the other difficult—to miss the mark easy, to hit it difficult); for these reasons also, then, excess and defect are characteristic of vice, and the mean of virtue;

For men are good in but one way, but bad in many.

Virtue, then, is a state of character concerned with choice, lying in a mean, i.e., the mean relative to us, this being determined by a rational principle, and by that principle by which the man of practical wisdom would determine it. Now it is a mean between two vices, that which depends on excess and that which depends on defect; and again it is a mean because the vices respectively fall short of or exceed what is right in both passions and actions, while virtue both finds and chooses that which is intermediate. Hence in respect of its substance and the definition which states its essence virtue is a mean, with regard to what is best and right an extreme.

But not every action nor every passion admits of a mean; for some have names that already imply badness, e.g., spite, shamelessness, envy, and in the case of actions adultery, theft, murder, for all of these and suchlike things imply by their names that they are themselves bad, and not the excesses or deficiencies of them. It is not possible, then, ever to be right with regard to them; one must always be wrong. Nor does goodness or badness with regard to such things depend on committing adultery with the right woman, at the right time, and in the right way, but simply to do any of them is to go wrong. It would be equally absurd, then, to expect that in unjust, cowardly, and voluptuous action there should be a mean, an excess, and a deficiency; for at that rate there would be a mean of excess and of deficiency, an excess of excess, and a deficiency of deficiency. But as there is no excess and deficiency of temperance and courage because what is intermediate is in a sense an extreme, so too of the actions we have mentioned there is no mean nor any excess and deficiency, but however they are done they are wrong; for in general there is neither a mean of excess and deficiency, nor excess and deficiency of a mean.

7   We must, however, not only make this general statement, but also apply it to the individual facts. For among statements about conduct those which are general apply more widely, but those which are particular are more genuine, since conduct has to do with individual cases, and our statements must harmonize with the facts in these cases. We may take these cases from our table. With regard to feelings of fear and confidence courage is the mean; of the people who exceed, he who exceeds in fearlessness has no name (many of the states have no name), while the man who exceeds in confidence is rash, and he who exceeds in fear and falls short in confidence is a coward. With regard to pleasures and pains—not all of them, and not so much with regard to the pains—the mean is temperance, the excess self-indulgence. Persons deficient with regard to the pleasures are not often found; hence such persons also have received no name. But let us call them "insensible." . . .

9   That moral virtue is a mean, then, and in what sense it is so, and that it is a mean between two vices, the one involving excess, the other deficiency, and that it is such because its character is to aim at what is intermediate in passions and in actions, has been sufficiently stated. Hence also it is no easy task to be good. For in everything it is no easy task to find the middle, e.g., to find the middle of a circle is not for everyone but for him who knows; so, too, any one can get angry—that is easy—or give or spend money; but to do this to the right person, to the right extent, the right time, with the right motive, and in the right way, *that* is not for every nor is it easy; wherefore goodness is both rare and laudable and noble.

t we must consider the things towards which we ourselves also are easily carry; for some of us tend to one thing, some to another, and this will be recognizable from the pleasure and the pain we feel. We must drag ourselves away to the contrary extreme; for we shall get into the intermediate state by drawing well away from error, as people do in straightening sticks that are bent.

Now in everything the pleasant or pleasure is most to be guarded against; for we do not judge it impartially. We ought, then, to feel towards pleasure as the elders of the people felt towards Helen, and in all circumstances repeat their saying; for if we dismiss pleasure thus we are less likely to go astray. It is by doing this, then (to sum the matter up), that we shall best be able to hit the mean.

But this is no doubt difficult, and especially in individual cases; for it is not easy to determine both how and with whom and on what provocation and how long one should be angry; for we too sometimes praise those who fall short and call them good-tempered, but sometimes we praise those who get angry and call them manly. The man, however, who deviates little from goodness is not blamed, whether he do so in the direction of the more or of the less, but only the man who deviates more widely; for *he* does not fail to be noticed. But up to what point and to what extent a man must deviate before he becomes blameworthy it is not easy to determine by reasoning, any more than anything else that is perceived by the senses; such things depend on particular facts, and the decision rests with perception. So much, then, is plain, that the intermediate state is in all things to be praised, but that we must incline sometimes towards the excess, sometimes towards the deficiency; for so shall we most easily hit the mean and what is right.

BOOK III

1   Since virtue is concerned with passions and actions, and on voluntary passions and actions praise and blame are bestowed, on those that are involuntary pardon, and sometimes also pity, to distinguish the voluntary and the involuntary is presumably necessary for those who are studying the nature of virtue, and useful also for legislators with a view to the assigning both of honours and of punishments.

Those things, then, are thought involuntary, which take place under compulsion or owing to ignorance; and that is compulsory of which the moving principle is outside, being a principle in which nothing is contributed by the person who is acting or is feeling the passion, e.g., if he were to be carried somewhere by a wind, or by men who had him in their power.

But with regard to the things that are done from fear of greater evils or for some noble object (e.g., if a tyrant were to order one to do something base, having one's parents and children in his power, and if one did the action they were to be saved, but otherwise would be put to death), it may be debated whether such actions are involuntary or voluntary. Something of the sort happens also with regard to the throwing of goods overboard in a storm; for in the abstract no one throws goods away voluntarily, but on condition of its securing the safety of himself and his crew any sensible man does so. Such actions, then, are mixed, but are more like voluntary actions; for they are worthy of choice at the time when they are done, and the end of an action is relative to the occasion. Both the terms, then, "voluntary" and "involuntary," must be used with reference to the moment of action. Now the man acts voluntarily; for the principle that moves the instrumental parts of the body in such actions is in him, and the things of which the moving principle is in a man himself are in his power to do or not to do. Such actions, therefore, are voluntary, but in the abstract perhaps involuntary; for no one would choose any such act in itself. . . .

What sort of acts, then, should be called compulsory? We answer that without qualification actions are so when the cause is in the external circumstances and the agent contributes nothing. But the things that in themselves are involuntary, but now and in return for these gains are worthy of choice, and whose moving principle is in the agent, are in themselves involuntary, but now and in return for these gains voluntary. They are more like voluntary acts; for actions are in the class of particulars; and the particular acts here are voluntary. What sort of things are to be chosen, and in return for what, it is not easy to state; for there are many differences in the particular cases.

But if some one were to say that pleasant and noble objects have a compelling power, forcing us from without, all acts would be for him compulsory; for it is for these objects that all men do everything they do. And those who act under compulsion and unwillingly act with pain, but those who do acts for their pleasantness and nobility do them with pleasure; it is absurd to make external circumstances responsible, and not oneself, as being caught by such attractions, and to make oneself responsible for noble acts but the pleasant objects responsible for base acts. The compulsory, then, seems to be that whose moving principle is outside, the person compelled contributing nothing.

Everything that is done by reason of ignorance is *not* voluntary; it is only what produces pain and repentance that is *in*voluntary. For the man who has done something owing to ignorance, and feels not the least vexation at his action, has not acted voluntarily, since he did not know what he was doing, nor yet involuntarily, since he is not pained. Of people, then, who act by reason of ignorance he who repents is thought an involuntary agent, and the man who does not repent may, since he is different, be called a not voluntary agent; for, since he differs from the other, it is better that he should have a name of his own.

Acting by reason of ignorance seems also to be different from acting *in* ignorance; for the man who is drunk or in a rage is thought to act as a result not of ignorance but of one of the causes mentioned, yet not knowingly but in ignorance.

Now every wicked man is ignorant of what he ought to do and what he ought to abstain from, and it is by reason of error of this kind that men become unjust and in general bad; but the term "involuntary" tends to be used not if a man is ignorant of what is to his advantage—for it is not mistaken purpose that causes involuntary ction (it leads rather to wickedness), nor ignorance of the universal (for *that* men blamed), but ignorance of particulars, i.e., of the circumstances of the action and objects with which it is concerned. For it is on these that both pity and pardon d, since the person who is ignorant of any of these acts involuntarily.

rhaps it is just as well, therefore, to determine their nature and number. A y be ignorant, then, of who he is, what he is doing, what or whom he is acting on, and sometimes also what (e.g, what instrument) he is doing it with, and to what end (e.g., he may think his act will conduce to some one's safety), and how he is doing it (e.g., whether gently or violently). Now of all of these no one could be ignorant unless he were mad, and evidently also he could not be ignorant of the agent; for how could he not know himself? But of what he is doing a man might be ignorant. . . . The ignorance may relate, then, to any of these things, i.e., of the circumstances of the action, and the man who was ignorant of any of these is thought to have acted involuntarily, and especially if he was ignorant on the most important points; and these are thought to be the circumstances of the action and its end. Further, the doing of an act that is called involuntary in virtue of ignorance of this sort must be painful and involve repentance.

Since that which is done under compulsion or by reason of ignorance is involuntary, the voluntary would seem to be that of which the moving principle is in the agent himself, he being aware of the particular circumstances of the action. Presumably acts done by reason of anger or appetite are not rightly called involuntary. For in the first place, on that showing none of the other animals will act voluntarily, nor will children; and secondly, is it meant that we do not do voluntarily *any* of the acts that are due to appetite or anger, or that we do the noble acts voluntarily and the base acts involuntarily? Is not this absurd, when one and the same thing is the cause? But it would surely be odd to describe as involuntary the things one ought to desire; and we ought both to be angry at certain things and to have an appetite for certain things, e.g., for health and for learning. Also what is involuntary is thought to be painful, but what is in accordance with appetite is thought to be pleasant. Again, what is the difference in respect of involuntariness between errors committed upon calculation and those committed in anger? Both are to be avoided, but the irrational passions are thought not less human than reason is, and therefore also the actions which proceed from anger or appetite are the man's actions. It would be odd, then, to treat them as involuntary.

2   Both the voluntary and the involuntary having been delimited, we must next discuss choice; for it is thought to be most closely bound up with virtue and to discriminate characters better than actions do.

Choice, then, seems to be voluntary, but not the same thing as the voluntary; the latter extends more widely. For both children and the lower animals share in voluntary action, but not in choice, and acts done on the spur of the moment we describe as voluntary, but not as chosen.

What, then, or what kind of thing is [choice]. . . ? It seems to be voluntary, but not all that is voluntary [is] an object of choice. Is it, then, what has been decided on by previous deliberation? At any rate choice involves a rational principle and thought. Even the name seems to suggest that it is what is chosen before other things.

3   Do we deliberate about everything, and is everything a possible subject of deliberation, or is deliberation impossible about some things? We ought presumably to call not what a fool or a madman would deliberate about, but what a sensible man

ould deliberate about, a subject of deliberation. Now about eternal things no one deliberates, e.g., about the material universe or the incommensurability of the diagonal and the side of a square. But no more do we deliberate about the things that involve movement but always happen in the same way, whether of necessity or by nature or from any other cause, e.g., the solstices and the risings of the stars; nor about things that happen now in one way, now in another, e.g., droughts and rains: nor about chance events, like the finding of treasure. But we do not deliberate even about all human affairs; for instance, no Spartan deliberates about the best constitution for the Scythians. For none of these things can be brought about by our own efforts.

Now every class of men deliberates about the things that can be done by their own efforts. And in the case of exact and self-contained sciences there is no deliberation, e.g., about the letters of the alphabet (for we have no doubt how they should be written); but the things that are brought about by our own efforts, but not always in the same way, are the things about which we deliberate, e.g., questions of medical treatment or of money-making. And we do so more in the case of the art of navigation than in that of gymnastics, inasmuch as it has been less exactly worked out, and again about other things in the same ratio, and more also in the case of the arts than in that of the sciences; for we have more doubt about the former. Deliberation is concerned with things that happen in a certain way for the most part, but in which the event is obscure, and with things in which it is indeterminate. We call in others to aid us in deliberation on important questions, distrusting ourselves as not being equal to deciding.

We deliberate not about ends but about means. For a doctor does not deliberate whether he shall heal, nor an orator whether he shall persuade, nor a statesman whether he shall produce law and order, nor does any one else deliberate about his end. They assume the end and consider how and by what means it is to be attained; and if it seems to be produced by several means they consider by which it is most easily and best produced, while if it is achieved by one only they consider how it will be achieved by this and by what means *this* will be achieved, till they come to the first cause, which in the order of discovery is last. . . . And if we come on an impossibility, we give up the search, e.g., if we need money and this cannot be got; but if a thing appears possible we try to do it. By "possible" things I mean things that might be brought about by our own efforts; and these in a sense include things that can be brought about by the efforts of our friends, since the moving principle is in ourselves. The subject of investigation is sometimes the instruments, sometimes the use of them; and similarly in the other cases—sometimes the means, sometimes the node of using it or the means of bringing it about. It seems, then, as has been said, at man is a moving principle of actions; now deliberation is about the things to be e by the agent himself, and actions are for the sake of things other than them- s. For the end cannot be a subject of deliberation, but only the means; nor in- an the particular facts be a subject of it, as whether this is bread or has been it should: for these are matters of perception. If we are to be always deliber- shall have to go on to infinity.

me thing is deliberated upon and is chosen, except that the object of eady determinate, since it is that which has been decided upon as a result of deliberation that is the object of choice. For every one ceases to inquire how he is to act when he has brought the moving principle back to himself and to the ruling part of himself; for this is what chooses. . . . The object of choice being one of the things in our own power which is desired after deliberation, choice will be deliberate desire of things in our own power, for when we have decided as a result of deliberation, we desire in accordance with our deliberation.

We may take it, then, that we have described choice in outline, and stated the nature of its objects and the fact that it is concerned with means.

5   The end, then, being what we wish for, the means what we deliberate about and choose, actions concerning means must be according to choice and voluntary. Now the exercise of the virtues is concerned with means. Therefore virtue also is in our own power, and so too vice. For where it is in our power to act it is also in our power not to act, and *vice versa*; so that, if to act, where this is noble, is in our power, not to act, which will be base, will also be in our power, and if not to act, where this is noble, is in our power, to act, which will be base, will also be in our power. Now if it is in our power to do noble or base acts, and likewise in our power not to do them, and this was what being good or bad meant, then it is in our power to be virtuous or vicious.

The saying that "no one is voluntarily wicked nor involuntarily happy" seems to be partly false and partly true; for no one is involuntarily happy, but wickedness is voluntary. . . .

Witness seems to be borne to this both by individuals in their private capacity and by legislators themselves; for these punish and take vengeance on those who do wicked acts (unless they have acted under compulsion or as a result of ignorance for which they are not themselves responsible), while they honour those who do noble acts, as though they meant to encourage the latter and deter the former. But no one is encouraged to do the things that are neither in our power nor voluntary; it is assumed that there is no gain in being persuaded not to be hot or in pain or hungry or the like, since we shall experience these feelings none the less. Indeed, we punish a man for his very ignorance, if he is thought responsible for the ignorance as when penalties are doubled in the case of drunkenness; for the moving principle is in the man himself, since he had the power of not getting drunk and his getting drunk was the cause of his ignorance. And we punish those who are ignorant of anything in the laws that they ought to know and that is not difficult, and so too in the case of anything else that they are thought to be ignorant of through carelessness; we assume that it is in their power not to be ignorant, since they have the power of taking care.

But perhaps a man is the kind of man not to take care. Still they are themselves by their slack lives responsible for becoming men of that kind, and men make themselves responsible for being unjust or self-indulgent, in the one case by cheating and in the other by spending their time in drinking bouts and the like; for it is activities exercised on particular objects that make the corresponding character. . . .

But not only are the vices of the soul voluntary, but those of the body also for some men, whom we accordingly blame; while no one blames those who are ugly by nature, we blame those who are so owing to want of exercise and care. So it is, too, with respect to weakness and infirmity; no one would reproach a man blind from birth or by disease or from a blow, but rather pity him, while every one would blame a man who was blind from drunkenness or some other form of self-indulgence. Of vices of the body, then, those in our own power are blamed, those not in our power are not. And if this be so, in the other cases also the vices that are blamed must be in our own power. . . .

. . . If, then, as is asserted, the virtues are voluntary (for we are ourselves somehow partly responsible for our states of character, and it is by being persons of a certain kind that we assume the end to be so and so), the vices also will be voluntary; for the same is true of them.

With regard to the virtues in *general* we have stated their genus in outline, viz., that they are means and that they are states of character and that they tend, and by their own nature, to the doing of the acts by which they are produced, and that they are in our power and voluntary, and act as the right rule prescribes. But actions and states of character are not voluntary in the same way; for we are masters of our actions from the beginning right to the end, if we know the particular facts, but though we control the beginning of our states of character the gradual progress is not obvious, any more than it is in illnesses; because it was in our power, however, to act in this way or not in this way, therefore the states are voluntary. . . .

BOOK V

1   With regard to justice and injustice we must consider (1) what kind of actions they are concerned with, (2) what sort of mean justice, is, and (3) between what extremes the just act is intermediate. Our investigation shall follow the same course as the preceding discussions.

We see that all men mean by justice that kind of state of character which makes people disposed to do what is just and makes them act justly and wish for what is just; and similarly by injustice that state which makes them act unjustly and wish for what is unjust. . . .

Now "justice" and "injustice" seem to be ambiguous. . . . Let us take as a starting-point, then, the various meanings of "an unjust man." Both the lawless man and the grasping and unfair man are thought to be unjust, so that evidently both the law-abiding and the fair man will be just. The just, then, is the lawful and the fair, the unjust the unlawful and the unfair. . . .

Since the lawless man was seen to be unjust and the law-abiding man just, evidently all lawful acts are in a sense just acts; for the acts laid down by the legislative art are lawful, and each of these, we say, is just. Now the laws in their enactments on all subjects aim at the common advantage either of all or of the best or of those who hold power, or something of the sort; so that in one sense we call those acts just that tend to produce and preserve happiness and its components for the political society. And the law bids us do both the acts of a brave man (e.g., not to desert our post nor take to flight nor throw away our arms), and those of a temperate man (e.g., not to commit adultery nor to gratify one's lust), and those of a good-tempered man (e.g., not to strike another nor to speak evil), and similarly with regard to the other virtues and forms of wickedness, commanding some acts and forbidding others; and the rightly-framed law does this rightly, and the hastily conceived one less well.

This form of justice, then, is complete virtue, but not absolutely, but in relation to our neighbour. And therefore justice is often thought to be the greatest of virtues. . . . And it is complete virtue in its fullest sense, because it is the actual exercise of complete virtue. It is complete because he who possesses it can exercise his virtue not only in himself but towards his neighbour also; for many men can exercise virtue in their own affairs, but not in their relations to their neighbour. . . . [J]ustice, alone of the virtues, is though to be "another's good," because it is related to our neighbour, for it does what is advantageous to another, either a ruler or a copartner. Now the worst man is he who exercises his wickedness both towards himself and towards his friends, and the best man is not he who exercises his virtue towards himself but he who exercises it towards another; for this is a difficult task. Justice in this sense, then, is not part of virtue but virtue entire, nor is the contrary injustice a part of vice but vice entire. What the difference is between virtue and justice in this sense is plain from what we have said; they are the same but their essence is not the same; what, as a relation to one's neighbour, is justice is, as a certain kind of state without qualification, virtue.

2   But at all events what we are investigating is the justice which is a *part* of virtue; for there is a justice of this kind, as we maintain. Similarly it is with injustice in the particular sense that we are concerned. . . .

It is clear, then, that there is more than one kind of justice, and that there is one which is distinct from virtue entire; we must try to grasp its genus and differentia.

The unjust has been divided into the unlawful and the unfair, and the just into the lawful and the fair. To the unlawful answers the aforementioned sense of injustice. But since the unfair and the unlawful are not the same, but are different as a part is from its whole (for all that is unfair is unlawful, but not all that is unlawful is unfair), the unjust and injustice in the sense of the unfair are not the same as but different from the former kind, as part from whole; for injustice in this sense is a part of injustice in the wide sense, and similarly justice in the one sense of justice in the other. Therefore we must speak also about particular justice and particular injustice, and similarly about the just and the unjust. The justice, then, which answers to the whole of virtue, and the corresponding injustice, one being the exercise of virtue as a whole, and the other that of vice as a whole, towards one's neighbour, we may leave on one side. And how the meanings of "just" and "unjust" which answer to these are to be distinguished is evident; for practically the majority of the acts commanded by the law are those which are prescribed from the point of view of virtue taken as a whole; for the law bids us practice every virtue and forbids us to practice any vice. And the things that tend to produce virtue taken as a whole are those of the acts prescribed by the law which have been prescribed with a view to education for the common good. . . .

Of particular justice and that which is just in the corresponding sense, (A) one kind is that which is manifested in distributions of honour or money or the other things that fall to be divided among those who have a share in the constitution (for in these it is possible for one man to have a share either unequal or equal to that of another), and (B) one is that which plays a rectifying part in transactions between man and man. Of this there are two divisions; of transactions (1) some are voluntary and (2) others involuntary—voluntary such transactions as sale, purchase, loan for consumption, pledging, loan for use, depositing, letting (they are called voluntary because the origin of these transactions is voluntary), while of the involuntary (a) some are clandestine, such as theft, adultery, poisoning, procuring, enticement of slaves, assassination, false witness, and (b) others are violent, such as assault, imprisonment, murder, robbery with violence, mutilation, abuse, insult.

3   . . . Now equality implies at least two things. The just, then, must be both intermediate and equal and relative (i.e., for certain persons). And *qua* intermediate it must be between certain things (which are respectively greater and less); *qua* equal, it involves two things; *qua* just, it is for certain people. The just, therefore, involves at least four terms; for the persons for whom it is in fact just are two, and the things in which it is manifested, the objects distributed, are two. And the same equality will exist between the persons and between the things concerned; for as the latter— the things concerned—are related, so are the former, if they are not equal, they will not have what is equal, but this is the origin of quarrels and complaints—when either equals have and are awarded unequal shares, or unequals equal shares. . . .

The just, then, is a species of the proportionate (proportion being not a property only of the kind of number which consists of abstract units, but of number in general). For proportion is equality of ratios, and involves four terms at least. . . .

This, then, is one species of the just.

4   The remaining one is the rectificatory, which arises in connexion with transactions both voluntary and involuntary. This form of the just has a different specific character from the former. . . . For it makes no difference whether a good man has defrauded a bad man or a bad man a good one, nor whether it is a good or a bad man that has committed adultery; the law looks only to the distinctive character of the injury, and treats the parties as equal, if one is in the wrong and the other is being wronged, and if one inflicted injury and the other has received it. Therefore, this kind of injustice being an inequality, the judge tries to equalize . . . things by means of the penalty, taking away from the gain of the assailant. For the term "gain" is applied generally to such cases, even if it be not a term appropriate to certain cases, e.g., to the person who inflicts a wound—and "loss" to the sufferer, at all events when the suffering has been estimated, the one is called loss and the other gain. . . . [C]orrective justice will be the intermediate between loss and gain. This is why, when people dispute, they take refuge in the judge; and to go to the judge is to go to justice; for the nature of the judge is to be a sort of animate justice; and they seek the judge as an intermediate, and in some states they call judges media-

tors, on the assumption that if they get what is intermediate they will get what is just. The just, then, is an intermediate, since the judge is so. Now the judge restores equality. . . .

6   . . . [Political justice] if found among men who share their life with a view to self-sufficiency, men who are free and either proportionately or arithmetically equal, so that between those who do not fulfill this condition there is no political justice but justice in a special sense and by analogy. For justice exists only between men whose mutual relations are governed by law; and law exists for men between whom there is injustice; for legal justice is the discrimination of the just and the unjust. And between men between whom there is injustice there is also unjust action (though there is not injustice between all between whom there is unjust action), and this is assigning too much to oneself of things good in themselves and too little of things evil in themselves. This is why we do not allow a *man* to rule, but *rational principle*, because a man behaves thus in his own interests and becomes a tyrant. The magistrate on the other hand is the guardian of justice, and, if of justice, then of equality also. And since he is assumed to have no more than his share, if he is just (for he does not assign to himself more of what is good in itself, unless such a share is proportional to his merits—so that it is for others that he labours, and it is for this reason that men, as we stated previously, say that justice is "another good"), therefore a reward must be given him, and this is honour and privilege; but those for whom such things are not enough become tyrants. . . .

7   Of political justice part is natural, part legal—natural, that which everywhere has the same force and does not exist by people's thinking this or that; legal, that which is originally indifferent, but when it has been laid down is not indifferent. . . .

Of things just and lawful each is related as the universal to its particulars; for the things that are done are many, but of *them* each is one, since it is universal.

There is a difference between the act of injustice and what is unjust, and between the act of justice and what is just; for a thing is unjust by nature or by enactment; and this very thing, when it has been done, is an act of injustice, but before it is done is not yet that but is unjust. So, too, with an act of justice. . . .

BOOK VI

2   What affirmation and negation are in thinking, pursuit and avoidance are in desire; so that since moral virtue is a state of character concerned with choice, and choice is deliberate desire, therefore both the reasoning must be true and the desire right, if the choice is to be good, and the latter must pursue just what the former asserts. . . .

The origin of action—its efficient, not its final cause—is choice, and that of choice is desire and reasoning with a view to an end. This is why choice cannot exist either without reason and intellect or without a moral state; for good action and its opposite cannot exist without a combination of intellect and character. Intellect itself, however, moves nothing, but only the intellect which aims at an end and is practical; for this rules the productive intellect as well, since every one who makes makes for an end, and that which is made is not an end in the unqualified sense (but only an end in a particular relation, and the end of a particular operation)—only that which is *done* is that; for good action is an end, and desire aims at this. Hence choice is either desiderative reason or ratiocinative desire, and such an origin of action is a man. (It is to be noted that nothing that is past is an object of choice, e.g., no one chooses to have sacked Troy; for no one *deliberates* about the past, but about what is future and capable of being otherwise. . . .)

5   Regarding *practical wisdom* we shall get at the truth by considering who are the persons we credit with it. Now it is thought to be the mark of a man of practical wisdom to be able to deliberate well about what is good and expedient for himself, not in some particular respect, e.g., about what sorts of thing conduce to health or to strength, but about what sorts of thing conduce to the good life in general. This is shown by the fact that we credit men with practical wisdom in some particular respect when they have calculated well with a view to some good end which is one of those that are not the object of any art. It follows that in the general sense also the man who is capable of deliberating has practical wisdom. Now no one deliberates about things that are invariable, nor about things that it is impossible for him to do. Therefore, since scientific knowledge involves demonstration, but there is no demonstration of things whose first principles are variable (for all such things might actually be otherwise), and since it is impossible to deliberate about things that are necessity, practical wisdom cannot be scientific knowledge nor art; not science because that which can be done is capable of being otherwise, not art because action and making are different kinds of thing. The remaining alternative, then, is that it is a true and reasoned state of capacity to act with regard to the things that are good or bad for man. For while making has an end other than itself, action cannot; for good action itself is its end. It is for this reason that we think Pericles and men like him have practical wisdom, viz., because they can see what is good for themselves and what is good for men in general; we consider that those can do this who are good at managing households or states. . . .

Practical wisdom, then, must be a reasoned and true state of capacity to act with regard to human goods. But further, while there is such a thing as excellence in art, there is no such thing as excellence in practical wisdom; and in art he who errs willingly is preferable, but in practical wisdom, as in the virtues, he is the reverse. Plainly, then, practical wisdom is a virtue and not an art. There being two parts of the soul that can follow a course of reasoning, it must be the virtue of one of the two, i.e., of that part which forms opinions; for opinion is about the variable and so is practical wisdom. But yet it is not only a reasoned state; this is shown by the fact that a state of that sort may be forgotten but practical wisdom cannot.

7   . . . Practical wisdom on the other hand is concerned with things human and things about which it is possible to deliberate; for we say this is above all the work of

the man of practical wisdom, to deliberate well, but no one deliberates about things invariable, nor about things which have not an end, and that a good that can be brought about by action. The man who is without qualification good at deliberating is the man who is capable of aiming in accordance with calculation at the best for man of things attainable by action. Nor is practical wisdom concerned with universals only—it must also recognize the particulars; for it is practical, and practice is concerned with particulars. This is why some who do not know, and especially those who have experience, are more practical than others who know; for if a man knew that light meats are digestible and wholesome, but did not know which sorts of meat are light, he would not produce health, but the man who knows that chicken is wholesome is more likely to produce health.

Now practical wisdom is concerned with action; therefore one should have both forms of it, or the latter in preference to the former. But of practical as of philosophic wisdom there must be a controlling kind.

8 . . . Further, error in deliberation may be either about the universal or about the particular; we may fail to know either that all water that weighs heavy is bad, or that this particular water weighs heavy. . . .

9 . . . But excellence in deliberation is a certain correctness of deliberation; hence we must first inquire what deliberation is and what it is about. And, there being more than one kind of correctness, plainly excellence in deliberation is not any and every kind; for (1) the incontinent man and the bad man, if he is clever, will reach as a result of his calculation what he sets before himself, so that he will have deliberated correctly, but he will have got for himself a great evil. Now to have deliberated well is thought to be a good thing; for it is this kind of correctness of deliberation that is excellence in deliberation, viz., that which tends to attain what is good. But (2) it is possible to attain even good by a false syllogism, and to attain what one ought to do but not by the right means, the middle term being false; so that this too is not yet excellence in deliberation—this state in virtue of which one attains what one ought but not by the right means. Again (3) it is possible to attain it by long deliberation while another man attains it quickly. Therefore in the former case we have not yet got excellence in deliberation, which is rightness with regard to the expedient—rightness in respect both of the end, the manner, and the time. (4) Further it is possible to have deliberated well either in the unqualified sense or with reference to a particular end. Excellence in deliberation in the unqualified sense, then, is that which succeeds with reference to what is the end in the unqualified sense, and excellence in deliberation in a particular sense is that which succeeds relatively to a particular end. If, then, it is characteristic of men of practical wisdom to have deliberated well, excellence in deliberation will be correctness with regard to what conduces to the end of which practical wisdom is the true apprehension.

11 What is called judgment, in virtue of which men are said to "be sympathetic judges" and to "have judgment," is the right discrimination of the equitable. This is

shown by the fact that we say the equitable man is above all others a man of sympathetic judgment, and identify equity with sympathetic judgment about certain facts. And sympathetic judgment is judgment which discriminates what is equitable and does so correctly; and correct judgment is that which judges what is true.

Now all the states we have considered converge, as might be expected, to the same point; for when we speak of judgment and understanding and practical wisdom and intuitive reason we credit the same people with possessing judgment and having reached years of reason and with having practical wisdom and understanding. For all these faculties deal with ultimates, i.e., with particulars; and being a man of understanding and of good or sympathetic judgment consists in being able to judge about the things with which practical wisdom is concerned; for the equities are common to all good men in relation to other men. Now all things which have to be done are included among particulars or ultimates; for not only must the man of practical wisdom know particular facts, but understanding and judgment are also concerned with things to be done, and these are ultimates. And intuitive reason is concerned with the ultimates in both directions; for both the first terms and the last are objects of intuitive reason and not of argument, and the intuitive reason which is presupposed by demonstrations grasps the unchangeable and first terms, while the intuitive reason involved in practical reasonings grasps the last and variable fact, i.e., the minor premise. For these variable facts are the starting-points for the apprehension of the end, since the universals are reached from the particulars; of these therefore we must have perception, and this perception is intuitive reason. . . .

BOOK X

7   If happiness is activity in accordance with virtue, it is reasonable that it should be in accordance with the highest virtue; and this will be that of the best thing in us. Whether it be reason or something else that is this element which is thought to be our natural ruler and guide and to take thought of things noble and divine, whether it be itself also divine or only the most divine element in us, the activity of this in accordance with its proper virtue will be perfect happiness. That this activity is contemplative we have already said.

Now this would seem to be in agreement both with what we said before and with the truth. For, firstly, this activity is the best (since not only is reason the best thing in us, but the objects of reason are the best of knowable objects); and, secondly, it is the most continuous, since we can contemplate truth more continuously than we can *do* anything. And we think happiness has pleasure mingled with it, but the activity of philosophic wisdom is admittedly the pleasantest of virtuous activities; at all events the pursuit of it is thought to offer pleasures marvelous for their purity and their enduringness, and it is to be expected that those who know will pass their time more pleasantly than those who inquire. And the self-sufficiency that is spoken of must belong most to the contemplative activity. For while a philosopher, as well as a just man or one possessing any other virtue, needs the necessaries of life, when they are sufficiently equipped with things of that sort the just man needs people towards whom and with whom he shall act justly, and the temperate man, the brave man, and each of the others is in the same case, but the philosopher, even when by himself, can contemplate truth, and the better the wiser he is; he can perhaps do so better if he has fellow-workers, but still he is the most self-sufficient. And this activity alone would seem to be loved for its own sake; for nothing arises from it apart from the contemplating, while from practical activities we gain more or less a part from the action. . . . [B]ut the activity of reason, which is contemplative, seems both to be superior in serious worth and to aim at no end beyond itself, and to have its pleasure proper to itself (and this augments the activity), and the self-sufficiency, leisureliness, unweariedness (so far as this is possible for man), and all the other attributes ascribed to the supremely happy man are evidently those connected with this activity, it follows that this will be the complete happiness of man, if it be allowed a complete term of life (for none of the attributes of happiness is *in*complete).

But such a life would be too high for man; for it is not in so far as he is man that he will live so, but in so far as something divine is present in him; and by so much as this is superior to our composite nature is its activity superior to that which is the exercise of the other kind of virtue. If reason is divine, then, in comparison with man, the life according to it is divine in comparison with human life. But we must not follow those who advise us, being men, to think of human things, and, being mortal, of mortal things, but must, so far as we can, make ourselves immortal, and strain every nerve to live in accordance with the best thing in us; . . . for man, therefore, the life according to reason is best and pleasantest, since reason more than anything else *is* man. This life therefore is also the happiest.

8   But in a secondary degree the life in accordance with the other kind of virtue is happy; for the activities in accordance with this befit our human estate. Just and brave acts, and other virtuous acts, we do in relation to each other, observing our respective duties with regard to contracts and services and all manner of actions and with regard to passions; and all of these seem to be typically human. Some of them seem even to arise from the body, and virtue of character to be in many ways bound up with the passions. Practical wisdom, too, is linked to virtue of character, and this to practical wisdom, since the principles of practical wisdom are in accordance with the moral virtues and rightness in morals is in accordance with practical wisdom. Being connected with the passions also, the moral virtues must belong to our composite nature; and the virtues of our composite nature are human; so, therefore, are the life and the happiness which correspond to these. The excellence of the reason is a thing apart. . . .

But that perfect happiness is a contemplative activity will appear from the following consideration as well. We assume the gods to be above all other beings blessed and happy; but what sort of actions must we assign to them? Acts of justice? Will not the gods seem absurd if they make contracts and return deposits, and so on? Acts of a brave man, then, confronting dangers and running risks because it is noble to do so? Or liberal acts? To whom will they give? It will be strange if they are really to have money or anything of the kind. And what would their temperate acts be? Is not such praise tasteless, since they have no bad appetites? If we were to run through them all, the circumstances of action would be found trivial and unworthy of gods. Still, every one supposes that they *live* and therefore that they are active; we cannot suppose them to sleep like Endymion. Now if you take away from a living being action, and still more production, what is left but contemplation? Therefore the activity of God, which surpasses all others in blessedness, must be contemplative; and of human activities, therefore, that which is most akin to this must be most of the nature of happiness.

This is indicated, too, by the fact that the other animals have no share in happiness, being completely deprived of such activity. For while the whole life of the gods is blessed, and that of men too in so far as some likeness of such activity belongs to them, none of the other animals is happy, since they in no way share in contemplation. Happiness extends, then, just so far as contemplation does, and those to whom contemplation more fully belongs are more truly happy, not as a mere concomitant but in virtue of the contemplation; for this is in itself precious. Happiness, therefore, must be some form of contemplation.

. . . Now he who exercises his reason and cultivates it seems to be both in the best state of mind and most dear to the gods. For if the gods have any care for human affairs, as they are thought to have, it would be reasonable both that they should delight in that which was best and most akin to them (i.e., reason) and that they should reward whose who love and honour this most, as caring for the things that are dear to them and acting both rightly and nobly. And that all these attributes belong most of all to the philosopher is manifest. He, therefore, is the dearest to the gods. And he who is that will presumably be also the happiest; so that in this way too the philosopher will more than any other be happy.

9   . . . And surely he who wants to make men, whether many or few, better by his care must try to become capable of legislating, if it is through laws that we can become good. For to get any one whatever—any one who is put before us—into the right condition is not for the first chance comer, if any one can do it, it is the man who knows, just as in medicine and all other matters which give scope for care and prudence.

SUGGESTIONS FOR DISCUSSION

1. Plato develops a "natural" as opposed to a "conventional" conception of moral value. What implications might this distinction have for deciding what is right to do in the case of social issues such as those discussed in Part III?

2. What views about justice does Plato criticize, and what views does he affirm? Would a Platonist endorse any of the contemporary views on distributive justice discussed in Chapter 5 (Rawls, Nozick, Smart)?

3. What are the kinds of justice Aristotle distinguishes? Are these distinctions pertinent to our contemporary conceptions of justice?

4. How, on Aristotle's view, are we to decide what it is virtuous to do when confronted by social problems of the sort discussed in Part III? Is this how we should make moral decisions?

FOR FURTHER READING

PLATO

Annas, J. *An Introduction to Plato's Republic.* Oxford: Oxford University Press, 1981.

Brumbaugh. R. *The Philosophers of Greece.* Albany: SUNY Press, 1981.

Cross, R. C., and Woozley, A. D. *Plato's Republic: A Philosophical Commentary.* London: Macmillan, 1964.

Gadamer, H-G. *Dialogue and Dialectic: Eight Hermeneutical Studies on Plato.* New Haven: Yale University Press, 1980.

Irwin, T. H. *Plato's Moral Theory: The Early and Middle Dialogues.* Oxford: Oxford University Press, 1977.

Nettleship, R. L. *Lectures on the Republic of Plato.* London: Macmillan, 1968.

Plato. *The Dialogues of Plato.* 4th ed. Trans. Benjamin Jowett. Oxford: Oxford University Press, 1892.

Vlastos, G. *Socrates: Ironist and Moral Philosopher.* Ithaca: Cornell University Press, 1991.

Vlastos, G., ed. *Plato I and II.* New York: Doubleday, 1971.

White, N. *A Companion to Plato's Republic.* Indianapolis: Hackett Publishing Company, 1979.

ARISTOTLE

Ackrill, J. L. *Aristotle's Ethics.* New York: Humanities Press, 1973.

Aristotle. *Politics.*

Broadie, S. *Ethics with Aristotle.* New York: Oxford University Press, 1991.

Guthrie, W.K.C. *History of Greek Philosophy.* Vol. III, (The Sophists and Socrates); Vols. IV and V (Plato); Vol. VI (Aristotle). Oxford: Clarendon Press, 1969.

Hardie, W.F.R. *Aristotle's Ethical Theory.* Oxford: Oxford University Press, 1981.

Irwin, T. H. *Aristotle's First Principles.* Oxford: Oxford University Press, 1990.

Kenny, A. *Aristotle's Theory of the Will.* New Haven: Yale University Press, 1979.

Lear, J. *Aristotle: The Desire to Understand.* Cambridge: Cambrige University Press, 1988.

Lloyd, G.E.R. *Aristotle.* London: Cambridge University Press, 1968.

Nussbaum, M. C. *The Fragility of Goodness: Luck and Ethics in Greek Tragedy and Philosophy.* Cambridge: Cambridge University Press, 1986.

Randall, J. A. *Aristotle.* New York: Random House, 1960.

Rorty, A., ed. *Essays on Aristotle's Ethics.* Berkeley: University of California Press, 1980.

Ross, W. D. *Aristotle.* Oxford: Oxford University Press, 1960.

Smith, J. A., and Ross, W. D., eds. *The Works of Aristotle.* Oxford, 1910–52.

Sorabji, R. *Necessity, Cause and Blame.* Ithaca: Cornell University Press, 1980.

CHAPTER TWO

HOBBES AND HUME

■ THOMAS HOBBES (1588–1679): THE STATE OF NATURE AND THE SOCIAL CONTRACT

Thomas Hobbes focused his philosophical attention upon an analysis of political power. He was particularly concerned, given the turmoil in seventeenth century England, to justify political arrangements in which citizens would be guaranteed security and peaceful coexistence. Hobbes's theory of power was deeply influenced by both the deductive method of Euclidean geometry and the new heliocentric (or "sun-centered") world view of contemporary scientists, especially that of Galileo (1564–1642). Hobbes set out to develop a deductive science of politics laid upon the foundation of fundamental first principles.

Hobbes's Premises   Hobbes assumed Galileo's antitraditional view that the primary state of all matter is motion, not rest. The principle of *human* self-motion was taken to be desire, and human beings were characterized in terms of two basic principles of voluntary action: appetites and aversions. Appetites were defined as attractions to motion or to what enables motion; and aversions, as repulsions from rest or from what leads to rest. Hobbes considered "good" to be any object of appetite, and "evil" as any object of aversion. Death is the worst of all evils because it is the end of all motion. It follows that the first principle of Hobbes's political theory is that all people fear death: the most basic desire of every person is to live a long life.

Hobbes admitted that there are particular differences, both mental and physical, between individuals. Nevertheless, he argued that human differences are not so great that weaker people could not overcome their natural disadvantages—by cunning, by complicity with others, or by taking up weapons. Further, most persons consider themselves more capable in some respects than everyone else. Hobbes inferred from this that although there are ("material") inequalities, persons can be generally assumed to be ("formally") equal. Hobbes thought that this equality is the foundation for the equality of *hope* among all individuals to obtain the objects of their wants. No matter their diversity, if they are rationally self-interested, the fact that people have these wants entails that they hope to satisfy their own desires. Given the underlying assumption that human desires as a whole are limitless, it follows that resources will be scarce; at some point there will be insufficient goods to satisfy demand for them. Hobbes concluded that the inevitable outcome is competition for scarce resources. With competition—at least in the absence of rules that are agreed upon and enforced—mistrust of others must arise.

Hobbes's State of Nature   This condition of general mistrust Hobbes called "warre." "Warre" would occur whenever there is no common power sufficiently strong to instill the fear of punishment and to maintain order. The state of "warre," elsewhere termed by Hobbes the *state of nature*, is not simply the actual battle of each individual against all the others. In the absence of laws and their adequate enforcement, it is sufficient that the will of some to attack and fight with others be publicly known or assumed. The hypothetical state of nature, then, is one of paranoia ("worry"). In this state, each has a right to everything, including the right to self-protection by whatever means deemed fit, physical strength and mental deception are the fundamental virtues, and the only property would be what one could keep by force or fraud. There would be no products of cooperation: no science, culture, or industry. Life, as Hobbes concluded pessimistically, would be "solitary, poor, nasty, brutish and short." A fundamental implication of this conception of the state of nature is that there is no natural sin or right conduct. Justice and injustice are laid out in laws, which are established by a chosen authority whose task it is to write the laws. On Hobbes's view, where there is no sovereign power there will be no written law.

The Prisoner's Dilemma   The concept of rationality at work in Hobbes's state of nature offers the classic illustration of Prisoner's Dilemma reasoning. Consider two prisoners, suspected of criminal complicity, who are confined in separate cells. The prosecutor confronts each individually with the following proposal: "Confess to the more serious charge and you will be treated leniently. Your partner in crime will be jailed for ten years, you for one. If you fail to confess but your partner does, the sentences will be reversed. Should both of you confess, each will be sentenced to five years. Yet should neither of you confess, evidence now suffices to convict both only on a lesser charge drawing three-year sentences each." If both prisoners are rational and committed to minimizing their own sentences, each will reason thus: "I don't want to confess, but the other person might. If he confesses and I do not, I get ten years and he one. So, I should confess. For then, if he fails to confess, I get one year, and if we both confess, we each get five." So, if rational, both will confess.

Laws of Nature and the Social Contract   Hobbes thought that everyone fears death and desires to live long. The state of nature is inconsistent with this desire. Rational self-interest suggests to each individual in the state of nature, as it might to a prisoner wanting to maximize self-interest in the Prisoner's Dilemma, a set of general principles to secure a peaceful social order. These rational principles, or what Hobbes called *laws of nature,* are general rules established by reason. They oblige rational persons to follow them, for the likelihood of a long life would thereby be increased. These laws of nature are to be distinguished from the *right of nature.* The latter is the freedom in the state of nature to do whatever satisfies one's desires. Most fundamentally, one has the right in the state of nature to defend oneself by any means available. Nevertheless, reason commands as the first *law* that one seek peace and preserve it, for this maximizes the possibility of self-preservation. The second law, crucial for peace, requires that one give up as many liberties in the state of nature as one demands that others give up. Here the motivation is twofold: to disadvantage neither oneself nor others, and to oblige all to cease random or self-interested acts of violence. Agents are not simply to renounce these rights but are to transfer them for safekeeping to a party consensually agreed to, a sovereign monarch or body of rulers. This common agreement or mutual promise between individuals in choosing a sovereign ruler is the *social contract.* Hobbes insisted that the designated sovereign ruler must be invested with sufficient power to guarantee security: the sovereign's word must become law. Justice (right) and injustice (wrong) are taken to be *relative* to the particular language of the sovereign at the particular time and place. The only rational grounds for citizens' objections would be the failure of the sovereign to secure social order and peace. Hobbes derived the rest of his nineteen laws of nature deductively from these first three.

Interpreting Hobbes   Hobbes's moral and political theories are usually characterized as a rationalization for authoritarianism, in so far as moral and political obligations and rights are made subject to the power of the sovereign. So Hobbes seems to offer a sophisticated and more plausible version of the Sophists' view that "might makes right." However, there is another way in which Hobbes's theory can be read. Here "reason" and the "laws of nature" to which reason gives rise bear the weight of Hobbes's theoretical construct. Reason demands that everyone be treated equally and justly, and that each give up only the *minimum* liberties necessary to guarantee peace. The sovereign is not subject to the particular laws made, for what the sovereign rules the sovereign can alter. Nevertheless, the sovereign or ruling body also consists of persons, and they similarly desire self-preservation. Thus the sovereign body is likewise subject to the rational constraints of the laws of nature. Reason demands that the sovereign restrict no more than what is *minimally* necessary to maintain peace. For example, if peace and security can be promoted without censorship (see Chapter 10) or capital punishment (see Chapter 14), then on this reading it would be irrational for the sovereign to require it. As generally recognized, Hobbes criticized the Natural Law tradition promoted by Aquinas. For Aquinas, natural law is a moral principle or standard established by the nature of things or by God, to which human laws and actions ought thereby to conform. Yet on this alternative interpretation, Hobbes's universal principles commanded by reason tend to undermine crude conceptions of justice that are linked to authoritarianism.

Thomas Hobbes

LEVIATHAN

Part I: Of Man

Chapter XIII
Of the Naturall Condition of Mankind,
As Concerning Their Felicity, and Misery

Men by nature Equall   Nature hath made men so equall, in the faculties of body, and mind; as that though there bee found one man sometimes manifestly stronger in body, or of quicker mind then another, yet when all is reckoned together, the difference between man, and man, is not so considerable, as that one man can thereupon claim to himselfe any benefit, to which another may not pretend, as well as he. For as to the strength of body, the weakest has strength enough to kill the strongest, either by secret machi-

From Thomas Hobbes, *Leviathan* (London, 1651).

nation, or by confederacy with others, that are in the same danger with himselfe.

And as to the faculties of the mind (setting aside the arts grounded upon words, and especially that skill of proceeding upon generall, and infallible rules, called Science; which very few have, and but in few things; as being not a native faculty, born with us; nor attained [as Prudence] while we look after somewhat else,) I find yet a greater equality amongst men, than that of strength. For Prudence, is but Experience; which equall time, equally bestowes on all men, in those things they equally apply themselves unto. That which may perhaps make such equality incredible, is but a vain conceipt of ones owne wisdome, which almost all men think they have in a greater degree, than the Vulgar, that is, than all men but themselves, and a few others, whom by Fame, or for concurring with themselves, they approve. For such is the nature of men, that howsoever they may acknowledge many others to be more witty, or more eloquent, or more learned; Yet they will hardly believe there be many so wise as themselves: For they see their own wit at hand, and other men's at a distance. But this proveth rather that men are in that point equall, than unequall. For there is not ordinarily a greater signe of the equall distribution of anything, than that every man is contented with his share.

From this equality of ability, ariseth equality of hope in the attaining of our Ends. And therefore if any two men desire the same thing, which neverthelesse they cannot both enjoy, they become enemies; and in the way to their End (which is principally their owne conservation, and sometimes their delectation only), endeavour to destroy, or subdue one an other. And from hence it comes to passe, that where an Invader hath no more to feare, than an other mans single power; if one plant, sow, build, or possesse a convenient Seat, others may probably be expected to come prepared with forces united, to dispossesse, and deprive him, not only of the fruit of his labour, but also of his life, or liberty. And the Invader again is in the like danger of another. *From Equality proceeds Dissidence*

And from this diffidence of one another, there is no way for any man to secure himselfe, so reasonable, as Anticipation; that is, by force, or wiles, to master the persons of all men he can, so long, till he see no other power great enough to endanger him: And this is no more than his own conservation requireth, and is generally allowed. Also because there be some, that taking pleasure in contemplating their own power in the acts of conquest, which they pursue farther than their security requires; if others, that otherwise would be glad to be at ease within modest bounds, should not by invasion increase their power, they would not be able, long time, by standing only on their defence, to subsist. And by consequence, such augmentation of dominion over men, being necessary to a mans conservation, it ought to be allowed him. *From Dissidence Warre*

Againe, men have no pleasure (but on the contrary a great deale of griefe) in keeping company, where there is no power able to over-awe them all. For every man looketh that his companion should value him, at the same rate he sets upon himselfe: And upon all signes of contempt, or undervaluing, naturally endeavours, as far as he dares (which amongst them that have no common power, to keep them in quiet, if far enough to make them destroy each other,) to extort a greater value from his contemners, by dommage; and from others, by the example.

So that in the nature of man, we find three principall causes of quarrell. First, Competition; Secondly, Diffidence; Thirdly, Glory.

62   The first, maketh men invade for Gain; the second, for Safety; and the third, for Reputation. The first use Violence, to make themselves Masters of other mens persons, wives, children, and cattell; the second, to defend them; the third, for trifles, as a word, a smile, a different opinion, and any other signe of undervalue, either direct in their Persons, or by reflexion in their Kindred, their Friends, their nation, their Profession, or their Name.

Out of Civil States, there is always Warre of every one against every one.   Hereby it is manifest, that during the time men live without a common Power to keep them all in awe, they are in that condition which is called Warre; and such a warre, as is of every man against every man. For Warre, consisteth not in Battell onely, or the act of fighting; but in a tract of time, wherein the Will to contend by Battell is sufficiently known; and therefore the notion of *Time*, is to be considered in the nature of Warre; as it is in the nature of Weather. For as the nature of Foule weather, lyeth not in a showre or two of rain; but in an inclination thereto of many dayes together: So the nature of War, consisteth not in actuall fighting; but in the known disposition thereto, during all the time there is no assurance to the contrary. All other time is Peace.

The Incommodities of such a Warre   Whatsoever therefore is consequent to a time of Warre, where every man is Enemy to every man; the same is consequent to the time, wherein men live without other security, than what their own strength, and their own invention shall furnish them withall. In such condition, there is no place for Industry; because the fruit thereof is uncertain: and consequently no Culture of the Earth; no Navigation, nor use of the commodities that may be imported by Sea; no commodious Building; no Instruments of moving, and removing such things as require much force; no Knowledge of the face of the Earth; no account of Time; no Arts; no Letters; no Society; and which is worst of all, continuall feare, and danger of violent death; And the life of man, solitary, poore, nasty, brutish, and short.

    It may seem strange to some man, that has not well weighed these things; that Nature should thus dissociate, and render men apt to invade, and destroy one another: and he may therefore, not trusting to this Inference, made from the Passions, desire perhaps to have the same confirmed by Experience. Let him therefore consider with himselfe, when taking a journey, he armes himselfe, and seeks to go well accompanied; when going to sleep, he locks his dores; when even in his house he lockes his chests; and this when he knows there bee Lawes, and publike Officers, armed, to revenge all injuries shall bee done him; what opinion he has of his fellow subjects, when he rides armed; of his fellow Citizens, when he locks his dores; and of his children, and servants, when he locks his chests. Does he not there as much accuse mankind by his actions, as I do by my words? But neither of us accuse mans nature in it. The Desires, and other Passions of man, are in themselves no Sin. No more are the Actions, that proceed from those Passions, till they know a Law that forbids them: which till Lawes be made they cannot know: nor can any Law be made, till they have agreed upon the Person that shall make it.

63   It may peradventure be thought, there was never such a time, nor condition of warre as this; and I believe it was never generally so, over all the world; but there are many places, where they live so now. For the savage people in many places of *America*, except the government of small Families, the concord whereof dependeth

on naturall lust, have no government at all; and live at this day in that brutish manner, as I said before. Howsoever, it may be perceived what manner of life there would be, where there were no common Power to feare; by the manner of life, which men that have formerly lived under a peacefull government, use to degenerate into, in a civill Warre.

But though there had never been any time, wherein particular men were in a condition of warre one against another, yet in all times, Kings, and Persons of Soveraigne authority, because of their Independency, are in continuall jealousies, and in the state and posture of Gladiators; having their weapons pointing, and their eyes fixed on one another; that is, their Forts, Garrisons, and Guns upon the Frontiers of their Kingdomes; and continuall Spyes upon their neighbours; which is a posture of War. But because they uphold thereby, the Industry of their Subjects; there does not follow from it, that misery, which accompanies the Liberty of particular men.

To this warre of every man against every man, this also is consequent; that nothing can be Unjust. The notions of Right and Wrong, Justice and Injustice have there no place. Where there is no common Power, there is no Law: where no Law, no Injustice. Force, and Fraud, are in warre the two Cardinall vertues. Justice, and Injustice are none of the Faculties neither of the Body, nor Mind. If they were, they might be in a man that were alone in the world, as well as his Senses, and Passions. They are Qualities, that relate to men in Society, not in Solitude. It is consequent also to the same condition, that there be no Propriety, no Dominion, no *Mine* and *Thine* distinct; but onely that to be every mans that he can get; and for so long, as he can keep it. And thus much for the ill condition, which man by meer Nature is actually placed in; though with a possibility to come out of it, consisting partly in the Passions, partly in his Reason. *In such a Warre, nothing is Unjust*

The Passions that incline men to Peace, are Feare of Death; Desire of such things as are necessary to commodious living; and a Hope by their industry to obtain them. And Reason suggesteth convenient Articles of Peace, upon which men may be drawn to agreement. These Articles, are they, which otherwise are called the Lawes of Nature: whereof I shall speak more particularly, in the two following Chapters. *The Passions that incline men to Peace*

Chapter XIV
Of the First and Second Naturall Lawes, and of Contracts

The Right of Nature, which Writers commonly call Jus Naturale, is the Liberty each man hath, to use his own power, as he will himselfe, for the preservation of his own Nature; that is to say, of his own Life; and consequently, of doing any thing, which in his own Judgement, and Reason, hee shall conceive to be the aptest means thereunto. *Right of Nature what*

By Liberty, is understood, according to the proper signification of the word, the absence of externall Impediments: which Impediments, may oft take away part of a mans power to do what hee would; but cannot hinder him from using the power left him, according as his judgement, and reason shall dictate to him. *Liberty what*

A Law of Nature (*Lex Naturalis*) is a Precept, or a generall Rule, found out by Reason, by which a man is forbidden to do, that, which is destructive of his life, or taketh away the means of preserving the same; and to omit, that by which he thinketh it may be best preserved. For though they that speak of this subject, use to confound *Jus*, and *Lex, Right* and *Law*; yet they ought to be distinguished; because Right, consisteth in liberty to do, or to forbeare; Whereas Law, determineth, and bindeth to one of them: so that Law, and Right, differ as much, as Obligation, and Liberty; which in one and the same matter are inconsistent.

*Natur-
ally
every
man has
Right to
every-
thing*   And because the condition of Man (as hath been declared in the precedent Chapter) is a condition of Warre of every one against every one; in which case every one is governed by his own Reason; and there is nothing he can make use of, that may not be a help unto him, in preserving his life against his enemyes; It followeth, that in such a condition, every man has a Right to every thing; even to one anothers body. And therefore, as long as this naturall Right of every man to every thing endureth, there can be no security to any man (how strong or wise soever he be) of living out the time, which Nature ordinarily alloweth men to live. And conse-

quently it is a precept, or generall rule of Reason, *That every man, ought to endeavour Peace, as farre as he has hope of obtaining it; and when he cannot obtain it, that he may seek, and use, all helps, and advantages of Warre.* The first branch of which Rule, containeth the first, and Fundamentall Law of Nature; which is, *to seek Peace, and follow it.* The Second, the summe of the Right of Nature; which is, *By all means we can, to defend our selves.*

From this Fundamentall Law of Nature, by which men are commanded to endeavour Peace, is derived this second Law; *That a man be willing, when others are so too, as farre-forth, as for Peace, and defence of himselfe he shall think it necessary, to lay down this right to all things; and be contented with so much liberty against other men, as he would allow other men against himselfe.* For as long as every man holdeth this Right, of doing any thing he liketh; so long are all men in the condition of Warre. But if other men will not lay down their Right, as well as he; then there is no Reason for any one, to devest himselfe of his: For that were to expose himselfe to Prey (which no man is bound to) rather than to dispose himselfe to Peace. This is that Law of the Gospell; *Whatsoever you require that others should do to you, that do ye to them.* And that Law of all men, *Quod tibi fieri non vis, alteri ne feceris.*

To *lay downe* a mans *Right* to any thing, is to *devest* himselfe of the *Liberty*, of hindring another of the benefit of his own Right to the same. For he that renounceth, or passeth away his Right, giveth not to any other man a Right which he had not before; because there is nothing to which every man had not Right by Nature: but onely standeth out of his way, that he may enjoy his own originall Right, without hindrance from him; not without hindrance from another. So that the effect which redoundeth to one man, by another mans defect of Right, is but so much diminution of impediments to the use of his own right originall.

*Renounc-
ing a Right
what it is*   Right is layd aside, either by simply Renouncing it; or by Transferring it to another. By Simply Renouncing; when he cares not to whom the benefit thereof redoundeth. By Transferring; when he intendeth the benefit thereof to some certain

person, or persons. And when a man hath in either manner abandoned, or granted *Transfer-*
away his Right, then is he said to be Obliged, or Bound, not to hinder those, to *ring Right*
whom such Right is granted, or abandoned, from the benefit of it: and that he *what*
Ought, and it is his Duty, not to make voyd that voluntary act of his own: and that *Obliga-*
such hindrance is Injustice, and Injury, as being *Sine Jure*; the Right being before re- *tion*
nounced, or transferred. So that *Injury*, or *Injustice*, in the controversies of the *Duty*
world, is somewhat like to that, which in the disputations of Scholers is called
Absurdity. For as it is there called an Absurdity, to contradict what one maintained
in the Beginning: so in the world, it is called Injustice, and Injury, voluntarily to *Injustice*
undo that, which from the beginning he had voluntarily done. . . .

The mutuall transferring of Right, is that which men call Contract.

There is difference, between transferring of Right to the Thing; and transferring, or tradition, that is, delivery of the Thing it selfe. For the Thing may be delivered together with the Translation of the Right; as in buying and selling with ready
money; or exchange of goods, or lands: and it may be delivered some time after.

Again, one of the Contractors, may deliver the Thing contracted for on his
part, and leave the other to perform his part at some determinate time after, and in
the mean time be trusted; and then the Contract on his part, is called Pact, or *Cove-*
Covenant: Or both parts may contract now, to performe hereafter: in which cases, *nant*
he that is to performe in time to come, being trusted, his performance is called *what*
Keeping of Promise, or Faith: and the fayling of performance (if it be voluntary)
Violation of Faith. . . .

Chapter XV
Of Other Lawes of Nature

From that law of Nature, by which we are obliged to transferre to another, such *The*
Rights, as being retained, hinder the peace of Mankind, there followeth a Third; *third*
which is this, *That men performe their Covenants made*; without which, Covenants *Law of*
are in vain, and but Empty words; and the Right of all men to all things remaining, *Nature,*
wee are still in the condition of Warre. *Justice*

And in this law of Nature, consisteth the Fountain and Originall of Justice. For *Justice*
where no Covenant hath preceded, there hath no Right been transferred, and every- *and*
man has right to every thing; and consequently, no action can be Unjust. But when a *Injustice*
Covenant is made, then to break it is *Unjust*: And the definition of Injustice, is no other *what*
than the *not Performance of Covenant*. And whatsoever is not Unjust, is *Just*. . . .

. . . And though this may seem too subtile a deduction of the Lawes of Na- *A Rule*
ture, to be taken notice of by all men; whereof the most part are too busie in getting *by which*
food, and the rest too negligent to understand; yet to leave all men unexcusable, *the*
they have been contracted into one easie sum, intelligible, even to the meanest *Lawes of*
capacity; and that is, *Do not that to another, which thou wouldest not have done to thy* *Nature*
selfe; which sheweth him, that he has no more to do in learning the Lawes of *may eas-*
Nature, but, when weighing the actions of other men with his own, they seem too *ily be*
heavy, to put them into the other part of the ballance, and his own into their place, *exam-*
ined

The Lawes
of Nature
oblige in
Conscience
alwayes,
but in
Effect then
onely when
there is
Security

that his own passions, and selfe-love, may adde nothing to the weight; and then there is none of these Lawes of Nature that will not appear unto him very reasonable.

The Lawes of Nature oblige *in foro interno*; that is to say, they bind to a desire they should take place: but *in foro externo*; that is, to the putting them in act, not alwayes. For he that should be modest, and tractable, and performe all he promises, in such time, and place where no man els should do so, should but make himselfe a prey to others, and procure his own certain ruine, contrary to the ground of all Lawes of Nature, which tend to Natures preservation. . . .

The Lawes
of Nature
are Eternal

The Lawes of Nature are Immutable and Eternall; For Injustice, Ingratitude, Arrogance, Pride, Iniquity, Acception of persons, and the rest, can never be made lawfull. For it can never be that Warre shall preserve life, and Peace destroy it.

And yet
Easie

The same Lawes, because they oblige onely to a desire, and endeavour, I mean an unfeigned and constant endeavour, are easie to be observed. For in that they require nothing but endeavour; he that endeavoureth their performance, fulfilleth them; and he that fulfilleth the Law, is Just.

■ DAVID HUME (1711–1776): A CRITIQUE OF MORAL REASON AND THE THEORY OF MORAL SENTIMENTS

Hobbes's theory was so provocative and his arguments so compelling that for a century and a half British philosophers, theologians, and political theorists felt constrained to address the issues he raised. Almost all British philosophers of the time devoted their philosophical energies largely to moral matters. David Hume was somewhat less concerned with moral matters than other British Moralists (as they have been named). Yet it is perhaps a mark of Hobbes's influence that Hume chose the title of his influential work *Treatise of Human Nature* (1739) from the title of Hobbes's book *Human Nature* (1650).

Hume's Critique Of Reason   Hume formulated a consistent critical attack upon the possibility of all forms of claimed knowledge. He raised deep questions about the possibility of acquiring scientific knowledge of the external world, especially of the relation between cause and effect, knowledge of the self, and religious knowledge of God. Hume's moral criticisms are part of this wider critical attack and they are directed primarily against the claims of moral objectivity, against moral knowledge of the distinction between right and wrong, and against claims of the universal scope of reason. Like Hume, one might wonder whether reason has universal force, commanding obedience to some abstract, context-independent principles reason alone is capable of identifying. Much as he argued that reason is incapable of establishing the relation between cause and effect, so Hume suggested that the distinction between good and evil cannot be deduced by reason.

The primary target of Hume's moral criticism, then, is the claim that reason is practical. Many philosophers had assumed that good and evil are to be distinguished by rational deliberation, and that to be moral actions must be commanded by practical reasoning. Accordingly, practical reasoning must conclude, as Aristotle noted, with an action (see Aristotle, Chapter 1).

Hume's attack on practical reasoning rests upon two arguments: that reason alone is incapable of motivating an action, and that reason alone cannot oppose the effect on the will of the passions.

For Hume, *impressions* and *ideas* together exhaust the contents of mind. The passions (like hunger or anger) are impressions or original impositions on the mind that motivate or excite the agent to action. Reason, by contrast, has to do only with relations of ideas or matters of fact. So reason is not capable on its own of moving one to action, for it has no impressive force upon the will. In short, while reason is inert and impotent, morality concerns virtuous *action*. Active principles cannot be prompted by inactive ones, and so moral action cannot be a function of reason alone, nor can immoral actions simply be ascribed to irrationality. Despite the claim of many British Moralists, moral rules cannot be conclusions to the deductions of reason, for then they would have no force on their own to affect behavior.

Hume held that, at most, reason can indicate the existence of some end that is desired (education, say), and especially the means best able to achieve that end. Reason is unable to recommend an end as desired or to originate the causal impulse that leads an agent to pursue or avoid something. For example, reason may suggest to me that the surest way to secure my graduation is to study hard; but on Hume's view reason cannot impress upon me the goal of graduation or create in me the desire to study. The originating impulse that disposes an agent to pursue or avoid some end arises from the agent's anticipation of the accompanying pleasure or pain. Only such an impulse can move the will to act or refrain from acting; in the example, to study or not. It follows that reason is also incapable of preventing the will from acting. Because of reason's impotence in the face of the passions, Hume drew his celebrated conclusion that "reason is, and ought to be the slave of the passions."

Fact and Value   Hume inferred a more general lesson from this line of argument. If moral claims are to impel action, they must prescribe behavior. They must command agents to do what they ought or to refrain from doing what they ought not. Moral prescriptions, by definition, involve value claims and so are not matters of fact. They cannot be reduced to factual claims about what is or is not the case. That I *ought* not to lie, say, cannot be derived from any *factual* claim about the harmful consequences of lying. We cannot, in short, deduce "ought" or value claims solely from "is" or factual ones.

Moral Sentiments   If reason is incapable of determining the distinction between virtue and vice or right and wrong, Hume had to argue that the source of these moral distinctions lies elsewhere. By circumscribing the effective power of reason, he evaded the claim that moral rules or judgments are objective, eternal, or universally obligatory. Rather, he took them to have their foundation in people's desires for what is in their common interest. In contrast to those who argued that moral judgments and knowledge of the moral distinctions stem from reason, Hume contended that they spring from ordinary sensations. These sensations he called the *moral sentiments* or moral passions, the most fundamental of which are *sympathy* and *antipathy*.

Hume's theory of sympathy was supposed to explain how an isolated individual with private experiences and feelings can care for the feelings of others. He held that moral sentiments are innate to human nature, and in spite of the seemingly local variations, human beings have a uniform tendency to sympathize with their fellows. As a consequence of social functioning, this results in sympathy for some kinds of objects and antipathy toward others. Hume suggested that we sympathize with the pleasure that we presume an object, quality, or character gives to an agent possessing it. This reflects the paradigm case of the pleasure that one experiences from some object, character, or quality that one owns. Sympathy amounts to—it is identical with—a pleasure (or in the case of antipathy, a pain) that we experience. For example, we approve of the courage exhibited by one who performs a daring rescue, for we have experienced the sort of pleasure arising from courageous action and so we can sympathize with the pleasure of the rescuer. Our approval is a function of the pleasure we feel in sympathizing with the rescuer's pleasure.

Hume presumed, with little supporting argument, that this transferred pleasure or pain will suffice to outweigh any direct pleasure or pain we might experience from a competing object, quality, or character directly in our possession—for example, that the rescuer is someone we otherwise despise. He supposed that overcoming this direct pleasure or pain is sufficient to arouse in us disapproval of any unjust self-serving action that we might be considering. Thus Hume rejected the idea, suggested perhaps by Hobbes's general moral law or by the Golden Rule of "doing unto others," that sympathy is a function of impartially imagining ourselves in another's place. In Hume's view, we do not sympathize with other members of our society because to do so is objectively or impartially right or just, commanded by reason, but because our social condition and custom have led us to love and identify with them.

Thus for both Hobbes and Hume social considerations play central though different roles in the determination of morality and how we ought to act on any given social issue. For Hobbes, the sovereign's prescription of moral rules and morally acceptable behavior is founded upon a social contract subject to certain rational constraints. For Hume, moral rules are established in accordance with social condition, custom, and common interests.

David Hume

A TREATISE OF HUMAN NATURE

BOOK II
OF THE PASSIONS.

Part III. Of the Will and Direct Passions

SECTION III.
OF THE INFLUENCING
MOTIVES OF THE WILL

Nothing is more usual in philosophy, and even in common life, than to talk of the combat of passion and reason, to give the preference to reason, and to assert that

From David Hume, A *Treatise of Human Nature*. First published in 1739 and 1740.

men are only so far virtuous as they conform themselves to its dictates. Every rational creature, 'tis said, is oblig'd to regulate his actions by reason; and if any other motive or principle challenge the direction of his conduct, he ought to oppose it, 'till it be entirely subdu'd, or at least brought to a conformity with that superior principle. On this method of thinking the greatest part of moral philosophy, ancient and modern, seems to be founded; nor is there an ampler field, as well for metaphysical arguments, as popular declamations, than this suppos'd pre-eminence of reason above passion. The eternity, invariableness, and divine origin of the former have been display'd to the best advantage: The blindness, unconstancy and deceitfulness of the latter have been as strongly insisted on. In order to shew the fallacy of all this philosophy, I shall endeavour to prove *first*, that reason alone can never be a motive to any action of the will; and *secondly*, that it can never oppose passion in the direction of the will.

The understanding exerts itself after two different ways, as it judges from demonstration or probability; as it regards the abstract relations of our ideas, or those relations of objects, of which experience only gives us information. I believe it scarce will be asserted, that the first species of reasoning alone is ever the cause of any action. As its proper province is the world of ideas, and as the will always places us in that of realities, demonstration and volition seem, upon that account, to be totally remov'd, from each other. Mathematics, indeed, are useful in all mechanical operations, and arithmetic in almost every art and profession: But 'tis not of themselves they have any influence. Mechanics are the art of regulating the motions of bodies *to some design'd end or purpose;* and the reason why we employ arithmetic in fixing the proportions of numbers, is only that we may discover the proportions of their influence and operation. A merchant is desirous of knowing the sum total of his accounts with any person: Why? but that he may learn what sum will have the same *effects* in paying his debt, and going to market, as all the particular articles taken together. Abstract or demonstrative reasoning, therefore, never influences any of our actions, but only as it directs our judgment concerning causes and effects; which leads us to the second operation of the understanding.

'Tis obvious, that when we have the prospect of pain or pleasure from any object, we feel a consequent emotion of aversion or propensity, and are carry'd to avoid or embrace what will give us this uneasiness or satisfaction. 'Tis also obvious, that this emotion rests not here, but making us cast our view on every side, comprehends whatever objects are connected with its original one by the relation of cause and effect. Here then reasoning takes place to discover this relation; and according as our reasoning varies, our actions receive a subsequent variation. But 'tis evident in this case, that the impulse arises not from reason, but is only directed by it. 'Tis from the prospect of pain or pleasure that the aversion or propensity arises towards any object: And these emotions extend themselves to the causes and effects of that object, as they are pointed out to us by reason and experience. It can never in the least concern us to know, that such objects are causes, and such others effects, if both the causes and effects be indifferent to us. Where the objects themselves do not affect us, their connexion can never give them any influence; and 'tis plain, that as reason is nothing but the discovery of this connexion, it cannot be by its means that the objects are able to affect us.

Since reason alone can never produce any action, or give rise to volition, I infer, that the same faculty is as incapable of preventing volition, or of disputing the preference with any passion or emotion. This consequence is necessary. 'Tis impossible reason cou'd have the latter effect of preventing volition, but by giving an impulse in a contrary direction to our passion; and that impulse, had it operated alone, wou'd have been able to produce volition. Nothing can oppose or retard the impulse of passion, but a contrary impulse; and if this contrary impulse ever arises from reason, that latter faculty must have an original influence on the will, and must be able to cause, as well as hinder any act of volition. But if reason has no original influence, 'tis impossible it can withstand any principle, which has such an efficacy, or ever keep the mind in suspense a moment. Thus it appears, that the principle, which opposes our passion, cannot be the same with reason, and is only call'd so in an improper sense. We speak not strictly and philosophically when we talk of the combat of passion and of reason. Reason is, and ought only to be the slave of the passions, and can never pretend to any other office than to serve and obey them. As this opinion may appear somewhat extraordinary, it may not be improper to confirm it by some other considerations.

A passion is an original existence, or, if you will, modification of existence, and contains not any representative quality, which renders it a copy of any other existence or modification. When I am angry, I am actually possest with the passion, and in that emotion have no more a reference to any other object, than when I am thirsty, or sick, or more than five foot high. 'Tis impossible, therefore, that this passion can be oppos'd by, or be contradictory to truth and reason; since this contradiction consists in the disagreement of ideas, consider'd as copies, with those objects, which they represent.

What may at first occur on this head, is, that as nothing can be contrary to truth or reason, except what has a reference to it, and as the judgments of our understanding only have this reference, it must follow, that passions can be contrary to reason only so far as they are *accompany'd* with some judgment or opinion. According to this principle, which is so obvious and natural, 'tis only in two senses, that any affection can be call'd unreasonable. First, When a passion, such as hope or fear, grief or joy, despair or security, is founded on the supposition of the existence of objects, which really do not exist. Secondly, When in exerting any passion in action, we chuse means insufficient for the design'd end, and deceive ourselves in our judgment of causes and effects. . . . In short, a passion must be accompany'd with some false judgment, in order to its being unreasonable; and even then 'tis not the passion, properly speaking, which is unreasonable, but the judgment.

The consequences are evident. Since a passion can never, in any sense, be call'd unreasonable, but when founded on a false supposition, or when it chuses means insufficient for the design'd end, 'tis impossible, that reason and passion can ever oppose each other, or dispute for the government of the will and actions. The moment we perceive the falshood of any supposition, or the insufficiency of any means our passions yield to our reason without any opposition. I may desire any fruit as of an excellent relish; but whenever you convince me of my mistake, my longing ceases. I may will the performance of certain actions as means of obtaining any desir'd good;

but as my willing of these actions is only secondary, and founded on the supposition that they are causes of the propos'd effect; as soon as I discover the falshood of that supposition, they must become indifferent to me.

BOOK III
OF MORALS.

Part I.
Of Virtue and Vice in General.

SECTION I
MORAL DISTINCTIONS
NOT DERIV'D FROM REASON.

. . . It has been observ'd, that nothing is ever present to the mind but its perceptions; and that all the actions of seeing, hearing, judging, loving, hating, and thinking, fall under this denomination. The mind can never exert itself in any action, which we may not comprehend under the term of *perception*; and consequently that term is no less applicable to those judgments, by which we distinguish moral good and evil, than to every other operation of the mind. To approve of one character, to condemn another, are only so many different perceptions.

Now as perceptions resolve themselves into two kinds, viz. *impressions* and *ideas*, this distinction gives rise to a question, with which we shall open up our present enquiry concerning morals, *Whether 'tis by means of our ideas or impressions we distinguish betwixt vice and virtue, and pronounce an action blameable or praiseworthy?* This will immediately cut off all loose discourses and declamations, and reduce us to something precise and exact on the present subject.

Those who affirm that virtue is nothing but a conformity to reason; that there are eternal fitnesses and unfitnesses of things, which are the same to every rational being that considers them; that the immutable measures of right and wrong impose an obligation, not only on human creatures, but also on the Deity himself: All these systems concur in the opinion, that morality, like truth, is discern'd merely by ideas, and by their juxtaposition and comparison. In order, therefore, to judge of these systems, we need only consider, whether it be possible, from reason alone, to distinguish betwixt moral good and evil, or whether there must concur some other principles to enable us to make that distinction.

If morality had naturally no influence on human passions and actions, 'twere in vain to take such pains to inculcate it; and nothing wou'd be more fruitless than that multitude of rules and precepts, with which all moralists abound. Philosophy is commonly divided into *speculative* and *practical*; and as morality is always comprehended under the latter division, 'tis supposed to influence our passions and actions, and to go beyond the calm and indolent judgments of the understanding. And this is confirm'd by common experience, which informs us, that men are often govern'd by their duties, and are deter'd from some actions by the opinion of injustice, and impell'd to others by that of obligation.

Since morals, therefore, have an influence on the actions and affections, it follows, that they cannot be deriv'd from reason; and that because reason alone, as we have already prov'd, can never have any such influence. Morals excite passions, and produce or prevent actions. Reason of itself is utterly impotent in this particular. The rules of morality, therefore, are not conclusions of our reason.

No one, I believe, will deny the justness of this inference; nor is there any other means of evading it, than by denying that principle, on which it is founded. As long as it is allow'd, that reason has no influence on our passions and actions, 'tis in vain to pretend, that morality is discover'd only by a deduction of reason. An active principle can never be founded on an inactive; and if reason be inactive in itself, it must remain so in all its shapes and appearances, whether it exerts itself in natural or moral subjects, whether it considers the powers of external bodies, or the actions of rational beings. . . .

Reason is the discovery of truth or falshood. Truth or falshood consists in an agreement or disagreement either to the *real* relations of ideas, or to *real* existence and matter of fact. Whatever, therefore, is not susceptible of this agreement or disagreement, is incapable of being true or false, and can never be an object of our reason. Now 'tis evident our passions, volitions, and actions, are not susceptible of any such agreement or disagreement; being original facts and realities, compleat in themselves, and implying no reference to other passions, volitions, and actions. 'Tis impossible, therefore, they can be pronounced either true or false, and be either contrary or conformable to reason.

This argument is of double advantage to our present purpose. For it proves *directly*, that actions do not derive their merit from a conformity to reason, nor their blame from a contrariety to it; and it proves the same truth more *indirectly*, by shewing us, that as reason can never immediately prevent or produce any action by contradicting or approving of it, it cannot be the source of moral good and evil, which are found to have that influence. Actions may be laudable or blameable; but they cannot be reasonable or unreasonable: Laudable or blameable, therefore, are not the same with reasonable or unreasonable. The merit and demerit of actions frequently contradict, and sometimes controul our natural propensities. But reason has no such influence. Moral distinctions, therefore, are not the offspring of reason. Reason is wholly inactive, and can never be the source of so active a principle as conscience, or a sense of morals. . . .

It has been observ'd, that reason, in a strict and philosophical sense, can have an influence on our conduct only after two ways: Either when it excites a passion by informing us of the existence of something which is a proper object of it; or when it discovers the connexion of causes and effects, so as to afford us means of exerting any passion. These are the only kinds of judgment, which can accompany our actions, or can be said to produce them in any manner, and it must be allow'd, that these judgments may often be false and erroneous. A person may be affected with passion, by supposing a pain or pleasure to lie in an object, which has no tendency to produce either of these sensations, or which produces the contrary to what is imagin'd. A person may also take false measures for the attaining his end, and may retard, by his foolish conduct, instead of forwarding the execution of any project. These false judgments may be thought to affect the passions and actions, which are connected with them, and may be said to render them unreasonable, in a figurative and improper way of speaking. But tho' this be acknowledg'd, 'tis easy to observe, that these errors are so far from being the source of all immorality, that they are commonly very innocent, and draw no manner of guilt upon the person who is so unfortunate as to fall into them. They extend not beyond a mistake of *fact*, which moralists have not generally suppos'd criminal, as being perfectly involuntary. I am more to be lamented than blam'd, if I am mistaken with regard to the influence of objects in producing pain or pleasure, or if I know not the proper means of satisfying my desires. No one can ever regard such errors as a defect in my moral character. A fruit, for instance, that is really disagreeable, appears to me at a distance, and thro' mistake I fancy it to be pleasant and delicious. Here is one error. I choose certain means of reaching this fruit, which are not proper for my end. Here is a second error; nor is there any third one, which can ever possibly enter into our reasonings concerning actions. I ask, therefore, if a man, in this situation, and guilty of these two errors, is to be regarded as vicious and criminal, however unavoidable they might have been? Or if it be possible to imagine, that such errors are the sources of all immorality? . . .

Shou'd it be pretended, that tho' a mistake of *fact* be not criminal, yet a mistake of *right* often is; and that this may be the source of immorality: I would answer, that 'tis impossible such a mistake can ever be the original source of immorality, since it supposes a real right and wrong; that is, a real distinction in morals, independent of these judgments. A mistake, therefore, of right may become a species of immorality; but 'tis only a secondary one, and is founded on some other, antecedent to it. . . .

Thus upon the whole, 'tis impossible, that the distinction betwixt moral good and evil, can be made by reason; since that distinction has an influence upon our actions, of which reason alone is incapable. Reason and judgment may, indeed, be the mediate cause of an action, by prompting, or by directing a passion: But it is not pretended, that a judgment of this kind, either in its truth or falshood, is attended with virtue or vice. And as to the judgments, which are caused by our judgments, they can still less bestow those moral qualities on the actions, which are their causes.

But to be more particular, and to shew, that those eternal immutable fitnesses and unfitnesses of things cannot be defended by sound philosophy, we may weigh the following considerations.

If the thought and understanding were alone capable of fixing the boundaries of right and wrong, the character of virtuous and vicious either must lie in some relations of objects, or must be a matter of fact, which is discovered by our reasoning. This consequence is evident. As the operations of human understanding divide themselves into two kinds, the comparing of ideas, and the inferring of matter of fact; were virtue discover'd by the understanding; it must be an object of one of these operations, nor is there any third operation of the understanding, which can discover it. There has been an opinion very industriously propagated by certain philosophers, that morality is susceptible of demonstration; and tho' no one has ever been able to advance a single step in those demonstrations; yet 'tis taken for granted, that this science may be brought to an equal certainty with geometry or algebra. Upon this supposition, vice and virtue must consist in some relations; since 'tis allow'd on all hands, that no matter of fact is capable of being demonstrated. . . .

If you assert, that vice and virtue consist in relations susceptible of certainty and demonstration, you must confine yourself to those *four* relations, which alone admit of that degree of evidence; and in that case you run into absurdities, from which you will never be able to extricate yourself. For as you make the very essence of morality to lie in the relations, and as there is no one of these relations but what is applicable, not only to an irrational, but also to an inanimate object; it follows, that even such objects must be susceptible of merit or demerit. *Resemblance, contrariety, degrees in quality,* and *proportions in quantity and number;* all these relations belong as properly to matter, as to our actions, passions, and volitions. 'Tis unquestionable, therefore, that morality lies not in any of these relations, nor the sense of it in their discovery. . . .

I must, therefore, on this occasion, rest contented with requiring the two following conditions of any one that wou'd undertake to clear up this system. *First,* As moral good and evil belong only to the actions of the mind, and are deriv'd from our situation with regard to external objects, the relations, from which these moral distinctions arise, must lie only betwixt internal actions, and external objects, and must not be applicable either to internal actions, compared among themselves, or to external objects, when placed in opposition to other external objects. For as morality is supposed to attend certain relations, if these relations cou'd belong to internal actions consider'd singly, it wou'd follow, that we might be guilty of crimes in ourselves, and independent of our situation, with respect to the universe: And in like manner, if these moral relations cou'd be apply'd to external objects, it wou'd follow, that even inanimate beings wou'd be susceptible of moral beauty and deformity. Now it seems difficult to imagine, that any relation can be discover'd betwixt our passions, volitions and actions, compared to external objects, which relation might not belong either to these passions and volitions, or to these, external objects, compar'd among *themselves.*

But it will be still more difficult to fulfil the *second* condition, requisite to justify this system. According to the principles of those who maintain an abstract rational difference betwixt moral good and evil, and a natural fitness and unfitness of things, 'tis not only suppos'd, that these relations, being eternal and immutable, are the same, when consider'd by every rational creature, but their *effects* are also suppos'd to be necessarily the same; and 'tis concluded they have no less, or rather a greater, influence in directing the will of the deity, than in governing the rational and virtuous of our own species. These two particulars are evidently distinct. 'Tis one thing to know virtue, and another to conform the will to it. In order, therefore, to prove, that the measures of right and wrong are eternal laws, *obligatory* on every rational mind, 'tis not sufficient to shew the relations upon which they are founded: We must also point out the connexion betwixt the relation and the will; and must prove that this connexion is so necessary, that in every well-disposed mind, it must take place and have its influence; tho' the difference betwixt these minds be in other respects immense and infinite. Now besides what I have already prov'd, that even in human nature no relation can ever alone produce any action; besides this, I say, it has been shewn, in treating of the understanding, that there is no connexion of cause and effect, such as this is suppos'd to be, which is discoverable otherwise than by experience, and of which we can pretend to have any security by the simple consideration of the objects. All beings in the universe, consider'd in themselves, appear entirely loose and independent of each other. 'Tis only by experience we learn their influence and connexion; and this influence we ought never to extend beyond experience.

Thus it will be impossible to fulfil the *first* condition required to the system of eternal rational measures of right and wrong; because it is impossible to shew those relations, upon which such a distinction may be founded: And 'tis as impossible to fulfil the *second* condition; because we cannot prove *a priori,* that these relations, if they really existed and were perceiv'd, wou'd be universally forcible and obligatory.

But to make these general reflexions more clear and convincing, we may illustrate them by some particular instances, wherein this character of moral good or evil is the most universally acknowledged. Of all crimes that human creatures are capable of committing, the most horrid and unnatural is ingratitude, especially when it is committed against parents, and appears in the more flagrant instances of wounds and death. This is acknowledg'd by all mankind, philosophers as well as the people; the question only arises among philosophers, whether the guilt or moral deformity of this action be discover'd by demonstrative reasoning, or be felt by an internal sense, and by means of some sentiment, which the reflecting on such an action naturally occasions. This question will soon be decided against the former opinion, if we can shew the same relations in other objects, without the notion of any guilt or iniquity attending them. Reason or science is nothing but the comparing of ideas, and the discovery of their relations; and if the same relations have different characters, it must evidently follow, that those characters are not discover'd merely by reason. . . .

But to chuse an instance, still more resembling; I would fain ask any one, why incest in the human species is criminal, and why the very same action, and the same relations in animals have not the smallest moral turpitude and deformity? If it be answer'd, that this action is innocent in animals, because they have not reason sufficient to discover its turpitude; but that man, being endow'd with that faculty, which *ought* to restrain him to his duty, the same action instantly becomes criminal to him; should this be said, I would reply, that this is evidently arguing in a circle. For before reason can perceive this turpitude, the turpitude must exist; and consequently is independent of the decisions of our reason, and is their object more properly than their effect. According to this system, then, every animal, that has sense, and appetite, and will; that is, every animal must be susceptible of all the same virtues and vices, for which we ascribe praise and blame to human creatures. All the difference is, that our superior reason may serve to discover the vice or virtue, and by that means may augment the blame or praise: But still this discovery supposes a separate being in these moral distinctions, and a being, which depends only on the will and appetite, and which, both in thought and reality, may be distinguish'd from the reason. Animals are susceptible of the same relations, with respect to each other, as the human species, and therefore wou'd also be susceptible of the same morality, if the essence of morality consisted in these relations. Their want of a sufficient degree of reason may hinder them from perceiving the duties and obligations of morality, but can never hinder these duties from existing; since they must antecedently exist, in order to their being perceiv'd. Reason must find them, and can never produce them. This argument deserves to be weigh'd, as being, in my opinion, entirely decisive.

Nor does this reasoning only prove, that morality consists not in any relations, that are the objects of science; but if examin'd, will prove with equal certainty, that it consists not in any *matter of fact*, which can be discover'd by the understanding. This is the *second* part of our argument; and if it can be made evident, we may conclude, that morality is not an object of reason. But can there be any difficulty in proving, that vice and virtue are not matters of fact, whose existence we can infer by reason? Take any action allow'd to be vicious: Wilful murder, for instance. Examine it in all lights, and see if you can find that matter of fact, or real existence, which you call *vice*. In which-ever way you take it, you find only certain passions, motives, volitions and thoughts. There is no other matter of fact in this case. The vice entirely escapes you, as long as you consider the object. You never can find it, till you turn your reflexion into your own breast, and find a sentiment of disapprobation, which arises in you, towards this action. Here is a matter of fact; but 'tis the object of feeling, not of reason. It lies in yourself, not in the object. So that when you pronounce any action or character to be vicious, you mean nothing, but that from the constitution of your nature you have a feeling or sentiment of blame from the contemplation of it. Vice and virtue, therefore, may be compar'd to sounds, colours, heat and cold, which, according to modern philosophy, are not qualities in objects, but perceptions in the mind: And this discovery in morals, like that other in physics, is to be regarded as a considerable advancement of the speculative sciences; tho', like that too, it has little or no influence on practice. Nothing can be more real, or concern us more, than our own sentiments of pleasure and uneasiness; and if these be favourable to virtue, and unfavourable to vice, no more can be requisite to the regulation of our conduct and behaviour.

I cannot forbear adding to these reasonings an observation, which may, perhaps, be found of some importance. In every system of morality, which I have hitherto met with, I have always remark'd, that the author proceeds for some time in the ordinary way of reasoning, and establishes the being of a God, or makes observations concerning human affairs; when of a sudden I am surpriz'd to find, that instead of the usual copulations of propositions, *is*, and *is not*, I meet with no proposition that is not connected with an *ought* or an *ought not*. This change is imperceptible; but is, however, of the last consequence. For as this *ought*, or *ought not*, expresses some new relation or affirmation, 'tis necessary that it shou'd be observ'd and explain'd; and at the same time that a reason should be given, for what seems altogether inconceivable, how this new relation can be a deduction from others, which are entirely different from it. But as authors do not commonly use this precaution, I shall presume to recommend it to the readers; and am persuaded, that this small attention wou'd subvert all the vulgar systems of morality, and let us see, that the distinction of vice and virtue is not founded merely on the relations of objects, nor is perceiv'd by reason.

SECTION II
MORAL DISTINCTIONS
DERIV'D FROM A MORAL SENSE

Thus the course of the argument leads us to conclude, that since vice and virtue are not discoverable merely by reason, or the comparison of ideas, it must be by means of some impression or sentiment they occasion, that we are able to mark the difference betwixt them. Our decisions concerning moral rectitude and depravity are evidently perceptions; and as all perceptions are either impressions or ideas, the exclusion of one is a convincing argument for the other. Morality, therefore, is more properly felt than judg'd of; tho' this feeling or sentiment is commonly so soft and gentle, that we are apt to confound it with an idea, according to our common custom of taking all things for the same, which have any near resemblance to each other.

The next question is, Of what nature are these impressions, and after what manner do they operate upon us? Here we cannot remain long in suspense, but must pronounce the impression arising from virtue, to be agreeable, and that proceeding from vice to be uneasy. Every moment's experience must convince us of this. There is no spectacle so fair and beautiful as a noble and generous action; nor any which gives us more abhorrence than one that is cruel and treacherous. No enjoyment equals the satisfaction we receive from the company of those we love and esteem; as the greatest of all punishments is to be oblig'd to pass our lives with those we hate or contemn. A very play or romance may afford us instances of this pleasure, which virtue conveys to us; and pain, which arises from vice.

Now since the distinguishing impressions, by which moral good or evil is known, are nothing but *particular* pains or pleasures; it follows, that in all enquiries concerning these moral distinctions, it will be sufficient to shew the principles, which make us feel a satisfaction or uneasiness from the survey of any character, in order to satisfy us why the character is laudable or blameable. An action, or sentiment, or character is virtuous or vicious; why? because its view causes a pleasure or uneasiness of a particular kind. In giving a reason, therefore, for the pleasure or uneasiness, we sufficiently explain the vice or virtue. To have the sense of virtue, is nothing but to *feel* a satisfaction of a particular kind from the contemplation of a character. The very *feeling* constitutes our praise or admiration. We go no farther; nor do we enquire into the cause of the satisfaction. We do not infer a character to be virtuous, because it pleases: But in feeling that it pleases after such a particular manner, we in effect feel that it is virtuous. The case is the same as in our judgments concerning all kinds of beauty, and tastes, and sensations. Our approbation is imply'd in the immediate pleasure they convey to us.

I have objected to the system, which establishes eternal rational measures of right and wrong, that 'tis impossible to shew, in the actions of reasonable creatures, any relations, which are not found in external objects; and therefore, if morality always attended these relations, 'twere possible for inanimate matter to become virtuous or vicious. Now it may, in like manner, be objected to the present system, that if virtue and vice be determin'd by pleasure and pain, these qualities must, in every case, arise from the sensations; and consequently any object, whether animate or inanimate, rational or irrational might become morally good or evil, provided it can excite a satisfaction or uneasiness. But tho' this objection seems to be the very same, it has by no means the same force, in the one case as in the other. For, *first*, 'tis evident, that under the term *pleasure*, we comprehend sensations, which are very different from each other, and which have only such a distant resemblance, as is requisite to make them be express'd by the same abstract term. A good composition of music and a bottle of good wine equally produce pleasure; and what is more, their goodness is determin'd merely by the pleasure. But shall we say upon that account, that the wine is harmonious, or the music of a good flavour? In like manner an inanimate object, and the character or sentiments of any person may, both of them, give satisfaction; but as the satisfaction is different, this keeps our sentiments concerning them from being confounded, and makes us ascribe virtue to the one, and not to the other. Nor is every sentiment of pleasure or pain, which arises from characters and actions, of that *peculiar* kind, which makes us praise or condemn. The good qualities of an enemy are hurtful to us; but may still command our esteem and respect. 'Tis only when a character is considered in general, without reference to our particular interest, that it causes such a feeling or sentiment, as denominates it morally good or evil. 'Tis true, those sentiments, from interest and morals, are apt to be confounded, and naturally run into one another. It seldom happens, that we do not think an enemy vicious, and can distinguish betwixt his opposition to our interest and real villainy or baseness. But this hinders not, but that the sentiments are, in themselves, distinct; and a man of temper and judgment may preserve himself from these illusions. In like manner, tho' 'tis certain a musical voice is nothing but one that naturally gives a *particular* kind of pleasure; yet 'tis difficult for a man to be sensible, that the voice of an enemy is agreeable, or allow it to be musical. But a person of a fine ear, who has the command of himself, can separate these feelings, and give praise to what deserves it.

Secondly, We may call to remembrance the preceding system of the passions in order to remark a still more considerable difference among our pains and pleasures. Pride and humility, love and hatred are excited, when there is any thing presented to us, that both bears a relation to the object of the passion, and produces a separate sensation related to the sensation of the passion. Now virtue and vice are attended with these circumstances. They must necessarily be plac'd either in ourselves or others, and excite either pleasure or uneasiness; and therefore must give rise to one of these four passions; which clearly distinguishes them from the pleasure and pain arising from inanimate objects, that often bear no relation to us: And this is, perhaps, the most considerable effect that virtue and vice have upon the human mind.

It may now be ask'd *in general*, concerning this pain or pleasure, that distinguishes moral good and evil, *From what principles is it derived, and whence does it arise in the human mind?* To this I reply, *first*, that 'tis absurd to imagine, that in every particular instance, these sentiments are produc'd by an *original* quality and *primary* constitution. For as the number of our duties is, in a manner, infinite, 'tis impossible that our original instincts should extend to each of them, and from our very first infancy impress on the human mind all that multitude of precepts, which are contain'd in the compleatest system of ethics. Such a method of proceeding is not conformable to the usual maxims, by which nature is conducted, where a few principles produce all that variety we observe in the universe, and every thing is carry'd on in the easiest and most simple manner. 'Tis necessary, therefore, to abridge these primary impulses, and find some more general principles, upon which all our notions of morals are founded.

But in the *second* place, should it be ask'd, Whether we ought to search for these principles in *nature*, or whether we must look for them in some other origin? I wou'd reply, that our answer to this question depends upon the definition of the word, Nature, than which there is none more ambiguous and equivocal. If *nature* be oppos'd to miracles, not only the distinction betwixt vice and virtue is natural but also every event, which has ever happen'd in the world, *excepting those miracles, on which our religion is founded.* In saying, then, that the sentiments of vice and virtue are natural in this sense, we make no very extraordinary discovery.

But *nature* may also be opposed to rare and unusual; and in this sense of the word, which is the common one, there may often arise disputes concerning what is natural or unnatural; and one may in general affirm, that we are not possess'd of any very precise standard, by which these disputes can be decided. Frequent and rare depend upon the number of examples we have observ'd; and as this number may gradually increase or diminish, 'twill be impossible to fix any exact boundaries betwixt them. We may only affirm on this head, that if ever there was any thing, which cou'd be call'd natural in this sense, the sentiments of morality certainly may; since there never was any nation of the world, nor any single person in any nation, who was utterly depriv'd of them, and who never, in any instance, shew'd the least approbation or dislike of manners. These sentiments are so rooted in our constitution and temper, that without entirely confounding the human mind by disease or a madness, 'tis impossible to extirpate and destroy them.

But *nature* may also be opposed to artifice, as well as to what is rare and unusual; and in this sense it may be disputed, whether the notions of virtue be natural or not. We readily forget, that the designs, and projects, and views of men are principles as necessary in their operation as heat and cold, moist and dry: But taking them to be free and entirely our own, 'tis usual for us to set them in opposition to the other principles of nature. Shou'd it, therefore, be demanded, whether the sense of virtue be natural or artificial, I am of opinion, that 'tis impossible for me at present to give any precise answer to this question. Perhaps it will appear afterwards, that our sense of some virtues is artificial, and that of others natural. . . .

Mean while it may not be amiss to observe from these definitions of *natural* and *unnatural,* that nothing can be more unphilosophical than those systems, which assert, that virtue is the same with what is natural, and vice with what is unnatural. For in the first sense of the word, Nature, as opposed to miracles, both vice and virtue are equally natural; and in the second sense, as oppos'd to what is unusual, perhaps virtue will be found to be the most unnatural. At least it must be own'd, that heroic virtue, being as unusual, is as little natural as the most brutal barbarity. As to the third sense of the word, 'tis certain, that both vice and virtue are equally artificial, and out of nature. For however it may be disputed, whether the notion of a merit or demerit in certain actions be natural or artificial, 'tis evident, that the actions themselves are artificial, and are perform'd with a certain design and intention; otherwise they cou'd never be rank'd under any of these denominations. 'Tis impossible, therefore, that the character of natural and unnatural can ever, in any sense, mark the boundaries of vice and virtue.

Part III
Of the Other Virtues and Vices

SECTION I.
OF THE ORIGIN OF THE
NATURAL VIRTUES AND VICES.

. . .The same principle produces, in many instances, our sentiments of morals, as well as those of beauty. No virtue is more esteem'd than justice, and no vice more detested than injustice; nor are there any qualities, which go farther to the fixing the character, either as amiable or odious. Now justice is a moral virtue, merely because it has that tendency to the good of mankind; and, indeed, is nothing but an artificial invention to that purpose. The same may be said of allegiance, of the laws of nations, of modesty, and of good-manners. All these are mere human contrivances for the interest of society. And since there is a very strong sentiment of morals, which in all nations, and all ages, has attended them, we must allow, that the reflecting on the tendency of characters and mental qualities, is sufficient to give us the sentiments of approbation and blame. Now as the means to an end can only be agreeable, where the end is agreeable; and as the good of society, where our own interest is not concern'd, or that of our friends, pleases only by sympathy: It follows, that sympathy is the source of the esteem, which we pay to all the artificial virtues.

Thus it appears, *that* sympathy is a very powerful principle in human nature, *that* it has a great influence on our taste of beauty, and *that* it produces our sentiment of morals in all the artificial virtues. From thence we may presume, that it also gives rise to many of the other virtues; and that qualities acquire our approbation, because of their tendency to the good of mankind. This presumption must become a certainty, when we find that most of those qualities, which we *naturally* approve of, have actually that tendency, and render a man a proper member of society: While the qualities, which we *naturally* disapprove of, have a contrary tendency, and render any intercourse with the person dangerous or disagreeable. For having found, that such tendencies have force enough to produce the strongest sentiment of morals, we can never reasonably, in these cases, look for any other cause of approbation or blame; it being an inviolable maxim in philosophy, that where any particular cause is sufficient for an effect, we ought to rest satisfied with it, and ought not to multiply causes without necessity. . . .

. . . The approbation of moral qualities most certainly is not deriv'd from reason, or any comparison of ideas; but proceeds entirely from a moral taste, and from certain sentiments of pleasure or disgust, which arise upon the contemplation and view of particular qualities or characters. Now 'tis evident, that those sentiments, whence-ever they are deriv'd, must vary according to the distance or contiguity of the objects; nor can I feel the same lively pleasure from the virtues of a person, who liv'd in *Greece* two thousand years ago, that I feel from the virtues of a familiar friend and acquaintance. Yet I do not say, that I esteem the one more than the other: And therefore, if the variation of the sentiment, without a variation of the esteem, be an objection, it must have equal force against every other system, as against that of sympathy. But to consider the matter a-right, it has no force at all. . . .

In general, all sentiments of blame or praise are variable, according to our situation of nearness or remoteness, with regard to the person blam'd or prais'd, and according to the present disposition of our mind. But these variations we regard not in our general decisions, but still apply the terms expressive of our liking or dislike, in the same manner, as if we remain'd in one point of view. Experience soon teaches us this method of correcting our sentiments, or at least, of correcting our language, where the sentiments are more stubborn and inalterable. Our servant, if diligent and faithful, may excite stronger sentiments of love and kindness than *Marcus Brutus*, as represented in history; but we say not upon that account, that the former character is more laudable than the latter. We know, that were we to approach equally near to that renown'd patriot, he wou'd command a much higher degree of affection and admiration. Such corrections are common with regard to all the senses; and indeed 'twere impossible we cou'd ever make use of language, or communicate our sentiments to one another, did we not correct the momentary appearances of things, and overlook our present situation. . . .

Thus, to take a general review of the present hypothesis: Every quality of the mind is denominated virtuous, which gives pleasure by the mere survey; as every quality, which produces pain, is call'd vicious. This pleasure and this pain may arise from four different sources. For we reap a pleasure from the view of a character, which is naturally fitted to be useful to others, or to the person himself, or which is agreeable to others, or to the person himself. One may, perhaps, be surpriz'd, that amidst all these interests and pleasures, we shou'd forget our own, which touch us so nearly on every other occasion. But we shall easily satisfy ourselves on this head, when we consider, that every particular person's pleasure and interest being different, 'tis impossible men cou'd ever agree in their sentiments and judgments, unless they chose some common point of view, from which they might survey their object, and which might cause it to appear the same to all of them. Now, in judging of characters, the only interest or pleasure, which appears the same to every spectator, is that of the person himself, whose character is examin'd; or that of persons, who have a connexion with him. And tho' such interests and pleasures touch us more faintly than our own, yet being more constant and universal, they counter-balance the latter even in practice, and are alone admitted in speculation as the standard of virtue and morality. They alone produce that particular feeling or sentiment, on which moral distinctions depend.

As to the good or ill desert of virtue or vice, 'tis an evident consequence of the sentiments of pleasure or uneasiness. These sentiments produce love or hatred; and love or hatred, by the original constitution of human passion, is attended with benevolence or anger; that is, with a desire of making happy the person we love, and miserable the person we hate.

SUGGESTIONS FOR DISCUSSION

1. Can all moral principles be established as a result of a social contract?

2. What policies would a Hobbesian sovereign adopt concerning capital punishment (see Chapter 14)?

3. Do facts play the decisive role in establishing what we ought morally to do in given circumstances?

4. What implications, if any, do Hume's positive views on morality have for setting social policy?

FOR FURTHER READING

HOBBES

Baumrin, B., ed. *Hobbes's Leviathan*. San Francisco: Wadsworth, 1969.

Chappell, V. C., ed. *Essays on Early Modern Philosophers, Vol. 5, Thomas Hobbes*. Hemden: Garland, 1992.

Collingwood, R. G. *The New Leviathan*. Oxford: Clarendon Press, 1942.

Gauthier, D. P. *The Logic of Leviathan*. Oxford: Clarendon Press, 1969.

Gert, B. *The Moral Rules*. New York: Harper & Row, 1970.

Goldsmith, M. M. *Hobbes's Science of Politics*. New York: Columbia University Press, 1966.

Hampton, J. *Hobbes and the Social Contract Tradition*. Cambridge: Cambridge University Press, 1986.

Johnston, D. *The Rhetoric of Leviathan*. Princeton: Princeton University Press, 1986.

Kavka, G. *Hobbesian Moral and Political Theory*. Princeton: Princeton University Press, 1986.

Macpherson, C. B. *The Political Theory of Possessive Individualism*. Oxford: Clarendon Press, 1962.

Oakeshott, M. *Rationalism in Politics and Other Essays*. New York: Basic Books, 1962.

Peters, R. *Hobbes*. London: Harmondsworth, 1962.

Rogers, G. A. J., and Ryan, A., eds. *Perspectives on Thomas Hobbes*. New York: Oxford University Press, 1988.

Strauss, L. *Political Philosophy of Hobbes*. Oxford: Clarendon Press, 1936.

Taylor, A. E. *Thomas Hobbes*. London: A. Constable, 1908.

Warrender, H. *The Political Philosophy of Hobbes*. Oxford: Clarendon Press, 1957.

Watkins, J. W. *Hobbes's System of Ideas*. New York: Hilary House, 1965.

HUME

Baier, A. *Postures of the Mind.* Minneapolis: University of Minnesota Press, 1985.

Bennett, J. *Locke, Berkeley and Hume.* Oxford: Oxford University Press, 1971.

Brand, W. *Hume's Theory of Moral Judgment.* Dordrecht: Kluwer, 1992.

Broad, C. D. *Five Types of Ethical Theory.* London: Routledge, 1930.

Capaldi, N. *Hume's Place in Moral Philosophy.* New York: Lang, 1989.

Chappell, V. C., ed. *Hume: A Collection of Critical Essays.* South Bend: University of Notre Dame Press, 1966.

Glathe, A. B. *Hume's Theory of the Passions and of Morals.* Berkeley: University of California Press, 1950.

Hume, D. *Enquiry Concerning Human Understanding.* London, 1751.

Kemp, J. *Ethical Naturalism: Hume and Hobbes.* London: Macmillan, 1970.

Pears, D. F., ed. *David Hume: A Symposium.* London: Macmillan, 1963.

Raphael, D. D., ed. *British Moralists, 1650–1800.* Oxford: Oxford University Press, 1979.

————. *The Moral Sense.* London: Oxford University Press, 1947.

Snare, F. *Morals, Motivation and Convention: Hume's Influential Doctrines.* New York: Cambridge University Press, 1991.

CHAPTER THREE

ROUSSEAU AND KANT

■ **JEAN-JACQUES ROUSSEAU (1712–1778):**
THE GENERAL WILL AND THE SOCIAL CONTRACT

Hobbes and Rousseau   Like Hobbes, Jean-Jacques Rousseau was primarily concerned with questions of political morality and the social institutions that would best secure legitimate government. Like Hobbes, again, Rousseau developed his philosophical analysis of legitimate government in terms of concepts like the *state of nature, right,* and the *social contract.* However, on Hobbes's conception of human nature individuals fear death, while on Rousseau's view they do not. Nor did Rousseau assume that in an economy of scarce resources, each individual equally desires simply to satisfy self-interests (see Hobbes, Chapter 2). Rather, Rousseau believed that the state of nature is one of abundance, that human beings are equally interested in and capable of achieving freedom, and that they are motivated by self-love.

Rousseau's State of Nature   Schematically, self-interest need not incorporate notions of self-respect and self-esteem, whereas the concept of self-love must include them. So, for its satisfaction, self-love requires recognition *by* others, while self-interest need not. Yet individuals in Rousseau's state of nature are indifferent to each other; they seek only what they find necessary for self-preservation. Accordingly, life in Rousseau's state of nature may not be short, nasty, and brutish, but it will lack human fulfillment because the benefits of social cooperation are lacking.

The Social Contract   Rousseau assumed that individuals desire to satisfy their fundamental needs and to fulfill their self-love. Each understands also that if he or she aimed only to satisfy self-interest, everyone would fare worse than if all cooperated. Rousseau held that satisfaction of self-love depends upon actions of others; satisfaction is ultimately possible only under conditions of social interdependence. Moreover, he assumed that each individual has a set of beliefs about the acceptability of claims that can be made upon him or her, and that this set conflicts with the relevant beliefs of others. Given these assumptions, Rousseau sought a form of social cooperation and association that protects the person and property of each while making individual development, education and expression possible. It must do so, however, while it maintains individual freedom, rights, and self-determination. The social contract was supposed to furnish this form of association.

For Rousseau, each individual knows that a conception of the "common good" or common interest is shared with all others. What differs among agents, if anything, is not this conception, but their particular views of how best to achieve the common good. That an institution, social arrangement, or law best guarantees the common good is considered by individuals as one among the possible reasons for accepting it. They comprehend that reason requires them to act for the sake of the common good, if they are reasonably confident others will also.

The General Will   Rousseau argued that self-protection, self-expression, and freedom would be maximized by a contractual agreement among members of the state of nature. After all, they share a conception of their common interest. This agreement establishes a *general will.* The general will is constituted by a contract whereby each individual will invests person and power in a common authority and common institutions. Authority is bestowed in the final analysis by the shared conception each contractor has of the good common to all. The general will commands the "supreme" direction, though not the only one. The contract that produces the general will promotes both individual freedom and self-love. Though the conception of the common good is shared, it is the agent's own; it is chosen autonomously. Each citizen accepts the law because in prescribing it for all, each prescribes it for himself or herself. So the rule of the general will is the rule of each individual will. Yet the general will differs from the *will of all;* that is, from the aggregate forces of all separate individuals. The social contract, Rousseau concluded, "leaves [contractors or citizens] as free as before." Further, it is only because the unanimous agreement is among rational agents with common interests that they are prepared to accept the contract. The satisfaction of common interest by contractual agreement, in turn, is a necessary condition for fulfilling self-love.

Morality and Socialization   Rousseau's justification of the general will in terms of the social contract depends upon an analysis of rationality, and the moral principles it identifies, that is independent of any appeal to empirical or factual experience of how the world is. Known as *a priori* analysis, it is to be distinguished from the account Rousseau offered of how citizens in fact acquire social and political principles as they become socialized. These potentially conflicting concerns with moral principles or right, on the one hand, and principles acquired in socialization, on the other, merged for Rousseau in the question of how citizens best acquire and act upon principles of right. Rousseau thought that socialization in a *democratic* state would engender in agents the conception of the general will. This conception was taken to provide citizens with the basis for establishing the principles of moral and political right. In this way, Rousseau merged moral and political inquiry: what it takes to be a moral person is what is required of a good citizen.

Jean-Jacques Rousseau

THE SOCIAL CONTRACT

BOOK I

Chapter 1
The Subject of Book I

Man was born free, and he is everywhere in chains. Those who think themselves the masters of others are indeed greater slaves than they. How did this transformation come about? I do not know. How can it be made legitimate? That question I believe I can answer.

If I were to consider only force and the effects of force, I should say: "So long as a people is constrained to obey, and obeys, it does well; but as soon as it can shake off the yoke, and shakes it off, it does better; for since it regains its freedom by the same right as that which removed it, a people is either justified in taking back its freedom, or there is no justifying those who took it away." But the social order is a sacred right which serves as a basis for all other rights. And as it is not a natural right, it must be one founded on covenants. The problem is to determine what those covenants are. . . .

Chapter 3
The Right of the Strongest

The strongest man is never strong enough to be master all the time, unless he transforms force into right and obedience into duty. Hence "the right of the strongest"—a "right" that sounds like something intended ironically, but is actually laid down as a principle. But shall we never have this phrase explained? Force is a physical power, I do not see how its effects could produce morality. To yield to force is an act of necessity, not of will; it is at best an act of prudence. In what sense can it be a moral duty?

Let us grant, for a moment, that this so-called right exists. I suggest it can only produce a tissue of bewildering nonsense; for once might is made to be right, cause and effect are reversed, and every force which overcomes another force inherits the right which belonged to the vanquished. As soon as man can disobey with impunity,

From Jean-Jacques Rousseau, *The Social Contract*. Trans. Maurice Cranston (Harmondsworth: Penguin Books, 1968). Reprinted by permission of the Peters Fraser and Dunlop Group Ltd.

his disobedience becomes legitimate; and as the strongest is always right, the only problem is how to become the strongest. But what can be the validity of a right which perishes with the force on which it rests? If force compels obedience, there is no need to invoke a duty to obey, and if force ceases to compel obedience, there is no longer any obligation. Thus the word "right" adds nothing to what is said by "force"; it is meaningless.

"Obey those in power." If this means "yield to force" the precept is sound, but superfluous; it has never, I suggest, been violated. All power comes from God, I agree; but so does every disease, and no one forbids us to summon a physician. If I am held up by a robber at the edge of a wood, force compels me to hand over my purse. But if I could somehow contrive to keep the purse from him, would I still be obliged in conscience to surrender it? After all, the pistol in the robber's hand is undoubtedly a *power*.

Surely it must be admitted then, that might does not make right, and that the duty of obedience is owed only to legitimate powers. . . .

Chapter 4
Slavery

Since no man has any natural authority over his fellows, and since force alone bestows no right, all legitimate authority among men must be based on covenants. . . .

Chapter 5
That We Must Always
Go Back to an Original Covenant

Even if I were to concede all that I have so far refuted, the champions of despotism would be no better off. There will always be a great difference between subduing a multitude and ruling a society. If one man successively enslaved many separate individuals no matter how numerous, he and they would never bear the aspect of anything but a master and his slaves, not at all that of a people and their ruler; an aggregation, perhaps, but certainly not an association, for they would neither have a common good nor be a body politic. Even if such a man were to enslave half the world, he would remain a private individual, and his interest, always at variance with that of the others, would never be more than a personal interest. When he died, the empire he left would be scattered for lack of any bond of union, even as an oak crumbles and falls into a heap of ashes when fire has consumed it.

"A people," says Grotius, "may give itself to a king." Therefore, according to Grotius a people is *a people* even before the gift to the king is made. The gift itself is a civil act; it presupposes public deliberation. Hence, before considering the act by which a people submits to a king, we ought to scrutinize the act by which people become a people, for that act, being necessarily antecedent to the other, is the real foundation of society.

Indeed, if there were no earlier agreement, then how, unless the election were unanimous, could there be any obligation on the minority to accept the decision of the majority? What right have the hundred who want to have a master to vote on behalf of the ten who do not? The law of majority-voting itself rests on a covenant, and implies that there has been on at least one occasion unanimity.

Chapter 6
The Social Pact

I assume that men reach a point where the obstacles to their preservation in a state of nature prove greater than the strength that each has to preserve himself in that state. Beyond this point, the primitive condition cannot endure, for then the human race will perish if it does not change its mode of existence.

Since men cannot create new forces, but merely combine and control those which already exist, the only way in which they can preserve themselves is by uniting their separate powers in a combination strong enough to overcome any resistance, uniting them so that their powers are directed by a single motive and act in concert.

Such a sum of forces can be produced only by the union of separate men, but as each man's own strength and liberty are the chief instruments of his preservation, how can he merge his with others' without putting himself in peril and neglecting the care he owes to himself? This difficulty, which brings me back to my present subject, may be expressed in these words:

"How to find a form of association which will defend the person and goods of each member with the collective force of all, and under which each individual, while uniting himself with the others, obeys no one but himself, and remains as free as before." This is the fundamental problem to which the social contract holds the solution.

The articles of this contract are so precisely determined by the nature of the act, that the slightest modification must render them null and void; they are such that, though perhaps never formally stated, they are everywhere tacitly admitted and recognized; and if ever the social pact is violated, every man regains his original rights and, recovering his natural freedom, loses that social freedom for which he exchanged it.

These articles of association, rightly understood, are reducible to a single one, namely the total alienation by each associate of himself and all his rights to the whole community. Thus, in the first place, as every individual gives himself absolutely, the conditions are the same for all, and precisely because they are the same for all, it is in no one's interest to make the conditions onerous for others.

Secondly, since the alienation is unconditional, the union is as perfect as it could be, and no individual associate has any longer any rights to claim; for if rights were left to individuals, in the absence of any higher authority to judge between them and the public, each individual, being his own judge in some causes, would soon demand to be his own judge in all; and in this way the state of nature would be kept in being, and the association inevitably become either tyrannical or void.

Finally, since each man gives himself to all, he gives himself to no one; and since there is no associate over whom he does not gain the same rights as others gain over him, each man recovers the equivalent of everything he loses, and in the bargain he acquires more power to preserve what he has.

If, then, we eliminate from the social pact everything that is not essential to it, we find it comes down to this: "Each one of us puts into the community his person and all his powers under the supreme direction of the general will; and as body, we incorporate every member as an indivisible part of the whole."

Immediately, in place of the individual person of each contracting party, this act of association creates an artificial and collective body composed of as many members as there are voters in the assembly, and by this same act that body acquires its unity, its common *ego*, its life and will. The public person thus formed by the union of all other persons was once called the *city*, and is now known as the *republic* or the *body politic*. . . .

Chapter 7
The Sovereign

This formula shows that the act of association consists of a reciprocal commitment between society and the individual, so that each person, in making a contract, as it were, with himself, finds himself doubly committed, first, as a member of the sovereign body in relation to individuals, and secondly as a member of the state in relation to the sovereign. Here there can be no invoking the principle of civil law which says that no man is bound by a contract with himself, for there is a great difference between having an obligation to oneself and having an obligation to something of which one is a member.

We must add that a public decision can impose an obligation on all the subjects towards the sovereign, by reason of the two aspects under which each can be seen, while, contrariwise, such decisions cannot impose an obligation on the sovereign towards itself; and hence it would be against the very nature of a political body for the Sovereign to set over itself a law which it could not infringe. The sovereign, bearing only one single and identical aspect, is in the position of a private person making a contract with himself, which shows that there neither is, nor can be, any kind of fundamental law binding on the people as a body, not even the social contract itself. This does not mean that the whole body cannot incur obligations to other nations, so long as those obligations do not infringe the contract; for in relation to foreign powers, the body politic is a simple entity, an individual.

However, since the body politic, or sovereign, owes its being to the sanctity of the contract alone, it cannot commit itself, even in treaties with foreign powers, to anything that would derogate from the original act of association; it could not, for example, alienate a part of itself or submit to another sovereign. To violate the act which has given it existence would be to annihilate itself; and what is nothing can produce nothing.

As soon as the multitude is united thus in a single body, no one can injure any one of the members without attacking the whole, still less injure the whole without each member feeling it. Duty and self-interest thus equally oblige the two contracting parties to give each other mutual aid; and the same men should seek to bring together in this dual relationship, all the advantages that flow from it.

Now, as the sovereign is formed entirely of the individuals who compose it, it has not, nor could it have, any interest contrary to theirs; and so the sovereign has no need to give guarantees to the subjects, because it is impossible for a body to wish to hurt all of its members, and, as we shall see, it cannot hurt any particular member. The sovereign by the mere fact that it is, is always all that it ought to be.

But this is not true of the relation of subject to sovereign. Despite their common interest, subjects will not be bound by their commitment unless means are found to guarantee their fidelity.

For every individual as a man may have a private will contrary to, or different from the general will that he has as a citizen. His private interest may speak with a very different voice from that of the public interest; his absolute and naturally independent existence may make him regard what he owes to the common cause as a gratuitous contribution, the loss of which would be less painful for others than the payment is onerous for him; and fancying that the artificial person which constitutes the state is a mere rational entity (since it is not a man), he might seek to enjoy the rights of a citizen without doing the duties of a subject. The growth of this kind of injustice would bring about the ruin of the body politic.

Hence, in order that the social pact shall not be an empty formula, it is tacitly implied in that commitment—which alone can give force to all others—that whoever refuses to obey the general will shall be constrained to do so by the whole body, which means nothing other than that he shall be forced to be free; for this is the condition which, by giving each citizen to the nation, secures him against all personal dependence, it is the condition which shapes both the design and the working of the political machine, and which alone bestows justice on civil contracts—without it, such contracts would be absurd, tyrannical and liable to the grossest abuse.

Chapter 8
Civil Society

The passing from the state of nature to the civil society produces a remarkable change in man; it puts justice as a rule of conduct in the place of instinct, and gives his actions the moral quality they previously lacked. It is only then, when the voice of duty has taken the place of physical impulse, and right that of desire, that man, who has hitherto thought only of himself, finds himself compelled to act on other principles, and to consult his reason rather than study his inclinations. And although in civil society man surrenders some of the advantages that belong to the state of nature, he gains in return far greater ones; his faculties are so exercised and developed, his mind is so enlarged, his sentiments so ennobled, and his whole spirit so elevated that, if the abuse of his new condition did not in many cases lower him to something worse than what he had left, he should constantly bless the happy hour that lifted him for ever from the state of nature and from a narrow, stupid animal made a creature of intelligence and a man.

Suppose we draw up a balance sheet, so that the losses and gains may be readily compared. What man loses by the social contract is his natural liberty and the absolute right to anything that tempts him and that he can take; what he gains by the social contract is civil liberty and the legal right of property in what he possesses. If we are to avoid mistakes in weighing the one side against the other, we must clearly distinguish between *natural* liberty, which has no limit but the physical power of the individual concerned, and *civil* liberty, which is limited by the general will; and we must distinguish also between *possession*, which is based only on force or "the right of the first occupant," and *property*, which must rest on a legal title.

We might also add that man acquires with civil society, moral freedom, which alone makes man the master of himself; for to be governed by appetite alone is slavery, while obedience to a law one prescribes to oneself is freedom. However, I have already said more than enough on this subject, and the philosophical meaning of the word "freedom" is no part of my subject here. . . .

BOOK II

Chapter 6
On Law

We have given life and existence to the body politic by the social pact; now it is a matter of giving it movement and will by legislation. For the primitive act by which the body politic is formed and united does not determine what it shall do to preserve itself.

What is good and in conformity with order is such by the very nature of things and independently of human agreements. All justice comes from God, who alone is its source; and if only we knew how to receive it from that exalted fountain, we should need neither governments nor laws. There is undoubtedly a universal justice which springs from reason alone, but if that justice is to be admitted among men it must be reciprocal. Humanly speaking, the laws of natural justice, lacking any natural sanction, are unavailing among men. In fact, such laws merely benefit the wicked and injure the just, since the just respect them while others do not do so in return. So there must be covenants and positive laws to unite rights with duties and to direct justice to its object. In the state of nature, where everything is common, I owe nothing to those to whom I have promised nothing, and I recognize as belonging to others only those things that are of no use to me. But this is no longer the case in civil society, where all rights are determined by law.

Yet what in the last analysis, is law? If we simply try to define it in terms of metaphysical ideas, we shall go on talking without reaching any understanding; and when we have said what natural law is, we shall still not know what the law of the state is.

I have already said that the general will cannot relate to any particular object. For such a particular object is either within the state or outside the state. If it is outside, then a will which is alien to it is not general with regard to it: if the object is within the state, it forms a part of the state. Then there comes into being a relationship between the whole and the part which involves two separate entities, the part being one, and the whole, less that particular part, being the other. But a whole less a particular part is no longer a whole; and so as long as this relationship exists there is no whole but only two unequal parts, from which it follows that the will of the one is no longer general with respect to the other.

But when the people as a whole makes rules for the people as a whole, it is dealing only with itself; and if any relationship emerges, it is between the entire body seen from one perspective and the same entire body seen from another, without any division whatever. Here the matter concerning which a rule is made is as general as the will which makes it. And *this* is the kind of act which I call a law.

When I say that the province of the law is always general, I mean that the law considers all subjects collectively and all actions in the abstract; it does not consider any individual man or any specific action. Thus the law may well lay down that there shall be privileges, but it may not nominate the persons who shall have those privileges; the law may establish several classes of citizen, and even specify the qualifications which shall give access to those several classes, but may not say that this man or that shall be admitted; the law may set up a royal government and a hereditary succession, but it may not elect a king or choose a royal family—in a word, no function which deals with the individual falls within the province of the legislative power.

On this analysis, it is immediately clear that we can no longer ask *who* is to make the laws, because laws are acts of the general will; no longer ask if the prince is above the law, because he is a part of the state; no longer ask if the law can be unjust, because no one is unjust to himself; and no longer ask how we can be both free and subject to laws, for the laws are but registers of what we ourselves desire.

It is also clear that since the law unites universality of will with universality of the field of legislation, anything that any man, no matter who, commands on his own authority is not a law; even what the sovereign itself commands with respect to a particular object is not a law but a decree, not an act of sovereignty but an act of government.

Any state which is ruled by law I call a "republic," whatever the form of its constitution; for then, and then alone, does the public interest govern and then alone is the "public thing"—the *res publica*—a reality. All legitimate government is "republican."*. . .

Laws are really nothing other than the conditions on which civil society exists. A people, since it is subject to laws, ought to be the author of them. The right of laying down the rules of society belongs only to those who form the society; but how can they exercise it? Is it to be by common agreement, by a sudden inspiration? Has the body politic an organ to declare its will? Who is to give it the foresight necessary to formulate enactments and proclaim them in advance, and how is it to announce them in the hour of need? How can a blind multitude, which often does not know what it wants, because it seldom knows what is good for it, undertake by itself an enterprise as vast and difficult as a system of legislation? By themselves the people always will what is good, but by themselves they do not always discern it. The general will is always rightful, but the judgment which guides it is not always enlightened. It must be made to see things as they are, and sometimes as they should be seen; it must be shown the good path which it is seeking, and secured against seduction by the desires of individuals; it must be given a sense of situation and season, so as to weigh immediate and tangible advantages against distant and hidden evils. Individuals see the good and reject it; the public desires the good but does not see it. Both equally need guidance. Individuals must be obliged to subordinate their will to their reason; the public must be taught to recognize what it desires. Such public enlightenment would produce a union of understanding and will in the social body, bring the parts into perfect harmony and lift the whole to its fullest strength. Hence the necessity of a lawgiver.

■ IMMANUEL KANT (1724–1804): SELF-DETERMINATION AND THE CATEGORICAL IMPERATIVE

Kant and Hume The German philosopher Immanuel Kant was deeply troubled by Hume's argument that reason is incapable of originating or inhibiting action. Hume's argument was designed to show that formal principles of reason cannot directly cause human action. These rational principles service socially formed and changing motivations. Hume's critique of reason effectively undermined the view that moral claims are objectively right or wrong (see Chapter 2).

---

* By this word I understand not only an aristocracy or democracy, but generally any government directed by the general will, which is law. If it is to be legitimate, the government must not be united with the sovereign, but must serve it as its ministry, so even a monarch can be a republic. . . .

Challenged by Hume's critique of reason, Kant appealed to Rousseau's insight that if morality is to be possible on its own terms, self-interest must be governed by moral reason. This required demonstrating that moral reason is necessarily self-motivating: moral reason must be independent of both self-interest and any such moral sentiment as benevolence or sympathy. Kant set out to establish the conditions that must hold for individual agents if moral reason is to provide them with its own motive to act.

He began by assuming that ordinary moral judgments in the Judeo-Christian tradition—for instance, that we ought to keep our promises or pay our debts—may legitimately claim to be true. He set out to establish the conditions that must hold for such claims to be true. Thus Kant represented his undertaking as moving from "common sense morality" to "philosophical morality." In other words, he aimed to show, against Hume, that pure reason can be practical or can cause action. Kant argued that reason is represented, in its application to practical affairs requiring action, by a single unchanging principle of right conduct. If agents are to be held responsible for acting on this morally binding principle, it cannot be imposed upon them by external forces. Thus Kant had to show that the principle of morality is freely chosen by agents themselves.

Morality and Rationality   Kant considered human beings to be only partly rational in constitution. Where sensuous inclinations such as desires or passions present goals or ends to be pursued, Kant acknowledged Hume's point that reason simply services the sensuous by identifying the best means to achieve the given ends. A supreme principle or single standard capable of determining the morality of any act, however, cannot be established empirically by observing actual human behavior. Descriptive psychology and anthropology reveal only facts, and they are unable to establish what acts *ought* to be done. Kant argued also that the Natural Law tradition is mistaken in taking morality to be derivable from human nature, for human nature in general changes over time. He insisted that only the formal or rational part of human nature is unchanging. Moral action is rational action, and the supreme principle of morality must apply to all rational beings by virtue of their rationality. Analysis of rationality was supposed to reveal how, although commanded by reason to act morally, rational agents nevertheless remain free and so rationally responsible for their acts.

The Good Will   Kant acknowledged that nature, including human nature, functions according to laws. For an act to be moral, it must accord with and be done for the sake of the moral law: duty must be done for duty's sake. Rational creatures differ from others in that they alone are capable of willing that their actions be done for the sake of the moral law. A will governed always by reason is a good will. A *good will,* for Kant, may be thought of as the self-conscious resolve to act in a way that is morally right, and to do so only for the reason that it is right. A will is not good because of any beneficial consequences; a good will has intrinsic moral worth independent of its advantages. Indeed, on Kant's view, the good will is the only thing that is good without qualification; it is necessary for the production of any other moral good, including happiness.

Imperatives   While the human will may be rational and so good, it is also subject to motivations that are not strictly rational. To the extent that it is motivated by nonrational inclinations like pleasure, the human will is less than perfectly good. So the human will experiences the laws of reason as commands or requirements of what it ought rationally to do. These commands or constraints of reason Kant called "imperatives." *Imperatives* are commands or requirements issued by reason to act in various ways that may or should be considered valuable. Examples of imperatives may include "Learn to speak Spanish," "You should go to sleep," and "Do not lie."

Hypothetical Imperatives Kant identified two general kinds of imperative, the *hypothetical* and the *categorical*. If an action is commanded as instrumentally necessary for bringing about some further end, the imperative is hypothetical; if it is required as good without qualification, the imperative is categorical. Kant distinguished two sorts of hypothetical imperatives. First, *imperatives of skill* are technical rules of skill necessary for bringing about a given end or goal. Whoever desires the end is rationally constrained to use the technical means appropriate to achieving it: If I wish to work in Argentina, I must become fluent in Spanish. Second, *pragmatic counsels of prudence* advise one how best to achieve those goals that are likely to make one happy. Happiness is indefinite, for it is an ideal of imagination rather than one of reason. Accordingly, the means to its attainment suffer a lack of precision. For example, if I am tired and wish to be rested, I should sleep. The goals specified in hypothetical imperatives depend upon each person's subjective desire. The means ordered by such imperatives reflect the uncertainty of the hypothetical goals. Should the ends alter, the particular conditional imperative will no longer rationally command the will: If I am no longer tired, reason will not command me to sleep.

The Categorical Imperative The *categorical imperative,* by contrast, commands unconditionally. It constrains all rational agents irrespective of their subjective goals; it commands unqualified obedience to the practical law formulated by reason. The principles of practical reason are universal, impartial, and objective. In commanding me to act in some way, reason requires every rational agent to act alike in suitably similar circumstances. Kant formulated a decision procedure for rational agents to establish what they have a *duty* or a moral obligation to do in each act-context. First, the subjective principle or *maxim* of the act must be specified. For example, I am considering whether to lie to the buyer of my house about the development of the neighboring lot. The maxim of my projected act may be formulated as follows: "I will lie to the buyer of my property in order to secure the success of the sale." Second, in circumstances where this kind of act (in our example, lying to secure personal advantage) is a relevant option, the agent must be willing to have everyone act on the maxim. Finally, the act will be required as a moral duty if and only if the maxim can be willed without inconsistency to be acted on by all those for whom this kind of act is a relevant option. I will have a duty to lie if and only if it can be willed consistently that all individuals lie when it is to their advantage. Kant argued that the maxim of lying to secure advantage cannot be consistently willed to be universally acted upon, for if everyone acted on it, there would be no institution of truth-telling that the maxim of lying must presuppose were it to be successful. Note that Kant is not appealing here to the bad consequences of lying for advantage. Rather, his argument turns on the claim that the projected consequences of everyone acting in this way are self-defeating. Just as I cannot consistently conceive a square circle, so I cannot conceive that my lie will be believed if people generally lied The contradiction is contained in any liar's conception *both* that the lie be successful *and* that, once universalized, the lie must fail. So Kant would insist that my advantageous lie, as with lying in general, must be wrong irrespective of its benefits. Thus there is a duty never to lie.

Kant insisted that only one categorical imperative or fundamental rule of morality exists, though he formulated it in various ways. The first formulation is that an act is moral, and so required, if the maxim can be willed rationally—that is, without inconsistency—to become a universal law, a duty for all. Kant's second suggestive formulation, which has been emphasized by commentators, is that rational beings must be treated with the *respect* due them as such. They must be treated, that is, as *ends in themselves* and not merely as means to one's own ends. Humanity, or rational nature in general, has unqualified value that cannot be compared to or traded for anything one otherwise deems beneficial. The capacity of rational beings to determine and pursue their own ends implies that they should be treated as autonomous agents, free to decide rationally what they wish to do as long as they respect the same freedom for others. Though open to considerable interpretation, the notion of *respect* is far less formalistic than the notion of *universalizability.* Accordingly, many philosophers have found it germane to the moral domain.

Kant stressed that there is only one categorical imperative or principle of moral law. One might wonder, then, why he offered various formulations of it. He claimed that the first formulation or universalizability principle is a pure law, a formula that can be universally applied. The alternative formulations are offered to render the moral law more accessible to our ordinary grasp or intuition, to demonstrate in terms more readily acceptable what duty requires of us.

Autonomy Thus Kant claimed to have met Hume's challenge. Duties, or the commands of pure reason in its practical application, constrain the will to undertake impartial action, to act as any rational agent would. Though constrained, actions done from duty are nevertheless free because the principles of duty are self-legislated. They are consistent universalizations of the agent's own motives. This is what Kant means by the claim that if duties are to be morally binding, they must be *autonomously* chosen: rational agents are free and self-determined. In legislating rationally for themselves, agents legislate for all other rational agents. Kant concluded that rationality is impartial and, against Hume, that it is practical or capable of motivating action. Rousseau's dictum of self-determination, interpreted from the standpoint of the individual rather than the body politic, echo through Kant's moral theory: "each one uniting with all obeys only himself and remains as free as before."

Kant rejected all teleological appeals, whether to beneficial ends, pleasure, or happiness, as the grounds for justifying moral claims. Any such appeal would sustain only hypothetical imperatives. In contrast to autonomously chosen moral principles, the latter are imposed upon the agent "heteronomously," that is, because of various and possibly inconsistent considerations external to acts. In contrast to teleological moral theories, Kant's system of morality is *deontological:* it sets out to establish what rational agents ought morally to do independent of the act's projected consequences, such as its production of goodness.

Kant's attempt to construct a philosophical justification for general moral principles in the Judeo-Christian tradition has exerted considerable and lasting influence upon modern moral philosophy. Contemporary ethics has come to consist largely in the theoretical debate, and its public policy implications, between Kantian-inspired moral philosophy and the view of utilitarianism that developed in the wake of Hume and Kant. It will be seen in the following chapter that utilitarianism is composed of interpretations of the principle that moral good consists of maximizing utility or goodness.

Immanuel Kant

GROUNDWORK OF
THE METAPHYSIC OF MORALS

Chapter I
Passage from Ordinary Rational
Knowledge of Morality to Philosophical

It is impossible to conceive anything at all in the world, or even out of it, which can be taken as good without qualification, except a *good will*. Intelligence, wit, judgment, and any other talents of the mind we may care to name, or courage, resolution, and constancy of purpose, as qualities of *temperament*, are without doubt good and desirable in many respects; but they can also be extremely bad and hurtful when the will is not good which has to make use of these gifts of nature, and which for this reason has the term "*character*" applied to its peculiar quality. It is exactly the same with *gifts of fortune*. Power, wealth, honor, even health and that complete well-being and contentment with one's state which goes by the name of "*happiness*," produce boldness, and as a consequence often over-boldness as well, unless a good will is present by which their influence on the mind—and so too the whole principle of action—may be corrected and adjusted to universal ends; not to mention that a rational and impartial spectator can never feel approval in contemplating the uninterrupted prosperity of a being graced by no touch of a pure and good will and that consequently a good will seems to constitute the indispensable condition of our very worthiness to be happy.

Some qualities are even helpful to this good will itself and can make its task very much easier. They have none the less no inner unconditioned worth, but rather presuppose a good will which sets a limit to the esteem in which they are rightly held and does not permit us to regard them as absolutely good. Moderation in affections and passions, self-control, and sober reflection are not only good in

Immanuel Kant, *Groundwork of the Metaphysic of Morals*, trans. H.J. Paton (London: Hutchinson, an imprint of Century Hutchinson). Reprinted by permission of the estate author.

many respects: they may even seem to constitute part of the *inner* worth of a person. Yet they are far from being properly described as good without qualification (however unconditionally they have been commended by the ancients). For without the principles of a good will they may become exceedingly bad; and the very coolness of a scoundrel makes him, not merely more dangerous, but also immediately more abominable in our eyes than we should have taken him to be without it.

A good will is not good because of what it effects or accomplishes—because of its fitness for attaining some proposed end: it is good through its willing alone—that is, good in itself. Considered in itself it is to be esteemed beyond comparison as far higher than anything it could ever bring about merely in order to favor some inclination or, if you like, the sum total of inclinations. Even if, by some special disfavor of destiny or by the niggardly endowment of step-motherly nature, this will is entirely lacking in power to carry out its intentions; if by its utmost effort it still accomplishes nothing, and only good will is left (not, admittedly, as a mere wish, but as the straining of every means so far as they are in our control); even then it would still shine like a jewel for its own sake as something which has its full value in itself. Its usefulness or fruitlessness can neither add to, nor subtract from, this value. Its usefulness would be merely, as it were, the setting which enables us to handle it better in our ordinary dealings or to attract the attention of those not yet sufficiently expert, but not to commend it to experts or to determine its value.

Yet in this Idea of the absolute value of a mere will, all useful results being left out of account in its assessment, there is something so strange that, in spite of all the agreement it receives even from ordinary reason, there must arise the suspicion that perhaps its secret basis is merely some high-flown fantasticality, and that we may have misunderstood the purpose of nature in attaching reason to our will as its governor. We will therefore submit our Idea to an examination from this point of view.

In the natural constitution of an organic being—that is, of one contrived for the purpose of life—let us take it as a principle that in it no organ is to be found for any end unless it is also the most appropriate to that end and the best fitted for it. Suppose now that for a being possessed of reason and a will the real purpose of nature were his *preservation*, his *welfare*, or in a word his *happiness*. In that case nature would have hit on a very bad arrangement by choosing reason in the creature to carry out this purpose. For all the actions he has to perform with this end in view, and the whole rule of his behavior, would have been mapped out for him far more accurately by instinct; and the end in question could have been maintained far more surely by instinct than it ever can be by reason. If reason should have been imparted to this favored creature as well, it would have had to serve him only for contemplating the happy disposition of his nature, for admiring it, for enjoying it, and for being grateful to its beneficent Cause—not for subjecting his power of appetition to such feeble and defective guidance or for meddling incompetently with the purposes of nature. In a word, *nature* would have prevented reason from striking out into a *practical use* and from presuming, with its feeble vision, to think out for itself a plan for happiness and for the means to its attainment. Nature would herself have taken over the choice, not only of ends, but also of means, and would with wise precaution have entrusted both to instinct alone. . . .

For since reason is not sufficiently serviceable for guiding the will safely as regards its objects and the satisfaction of all our needs (which it in part even multiplies)—a purpose for which an implanted natural instinct would have led us much more surely; and since none the less reason has been imparted to us as a practical power—that is, as one which is to have influence on the *will;* its true function must be to produce a *will* which is *good* not as a *means* to some further end, but *in itself;* and for this function reason was absolutely necessary in a world where nature, in distributing her aptitudes, has everywhere else gone to work in a purposive manner. Such a will need not on this account be the sole and complete good, but it must be the highest good and the condition of all the rest, even of all our demands for happiness. In that case we can easily reconcile with the wisdom of nature our observation that the cultivation of reason which is required for the first and unconditioned purpose may in many ways, at least in this life, restrict the attainment of the second purpose—namely, happiness—which is always conditioned; and indeed that it can even reduce happiness to less than zero without nature proceeding contrary to its purpose; for reason, which recognizes as its highest practical function the establishment of a good will, in attaining this end is capable only of its own peculiar kind of contentment—contentment in fulfilling a purpose which in turn is determined by reason alone, even if this fulfillment should often involve interference with the purposes of inclination.

We have now to elucidate the concept of a will estimable in itself and good apart from any further end. This concept, which is already present in a sound natural understanding and requires not so much to be taught as merely to be clarified, always holds the highest place in estimating the total worth of our actions and constitutes the condition of all the rest. We will therefore take up the concept of *duty,* which includes that of a good will, exposed, however, to certain subjective limitations and obstacles. These, so far from hiding a good will or disguising it, rather bring it out by contrast and make it shine forth more brightly.

I will here pass over all actions already recognized as contrary to duty, however useful they may be with a view to this or that end; for about these the question does not even arise whether they could have been done *for the sake of duty* inasmuch as they are directly opposed to it. I will also set aside actions which in fact accord with duty, yet for which men have *no immediate inclination,* but perform them because impelled to do so by some other inclination. For there it is easy to decide whether the action which accords with duty has been done *from duty* or from some purpose of self-interest. This distinction is far more difficult to perceive when the action accords with duty and the subject has in addition an *immediate* inclination to the action. For example, it certainly accords with duty that a grocer should not overcharge his inexperienced customer; and where there is much competition a sensible shopkeeper refrains from so doing and keeps to a fixed and general price for everybody so that a child can buy from him just as well as anyone else. Thus people are served *honestly:* but this is not nearly enough to justify us in believing that the shopkeeper has acted in this way from duty or from principles of fair dealing; his interests required him to do so. We cannot assume him to have in addition an immediate inclination toward his customers, leading him, as it were out of love, to give no man preference over another in the matter of price. Thus the action was done neither from duty nor from immediate inclination, but solely from purposes of self-interest.

On the other hand, to preserve one's life is a duty, and besides this every one has also an immediate inclination to do so. But on account of this the often anxious precautions taken by the greater part of mankind for this purpose have no inner worth, and the maxim of their action is without moral content. They do protect their lives in *conformity with duty*, but not *from the motive of duty*. When on the contrary, disappointments and hopeless misery have quite taken away the taste for life; when a wretched man, strong in soul and more angered at his fate than faint-hearted or cast down, longs for death and still preserves his life without loving it—not from inclination or fear but from duty; then indeed his maxim has a moral content.

To help others where one can is a duty, and besides this there are many spirits of so sympathetic a temper that, without any further motive of vanity or self-interest, they find an inner pleasure in spreading happiness around them and can take delight in the contentment of others as their own work. Yet I maintain that in such a case an action of this kind, however right and however amiable it may be, has still no genuinely moral worth. It stands on the same footing as other inclinations—for example, the inclination for honor, which if fortunate enough to hit on something beneficial and right and consequently honorable, deserves praise and encouragement, but not esteem; for its maxim lacks moral content, namely, the performance of such actions, not from inclination, but *from duty*. Suppose then the mind of this friend of man were overclouded by sorrows of his own which extinguished all sympathy with the fate of others, but that he still had power to help those in distress, though no longer stirred by the need of others because sufficiently occupied with his own; and suppose that, when no longer moved by any inclination, he tears himself out of this deadly insensibility and does the action without any inclination for the sake of duty alone; then for the first time his action has its genuine moral worth. Still further: if nature had implanted little sympathy in this or that man's heart; if (being in other respects an honest fellow) he were cold in temperament, and indifferent to the sufferings of others—perhaps because, being endowed with the special gift of patience and robust endurance in his own sufferings, he assumed the like in others or even demanded it; if such a man (who would in truth not be the worst product of nature) were not exactly fashioned by her to be a philanthropist, would he not still find in himself a source from which he might draw a worth far higher than any that a good-natured temperament can have? Assuredly he would. It is precisely in this that the worth of character begins to show—a moral worth and beyond all comparison the highest—namely, that he does good, not from inclination, but from duty.

To assure one's own happiness is a duty (at least indirectly); for discontent with one's state, in a press of cares and amidst unsatisfied wants, might easily become a great *temptation to the transgression of duty*. But here also, apart from regard to duty, all men have already of themselves the strongest and deepest inclination toward happiness, because precisely in this Idea of happiness all inclinations are combined into a sum total. The prescription for happiness is, however, often so constituted as greatly to interfere with some inclinations, and yet men cannot form under the name of "happiness" any determinate and assured conception of the satisfaction of all inclinations as a sum. Hence it is not to be wondered at that a single inclination which is determinate as to what it promises and as to the time of its satisfaction may outweigh a wavering Idea; and that a man, for example, a sufferer from gout, may choose to enjoy what he fancies and put up with what he can—on the ground that on balance he has here at least not killed the enjoyment of the present moment because of some possibly groundless expectations of the good fortune supposed to attach to soundness of health. But in this case also, when the universal inclination toward happiness has failed to determine his will, when good health, at least for him has not entered into his calculations as so necessary, what remains over, here as in other cases, is a law—the law of furthering his happiness, not from inclination but from duty; and in this for the first time his conduct has a real moral worth.

It is doubtless in this sense that we should understand too the passages from Scripture in which we are commanded to love our neighbor and even our enemy. For love out of inclination cannot be commanded; but kindness done from duty— although no inclination impels us, and even although natural and unconquerable disinclination stands in our way—is *practical* and not *pathological* love, residing in the will and not in the propensions of feeling, in principles of action and not of melting compassion; and it is this practical love alone which can be an object of command.

Our second proposition is this: An action done from duty has its moral worth, *not in the purpose* to be attained by it, but in the maxim in accordance with which it is decided upon; it depends therefore, not on the realization of the object of the action, but solely on the *principle of volition* in accordance with which, irrespective of all objects of the faculty of desire, the action has been performed. That the purposes we may have in our actions, and also their effects considered as ends and motives of the will, can give to actions no unconditioned and moral worth is clear from what has gone before. Where then can this worth be found if we are not to find it in the will's relation to the effect hoped for from the action? It can be found nowhere but *in the principle of the will* irrespective of the ends which can be brought about by such an action; for between its *a priori* principle, which is formal, and its *a posteriori* motive, which is material, the will stands, so to speak, at a parting of the ways; and since it must be determined by some principle, it will have to be determined by the formal principle of volition when an action is done from duty, where, as we have seen, every material principle is taken away from it.

Our third proposition, as an inference from the two preceding I would express thus: *Duty is the necessity to act out of reverence for the law*. For an object as the effect of my proposed action I can have an *inclination*, but *never reverence*, precisely because it is merely the effect, and not the activity, of a will. Similarly for inclination as such, whether my own or that of another, I cannot have reverence: I can at most in the first case approve, and in the second case sometimes even love—that is, regard it as favorable to my own advantage. Only something which is conjoined with my will solely as a ground and never as an effect—something which does not serve my inclination, but outweighs it or at least leaves it entirely out of account in my choice—and therefore only bare law for its own sake, can be an object of reverence and therewith a command. Now an action done from duty has to set aside altogether the influence of inclination, and along with inclination every object of the will; so there is nothing left able to determine the will except objectively the *law* and subjectively *pure reverence* for this practical law, and therefore the maxim* of obeying this law even to the detriment of all my inclinations.

Thus the moral worth of an action does not depend on the result expected from it, and so too does not depend on any principle of action that needs to borrow its motive from this expected result. For all these results (agreeable states and even the promotion of happiness in others) could have been brought about by other causes as well, and consequently their production did not require the will of a rational being, in which, however, the highest and unconditioned good can alone be found. Therefore nothing but the *idea of the law* in itself, *which admittedly is present only in a rational being*—so far as it, and not an expected result, is the ground determining the will—can constitute that pre-eminent good which we call moral, a good which is already present in the person acting on this idea and has not to be awaited merely from the result.

But what kind of law can this be the thought of which, even without regard to the results expected from it, has to determine the will if this is to be called good absolutely and without qualification? Since I have robbed the will of every inducement that might arise for it as a consequence of obeying any particular law, nothing is left but the conformity of actions to universal law as such, and this alone must serve the will as its principle. That is to say, I ought never to act except in such a way *that I can also will that my maxim should become a universal law.* Here bare conformity to universal law as such (without having as its base any law prescribing particular actions) is what serves the will as its principle, and must so serve it if duty is not to be everywhere an empty delusion and a chimerical concept. The ordinary reason of mankind also agrees with this completely in its practical judgments and always has the aforesaid principle before its eyes.

Take this question, for example. May I not, when I am hard pressed, make a promise with the intention of not keeping it? Here I readily distinguish the two senses which the question can have—Is it prudent, or is it right, to make a false promise? The first no doubt can often be the case. I do indeed see that it is not enough for me to extricate myself from present embarrassment by this subterfuge: I have to consider whether from this lie there may not subsequently accrue to me much greater inconvenience than that from which I now escape, and also—since, with all my supposed *astuteness*, to foresee the consequences is not so easy that I can be sure there is no chance, once confidence in me is lost, of this proving far more disadvantageous than all the ills I now think to avoid—whether it may not be a *more prudent* action to proceed here on a general maxim and make it my habit not to give a promise except with the intention of keeping it. Yet it becomes clear to me at

---

* A *maxim* is the subjective principle of a volition: an objective principle (that is, one which would also serve subjectively as a practical principle for all rational beings if reason had full control over the faculty of desire) is a practical law.

once that such a maxim is always founded solely on fear of consequences. To tell the truth for the sake of duty is something entirely different from doing so out of concern for inconvenient results; for in the first case the concept of the action already contains in itself a law for me, while in the second case I have first of all to look around elsewhere in order to see what effects may be bound up with it for me. When I deviate from the principle of duty, this is quite certainly bad; but if I desert my prudential maxim, this can often be greatly to my advantage, though it is admittedly safer to stick to it. Suppose I seek, however, to learn in the quickest way and yet unerringly how to solve the problem "Does a lying promise accord with duty?" I have then to ask myself "Should I really be content that my maxim (the maxim of getting out of a difficulty by a false promise) should hold as a universal law (one valid both for myself and others)? And could I really say to myself that every one may make a false promise if he finds himself in a difficulty from which he can extricate himself in no other way?" I then become aware at once that I can indeed will to lie, but I can by no means will a universal law of lying; for by such a law there could properly be no promises at all, since it would be futile to profess a Will for future action to others who would not believe my profession or who, if they did so over-hastily, would pay me back in like coin; and consequently my maxim, as soon as it was made a universal law, would be bound to annul itself.

Thus I need no far-reaching ingenuity to find out what I have to do in order to possess a good will. Inexperienced in the course of world affairs and incapable of being prepared for all the chances that happen in it, I ask myself only "Can you also will that your maxim should become a universal law?" Where you cannot, it is to be rejected, and that not because of a prospective loss to you or even to others, but because it cannot fit as a principle into a possible enactment of universal law. For such an enactment reason compels my immediate reverence, into whose grounds (which the philosopher may investigate) I have as yet no *insight*, although I do at least understand this much: reverence is the assessment of a worth which far outweighs all the worth of what is commended by inclination, and the necessity for me to act out of *pure* reverence for the practical law is what constitutes duty, to which every other motive must give way because it is the condition of a will good *in itself*, whose value is above all else. . . .

Chapter II
Passage from Popular Moral
Philosophy to a Metaphysic of Morals

. . . Everything in nature works in accordance with laws. Only a rational being has the power to act *in accordance with his idea* of laws—that is, in accordance with principles—and only so has he a *will*. Since *reason* is required in order to derive actions from laws, the will is nothing but practical reason. If reason infallibly determines the will, then in a being of this kind the actions which are recognized to be objectively necessary are also subjectively necessary—that is to say, the will is then a power to choose *only that* which reason independently of inclination recognizes to be practically necessary, that is, to be good. But if reason solely by itself is not sufficient to determine the will; if the will is exposed also to subjective conditions (certain impulsions) which do not always harmonize with the objective ones; if, in a word, the will is not *in itself* completely in accord with reason (as actually happens in the case of men); then actions which are recognized to be objectively necessary are subjectively contingent, and the determining of such a will in accordance with objective laws is *necessitation*. That is to say, the relation of objective laws to a will not good through and through is conceived as one in which the will of a rational being, although it is determined by principles of reason, does not necessarily follow these principles in virtue of its own nature.

The conception of an objective principle so far as this principle is necessitating for a will is called a command (of reason), and the formula of this command is called an *Imperative*.

All imperatives are expressed by an *"ought"* (*Sollen*). By this they mark the relation of an objective law of reason to a will which is not necessarily determined by this law in virtue of its subjective constitution (the relation of necessitation). They say that something would be good to do or to leave undone; only they say it to a will which does not always do a thing because it has been informed that this is a good thing to do. The practically *good* is that which determines the will by concepts of reason, and therefore not by subjective causes, but objectively—that is, on grounds valid for every rational being as such. It is distinguished from the *pleasant* as that which influences the will, not as a principle of reason valid for every one, but solely through the medium of sensation by purely subjective causes valid only for the senses of this person or that.

A perfectly good will would thus stand quite as much under objective laws (laws of the good), but it could not on this account be conceived as *necessitated* to act in conformity with law, since of itself, in accordance with its subjective constitution, it can be determined only by the concept of the good. Hence for the *divine* will, and in general for a *holy* will, there are no imperatives: "I ought" is here out of place, because "I will" is already of itself necessarily in harmony with the law. Imperatives are in consequence only formulae for expressing the relation of objective laws of willing to the subjective imperfection of the will of this or that rational being— for example, of the human will.

All *imperatives* command either *hypothetically* or *categorically*. Hypothetical imperatives declare a possible action to be practically necessary as a means to the attainment of something else that one wills (or that one may will). A categorical imperative would be one which represented an action as objectively necessary in itself apart from its relation to a further end.

Every practical law represents a possible action as good and therefore as necessary for a subject whose actions are determined by reason. Hence all imperatives are formulae for determining an action which is necessary in accordance with the principle of a will in some sense good. If the action would be good solely as a means *to something else*, the imperative is *hypothetical*; if the action is represented as good *in itself* and therefore as necessary, in virtue of its principle, for a will which of itself accords with reason, then the imperative is *categorical*.

An imperative therefore tells me which of my possible actions would be good; and it formulates a practical rule for a will that does not perform an action straight away because the action is good—whether because the subject does not always know that it is good or because, even if he did know this, he might still act on maxims contrary to the objective principles of practical reason.

A hypothetical imperative thus says only that an action is good for some purpose or other, either *possible* or *actual*. In the first case it is a *problematic* practical principle; in the second case an *assertoric* practical principle. A categorical imperative, which declares an action to be objectively necessary in itself without reference to some purpose—that is, even without any further end—ranks as an *apodeictic* practical principle.

Everything that is possible only through the efforts of some rational being can be conceived as a possible purpose of some will; and consequently there are in fact innumerable principles of action so far as action is thought necessary in order to achieve some possible purpose which can be effected by it. All sciences have a practical part consisting of problems which suppose that some end is possible for us and of imperatives which tell us how it is to be attained. Hence the latter can in general be called imperatives of *skill*. Here there is absolutely no question about the rationality or goodness of the end, but only about what must be done to attain it. A prescription required by a doctor in order to cure his man completely and one required by a poisoner in order to make sure of killing him are of equal value so far as each serves to effect its purpose perfectly. Since in early youth we do not know what ends may present themselves to us in the course of life, parents seek above all to make their children learn things of *many kinds*; they provide carefully for *skill* in the use of means to all sorts of arbitrary ends, of none of which can be certain that it could not in the future become an actual purpose of their ward, while it is ways *possible* that he might adopt it. Their care in this matter is so great that they commonly neglect on this account to form and correct the judgment of their children about the worth of the things which they might possibly adopt as ends.

There is, however, *one* end that can be presupposed as actual in all rational beings (so far as they are dependent beings to whom imperatives apply); and thus there is one purpose which they not only *can* have, but which we can assume with certainty that they all *do* have by a natural necessity—the purpose, namely of *happiness*. A hypothetical imperative which affirms the practical necessity of an action as a means to the furtherance of happiness is *assertoric*. We may represent it, not simply as necessary to an uncertain, merely possible purpose, but as necessary to a purpose which we can presuppose *a priori* and with certainty to be present in every man because it belongs to his very being. Now skill in the choice of means to one's own greatest well-being can be called *prudence** in the narrowest sense. Thus an

---

* The word "prudence" (*Klugheit*) is used in a double sense: in one sense it can have the name of "worldly wisdom" (*Weltklugheit*); in a second sense that of "personal wisdom" (*Privatklugheit*). The first is the skill of a man in influencing others in order to use them for his own ends. The second is sagacity in combining all these ends to his own lasting advantage. The latter is properly that to which the value of the former can itself be traced; and of him who is prudent in the first sense, but not in the second, we might better say that he is clever and astute, but on the whole imprudent.

imperative concerned with the choice of means to one's own happiness—that is, a precept of prudence—still remains *hypothetical*: an action is commanded, not absolutely, but only as a means to a further purpose.

Finally, there is an imperative which, without being based on, and conditioned by, any further purpose to be attained by a certain line of conduct, enjoins this conduct immediately. This imperative is *categorical*. It is concerned, not with the matter of the action and its presumed results, but with its form and with the principle from which it follows; and what is essentially good in the action consists in the mental disposition, let the consequences be what they may. This imperative may be called the imperative of *morality*.

Willing in accordance with these three kinds of principle is also sharply distinguished by a *dissimilarity* in the necessitation of the will. To make this dissimilarity obvious we should, I think, name these kinds of principle most appropriately in their order if we said they were either *rules* of skill or *counsels* of prudence or *commands (laws)* of morality. For only *law* carries with it the concept of an *unconditioned*, and yet objective and so universally valid, *necessity*; and commands are laws which must be obeyed—that is, must be followed even against inclination. *Counsel* does indeed involve necessity, but necessity valid only under a subjective and contingent condition—namely, if this or that man counts this or that as belonging to his happiness. As against this, a categorical imperative is limited by no condition and can quite precisely be called a command, as being absolutely, although practically, necessary. We could also call imperatives of the first kind *technical* (concerned with art); of the second kind *pragmatic* (concerned with well-being); of the third kind *moral* (concerned with free conduct as such—that is, with morals).

The question now arises "How are all these imperatives possible?" This question does not ask how we can conceive the execution of an action commanded by the imperative, but merely how we can conceive the necessitation of the will expressed by the imperative in setting us a task. How an imperative of skill is possible requires no special discussion. Who wills the end, wills (so far as reason has decisive influence on his actions) also the means which are indispensably necessary and in his power. So far as willing is concerned, this proposition is analytic: for in my willing of an object as an effect there is already conceived the causality of myself as an acting cause—that is, the use of means; and from the concept of willing an end the imperative merely extracts the concept of actions necessary to this end. (Synthetic propositions are required in order to determine the means to a proposed end, but these are concerned, not with the reason for performing the act of will, but with the cause which produces the object.) That in order to divide a line into two equal parts on a sure principle I must from its ends describe two intersecting arcs—this is admittedly taught by mathematics only in synthetic propositions; but when I know that the aforesaid effect can be produced only by such an action, the proposition "If I fully will the effect, I also will the action required for it" is analytic; for it is one and the same thing to conceive something as an effect possible in a certain way through me and to conceive myself as acting in the same way with respect to it.

If it were only as easy to find a determinate concept of happiness, the imperatives of prudence would agree entirely with those of skill and would be equally analytic. From here as there it could alike be said "Who wills the end, wills also (necessarily, if he accords with reason) the sole means which are in his power." Unfortunately, however, the concept of happiness is so indeterminate a concept that although every man wants to attain happiness, he can never say definitely and in unison with himself what it really is that he wants and wills. The reason for this is that all the elements which belong to the concept of happiness are without exception empirical—that is, they must be borrowed from experience; but that none the less there is required for the Idea of happiness an absolute whole, a maximum of well-being in my present, and in every future, state. Now it is impossible for the most intelligent, and at the same time most powerful, but nevertheless finite, being to form here a determinate concept of what he really wills. Is it riches that he wants? How much anxiety, envy and pestering might he not bring in this way on his own head! Is it knowledge and insight? This might perhaps merely give him an eye so sharp that it would make evils at present hidden from him and yet unavoidable seem all the more frightful, or would add a load of still further needs to the desires which already give him trouble enough. Is it long life? Who will guarantee that it would not be a long misery? Is it at least health? How often has infirmity of body kept a man from excesses into which perfect health would have let him fall!—and so on. In short, he has no principle by which he is able to decide with complete certainty what will make him truly happy, since for this he would require omniscience. Thus we cannot act on determinate principles in order to be happy, but only on empirical counsels, for example, of diet, frugality, politeness, reserve, and so on—things which experience shows contribute most to well-being on the average. From this it follows that imperatives of prudence, peaking strictly, do not command at all—that is, cannot exhibit actions objectively as practically *necessary*; that they are rather to be taken as recommendations (*consilia*), than as commands (*praecepta*), of reason; that the problem of determining certainly and universally what action will promote the happiness of a rational being is completely insoluble; and consequently that in regard to this there is no imperative possible which in the strictest sense could command us to do what will make us happy, since happiness is an Ideal, not of reason, but of imagination—an Ideal resting merely on empirical grounds, of which it is vain to expect that they should determine an action by which we could attain the totality of a series of consequences which is in fact infinite. Nevertheless, if we assume that the means to happiness could be discovered with certainty, this imperative of prudence would be an analytic practical proposition; for it differs from the imperative of skill only in this—that in the latter the end is merely possible, while in the former the end is given. In spite of this difference, since both command solely the means to something assumed to be willed as an end, the imperative which commands him who wills the end to will the means is in both cases analytic. Thus there is likewise no difficulty in regard to the possibility of an imperative of prudence.

Beyond all doubt, the question "How is the imperative of *morality* possible?" is the only one in need of a solution; for it is in no way hypothetical, and consequently we cannot base the objective necessity which it affirms on any presupposition, as we can with hypothetical imperatives. Only we must never forget here that it is impossible to settle *by an example*, and so empirically, whether there is any imperative of this kind at all: we must rather suspect that all imperatives which seem to be categorical may none the less be covertly hypothetical. Take, for example, the saying "Thou shalt make no false promises." Let us assume that the necessity for this abstention is no mere advice for the avoidance of some further evil—as it might be said "You ought not to make a lying promise lest, when this comes to light, you destroy your credit." Let us hold, on the contrary, that an action of this kind must be considered as bad in itself, and that the imperative of prohibition is therefore categorical. Even so, we cannot with any certainty show by an example that the will is determined here solely by the law without any further motive, although it may appear to be so; for it is always possible that fear of disgrace, perhaps also hidden dread of other risks, may unconsciously influence the will. Who can prove by experience that a cause is not present? Experience shows only that it is not perceived. In such a case, however, the so-called moral imperative, which as such appears to be categorical and unconditioned, would in fact be only a pragmatic prescription calling attention to our advantage and merely bidding us take this into account.

We shall thus have to investigate the possibility of a *categorical* imperative entirely *a priori*, since here we do not enjoy the advantage of having its reality given in experience and so of being obliged merely to explain, and not to establish, its possibility. So much, however, can be seen provisionally—that the categorical imperative alone purports to be a practical *law*, while all the rest may be called *principles* of the will but not laws; for an action necessary merely in order to achieve an arbitrary purpose can be considered as in itself contingent, and we can always escape from the precept if we abandon the purpose; whereas an unconditioned command does not leave it open to the will to do the opposite at its discretion and therefore alone carries with it that necessity which we demand from a law. . . .

In this task we wish first to inquire whether perhaps the mere concept of a categorical imperative may not also provide us with the formula containing the only proposition that can be a categorical imperative, for even when we know the purport of such an absolute command, the question of its possibility will still require a special and troublesome effort, which we postpone to the final chapter.

When I conceive a *hypothetical* imperative in general, I do not know beforehand what it will contain—until its condition is given. But if I conceive a *categorical* imperative, I know at once what it contains. For since besides the law this imperative contains only the necessity that our maxim* should conform to this law, while the law, as we have seen, contains no condition to limit it, there remains nothing over to which the maxim has to conform except the universality of a law as such; and it is this conformity alone that the imperative properly asserts to be necessary.

---

* A *maxim* is a subjective principle of action and must be distinguished from an *objective principle*—namely, a practical law. The former contains a practical rule determined by reason in accordance with the conditions of the subject (often his ignorance or again his inclinations): it is thus a principle on which the subject *acts*. A law, on the other hand, is an objective principle valid for every rational being; and it is a principle on which he *ought to act*—that is, an imperative.

There is therefore only a single categorical imperative and it is this: *"Act only on the maxim through which you can at the same time will that it should become a universal law."*

. . . [T]he universal imperative of duty may also run as follows: *"Act as if the maxim of your action were to become through your will a universal law of nature."*

We will now enumerate a few duties, following their customary division into duties toward self and duties toward others and into perfect and imperfect duties.*

1. A man feels sick of life as the result of a series of misfortunes that has mounted to the point of despair, but he is still so far in possession of his reason as to ask himself whether taking his own life may not be contrary to his duty to himself. He now applies the test "Can the maxim of my action really become a universal law of nature?" His maxim is "From self-love I make it my principle to shorten my life if its continuance threatens more evil than it promises pleasure." The only further question to ask is whether this principle of self-love can become a universal law of nature. It is then seen at once that a system of nature by whose law the very same feeling whose function (*Bestimmung*) is to stimulate the furtherance of life should actually destroy life would contradict itself and consequently could not subsist as a system of nature. Hence this maxim cannot possibly hold as a universal law of nature and is therefore entirely opposed to the supreme principle of all duty.

2. Another finds himself driven to borrowing money because of need. He well knows that he will not be able to pay it back; but he sees too that he will get no loan unless he gives a firm promise to pay it back within a fixed time. He is inclined to make such a promise; but he has still enough conscience to ask "Is it not unlawful and contrary to duty to get out of difficulties in this way?" Supposing, however, he did resolve to do so, the maxim of his action would run thus: "Whenever I believe myself short of money, I will borrow money and promise to pay it back, though I know that this will never be done." Now this principle of self-love or personal advantage is perhaps quite compatible with my own entire future welfare; only there remains the question "Is it right?" I therefore transform the demand of self-love into a universal law and frame my question thus: "How would things stand if my maxim became a universal law?" I then see straight away that this maxim can never rank as a universal law of nature and be self-consistent, but must necessarily contradict itself. For the universality of a law that every one believing himself to be in need can make any promise he pleases with the intention not to keep it would make promising, and the very purpose of promising, itself impossible, since no one would believe he was being promised anything, but would laugh at utterances of this kind as empty shams.

3. A third finds in himself a talent whose cultivation would make him a useful man for all sorts of purposes. But he sees himself in comfortable circumstances, and he prefers to give himself up to pleasure rather than to bother about increasing and improving his fortunate natural aptitudes. Yet he asks himself further "Does my

---

* . . . I understand here by a perfect duty one which allows no exception in the interests of inclination, and so I recognize among perfect duties, not only outer ones, but also inner.

maxim of neglecting my natural gifts, besides agreeing in itself with my tendency to indulgence, agree also with what is called duty?" He then sees that a system of nature could indeed always subsist under such a universal law, although (like the South Sea Islanders) every man should let his talents rust and should be bent on devoting his life solely to idleness, indulgence, procreation, and, in a word, to enjoyment. Only he cannot possibly *will* that this should become a universal law of nature or should be implanted in us as such a law by a natural instinct. For as a rational being he necessarily wills that all his powers should be developed, since they serve him, and are given him, for all sorts of possible ends.

4. Yet *a fourth* is himself flourishing, but he sees others who have to struggle with great hardships (and whom he could easily help); and he thinks "What does it matter to me? Let every one be as happy as Heaven wills or as he can make himself; I won't deprive him of anything; I won't even envy him; only I have no wish to contribute anything to his well-being or to his support in distress." Now admittedly if such an attitude were a universal law of nature, mankind could get on perfectly well—better no doubt than if everybody prates about sympathy and goodwill, and even takes pains, on occasion, to practice them, but on the other hand cheats where he can, traffics in human rights, or violates them in other ways. But although it is possible that a universal law of nature could subsist in harmony with this maxim, yet it is impossible to *will* that such a principle should hold everywhere as a law of nature. For a will which decided in this way would be in conflict with itself, since many a situation might arise in which the man needed love and sympathy from others, and in which, by such a law of nature sprung from his own will, he would rob himself of all hope of the help he wants for himself.

These are some of the many actual duties—or at least of what we take to be such—whose derivation from the single principle cited above leaps to the eye. We must *be able to will* that a maxim of our action should become a universal law—this is the general canon for all moral judgment of action. Some actions are so constituted that their maxim cannot even be *conceived* as a universal law of nature without contradiction, let alone be *willed* as what *ought* to become one. In the case of others we do not find this inner impossibility, but it is still impossible to *will* that their maxim should be raised to the universality of a law of nature, because such a will would contradict itself. It is easily seen that the first kind of action is opposed to strict or narrow (rigorous) duty, the second only to wider (meritorious) duty; and thus that by these examples all duties—so far as the type of obligation is concerned (not the object of dutiful action)—are fully set out in their dependence on our single principle.

If we now attend to ourselves whenever we transgress a duty, we find that we in fact do not will that our maxim should become a universal law—since this is impossible for us—but rather that its opposite should remain a law universally: we only take the liberty of making an *exception* to it for ourselves (or even just for this once) to the advantage of our inclination. Consequently if we weighed it all up from one and the same point of view—that of reason—we should find a contradiction in our own will, the contradiction that a certain principle should be objectively necessary as a universal law and yet subjectively should not hold universally but should admit of exceptions. Since, however, we first consider our action from the point of view of a will wholly in accord with reason, and then consider precisely the same action from the point of view of a will affected by inclination, there is here actually no contradiction, but rather an opposition of inclination to the precept of reason (*antagonismus*), whereby the universality of the principle (*universalitas*) is turned into a mere generality (*generalitas*) so that the practical principle of reason may meet our maxim half-way. This procedure, though in our own impartial judgment it cannot be justified, proves none the less that we in fact recognize the validity of the categorical imperative and (with all respect for it) merely permit ourselves a few exceptions which are, as we pretend, inconsiderable and apparently forced upon us. . . .

The will is conceived as a power of determining oneself to action *in accordance with the idea of certain laws*. And such a power can be found only in rational beings. Now what serves the will as a subjective ground of its self-determination is an end; and this, if it is given by reason alone, must be equally valid for all rational beings. What, on the other hand, contains merely the ground of the possibility of an action whose effect is an end is called a *means*. The subjective ground of a desire is an *impulsion*. . . ; the objective ground of a volition is a *motive*. . . . Hence the difference between subjective ends, which are based on impulsions, and objective ends, which depend on motives valid for every rational being. Practical principles are *formal* if they abstract from all subjective ends; they are *material*, on the other hand, if they are based on such ends and consequently on certain impulsions. Ends that a rational being adopts arbitrarily as *effects* of his action (material ends) are in every case only relative; for it is solely their relation to special characteristics in the subject's power of appetition which gives them their value. Hence this value can provide no universal principles, no principles valid and necessary for all rational beings and also for every volition—that is, no practical laws. Consequently all these relative ends can be the ground only of hypothetical imperatives.

Suppose, however, there were something *whose existence* has *in itself* an absolute value, something which as *an end in itself* could be a ground of determinate laws; then in it, and in it alone, would there be the ground of a possible categorical imperative—that is, of a practical law.

Now I say that man, and in general every rational being, *exists* as an end in himself, *not merely as a means* for arbitrary use by this or that will: he must in all his actions, whether they are directed to himself or to other rational beings, always be viewed *at the same time as an end*. All the objects of inclination have only a conditioned value; for if there were not these inclinations and the needs grounded on them, their object would be valueless. Inclinations themselves, as sources of needs, are so far from having an absolute value to make them desirable for their own sake that it must rather be the universal wish of every rational being to be wholly free from them. Thus the value of all objects that can *be produced* by our action is always conditioned. Beings whose existence depends, not on our will, but on nature, have none the less, if they are non-rational beings, only a relative value as means and are consequently called *things*. Rational beings, on the other hand, are called *persons* because their nature already marks them out as ends in themselves—that is, as something which ought not to be used merely as a means—and consequently imposes to that extent a limit on all arbitrary treatment of them (and is an object of reverence). Persons, therefore, are not merely subjective ends whose existence as an object of our actions has a value *for us:* they are *objective ends*—that is, things whose existence is in itself an end, and indeed an end such that in its place we can put no other end to which they should serve *simply* as means; for unless this is so, nothing at all of *absolute* value would be found anywhere. But if all value were conditioned—that is, contingent—then no supreme principle could be found for reason at all.

If then there is to be a supreme practical principle and—so far as the human will is concerned—a categorical imperative, it must be such that from the idea of something which is necessarily an end for every one because it is an *end in itself* it forms an *objective* principle of the will and consequently can serve as a practical law. The ground of this principle is: *Rational nature exists as an end in itself*. This is the way in which a man necessarily conceives his own existence: it is therefore so far a *subjective* principle of human actions. But it is also the way in which every other rational being conceives his existence on the same rational ground which is valid also for me; hence it is at the same time an objective principle, from which, as a supreme practical ground, it must be possible to derive all laws for the will. The practical imperative will therefore be as follows: *Act in such a way that you always treat humanity, whether in your own person or in the person of any other, never simply as a means but always at the same time as an end. . . .*

This principle of humanity, and in general of every rational agent, *as an end in itself* (a principle which is the supreme limiting condition of every man's freedom of action) is not borrowed from experience; firstly, because it is universal, applying as it does to all rational beings as such, and no experience is adequate to determine universality; secondly, because in it humanity is conceived, not as an end of man (subjectively)—that is, as an object which, as a matter of fact, happens to be made an end—but as an objective end—one which, be our ends what they may, must, as a law, constitute the supreme limiting condition of all subjective ends and so must spring from pure reason. That is to say, the ground for every enactment of practical law lies *objectively in the rule* and in the form of universality which (according to our first principle) makes the rule capable of being a law (and indeed a law of nature); *subjectively,* however, it lies in the *end;* but (according to our second principle) the subject of all ends is to be found in every rational being as an end in himself. From this there now follows our third practical principle for the will—as the supreme condition of the will's conformity with universal practical reason—namely, the Idea of the *will of every rational being as a will which makes universal law.*

By this principle all maxims are repudiated which cannot accord with the will's own enactment of universal law. The will is therefore not merely subject to the law, but is so subject that it must be considered as also *making the law* for itself and precisely on this account as first of all subject to the law (of which it can regard itself as the author). . . .

. . . [A] will *which is subject to law* may be bound to this law by some interest, nevertheless a will which is itself a supreme lawgiver cannot possibly as such depend on any interest; for a will which is dependent in this way would itself require yet a further law in order to restrict the interest of self-love to the condition that this in-terest should itself be valid as a universal law.

Thus the *principle* that every human will is *a will which by all its maxims enacts universal law*—provided only that it were right in other ways—would be *well suited* to be a categorical imperative in this respect: that precisely because of the Idea of making universal law it is *based on no interest* and consequently can alone among all possible imperatives be *unconditioned*. Or better still—to convert the proposition—if there is a categorical imperative (that is, a law for the will of every rational being), it can command us only to act always on the maxim of such a will in us as can at the same time look upon itself as making universal law; for only then is the practical principle and the imperative which we obey unconditioned, since it is wholly im-possible for it to be based on any interest.

We need not now wonder, when we look back upon all the previous efforts that have been made to discover the principle of morality, why they have been made to discover the principle of morality, why they have one and all been bound to fail. Their authors saw man as tied to laws by his duty, but it never occurred to them that he is subject only to *laws which are made by himself* and yet are *universal*, and that he is bound only to act in conformity with a will which is his own but has as nature's purpose for it the function of making universal law. For when they thought of man merely as subject to a law (whatever it might be), the law had to carry with it some interest in order to attract or compel, because it did not spring as a law from *his own* will: in order to conform with the law his will had to be necessitated by *something else* to act in a certain way. This absolutely inevitable conclusion meant that all the labor spent in trying to find a supreme principle of duty was lost beyond recall; for what they discovered was never duty, but only the necessity of acting from a certain interest. This interest might be one's own or another's; but on such a view the im-perative was bound to be always a conditioned one and could not possibly serve as a moral law. I will therefore call my principle the principle of the *Autonomy* of the will in contrast with others, which I consequently class under *Heteronomy*.

The concept of every rational being as one who must regard himself as making universal law by all the maxims of his will, and must seek to judge himself and his actions from this point of view, leads to a closely connected and very fruitful con-cept—namely, that of *a kingdom of ends*.

I understand by a "*kingdom*" a systematic union of different rational beings under common laws. Now since laws determine ends as regards their universal va-lidity, we shall be able—if we abstract from the personal differences between rational beings, and also from all the content of their private ends—to conceive a whole of all ends in systematic conjunction (a whole both of rational beings as ends in them-selves and also of the personal ends which each may set before himself); that is, we shall be able to conceive a kingdom of ends which is possible in accordance with the above principles.

For rational beings all stand under the *law* that each of them should treat him-self and all others, *never merely as a means*, but always *at the same time as an end in himself*. But by so doing there arises a systematic union of rational beings under common objective laws—that is, a kingdom. Since these laws are directed precisely to the relation of such beings to one another as ends and means, this kingdom can be called a kingdom of ends (which is admittedly only an Ideal).

A rational being belongs to the kingdom of ends as a *member*, when, although he makes its universal laws, he is also himself subject to these laws. He belongs to it as its *head*, when as the maker of laws he is himself subject to the will of no other.

A rational being must always regard himself as making laws in a kingdom of ends which is possible through freedom of the will—whether it be as member or as head. The position of the latter he can maintain, not in virtue of the maxim of his will alone, but only if he is a completely independent being, without needs and with an unlimited power adequate to his will.

Thus morality consists in the relation of all action to the making of laws whereby alone a kingdom of ends is possible. This making of laws must be found in every rational being himself and must be able to spring from his will. The principle of his will is therefore never to perform an action except on a maxim such as can also be a universal law, and consequently such *that the will can regard itself as at the same time making universal law by means of its maxim*. Where maxims are not already by their very nature in harmony with this objective principle of rational beings as makers of universal law, the necessity of acting on this principle is practical necessitation—that is, *duty*. Duty does not apply to the head in a kingdom of ends, but it does apply to every member and to all members in equal measure.

The practical necessity of acting on this principle—that is, duty—is in no way based on feelings, impulses, and inclinations, but only on the relation of rational beings to one another, a relation in which the will of a rational being must always be regarded as *making universal law*, because otherwise he could not be conceived as *an end in himself*. Reason thus relates every maxim of the will, considered as making universal law, to every other will and also to every action toward oneself: it does so, not because of any further motive or future advantage, but from the Idea of the *dignity* of a rational being who obeys no law other than that which he at the same time enacts himself. . . .

What is it then that entitles a morally good attitude of mind—or virtue—to make claims so high? It is nothing less than the *share* which it affords to a rational being *in the making of universal law*, and which therefore fits him to be a member in a possible kingdom of ends. For this he was already marked out in virtue of his own proper nature as an end in himself and consequently as a maker of laws in the kingdom of ends—as free in respect of all laws of nature, obeying only those laws which he makes himself and in virtue of which his maxims can have their part in the making of universal law (to which he at the same time subjects himself). For nothing can have a value other than that determined for it by the law. But lawmaking which determines all value must for this reason have a dignity—that is, an unconditioned and incomparable worth—for the appreciation which, as necessarily given by a rational being, the word "*reverence*" is the only becoming expression. *Autonomy* is therefore the ground of the dignity of human nature and of every rational nature. . . .

From what was said a little time ago we can now easily explain how it comes about that, although in the concept of duty we think of subjection to the law, yet we also at the same time attribute to the person who fulfills all his duties a certain sub-limity and *dignity*. For it is not in so far as he is *subject* to the law that he has sublim-ity, but rather in so far as, in regard to this very same law, he is at the same time its *author* and is subordinated to it only on this ground. We have also shown above how neither fear nor inclination, but solely reverence for the law, is the motive which can give an action moral worth. Our own will, provided it were to act only under the condition of being able to make universal law by means of its maxims—this ideal will which can be ours is the proper object of reverence; and the dignity of man consists precisely in his capacity to make universal law, although only on con-dition of being himself also subject to the law he makes.

Autonomy of the Will
as the supreme principle of morality

Autonomy of the will is the property the will has of being a law to itself (indepen-dently of every property belonging to the objects of volition). Hence the principle of autonomy is "Never to choose except in such a way that in the same volition the maxims of your choice are also present as universal law.". . . [B]y mere analysis of the concepts of morality we can quite well show that the above principle of autonomy is the sole principle of ethics. For analysis finds that the principle of morality must be a categorical imperative, and that this in turn commands nothing more nor less than precisely this autonomy.

Heteronomy of the Will
as the source of all spurious principles of morality

If the will seeks the law that is to determine it *anywhere else* than in the fitness of its maxims for its own making of universal law—if therefore in going beyond itself it seeks this law in the character of any of its objects—the result is always *heteronomy*. In that case the will does not give itself the law, but the object does so in virtue of its relation to the will. This relation, whether based on inclination or on rational ideas, can give rise only to hypothetical imperatives: "I ought to do something *because I will something else*." As against this, the moral, and therefore categorical, imperative, says: "I ought to will thus or thus, although I have not willed something else." For example, the first says: "I ought not to lie if I want to maintain my reputation"; while the second says: "I ought not to lie even if so doing were to bring me not the slightest disgrace." The second imperative must therefore abstract from all objects to this extent—they should be without any *influence* at all on the will so that prac-tical reason (the will) may not merely administer an alien interest but may simply manifest its own sovereign authority as the supreme maker of the law. Thus, for ex-ample, the reason why I ought to promote the happiness of others is not because the realization of their happiness is of consequence to myself (whether on account of immediate inclination or on account of some satisfaction gained indirectly through reason), but solely because a maxim which excludes this cannot also be present in one and the same volition as a universal law.

SUGGESTIONS FOR DISCUSSION

1. What are the basic differences between Rousseau's conception of the social contract and that of Hobbes? Do these differences have implications for social policy?

2. Does Rousseau's conception of the "general will" establish a basis for deciding what ought properly to be done in respect to such social questions as affirmative action (see Chapter 9) and censorship (Chapter 10)?

3. John Stuart Mill argues that Kant's practical application of the categorical imperative does not show that immoral rules of conduct rest on contradictions. It shows rather, Mill claims, that no rational person would be prepared to accept the consequences of the universal adoption of immoral rules. Why does Mill's point amount to a criticism of Kant's theory of morality? Can Kant's view be defended against Mill's attack?

4. How would Kant's fundamental moral principle oblige us to act when applied to a case of capital punishment (Chapter 14) or euthanasia (see Chapter 13) or in relation to someone who has tested HIV positive (Chapter 12)?

FOR FURTHER READING

ROUSSEAU

Cassirer, E. *The Question of Jean-Jacques Rousseau.* Trans. P. W. Gay. Bloomington: Indiana University Press, 1963.

Cohen, J. "Reflections on Rousseau: Autonomy and Democracy." *Philosophy and Public Affairs* 15, 3 (Summer 1986): 275–97.

Gildin, H. *Rousseau's Social Contract.* Chicago: University of Chicago Press, 1983.

Miller, J. *Rousseau: Dreamer of Democracy.* New Haven: Yale University Press, 1984.

Rousseau, J.-J. *The Social Contract.* Trans. M. Cranston. London: Penguin Classics, 1968.

———. *The 1st and 2nd Discourses.* Trans. R. and J. Masters. New York: St. Martin's Press, 1978.

Shklar, J. *Men and Citizens: A Study in Rousseau's Social Theory.* 2nd ed. Cambridge: Cambridge University Press, 1985.

KANT

Allison, H. *Kant's Theory of Freedom.* Cambridge: Cambridge University Press, 1990.

Aune, B. *Kant: Theory of Morals.* Princeton: Princeton University Press, 1979.

Auxter, T. *Kant's Moral Teleology.* Macon, Ga.: Mercer University Press, 1982.

Bernstein, J. A. *Shaftesbury, Rousseau, and Kant.* London: Associated University Presses, 1980.

Donagan, A. *The Theory of Morality.* Chicago: University of Chicago Press, 1977.

Herman, B. *The Practice of Moral Judgment.* Cambridge: Harvard University Press, 1993.

———. "Mutual Aid and Respect for Persons." *Ethics* 94 (July 1984): 577–602.

Hill, T. E., Jr. *Dignity and Practical Reason in Kant's Moral Theory.* Ithaca: Cornell University Press, 1992.

Kant, I. *Critique of Practical Reason.* Trans. L.W. Beck. Indianapolis: Bobbs-Merrill, 1956.

———. *The Metaphysical Elements of Justice.* Trans. J. Ladd, Indianapolis: Bobbs-Merrill, 1965.

———. *The Doctrine of Virtue.* Trans. M. Gregor. Philadelphia: University of Pennsylvania Press, 1971.

————— . *Lectures on Ethics.* Trans. L. Infield. Indianapolis: Hackett Publishing, 1980.

Körner, S. *Kant.* New Haven: Yale University Press, 1982.

Murphy, J. *Kant: The Philosophy of Right.* London: St. Martin's Press, 1970.

Nell, O. *Acting on Principle: An Essay on Kantian Ethics.* New York: Columbia University Press, 1975.

O'Neill, O. *Construction of Reason: Explorations of Kant's Practical Philosophy.* New York: Cambridge University Press, 1989.

Paton, H. J. *The Categorical Imperative: A Study in Kant's Moral Philosophy.* Philadelphia: University of Pennsylvania Press, 1971.

Schneewind, J., and Hoy, D., eds. *Kantian Ethical Thought.* Tallahassee: Council of Philosophical Studies, 1984.

Scruton, R. *Kant.* Oxford: Oxford University Press, 1982.

Sullivan, R. J. *Immanuel Kant's Moral Theory.* Cambridge: Cambridge University Press, 1989.

Wolff, R. P., ed. *Kant: A Collection of Critical Essays.* South Bend: University of Notre Dame Press, 1968.

──────────────────────────

CHAPTER FOUR

BENTHAM AND MILL

Utilitarianism   Jeremy Bentham and John Stuart Mill are regarded commonly as the founders of the ethical theory known as *utilitarianism*. Utilitarianism defines the moral rightness or wrongness of an act, rule, principle, or policy in terms of the balance in each case of good or bad *consequences*. The value assigned by utilitarianism to an act in producing these consequences is termed its *utility* or *disutility*. A variety of utilitarian views exist, in part reflecting the differences between the "classical" views of Bentham and Mill and those of more contemporary utilitarians (see, for example, R. M. Hare, Chapter 12). In general, the various utilitarian theories may be distinguished in two ways: according to the interpretation each assigns to the concept of "utility" and according to whether it is the consequences of individual acts or types of acts that are to be assessed.

■ JEREMY BENTHAM (1748–1832): CLASSICAL UTILITARIANISM

Bentham's Principle of Utility   David Hume and others used the term *utility* in their moral writings. Nevertheless, Bentham was the first to formulate an explicitly utilitarian moral theory, although it seems that his student John Stuart Mill actually coined the term *utilitarianism* to refer to this account of morality. Bentham's primary interests lay in instituting legal, political, and social reforms. He wanted to provide a rational basis for identifying and justifying widespread reforms, and to remove the hold that the clerics exercised on moral justification, by offering a way of analyzing morality in secular terms. He developed a simple *moral calculus* for specifying the right action to be done in any act-context a person might face. Bentham's science of ethics consisted of formulating a simple but universal basic moral rule and demonstrating its application in widely varying contexts. Bentham called this single moral standard the *principle of utility*.

The principle of utility claims that any act or institution is good if and only if it tends to produce the greatest amount of happiness. In particular, an act will be good if and only if it tends to increase the happiness of all those likely to be affected by it (including the person acting) more than any other act or, failing this, if it tends to diminish unhappiness more than any other act. Bentham interpreted happiness (or utility) strictly as pleasure and unhappiness as pain. In terms of this moral calculus, each individual is considered to be equal, and no act is deemed superior in kind to any other. The sole consideration in what he called the *hedonic* or *felicific calculus* is the balance in *quantity* of pleasure and pain (to be) experienced. As Bentham so eloquently concluded, "Quantity of pleasure being equal, pushpin is as good as poetry." (Pushpin is a simple children's game.) Bentham assumed that pleasure and pain are the sole direct causes of human action, and he claimed in this way to provide a common explanation both for how individuals *do* act and how they *ought* to act.

Measuring Pleasure and Pain   In Bentham's view, the rightness or wrongness of any act or type of act is determined by the balance of immediate and distant pleasure or pain this act or type of act tends to produce for all persons it affects. Pleasures and pains are to be measured quantitatively in terms of their intensity, the span of time they last, their certainty of occurrence, and their immediacy or remoteness. Bentham perhaps thought that the more immediate the pleasure or pain, the more assured one is that it will occur, and that this should be reflected in the calculus. To these criteria must be added the tendency of the act or type of act to bring about further pleasurable or painful acts. Consider an act of promise breaking. Measured in these terms, utilitarians sum up the utilities or disutilities for all persons that a broken promise might create. If the total pleasure outweighs the total pain, and tends to outweigh the pleasures that would be produced by any other appropriate act (or type) in the circumstances, then it is right (that is, a person would thus have *a duty* to break the promise). Where, on balance, as much pleasure would be produced by breaking the promise as by some other appropriate act, it will be *permissible*—though not required—to act in this way. Where more pain is produced, on balance, the act or type will be *im*permissible.

Criticisms   Bentham's theory has been criticized in various ways. In his view, a society could be required to institute slavery if it turned out that the pleasure produced by it really outweighed the sum of individual pains and the social disutilities it caused. Yet there are reasons having nothing to do with the hedonic calculus that commit us to rejecting slavery, even if the pleasure from it proved to be greater than the painful consequences. Bentham's contemporary critics raised a related difficulty for the hedonic calculus concerning its requirement that the measure of pleasure and pain be strictly quantitative. They argued that because some pleasures are inherently better than others (getting an education, say, is better than getting drunk), they are intrinsically more worthy of human pursuit. If we accept the claim that some acts or goals have inherent worth that makes them desirable, it throws in question the very possibility of a hedonic calculus: it would mean that pleasure and pain are no longer considered the basic units in terms of which the worth of all acts or goals are to be measured. These considerations prompted John Stuart Mill to reformulate the theory of utilitarianism.

Jeremy Bentham

AN INTRODUCTION TO THE PRINCIPLES OF MORALS AND LEGISLATION

Chap. I—Of the Principle of Utility

I. Nature has placed mankind under the governance of two sovereign masters, *pain* and *pleasure*. It is for them alone to point out what we ought to do, as well as to determine what we shall do. On the one hand the standard of right and wrong, on the other the chain of causes and effects, are fastened to their throne They govern us in all we do, in all we say, in all we think: every effort we can make to throw off our subjection, will serve but to demonstrate and confirm it. In words a man may pretend to abjure their empire: but in reality he will remain subject to it all the while. The *principle of utility** recognizes this subjection, and assumes it for the foundation of that system, the object of which is to rear the fabric of felicity by the hands of reason and of law. . . .

II. The principle of utility is the foundation of the present work: it will be proper therefore at the outset to give an explicit and determinate account of what is meant by it. By the principle** of utility is meant that principle which approves or disapproves of every action whatsoever, according to the tendency which it appears

---

* Note by the Author, July 1822.

To this denomination has of late been added, or substituted, the greatest happiness or greatest felicity principle: this for shortness. instead of saying at length that principle which states the greatest happiness of all those whose interest is in question, as being the right and proper and only right and proper and universally desirable, end of human action: of human action in every situation, and in particular in that of a functionary or set of functionaries exercising the powers of Government. The word utility does not so clearly point to the ideas of pleasure and pain as the words happiness and felicity do: nor does it lead us to the consideration of the number, of the interests affected; to the number, as being the circumstance, which contributes, in the largest proportion, to the formation of the standard here in question; the standard of right and wrong, by which alone the propriety of human conduct, in every situation, can with propriety be tried. This want of a sufficiently manifest connection between the ideas of happiness and pleasure on the one hand, and the idea of utility on the other, I have every now and then found operating, and with but too much efficiency, as a bar to the acceptance, that might otherwise have been given, to this principle.

** [Principle] . . . The principle here in question may be taken for an act of the mind; a sentiment of approbation; a sentiment which, when applied to an action, approves of its utility, as that quality of it by which the measure of approbation or disapprobation bestowed upon it ought to be governed.

From Jeremy Bentham, *An Introduction to the Principles of Morals and Legislation*, revised edition (1823).

to have to augment or diminish the happiness of the party whose interest is in question or, what is the same thing in other words, to promote or to oppose that happiness I say of every action whatsoever, and therefore not only of every action of a private individual, but of every measure of government.

III. By utility is meant that property in any object, whereby it tends to produce benefit, advantage, pleasure, good, or happiness, (all this in the present case comes to the same thing) or (what comes again to the same thing) to prevent the happening of mischief, pain, evil, or unhappiness to the party whose interest is considered: if that party be the community in general, then the happiness of the community: if a particular individual, then the happiness of that individual.

IV. . . . The community is a fictitious *body*, composed of the individual persons who are considered as constituting as it were its *members*. The interest of the community then is, what?—the sum of the interests of the several members who compose it.

V. . . . A thing is said to promote the interest, or to be *for* the interest, of an individual, when it tends to add to the sum total of his pleasures: or, what comes to the same thing, to diminish the sum total of his pains.

VI. An action then may be said to be conformable to the principle of utility, or, for shortness sake, to utility (meaning with respect to the community at large), when the tendency it has to augment the happiness of the community is greater than any it has to diminish it.

VII. A measure of government (which is but a particular kind of action, performed by a particular person or persons) may be said to be conformable to or dictated by the principle of utility, when in like manner the tendency which it has to augment the happiness of the community is greater than any which it has to diminish it.

VIII. When an action, or in particular a measure of government, is supposed by a man to be conformable to the principle of utility, it may be convenient, for the purposes of discourse, to imagine a kind of law or dictate, called a law or dictate of utility: and to speak of the action in question. as being conformable to such law or dictate.

IX. A man may be said to be a partisan of the principle of utility, when the approbation or disapprobation he annexes to any action, or to any measure, is determined by, and proportioned to the tendency which he conceives it to have to augment or to diminish the happiness of the community: or in other words, to its conformity or unconformity to the laws or dictates of utility.

X. Of an action that is conformable to the principle of utility, one may always say either that it is one that ought to be done, or at least that it is not one that ought not to be done. One may say also, that it is right it should be done; at least that it is not wrong it should be done: that it is a right action; at least that it is not a wrong action. When thus interpreted, the words *ought*, and *right* and *wrong*, and others of that stamp, have a meaning: when otherwise, they have none.

XI. Has the rectitude of this principle been ever formally contested? It should seem that it had, by those who have not known what they have been meaning. Is it susceptible of any direct proof? It should seem not: for that which is used to prove every thing else, cannot itself be proved: a chain of proofs must have their commencement somewhere. To give such proof is as impossible as it is needless. . . .

XIII. When a man attempts to combat the principle of utility, it is with reasons drawn, without his being aware of it, from that very principle itself.* His arguments, if they prove any thing, prove not that the principle is *wrong*, but that according to the applications he supposes to be made of it, it is *misapplied*. . . .

XIV. To disprove the propriety of it by arguments is impossible; but, from the causes that have been mentioned, or from some confused or partial view of it, a man may happen to be disposed not to relish it. Where this is the case, if he thinks the settling of his opinions on such a subject worth the trouble, let him take the following steps, and at length, perhaps, he may come to reconcile himself to it.

1. Let him settle with himself, whether he would wish to discard this principle altogether; if so, let him consider what it is that all his reasonings (in matters of politics especially) can amount to?

2. If he would, let him settle with himself, whether he would judge and act without any principle, or whether there is any other he would judge and act by?

3. If there be, let him examine and satisfy himself whether the principle he thinks he has found is really any separate intelligible principle; or whether it be not a mere principle in words, a kind of phrase, which at bottom expresses neither more nor less than the mere averment of his own unfounded sentiments; that is, what in another person he might be apt to call caprice?

4. If he is inclined to think that his own approbation or disapprobation, annexed to the idea of an act, without any regard to its consequences, is a sufficient foundation for him to judge and act upon, let him ask himself whether his sentiment is to be a standard of right and wrong, with respect to every other man, or whether every man's sentiment has the same privilege of being a standard to itself?

5. In the first case, let him ask himself whether his principle is not despotical, and hostile to all the rest of the human race?

6. In the second case, whether it is not anarchical, and whether at this rate there are not as many different standards of right and wrong as there are men? and whether even to the same man, the same thing, which is right to-day, may not (without the least change in its nature) be wrong to-morrow? and whether the same thing is not right and wrong in the same place at the same time? and in either case, whether all argument is not at an end? and whether, when two men have said, "I like this," and "I don't like it," they can (upon such a principle) have any thing more to say?

7. If he should have said to himself, No: for that sentiment which he proposes as a standard must be grounded on reflection, let him say on what particulars the reflection is to turn? If on particulars having relation to the utility of the act, then let him say whether this is not deserting his own principle, and borrowing assistance

---

* "The principle of utility (I have heard it said) is a dangerous principle: it is dangerous on certain occasions to consult it." This is as much as to say, what? that it is not consonant to utility, to consult utility: in short, that it is not consulting it, to consult it.

from that very one in opposition to which he sets it up: or if not on those particulars, on what other particulars?

8. If he should be for compounding the matter, and adopting his own principle in part, and the principle of utility in part, let him say how far he will adopt it?

9. When he has settled with himself where he will stop, then let him ask himself how he justifies to himself the adopting it so far? and why he will not adopt it any farther?

10. Admitting any other principle than the principle of utility to be a right principle, a principle that it is right for a man to pursue; admitting (what is not true) that the word *right* can have a meaning without reference to utility, let him say whether there is any such thing as a motive that a man can have to pursue the dictates of it: if there is, let him say what that *motive* is, and how it is to be distinguished from those which enforce the dictates of utility: if not, then lastly let him say what it is this other principle can be good for?

Chap. II—Of Principles Adverse to That of Utility

I. If the principle of utility be a right principle to be governed by, and that in all cases, it follows from what has been just observed, that whatever principle differs from it in any case must necessarily be a wrong one. To prove any other principle, therefore, to be a wrong one, there needs no more than just to show it to be what it is, a principle of which the dictates are in some point or other different from those of the principle of utility: to state it is to confute it.

II. A principle may be different from that of utility in two ways: 1. By being constantly opposed to it: this is the case with a principle which may be termed the principle of *asceticism*. 2. By being sometimes opposed to it, and sometimes not, as it may happen: this is the case with another, which may be termed the principle of *sympathy* and *antipathy*.

III. By the principle of asceticism I mean that principle, which, like the principle of utility, approves or disapproves of any action, according to the tendency which it appears to have to augment or diminish the happiness of the party whose interest is in question; but in an inverse manner: approving of actions in as far as they tend to diminish his happiness; disapproving of them in as far as they tend to augment it. . . .

IX. The principle of asceticism seems originally to have been the reverie of certain hasty speculators, who having perceived, or fancied, that certain pleasures, when reaped in certain circumstances, have, at the long run, been attended with pains more than equivalent to them, took occasion to quarrel with every thing that offered itself under the name of pleasure. Having then got thus far, and having forgot the point which they set out from, they pushed on, and went so much further as to think it meritorious to fall in love with pain. Even this, we see, is at bottom but the principle of utility misapplied.

X. The principle of utility is capable of being consistently pursued; and it is but tautology to say, that the more consistently it is pursued, the better it must ever be for human-kind. The principle of asceticism never was, nor ever can be, consistently pursued by any living creature. Let but one tenth part of the inhabitants of this earth pursue it consistently, and in a day's time they will have turned it into a hell.

XI. Among principles adverse to that of utility, that which at this day seems to have most influence in matters of government, is what may be called the principle of sympathy and antipathy. By the principle of sympathy and antipathy, I mean that principle which approves or disapproves of certain actions, not on account of their tending to augment the happiness, nor yet on account of their tending to diminish the happiness of the party whose interest is in question, but merely because a man finds himself disposed to approve or disapprove of them: holding up that approbation or disapprobation as a sufficient reason for itself, and disclaiming the necessity of looking out for any extrinsic ground.

XII. It is manifest, that this is rather a principle in name than in reality: it is not a positive principle of itself, so much as a term employed to signify the negation of all principle. What one expects to find in a principle is something that points out some external consideration, as a means of warranting and guiding the internal sentiments of approbation and disapprobation: this expectation is but ill fulfilled by a proposition, which does neither more nor less than hold up each of those sentiments as a ground and standard for itself. . . .

XIV. The various systems that have been formed concerning the standard of right and wrong, may all be reduced to the principle of sympathy and antipathy. One account may serve for all of them. They consist all of them in so many contrivances for avoiding the obligation of appealing to any external standard, and for prevailing upon the reader to accept of the author's sentiment or opinion as a reason for itself. The phrases different, but the principle the same.*. . .

XVIII. It may be wondered, perhaps, that in all this while no mention has been made of the *theological* principle; meaning that principle which professes to recur for the standard of right and wrong to the will of God. But the case is, this is not in fact a distinct principle. It is never any thing more or less than one or other of the three before-mentioned principles presenting itself under another shape. The *will* of God

---

* A great multitude of people are continually talking of the Law of Nature; and then they go on giving you their sentiments about what is right and what is wrong: and these sentiments, you are to understand, are so many chapters and sections of the Law of Nature.

Instead of the phrase, Law of Nature, you have sometimes, Law of Reason, Right Reason, Natural Justice, Natural Equity, Good Order. Any of them will do equally well. This latter is most used in Politics. The three last are much more tolerable than the others, because they do not very explicitly claim to be any thing more than phrases: they insist but feebly upon the being looked upon as so many positive standards of themselves, and seem content to be taken, upon occasion, for phrases expressive or the conformity of the thing in question to the proper standard, whatever that may be. On most occasions, however, it will be better to say *utility: utility* is clearer, as referring more explicitly to pain and pleasure.

here meant cannot be his revealed will, as contained in the sacred writings: for that is a system which nobody ever thinks of recurring to at this time of day, for the details of political administration: and even before it can be applied to the details of private conduct, it is universally allowed, by the most eminent divines of all persuasions, to stand in need of pretty ample interpretations; else to what use are the works of those divines? And for the guidance of these interpretations, it is also allowed, that some other standard must be assumed. The will then which is meant on this occasion, is that which may be called the *presumptive* will; that is to say, that which is presumed to be his will on account of the conformity of its dictates to those of some other principle. What then may be this other principle? It must be one or other of the three mentioned above: for there cannot, as we have seen, be any more. It is plain, therefore, that, setting revelation out of the question, no light can ever be thrown upon the standard of right and wrong, by any thing that can be said upon the question, what is God's will? We may be perfectly sure, indeed, that whatever is right is conformable to the will of God: but so far is that from answering the purpose of showing us what is right, that it is necessary to know first whether a thing is right, in order to know from thence whether it be conformable to the will of God.*

XIX. There are two things which are very apt to be confounded, but which it imports us carefully to distinguish:—the motive or cause, which, by operating on the mind of an individual, is productive of any act: and the ground or reason which warrants a legislator, or other by-stander, in regarding that act with an eye of approbation. When the act happens, in the particular instance in question, to be productive of effects which we approve of, much more if we happen to observe that the same motive may frequently be productive, in other instances, of the like effects, we are apt to transfer our approbation to the motive itself, and to assume, as the just ground for the approbation we bestow on the act, the circumstance of its originating from that motive. It is in this way that the sentiment of antipathy has often been considered as a just ground of action. Antipathy, for instance, in such or such a case, is the cause of an action which is attended with good effects: but this does not make it a right ground of action in that case, any more than in any other. Still farther. Not only the effects are good, but the agent sees beforehand that they will be so. This

---

* The principle of theology refers every thing to God's pleasure. But what is God's pleasure? God does not, he confessedly does not now, either speak or write to us. How then are we to know what is his pleasure? By observing what is our own pleasure, and pronouncing it to be his. Accordingly, what is called the pleasure of God, is and must necessarily be (revelation apart) neither more nor less than the good pleasure of the person, whoever he be, who is pronouncing what he believes, or pretends, to be God's pleasure. How know you it to be God's pleasure that such or such an act should be abstained from? whence come you even to suppose as much? "Because the engaging in it would, I imagine, be prejudicial upon the whole to the happiness of mankind"; says the partisan of the principle of utility; "Because the commission of it is attended with a gross and sensual, or at least with a trifling and transient satisfaction"; says the partisan of the principle of asceticism: "Because I detest the thoughts of it; and I cannot, neither ought I to be called upon to tell why"; says he who proceeds upon the principle of antipathy. In the words of one or other of these must that person necessarily answer (revelation apart) who professes to take for his standard the will of God.

may make the action indeed a perfectly right action: but it does not make antipathy a right ground of action. For the same sentiment of antipathy, if implicitly deferred to, may be, and very frequently is, productive of the very worst effects. Antipathy, therefore, can never be a right ground of action. No more, therefore, can resentment, which . . . is but a modification of antipathy. The only right ground of action, that can possibly subsist, is, after all, the consideration of utility, which, if it is a right principle of action, and of approbation, in any one case, is so in every other. Other principles in abundance, that is, other motives, may be the reasons why such and such an act has been done: that is, the reasons or causes of its being done: but it is this alone that can be the reason why it might or ought to have been done. Antipathy or resentment requires always to be regulated, to prevent its doing mischief: to be regulated by what? always by the principle of utility. The principle of utility neither requires nor admits of any other regulator than itself. . . .

Chap. IV—Value of a Lot of Pleasure or Pain, How to Be Measured

I. Pleasures then, and the avoidance of pains, are the *ends* which the legislator has in view: it behooves him therefore to understand their *value*. Pleasures and pains are the *instruments* he has to work with: it behooves him therefore to understand their force, which is again, in other words, their value.

II. To a person considered *by himself*, the value of a pleasure or pain considered *by itself*, will be greater or less, according to the four following circumstances:

1. Its *intensity*.
2. Its *duration*.
3. Its *certainty* or *uncertainty*.
4. Its *propinquity* or *remoteness*.

III. These are the circumstances which are to be considered in estimating a pleasure or a pain considered each of them by itself. But when the value of any pleasure or pain is considered for the purpose of estimating the tendency of any *act* by which it is produced, there are two other circumstances to be taken into the account; these are,

5. Its *fecundity*, or the chance it has of being followed by sensations of the same kind; that is, pleasures, if it be a pleasure: pains, if it be a pain.

6. Its *purity*, or the chance it has of *not* being followed by sensations of the *opposite* kind: that is, pains, if it be a pleasure: pleasures, if it be a pain. These two last, however, are in strictness scarcely to be deemed properties of the pleasure or the pain itself; they are not, therefore, in strictness to be taken into the account of the value of that pleasure or that pain. They are in strictness to be deemed properties only of the act, or other event, by which such pleasure or pain has been produced; and accordingly are only to be taken into the account of the tendency of such act or such event.

IV. To a *number* of persons, with reference to each of whom the value of a pleasure or a pain is considered, it will be greater or less, according to seven circumstances: to wit, the six preceding ones; viz.

1. Its *intensity*.
2. Its *direction*.
3. Its *certainty* or *uncertainty*.
4. Its *propinquity* or *remoteness*.
5. Its *fecundity*.
6. Its *purity*.

And one other, to wit:

7. Its *extent*; that is, the number of persons to whom it *extends*; or (in other words) who are affected by it.

V. To take an exact account then of the general tendency of any act, by which the interests of a community are affected, proceed as follows. Begin with any one person of those whose interests seem most immediately to be affected by it: and take an account,

1. Of the value of each distinguishable *pleasure* which appears to be produced by it in the *first* instance.

2. Of the value of each *pain* which appears to be produced by it in the *first* instance.

3. Of the value of each *pleasure* which appears to be produced by it *after* the first. This constitutes the *fecundity* of the first *pleasure* and the *impurity* of the first *pain*.

4. Of the value of each *pain* which appears to be produced by it after the first. This constitutes the *fecundity* of the first *pain*, and the *impurity* of the first pleasure.

5. Sum up all the values of all of the *pleasures* on the one side, and those of all the pains on the other. The balance, if it be on the side of pleasure, will give the *good* tendency of the act upon the whole, with respect to the interests of that *individual* person; if on the side of pain, the bad tendency of it upon the whole.

6. Take an account of the *number* of persons whose interests appear to be concerned; and repeat the above process with respect to each. *Sum up* the numbers expressive of the degrees of *good* tendency, which the act has, with respect to each individual, in regard to whom the tendency of it is *good* upon the whole: do this again with respect to each individual, in regard to whom the tendency of it is *bad* upon the whole. Take the *balance*; which, if on the side of *pleasure* will give the general *good tendency* of the act, with respect to the total number or community of individuals concerned; if on the side of pain, the general *evil tendency*, with respect to the same community.

VI. It is not to be expected that this process should be strictly pursued previously to every moral judgment, or to every legislative or judicial operation. It may, however, be always kept in view: and as near as the process actually pursued on these occasions approaches to it, so near will such process approach to the character of an exact one.

VII. The same process is alike applicable to pleasure and pain, in whatever shape they appear: and by whatever denomination they are distinguished: to pleasure, whether it be called *good* (which is properly the cause or instrument of pleasure) or *profit* (which is distant pleasure, or the cause or instrument of distant pleasure,) or *convenience*, or *advantage*, *benefit*, *emolument*, *happiness*, and so forth: to pain, whether it be called *evil* (which corresponds to *good*) or *mischief*; or *inconvenience*, or *disadvantage*, or *loss*, or *unhappiness*, and so forth.

VIII. Nor is this a novel and unwarranted, any more than it is a useless theory. In all this there is nothing but what the practice of mankind, wheresoever they have a clear view of their own interest, is perfectly conformable to. An article of property, an estate in land, for instance, is valuable, on what account? On account of the pleasures of all kinds which it enables a man to produce, and, what comes to the same thing, the pains of all kinds which it enables him to avert. But the value of such an article of property is universally understood to rise or fall according to the length or shortness of the time which a man has in it: the certainty or uncertainty of its coming into possession: and the nearness or remoteness of the time at which, if at all, it is to come into possession. As to the *intensity* of the pleasures which a man may derive from it, this is never thought of, because it depends upon the use which each particular person may come to make of it; which cannot be estimated till the particular pleasures he may come to derive from it, or the particular pains he may come to exclude by means of it, are brought to view. For the same reason neither does he think of the *fecundity* or *purity* of those pleasures.

JOHN STUART MILL (1806–1873): REVISED UTILITARIANISM

Bentham and Mill   In the principle of utility, Bentham perceived a universal criterion for distinguishing good government from bad. Mill found in this principle a foundation for his philosophical arguments in support of maximizing individual and social freedoms. Good government, for Mill, is one that would guarantee the fullest range of individual liberties for all citizens. Mill set about his defense of utilitarianism by conceiving the principle of utility as Bentham had: happiness alone is desirable as an end, and it consists in pleasure and freedom from pain. Acts are right insofar as they tend to promote pleasure and wrong in tending to prompt pain. From the social point of view, acts are right in tending to add to the sum of happiness or, failing this, to diminish pain. Thus pleasure is the only thing that is inherently good, pain the only thing inherently bad.

Higher and Lower Pleasures   However, Mill considered it self-evident that pushpin, foolishness, or selfishness are inferior to poetry, intelligence, or generosity. Mill admitted that some goods (generally, the intellectual) are by their nature more valuable, and so more worthy of human pursuit, than others (generally, the bodily). The way Mill put this is that pleasures and pains are to be measured not only in terms of their *quantities* but also in terms of their *qualities,* though he never makes clear how. But if the "higher" and "lower" pleasures are distinguished in this way, it appears to undermine Bentham's claim that the utility principle is at basis empirical in its appeal to what people actually find pleasurable. Mill took two steps to save this empirical or factual appeal underlying the utility principle. First, he argued, that human beings in fact mostly prefer the higher pleasures. Second, he urged that what counts as a higher or lower pleasure is to be decided by the majority decision of those having experience of *both* sorts of pleasure. Mill thought that almost all with such common experience would agree with his famous summary: "It is better to be a human being dissatisfied than a pig satisfied: better to be Socrates dissatisfied than a fool satisfied."

Mill's Revisions   Bentham held that the principle of utility is incapable of proof: the standard of proof itself cannot be proved. He suggested, nevertheless, that the principle of utility could be denied only by experiencing the personal displeasure caused by its misapplication and so by actually appealing to the principle denied. Similarly, Mill argued that any attempt, like Kant's, to avoid consequences by deriving moral rules strictly from the commands of reason must inevitably appeal to the benevolent consequences of those rules in order to justify their rightness (see Kant, Chapter 3). Mill added that each person desires his or her own happiness. So, by aggregation, happiness must be generally desirable as a good for all. Mill acknowledged that intrinsically good ends like virtue are desirable for their own sakes, not for the happiness they effect. He insisted, though, that in being desired as ends in themselves and not merely as means to happiness, these intrinsic goods are desired as *parts* or representatives of happiness. Mill countered in like manner the criticism that the principle of utility is unable to account for our common intuition, that acts such as promise-breaking or slavery are intrinsically immoral. Acts of some kinds, he argued, are commonly experienced as *tending* to create more pain than pleasure. A particular act of the kind can be presumed wrong because of this general tendency. For example, breaking a promise tends overwhelmingly to undermine trust, and so as a rule it is unacceptable. Yet the utility generated by breaking a promise under some specific conditions may be sufficiently great that breaking a promise would be morally required in the exceptional circumstance.

Act- and Rule-Utilitarianism   Considerations of this sort have encouraged philosophers more recently to distinguish between two kinds of utilitarianism. *Act-utilitarianism* holds that what is morally right in any situation is established by assessing which of the available acts would maximize the general sum of good over bad. Act-utilitarians are not concerned to assess the utility of *kinds* of acts (such as truth telling or stealing), nor are they concerned with the effects on utility of everyone acting in a given way. Whether the balance of good over bad is maximized must be directly assessed for each of the *particular acts* under consideration. If some act of lying or stealing maximizes the good, act-utilitarianism will consider it to be obligatory. It may be that among the alternatives, no act produces positive utility; here the act that produces the least disutility or evil will be required.

    Rule-utilitarianism holds that moral right is to be determined by assessing what applicable principle or social practice would maximize the sum of the general good. Here the question is not whether one's individual act would maximize goodness, but whether goodness would be maximized if everyone did the act. The principle of utility applies in establishing what the rules, principles, or practices should be. Social rules or practices are chosen or changed solely on the grounds of their utility. Whether an act is required in a specific situation would depend upon whether it is obliged by a rule or practice whose application in the context is considered to maximize the good. Rule-utilitarianism seeks to justify the intuition that what as a rule or practice is considered moral may sometimes override a particular act that would maximize utility. The general good of the rule or practice that promises should not be broken, say, would require rule-utilitarians always to keep their promises, even though breaking a promise in some particular circumstance may maximize the general utility. Act utilitarians, by contrast, may use rules of thumb as general guides to acts that tend to maximize utility. But if it is found that a particular act, like one of promise breaking, would create greater good than an act required by a rule like promise keeping, then an act-utilitarian would be obliged to break the promise.

Ideal Rule-Utilitarianism   We can distinguish also between two types of rule-utilitarianism. The first assesses the utility of the actual rules, principles, or practices of a society; the second sets out to establish those *ideal* rules that would maximize goodness. Richard Brandt develops a form of the latter, which he calls "ideal moral code rule-utilitarianism." Here an act is right if and only if the ideal moral code for the society does not prohibit it. A moral code is ideal for a society if its acceptance by the vast majority of the society's members (at least 90 percent, say) would produce more good per person than any competing moral code. The moral code is made up of general rules—such as "Keep promises" or "Do not harm"—rather than particular institutional principles—such as those concerning the repayment of government loans or police brutality. Thus the moral acceptability of particular institutional rules may be judged on the basis of the ideal moral code. An institutional principle allowing politicians to renege on repaying campaign loans may be deemed immoral if the ideal code commands keeping promises (a loan involves a promise to repay), and a law enforcement principle that permitted police generally "to shoot first and ask questions later" may entail violation of a moral rule not to harm.

Aggregate and Average Utilitarianism   It remains open to interpretation whether Bentham and Mill were act- or rule-utilitarians. Nevertheless, both clearly emphasized that happiness or pleasure is to be maximized. But an ambiguity may be evident here, too. In Bentham's classical utilitarianism, the mark of morality is the sum total or *aggregate* utility that might be produced. Mill and contemporary utilitarians have suggested that the criterion should not be the greatest aggregate happiness produced for all, but the maximizing of *average* utility, the total *per person,* resulting from the act or rule. (Brandt endorses such an interpretation.) This requires that not only must total utility be maximized, but the number of people whom utility benefits must be maximized. Attempts to combine the criteria of aggregate and average utility may cause conflict: Cases may rise where an act or rule that maximizes utility by greatly satisfying a few people clashes with one that maximizes the number of those experiencing some modest or small amount of satisfaction. For example, it must be decided whether a tax increase that greatly benefits 10 percent of the population but has minimal benefits for the rest is preferable to one that benefits all members of the population equally but in modest ways. Cases of this sort require utilitarians to indicate which criterion they take to be primary.

The appeal of utilitarianism has been a function of its simplicity, egalitarianism, and comprehensiveness, as well as the fact that we do value the good or happiness or pleasure. Utilitarianism has held out the promise of a single, simple, and general quantitative calculus for ethics, government, economics, and the law. Historically, hedonic utilitarianism encountered difficulties in establishing an acceptable unit of quantitative measurement for the calculus: specific weights are not assignable to pleasures and pains in every—some might argue—in any occurrence. Despite this, utilitarianism has continued to offer a method for determining efficient rules for law, politics, and economic distributions. Contemporary utilitarians no longer interpret *utility* simply as pleasure or happiness. The calculus is conducted more technically now in terms of preferences, interests, benefits, or welfare. Instead of evaluating the consequences of acts or rules in terms of maximizing pleasure and pain, *preference utilitarianism* seeks to evaluate their acceptability in terms of maximizing the satisfaction of desires and preferences. Yet whether the notion of utilitarian efficiency furnishes the fundamental criterion of morality remains an open question.

John Stuart Mill

UTILITARIANISM

Chapter I
General Remarks

To inquire . . . to what extent the moral beliefs of mankind have been vitiated or made uncertain by the absence of any distinct recognition of an ultimate standard, would imply a complete survey and criticism of past and present ethical doctrine. It would, however, be easy to show that whatever steadiness or consistency these moral beliefs have attained, has been mainly due to the tacit influence of a standard not recognized. Although the nonexistence of an acknowledged first principle has made ethics not so much a guide as a consecration of men's actual sentiments, still, as men's sentiments, both of favor and of aversion, are greatly influenced by what they suppose to be the effects of things upon their happiness, the principle of utility, or as Bentham latterly called it, the greatest happiness principle, has had a large share in forming the moral doctrines even of those who most scornfully reject its authority. Nor is there any school of thought which refuses to admit that the influence of actions on happiness is a most material and even predominant consideration in many of the details of morals, however unwilling to acknowledge it as the fundamental principle of morality, and the source of moral obligation. I might go much further, and say that to all those *a priori* moralists who deem it necessary to argue at

From John Stuart Mill, *Utilitarianism* (1863).

all, utilitarian arguments are indispensable. It is not my present purpose to criticize these thinkers; but I cannot help referring, for illustration, to a systematic treatise by one of the most illustrious of them, the *Metaphysics of Ethics*, by Kant. This remarkable man, whose system of thought will long remain one of the landmarks in the history of philosophical speculation, does, in the treatise in question, lay down a universal first principle as the origin and ground of moral obligation; it is this:—"So act, that the rule on which thou actest would admit of being adopted as a law by all rational beings." But when he begins to deduce from this precept any of the actual duties of morality, he fails, almost grotesquely, to show that there would be any contradiction, any logical (not to say physical) impossibility, in the adoption by all rational beings of the most outrageously immoral rules of conduct. All he shows is that the *consequences* of their universal adoption would be such as no one would choose to incur.

On the present occasion, I shall, without further discussion of the other theories, attempt to contribute something toward the understanding and appreciation of the Utilitarian or Happiness theory, and toward such proof as it is susceptible of. It is evident that this cannot be proof in the ordinary and popular meaning of the term. Questions of ultimate ends are not amenable to direct proof. Whatever can be proved to be good, must be so by being shown to be a means to something admitted to be good without proof. The medical art is proved to be good, by its conducing to health; but how is it possible to prove that health is good? The art of music is good, for the reason, among others, that it produces pleasure; but what proof is it possible to give that pleasure is good? If, then, it is asserted that there is a comprehensive formula, including all things which are in themselves good, and that what ever else is good, is not so as an end, but as a mean, the formula may be accepted or rejected, but is not a subject of what is commonly understood by proof. We are not, however, to infer that its acceptance or rejection must depend on blind impulse, or arbitrary choice. There is a larger meaning of the word proof, in which this question is as amenable to it as any other of the disputed questions of philosophy. The subject is within the cognizance of the rational faculty; and neither does that faculty deal with it solely in the way of intuition. Considerations may be presented capable of determining the intellect either to give or withhold its assent to the doctrine; and this is equivalent to proof. . . .

Chapter II
What Utilitarianism Is

. . . The creed which accepts as the foundation of morals, Utility, or the Greatest Happiness Principle, holds that actions are right in proportion as they tend to promote happiness, wrong as they tend to produce the reverse of happiness. By happiness is intended pleasure, and the absence of pain; by unhappiness, pain, and the privation of pleasure. To give a clear view of the moral standard set up by the theory, much more requires to be said; in particular, what things it includes in the ideas of pain and pleasure; and to what extent this is left an open question. But these supplementary explanations do not affect the theory of life on which this theory of morality is grounded—namely, that pleasure, and freedom from pain, are the only things desirable as ends; and that all desirable things (which are as numerous in the utilitarian as in any other scheme) are desirable either for the pleasure inherent in themselves, or as means to the promotion of pleasure and the prevention of pain.

Now, such a theory of life excites in many minds, and among them in some of the most estimable in feeling and purpose, inveterate dislike. To suppose that life has (as they express it) no higher end than pleasure—no better and nobler object of desire and pursuit—they designate as utterly mean and grovelling, as a doctrine worthy only of swine, to whom the followers of Epicurus were, at a very early period, contemptuously likened. . . . The comparison of the Epicurean life to that of beasts is felt as degrading, precisely because a beast's pleasures do not satisfy a human beings conceptions of happiness. Human beings have faculties more elevated than the animal appetites, and when once made conscious of them, do not regard anything as happiness which does not include their gratification. I do not indeed consider the Epicureans to have been by any means faultless in drawing on their scheme of consequences from the utilitarian principle. To do this in any sufficient manner, many Stoic, as well as Christian elements require to be included. But there is no known Epicurean theory of life which does not assign to the pleasures of the intellect, of the feelings and imagination, and of the moral sentiments, a much higher value as pleasures than to those of mere sensation. It must be admitted, however, that utilitarian writers in general have placed the superiority of mental over bodily pleasures chiefly in the greater permanency, safety, uncostliness, of the former—that is, in their circumstantial advantages rather than in their intrinsic nature. And on all these points utilitarians have fully proved their case; but they might have taken the other, and, as it may be called, higher ground, with entire consistency. It is quite compatible with the principle of utility to recognize the fact, that some *kinds* of pleasure are more desirable and more valuable than others. It would be absurd that while, in estimating all other things, quality is considered as well as quantity, the estimation of pleasures should be supposed to depend on quantity alone.

If I am asked, what I mean by difference of quality in pleasures, or what makes one pleasure more valuable than another, merely as a pleasure, except its being greater in amount, there is but one possible answer. Of two pleasures, if there be one to which all or almost all who have experience of both give a decided preference, irrespective of any feeling of moral obligation to prefer it, that is the more desirable pleasure. If one of the two is, by those who are competently acquainted with both, placed so far above the other that they prefer it, even though knowing it to be attended with a greater amount of discontent, and would not resign it for any quantity of the other pleasure which their nature is capable of, we are justified in ascribing to the preferred enjoyment a superiority in quality, so far outweighing quantity as to render it, in comparison, of small account.

Now it is an unquestionable fact that those who are equally acquainted with, and equally capable of appreciating and enjoying, both, do give a most marked preference to the manner of existence which employs their higher faculties. Few human creatures would consent to be changed into any of the lower animals, for a promise of the fullest allowance of a beast's pleasures; no intelligent human being would consent to be a fool, no instructed person would be an ignoramus, no person of feeling and conscience would be selfish and base, even though they should be persuaded that the fool, the dunce, or the rascal is better satisfied with his lot than they are with theirs. They would not resign what they possess more than he, for the most complete satisfaction of all the desires which they have in common with him. If they ever fancy they would, it is only in cases of unhappiness so extreme, that to escape from it they would exchange their lot for almost any other, however undesirable in their own eyes. A being of higher faculties requires more to make him happy, is capable probably of more acute suffering, and is certainly accessible to it at more points, than one of an inferior type; but in spite of these liabilities, he can never really wish to sink into what he feels to be a lower grade of existence. We may give what explanation we please of this unwillingness; . . . but its most appropriate appellation is a sense of dignity, which all human beings possess in one form or other, and in some, though by no means in exact, proportion to their higher faculties, and which is so essential a part of the happiness of those in whom it is strong that nothing which conflicts with it could be, otherwise than momentarily, an object of desire to them. Whoever supposes that this preference takes place at a sacrifice of happiness—that the superior being, in anything like equal circumstances, is not happier than the inferior—confounds the two very different ideas, of happiness, and content. It is indisputable that the being whose capacities of enjoyment are low, has the greatest chance of having them fully satisfied, and a highly-endowed being will always feel that any happiness which he can look for, as the world is constituted, is imperfect. But he can learn to bear its imperfections, if they are at all bearable; and they will not make him envy the being who is indeed unconscious of the imperfections, but only because he feels not at all the good which those imperfections qualify. It is better to be a human being dissatisfied than a pig satisfied; better to be Socrates dissatisfied than a fool satisfied. And if the fool, or the pig, is of a different opinion, it is because they only know their own side of the question. The other party to the comparison knows both sides.

It may be objected, that many who are capable of the higher pleasures, occasionally, under the influence of temptation, postpone them to the lower. But this is quite compatible with a full appreciation of the intrinsic superiority of the higher. Men often, from infirmity of character, make their election for the nearer good, though they know it to be the less valuable; and this no less when the choice is between two bodily pleasures, than when it is between bodily and mental. They pursue sensual indulgences to the injury of health, though perfectly aware that health is the greater good. It may be further objected, that many who begin with youthful enthusiasm for everything noble, as they advance in years sink into indolence and selfishness. But I do not believe that those who undergo this very common change, voluntarily choose the lower description of pleasures in preference to the higher. I believe that before they devote themselves exclusively to the one, they have already become incapable of the other. Capacity for the nobler feelings is in most natures a very tender plant, easily killed, not only by hostile influences, but by mere want of sustenance; and in the majority of young persons it speedily dies away if the occupations to which their position in life has devoted them, and society into which it has thrown them, are not favorable to keeping that higher capacity in exercise. Men lose their high aspirations as they lose their intellectual tastes, because they have not time or opportunity for indulging them; and they addict themselves to inferior pleasures, not because they deliberately prefer them, but because they are either the only ones to which they have access, or the only ones which they are any longer capable of enjoying. It may be questioned whether any one who has remained equally susceptible to both classes of pleasures, ever knowingly and calmly preferred the lower; though many, in all ages, have broken down in an ineffectual attempt to combine both.

From this verdict of the only competent judges, I apprehend there can be no appeal. On a question which is the best worth having of two pleasures, or which of two modes of existence is the most grateful to the feelings, apart from its moral attributes and from its consequences, the judgment of those who are qualified by knowledge of both, or, if they differ, that of the majority among them, must be admitted as final. And there needs be the less hesitation to accept this judgment respecting the quality of pleasures, since there is no other tribunal to be referred even on the question of quantity. What means are there of determining which is the acutest of two pains, or the intensest of two pleasurable sensations, except the general suffrage of those who are familiar with both? Neither pains nor pleasures are homogeneous, and pain is always heterogeneous with pleasure. What is there to decide whether a particular pleasure is worth purchasing at the cost of a particular pain, except the feelings and judgment of the experienced? When, therefore, those feelings and judgment declare the pleasures derived from the higher faculties to be preferable *in kind,* apart from the question of intensity, to those of which the animal nature, disjoined from the higher faculties, is susceptible, they are entitled on this subject to the same regard.

I have dwelt on this point, as being a necessary part of a perfectly just conception of Utility or Happiness, considered as the directive role of human conduct. But it is by no means an indispensable condition to the acceptance of the utilitarian standard; for that standard is not the agent's own greatest happiness, but the greatest amount of happiness altogether; and if it may possibly be doubted whether a noble character is always the happier for its nobleness, there can be no doubt that it makes other people happier, and that the world in general is immensely a gainer by it. Utilitarianism, therefore, could only attain its end by the general cultivation of nobleness of character, even if each individual were only benefited by the nobleness of others, and his own, so far as happiness is concerned, were a sheer deduction from the benefit. But the bare enunciation of such an absurdity as this last, renders refutation superfluous.

According to the Greatest Happiness Principle, as above explained, the ultimate end, with reference to and for the sake of which all other things are desirable (whether we are considering our own good or that of other people), is an existence exempt as far as possible from pain, and as rich as possible in enjoyments, both in point of quantity and quality; the test of quality, and the rule for measuring it against quantity, being the preference felt by those who, in their opportunities of experience, to which must be added their habits of self consciousness and self-observation, are best furnished with the means of comparison. This, being, according to the utilitarian opinion, the end of human action, is necessarily also the standard of morality; which may accordingly be defined, the rules and precepts for human conduct, by the observance of which an existence such as has been described might be, to the greatest extent possible, secured to all mankind; and not to them only, but, so far as the nature of things admits, to the whole sentient creation. . . .

. . . [T]he assailants of utilitarianism seldom have the justice to acknowledge, that the happiness which forms the utilitarian standard of what is right in conduct, is not the agent's own happiness, but that of all concerned. As between his own happiness and that of others, utilitarianism requires him to be as strictly impartial as a disinterested and benevolent spectator. In the golden rule of Jesus of Nazareth, we read the complete spirit of the ethics of utility. To do as one would be done by, and to love one's neighbor as oneself, constitute the ideal perfection of utilitarian morality. As the means of making the nearest approach to this ideal, utility would enjoin, first, that laws and social arrangements should place the happiness, or (as speaking practically it may be called) the interest, of every individual, as nearly as possible in harmony with the interest of the whole; and secondly, that education and opinion, which have so vast a power over human character, should so use that power as to establish in the mind of every individual an indissoluble association between his own happiness and the good of the whole; especially between his own happiness and the practice of such modes of conduct, negative and positive, as regard for the universal happiness prescribes: so that not only he may be unable to conceive the possibility of happiness to himself, consistently with conduct opposed to the general good, but also that a direct impulse to promote the general good may be in every individual one of the habitual motives of action, and the sentiments connected therewith may fill a large and prominent place in every human being's sentient existence. If the impugners of the utilitarian morality represented it to their Own minds in this its true character, I know not what recommendation possessed by any other morality they could possibly affirm to be wanting to it: what more beautiful or more exalted developments of human nature any other ethical system can be supposed to foster, or what springs of action, not accessible to the utilitarian, such systems rely on for giving effect to their mandates.

The objectors to utilitarianism . . . who entertain anything like a just idea of its disinterested character, sometimes find fault with its standard as being too high for humanity. They say it is exacting too much to require that people shall always act from the inducement of promoting the general interests of society. But this is to mistake the very meaning of a standard of morals, and to confound the rule of action with the motive of it. It is the business of ethics to tell us what are our duties, or by what test we may know them; but no system of ethics requires that the sole motive of all we do shall be a feeling of duty; on the contrary, ninety-nine hundredths of all our actions are done from other motives, and rightly so done, if the rule of duty does not condemn them. It is the more unjust to utilitarianism that this particular misapprehension should be made a ground of objection to it, inasmuch as utilitarian moralists have gone beyond almost all others in affirming that the motive has nothing to do with the morality of the action, though much with the worth of the agent. He who saves a fellow creature from drowning does what is morally right, whether his motive be duty, or the hope of being paid for his trouble: he who betrays the friend that trusts him, is guilty of a crime, even if his object be to serve another friend to whom he is under greater obligations.* But to speak only of actions done from the motive of duty, and in direct obedience to principle: it is a misapprehension of the utilitarian mode of thought, to conceive it as implying that people should fix their minds upon so wide a generality as the world, or society at large. The great majority of good actions are intended, not for the benefit of the world, but for that of individuals, of which the good of the world is made up; and the thoughts of the most virtuous man need not on these occasions travel beyond the particular persons concerned, except so far as is necessary to assure himself that in benefiting them he is not violating the rights—that is, the legitimate and authorized expectations—of any one else. The multiplication of happiness is, according to the utilitarian ethics, the object of virtue: the occasions on which any person (except one in a thousand) has it in his power to do this on an extended scale, in other words, to be a public benefactor, are but exceptional; and on these occasions alone is he called on to consider public utility; in every other case, private utility, the interest or happiness of some few persons, is all he has to attend to. Those alone the influence of whose actions extends to society in general, need concern themselves habitually about so large an object. In the case of abstinences indeed—of things which people forbear to do, from moral considerations, though the consequences in the particular

---

* An opponent, whose intellectual and moral fairness it is a pleasure to acknowledge (the Rev. J. Llewellyn Davies), has objected to this passage, saying, "Surely the rightness or wrongness of saving a man from drowning does depend very much upon the motive with which it is done. Suppose that a tyrant, when his enemy jumped into the sea to escape from him, saved him from drowning simply in order that he might inflict upon him more exquisite tortures, would it tend to clearness to speak of that rescue as 'a morally right action?' Or suppose again, according to one of the stock illustrations of ethical inquiries, that a man betrayed a trust received from a friend, because the discharge of it would fatally injure that friend himself or some one belonging to him, would utilitarianism compel one to call the betrayal 'a crime' as much as if it had been done from the meanest motive?"

I submit, that he who saves another from drowning in order to kill him by torture afterwards, does not differ only in motive from him who does the same thing from duty or benevolence; the act itself is different. The rescue of the man is, in the case supposed, only the necessary first step of an act far more atrocious than leaving him to drown would have been. Had Mr. Davies said, "The rightness or wrongness of saving a man from drowning does depend very much"—not upon the motive, but—"upon the *intention*," no utilitarian would have differed from him. Mr. Davies, by an oversight too common not to be quite venial, has in this case confounded the very different ideas of Motive and Intention. There is no point which utilitarian thinkers (and Bentham preeminently) have taken more pains to illustrate than this. The morality of the action depends entirely upon the intention—that is, upon what the agent *wills to do*. But the motive, that is, the feeling which makes him will so to do, when it makes no difference in the act, makes none in the morality: though it makes a great difference in our moral estimation of the agent, especially if it indicates a good or a bad habitual *disposition*—a bent of character from which useful, or from which hurtful actions are likely to arise.

case might be beneficial—it would be unworthy of an intelligent agent not to be consciously aware that the action is of a class which, if practiced generally, would be generally injurious, and that this is the ground of the obligation to abstain from it. The amount of regard for the public interest implied in this recognition, is no greater than is demanded by every system of morals; for they all enjoin to abstain from whatever is manifestly pernicious to society.

The same considerations dispose of another reproach against the doctrine of utility, founded on a still grosser misconception of the purpose of a standard of morality, and of the very meaning of the words right and wrong. It is often affirmed that utilitarianism renders men cold and unsympathizing; that it chills their moral feelings toward individuals; that it makes them regard only the dry and hard consideration of the consequences of actions, not taking into their moral estimate the qualities from which those actions emanate. If the assertion means that they do not allow their judgment respecting the rightness or wrongness of an action to be influenced by their opinion of the qualities of the person who does it, this is a complaint not against utilitarianism, but against having any standard of morality at all; for certainly no known ethical standard decides an action to be good or bad because it is done by a good or a bad man, still less because done by an amiable, a brave, or a benevolent man, or the contrary. These considerations are relevant, not to the estimation of actions, but of persons, and there is nothing in the utilitarian theory inconsistent with the fact that there are other things which interest us in persons besides the rightness and wrongness of their actions. The Stoics, indeed, with the paradoxical misuse of language which was part of their system, and by which they strove to raise themselves above all concern about anything but virtue, were fond of saying that he who has that has everything; that he, and only he, is rich, is beautiful, is a king. But no claim of this description is made for the virtuous man by the utilitarian doctrine. Utilitarians are quite aware that there are other desirable possessions and qualities besides virtue, and are perfectly willing to allow to all of them their full worth. They are also aware that a right action does not necessarily indicate a virtuous character, and that actions which are blameable often proceed from qualities entitled to praise. When this is apparent in any particular case, it modifies their estimation, not certainly of the act, but of the agent. I grant that they are, notwithstanding, of opinion, that in the long run the best proof of a good character is good actions; and resolutely refuse to consider any mental disposition as good, of which the predominant tendency is to produce bad conduct. This makes them unpopular with many people; but it is an unpopularity which they must share with every one who regards the distinction between right and wrong in a serious light; and the reproach is not one which a conscientious utilitarian need be anxious to repel.

If no more be meant by the objection than that many utilitarians look on the morality of actions, as measured by the utilitarian standard, with too exclusive a regard, and do not lay sufficient stress upon the other beauties of character which go toward making a human being lovable or admirable, this may be admitted. Utilitarians who have cultivated their moral feelings, but not their sympathies nor their artistic perceptions, do fall into this mistake; and so do all other moralists under the same conditions. What can be said in excuse for other moralists is equally available for them, namely, that if there is to be any error, it is better that it should be on that side. As a matter of fact, we may affirm that among utilitarians as among adherents of other systems, there is every imaginable degree of rigidity and of laxity in the application of their standard: some are even puritanically rigorous, while others are as indulgent as can possibly be desired by sinner or by sentimentalist. But on the whole, a doctrine which brings prominently forward the interest that mankind have in the repression and prevention of conduct which violates the moral law, is likely to be inferior to no other in turning the sanctions of opinion against such violations. It is true, the question, What does violate the moral law? is one on which those who recognize different standards of morality are likely now and then to differ. But difference of opinion on moral questions was not first introduced into the world by utilitarianism, while the doctrine does supply, if not always an easy, at all events a tangible and intelligible mode of deciding such differences. . . .

Again, Utility is often summarily stigmatized as an immoral doctrine by giving it the name of Expediency, and taking advantage of the popular use of that term to contrast it with Principle. But the Expedient, in the sense in which it is opposed to the Right, generally means that which is expedient for the particular interest of the agent himself; as when a minister sacrifices the interest of his country to keep himself in place. When it means anything better than this, it means that which is expedient for some immediate object, some temporary purpose, but which violates a rule whose observance is expedient in a much higher degree. The Expedient, in this sense, instead of being the same thing with the useful, is a branch of the hurtful. Thus, it would often be expedient, for the purpose of getting over some momentary embarrassment, or attaining some object immediately useful to ourselves or others, to tell a lie. But inasmuch as the cultivation in ourselves of a sensitive feeling on the subject of veracity, is one of the most useful, and the enfeeblement of that feeling one of the most hurtful, things to which our conduct can be instrumental; and inasmuch as any, even unintentional, deviation from truth, does that much toward weakening the trustworthiness of human assertion, which is not only the principal support of all present social well-being, but the insufficiency of which does more than any one thing that can be named to keep back civilization, virtue, everything on which human happiness on the largest scale depends; we feel that the violation, for a present advantage, of a rule of such transcendent expediency, is not expedient, and that he who, for the sake of a convenience to himself or to some other individual, does what depends on him to deprive mankind of the good, and inflict upon them the evil, involved in the greater or less reliance which they can place in each other's word, acts the part of one of their worst enemies. Yet that even this rule, sacred as it is, admits of possible exceptions, is acknowledged by all moralists; the chief of which is when the withholding of some fact (as of information from a malefactor, or of bad news from a person dangerously ill) would preserve some one (especially a person other than oneself) from great and unmerited evil, and when the withholding can only be effected by denial. But in order that the exception may not extend itself beyond the need, and may have the least possible effect in weakening reliance on veracity, it ought to be recognized, and, if possible, its limits defined; and if the principle of utility is good for anything, it must be good for weighing these conflicting utilities against one another, and marking out the region within which one or the other preponderates.

Again, defenders of utility often find themselves called upon to reply to such objections as this—that there is not time, previous to action, for calculating and weighing the effects of any line of conduct on the general happiness. This is exactly as if any one were to say that it is impossible to guide our conduct by Christianity, because there is not time, on every occasion on which anything has to be done, to read through the Old and New Testaments. The answer to the objection is, that there has been ample time, namely, the whole past duration of the human species. During all that time mankind have been learning by experience the tendencies of actions; on which experience all the prudence, as well as all the morality of life, is dependent. People talk as if the commencement of this course of experience had hitherto been put off, and as if, at the moment when some man feels tempted to meddle with the property or life of another, he had to begin considering for the first time whether murder and theft are injurious to human happiness. Even then I do not think that he would find the question very puzzling; but, at all events, the matter is now done to his hand. It is truly a whimsical supposition that if mankind were agreed in considering utility to be the test of morality, they would remain without any agreement as to what *is* useful, and would take no measures for having their notions on the subject taught to the young, and enforced by law and opinion. There is no difficulty in proving any ethical standard whatever to work ill, if we suppose universal idiocy to be conjoined with it; but on any hypothesis short of that, mankind must by this time have acquired positive beliefs as to the effects of some actions on their happiness; and the beliefs which have thus come down are the rules of morality for the multitude, and for the philosopher until he has succeeded in finding better. That philosophers might easily do this, even now, on many subjects; that the received code of ethics is by no means of divine right; and that mankind have still much to learn as to the effects of actions on the general happiness, I admit, or rather, earnestly maintain. The corollaries from the principle of utility, like the precepts of every practical art, admit of indefinite improvement, and, in a progressive state of the human mind, their improvement is perpetually going on, but to consider the rules of morality as improvable, is one thing; to pass over the intermediate generalizations entirely, and endeavor to test each individual action directly by the first principle, is another. It is a strange notion that the acknowledgment of a first principle is inconsistent with the admission of secondary ones. . . . Whatever we adopt as the fundamental principle of morality, we require subordinate principles to apply it by: the impossibility of doing without them, being common to all systems, can afford no argument against any one in particular: but gravely to argue as if no such secondary principles could be had, and as if mankind had remained till now, and always must remain, without drawing any general conclusions from the experience of human life, is as high a pitch, I think, as absurdity has ever reached in philosophical controversy.

The remainder of the stock arguments against utilitarianism mostly consist in laying to its charge the common infirmities of human nature, and the general difficulties which embarrass conscientious persons in shaping their course through life. We are told that a utilitarian will be apt to make his own particular case an exception to moral rules, and, when under temptation, will see a utility in the breach of rule, greater than he will see in its observance. But is utility the only creed which is able to furnish us with excuses for evil doing, and means of cheating our own conscience? They are afforded in abundance by all doctrines which recognize as a fact in morals the existence of conflicting considerations; which all doctrines do, that have been believed by sane persons. It is not the fault of any creed, but of the complicated nature of human affairs, that rules of conduct cannot be so framed as to require no exceptions, and that hardly any kind of action can safely be laid down as either always obligatory or always condemnable. There is no ethical creed which does not temper the rigidity of its laws, by giving a certain latitude, under the moral responsibility of the agent, for accommodation to peculiarities of circumstances; and under every creed, at the opening thus made, self-deception and dishonest casuistry get in. There exists no moral system under which there do not arise unequivocal cases of conflicting obligation. These are the real difficulties, the knotty points both in the theory of ethics, and in the conscientious guidance of personal conduct. They are overcome practically with greater or with less success according to the intellect and virtue of the individual; but it can hardly be pretended that any one will be the less qualified for dealing with them, from possessing an ultimate standard to which conflicting rights and duties can be referred. If utility is the ultimate source of moral obligations, utility may be invoked to decide between them when their demands are incompatible. Though the application of the standard may be difficult, it is better than none at all: while in other systems, the moral laws all claiming independent authority, there is no common umpire entitled to interfere between them; their claims to precedence one over another rest on little better than sophistry, and unless determined, as they generally are, by the unacknowledged influence of considerations of utility, afford a free scope for the action of personal desires and partialities. We must remember that only in these cases of conflict between secondary principles is it requisite that first principles should be appealed to. There is no case of moral obligation in which some secondary principle is not involved; and if only one, there can seldom be any real doubt which one it is, in the mind of any person by whom the principle itself is recognized.

Chapter IV
Of What Sort of Proof
the Principle of Utility Is Susceptible

It has already been remarked, that questions of ultimate ends do not admit of proof, in the ordinary acceptation of the term. To be incapable of proof by reasoning is common to all first principles; to the first premises of our knowledge, as well as to those of our conduct. But the former, being matters of fact, may be the subject of a direct appeal to the faculties which judge of fact—namely, our senses, and our internal consciousness. Can an appeal be made to the same faculties on questions of practical ends? Or by what other faculty is cognizance taken of them?

Questions about ends are, in other words, questions about what things are desirable. The utilitarian doctrine is, that happiness is desirable, and the only thing desirable, as an end; all other things being only desirable as means to that end. What ought to be required of this doctrine—what conditions is it requisite that the doctrine should fulfill—to make good its claim to be believed?

The only proof capable of being given that an object is visible, is that people actually see it. The only proof that a sound is audible, is that people hear it: and so of the other sources of our experience. In like manner, I apprehend, the sole evidence it is possible to produce that anything is desirable, is that people do actually desire it. If the end which the utilitarian doctrine proposes to itself were not, in theory and in practice, acknowledged to be an end, nothing could ever convince any person that it was so. No reason can be given why the general happiness is desirable, except that each person, so far as he believes it to be attainable, desires his own happiness. This, however, being a fact, we have not only all the proof which the case admits of, but all which it is possible to require, that happiness is a good: that each person's happiness is a good to that person and the general happiness, therefore, a good to the aggregate of all persons. Happiness has made out its title as *one* of the ends of conduct, and consequently one of the criteria of morality.

But it has not, by this alone, proved itself to be the sole criterion. To do that, it would seem, by the same rule, necessary to show, not only that people desire happiness, but that they never desire anything else. . . .

. . . The ingredients of happiness are very various, and each of them is desirable in itself, and not merely when considered as swelling an aggregate. The principle of utility does not mean that any given pleasure, as music, for instance, or any given exemption from pain, as for example health, are to be looked upon as means to a collective something termed happiness, and to be desired on that account. They are desired and desirable in and for themselves; besides being means, they are a part of end. Virtue, according to the utilitarian doctrine, is not naturally and originally part of the end, but it is capable of becoming so; and in those who love it disinterestedly it has become so, and is desired and cherished, not as a means to happiness, but as a part of their happiness. . . .

We have now, then, an answer to the question, of what sort of proof the principle of utility is susceptible. If the opinion which I have now stated is psychologically true—if human nature is so constituted as to desire nothing which is not either a part of happiness or a means of happiness, we can have no other proof, and we require no other, that these are the only things desirable. If so, happiness is the sole end of human action, and the promotion of it the test by which to judge of all human conduct; from whence it necessarily follows that it must be the criterion of morality, since a part is included in the whole.

And now to decide whether this is really so; whether mankind do desire nothing for itself but that which is a pleasure to them, or of which the absence is a pain; we have evidently arrived at a question of fact and experience, dependent, like all similar questions, upon evidence. It can only be determined by practiced self-consciousness and self-observation, assisted by observation of others. I believe that these sources of evidence, impartially consulted, will declare that desiring a thing and finding it pleasant, aversion to it and thinking of it as painful, are phenomena entirely inseparable, or rather two parts of the same phenomenon, in strictness of language, two different modes of naming the same psychological fact: that to think of an object as desirable (unless for the sake of its consequences), and to think of it as pleasant, are one and the same thing; and that to desire anything, except in proportion as the idea of it is pleasant, is a physical and metaphysical impossibility.

So obvious does this appear to me, that I expect it will hardly be disputed: and the objection made will be, not that desire can possibly be directed to anything ultimately except pleasure and exemption from pain, but that the will is a different thing from desire; that a person of confirmed virtue, or any other person whose purposes are fixed, carries out his purposes without any thought of the pleasure he has in contemplating them, or expects to derive from their fulfillment; and persists in acting on them, even though these pleasures are much diminished, by changes in his character or decay of his passive sensibilities, or are outweighed by the pains which the pursuit of the purposes may bring upon him. All this I fully admit, and have stated it elsewhere, as positively and emphatically as any one. Will, the active phenomenon, is a different thing from desire, the state of passive sensibility, and though originally an offshoot from it, may in time take root and detach itself from the parent stock; so much so, that in the case of an habitual purpose, instead of willing the thing because we desire it, we often desire it only because we will it. This, however, is but an instance of that familiar fact, the power of habit, and is nowise confined to the case of virtuous actions. Many indifferent things, which men originally did from a motive of some sort, they continue to do from habit. Sometimes this is done unconsciously, the consciousness coming only after the action: at other times with conscious volition, but volition which has become habitual, and is put into operation by the force of habit, in opposition perhaps to the deliberate preference, as often happens with those who have contracted habits of vicious or hurtful indulgence. Third and last comes the case in which the habitual act of will in the individual instance is not in contradiction to the general intention prevailing at other times, but in fulfillment of it; as in the case of the person of confirmed virtue, and of all who pursue deliberately and consistently any determinate end. The distinction between will and desire thus understood, is an authentic and highly important psychological fact; but the fact consists solely in this—that will, like all other parts of our constitution, is amenable to habit, and that we may will from habit what we no longer desire for itself, or desire only because we will it. It is not the less true that will, in the beginning, is entirely produced by desire; including in that term the repelling influence of pain as well as the attractive one of pleasure. Let us take into consideration, no longer the person who has a confirmed will to do right, but him in whom that virtuous will is still feeble, conquerable by temptation, and not to be fully relied on; by what means can it be strengthened? How can the will be virtuous, where it does not exist in sufficient force, be implanted or awakened? Only by making the person *desire* virtue—by making him think of it in a pleasurable light, or of its absence in a painful one. It is by associating the doing right with pleasure, or the doing wrong with pain, or by eliciting and impressing and bringing home to the person's experience the pleasure naturally involved in the one or the pain in the other, that it is possible to call forth that will to be virtuous, which, when confirmed, acts without any thought of either pleasure or pain. Will is the child of desire, and passes out of the dominion of its parent only to come under that of habit. That which is the result of habit affords no presumption of being intrinsically good; and there would be no reason for wishing that the purpose of virtue should become independent of pleasure and pain, were it not that the influence of the pleasurable and painful associations which prompt to virtue is not sufficiently to be depended on for unerring constancy of action until it has acquired the support of habit. Both in feeling and in conduct, habit is the only thing which imparts certainty; and it is because of the importance to others of being able to rely absolutely on one's feelings and conduct, and to oneself of being able to rely on one's own, that the will to do right ought to be cultivated into this habitual independence. In other words, this state of the will is a means to good, not intrinsically a good; and does not contradict the doctrine that nothing is a good to human beings but in so far as it is either itself pleasurable, or a means of attaining pleasure or averting pain.

But if this doctrine be true, the principle of utility is proved. Whether it is so or not, must now be left to the consideration of the thoughtful reader.

ON LIBERTY

The object of this Essay is to assert one very simple principle, as entitled to govern absolutely the dealings of society with the individual in the way of compulsion and control, whether the means used be physical force in the form of legal penalties, or the moral coercion of public opinion. That principle is, that the sole end for which mankind are warranted, individually or collectively, in interfering with the liberty of action of any of their number, is self-protection. That the only purpose for which power can be rightfully exercised over any member of a civilized community, against his will, is to prevent harm to others. His own good, either physical or moral, is not a sufficient warrant. He cannot rightfully be compelled to do or forbear because it will be better for him to do so, because it will make him happier, because, in the opinions of others, to do so would be wise, or even right. These are good reasons for remonstrating with him, or reasoning with him, or persuading him, or entreating him, but not for compelling him, or visiting him with any evil in case he do other-

From John Stuart Mill, *On Liberty* (1859).

wise. To justify that, the conduct from which it is desired to deter him, must be calculated to produce evil to some one else. The only part of the conduct of any one, for which he is amenable to society, is that which concerns others. In the part which merely concerns himself, his independence is, of right, absolute. Over himself, over his own body and mind, the individual is sovereign.

It is, perhaps, hardly necessary to say that this doctrine is meant to apply only to human beings in the maturity of their faculties. We are not speaking of children, or of young persons below the age which the law may fix as that of manhood and womanhood. Those who are still in a state to require being taken care of by others, must be protected against their own actions as well as against external injury. . . .

There is a sphere of action in which society, as distinguished from the individual, has, if any, only an indirect interest, comprehending all that portion of a person's life and conduct which affects only himself, or if it also affects others, only with their free, voluntary, and undeceived consent and participation. When I say only himself, I mean directly, and in the first instance: for whatever affects himself, may affect others *through* himself; and the objection which may be grounded on this contingency, will receive consideration in the sequel. This, then, is the appropriate region of human liberty. It comprises, first, the inward domain of consciousness; demanding liberty of conscience, in the most comprehensive sense; liberty of thought and feeling; absolute freedom of opinion and sentiment on all subjects, practical or speculative, scientific, moral, or theological. The liberty of expressing and publishing opinions may seem to fall under a different principle, since it belongs to that part of the conduct of an individual which concerns other people; but, being almost of as much importance as the liberty of thought itself, and resting in great part on the same reasons, is practically inseparable from it. Secondly, the principle requires liberty of tastes and pursuits; of framing the plan of our life to suit our own character, of doing as we like, subject to such consequences as may follow; without impediment from our fellow-creatures, so long as what we do does not harm them, even though they should think our conduct foolish, perverse, or wrong. Thirdly, from this liberty of each individual, follows the liberty, within the same limits, of combination among individuals; freedom to unite, for any purpose not involving harm to others: the persons combining being supposed to be of full age, and not forced or deceived.

No society in which these liberties are not, on the whole, respected, is free, whatever may be its form of government; and none is completely free in which they do not exist absolute and unqualified. The only freedom which deserves the name, is that of pursuing our own good in our own way, so long as we do not attempt to deprive others of theirs, or impede their efforts to obtain it. Each is the proper guardian of his own health, whether bodily, or mental and spiritual. Mankind are greater gainers by suffering each other to live as seems good to themselves, than by compelling each to live as seems good to the rest. . . .

Again, there are many acts which, being directly injurious only to the agents themselves, ought not to be legally interdicted, but which, if done publicly, are a violation of good manners, and coming thus within the category of offenses against others, may rightfully be prohibited. Of this kind are offenses against decency; on which it is unnecessary to dwell, the rather as they are only connected indirectly with our subject, the objection to publicity being equally strong in the case of many actions not in themselves condemnable, nor supposed to be so.

SUGGESTIONS FOR DISCUSSION

1. Should utilitarianism be concerned to bring about the greatest amount of happiness or to maximize the number of people who are happy?
2. Should a doctor's decision to remove a terminal patient's life-support system (see Chapter 13) or to abort a fetus (see Chapter 12) be decided on the basis of whether the act will maximize pleasure or minimize pain?
3. Justices Stewart, Powell, and Stevens argued that the majority of Americans support capital punishment. Justice Marshall countered that if the American people were fully informed about all the considerations concerning capital punishment, they would not support it (see Chapter 14). Are each of these contesting views utilitarian at basis? Should utilitarian considerations determine whether capital punishment is socially and morally acceptable?
4. Compare an act-utilitarian argument for affirmative action (see Chapter 9) or against mandatory AIDS testing (see Chapter 11) with a nonutilitarian one. Which of the arguments is more compelling?

FOR FURTHER READING

UTILITARIANISM

Bayles, M., ed. *Contemporary Utilitarianism.* New York: Doubleday, 1962.

Bentham, J. *An Introduction to the Principles of Morals and Legislation.* Oxford: Clarendon Press, 1948.

Brandt, R. B. *Ethical Theory.* Englewood Cliffs, N.J.: Prentice-Hall, 1959.

———— . *A Theory of the Good and the Right.* Oxford: Oxford University Press, 1979.

———— . *Morality, Utilitarianism, and Rights.* New York: Cambridge University Press, 1992.

Campos-Boralevi, L. *Bentham and the Oppressed.* New York: De Gruyter, 1990.

Donner, W. *The Liberal Self: John Stuart Mill's Moral and Political Philosophy.* Ithaca: Cornell University Press, 1991.

Frey, R., ed. *Utility and Rights.* Minneapolis: University of Minnesota Press, 1984.

Gray, J., and Smith, G. W., eds. *J. S. Mill's "On Liberty" in Focus.* New York: Routledge, 1991.

Griffin, J. *Well-Being: Its Meaning, Measurement and Social Importance.* Oxford: Clarendon Press. 1987.

Hare, R. M. *Freedom and Reason.* London: Oxford University Press, 1963.

———— . *Applications of Moral Philosophy.* London: Macmillan, 1972.

———— . *Essays on the Moral Concepts.* London: Macmillan, 1972.

Lyons, D. *In the Interests of the Governed: A Study in Bentham's Philosophy of Utility and Law.* Revised ed., New York: Oxford University Press, 1991.

———— . *Forms and Limits of Utilitarianism.* Oxford: Oxford University Press, 1965.

Rawls, J. "Two Concepts of Rules," *Philosophical Review* 64 (1955): 3-32.

Ryan, A. *The Philosophy of John Stuart Mill.* 2nd ed. Atlantic Highlands: Humanities Press, 1990.

Sen, A., and Williams, B., eds. *Utilitarianism and Beyond.* Cambridge: Cambridge University Press, 1982.

Sidgwick, H. *Methods of Ethics.* 7th ed. London: Macmillan, 1962.

Singer, M. G. *Generalization in Ethics.* New York: Knopf, 1961.

Smart, J. J. C., and Williams, B. *Utilitarianism: For and Against.* Cambridge: Cambridge University Press, 1973.

Warnock, M., ed. *Utilitarianism, by J. S. Mill.* London: Fontana, 1962.

PART TWO

CONTEMPORARY
ETHICAL THEORY

INTRODUCTION

Twentieth-century ethical theory has been rich and varied. A concern with metaethics prevailed in the first half of this century: theoretical analysis focused overwhelmingly upon the meanings of moral terms and on the logical form of ethical reasoning and justification. More recently, ethical theory has consisted largely of challenging the major ethical traditions, recasting them in new and more acceptable terms, or drawing out their normative implications for determining the right thing to do when applied in different act and institutional contexts. The formative debate in contemporary ethical theory has taken place mostly between proponents and critics of liberalism and within liberalism between revised interpretations of utilitarianism (see Chapter 4), reconstructions of Kantianism (see Chapter 3), and libertarianism. Among critics of ethical liberalism, communitarians and feminists are the most visible. Part II is divided accordingly into chapters on contemporary liberalism, communitarianism, and feminism.

CHAPTER FIVE

LIBERALISM

In spite of deep philosophical differences between them, liberals are united by a core set of common general principles that are taken at once as basic presuppositions and ideals. Thus liberalism is committed first to individualism, for it takes as basic the moral, political, and legal claims of the individual in contest with the claims of the collective. Second, liberalism seeks foundations in universal principles applicable to all human beings or rational agents in virtue of their humanity or rationality. In this, liberalism seeks to transcend particular historical, social, and cultural differences. It is concerned with broad identities, which it sees uniting persons on moral grounds, rather than with those identities that divide politically, culturally, geographically, or temporally. The philosophical basis of this broad human identity, of an essentially human nature, is presumed to lie in a rational core common to each individual, and so in the (potential) capacity to be moved by reason. Third, liberalism presupposes that all social arrangements may be ameliorated by rational reform. Moral, political, economic, and cultural progress is to be established through carefully planned institutional improvement, subject always to the satisfaction of individual rights. So, progress is measured against the extent to which institutional improvement serves to extend people's liberty, for example, by opening up or extending spaces for free expression. Fourth, liberalism is committed to the equality of individuals. Liberalism recognizes all human beings to enjoy a common moral standing, no matter individual differences. This commitment is open to a wide range of interpretations the particular nature of which distinguishes one liberalism from another. Contemporary utilitarians, recall, construe the rightness or wrongness of acts or rules no longer simply in terms of pleasure and pain, but in terms of preferences; each individual preference maximizer is to be treated as one and only one (see Chapter 4); Kantians reject the claim that the rightness or wrongness of acts is a function of their good or bad consequences, extending to individuals equal respect (see Chapter 3); while libertarians assess moral and political arrangements in terms of their implications for promoting everyone's liberty, defined as maximal freedom from coercion.

Liberty and Equality   A fundamental tension facing liberal theories of justice, indeed, facing moral and political theories generally, involves the conflict between the respective demands of liberty and equality. This tension is especially pronounced in concerns pertaining to the distribution of social resources and by extension in matters of taxation and welfare. Some (called *libertarians*) argue that the only acceptable ground for distributing or accumulating resources is individual liberty of choice. In this view, it is a violation of my liberty to take from me against my will the wealth or property I have accumulated by my own efforts and without coercion. Others (called *egalitarians*) insist that income, wealth, and power should be distributed equally, although they usually recognize that it is unreasonable for a family of two, say, to receive a quantity of goods equal to that of a family of five. Thus the standard of equality requires qualification according to relevant need.

Nevertheless, it is clear that liberty and equality may conflict—increasing either in some cases militates against the other. Moreover, liberties of one individual often conflict with another's, and one kind of liberty with some other kind. For example, one's liberty to accumulate the only available food may conflict with another's, and one's liberty to enjoy one's wealth as one pleases may conflict with another's liberty not to be harmed by what one does with one's wealth. Accordingly, libertarians are committed to a minimal state, that is, to those institutional arrangements only that would guarantee the absence of unjustified coercion and constraint of individuals. Like general taxation (as opposed, say, to user fees), welfare programs are rejected generally by libertarians as requiring coercion. Libertarians are committed to a view of property as an extension of the self. This view sustains so firm a right to property that it disables any less than freely supported redistribution to benefit others. Egalitarians would find acceptable much greater state intervention, for they are committed to institute equality through redistributive mechanisms. By contrast to both libertarians and egalitarians, some argue for an intermediate principle of distributive justice that undertakes to combine liberty and equality. These theorists endorse the optimal set of distributions that is seen to maximize correlative individual liberties and equality in specific sociohistorical circumstances.

Each of these views tends to correlate with an idealized socioeconomic system generally considered to encourage institution of the distributive principle endorsed. The libertarian view usually sanctions free market or *laissez faire* capitalism with minimal state interference. Those who attempt to integrate liberty and equality tend to support welfare state capitalism. Strict egalitarians tend to esteem socialism.

■ JOHN RAWLS (1921–): CONTRACTARIANISM

Contract Theory   For John Rawls, a just or fair social arrangement of the basic socioeconomic institutions for a modern constitutional democracy is one all social members would agree to, though they are ignorant of any personal effects the chosen arrangement would have on themselves. Rawls reconstructs the idea of a social contract as formulated by Hobbes, Locke, and Rousseau. In the social contract theories of the seventeenth and eighteenth centuries, isolated individuals were considered to live originally in a "state of nature" lacking all social institutions. The poverty of life here encouraged them to contract with each other to form a structured society (see Hobbes, Chapter 2, and Rousseau, Chapter 3). The central claim of the doctrine of contractarianism is that the principles of morality and justice are just those that would be agreed to by rational agents. The contractual agreement is reached by persons deciding what moral and political principles it is in their rational self-interest to have rule their social institutions. Each person as party to the contract must be subject to the same impartial constraints or limitations on his or her rational decision making as all others.

The Veil of Ignorance   Rawls reinterprets the "state of nature" as an *original position* from which individuals are to choose the basic institutional structure of their society. People are to agree in the original position to the fundamental principles of justice that will order their cooperative social relations with each other. Every individual is conceived as rational and self-interested: the principles each chooses will be those that would most probably maximize his or her individual self-interest. Yet the original choice or agreement is governed by a *veil of ignorance:* individuals choosing the basic principles are not to have any information about themselves or others that is likely to advantage themselves or disadvantage others in respect to the principles agreed to.

The Limits on Information   So, Rawls places constraints upon agents' information about characteristics or abilities that might advantage themselves in choosing principles of justice or disadvantage others. This limit on information in the original position behind the veil of ignorance includes knowledge of one's own and others' sex, age, race, class, nationality, and religion, but also of such characteristics as health status, height, and talents. Any accidental advantages or past influences are to be discounted in the initial institutional choices. In deciding originally what institutional principles should rationally order their lives, individuals know only general information about the world. Rawls's underlying moral assumption here is that individuals should not be advantaged by their natural talents or social position, nor suffer their lack of talent or social condition; these are features of life for which individuals are not themselves responsible. Thus, in choosing basic institutions that would maximize self-interest, any individual is actually choosing a basic structure of society that is most likely to maximize benefits for all. It follows that any rational individual would agree to impartial principles of justice, for given the constraints on information, they are principles self-interested rationality demands each person choose. Nobody would agree to a distributive principle that is race- or sex-biased, for when the constraints on information about one's own race or sex are lifted, it may turn out that one has chosen a principle that disadvantages oneself, and to do so would be irrational.

The Universalistic Conception of Rationality   In Rawls's view, contractual agreement is ensured by a universalistic conception of rationality. Not only do individuals use the same formal procedures to make rational decisions, but the informational input is also identical. Differences between persons are eliminated by restricting information all have about themselves. Rational choice is universal: the choice of any individual would be the same as every individual's, given identity of information. Rawls is interested in establishing what principles of justice would be agreed to, rather than in deriving moral rules from nonmoral premises. Rawls thus builds moral presuppositions into the universalistic conception of rationality.

Persons, in Rawls's view, are to choose ideal principles of institutional justice against a background of *primary goods.* These are goods every rational self-interested agent would desire, if she or he desired anything. Primary goods include basic rights and liberties, powers and opportunities, income and wealth, and self-respect. Rawls argues that, from the standpoint of equality, individuals would agree to two basic principles. They would agree, first, to maximum liberty for themselves, compatible with a like liberty for all. Second, they would accept the *difference principle.* This justifies differential distributions in favor of some if and only if such inequality benefits most the least advantaged in the social arrangement. Injustices, then, are inequalities that fail to benefit all. Satisfaction of the difference principle presupposes satisfying the equal liberty principle. Unlike utilitarianism (see Chapter 4), it will never be permissible to sacrifice liberty—by giving up power, say—for some economic benefit. Yet, it would not be permissible for any person to have greater liberty than any other.

It has been suggested that Rawls's principles are consistent with socialism. Benefits relevant to the difference principle involve increases in all the primary goods, including self-respect. Self-respect may be interpreted as requiring worker self-determination for its fulfillment. However, Rawls's contractarianism has been widely considered to offer a defense of welfare state capitalism in a constitutional democracy. (Rawls himself has argued that his theory supports any just constitutional structure, not only a liberal one.) Rawls's principles are ideals for directing only new distributions; they presuppose, by applying to, currently established inequalities. (In more recent work, Rawls has moved to separate the focus of the political from universal moral theory. Thus, his focal question now is what form of political constitution could serve as a just social structure in a multicultural, pluralistic society comprised of a wide range of comprehensive views or ideologies. He calls his theory of "overlapping consensus" offered in response to this question "political liberalism.")

John Rawls

A THEORY OF JUSTICE

THE MAIN IDEA OF THE THEORY OF JUSTICE

My aim is to present a conception of justice which generalizes and carries a higher level of abstraction the familiar theory of the social contract as found, say, in Locke, Rousseau, and Kant.* In order to do this we are not to think of the original contract

---

* As the text suggests, I shall regard Locke's *Second Treatise of Government*, Rousseau's *The Social Contract*, and Kant's ethical works beginning with *The Foundations of the Metaphysics of Morals* as definitive of the contract tradition. For all of its greatness, Hobbes's *Leviathan* raises special problems. A general historical survey is provided by J. W. Gough, *The Social Contract*, 2d ed. (Oxford: Clarendon Press, 1957), and Otto Gierke, *Natural Law and the Theory of Society*, trans. with an introduction by Ernest Barker (Cambridge: University Press, 1934). A presentation of the contract view as primarily an ethical theory is to be found in G. R. Grice, *The Grounds of Moral Judgment* (Cambridge: University Press, 1967).

as one to enter a particular society or to set up a particular form of government. Rather, the guiding idea is that the principles of justice for the basic structure of society are the object of the original agreement. They are the principles that free and rational persons concerned to further their own interests would accept in an initial position of equality as defining the fundamental terms of their association. These principles are to regulate all further agreements; they specify the kinds of social cooperation that can be entered into and the forms of government that can be established. This way of regarding the principles of justice I shall call justice as fairness.

Thus we are to imagine that those who engage in social cooperation choose together, in one joint act, the principles which are to assign basic rights and duties and to determine the division of social benefits. Men are to decide in advance how they are to regulate their claims against one another and what is to be the foundation character of their society. Just as each person must decide by rational reflection what constitutes his good, that is, the system of ends which it is rational for him to pursue, so a group of persons must decide once and for all what is to count among them as just and unjust. The choice which rational men would make in this hypothetical situation of equal liberty, assuming for the present that this choice problem has a solution, determines the principles of justice.

In justice as fairness the original position of equality corresponds to the state of nature in the traditional theory of the social contract. This original position is not, of course, thought of as an actual historical state of affairs, much less as a primitive condition of culture. It is understood as a purely hypothetical situation characterized so as to lead to a certain conception of justice. Among the essential features of this situation is that no one knows his place in society, his class position or social status, nor does any one know his fortune in the distribution of natural assets and abilities, his intelligence, strength, and the like. I shall even assume that the parties do not know their conceptions of the good or their special psychological propensities. The principles of justice are chosen behind a veil of ignorance. This ensures that no one is advantaged or disadvantaged in the choice of principles by the outcome of natural chance or the contingency of social circumstances. Since all are similarly situated and no one is able to design principles to favor his particular condition, the principles of justice are the result of a fair agreement or bargain. For given the circumstances of the original position, the symmetry of everyone's relations to each other, this initial situation is fair between individuals as moral persons, that is, as rational beings with their own ends and capable, I shall assume, of a sense of justice. The original position is, one might say, the appropriate initial status quo, and thus the fundamental agreements reached in it are fair. This explains the propriety of the name "justice as fairness": it conveys the idea that the principles of justice are agreed to in an initial situation that is fair. The name does not mean that the concepts of justice and fairness are the same, any more than the phrase "poetry as metaphor" means that the concepts of poetry and metaphor are the same.

Justice as fairness begins, as I have said, with one of the most general of all choices which persons might make together, namely, with the choice of the first principles of a conception of justice which is to regulate all subsequent criticism and reform of institutions. Then, having chosen a conception of justice, we can suppose that they are to choose a constitution and a legislature to enact laws, and so on, all in accordance with the principles of justice initially agreed upon. Our social situation is just if it is such that by this sequence of hypothetical agreements we would have contracted into the general system of rules which defines it. Moreover, assuming that the original position does determine a set of principles (that is, that a particular conception of justice would be chosen), it will then be true that whenever social institutions satisfy these principles those engaged in them can say to one another that they are cooperating on terms to which they would agree if they were free and equal persons whose relations with respect to one another were fair. They could all view their arrangements as meeting the stipulations which they would acknowledge in an initial situation that embodies widely accepted and reasonable constraints on the choice of principles. The general recognition of this fact would provide the basis for a public acceptance of the corresponding principles of justice. No society can, of course, be a scheme of cooperation which men enter voluntarily in a literal sense; each person finds himself placed at birth in some particular position in some particular society, and the nature of this position materially affects his life prospects. Yet a society satisfying the principles of justice as fairness comes as close as a society can to being a voluntary scheme, for it meets the principles which free and equal persons would assent to under circumstances that are fair. In this sense its members are autonomous and the obligations they recognize self-imposed.

One feature of justice as fairness is to think of the parties in the initial situation as rational and mutually disinterested. This does not mean that the parties are egoists, that is, individuals with only certain kinds of interests, say in wealth, prestige, and domination. But they are conceived as not taking an interest in one another's interests. They are to presume that even their spiritual aims may be opposed, in the way that the aims of those of different religions may be opposed. Moreover, the concept of rationality must be interpreted as far as possible in the narrow sense, standard in economic theory, of taking the most effective means to given ends. I shall modify this concept to some extent, . . . but one must try to avoid introducing into it any controversial ethical elements. The initial situation must be characterized by stipulations that are widely accepted.

In working out the conception of justice as fairness one main task clearly is to determine which principles of justice would be chosen in the original position. To do this we must describe this situation in some detail and formulate with care the problem of choice which it presents. . . . It may be observed, however, that once the principles of justice are thought of as arising from an original agreement in a situation of equality, it is an open question whether the principle of utility would be acknowledged. Offhand it hardly seems likely that persons who view themselves as equals, entitled to press their claims upon one another, would agree to a principle which may require lesser life prospects for some simply for the sake of a greater sum of advantages enjoyed by others. Since each desires to protect his interests, his capacity to advance his conception of the good, no one has a reason to acquiesce in an enduring loss for himself in order to bring about a greater net balance of satisfaction. In the absence of strong and lasting benevolent impulses, a rational man would not accept a basic structure merely because it maximized the algebraic sum of advantages irrespective of its permanent effects on his own basic rights and interests. Thus it seems that the principle of utility is incompatible with the conception of social cooperation among equals for mutual advantages. It appears to be inconsistent with the idea of reciprocity implicit in the notion of a well-ordered society. . . .

I shall maintain instead that the persons in the initial situation would choose two rather different principles: the first requires equality in the assignment of basic rights and duties, while the second holds that social and economic inequalities, for example inequalities of wealth and authority, are just only if they result in compensating benefits for everyone, and in particular for the least advantaged members of society. These principles rule out justifying institutions on the grounds that the hardships of some are offset by a greater good in the aggregate. It may be expedient but it is not just that some should have less in order that others may prosper. But there is no injustice in the greater benefits earned by a few provided that the situation of persons not so fortunate is thereby improved. The intuitive idea is that since everyone's well-being depends upon a scheme of cooperation without which no one could have a satisfactory life, the division of advantages should be such as to draw forth the willing cooperation of everyone taking part in it, including those less well situated. Yet this can be expected only if reasonable terms are proposed. The two principles mentioned seem to be a fair agreement on the basis of which those better endowed, or more fortunate in their social position, neither of which we can be said to deserve, could expect the willing cooperation of others when some workable scheme is a necessary condition of the welfare of all. Once we decide to look for a conception of justice that nullifies the accidents of natural endowment and the contingencies of social circumstances as counters in quest for political and economic advantage, we are led to these principles. They express the result of leaving aside those aspects of the social world that seem arbitrary from a moral point of view. . . .

TWO PRINCIPLES OF JUSTICE

I shall now state in a provisional form the two principles of justice that I believe would be chosen in the original position. In this section I wish to make only the most general comments, and therefore the first formulation of these principles is tentative. . . .

The first statement of the two principles reads as follows:

> First: each person is to have an equal right to the most extensive basic liberty compatible with a similar liberty for others.
> Second: social and economic inequalities are to be arranged so that they are both (a) reasonably expected to be to everyone's advantage, and (b) attached to positions and offices open to all. . . .

By way of general comment, these principles primarily apply, as I have said, to the basic structure of society. They are to govern the assignment of rights and duties and to regulate the distribution of social and economic advantages. As their formulation suggests, these principles presuppose that the social structure can be divided into two more or less distinct parts, the first principle applying to the one, and the second to the other. They distinguish between those aspects of the social system that define and secure the equal liberties of citizenship and those that specify and establish social and economic inequalities. The basic liberties of citizens are, roughly speaking, political liberty (the right to vote and to be eligible for public office) together with freedom of speech and assembly; liberty of conscience and freedom of thought; freedom of the person along with the right to hold (personal) property; and freedom from arbitrary arrest and seizure as defined by the concept of the rule of law. These liberties are all required to be equal by the first principle, since citizens of a just society are to have the same basic rights.

The second principle applies, in the first approximation, to the distribution of income and wealth and to the design of organizations that make use of differences in authority and responsibility, or chains of command. While the distribution of wealth and income need not be equal, it must be to everyone's advantage, and at the same time, positions of authority and offices of command must be accessible to all. One applies the second principle by holding positions open, and then, subject to this constraint, arranges social and economic inequalities so that everyone benefits.

These principles are to be arranged in a serial order with the first principle prior to the second. This ordering means that a departure from the institutions of equal liberty required by the first principle cannot be justified, or compensated for, by greater social and economic advantages. The distribution of wealth and income, and the hierarchies of authority, must be consistent with both the liberties of equal citizenship and equality of opportunity.

It is clear that these principles are rather specific in their content, and their acceptance rests on certain assumptions that I must eventually try to explain and justify. A theory of justice depends upon a theory of society in ways that will become evident as we proceed. For the present, it should be observed that the two principles (and this holds for all formulations) are a special case of a more general conception of justice that can be expressed as follows.

> All social values—liberty and opportunity, income and wealth, and the bases of self-respect—are to be distributed equally unless an unequal distribution of any, or all, of these values is to everyone's advantage.

Injustice, then, is simply inequalities that are not to the benefit of all. Of course, this conception is extremely vague and requires interpretation.

As a first step, suppose that the basic structure of society distributes certain primary goods, that is, things that every rational man is presumed to want. These goods normally have a use whatever a person's rational plan of life. For simplicity, assume that the chief primary goods at the disposition of society are rights and liberties, powers and opportunities, income and wealth. . . . These are the social primary goods. Other primary goods such as health and vigor, intelligence and imagination, are natural goods; although their possession is influenced by the basic structure, they are not so directly under its control. Imagine, then, a hypothetical initial arrangement in which all the social primary goods are equally distributed, everyone has

similar rights and duties, and income and wealth are evenly shared. This state of affairs provides a benchmark for judging improvements. If certain inequalities of
wealth and organizational powers would make everyone better off than in this hypothetical starting situation, then they accord with the general conception.

Now it is possible, at least theoretically, that by giving up some of their fundamental liberties men are sufficiently compensated by the resulting social and economic gains. The general conception of justice imposes no restrictions on what sort
of inequalities are permissible; it only requires that everyone's position be improved.
We need not suppose anything so drastic as consenting to a condition of slavery.
Imagine instead that men forego certain political rights when the economic returns
are significant and their capacity to influence the course of policy by the exercise of
these rights would be marginal in any case. It is this kind of exchange which the two
principles as stated rule out; being arranged in serial order they do not permit ex-
changes between basic liberties and economic and social gains. The serial ordering
of principles expresses an underlying preference among primary social goods. When
this preference is rational so likewise is the choice of these principles in this order.

In developing justice as fairness I shall, for the most part, leave aside the general
conception of justice and examine instead the special case of the two principles in
serial order. The advantage of this procedure is that from the first the matter of priorities is recognized and an effort made to find principles to deal with it. One is led
to attend throughout to the conditions under which the acknowledgment of the absolute weight of liberty with respect to social and economic advantages, as defined
by the lexical order of the two principles, would be reasonable. Offhand, this ranking appears extreme and too special a case to be of much interest; but there is more
justification for it than would appear at first sight. . . . Furthermore, the distinction
between fundamental rights and liberties and economic and social benefits marks a
difference among primary social goods that one should try to exploit. It suggests an
important division in the social system. Of course, the distinctions drawn and the
ordering proposed are bound to be at best only approximations. There are surely circumstances in which they fail. But it is essential to depict clearly the main lines of a
reasonable conception of justice; and under many conditions anyway, the two principles in serial order may serve well enough. When necessary we can fall back on the
more general conception.

The fact that the two principles apply to institutions has certain consequences.
Several points illustrate this. First of all, the rights and liberties referred to by these
principles are those which are defined by the public rules of the basic structure.
Whether men are free is determined by the rights and duties established by the
major institutions of society. Liberty is a certain pattern of social forms. The first
principle simply requires that certain sorts of rules, those defining basic liberties,
apply to everyone equally and that they allow the most extensive liberty compatible
with a like liberty for all. The only reason for circumscribing the rights defining liberty and making men's freedom less extensive than it might otherwise be is that
these equal rights as institutionally defined would interfere with one another.

Another thing to bear in mind is that when principles mention persons, or require that everyone gain from an inequality, the reference is to representative per-

sons holding the various social positions, or offices, or whatever, established by the basic structure. Thus in applying the second principle I assume that it is possible to assign an expectation of well-being to representative individuals holding these positions. This expectation indicates their life prospects as viewed from their social station. In general, the expectations of representative persons depend upon the distribution of rights and duties throughout the basic structure. When this changes, expectations change. I assume, then, that expectations are connected: by raising the prospects of the representative man in one position we presumably increase or decrease the prospects of representative men in other positions. Since it applies to institutional forms, the second principle (or rather the first part of it) refers to the expectations of representative individuals. . . . [N]either principle applies to distributions of particular goods to particular individuals who may be identified by their proper names. The situation where someone is considering how to allocate certain commodities to needy persons who are known to him is not within the scope of the principles. They are meant to regulate basic institutional arrangements. We must not assume that there is much similarity from the standpoint of justice between an administrative allotment of goods to specific persons and the appropriate design of society. Our common sense intuitions for the former may be a poor guide to the latter.

Now the second principle insists that each person benefit from permissible inequalities in the basic structure. This means that it must be reasonable for each relevant representative man defined by this structure, when he views it as a going concern, to prefer his prospects with the inequality to his prospects without it. One is not allowed to justify differences in income or organizational powers on the ground that the disadvantages of those in one position are outweighed by the greater advantages of those in another. Much less can infringements of liberty be counterbalanced in this way. Applied to the basic structure, the principle of utility would have us maximize the sum of expectations of representative men (weighted by the number of persons they represent, on the classical view); and this would permit us to compensate for the losses of some by the gains of others. Instead, the two principles require that everyone benefit from economic and social inequalities. It is obvious, however, that there are definitely many ways in which all may be advantaged when the initial arrangement of equality is taken as a benchmark. How then are we to choose among these possibilities? The principles must be specified so that they yield a determinate conclusion.

■ **ROBERT NOZICK (1938–): ENTITLEMENT THEORY**

Justice, on Robert Nozick's *libertarian* conception, does not necessitate any preordained "pattern" or structure of distribution. Economic arrangements would be just if they were consented to freely and involved no fraud or coercion. In contrast to a *patterned* conception of just distribution, Nozick holds that any person's "holdings" at a specific time would be just, provided that neither the original historical acquisition of goods held nor any subsequent transfer involved coercion. If acquisition of goods is just in the sense specified, the title-holder is *entitled* to the goods held, no matter the quantity. A patterned approach specifying some *end-state* or predefined arrangement that the distribution is to achieve is likely to be unjust in Nozick's view. It will tend to deny people goods to which Nozick thinks they are "historically" entitled. Nozick's principle of distributive justice holds a distribution *D* to be just if and only if all people are *entitled* to their possessions, and *D* renders none worse off than they would have been without it. The libertarian is concerned to maximize liberty, negatively conceived as freedom *from* constraint, and in particular from the coercive power of government. Nozick argues that taking liberty seriously will upset any pattern of distribution, especially equalitarian ones. However, Nozick admits that any justifiable libertarian conception of justice in appropriation will be qualified by what he calls the "Lockean proviso." Nozick's formulation of the proviso allows that an initial appropriation of something unowned will be justified so long as it does not render the situation of others worse than it would have been had the object continued to be generally available. If the prospects of all others are left unchanged or bettered by the appropriation, the holding would be considered just.

Robert Nozick

THE ENTITLEMENT THEORY

The subject of justice in holdings consists of three major topics. The first is the *original acquisition of holdings*, the appropriation of unheld things. This includes the issues of how unheld things may come to be held, the process, or processes, by which unheld things may come to be held, the things that may come to be held by these processes, the extent of what comes to be held by a particular process, and so on. We shall refer to the complicated truth about this topic, which we shall not formulate here, as the principle of justice in acquisition. The second topic concerns the *transfer of holdings* from one person to another. By what processes may a person transfer holdings to another? How may a person acquire a holding from another who holds it? Under this topic come general descriptions of voluntary exchange, and gift and (on the other hand) fraud, as well as reference to particular conventional details fixed upon in a given society. The complicated truth about this subject (with place-holders for conventional details) we shall call the principle of justice in transfer.

(And we shall suppose it also includes principles governing how a person may divest himself of a holding, passing it into an unheld state.)

If the world were wholly just, the following inductive definition would exhaustively cover the subject of justice in holdings.

1. A person who acquires a holding in accordance with the principle of justice in acquisition is entitled to that holding.
2. A person who acquires a holding in accordance with the principle of justice in transfer, from someone else entitled to the holding, is entitled to the holding.
3. No one is entitled to a holding except by (repeated) applications of 1 and 2.

The complete principle of distributive justice would say simply that a distribution is just if everyone is entitled to the holdings they possess under the distribution.

A distribution is just if it arises from another just distribution by legitimate means. The legitimate means of moving from one distribution to another are specified by the principle of justice in transfer. The legitimate first "moves" are specified by the principle of justice in acquisition. Whatever arises from a just situation by just steps is itself just. The means of change specified by the principle of justice in transfer preserve justice. . . .

HISTORICAL PRINCIPLES AND END-RESULT PRINCIPLES

The general outlines of the entitlement theory illuminate the nature and defects of other conceptions of distributive justice. The entitlement theory of justice in distribution is *historical;* whether a distribution is just depends upon how it came about. In contrast, *current time-slice principles* of justice hold that the justice of a distribution is determined by how things are distributed (who has what) as judged by some *structural* principle(s) of just distribution. A utilitarian who judges between any two distributions by seeing which has the greater sum of utility and, if the sums tie, applies some fixed equality criterion to choose the more equal distribution, would hold a current time-slice principle of justice. As would someone who had a fixed schedule of trade-offs between the sum of happiness and equality. According to a current time-slice principle, all that needs to be looked at, in judging the justice of a distribution, is who ends up with what; in comparing any two distributions one need look only at the matrix presenting the distributions. No further information need be fed into a principle of justice. It is a consequence of such principles of justice that any two structurally identical distributions are equally just. (Two distributions are structurally identical if they present the same profile, but perhaps have different persons occupying the particular slots. My having ten and your having five, and my having five and your having ten, are structurally identically distributions.) Welfare economics is the theory of current time-slice principles of justice. . . .

We construe the position we discuss too narrowly by speaking of *current* time-slice principles. Nothing is changed if structural principles operate upon a time sequence of current time-slice profiles and, for example, give someone more now to counterbalance the less he has had earlier. A utilitarian or an egalitarian or any mixture of the two over time will inherit the difficulties of his more myopic comrades. He is not helped by the fact that *some* of the information others consider relevant in assessing a distribution is reflected, unrecoverably, in past matrices. Henceforth, we shall refer to such unhistorical principles of distributive justice, including the current time-slice principles, as *end-result principles* or *end-state principles*.

In contrast to end-result principles of justice, *historical principles* of justice hold that past circumstances or actions of people can create differential entitlements or differential deserts to things. An injustice can be worked by moving from one distribution to another structurally identical one, for the second, in profile the same, may violate people's entitlements or deserts; it may not fit the actual history.

PATTERNING

The entitlement principles of justice in holdings that we have sketched are historical principles of justice. To better understand their precise character, we shall distinguish them from another subclass of the historical principles. . . . Let us call a principle of distribution *patterned* if it specifies that a distribution is to vary along with some natural dimension, weighted sum of natural dimensions, or lexicographic ordering of natural dimensions. And let us say a distribution is patterned if it accords with some patterned principle. . . . The principle of distribution in accordance with moral merit is a patterned historical principle, which specifies a patterned distribution. "Distribute according to I.Q." is a patterned principle that looks to information not contained in distributional matrices. It is not historical, however, in that it does not look to any past actions creating differential entitlements to evaluate a distribution; it requires only distributional matrices whose columns are labeled by I.Q. scores. The distribution in a society, however, may be composed of such simple patterned distributions, without itself being simply patterned. Different sectors may operate different patterns, or some combination of patterns may operate in different proportions across a society. A distribution composed in this manner, from a small number of patterned distributions, we also shall term "patterned." And we extend the use of "pattern" to include the overall designs put forth by combinations of end-state principles.

Almost every suggested principle of distributive justice is patterned: to each according to his moral merit or needs, or marginal product, or how hard he tries, or the weighted sum of the foregoing, and so on. The principle of entitlement we have sketched is not patterned. There is no one natural dimension or weighted sum or combination of a small number of natural dimensions that yields the distributions generated in accordance with the principle of entitlement. The set of holdings that results when some persons receive their marginal products, others win at gambling, others receive a share of their mate's income, others receive gifts from foundations, others receive interest on loans, others receive gifts from admirers, others receive returns on investment, others make for themselves much of what they have, others find things, and so on, will not be patterned. Heavy strands of patterns will run through it; significant portions of the variance in holdings will be accounted for by pattern-variables. If most people most of the time choose to transfer some of their entitlements to others only in exchange for something from them, then a large part of what many people hold will vary with what they held that others wanted. More details are provided by the theory of marginal productivity. But gifts to relatives, charitable donations, bequests to children, and the like, are not best conceived, in the first instance, in this manner. Ignoring the strands of pattern, let us suppose for the moment that a distribution actually arrived at by the operation of the principle of entitlement is random with respect to any pattern. Though the resulting set of holdings will be unpatterned, it will not be incomprehensible, for it can be seen as arising from the operation of a small number of principles. These principles specify how an initial distribution may arise (the principle of acquisition of holdings) and how distributions may be transformed into others (the principle of transfer of holdings). The process whereby the set of holdings is generated will be intelligible, though the set of holdings itself that results from this process will be unpatterned. . . .

To think that the task of a theory of distributive justice is to fill in the blank in "to each according to his _____" is to be predisposed to search for a pattern; and the separate treatment of "from each according to his _____" treats production and distribution as two separate and independent issues. On an entitlement view these are *not* two separate questions. Whoever makes something, having bought or contracted for all other held resources used in the process (transferring some of his holdings for these cooperating factors), is entitled to it. The situation is *not* one of something's getting made, and there being an open question of who is to get it. Things come into the world already attached to people having entitlements over them. From the point of view of the historical entitlement conception of justice in holdings, those who start afresh to complete "to each according to his _____" treat objects as if they appeared from nowhere, out of nothing. A complete theory of justice might cover this limit case as well; perhaps here is a use for the usual conceptions of distributive justice.

So entrenched are maxims of the usual form that perhaps we should present the entitlement conception as a competitor. Ignoring acquisition and rectification, we might say:

> From each according to what he chooses to do, to each according to what he makes for himself (perhaps with the contracted aid of others) and what others choose to do for him and choose to give him of what they've been given previously (under this maxim) and haven't yet expended or transferred.

This, the discerning reader will have noticed, has its defects as a slogan. So as a summary and great simplification (and not as a maxim with any independent meaning) we have:

> *From each as they choose, to each as they are chosen.*

HOW LIBERTY UPSETS PATTERNS

It is not clear how those holding alternative conceptions of distributive justice can reject the entitlement conception of justice in holdings. For suppose a distribution favored by one of these nonentitlement conceptions is realized. Let us suppose it is your favorite one and let us call this distribution D1; perhaps everyone has an equal share, perhaps shares vary in accordance with some dimension you treasure. Now suppose that Wilt Chamberlain is greatly in demand by basketball teams, being a great gate attraction. (Also suppose contracts run only for a year, with players being free agents.) He signs the following sort of contract with a team: In each home game, twenty-five cents from the price of each ticket of admission goes to him. (We ignore the question of whether he is "gouging" the owners, letting them look out for themselves.) The season starts, and people cheerfully attend his team's games; they buy their tickets, each time dropping a separate twenty-five cents of their admission price into a special box with Chamberlain's name on it. They are excited about seeing him play; it is worth the total admission price to them. Let us suppose that in one season one million persons attend his home games, and Wilt Chamberlain winds up with $250,000, a much larger sum than the average income and larger even than anyone else has. Is he entitled to this income? Is this new distribution D2, unjust? If so, why? There *is no* question about whether each of the people was entitled to the control over the resources they held in D1; because that was the distribution (your favorite) that (for the purposes of argument) we assumed was acceptable. Each of these persons *chose* to give twenty-five cents of their money to Chamberlain. They could have spent it on going to the movies, or on candy bars, or on copies of *Dissent* magazine, or of *Monthly Review*. But they all, at least one million of them, converged on giving it to Wilt Chamberlain in exchange for watching him play basketball. If D1 was a just distribution, and people voluntarily moved from it to D2, transferring parts of their shares they were given under D1 (what was it for if not to do something with?), isn't D2 also just? If the people were entitled to dispose of the resources to which they were entitled (under D1), didn't this include their being entitled to give it to, or exchange it with, Wilt Chamberlain? Can anyone else complain on grounds of justice? Each other person already has his legitimate share under D1. Under D1, there is nothing that anyone has that anyone else has a claim of justice against. After someone transfers something to Wilt Chamberlain, third parties *still* have their legitimate shares; *their* shares are not changed. By what process could such a transfer among two persons give rise to a legitimate claim of distributive justice on a portion of what was transferred, by a third party who had no claim of justice on any holding of the others *before* the transfer? To cut off objections irrelevant here, we might imagine the exchanges occurring in a socialist society, after hours. After playing whatever basketball he does in his daily work, or doing whatever other daily work he does, Wilt Chamberlain decides to put in *overtime* to earn additional money. (First his work quota is set; he works time over that.) Or imagine it is a skilled juggler people like to see, who puts on shows after hours.

Why might someone work overtime in a society in which it is assumed their needs are satisfied? Perhaps because they care about things other than needs. I like to write in books that I read, and to have easy access to books for browsing at odd hours. It would be very pleasant and convenient to have the resources of Widener Library in my back yard. No society, I assume, will provide such resources close to each person who would like them as part of his regular allotment (under D1). Thus, persons either must do without some extra things that they want, or be allowed to do something extra to get some of these things. On what basis could the inequalities that would eventuate be forbidden? Notice also that small factories would spring up in a socialist society, unless forbidden. I melt down some of my personal possessions (under D1) and build a machine out of the material. I offer you, and others, a philosophy lecture once a week in exchange for your cranking the handle on my machine, whose products I exchange for yet other things, and so on. (The raw materials used by the machine are given to me by others who possess them under D1, in exchange for hearing lectures.) Each person might participate to gain things over and above their allotment under D1. Some persons even might want to leave their job in socialist industry and work full time in this private sector. I shall say something more about these issues in the next chapter. Here I wish merely to note how private property even in means of production would occur in a socialist society that did not forbid people to use as they wished some of the resources they are given under the socialist distribution D1. The socialist society would have to forbid capitalist acts between consenting adults.

The general point illustrated by the Wilt Chamberlain example and the example of the entrepreneur in a socialist society is that no end-state principle or distributional patterned principle of justice can be continuously realized without continuous interference with people's lives. Any favored pattern would be transformed into one unfavored by the principle, by people choosing to act in various ways; for example, by people exchanging goods and services with other people, or giving things to other people, things the transferrers are entitled to under the favored distributional pattern. To maintain a pattern one must either continually interfere to stop people from transferring resources as they wish to, or continually (or periodically) interfere to take from some persons resources that others for some reason chose to transfer to them. (But if some time limit is to be set on how long people may keep resources others voluntarily transfer to them, why let them keep these resources for *any* period of time? Why not have immediate confiscation?) It might be objected that all persons voluntarily will choose to refrain from actions which would upset the pattern. This presupposes unrealistically (1) that all will most want to maintain the pattern (are those who don't to be "reeducated" or forced to undergo "self-criticism"?), (2) that each can gather enough information about his own actions and the ongoing activities of others to discover which of his actions will upset the pattern, and (3) that diverse and far-flung persons can coordinate their actions to dovetail into the pattern. Compare the manner in which the market is neutral among persons' desires, as it reflects and transmits widely scattered information via prices, and coordinates persons' activities.

It puts things perhaps a bit too strongly to say that every patterned (or end-state) principle is liable to be thwarted by the voluntary actions of the individual parties transferring some of their shares they receive under the principle. For perhaps some very weak patterns are not so thwarted. . . . Any distributional pattern with any egalitarian component is overturnable by the voluntary actions of individual persons over time; as is every patterned condition with sufficient content so as actually to have been proposed as presenting the central core of distributive justice. Still, given the possibility that some weak conditions or patterns may not be unstable in this way, it would be better to formulate an explicit description of the kind of interesting and contentful patterns under discussion, and to prove a theorem about their instability. Since the weaker the patterning, the more likely it is that the entitlement system itself satisfies it, a plausible conjecture is that any patterning either is unstable or is satisfied by the entitlement system.

LOCKE'S THEORY OF ACQUISITION

Before we turn to consider other theories of justice in detail, we must introduce an additional bit of complexity into the structure of the entitlement theory. This is best approached by considering Locke's attempt to specify a principle of justice in acquisition. Locke views property rights in an unowned object as originating through someone's mixing his labor with it. This gives rise to many questions. What are the boundaries of what labor is mixed with? If a private astronaut clears a place on Mars, has he mixed his labor with (so that he comes to own) the whole planet, the whole uninhabited universe, or just a particular plot? Which plot does an act bring under ownership? The minimal (possibly disconnected) area such that an act decreases entropy in that area, and not elsewhere? Can virgin land (for the purposes of ecological investigation by high-flying airplane) come under ownership by a Lockean process? Building a fence around a territory presumably would make one the owner of only the fence (and the land immediately underneath it).

Why does mixing one's labor with something make one the owner of it? Perhaps because one owns one's labor, and so one comes to own a previously unowned thing that becomes permeated with what one owns. Ownership seeps over into the rest. But why isn't mixing what I own with what I don't own a way of losing what I own rather than a way of gaining what I don't? If I own a can of tomato juice and spill it in the sea so that its molecules (made radioactive, so I can check this) mingle evenly throughout the sea, do I thereby come to own the sea, or have I foolishly dissipated my tomato juice? Perhaps the idea, instead, is that laboring on something improves it and makes it more valuable; and anyone is entitled to own a thing whose value he has created. (Reinforcing this, perhaps, is the view that laboring is unpleasant. If some people made things effortlessly, as the cartoon characters in *The Yellow Submarine* trail flowers in their wake, would they have lesser claim to their own products whose making didn't *cost* them anything?) Ignore the fact that laboring on something may make it less valuable (spraying pink enamel paint on a piece of driftwood that you have found). Why should one's entitlement extend to the whole object rather than just to the *added value* one's labor has produced? (Such reference to value might also serve to delimit the extent of ownership; for example, substitute "increases the value of" for "decreases entropy in" in the above entropy criterion.) No workable or coherent value-added property scheme has yet been devised, and any such scheme presumably would fall to objections (similar to those) that fell the theory of Henry George.

It will be implausible to view improving an object as giving full ownership to it, if the stock of unowned objects that might be improved is limited. For an object's coming under one person's ownership changes the situation of all others. Whereas previously they were at liberty (in Hohfeld's sense) to use the object, they now no longer are. This change in the situation of others (by removing their liberty to act on a previously unowned object) need not worsen their situation. If I appropriate a grain of sand from Coney Island, no one else may now do as they will with *that* grain of sand. But there are plenty of other grains of sand left for them to do the same with. Or if not grains of sand, then other things. Alternatively, the things I do with the grain of sand I appropriate might improve the position of others, counterbalancing their loss of the liberty to use that grain. The crucial point is whether appropriation of an unowned object worsens the situation of others.

Locke's proviso that there be "enough and as good left in common for others" (sect. 27) is meant to ensure that the situation of others is not worsened. (If this proviso is met is there any motivation for his further condition of nonwaste?) It is often said that this proviso once held but now no longer does. But there appears to be an argument for the conclusion that if the proviso no longer holds, then it cannot ever have held so as to yield permanent and inheritable property rights. Consider the first person Z for whom there is not enough and as good left to appropriate. The last person Y to appropriate left Z without his previous liberty to act on an object, and so worsened Z's situation. So Y's appropriation is not allowed under Locke's proviso. Therefore the next to last person X to appropriate left Y in a worse position, for X's act ended permissible appropriation. Therefore X's appropriation wasn't permissible. But then the appropriator two from last, W, ended permissible appropriation and so, since it worsened X's position, W's appropriation wasn't permissible. And so on back to the first person A to appropriate a permanent property right.

This argument, however, proceeds too quickly. Someone may be made worse off by another's appropriation in two ways: first, by losing the opportunity to improve his situation by a particular appropriation or any one; and second, by no longer being able to use freely (without appropriation) what he previously could. A *stringent* requirement that another not be made worse off by an appropriation would exclude the first way if nothing else counterbalances the diminution in opportunity, as well as the second. A *weaker* requirement would exclude the second way, though not the first. With the weaker requirement, we cannot zip back so quickly from Z to A, as in the above argument; for though person Z can no longer *appropriate*, there may remain some for him to *use* as before. In this case Y's appropriation would not violate the weaker Lockean condition. (With less remaining that people are at liberty to use, users might face more inconvenience, crowding, and so on; in that way the situation of others might be worsened, unless appropriation stopped far short of such a point.) It is arguable that no one legitimately can complain if the weaker provision is satisfied. However, since this is less clear than in the case of the more stringent proviso, Locke may have intended this stringent proviso by "enough and as good" remaining, and perhaps he meant the nonwaste condition to delay the end point from which the argument zips back.

Is the situation of persons who are unable to appropriate (there being no more accessible and useful unowned objects) worsened by a system allowing appropriation and permanent property? Here enter the various familiar social considerations favoring private property: it increases the social product by putting means of production in the hands of those who can use them most efficiently (profitably); experimentation is encouraged, because with separate persons controlling resources, there is no one person or small group whom someone with a new idea must convince to try it out; private property enables people to decide on the pattern and types of risks they wish to bear, leading to specialized types of risk bearing; private property protects future persons by leading some to hold back resources from current consumption for future markets; it provides alternate sources of employment for unpopular persons who don't have to convince any one person or small group to hire them, and so on. These considerations enter a Lockean theory to support the claim that appropriation of private property satisfies the intent behind the "enough and as good left over" proviso, not as a utilitarian justification of property. They enter to rebut the claim that because the proviso is violated no natural right to private property can arise by a Lockean process. The difficulty in working such an argument to show that the proviso is satisfied is in fixing the appropriate base line for comparison. Lockean appropriation makes people no worse off than they would be *how?* This question of fixing the baseline needs more detailed investigation than we are able to give it here. It would be desirable to have an estimate of the general economic importance of original appropriation in order to see how much leeway there is for differing theories of appropriation and of the location of the baseline. Perhaps this importance can be measured by the percentage of all income that is based upon untransformed raw materials and given resources (rather than upon human actions), mainly rental income representing the unimproved value of land, and the price of raw material in situ, and by the percentage of current wealth which represents such income in the past. . . .

We should note that it is not only persons favoring private property who need a theory of how property rights legitimately originate. Those believing in collective property, for example those believing that a group of persons living in an area jointly own the territory, or its mineral resources, also must provide a theory of how such property rights arise; they must show why the persons living there have rights to determine what is done with the land and resources there that persons living elsewhere don't have (with regard to the same land and resources).

THE PROVISO

Whether or not Locke's particular theory of appropriation can be spelled out so as to handle various difficulties, I assume that any adequate theory of justice in acquisition will contain a proviso similar to the weaker of the ones we have attributed to Locke. A process normally giving rise to a permanent bequeathable property right in a previously unowned thing will not do so if the position of others no longer at liberty to use the thing is thereby worsened. It is important to specify this particular mode of worsening the situation of others, for the proviso does not encompass other modes. It does not include the worsening due to more limited opportunities to appropriate (the first way above, corresponding to the more stringent condition), and it does not include how I "worsen" a seller's position if I appropriate materials to make some of what he is selling, and then enter into competition with him. Someone whose appropriation otherwise would violate the proviso still may appropriate provided he compensates the others so that their situation is not thereby worsened; unless he does compensate these others, his appropriation will violate the proviso of the principle of justice in acquisition and will be an illegitimate one. . . . A theory of appropriation incorporating this Lockean proviso will handle correctly the cases (objections to the theory lacking the proviso) where someone appropriates the total supply of something necessary for life.[*]

A theory which includes this proviso in its principle of justice in acquisition must also contain a more complex principle of justice in transfer. Some reflection of the proviso about appropriation constrains later actions. If my appropriating all of a certain substance violates the Lockean proviso, then so does my appropriating some and purchasing all the rest from others who obtained it without otherwise violating the Lockean proviso. If the proviso excludes someone's appropriating all the drinking water in the world, it also excludes his purchasing it all. (More weakly, and messily, it may exclude his charging certain prices for some of his supply.) This proviso (almost?) never will come into effect; the more someone acquires of a scarce substance which others want, the higher the price of the rest will go, and the more difficult it will become for him to acquire it all. But still, we can imagine, at least, that something like this occurs: someone makes simultaneous secret bids to the separate owners of a substance, each of whom sells assuming he can easily purchase more from the other owners; or some natural catastrophe destroys all of the supply of something except that in one person's possession. The total supply could not be permissibly appropriated by one person at the beginning. His later acquisition of it all does not show that the original appropriation violated the proviso (even by a reverse argument similar to the one above that tried to zap back from Z to A). Rather, it is the combination of the original appropriation plus all the later transfers and actions that violates the Lockean proviso.

---

[*] For example, Rashdall's case of someone who comes upon the only water in the desert several miles ahead of others who also will come to it and appropriates it all. Hastings Rashdall, "The Philosophical Theory of Property," in *Property, Its Duties and Rights* (London: MacMillan, 1915).

We should note Ayn Rand's theory of property rights ("Man's Rights" in *The Virtue of Selfishness* [New York: New American Library, 1964], p. 94), wherein these follow from the right to life, since people need physical things to live. But a right to life is not a right to whatever one needs to live; other people may have rights over these other things (see Chapter 3 of this book). At most, a right to life would be a right to have or strive for whatever one needs to live, provided that having it does not violate anyone else's rights. With regard to material things, the question is whether having it does violate any right of others. (Would appropriation of all unowned things do so? Would appropriating the water hole in Rashdall's example?) Since special considerations (such as the Lockean proviso) may enter with regard to material property, one first needs a theory of property rights before one can apply any supposed right to life (as amended above). Therefore the right to life cannot provide the foundation for a theory of property rights.

Each owner's title to his holding includes the historical shadow of the Lockean proviso on appropriation. This excludes his transferring it into an agglomeration that does violate the Lockean proviso and exclude his using it in a way, in coordination with others or independently of them, so as to violate the proviso by making the situation of others worse than their baseline situation. Once it is known that someone's ownership runs afoul of the Lockean proviso, there are stringent limits on what he may do with (what it is difficult any longer unreservedly to call) "his property." Thus a person may not appropriate the only water hole in a desert and charge what he will. Nor may he charge what he will if he possesses one, and unfortunately it happens that all the water holes in the desert dry up, except for his. This unfortunate circumstance, admittedly no fault of his, brings into operation the Lockean proviso and limits his property rights.* Similarly, an owner's property right in the only island in an area does not allow him to order a castaway from a shipwreck off his island as a trespasser, for this would violate the Lockean proviso.

Notice that the theory does not say that owners do have these rights, but that the rights are overridden to avoid some catastrophe. (Overridden rights do not disappear; they leave a trace of a sort absent in the cases under discussion.) There is no such external (and *ad hoc?*) overriding. Considerations internal to the theory of property itself, to its theory of acquisition and appropriation, provide the means for handling such cases. The results, however, may be coextensive with some condition about catastrophe, since the baseline for comparison is so low as compared to the productiveness of a society with private appropriation that the question of the Lockean proviso being violated arises only in the case of catastrophe (or a desert-island situation).

The fact that someone owns the total supply of something necessary for others to stay alive does *not* entail that his (or anyone's) appropriation of anything left some people (immediately or later) in a situation worse than the baseline one. A medical researcher who synthesizes a new substance that effectively treats a certain disease and who refuses to sell except on his terms does not worsen the situation of others by depriving them of whatever he has appropriated. The others easily can possess the same materials he appropriated; the researcher's appropriation or purchase of chemicals didn't make those chemicals scarce in a way so as to violate the Lockean proviso. Nor would someone else's purchasing the total supply of the synthesized substance from the medical researcher. The fact that the medical researcher uses easily available chemicals to synthesize the drug no more violates the Lockean proviso than does the fact that the only surgeon able to perform a particular operation eats easily obtainable food in order to stay alive and to have the energy to work. This shows that the Lockean proviso is not an "end-state principle"; it focuses on a particular way that appropriate actions affect others, and not on the structure of the situation that results.

---

* The situation would be different if his water hole didn't dry up, due to special precautions he took to prevent this. Compare our discussion of the case in the text with Hayek, *The Constitution of Liberty*, 136, and also with Ronald Hamowy, "Hayek's Concept of Freedom; A Critique," *New Individualist Review*. April 1961, 28–31.

Intermediate between someone who takes all of the public supply and someone who makes the total supply out of easily obtainable substances is someone who appropriates the total supply of something in a way that does not deprive the others of it. For example, someone finds a new substance in an out-of-the-way place. He discovers that it effectively treats a certain disease and appropriates the total supply. He does not worsen the situation of others; if he did not stumble upon the substance no one else would have, and the others would remain without it. However, as time passes, the likelihood increases that others would have come across the substance; upon this fact might be based a limit to his property right in the substance so that others are not below their baseline position; for example, its bequest might be limited. The theme of someone worsening another's situation by depriving him of something he otherwise would possess may also illuminate the example of patents. An inventor's patent does not deprive others of an object which would not exist if not for the inventor. Yet patents would have this effect on others who independently invent the object. Therefore, these independent inventors, upon whom the burden of proving independent discovery may rest, should not be excluded from utilizing their own invention as they wish (including selling it to others). Furthermore, a known inventor drastically lessens the chances of actual independent invention. For persons who know of an invention usually will not try to reinvent it, and the notion of independent discovery here would be murky at best. Yet we may assume that in the absence of the original invention, sometime later someone else would have come up with it. This suggests placing a time limit on patents, as a rough rule of thumb to approximate how long it would have taken, in the absence of knowledge of the invention, for independent discovery.

I believe that the free operation of a market system will not actually run afoul of the Lockean proviso. (Recall that crucial to our story in Part I of how a protective agency becomes dominant and a *de facto* monopoly is the fact that it wields force in situations of conflict, and is not merely in competition, with other agencies. A similar tale cannot be told about other businesses.) If this is correct, the proviso will not play a very important role in the activities of protective agencies and will not provide a significant opportunity for future state action. Indeed, were it not for the effects of previous *illegitimate* state action, people would not think the possibility of the proviso's being violated as of more interest than any other logical possibility. (Here I make an empirical historical claim; as does someone who disagrees with this.) This completes our indication of the complication in the entitlement theory introduced by the Lockean proviso.

■ J. L. MACKIE (1917–1982): RIGHTS-BASED ETHICS

Rights, Duties, and Goals   J. L. Mackie noted that ethical theories can be classified into three basic kinds: goal-based, duty-based, and right-based. Utilitarianism derives duties and rights from their utility or consequential good. Kant, by contrast, attempted to show that goals and rights are derivable from one fundamental duty. Mackie argues that the appeal of rights-discourse and the difficulties with duty-based and goal-based theories encourage the formulation of a rights-based view. Rights are basic to legal language and to political relations: they are legislated, enacted by government executives, ruled upon judicially, and demanded politically. Rights are more popular than duties: people want rights for their own sake, whereas duties are impositions tolerated to secure morality and freedom. Mackie rejects utilitarianism, the leading goal-based theory, for being committed in some cases to morally unacceptable judgments.

The Basic Right   For Mackie, any adequate goal-based morality must assume the basic goal to be an activity. This implies that there is not simply one but indefinitely many diverse goals, as many as there are valued activities. These goals cannot be an object of a single conclusive choice; they involve a range of successive choices. Thus, on a goal-based theory, what must be considered central are "the *rights* of persons progressively to choose how they shall live." Goal-based theories invariably have this fundamental right as their basis. Mackie concluded that the only acceptable moral theories must be rights-based.

A person's right to do X is understood, minimally, as the conjunction of the freedom to do X, if she so chooses, and a claim in so doing to protection from interference by others. Duties and goals are both derivable from this right. If the agent has a right to do X, others have a duty to refrain from interfering. Moreover, if she really has the right, circumstances must be such as to enable her to fulfill it. Mackie concluded that goals may be interpreted as necessary conditions for the fulfillment of rights, and so derivative from these rights. Rights may be derived also from other rights. If an agent has a right to do X, and X causally requires doing Y, then there is a right to Y in the absence of other mitigating circumstances. For example, if a person has a right to defend himself when under harmful attack, and in some circumstances this necessitates injuring the assailant, then the defendant has the right here to cause injury. Mackie insisted that the fundamental right to choose how to lead one's life is universal: all persons are to have it, and to have it equally. Thus, unlike utilitarianism, no individual's or group's rights to life, liberty, and the pursuit of happiness can be sacrificed for the advantage of others.

Conflicts and Prima Facie Rights   The major difficulty facing this view is that specific rights of different individuals derived in historically determinate contexts may conflict. One person's right to express himself freely in a racist or sexist manner may conflict with another's right not to be harmed (see Chapter 10). Mackie aimed to resolve this by interpreting conflicting rights as no more than "*prima facie* rights," namely, those rights that hold before or in the absence of any other overriding or competing considerations. The "final rights" that people in practice actually end up with are the results of compromises worked out by the parties whose *prima facie* rights conflict. These historically determinate agreements are always subject to the condition of equality of the fundamental right.

J. L. Mackie

CAN THERE BE A RIGHT-BASED MORAL THEORY?

In the course of a discussion of Rawls's theory of justice, Ronald Dworkin suggests a "tentative initial classification" of political theories into goal-based, right-based, and duty-based theories.[1] Though he describes this, too modestly, as superficial and trivial ideological sociology, it in fact raises interesting questions. In particular, does some such classification hold for moral as well as for political theories? We are familiar with goal-based or consequentialist moral views and with duty-based or deontological ones; but it is not so easy to find right-based examples, and in discussions of consequentialism and deontology this third possibility is commonly ignored. Dworkin's own example of a right-based theory is Tom Paine's theory of revolution; another, recent, example might be Robert Nozick's theory of the minimal state.[2] But each of these is a political theory; the scope of each is restricted to the criticism of some political structures and policies and the support of others; neither is a fully developed general moral theory. If Rawls's view is, as Dworkin argues, fundamentally right-based, it may be the only member of this class. Moreover, it is only for Rawls's "deep theory" that Dworkin can propose this identification: as explicitly formulated, Rawls's moral philosophy is not right-based. The lack of any convincing and decisive example leaves us free to ask the abstract question, "Could there be a right-based general moral theory, and, if there were one, what would it be like?"

It is obvious that most ordinary moral theories include theses about items of all three kinds, goals, duties, and rights, or, equivalently, about what is good as an end, about what is obligatory or about what ought or ought not to be done or must or must not be done, and about what people are entitled to have or receive or do. But it is also obvious that moral theories commonly try to derive items of some of these sorts from items of another of them. It is easy to see how a consequentialist, say a utilitarian, may derive duties and rights from his basic goal. There are certain things that people must or must not do if the general happiness is to be maximized. Equally, the securing for people of certain entitlements and protections, and therefore of areas of freedom in which they can act as they choose, is, as Mill says, something which concerns the essentials of human well-being more nearly, and is therefore of more absolute obligation, than any other rules for the guidance of life.[3]

Again, it is possible to derive both goals and rights from duties. Trivially, there could just be a duty to pursue a certain end or to respect and defend a certain right.

From *Midwest Studies in Philosophy,* edited by Peter French, Theodore Uehling, and Howard Wettstein (Minneapolis: The University of Minnesota Press, 1978). Reprinted by permission of the editors, The University of Minnesota Press, and Mrs. Joan Mackie. Copyright 1980 by The University of Minnesota Press.

More interestingly, though more obscurely, it is conceivable that sets of goals and rights should follow from a single fundamental duty. Kant, for example, attempts to derive the principle of treating humanity as an end from the categorical imperative, "Act only on that maxim through which you can at the same time will that it should become a universal law."[4] Taken as literally as it can be taken, the principle of treating humanity—that is, persons, or more generally rational beings—as an end would seem to set up a goal. But it could well be interpreted as assigning rights to persons. Alternatively it could be argued that some general assignment of rights would follow directly from the choice of maxims which one could will to be universal. In either of these ways rights might be derived from duties.

But is it possible similarly to derive goals and duties from rights? And, if we are seeking a systematic moral theory, is it possible to derive a multiplicity of rights from a single fundamental one or from some small number of basic rights?

A right, in the most important sense, is the conjunction of a freedom and a claim-right. That is, if someone, A, has the moral right to do X, not only is he entitled to do X if he chooses—he is not morally required not to do X—but he is also protected in his doing of X—others are morally required not to interfere or prevent him. This way of putting it suggests that duties are at least logically prior to rights: this sort of right is built up out of two facts about duties, that A does not have a duty not to do X and that others have a duty not to interfere with A of X. But we could look at it the other way round: what is primary is A's having this right in a sense indicated by the prescription "Let A be able to do X if he chooses," and the duty of others not to interfere follows from this (as does the absence of a duty for A not to do X). Here we have one way, at least, in which duties (and negations of duties) may be derived from rights.

I cannot see any way in which the mere fact of someone's having a certain right would in itself entail that anyone should take something as a goal. Nor does someone's having a right in itself require the achievement or realization of any goal. But the achievement of certain things as goals, or of things that may be taken as goals, may well be a necessary condition for the exercise of a right. Things must be thus and so if A is really to be able to do X; his merely having the right is not in itself sufficient. In this way a goal may be derived from a right, as a necessary condition of its exercise.

Rights can be derived from other rights in fairly obvious logical ways. For example, if I have a right to walk from my home to my place of work by the most direct route, and the most direct route is across Farmer Jones's potato field, then I have a right to walk across Farmer Jones's potato field. Again, there may be a right to create rights—in Hohfeld's terminology, a power. If someone has a certain power, and exercises it appropriately, then it follows that there will be the rights he has thus created. But what may be of more interest is a causal derivation of rights from rights. Suppose that A has a right to do X, but it is causally impossible for him to do X unless he does Y. It does not follow from this alone that he has a right to do Y, and in many cases we may have other grounds for denying him the right to do Y. But at least a prima facie case for his having the right to do Y could be based on the fact that doing Y is causally necessary for doing X, which he already has the right to do.

It seems, then, to be at least formally possible to have a system of moral ideas in which some rights are fundamental and other rights, and also goals and duties, are derived from these. But is it substantially possible? Are rights really the sort of thing that could be fundamental?

It is true that rights are not plausible candidates for objective existence. But neither are goods or intrinsic goals, conceived as things whose nature in itself requires that they should be pursued, or duties taken as intrinsic requirements, as constituting something like commands for which there need be, and is, no commander, which issue from no source. A belief in objective prescriptivity has flourished within the tradition of moral thinking, but it cannot in the end be defended.[5] So we are not looking for objective truth or reality in a moral system. Moral entities—values or standards or whatever they may be—belong within human thinking and practice: they are either explicitly or implicitly posited, adopted, or laid down. And the positing of rights is no more obscure or questionable than the positing of goals or obligations.

We might, then, go on to consider what rights to posit as fundamental. But it will be better, before we do this, to consider the comparative merits of right-based, goal-based, and duty-based theories. When we know what advantages a right-based theory might secure, we shall be better able to specify the rights that would secure them.

Rights have obvious advantages over duties as the basis and ground of morality. Rights are something that we may well want to have; duties are irksome. We may be glad that duties are imposed on others, but only (unless we are thoroughly bloody-minded) for the sake of the freedom, protection, or other advantages that other people's duties secure for us and our friends. The point of there being duties must lie elsewhere. Duty for duty's sake is absurd, but rights for their own sake are not. Duty is, as Wordsworth says, the stern daughter of the voice of God, and if we deny that there is a god, her parentage becomes highly dubious. Even if we accept a god, we should expect his commands to have some further point, though possibly one not known to us; pointless commands, even from a god, would be gratuitous tyranny. Morality so far as we understand it might conceivably be thus based on divine commands, and therefore have, for us, a duty-based form; but if we reject this mythology and see morality as a human product we cannot intelligibly take duties as its starting point. Despite Kant, giving laws to oneself is not in itself a rational procedure. For a group to give laws to its members may be, but not for the sake of the restrictions they impose, or even for the sake of the similarity of those restrictions, but only for the sake of the correlative rights they create or the products of the cooperation they maintain.

However, such points as these can be and commonly are made against duty-based theories on behalf of goal-based ones. When duties have been eliminated from the contest, is there anything to be said for rights as against goals?

A central embarrassment for the best-known goal-based theories, the various forms of utilitarianism, is that they not merely allow but positively require, in certain circumstances, that the well-being of one individual should be sacrificed, without limits, for the well-being of others. It is not that these theories are collectivist in principle; it is not that the claims of individual welfare are overridden by those of some unitary communal welfare. They can and usually do take utility to be purely a resultant of individual satisfactions and frustrations. It is, quite literally, to other individuals that they allow one individual to be sacrificed. If some procedure produces a greater sum of happiness made up of the enjoyments experienced separately by B and C and D and so on than the happiness that this procedure takes away from A— or a sum greater than that needed to balance the misery that this procedure imposes on A—then, at least on a simple utilitarian view, that procedure is to be followed. And of course this holds whether the quantity to be maximized is total or average utility.

I have called this an embarrassment for utilitarianism, and it is no more than this. There are at least three well known possible reactions to it. The tough-minded act utilitarian simply accepts this consequence of his principles, and is prepared to dismiss any contrary "intuitions." Indirect utilitarianism, of which rule utilitarianism is only one variety, distinguishes two levels of moral thinking.[6] At the level of ordinary practical day-to-day thinking, actions and choices are to be guided by rules, principles, dispositions (virtues), and so on, which will indeed protect the welfare of each individual against the claims of the greater happiness of others: rights, in fact, will be recognized at this level. But at a higher level of critical or philosophical thinking these various provisions are to be called in question, tested, explained, justified, amended, or rejected by considering how well practical thinking that is guided by them is likely to promote the general happiness. Such intermediate devices, interposed between practical choices and the utilitarian goal, may for various reasons do more for that goal than the direct application of utility calculations to everyday choices. But in this goal itself, the general happiness which constitutes the ultimate moral aim and the final test in critical moral thought, the well-being of all individuals is simply aggregated, and the happiness of some can indeed compensate for the misery (even the undeserved misery) of others. This, then, is the second possible reaction. The third says that the difficulty or embarrassment results, not because utilitarianism is a goal-based theory, but because it is a purely aggregative one, and that what is required is the addition to it of a distributive principle that prescribes fairness in the distribution of happiness. It is not fair to sacrifice one individual to others.

Of these three reactions, the first would be attractive only if there were some strong prima facie case for adopting a simple utilitarian morality; but there is not.[7] The indirect view also has to assume that there are good general grounds for taking a sheer aggregate of happiness as the ultimate moral aim. But its great difficulty lies in maintaining the two levels of thinking while keeping them insulated from one another. There is, I admit, no difficulty in distinguishing them. The problem is rather the practical difficulty, for someone who is for part of the time a critical moral philosopher in this utilitarian style, to keep this from infecting his everyday moral thought and conduct. It cannot be easy for him to retain practical dispositions of honesty, justice, and loyalty if in his heart of hearts he feels that these don't really matter, and sees them merely as devices to compensate for the inability of everyone, himself included, to calculate reliably and without bias in terms of aggregate utility.

And a thinker who does achieve this is still exposed to the converse danger that his practical morality may weaken his critical thinking. He will be tempted to believe that the virtues built into his own character, the principles to which he automatically appeals in practice, are the very ones that will best promote the general happiness, not because he has reached this conclusion by cogent reasoning, but just because this belief reconciles his theory with his practice. He may come to cultivate a quite artificial distrust of his own ability to work out the consequences of actions for the general happiness. And what happens if the two levels cannot be kept apart? If the critical thinkers let their higher level thinking modify their own day-to-day conduct, the division will cease to be between two levels of thinking for at least some people, and become a division between two classes of people, those who follow a practical morality devised for them by others, and those who devise this but themselves follow a different, more directly utilitarian, morality. If, alternatively, the critical thinkers let their practical morality dominate their criticism, there can indeed be the same moral system for everyone, but it will have ceased to be a goal-based one. The derivation of the working principles from utility will have become a mere rationalization. Altogether, then, indirect utilitarianism is a rather unhappy compromise. And it is inadequately motivated. Why should it not be a fundamental moral principle that the well-being of one person cannot be simply replaced by that of another? There is no cogent proof of purely aggregative consequentialism at any level.[8]

Is the remedy, then, to add a distributive principle? This is still not quite what we need. If one individual is sacrificed for advantages accruing to others, what is deplorable is the ill-treatment of this individual, the invasion of his rights, rather than the relational matter of the unfairness of his treatment in comparison with others. Again, how are we to understand fairness itself? Within a purely goal-based theory it would have to be taken as an end or good, presumably a collective good, a feature of multiperson distributions which it is good to have in a group, or perhaps good for the group, though not good for any one member. And this would be rather mysterious. Further, within a goal-based theory it would be natural to take fairness, if it were recognized, as one additional constituent of utility, and then, unless it were given an infinite utility value, it in turn could be outweighed by a sufficient aggregate of individual satisfactions. There could still be a moral case for sacrificing not only A's welfare but also fairness along with it to the greater utility summed up in the welfare of B and C and so on.

Fairness as a distributive principle, added to an otherwise aggregative theory, would prescribe some distribution of utility. But what distribution? Presumably an equal one would be the ideal, to which distributions in practice would be expected to approximate as closely as was reasonably possible. But though extreme inequalities of satisfaction are deplorable, it is not clear that simple equality of satisfaction is the ideal. We surely want to leave it open to people to make what they can of their lives. But then it is inevitable that some will do better for themselves than others. This same point can be made about groups rather than individuals. Consider a society containing two groups, A and B, where the members of each group are in contact mainly with co-members of their own group. Suppose that the members of A are more cooperative, less quarrelsome, and so more successful in coordinating various activities than the members of B. Then the members of A are likely to do better, achieve more satisfaction, than the members of B. And why shouldn't they? Would there be any good reason for requiring an equal distribution of welfare in such circumstances? There is, of course, no need to adopt the extravagances and the myths of sturdy individualism, above all no ground for supposing that all actual inequalities of satisfaction result from some kind of merit and are therefore justified. All I am suggesting is that inequalities may be justified, and in particular that we should think of protecting each individual in an opportunity to do things rather than of distributing satisfactions.

Perhaps when fairness is added to an otherwise goal-based theory it should be thought of as a duty-based element. But then the arguments against duty-based systems apply to this element. What merit has even the duty to be fair for its own sake? It would be easier to endorse something like fairness as a right-based element, giving us a partly goal-based and partly right-based system.

But even this is not enough. A plausible goal, or good for man, would have to be something like Aristotle's *eudaimonia*: it would be in the category of activity. It could not be just an end, a possession, a termination of pursuit. The absurdity of taking satisfaction in the sense in which it is such a termination as the moral goal is brought out by the science-fictional pleasure machine described by Smart.[9] But Aristotle went wrong in thinking that moral philosophy could determine that a particular sort of activity constitutes the good for man in general, and is objectively and intrinsically the best way of life. People differ radically about the kinds of life that they choose to pursue. Even this way of putting it is misleading: in general people do not and cannot make an overall choice of a total plan of life. They choose successively to pursue various activities from time to time, not once and for all. And while there is room for other sorts of evaluation of human activities, morality as a source of constraints on conduct cannot be based on such comparative evaluations.[10] I suggest that if we set out to formulate a goal-based moral theory, but in identifying the goal to try to take adequate account of these three factors, namely that the "goal" must belong to the category of activity, that there is not one goal but indefinitely many diverse goals, and that they are the objects of progressive (not once-for-all or conclusive) choices, then our theory will change insensibly into a right-based one. We shall have to take as central the right of persons progressively to choose how they shall live.

This suggestion is dramatically illustrated by some of the writings of the best known of utilitarian moralists, John Stuart Mill. When he reiterates, in *On Liberty*, that he regards utility "as the ultimate appeal on all ethical questions," he hastens to add that "it must be utility in the largest sense, grounded on the permanent interests of a man as a progressive being." Not, as it is sometimes misquoted, "of man as a progressive being": that would imply a collectivist view, but here the stress is on the claims of each individual. "These interests, I contend, authorize the subjection of individual spontaneity to external control, only in respect to those actions of each, which concern the interest of other people." And the next few lines make it clear that he is thinking not of any interests of other people, but particularly of their rights and the defense of their rights. It is at least as plausible to say that the deep theory of *On Liberty* is right-based as that this holds of Rawls's *A Theory of Justice*.[11] The same point emerges from a close examination of the last chapter of *Utilitarianism*, "On the Connection between Justice and Utility." There Mill argues that what is morally required or obligatory is included in but not coextensive with what is expedient or worthy, and that what is just (or rather, what is required for justice) is similarly a proper sub-class of what is obligatory. By "justice" he makes it clear that he means the body of rules which protect rights which "reside in persons." They are "The moral rules which forbid mankind to hurt one another (in which we must never forget to include wrongful interference with each other's freedom)" and "are more vital to human well-being than any maxims, however important, which only point out the best way of managing some department of human affairs." And though he still says that general utility is the reason why society ought to defend me in the possession of these rights, he explains that it is an "extraordinarily important and impressive kind of utility which is concerned." "Our notion, therefore, of the claim we have on our fellow-creatures to join in making safe for us the very groundwork of our existence, gathers feelings around it so much more intense than those concerned in any of the more common cases of utility, that the difference in degree . . . becomes a real difference in kind." In such passages as these we can see Mill, while still working within the framework of a goal-based theory, moving toward a right-based treatment of at least the central part of morality.

When we think it out, therefore, we see that not only can there be a right-based moral theory, there cannot be an acceptable moral theory that is not right-based. Also, in learning why this approach is superior to those based either on duties or on goals, we have at least roughly identified what we may take as the fundamental rights. If we assume that, from the point of view of the morality we are constructing, what matters in human life is activity, but diverse activities determined by successive choices, we shall, as I have said, take as central the right of persons progressively to choose how they shall live. But this is only a rough specification, and at once raises problems. Who is to have this right? Let us make what is admittedly a further decision and say that all persons are to have it, and all equality. It is true that this leaves in a twilight zone sentient and even human beings that are not and never will be persons; let us simply admit that there are problems here, but postpone them to another occasion.[12] Other problems are more pressing. The rights we have assigned to all persons will in practice come into conflict with one another. One person's choice of how to live will constantly be interfering with the choices of others. We have come close to Jefferson's formulation of fundamental rights to life, liberty, and the pursuit of happiness. But one person's pursuit of happiness will obstruct another's, and diverse liberties, and even the similar liberties of different people, are notoriously incompatible. Liberty is an all-purpose slogan: in all wars and all revolutions both sides have been fighting for freedom. This means that the rights we have called fundamental can be no more than prima facie rights: the rights that in the end people have, their final rights, must result from compromises between their initially conflicting rights. These compromises will have to be worked out in practice, but will be morally defensible only insofar as they reflect the equality of the prima facie rights. This will not allow the vital interests of any to be sacrificed for the advantage of others, to be outweighed by an aggregate of less vital interests. Rather we might think in terms of a model in which each person is represented by a point-center of force, and the forces (representing prima facie rights) obey an inverse square law, so that a right decreases in weight with the remoteness of the matter on which it bears from the person whose right it is. There will be some matters so close to each person that, with respect to them, his rights will nearly always outweigh any aggregate of other rights, though admittedly it will sometimes happen that issues arise in which the equally vital interests of two or more people clash. . . .

Any right-based moral or political theory has to face the issue whether the rights it endorses are "natural" or "human" rights, universally valid and determinable a priori by some kind of reason, or are historically determined in and by the concrete institutions of a particular society, to be found out by analysis of its actual laws and practices. However, the view I am suggesting straddles this division. The fundamental right is put forward as universal. On the other hand I am not claiming that it is objectively valid, or that its validity can be found only by reason: I am merely adopting it and recommending it for general adoption as a moral principle. Also, I have argued that this fundamental right has to be formulated only as a prima facie right. Derived specific rights (which can be final, not merely prima facie) will be historically determined and contingent upon concrete circumstances and upon the interplay of the actual interests and preferences that people have. But the fact that something is an institutional right, recognized and defended by the laws and practices of a particular society, does not necessarily establish it as a moral right. It can be criticized from the moral point of view by considering how far the social interactions which have generated and maintain this institutional right express the fundamental right of persons progressively to choose how they shall live, interpreted along the lines of our model of centers of force, and to what extent they violate it. Our theory could have conservative implications in some contexts, but equally it could have reforming or revolutionary implications in others.

It may be asked whether this theory is individualist, perhaps too individualist. It is indeed individualist in that individual persons are the primary bearers of rights, and the sole bearers of fundamental rights, and one of its chief merits is that, unlike aggregate goal-based theories, it offers a persistent defense of some interests of each individual. It is, however, in no way committed to seeing individuals as spontaneous originators of their thoughts and desires. It can recognize that the inheritance of cultural traditions and being caught up in movements help to make each individual what he is, and that even the most independent individuals constitute their distinctive characters not by isolating themselves or by making "existential" choices but by working with and through inherited traditions. Nor need it be opposed to cooperation or collective action. I believe that Rousseau's description of a community with a general will, general "both in its object and in its essence," that is, bearing in its expression upon all members alike and located in every member of the community, provides a model of a conceivable form of association, and there is nothing in our theory that would be hostile to such genuine cooperation. But I do not believe that there could actually be a community with a genuine, not fictitious, general will of this sort of the size of an independent political unit, a sovereign state. The fundamental individual rights could, however, be expressed in joint activity or communal life on a smaller scale, and organizations of all sorts can have derived, though not fundamental, moral rights. Our theory, therefore, is not anti-collectivist; but it will discriminate among collectivities, between those which express and realize the rights of their members and those which sacrifice some or even most of their members to a supposed collective interest, or to the real interest of some members, or even to some maximized aggregate of interests.

I hope I have not given the impression that I think it an easy matter to resolve conflicts of rights and to determine, in concrete cases, what the implications of our theory will be. What I have offered is not an algorithm or decision procedure, but only, as I said, a model, an indication of a framework of ideas within which the discussion of actual specific issues might go on. And in general this paper is no more than a tentative initial sketch of a right-based moral theory. I hope that others will think it worth further investigation.

NOTES

1. R. Dworkin, *Taking Rights Seriously* (London, 1977), ch. 6 "Justice and Rights," esp. 171–172. This chapter appeared first as an article, "The Original Position," University of Chicago Law Review 40 (1973), reprinted as ch. 2 in N. Daniels, ed., *Reading Rawls* (Oxford, 1975).

2. R. Nozick, *Anarchy, State and Utopia* (New York and Oxford, 1974).

3. J. S. Mill, *Utilitarianism*, ch. 5.

4. I. Kant, *Groundwork of the Metaphysic of Morals*, sect. 2.

5. This is argued at length in ch. 1 of my *Ethics, Inventing Right and Wrong* (Harmondsworth, 1977).

6. For example, R. M. Hare, "Ethical Theory and Utilitarianism," in *Contemporary British Philosophy—Personal Statements*, ed. H. D. Lewis (London, 1976).

7. I have tried to show this in ch. 6 of *Ethics, Inventing Right and Wrong*, appealing to radical weaknesses in anything like Mill's proof of utility.

8. The discussion referred to in note 7 applies here also.

9. J. J. C. Smart and B. Williams, *Utilitarianism, For and Against* (Cambridge, 1973), 18–21.

10. I am speaking here of what I call morality in the narrow sense in *Ethics, Inventing Right and Wrong*, ch. 5.

11. Dworkin makes this point, at least implicitly, in ch. 11, "Liberty and Liberalism," of *Taking Rights Seriously*.

12. I have touched on it in ch. 8, sect. 8, of *Ethics, Inventing Right and Wrong*.

■ RICHARD RORTY (1931–): POSTMODERN ETHICS

Richard Rorty has been instrumental in promoting criticism of a basic feature of liberal ethical theory. Philosophical liberalism, recall, is committed historically to universal principles of reason and moral value. These commitments, Rorty argues, presuppose universal ideas like intrinsic humanity, human dignity, and human rights—values that are thought to characterize the very humanity of individuals. But, Rorty insists, there is no transhistorical or supersocial godly view on which such universal moral principles can be grounded or from which they might be derived. Rather, moral concepts are necessarily those of some historically specific community. So, individual moral responsibility is responsibility not to the commands of some abstract universal moral law (Kant's commands of reason) but to that individual's society, to its best traditions and principles.

Postmodernist Bourgeois Liberalism   In the contemporary context of the United States, Rorty concedes that the social tradition is philosophical liberalism. Nevertheless, he defends such liberalism not by appeal to universal Kantian principles of morality, but on the basis of their importance in the historical formation of this society. He characterizes this position as *postmodernist bourgeois liberalism*. It is *postmodernist* because it refuses any justificatory appeal to universal and absolute principles beyond those of specific historical communities; it is *bourgeois* because this signifies its specific sociohistorical and economic context; and it is *liberal* because the particular ethical commitments (for example, maximizing individual liberty), in contrast to the justification of the principles, are those of traditional liberalism.

Rorty defends this view against charges of relativism by arguing that we can only—and do—make moral judgments exclusively from within the tradition of moral notions of the society in which we stand. So, we judge racism, say, immoral from our point of view without appealing to Kantian notions of the intrinsic dignity of all human beings.

Richard Rorty

POSTMODERNIST BOURGEOIS LIBERALISM

Complaints about the social irresponsibility of the intellectuals typically concern the intellectual's tendency to marginalize herself, to move out from one community by interior identification of herself with some other community—for example, another country or historical period, an invisible college, or some alienated subgroup within the larger community. Such marginalization is, however, common to intel-

The Journal of Philosophy, LXXX, 10 (October) 1983: 583–9. Reprinted by permission of *The Journal of Philosophy* and Richard Rorty.

lectuals and to miners. In the early days of the United Mine Workers its members rightly put no faith in the surrounding legal and political institutions and were loyal only to each other. In this respect they resembled the literary and artistic avant-guard between the wars.

It is not clear that those who thus marginalize themselves can be criticized for social irresponsibility. One cannot be irresponsible toward a community of which one does not think of oneself as a member. Otherwise runaway slaves and tunnelers under the Berlin Wall would be irresponsible. If such criticism were to make sense there would have to be a supercommunity one *had to* identify with—humanity as such. Then one could appeal to the needs of that community when breaking with one's family or tribe or nation, and such groups could appeal to the same thing when criticizing the irresponsibility of those who break away. Some people believe that there is such a community. These are the people who think there are such things as intrinsic human dignity, intrinsic human rights, and an ahistorical distinction between the demands of morality and those of prudence. Call these people "Kantians." They are opposed by people who say that "humanity" is a biological rather than a moral notion, that there is no human dignity that is not derivative from the dignity of some specific community, and no appeal beyond the relative merits of various actual or proposed communities to impartial criteria which will help us weigh those merits. Call these people "Hegelians." Much of contemporary social philosophy in the English-speaking world is a three-cornered debate between Kantians (like John Rawls and Ronald Dworkin) who want to keep an ahistorical morality-prudence distinction as a buttress for the institutions and practices of the surviving democracies, those (like the post-Marxist philosophical left in Europe, Roberto Unger, and Alasdair MacIntyre) who want to abandon these institutions both because they presuppose a discredited philosophy and for other, more concrete, reasons, and those (like Michael Oakeshott and John Dewey) who want to preserve the institutions while abandoning their traditional Kantian backup. These last two positions take over Hegel's criticism of Kant's conception of moral agency, while either naturalizing or junking the rest of Hegel.

If the Hegelians are right, then there are no ahistorical criteria for deciding when it is or is not a responsible act to desert a community, any more than for deciding when to change lovers or professions. The Hegelians see nothing to be responsible to except persons and actual or possible historical communities; so they view the Kantians' use of 'social responsibility' as misleading. For that use suggests not the genuine contrast between, for example, Antigone's loyalties to Thebes and to her brother, or Alcibiades' loyalties to Athens and to Persia, but an illusory contrast between loyalty to a person or a historical community and to something "higher" than either. It suggests that there is a point of view that abstracts from any historical community and adjudicates the rights of communities vis-a-vis those of individuals.

Kantians tend to accuse of social irresponsibility those who doubt that there is such a point of view. So when Michael Walzer says that "A given society is just if its substantive life is lived in . . . a way faithful to the shared understandings of the members," Dworkin calls this view "relativism." "Justice," Dworkin retorts, "cannot be left to convention and anecdote." Such Kantian complaints can be defended using the Hegelian's own tactics, by noting that the very American society which Walzer wishes to commend and to reform is one whose self-image is bound up with the Kantian vocabulary of "inalienable rights" and "the dignity of man." Hegelian defenders of liberal institutions are in the position of defending, on the basis of solidarity alone, a society which has traditionally asked to be based on something more than mere solidarity. Kantian criticism of the tradition that runs from Hegel through Marx and Nietzsche, a tradition which insists on thinking of morality as the interest of a historically conditioned community rather than "the common interest of humanity," often insists that such a philosophical outlook is—if one values liberal practices and institutions—irresponsible. Such criticism rests on a prediction that such practices and institutions will not survive the removal of the traditional Kantian buttresses, buttresses which include an account of "rationality" and "morality" as transcultural and ahistorical.

I shall call the Hegelian attempt to defend the institutions and practices of the rich North Atlantic democracies without using such buttresses "postmodernist bourgeois liberalism." I call it "bourgeois" to emphasize that most of the people I am talking about would have no quarrel with the Marxist claim that a lot of those institutions and practices are possible and justifiable only in certain historical, and especially economic, conditions. I want to contrast bourgeois liberalism, the attempt to fulfill the hopes of the North Atlantic bourgeoisie, with philosophical liberalism, a collection of Kantian principles thought to justify us in having those hopes. Hegelians think that these principles are useful for summarizing these hopes, but not for justifying them (a view Rawls himself verges upon in his Dewey Lectures). I use "postmodernist" in a sense given to this term by Jean-Francois Lyotard, who says that the postmodern attitude is that of "distrust of metanarratives," narratives which describe or predict the activities of such entities as the noumenal self or the Absolute Spirit or the Proletariat. These metanarratives are stories which purport to justify loyalty to, or breaks with, certain contemporary communities, but which are neither historical narratives about what these or other communities have done in the past nor scenarios about what they might do in the future.

"Postmodernist bourgeois liberalism" sounds oxymoronic. This is partly because, for local and perhaps transitory reasons, the majority of those who think of themselves as beyond metaphysics and metanarratives also think of themselves as having opted out of the bourgeoisie. But partly it is because it is hard to disentangle bourgeois liberal institutions from the vocabulary that these institutions inherited from the Enlightenment—e.g., the eighteenth-century vocabulary of natural rights, which judges, and constitutional lawyers such as Dworkin, must use *ex officiis*. This vocabulary is built around a distinction between morality and prudence. In what follows I want to show how this vocabulary, and in particular this distinction, might be reinterpreted to suit the needs of us postmodernist bourgeois liberals. I hope thereby to suggest how such liberals might convince our society that loyalty to itself is morality enough, and that such loyalty no longer needs an ahistorical backup. I think they should try to clear themselves of charges of irresponsibility by convincing our society that it need be responsible only to its own traditions, and not to the moral law as well.

The crucial move in this reinterpretation is to think of the moral self, the embodiment of rationality, not as one of Rawls's original choosers, somebody who can distinguish her *self* from her talents and interests and views about the good, but as a network of beliefs, desires, and emotions with nothing behind it—no substrate behind the attributes. For purposes of moral and political deliberation and conversation, a person just is that network, as for purposes of ballistics she is a point-mass, or for purposes of chemistry a linkage of molecules. She is a network that is constantly reweaving itself in the usual Quinean manner—that is to say, not by reference to general criteria (e.g., "rules of meaning" or "moral principles") but in the hit-or-miss way in which cells readjust themselves to meet the pressures of the environment. On a Quinean view, rational behavior is just adaptive behavior of a sort which roughly parallels the behavior, in similar circumstances, of the other members of some relevant community. Irrationality, in both physics and ethics, is a matter of behavior that leads one to abandon, or be stripped of, membership in some such community. For some purposes this adaptive behavior is aptly described as "learning" or "computing" or "redistribution of electrical charges in neural tissue," and for others as "deliberation" or "choice." None of these vocabularies is privileged over against another.

What plays the role of "human dignity" on this view of the self? The answer is well expressed by Michael Sandel, who says that we cannot regard ourselves as Kantian subjects "capable of constituting meaning on our own," as Rawlsian choosers,

> . . . without great cost to those loyalties and convictions whose moral force consists partly in the fact that living by them is inseparable from understanding ourselves as the particular people we are—as members of this family or community or nation or people, as bearers of this history, as sons and daughters of that revolution, as citizens of this republic.[1]

I would argue that the moral force of such loyalties and convictions consists *wholly* in this fact, and that nothing else has any moral force. There is no "ground" for such loyalties and convictions save the fact that the beliefs and desires and emotions which buttress them overlap those of lots of other members of the group with which we identify for purposes of moral or political deliberations, and the further fact that these are *distinctive* features of that group, features which it uses to construct its self-image through contrasts with other groups. This means that the naturalized Hegelian analogue of "intrinsic human dignity" is the comparative dignity of a group with which a person identifies herself. Nations or churches or movements are, on this view, shining historical examples not because they reflect rays emanating from a higher source, but because of contrast-effects—comparisons with other, worse communities. Persons have dignity not as an interior luminescence, but because they share in such contrast-effects. It is a corollary of this view that the moral justification of the institutions and practices of one's group—e.g., of the contemporary bourgeoisie—is mostly a matter of historical narratives (including scenarios about what is likely to happen in certain future contingencies), rather than of philosophical metanarratives. The principal backup for historiography is not philosophy but the arts, which serve to develop and modify a group's self-image by, for example, apotheosizing its heroes, diabolizing its enemies, mounting dialogues among its members, and refocusing its attention.

A further corollary is that the morality/prudence distinction now appears as a distinction between appeals to two parts of the network that is the self—parts separated by blurry and constantly shifting boundaries. One part consists of those beliefs and desires and emotions which overlap with those of most other members of some community with which, for purposes of deliberation, she identifies herself, and which contrast with those of most members of other communities with which hers contrasts itself. A person appeals to morality rather than prudence when she appeals to this overlapping, shared part of herself, those beliefs and desires and emotions which permit her to say "WE do not do this sort of thing." Morality is, as Wilfrid Sellars has said, a matter of "we-intentions." Most moral dilemmas are thus reflections of the fact that most of us identify with a number of different communities and are equally reluctant to marginalize ourselves in relation to any of them. This diversity of identifications increases with education, just as the number of communities with which a person may identify increases with civilization.

Intra-societal tensions, of the sort which Dworkin rightly says mark our pluralistic society, are rarely resolved by appeals to general principles of the sort Dworkin thinks necessary. More frequently they are resolved by appeals to what he calls "convention and anecdote." The political discourse of the democracies, at its best, is the exchange of what Wittgenstein called "reminders for a particular purpose"—anecdotes about the past effects of various practices and predictions of what will happen if, or unless, some of these are altered. The moral deliberations of the postmodernist bourgeois liberal consists largely in this same sort of discourse, avoiding the formulation of general principles except where the situation may require this particular tactic—as when one writes a constitution, or rules for young children to memorize. It is useful to remember that this view of moral and political deliberation was a commonplace among American intellectuals in the days when Dewey—a postmodernist before his time—was the reigning American philosopher, days when "legal realism" was thought of as desirable pragmatism rather than unprincipled subjectivism.

It is also useful to reflect on why this tolerance for anecdote was replaced by a reattachment to principles. Part of the explanation, I think, is that most American intellectuals in Dewey's day still thought their country was a shining historical example. They identified with it easily. The largest single reason for their loss of identification was the Vietnam War. The War caused some intellectuals to marginalize themselves entirely. Others attempted to rehabilitate Kantian notions in order to say, with Chomsky, that the War not merely betrayed America's hopes and interests and self-image, but was *immoral*, one which we had had no *right* to engage in in the first place.

Dewey would have thought such attempts at further self-castigation pointless. They may have served a useful cathartic purpose, but their long-run effect has been to separate the intellectuals from the moral consensus of the nation rather than to alter that consensus. Further, Dewey's naturalized Hegelianism has more overlap with the belief-systems of the communities we rich North American bourgeois need to talk with that does a naturalized Kantianism. So a reversion to the Deweyan out-look might leave us in a better position to carry on whatever conversation between nations may still be possible, as well as leaving American intellectuals in a better position to converse with their fellow citizens.

I shall end by taking up two objections to what I have been saying. The first ob-jection is that on my view a child found wandering in the woods, the remnant of a slaughtered nation whose temples have been razed and whose books have been burned, has no share in human dignity. This is indeed a consequence, but it does not follow that she may be treated like an animal. For it is part of the tradition of *our* community that the human stranger from whom all dignity has been stripped is to be taken in, to be reclothed with dignity. This Jewish and Christian element in our tradition is gratefully invoked by free-loading atheists like myself, who would like to let differences like that between the Kantian and the Hegelian remain "merely philosophical." The existence of human rights, in the sense in which it is at issue in this meta-ethical debate, has as much or as little relevance to our treatment of such a child as the question of the existence of God. I think both have equally little rele-vance.

The second objection is that what I have been calling "postmodernism" is bet-ter named "relativism," and that relativism is self-refuting. Relativism certainly is self-refuting, but there is a difference between saying that every community is as good as every other and saying that we have to work out from the networks we are, from the communities with which we presently identify. Postmodernism is no more relativistic than Hilary Putnam's suggestion that we stop trying for a "God's-eye view" and realize that "We can only hope to produce a more rational conception of rationality or a better conception of morality if we operate from within our tradi-tion."[2] The view that every tradition is as rational or as moral as every other could be held only by a god, someone who had no need to use (but only to mention) the terms "rational" or "moral," because she had no need to inquire or deliberate. Such a being would have escaped from history and conversation into contemplation and metanarrative. To accuse postmodernism of relativism is to try to put a metanarra-tive in the postmodernist's mouth. One will do this if one identifies "holding a philosophical position" with having a metanarrative available. If we insist on such a definition of "philosophy," then post-modernism is post-philosophical. But it would be better to change the definition.[3]

NOTES

1. *Liberalism and the Limits of Justice* (New York: Cambridge, 1982), p. 179. San-del's remarkable book argues masterfully that Rawls cannot naturalize Kant and still retain the meta-ethical authority of Kantian "practical reason."

2. *Reason, Truth and History* (New York: Cambridge, 1981), p. 216.

3. I discuss such redefinition in the Introduction to *Consequences of Pragmatism* (Minneapolis: Univ. of Minnesota Press, 1982), and the issue of relativism in "Ha-bermas and Lyotard on Postmodernity," forthcoming in *Praxis International* and in "Solidarite ou Objectivite?" forthcoming in *Critique*.

SUGGESTIONS FOR DISCUSSION

1. Are the principles of distributive justice to be established by way of a social contract? In what ways would distributive principles established by a social contract (Rawls) differ from Aristotelian principles of distribution (see Chapter 1)?

2. Should the liberty to accumulate holdings be regarded as a social value more fundamental than the principle of equality, or should egalitarianism be regarded as a "liberty-limiting principle"?

3. Political economies may be judged morally on economic and political grounds. Does free market capitalism or liberal welfare state capitalism or socialism best meet the joint constraint of distributive justice and guaranteeing rights?

4. Both pro- and antiabortion arguments are often based on appeals to rights—for example, the right of the woman to choose, or the right to life of the fetus (see Chapter 12). Would Mackie consider these conflicting claims to be prima facie rights? How, on Mackie's view, would one of these become the actual right? Is this how rights are actualized?

5. Karl Marx attacks rights as bourgeois fictions. What might be Mackie's defense against such an attack?

6. How does an act utilitarian differ theoretically from a contractarian like Rawls and from an entitlement theorist like Nozick? Would an act utilitarian insist that doctors have a duty to treat patients suffering complications from the AIDS virus, or would doctors ever have a right to withhold such treatment on utilitarian grounds (see Chapter 11)?

7. How does Rorty criticize the liberal philosophical tradition? In what sense does Rorty consider himself a liberal? Would Rorty endorse or condemn a campus hate speech code like that followed at Stanford University (see Chapter 10)?

FOR FURTHER READING

Baier, K. *The Moral Point of View.* Ithaca: Cornell University Press, 1958.

Brandt, R. J. *Ethical Theory.* Englewood Cliffs, N.J.: Prentice-Hall, 1959.

———. *A Theory of the Right and the Good.* Oxford: Oxford University Press, 1979.

Corlett, J. A., ed. *Equality and Liberty: Analyzing Rawls and Nozick.* London: Macmillan, 1991.

Dworkin, R. *Taking Rights Seriously.* Cambridge: Harvard University Press, 1977.

Elster, J. *Sour Grapes: Studies in the Subversion of Rationality.* Cambridge: Cambridge University Press, 1985.

Feinberg, J. *Social Philosophy.* Englewood Cliffs, N.J.: Prentice-Hall, 1973.

Foot, P. *Virtues and Vices.* Oxford: Oxford University Press, 1977.

Frey, R. G., ed. *Utility and Rights.* Minneapolis: University of Minnesota Press, 1984.

Friedman, M. *Capitalism and Freedom.* Chicago: University of Chicago Press, 1958.

Gauthier., D. *Morals by Agreement.* New York: Oxford University Press, 1986.

Gray, J. *Liberalism.* Minneapolis: University of Minnesota Press, 1986.

Hare, R. M. *Essays on the Moral Concepts.* London: Macmillan, 1972.

Harsanyi, J. C. *Rational Behavior and Bargaining Equilibrium in Games and Social Institutions.* Cambridge: Cambridge University Press, 1977.

Hayek, F. A. *The Constitution of Liberty.* Chicago: University of Chicago Press, 1960.

Held, V., ed. *Property, Profits and Economic Justice.* Belmont, Calif.: Wadsworth, 1980.

Kukathas, C. and Pettit, P. *Rawls: A Theory of Justice and Its Critics.* Oxford: Polity Press, 1990.

Lucash, F., ed. *Justice and Equality Here and Now.* Ithaca: Cornell University Press, 1986.

Mackie, J. *Ethics: Inventing Right and Wrong.* Harmondsworth: Penguin Books, 1977.

Nagel, T. "Moral Conflict and Political Legitimacy," *Philosophy and Public Affairs,* 1987: 215–40.

———. *Moral Questions.* Cambridge: Cambridge University Press, 1979.

Nielsen, K. *Equality and Liberty: A Defense of Radical Egalitarianism.* Totowa, N.J.: Rowman and Littlefield, 1984.

Nozick, R. *Anarchy, State, and Utopia.* New York: Basic Books, 1974.

Parfit, D. *Reasons and Persons.* Oxford: Oxford University Press, 1984.

Rawls, J. *A Theory of Justice.* Cambridge: Harvard University Press, 1971.

———. *Political Liberalism.* New York: Columbia University Press, 1993.

Rosenblum, N., ed., *Liberalism and the Moral Life.* Cambridge: Harvard University Press, 1989.

Reiman, J. "The Fallacy of Libertarian Capitalism." *Ethics* (October 1981): 85–95.

Ross, W. D. *The Right and the Good.* Oxford: Oxford University Press, 1930.

Sen, A., and Williams, B., eds. *Utilitarianism and Beyond.* Cambridge: Cambridge University Press, 1984.

Shue, H. *Basic Rights.* Princeton: Princeton University Press, 1980.

Sterba, J., ed. *Justice: Alternative Political Perspectives.* Belmont, Calif.: Wadsworth, 1980.

Williams, B. *Moral Luck.* Cambridge: Cambridge University Press, 1981.

———. *Ethics and the Limits of Philosophy.* Cambridge: Harvard University Press, 1984.

CHAPTER SIX

COMMUNITARIANISM

Liberalism, as we saw in Chapter 5, is wedded strongly to a conception of sovereign yet atomistic and isolated individuals freely choosing their own commitments, endeavours, and actions. The space of the sovereign individual is taken to be protected by rights delimiting incursion by others, institutions, and the state. Communitarianism is defined in terms of a critique of this liberal view of the self, holding that human beings acquire an identity—we are what we are—largely in virtue of the historically defined communities to which we belong. Individual conceptions of the good—of what ought to be pursued as a matter of morality or value—are not self-defined so much as they are acquired by way of our necessary socialization in a community. Communitarianism considers persons to be situated in specific social contexts, sharing moral values, a common conception of the good, and mutual goals acquired in and through community membership. Communitarians vary, then, according to how strongly they stress a range of priorities: of the community in contrast to the individual; of historically defined and socially specific values over purportedly universal ones; of the good over the right, or virtues over rights.

■ ALASDAIR MACINTYRE (1929–): THE DOCTRINE OF THE VIRTUES

Alasdair MacIntyre embraces a sweeping Nietzschean indictment of modern moral philosophy. Like Richard Rorty, he attacks as illusion the supposition of universality central to moral thinking, especially in the Kantian and utilitarian accounts. MacIntyre argues that this ahistorical, traditionless conception of universality replaced the Aristotelian doctrine of the virtues (see Chapter 1) that had been rejected by post-medieval philosophers. He suggests that Nietzsche alone comprehended the consequences for modern moral theory of this rejection of Aristotle's view. Unlike Rorty, however, MacIntyre offers a revised Aristotelianism as an alternative. He accepts Aristotle's doctrine of virtue, and the conceptual structure upon which it rests, as the basis of morality. Virtue-based theories reject duties or rights as the fundamental moral concepts. The basic concern of virtue-based theories is not with how we ought or have a right to act but with establishing what sort of moral character persons should develop.

The Structure of Virtues Central to MacIntyre's analysis is the attempt to show that the differing historical accounts of the virtues presuppose a unified conceptual structure. A virtue consists of three conceptual elements: a practice, a narrative order of a single life, and a moral tradition. A practice is the most basic. MacIntyre defines this as a complex form of cooperative social activity specified by standards of excellence. These standards establish goods internal rather than goods external to a practice. Internal goods are those that can be specified only in terms of, and achieved by participating in, the practice. External goods are those that are identifiable independent of the practice, only contingently related to it, and achievable by a range of alternative means. The game of basketball is a practice; money earned by playing it is an external good; and graceful proficiency at scoring field goals is an internal good. A practice involves historically defined standards of excellence, obedience to rules, and achievement of goals. The standards for the practice set the criteria in terms of which the participants' performances will be judged. External goods are always possessed by someone, thereby limiting the quantity available to others; achieving internal goods, by contrast, benefits all participants in the practice.

Virtues and Practices   MacIntyre defines virtue in terms of practices. A virtue is a human quality acquired in practices. Virtues make possible bringing about goods internal to practices; their lack bars such accomplishment (see Aristotle, Chapter 1). Thus virtues are historically specific, altering relative to social complex. MacIntyre argues that a small set of virtues are nevertheless necessary qualities of any practice. These include the Aristotelian virtues of justice, courage, and honesty. They are qualities required for achieving excellence in all social relations. Justice and honesty are conditions for the principled equality with which all participants in the practice are to be treated. Courage is the capacity to risk harm to oneself for the sake of others; it reveals care and concern. These, then, are standards of excellence characteristic of human activity, irrespective of private moral standpoints. Lack of these virtues simply reveals that a character has failed in some way or another. It indicates that the entire character is defective.

MacIntyre stresses that these core virtues, and the standards of human excellence they represent, are open to interpretations relative to time and place. He insists also that virtuous activity by a person in some respect does not preclude vicious activity in another. However, the success of vicious activity depends upon the virtues of others. So MacIntyre offers a complex historical conception of morality, relativized to time and place, as an alternative to the major traditions of contemporary ethical theorizing.

Alasdair MacIntyre

THE VIRTUES, THE UNITY OF A HUMAN LIFE, AND THE CONCEPT OF A TRADITION

. . . We thus have at least three very different conceptions of a virtue to confront: a virtue is a quality which enables an individual to discharge his or her social role

From *After Virtue: A Study in Moral Theory*, 2nd ed., by Alasdair MacIntyre. Copyright © 1984 University of Notre Dame Press. Used by permission of University of Notre Dame Press and Alasdair MacIntyre.

(Homer), a virtue is a quality which enables an individual to move toward the achievement of the specifically human *telos*, whether natural or supernatural Aristotle, the New Testament, and Aquinas); a virtue is a quality which has utility in achieving earthly and heavenly success (Franklin). Are we to take these as three different things? Perhaps the moral structures in archaic Greece, in fourth-century Greece, and in eighteenth-century Pennsylvania were so different from each other that we should treat them as embodying quite different concepts, whose difference is initially disguised from us by the historical accident of an inherited vocabulary which misleads us by linguistic resemblance long after conceptual identity and similarity have failed. Our initial question has come back to us with redoubled force. . . .

The question can therefore now be posed directly: are we or are we not able to disentangle from these rival and various claims a unitary core concept of the virtues of which we can give a more compelling account than any of the other accounts so far? I am going to argue that we can in fact discover such a core concept and that it turns out to provide the tradition of which I have written the history with its conceptual unity. It will indeed enable us to distinguish in a clear way those beliefs about the virtues which genuinely belong to the tradition from those which do not. Unsurprisingly perhaps it is a complex concept, different parts of which drive from different stages in the development of the tradition. Thus the concept itself in some sense embodies the history of which it is the outcome.

One of the features of the concept of a virtue which has emerged with some clarity from the argument so far is that it always requires for its application the acceptance for some prior account of certain features of social and moral life in terms of which it has to be defined and explained. So in the Homeric account the concept of a virtue is secondary to that of a *social role*, in Aristotle's account it is secondary to that of *the good life for man* conceived as the *telos* of human action, and in Franklin's much later account it is secondary to that of utility. What is it in the account which I am about to give which provides in a similar way the necessary background against which the concept of a virtue has to be made intelligible? It is in answering this question that the complex, historical, multi-layered character of the core concept of virtue becomes clear. For there are no less than three stages in the logical development of the concept which have to be identified in order, if the core conception of a virtue is to be understood, and each of these stages has its own conceptual background. The first stage requires a background account of what I shall call a practice, the second an account of what I have already characterized as the narrative order of a single human life, and the third an account a good deal fuller than I have given up to now of what constitutes a moral tradition. Each later stage presupposes the earlier, but not *vice versa*. Each earlier stage is both modified by and reinterpreted in the light of, but also provides an essential constituent of each later stage. The progress in the development of the concept is closely related to, although it does not recapitulate in any straightforward way, the history of the tradition of which it forms the core.

In the Homeric account of the virtues—and in heroic societies more generally—the exercise of a virtue exhibits qualities which are required for sustaining a social role and for exhibiting excellence in some well-marked area of social practice:

to excel is to excel at war or in the games, as Achilles does, in sustaining a household, as Penelope does, in giving counsel in the assembly, as Nestor does, in the telling of a tale, as Homer himself does. When Aristotle speaks of excellence in human activity, he sometimes though not always, refers to some well-defined type of human practice: flute-playing, or war, or geometry. I am going to suggest that this notion of a particular type of practice as providing the arena in which the virtues are exhibited and in terms of which they are to receive their primary, if incomplete, definition is crucial to the whole enterprise of identifying a core concept of the virtues. . . .

By a "practice" I am going to mean any coherent and complex form of socially established cooperative human activity through which goods internal to that form of activity are realized in the course of trying to achieve those standards of excellence which are appropriate to, and partially definitive of, that form of activity, with the result that human powers to achieve excellence, and human conceptions of the ends and goods involved, are systematically extended. Tic-tac-toe is not an example of a practice in this sense, nor is throwing a football with skill; but the game of football is, and so is chess. Bricklaying is not a practice; architecture is. Planting turnips is not a practice; farming is. So are the inquiries of physics, chemistry, and biology, and so is the work of the historian, and so are painting and music. In the ancient and medieval worlds the creation and sustaining of human communities—of households, cities, nations—is generally taken to be a practice in the sense in which I have defined it. Thus the range of practices is wide: arts, sciences, games, politics in the Aristotelian sense, the making and sustaining of family life, all fall under the concept. But the question of the precise range of practices is not at this stage of the first importance. Instead let me explain some of the key terms involved in my definition, beginning with the notion of goods internal to a practice.

Consider the example of a highly intelligent seven-year-old child whom I wish to teach to play chess, although the child has no particular desire to learn the game. The child does however have a very strong desire for candy and little chance of obtaining it. I therefore tell the child that if the child will play chess with me once a week I will give the child 50 cents worth of candy; moreover I tell the child that I will always play in such a way that it will be difficult, but not impossible, for the child to win and that, if the child wins, the child will receive an extra 50 cents worth of candy. Thus motivated the child plays and plays to win. Notice however that, so long as it is the candy alone which provides the child with a good reason for playing chess, the child has no reason not to cheat and every reason to cheat, provided he or she can do so successfully. But, so we may hope, there will come a time when the child will find in those goods specific to chess, in the achievement of a certain highly particular kind of analytical skill, strategic imagination and competitive intensity, a new set of reasons, reasons not just for winning on a particular occasion, but for trying to excel in whatever way the game of chess demands. Now if the child cheats, he or she will be defeating not me, but himself or herself.

There are thus two kinds of good possibly to be gained by playing chess. On the one hand there are those goods externally and contingently attached to chess-playing and to other practices by the accidents of social circumstances—in the case of the imaginary child candy, in the case of real adults such goods as prestige, status, and money. There are always alternative ways for achieving such goods, and their achievement is never to be had *only* by engaging in some particular kind of practice. On the other hand there are the goods internal to the practice of chess which cannot be had in any way but by playing chess or some other game of that specific kind. We call them internal for two reasons: first, as I have already suggested, because we can only specify them in terms of chess or some other game of that specific kind and by means of examples from such games . . . ; and secondly because they can only be identified and recognized by the experience of participating in the practice in question. Those who lack the relevant experience are incompetent thereby as judges of internal goods.

A practice involves standards of excellence and obedience to rules as well as the achievement of goods. To enter into a practice is to accept the authority of those standards and the inadequacy of my own performance as judged by them. It is to subject my own attitudes, choices, preferences, and tastes to the standards which currently and partially define the practice. Practices of course, as I have just noticed, have a history: games, sciences, and arts all have histories. Thus the standards are not themselves immune from criticism, but nonetheless we cannot be initiated into a practice without accepting the authority of the best standards realized so far. . . .

We are now in a position to notice an important difference between what I have called internal and what I have called external goods. It is characteristic of what I have called external goods that when achieved they are always some individual's property and possession. Moreover characteristically they are such that the more someone has of them, the less there is for other people. This is sometimes necessarily the case, as with power and fame, and sometimes the case by reason of contingent circumstance as with money. External goods are therefore characteristically objects of competition in which there must be losers as well as winners. Internal goods are indeed the outcome of competition to excel, but it is characteristic of them that their achievement is a good for the whole community who participate in the practice. . . .

But what does all or any of this have to do with the concept of the virtues? It turns out that we are now in a position to formulate a first, even if partial and tentative definition of a virtue: A *virtue is an acquired human quality the possession and exercise of which tends to enable us to achieve those goods which are internal to practices and the lack of which effectively prevents us from achieving any such goods.* Later this definition will need amplification and amendment. But as a first approximation to an adequate definition it already illuminates the place of the virtues in human life. For it is not difficult to show for a whole range of key virtues that without them the goods internal to practices are barred to us, but not just barred to us generally, barred in a very particular way.

It belongs to the concept of a practice as I have outlined it—and as we are all familiar with it already in our actual lives, whether we are painters or physicists or quarterbacks or indeed just lovers of good painting or first-rate experiments or a well-thrown pass—that its goods can only be achieved by subordinating ourselves within the practice in our relationship to other practitioners. We have to learn to recognize what is due to whom; we have to be prepared to take whatever self-endangering risks are demanded along the way; and we have to listen carefully to what we are told about our own inadequacies and to reply with the same carefulness for the facts. In other words we have to accept as necessary components of any practice with internal goods and standards of excellence the virtues of justice, courage, and honesty. For not to accept these, to be willing to cheat as our imagined child was willing to cheat in his or her early days at chess, so far bars us from achieving the standards of excellence or the goods internal to the practice that it renders the practice pointless except as a device for achieving external goods.

We can put the same point in another way. Every practice requires a certain kind of relationship between those who participate in it. Now the virtues are those goods by reference to which, whether we like it or not, we define our relationships to those other people with whom we share the kind of purposes and standards which inform practices. . . .

I take it then that from the standpoint of those types of relationship without which practices cannot be sustained truthfulness, justice, and courage—and perhaps some others—are genuine excellences, are virtues in the light of which we have to characterize ourselves and others, whatever our private moral standpoint or our society's particular codes may be. For this recognition that we cannot escape the definition of our relationships in terms of such goods is perfectly compatible with the acknowledgment that different societies have and have had different codes of truthfulness, justice, and courage. Lutheran pietists brought up their children to believe that one ought to tell the truth to everybody at all times, whatever the circumstances or consequences, and Kant was one of their children. Traditional Bantu parents brought up their children not to tell the truth to unknown strangers, since they believed that this could render the family vulnerable to witchcraft. In our culture many of us have been brought up not to tell the truth to elderly great-aunts who invite us to admire their new hats. But each of these codes embodies an acknowledgment of the virtue of truthfulness. So it is also with varying codes of justice and of courage.

Practices then might flourish in societies with very different codes; what they could not do is flourish in societies in which the virtues were not valued, although institutions and technical skills serving unified purposes might well continue to flourish. . . .

. . . It is no part of my thesis that great violinists cannot be vicious or great chess-players mean-spirited. Where the virtues are required, the vices also may flourish. It is just that the vicious and mean-spirited necessarily rely on the virtues of others for the practices in which they engage to flourish and also deny themselves the experience of achieving those internal goods which may reward even not very good chess-players and violinists.

To situate the virtues any further within practices it is necessary now to clarify a little further the nature of a practice by drawing two important contrasts. The discussion so far I hope makes it clear that a practice, in the sense intended, is never just a set of technical skills, even when directed toward some unified purpose and even if the exercise of those skills can on occasion be valued or enjoyed for their own sake. What is distinctive in a practice is in part the way in which conceptions of the relevant goods and ends which the technical skills serve—and every practice does require the exercise of technical skills—are transformed and enriched by these extensions of human powers and by that regard for its own internal goods which are partially definitive of each particular practice or type of practice. Practices never have a goal or goals fixed for all time—painting has no such goal nor has physics—but the goals themselves are transmuted by the history of the activity. It therefore turns out not to be accidental that every practice has its own history and a history which is more and other than that of the improvement of the relevant technical skills. This historical dimension is crucial in relation to the virtues.

To enter into a practice is to enter into a relationship not only with its contemporary practitioners, but also with those who have preceded us in the practice, particularly those whose achievements extended the reach of the practice to its present point. It is thus the achievement, and *a fortiori* the authority, of a tradition which I then confront and from which I have to learn. And for this learning and the relationship to the past which it embodies the virtues of justice, courage, and truthfulness are prerequisite in precisely the same way and for precisely the same reasons as they are in sustaining present relationships within practices.

It is not only of course with sets of technical skills that practices ought to be contrasted. Practices must not be confused with institutions. Chess, physics and medicine are practices; chess clubs, laboratories, universities, and hospitals are institutions. Institutions are characteristically and necessarily concerned with what I have called external goods. They are involved in acquiring money and other material goods; they are structured in terms of power and status, and they distribute money, power, and status as rewards. Nor could they do otherwise if they are to sustain not only themselves, but also the practices of which they are the bearers. For no practices can survive for any length of time unsustained by institutions. Indeed so intimate is the relationship of practices to institutions—and consequently of the goods external to the goods internal to the practices in question—that institutions and practices characteristically form a single causal order in which the ideals and the creativity of the practice are always vulnerable to the acquisitiveness of the institution, in which the cooperative care for common goods of the practice is always vulnerable to the competitiveness of the institution. In this context the essential function of the virtues is clear. Without them, without justice, courage, and truthfulness, practices could not resist the corrupting power of institutions.

Yet if institutions do have corrupting power, the making and sustaining of forms of human community—and therefore of institutions—itself has all the characteristics of a practice, and moreover of a practice which stands in a peculiarly close relationship to the exercise of the virtues in two important ways. The exercise of the virtues is itself apt to require a highly determinate attitude to social and political issues; and it is always within some particular community with its own specific institutional forms that we learn to fail to learn to exercise the virtues. . . . If my account of the complex relationship of virtues to practices and to institutions is correct, it follows that we shall be unable to write a true history of practices and institutions unless that history is also one of the virtues and vices. For the ability of a practice to retain its integrity will depend on the way in which the virtues can be and are exercised in sustaining the institutional forms which are the social bearers of the practice. The integrity of a practice causally requires the exercise of the virtues by at least some of the individuals who embody it in their activities; and conversely the corruption of institutions is always in part at least an effect of the vices. . . .

The time has come to ask the question of how far this partial account of a core conception of the virtues—and I need to emphasize that all that I have offered so far is the first stage of such an account—is faithful to the tradition which I delineated. How far, for example, and in what ways is it Aristotelian? It is—happily—not Aristotelian in two ways in which a good deal of the rest of the tradition also dissents from Aristotle. First, although this account of the virtues is teleological, it does not require any allegiance to Aristotle's metaphysical biology. And secondly, just because of the multiplicity of human practices and the consequent multiplicity of goods in the pursuit of which the virtues may be exercised—goods which will often be contingently incompatible and which will therefore make rival claims upon our allegiance—conflict will not spring solely from flaws in individual character. But it was just on these two matters that Aristotle's account of the virtues seemed most vulnerable; hence if it turns out to be the case that this socially teleological account can support Aristotle's general account of the virtues as well as does his own biologically teleological account, these differences from Aristotle himself may well be regarded as strengthening rather than weakening the case for a generally Aristotelian standpoint.

There are at least three ways in which the account that I have given *is* clearly Aristotelian. First it requires for its completion a cogent elaboration of just those distinctions and concepts which Aristotle's account requires: voluntariness, the distinction between the intellectual virtues and the virtues of character, the relationship of both to natural abilities and to the passions and the structure of practical reasoning. On every one of these topics something very like Aristotle's view has to be defended, if my own account is to be plausible.

Secondly my account can accommodate an Aristotelian view of pleasure and enjoyment, whereas it is interestingly irreconcilable with any utilitarian view and more particularly with Franklin's account of the virtues.

. . . Utilitarianism cannot accommodate the distinction between goods internal to and goods external to a practice. Not only is that distinction marked by none of the classical utilitarians—it cannot be found in Bentham's writings nor in those of either of the Mills or of Sidgwick—but internal goods and external goods are not commensurable with each other. Hence the notion of summing goods—and *a fortiori* in the light of what I have said about kinds of pleasure and enjoyment the notion of summing happiness—in terms of one single formula or conception of utility, whether it is Franklin's or Bentham's or Mill's, makes no sense. Nonetheless we ought to note that although *this* distinction is alien to J. S. Mill's thought, it is plausible and in no way patronizing to suppose that something like this is the distinction which he was trying to make in *Utilitarianism* when he distinguished between "higher" and "lower" pleasures. . . .

Thirdly my account is Aristotelian in that it links evaluation and explanation in a characteristically Aristotelian way. From an Aristotelian standpoint to identify certain actions as manifesting or failing to manifest a virtue or virtues is never only to evaluate; it is also to take the first step toward explaining why those actions rather than some others were performed. Hence for an Aristotelian quite as much as for a Platonist the fate of a city or an individual can be explained by citing the injustice of a tyrant or the courage of its defenders. Indeed without allusion to the place that justice and injustice, courage and cowardice play in human life very little will be genuinely explicable. . . .

I stressed earlier that any account of the virtues in terms of practices could only be a partial and first account. What is required to complement it? The most notable difference so far between my account and any account that could be called Aristotelian is that although I have in no way restricted the exercise of the virtues to the context of practices, it is in terms of practices that I have located their point and function. Whereas Aristotle locates that point and function in terms of the notion of a type of whole human life which can be called good. And it does seem that the question "What would a human being lack who lacked the virtues?" must be given a kind of answer which goes beyond anything which I have said so far. For such an individual would not merely fail *in a variety of particular ways* in respect of the kind of excellence which can be achieved through participation in practices and in respect of the kind of relationship required to sustain such excellence. His own life *viewed as a whole* would perhaps be defective; it would not be the kind of life which someone would describe in trying to answer the question "What is the best kind of life for this kind of man or woman to live?" And that question cannot be answered without at least raising Aristotle's own question, "What is the good life for man?" Consider three ways in which human life informed only by the conception of the virtues sketched so far would be defective.

It would be pervaded, first of all, by *too many* conflicts and *too much* arbitrariness. . . .

Secondly without an overriding conception of the *telos* of a whole human life, conceived as a unity, our conception of certain individual virtues has to remain partial and incomplete. . . .

I have suggested so far that unless there is a *telos* which transcends the limited goods of practices by constituting the good of a whole human life, the good of a human life conceived as a unity, it will *both* be the case that a certain subversive arbitrariness will invade the moral life *and* that we shall be unable to specify the context of certain virtues adequately. These two considerations are reinforced by a third: that there is at least one virtue recognized by the tradition which cannot be specified at all except with reference to the wholeness of a human life—the virtue of integrity or constancy. "Purity of heart," said Kierkegaard, "is to will one thing." This notion of singleness of purpose in a whole life can have no application unless that of a whole life does.

It is clear therefore that my preliminary account of the virtues in terms of practices captures much, but very far from all, of what the Aristotelian tradition taught about the virtues. It is also clear that to give an account that is at once more fully adequate to the tradition and rationally defensible, it is necessary to raise a question to which the Aristotelian tradition presupposed an answer, an answer so widely shared in the pre-modern world that it never had to be formulated explicitly in any detailed way. This question is: is it rationally justifiable to conceive of each human life as a unity, so that we may try to specify each such life as having its good and so that we may understand the virtues as having their function in enabling an individual to make of his or her life one kind of unity rather than another?

■ MICHAEL WALZER (1935–): CRITICAL COMMUNITARIANISM

Liberalism and Communitarianism   Liberalism, we have seen, is committed to the overriding importance of the individual. Communitarianism, by contrast, considers the community to be of paramount theoretical and social consideration. Michael Walzer suggests that the theory of communitarianism accordingly owes its salience to the excesses of philosophical liberalism; communitarianism appears as a recurrent critique of liberal commitments. Walzer distinguishes between two communitarian criticisms of liberalism.

First Criticism   Communitarians concede that liberal political theory accurately represents liberal social practice. Liberal capitalist society actually consists of the radically isolated individuals, the rational egoists separated from community, that are represented classically by Thomas Hobbes (see Chapter 2) and characterized as alienated by Karl Marx. Liberalism is committed to protecting individual freedoms against collective invasion precisely because it denies the possibility of social consensus between all individuals concerning the nature of the social good. The liberal state insists on remaining neutral between competing conceptions of the good. Here, the object of communitarian critique is social conditions—liberal capitalist society, as much as it is philosophical liberalism that accurately represents these conditions.

Second Criticism   Communitarians criticize liberal theory for radically misrepresenting social life. There could be no *human* life totally separated from all others, radically isolated and self-directed, with no social relations and common standards. Thus, the underlying structure even of liberal society must be communitarian: individuals are conceivable only against the background of the communities in terms of which they acquire their specific identities. In denying this, liberalism denies the reality of human experience.

Walzer argues that each of the criticisms involves a partial truth, but that they are deeply inconsistent: the validity of each undercuts that of the other. If liberalism captures the spirit of radical individualism, then it cannot misrepresent social relations. By way of resolving this tension, Walzer insists, first, that a society like the United States is characterized by considerable individualist isolation. The separation of individuals is promoted by what he calls the Four Mobilities: geographical, social, marital, and political mobility. These features of social life entail a loosening of community ties, a demotion of neighborliness. Liberalism is the theoretical justification of this mobility in terms of individual liberty, but it also licenses the miseries of separation and dislocation. The second criticism, suggests Walzer, captures the fact that we are creatures of community. We are much more concerned to work together in association than we are merely to get by on our own, as the first criticism suggests. Thus liberalism is a doctrine that continuously subverts itself, for it always produces attempts to foster a community that would not be so alien and social ties that would bind.

Resolving the Critical Tension   Walzer thinks that the truths within each of the criticisms may be rendered compatible by recognizing that in a society like the United States there are only liberal individuals who nevertheless need to understand that they are social beings. There is no superliberal, utopian community waiting to be unveiled. In so far as liberalism tends toward instability and dissociation, it necessitates periodic communitarian correction. Walzer argues that resolution of the two critiques is achievable on the basis of the liberal idea of voluntary association. The fragility of voluntary association in a liberal society is to be mitigated by a state engaged in fostering associative practices, in aiding its members into helpful (communitarian) associations. The liberal tradition of U.S. society would opt, he thinks, for a *liberal* state committed to and promoting liberal principles of association. Any further insistence upon communitarian social institutions could come only at the unacceptable cost of artificially restricting social mobility and voluntary action.

Michael Walzer

THE COMMUNITARIAN CRITIQUE OF LIBERALISM

I

Intellectual fashions are notoriously short-lived very much like fashions in popular music, art, or dress. But there are certain fashions that seem regularly to reappear. Like pleated trousers or short skirts they are inconstant features of a larger and more steadily prevailing phenomenon—in this case a certain way of dressing. They have brief but recurrent lives; we know their transience and expect their return. Needless to say there is no afterlife in which trousers will be permanently pleated or skirts forever short. Recurrence is all.

Although it operates at a much higher level (an infinitely higher level?) of cultural significance, the communitarian critique or liberalism is like the pleating of

Author's Note: This essay was first given as the John Dewey lecture at Harvard Law School in September 1989. *Political Theory*, vol. 18, no. 1, February 1990, 6–23. Copyright 1990 Sage Publications, Inc. Reprinted by permission of Michael Walzer and Sage Publications.

trousers: transient but certain to return. It is a consistently intermittent feature of liberal politics and social organization. No liberal success will make it permanently unattractive. At the same time no communitarian critique however penetrating will ever be anything more than an inconstant feature of liberalism. Someday perhaps there will be a larger transformation like the shift from aristocratic knee-breeches to plebeian pants, rendering liberalism and its critics alike irrelevant. But I see no present signs or anything like that nor am I sure that we should look forward to it. For now, there is much to be said for a recurrent critique whose protagonists hope only for small victories, partial incorporations, and when they are rebuked or dismissed or coopted, fade away for a time only to return.

Communitarianism is usefully contrasted with social democracy which has succeeded in establishing a permanent presence alongside of and sometimes conjoined with liberal politics. Social democracy has its own intermittently fashionable critics, largely anarchist and libertarian in character. Since it sponsors certain sorts of communal identification it is less subject to communitarian criticism than liberalism is. But it can never escape such criticism entirely for liberals and social democrats alike share a commitment to economic growth and cope (although in different ways) with the deracinated social forms that growth produces. Community itself is largely an ideological presence in modern society; it has no recurrent critics of its own. It is intermittently fashionable only because it no longer exists in anything like full strength and it is criticized only when it is fashionable.

The communitarian critique is nonetheless a powerful one; it would not recur if it were not capable of engaging our minds and feelings. In this essay, I want to investigate the power of its current American versions and then offer a version of my own—less powerful perhaps than the ones with which I shall begin but more available for incorporation within liberal (or social democratic) politics. I do not mean (I hardly have the capacity) to lay communitarianism to rest, although I would willingly wait for its reappearance in a form more coherent and incisive than that in which it currently appears. The problem with communitarian criticism today—I am not the first to notice this—is that it suggests two different, and deeply contradictory, arguments against liberalism. One of these arguments is aimed primarily at liberal practice, the other primarily at liberal theory, but they cannot both be right. It is possible that each one is partly right—indeed, I shall insist on just this partial validity—but each of the arguments is right in a way that undercuts the value of the other.

I I

The first argument holds that liberal political theory accurately represents liberal social practice. As if the Marxist account of ideological reflection were literally true and exemplified here, contemporary Western societies (American society especially) are taken to be the home of radically isolated individuals, rational egotists, and existential agents, men and women protected and divided by their inalienable rights. Liberalism tells the truth about the asocial society that liberals create—not, in fact, ex nihilo as their theory suggests, but in a struggle against traditions and communities and authorities that are forgotten as soon as they are escaped, so that liberal practices seem to have no history. The struggle itself is ritually celebrated but rarely reflected on. The members of liberal society share no political or religious traditions; they can tell only one story about themselves and that is the story of ex nihilo creation, which begins in the state of nature or the original position. Each individual imagines himself absolutely free, unencumbered, and on his own—and enters society accepting its obligations only in order to minimize his risks. His goal is security, and security is, as Marx wrote, "the assurance of his egoism." And as he imagines himself, so he really is, that is, an individual separated from the community, withdrawn into himself, wholly preoccupied with his private interest and acting in accordance with his private caprice. . . . The only bond between men is natural necessity, need, and private interest.[1] (I have used masculine pronouns in order to fit my sentences to Marx's. But it is an interesting question, not addressed here, whether this first communitarian critique speaks to the experience of women: Are necessity and private interest their only bonds with one another?)

The writings of the young Marx represent one of the early appearances of communitarian criticism, and his argument, first made in the 1840s is powerfully present today. Alasdair MacIntyre's description of the incoherence of modern intellectual and cultural life and the toss of narrative capacity makes a similar point in updated, state-of-the-art, theoretical language.[2] But the only theory that is necessary to the communitarian critique of liberalism is liberalism itself. All that the critics have to do, so they say, is to take liberal theory seriously. The self-portrait of the individual constituted only by his willfulness, liberated from all connection, without common values, binding ties, customs, or traditions—sans eyes, sans teeth, sans taste, sans everything—need only be evoked in order to be devalued: It is already the concrete absence of value. What can the real life of such a person be like? Imagine him maximizing his utilities, and society is turned into a war of all against all, the familiar rat race, in which, as Hobbes wrote, there is "no other goal, nor other garland, but being foremost."[3] Imagine him enjoying his rights and society is reduced to the coexistence of isolated selves, for liberal rights, according to this first critique, have more to do with "exit" than with "voice."[4] They are concretely expressed in separation, divorce, withdrawal, solitude, privacy, and political apathy. And finally, the very fact that individual life can be described in these two philosophical languages, the language of utilities and the language of rights, is a further mark, says MacIntyre, of its incoherence: Men and women in liberal society no longer have access to a single moral culture within which they can learn how they ought to live.[5] There is no consensus, no public meeting-of-minds, on the nature or the good life, hence the triumph of private caprice, revealed, for example, in Sartrean existentialism, the ideological reflection of everyday capriciousness.

We liberals are free to choose, and we have a right to choose, but we have no criteria to govern our choices except our own wayward understanding of our wayward interests and desires. And so our choices lack the qualities of cohesion and consecutiveness. We can hardly remember what we did yesterday; we cannot with any assurance predict what we will do tomorrow. We cannot give a proper account of ourselves. We cannot sit together and tell comprehensible stories, and we recognize ourselves in the stories we read only when these are fragmented narratives, without plots, the literary equivalent of atonal music and nonrepresentational art.

Liberal society, seen in the light of this first communitarian critique is fragmentation in practice; and community is the exact opposite, the home of coherence, connection, and narrative capacity. But I am less concerned here with the different accounts that might be provided of this lost Eden than I am with the repeated insistence on the reality of fragmentation after the toss. This is the common theme of all contemporary communitarianisms: neoconservative lamentation, neo-Marxist indictment, and neoclassical or republican hand-wringing. (The need for the prefix "neo" suggests again the intermittent or recurrent character of communitarian criticism.) I should think it would be an awkward theme, for if the sociological argument of liberal theory is right, if society is actually decomposed, without residue, into the problematic coexistence of individuals, then we might well assume that liberal politics is the best way to deal with the problems of decomposition. If we have to create an artificial and ahistorical union out of a multitude of isolated selves, why not take the state of nature or the original position as our conceptual starting point? Why not accept, in standard liberal fashion, the priority of procedural justice over substantive conceptions of the good, since we can hardly expect, given our fragmentation, to agree about the good? Michael Sandel asks whether a community of those who put justice first can ever be more than a community of strangers.[6] The question is a good one, but its reverse form is more immediately relevant: If we really are a community of strangers, how can we do anything else but put justice first?

I I I

We are saved from this entirely plausible line of argument by the second communitarian critique of liberalism. The second critique holds that liberal theory radically misrepresents real life. The world is not like that nor could it be. Men and women cut loose from all social ties, literally unencumbered, each one the one and only inventor of his or her own life, with no criteria, no common standards, to guide the invention—these are mythical figures. How can any group of people be strangers to one another when each member of the group is born with parents, and when these parents have friends, relatives, neighbors, comrades at work, coreligionists, and fellow citizens—connections, in fact, which are not so much chosen as passed on and inherited? Liberalism may well enhance the significance of purely contractual ties, but it is obviously false to suggest, as Hobbes sometimes seemed to do, that all our connections are mere "market friendships," voluntarist and self-interested in character, which cannot outlast the advantages they bring.[7] It is the very nature of a human society that individuals bred within it will find themselves caught up in patterns of relationship, networks of power, and communities of meaning. That quality of being caught up is what makes them persons of a certain sort. And only then can they make themselves persons of a (marginally) different sort by reflecting on what they are and by acting in more or less distinctive ways within the patterns, networks, and communities that are willy-nilly theirs.

The burden of the second critique is that the deep structure even of liberal society is in fact communitarian. Liberal theory distorts this reality and, insofar as we adopt the theory, deprives us of any ready access to our own experience of communal embeddedness. The rhetoric of liberalism—this is the argument of the authors of *Habits of the Heart*—limits our understanding of our own hearts' habits, and give us no way to formulate the convictions that hold us together as persons and that bind persons together into a community.[8] The assumption here is that we are in fact persons and that we are in fact bound together. The liberal ideology of separatism cannot take personhood and bondedness away from us. What it does take away is the sense of our personhood and bondedness, and this deprivation is then reflected in liberal politics. It explains our inability to form cohesive solidarities, stable movements and parties, that might make our deep convictions visible and effective in the world. It also explains our radical dependence (brilliantly foreshadowed in Hobbes's *Leviathan*) on the central state.

But how are we to understand this extraordinary disjunction between communal experience and liberal ideology, between personal conviction and public rhetoric, and between social bondedness and political isolation? That question is not addressed by communitarian critics of the second sort. If the first critique depends on a vulgar Marxist theory of reflection, the second critique requires an equally vulgar idealism. Liberal theory now seems to have a power over and against real life that has been granted to few theories in human history. Plainly, it has not been granted to communitarian theory, which cannot, on the first argument, overcome the reality of liberal separatism and cannot, on the second argument, evoke the already existing structures of social connection. In any case, the two critical arguments are mutually inconsistent; they cannot both be true. Liberal separatism either represents or misrepresents the conditions of everyday life. It might, of course, do a little of each—the usual muddle—but that is not a satisfactory conclusion from a communitarian standpoint. For if the account of dissociation and separatism is even partly right, then we have to raise questions about the depth, so to speak, of the deep structure. And if we are all to some degree communitarians under the skin, then the portrait of social incoherence loses its critical force.

I V

But each of the two critical arguments is partly right. I will try to say what is right about each, and then ask if something plausible can be made of the parts. First, then, there cannot be much doubt that we (in the United States) live in a society where individuals are relatively dissociated and separated from one another, or better, where they are continually separating from one another—continually in motion, often in solitary and apparently random motion, as if in imitation of what physicists call Brownian movement. Hence we live in a profoundly unsettled society. We can best see the forms of unsettlement if we track the most important moves. So, consider (imitating the Chinese style) the Four Mobilities:

1. Geographic mobility. Americans apparently change their residence more often than any people in history, at least since the barbarian migrations, excluding

only nomadic tribes and families caught up in civil or foreign wars. Moving people and their possessions from one city or town to another is a major industry in the United States, even though many people manage to move themselves. In another sense, of course, we are all self-moved, not refugees but voluntary migrants. The sense of place must be greatly weakened by this extensive geographic mobility, although I find it hard to say whether it is superseded by mere insensitivity or by a new sense of many places. Either way, communitarian feeling seems likely to decline in importance. Communities are more than just locations, but they are most often successful when they are permanently located.

2. Social mobility. This article will not address the arguments about how best to describe social standing or how to measure changes, whether by income, education, class membership, or rank in the status hierarchy. It is enough to say that fewer Americans stand exactly where their parents stood or do what they did than in any society for which we have comparable knowledge. Americans may inherit many things from their parents, but the extent to which they make a different life, if only by making a different living, means that the inheritance of community, that is, the passing on of beliefs and customary ways, is uncertain at best. Whether or not children are thereby robbed of narrative capacity, they seem likely to tell different stories than their parents told.

3. Marital mobility. Rates of separation, divorce, and remarriage are higher today than they have ever been in our society and probably higher than they have ever been in any other (except perhaps among Roman aristocrats, although I know of no statistics from that time, only anecdotes). The first two mobilities, geographic and social, also disrupt family life, so that siblings, for example, often live at great distances from one another, and later as uncles and aunts, they are far removed from nephews and nieces. But what we call "broken homes" are the product of marital breaks, of husbands or wives moving out—and then, commonly, moving on to new partners. Insofar as home is the first community and the first school of ethnic identity and religious conviction, this kind of breakage must have countercommunitarian consequences. It means that children often do not hear continuous or identical stories from the adults with whom they live. (Did the greater number of children ever hear such stories? The death of one spouse and the remarriage of the other may once have been as common as divorce and remarriage are today. But, then, other sorts of mobility have to be considered: Both men and women are more likely today to marry across class, ethnic, and religious lines; remarriage will therefore often produce extraordinarily complex and socially diverse families—which probably are without historical precedent.)

4. Political mobility. Loyalty to leaders, movements, parties, clubs, and urban machines seems to decline rapidly as place and social standing and family membership become less central in the shaping of personal identity. Liberal citizens stand outside all political organizations and then choose the one that best serves their ideals or interests. They are, ideally, independent voters, that is, people who move around; they choose for themselves rather than voting as their parents did, and they choose freshly each time rather than repeating themselves. As their numbers increase, they make for a volatile electorate and hence for institutional instability,

particularly at the local level where political organization once served to reinforce communal ties.

The effects of the Four Mobilities are intensified in a variety of ways by other social developments which we are likely to talk about in the common metaphor of movement: the advance of knowledge, technological progress, and so on. But I am concerned here only with the actual movement of individuals. Liberalism is, most simply, the theoretical endorsement and justification of this movement.[9] In the liberal view, then, the Four Mobilities represent the enactment of liberty, and the pursuit of (private or personal) happiness. And it has to be said that, conceived in this way, liberalism is a genuinely popular creed. Any effort to curtail mobility in the four areas described here would require a massive and harsh application of state power. Nevertheless, this popularity has an underside of sadness and discontent that are intermittently articulated, and communitarianism is, most simply, the intermittent articulation of these feelings. It reflects a sense of loss, and the loss is real. People do not always leave their old neighborhoods or hometowns willingly or happily. Moving may be a personal adventure in our standard cultural mythologies, but it is as often a family trauma in real life. The same thing is true of social mobility, which carries people down as well as up and requires adjustments that are never easy to manage. Marital breaks may sometimes give rise to new and stronger unions, but they also pile up what we might think of as family fragments: single-parent households, separated and lonely men and women, and abandoned children. And independence in politics is often a not-so-splendid isolation: Individuals with opinions are cut loose from groups with programs. The result is a decline in "the sense of efficacy," with accompanying effects on commitment and morale.

All in all, we liberals probably know one another less well, and with less assurance, than people once did, although we may see more aspects of the other than they saw, and recognize in him or her a wider range of possibilities (including the possibility of moving on). We are more often alone than people once were, being without neighbors we can count on, relatives who live nearby or with whom we are close, or comrades at work or in the movement. This is the truth of the first communitarian argument. We must now fix the limits of this truth by seeking what is true in the second argument.

In its easiest version, the second argument—that we are really, at bottom, creatures of community—is certainly true but of uncertain significance. The ties of place, class or status, family, and even politics survive the Four Mobilities to a remarkable extent. To take just one example, from the last of the Four: It remains true, even today in this most liberal and mobile of societies, that the best predictor of how people will vote is our knowledge of how their parents voted.[10] All those dutifully imitative young Republicans and Democrats testify to the failure of liberalism to make independence or waywardness of mind the distinctive mark of its adherents. The predictive value of parental behavior holds even for independent voters: They are simply the heirs of independence. But we do not know to what extent inheritances of this sort are a dwindling communal resource; it may be that each generation passes on less than it received. The full liberalization of the social order, the production and reproduction of self-inventing individuals, may take a long time, much longer, indeed, than liberals themselves expected. There is not much comfort here for communitarian critics, however; while they can recognize and value the survival or older ways of life, they cannot count on, and they must have anxieties about, the vitality of those ways.

But there is another approach to the truth of the second critical argument. Whatever the extent of the Four Mobilities, they do not seem to move us so far apart that we can no longer talk with one another. We often disagree, of course, but we disagree in mutually comprehensible ways. I should think it fairly obvious that the philosophical controversies that MacIntyre laments are not in fact a mark of social incoherence. Where there are philosophers, there will be controversies, just as where there are knights, there will be tournaments. But these are highly ritualized activities, which bear witness to the connection, not the disconnection, of their protagonists. Even political conflict in liberal societies rarely takes forms so extreme as to set its protagonists beyond negotiation and compromise, procedural justice, and the very possibility of speech. The American civil rights struggle is a nice example of a conflict for which our moral/political language was and is entirely adequate. The fact that the struggle has had only partial success does not reflect linguistic inadequacy but rather political failures and defeats.

Martin Luther King's speeches evoked a palpable tradition, a set of common values such that public disagreement could focus only on how (or how quickly) they might best be realized.[11] But this is not, so to speak, a traditionalist tradition, a *Gemeinschaft* tradition, a survival of the preliberal past. It is a liberal tradition modified, no doubt, by survivals of different sorts. The modifications are most obviously Protestant and Republican in character, though by no means exclusively so: The years of mass immigration have brought a great variety of ethnic and religious memories to bear on American politics. What all of them bear on, however, is liberalism. The language of individual rights—voluntary association, pluralism, toleration, separation, privacy, free speech, the career open to talents, and so on—is simply inescapable. Who among us seriously attempts to escape? If we really are situated selves, as the second communitarian critique holds, then our situation is largely captured by that vocabulary. This is the truth of the second critique. Does it make any sense then to argue that liberalism prevents us from understanding or maintaining the ties that bind us together?

It makes some sense, because liberalism is a strange doctrine, which seems continually to undercut itself, to disdain its own traditions, and to produce in each generation renewed hopes for a more absolute freedom from history and society alike. Much of liberal political theory, from Locke to Rawls, is an effort to fix and stabilize the doctrine in order to end the endlessless of liberal liberation. But beyond every current version of liberalism, there is always a super liberalism, which, as Roberto Unger says of his own doctrine, "pushes the liberal premises about state and society, about freedom from dependence and governance of social relations by the will, to the point at which they merge into a large ambition: the building of a social world less alien to a self that can always violate the generative rules of its own mental or social constructs."[12] Although Unger was once identified as a communitarian, this ambition—large indeed!—seems designed to prevent not only any stabilization of liberal doctrine but also any recovery or creation of community. For there is no imaginable community that would not be alien to the eternally transgressive self. If the ties that bind us together do not bind us, there can be no such thing as a community. If it is anything at all, communitarianism is antithetical to transgression. And the transgressive self is antithetical even to the liberal community which is its creator and sponsor.[13]

Liberalism is a self-subverting doctrine; for that reason, it really does require periodic communitarian correction. But it is not a particularly helpful form of correction to suggest that liberalism is literally incoherent or that it can be replaced by some preliberal or antiliberal community waiting somehow just beneath the surface or just beyond the horizon. Nothing is waiting; American communitarians have to recognize that there is no one out there but separated, rights-bearing, voluntarily associating, freely speaking, liberal selves. It would be a good thing, though, if we could teach those selves to know themselves as social beings, the historical products of, and in part the embodiments of, liberal values. For the communitarian correction of liberalism cannot be anything other than a selective reinforcement of those same values or, to appropriate the well-known phrase of Michael Oakeshott, a pursuit of the intimations of community within them.

V

The place to begin the pursuit is with the liberal idea of voluntary association, which is not well-understood, it seems to me, either among liberals or among their communitarian critics. In both its theory and its practice, liberalism expresses strong associative tendencies alongside its dissociative tendencies: Its protagonists from groups as well as split off from the groups they form; they join up and resign, marry and divorce. Nevertheless, it is a mistake, and a characteristically liberal mistake, to think that the existing patterns of association are entirely or even largely voluntary and contractual, that is, the product of will alone. In a liberal society, as in every other society, people are born into very important sorts of groups, born with identities, male or female, for example, working class, Catholic or Jewish, black, democrat, and so on. Many of their subsequent associations (like their subsequent careers) merely express these underlying identities, which, again, are not so much chosen as enacted.[14] Liberalism is distinguished less by the freedom to form groups on the basis of these identities than the freedom to leave the groups and sometimes even the identities behind. Association is always at risk in a liberal society. The boundaries of the group are not policed; people come and go, or they just fade into the distance without ever quite acknowledging that they have left. That is why liberalism is plagued by free-rider problems—by people who continue to enjoy the benefits of membership and identity while no longer participating in the activities that produce those benefits.[15] Communitarianism, by contrast, is the dream of a perfect free-riderlessness.

At its best, the liberal society is the social union of social unions that John Rawls described: a pluralism of groups bonded by shared ideas of toleration and democracy.[16] But if all the groups are precarious, continually on the brink of dissolution or abandonment, then the larger union must also be weak and vulnerable. Or, alternatively, its leaders and officials will be driven to compensate for the failures of association elsewhere by strengthening their own union, that is, the central state, beyond the limits that liberalism has established. These limits are best expressed in terms of individual rights and civil liberties, but they also include a prescription for state neutrality. The good life is pursued by individuals, sponsored by groups; the state presides over the pursuit and the sponsorship but does not participate in either. Presiding is singular in character; pursuing and sponsoring are plural. Hence it is a critical question for liberal theory and practice whether the associative passions and energies of ordinary people are likely over the long haul to survive the Four Mobilities and prove themselves sufficient to the requirements of pluralism. There is at least some evidence that they will not prove sufficient—without a little help. But, to repeat an old question, whence cometh our help? A few of the existing social unions live in the expectation of divine assistance. For the rest, we can only help one another, and the agency through which help of that sort comes most expeditiously is the state. But what kind of a state is it that fosters associative activities? What kind of a social union is it that includes without incorporating a great and discordant variety of social unions?

Obviously, it is a liberal state and social union; any other kind is too dangerous for communities and individuals alike. It would be an odd enterprise to argue in the name of communitarianism for an alternative state, for that would be to argue against our own political traditions and to repudiate whatever community we already have. But the communitarian correction does require a liberal state of a certain sort, conceptually though not historically unusual: a state that is, at least over some part of the terrain of sovereignty, deliberately nonneutral. The standard liberal argument for neutrality is an induction from social fragmentation. Since dissociated individuals will never agree on the good life, the state must allow them to live as they think best, subject only to John Stuart Mill's harm principle, without endorsing or sponsoring any particular understanding of what "best" means. But there is a problem here: The more dissociated individuals are, the stronger the state is likely to be, since it will be the only or the most important social union. And then membership in the state, the only good that is shared by all individuals, may well come to seem the good that is "best."

This is only to repeat the first communitarian critique, and it invites a response like the second critique: that the state is not in fact the only or even, for ordinary people in their everyday lives, the most important social union. All sorts of other groups continue to exist and to give shape and purpose to the lives of their members, despite the triumph of individual rights, the Four Mobilities in which that triumph is manifest, and the free-riding that it makes possible. But these groups are continually at risk. And so the state, if it is to remain a liberal state, must endorse and sponsor some of them, namely, those that seem most likely to provide shapes and purposes congenial to the shared values of a liberal society.[17] No doubt, there are problems here too, and I do not mean to deny their difficulty. But I see no way to avoid some such formulation—and not only for theoretical reasons. The actual history of the best liberal states, as of the best social democratic states (and these lend increasingly to be the same states), suggest that they behave in exactly this way, although often very inadequately.

Let me give three relatively familiar examples of state behavior of this kind. First, the Wagner Act of the 1930s: This was not a standard liberal law, hindering the hindrances to union organization, for it actively fostered union organization, and it did so precisely by solving the free-rider problem. By requiring collective bargaining whenever there was majority support (but not necessarily unanimous support) for the union, and then by allowing union shops. The Wagner Act sponsored the creation of strong unions capable, at least to some degree, of determining the shape of industrial relations.[18] Of course, there could not be strong unions without working class solidarity; unionization is parasitic on underlying communities of feeling and belief. But those underlying communities were already being eroded by the Four Mobilities when the Wagner Act was passed, and so the Act served to counter the dissociative tendencies of liberal society. It was nevertheless a liberal law, for the unions that it helped create enhanced the lives of individual workers and were subject to dissolution and abandonment in accordance with liberal principles should they ever cease to do that.

The second example is the use of tax exemptions and matching grants of tax money to enable different religious groups to run extensive systems of day-care centers, nursing homes, hospitals, and so on—welfare societies inside the welfare state. I do not pretend that these private and pluralist societies compensate for the shoddiness of the American welfare state. But they do improve the delivery of services by making it a more immediate function of communal solidarity. The state's role here, beside establishing minimal standards, is to abate, since in this case it cannot entirely solve the free-rider problem. If some number of men and women end up in a Catholic nursing home, even though they never contributed to a Catholic charity, they will at least have paid their taxes. But why not nationalize the entire welfare system and end free-ridership? The liberal response is that the social union of social unions must always operate at two levels: A welfare system run entirely by private, nonprofit associations would be dangerously inadequate and inequitable in its coverage; and a totally nationalized system would deny expression to local and particularist solidarities.[19]

The third example is the passage of plant-closing laws designed to afford some protection to local communities of work and residence. Inhabitants are insulated, although only for a time, against market pressure to move out of their old neighborhoods and search for work elsewhere. Although the market "needs" a highly mobile work force, the state takes other needs into account, not only in a welfarist way (through unemployment insurance and job retraining programs) but also in a communitarian way. But the state is not similarly committed to the preservation of every neighborhood community. It is entirely neutral toward communities of ethnicity and residence, offering no protection against strangers who want to move in. Here, geographic mobility remains a positive value, one of the rights of citizens.

Unions, religious organizations, and neighborhoods each draw on feelings and beliefs that, in principle if not always in history, predate the emergence of the liberal state. How strong these feelings and beliefs are, and what their survival value is, I cannot say. Have the unions established such a grip on the imaginations of their members so to make for good stories? There are some good stories, first told, then retold, and sometimes even re-enacted. But the narrative line does not seem sufficiently compelling to younger workers to sustain anything like the old working class solidarity. Nor is it sufficient for a religious organization to provide life cycle services for its members if they are no longer interested in its religious services. Nor are neighborhoods proof for long against market pressure. Still, communal feeling and belief seem considerably more stable than we once thought they would be, and the proliferation of secondary associations in liberal society is remarkable—even if many of them have short lives and transient memberships. One has a sense of people working together and trying to cope, and not, as the first communitarian critique suggests, just getting by on their own, by themselves, one by one.

V I

. . . The central issue for political theory is not the constitution of the self but the connection of constituted selves, the pattern of social relations. Liberalism is best understood as a theory of relationship, which has voluntary association at its center and which understands voluntariness as the right of rupture or withdrawal. What makes a marriage voluntary is the permanent possibility of divorce. What makes any identity or affiliation voluntary is the easy availability of alternative identities and affiliations. But the easier this easiness is, the less stable all our relationships are likely to become. The Four Mobilities take hold and society seems to be in perpetual motion, so that the actual subject of liberal practice, it might be said, is not a presocial but a postsocial self, free at last from all but the most temporary and limited alliances. Now, the liberal self reflects the fragmentation of liberal society: It is radically underdetermined and divided, forced to invent itself anew for every public occasion. Some liberals celebrate its freedom and self-invention; all communitarians lament its arrival, even while insisting that it is not a possible human condition.

    I have argued that insofar as liberalism tends toward instability and dissociation, it requires periodic communitarian correction. Rawls's "social union of social unions" reflects and builds on an earlier correction of this kind, the work of American writers like Dewey, Randolph Bourne, and Horace Kallen. Rawls has given us a generalized version of Kallen's argument that America, after the great immigration, was and should remain a "nation of nationalities."[20] In fact, however, the erosion of nationality seems to be a feature of liberal social life, despite intermittent ethnic revivals like that of the late 1960s and 1970s. We can generalize from this to the more or less steady attenuation of all the underlying bonds that make social unions possible. There is no strong or permanent remedy for communal attenuation short of an antiliberal curtailment of the Four Mobilities and the rights of rupture and divorce on which they rest. Communitarians sometimes dream of such a curtailment, but they rarely advocate it. The only community that most of them actually know, after all, is just this liberal union of unions, always precarious and always at risk. They cannot triumph over this liberalism; they can only, sometimes, reinforce its internal associative capacities. The reinforcement is only temporary, because the capacity for dissociation is also strongly internalized and highly valued. That is why communitarianism criticism is doomed—it probably is not a terrible fate—to eternal recurrence.

NOTES

1. Karl Marx, "On the Jewish Question," in *Early Writings*, ed. by T. B. Bottomore (London: C. A. Watts, 1963), p. 26.

2. Alasdair MacIntyre, *After Virtue* (Notre Dame: University of Notre Dame Press, 1981).

3. Thomas Hobbes, *The Elements of Law*, Part I, ch. 9, para. 21. I have noticed that the two favorite writers of communitarian critics of this first kind are Hobbes and Sartre. Is it possible that the essence of liberalism is best revealed by these two, who were not, in the usual sense of the term, liberals at all?

4. See Albert Hirschman's *Exit, Voice, and Loyalty* (Cambridge, MA: Harvard University Press, 1970).

5. MacIntyre, *After Virtue*, chs. 2, 17.

6. This is Richard Rorty's summary of Sandel's argument: "The Priority of Democracy to Philosophy," in *The Virginia Statute for Religious Freedom*, ed. by Merrill D. Peterson and Robert C. Vaughan (Cambridge: Cambridge University Press, 1988), p. 273; see Sandel, *Liberalism and the Limits of Justice* (Cambridge: Cambridge University Press, 1982).

7. Thomas Hobbes, *De Cive*, ed. by Howard Warrender (Oxford: Oxford University Press, 1983), Part I, ch. 1.

8. Robert Bellah, et al., *Habits of the Heart* (Berkeley: University of California Press, 1985), pp. 21, 290; see Rorty's comment, "Priority," p. 275, n. 12.

9. And also its practical working out, in the career open to talents, the right of free movement, legal divorce, and so on.

10. See A. Campbell et al., *The American Voter* (New York: Wiley, 1960), pp. 147–148.

11. See the evocation of King in *Habits of the Heart*, pp. 249, 252.

12. Roberto Mangabeira Unger, *The Critical Legal Studies Movement* (Cambridge, MA: Harvard University Press, 1986), p. 41.

13. Cf. Buff-Coat (Robert Everard) in the Putney debates: "Whatsoever . . . obligations I should be bound unto, if afterwards God should reveal himself, I would break it speedily, if it were an hundred a day." In *Puritanism and Liberty*, ed. by A. S. P. Woodhouse (London: J. M. Dent, 1938), p. 34. Is Buff-Coat the first superliberal or Unger a latterday Puritan saint?

14. I do not intend a determinist argument here. We mostly move around within inherited worlds because we find such worlds comfortable and even life-enhancing; but we also move out when we find them cramped—and liberalism makes the escape much easier than it was in preliberal societies.

15. I describe how free-ridership works in ethnic groups in "Pluralism: A Political Perspective," in the *Harvard Encyclopedia of American Ethnic Groups*, ed. by Stephan Thernstrom (Cambridge, MA: Harvard University Press, 1980), pp. 781–787.

16. John Rawls, *A Theory of Justice* (Cambridge, MA: Harvard University Press, 1971), pp. 527ff.
17. See the argument for a modest "perfectionism" (rather than neutrality) in Joseph Raz, *The Morality of Freedom* (Oxford: Clarendon Press, 1986), chs. 5 and 6.
18. Irving Bernstein, *Turbulent Years: A History of the American Worker, 1933–1941* (Boston: Houghton Mifflin, 1970), ch. 7.
19. See my essay on "Socializing the Welfare State" in *Democracy and the Welfare State*, ed. by Amy Gutmann (Princeton, NJ: Princeton University Press, 1988), pp. 13–26.
20. Kallen, *Culture and Democracy in the United States* (New York: Boni & Liveright, 1924).

SUGGESTIONS FOR DISCUSSION

1. What are MacIntyre's criticisms of the modern moral tradition? If effective, do MacIntyre's criticisms preclude morally informed decisions about censoring hate speech (see Chapter 10) or about abortion (see Chapter 12) or about capital punishment (see Chapter 14)?
2. In what ways is MacIntyre's view of the virtues influenced by Aristotle (see Chapter 1)? Would MacIntyre's view commit him to an account of the permissibility of euthanasia (see Chapter 13)?
3. What are Walzer's criticisms of liberalism? How, if at all, do you think a communitarian's views on the rights and obligations of citizenship (Chapter 8) might differ from a liberal's?

FOR FURTHER READING

Bellah, R., Madsen, R., Sullivan, W., Swidler, A., and Tipton, S. *Habits of the Heart.* Berkeley: University of California Press, 1985.

Baynes, K. "The Liberal/Communitarian Controversy and Communicative Ethics." *Philosophy and Social Criticism* 14, 3–4 (1988): 292–313.

Buchanan, A. "Assessing the Communitarian Critique of Liberalism." *Ethics* 99 (1989): 852–92.

Doppelt, G. "Beyond Liberalism and Communitarianism: Towards a Critical Theory of Social Justice." *Philosophy and Social Criticism* 14, 3–4 (1988): 271–92.

Ellis, R. D. "Toward a Reconciliation of Liberalism and Communitarianism." *Journal of Value Inquiry* 25 (1991): 55–64.

Etzioni, A. *A Responsive Society.* San Francisco: Jossey-Bass, 1991.

———. *The Moral Dimension: Toward a New Economics.* New York: The Free Press, 1988.

Feinberg, J. "Liberalism, Community, and Tradition." *Tikkun* vol. 3, no. 3 (May–June 1988).

Kymlicka, W. *Liberalism, Community and Culture.* Oxford: Oxford University Press, 1991.

———. "Liberalism and Communitarianism," *Canadian Journal of Philosophy* 18 (1988): 190–92.

MacIntyre, A. *After Virtue: A Study in Moral Theory.* South Bend: University of Notre Dame Press, 1981.

————. *Whose Justice? Which Rationality?* South Bend: University of Notre Dame Press, 1988.

Mulhall, S. *Liberals and Communitarians: An Introduction.* Oxford: Basil Blackwell, 1992.

Peden, C., and Hudson, Y., eds. *Communitarianism, Liberalism, and Social Responsibility.* Lewiston: Edwin Mellen, 1991.

Rasmussen, D. *Universalism vs. Communitarianism: Contemporary Debates in Ethics.* Boston: MIT Press, 1990.

Rosenblum, N. ed. *Liberalism and the Moral Life.* Boston: Harvard University Press, 1989.

Sandel, M. *Liberalism and the Limits of Justice.* Cambridge: Cambridge University Press, 1982.

Sandel, M., ed. *Liberalism and Its Critics.* New York: New York University Press, 1984.

Taylor, C. *Sources of the Self: The Making of Modern Identity.* Cambridge: Harvard University Press, 1989.

Walzer, M. *Spheres of Justice: A Defense of Pluralism and Equality.* New York: Basic Books, 1984.

CHAPTER SEVEN

FEMINISM

As Alison Jaggar indicates in the selection that follows, what has come to be referred to as "feminist ethics" consists of a wide variety of views, often deeply in conflict and so irreducible to any specific range of claims, topics, methods, or orthodoxy. What unites them under the rubric of a uniquely *feminist* ethic is their commitment to analyzing critically and challenging the ways ethics in the western philosophical traditional has excluded women, licensed their oppression, and rationalized their subordination. Jaggar articulates three broad conditions an ethic must meet to be counted as feminist. First, it must guide action for challenging and undoing rather than extending women's subordination. In this sense, a feminist ethic is practical and has political implications. For example, while some women who may characterize themselves as feminist oppose abortion, feminists very largely tend to be actively pro-abortion, for reasons having to do with the control of women's bodies. Second, a feminist ethic must furnish a conceptual apparatus capable of addressing moral issues in both the public and private domains. Concepts like impartiality that are fashioned in relation to the public domain should not be thought to apply necessarily to private domain issues like intimacy, affection, sexuality, and indeed abortion (see Chapter 12). Third, because the moral and social experiences of women differ a good deal from those of men, as well as among women themselves in terms of conditions like class, race ethnicity, and age, a feminist ethic must take these particular experiences of women seriously.

Thus, what is refreshing about feminist ethical theory is its direct concern with practical matters. This concern has raised new ethical dilemmas concerning women. For instance, new reproductive technologies have raised questions about surrogacy. The questions surrounding surrogacy faced by women often differ, however, from those faced by men: If men are free to sell their sperm, why should women not be free to trade rights to their bodies or bodily products? Feminists are quick to point out, nevertheless, that such trade "commodifies" the female body, opening it up to commercial transaction, and so once more diminishing women's self-determination. Feminists who cast themselves more conservatively respond differently to such questions than feminists committed to an ethic of care, as well as from more radical feminists. Indeed, the latter might well question whether there is not something paradoxical about conservative feminism.

■ NEL NODDINGS (1929–): ETHICS OF CARE

Among feminist theories of morality, the most prominent is an "ethics of care." Proponents of an "ethics of care" contrast it with the prevailing philosophical view that conceives morality in terms of a set of rationally grounded principles universally and impartially applicable to all — human beings. An ethic of care, rather, emphasizes the responsibilities that arise from the particular relations we have with those we care about. It is a feminist view because the experience of caring is considered to be more central to women's social position and experience than to men's. Nel Noddings is a principal exponent of an ethics of care.

Noddings responds to fears feminists have raised theoretically and politically about an ethics of care. The greatest and most general fear expressed by feminist critics is that any theoretical position resting on a claim of difference between men and women will likely disadvantage women by licensing their under- or devaluation. More specific fears hold that the emphasis on experience over principles in an ethics of care will encourage men again to stress the traditionally sexist charge that women cannot use principles. Moreover, some feminists have worried that considering relatedness to be basic in ethics may lead women to sacrifice their autonomy in the name of connection, caring, and response. Finally, some worry that rejection by an ethics of care of the principle of impartiality, deemed in mainstream moral theorizing to be identified overwhelmingly with the moral point of view, may be construed as rejecting morality itself.

In response to the general fear, Noddings first emphasizes that women's differences from men, especially in relation to social power, are not a matter of an essential female nature but of the set of experiences and conditions historically more usual to women. Women's traditional experiences are not only those of oppression. Cherished moral values are to be identified in women's traditional experience and differentiated from those to be abandoned. These cherished values are precisely the ones central to women's prevailing experience with relationship and care.

Noddings responds to the concern about women's use of principles by arguing first that principles are only minimally and not exhaustively necessary in ethical deliberation and action, and second that reasoning includes the direct reflective response to human need and feeling largely without recourse to principle. While principles may be used as general guides to reliable behavior, there is no Kantian-like algorithm for determining what or whom to care for or about and no principled directions how to care.

Noddings distinguishes between different meanings of autonomy and argues that rejecting the notion of autonomy as reason-defined impartiality does not entail rejecting the understanding of autonomy as the human right of self-directedness. In being committed to autonomy as the moral ideal of impartiality, Kantians are concerned with "generalized others," that is, with abstract universal selves rather than with the specific needs "particular others" may have to be cared for. Noddings suggests that the universalistic rationality of traditional Kantian morality be replaced by a "rationality of caring" or "responsibility reasoning." While the ethics of caring promotes sensitivity to the concerns and situation of each individual to whom one is related, it is not radically relativistic for it is based on the universal desire for connectedness.

Finally, Noddings points out that those committed to an ethics of care are not alone among ethical theorists in rejecting the centrality of impartiality to morality. Communitarians like MacIntyre (see Chapter 6) have also advanced this criticism, and no one reasonably accuses them of rejecting morality itself. At issue here is that a commitment to the principle of impartiality is thought to underpin the abstraction and alienated distance of dealing morally with "generalized others," and this often licenses the arrogant dismissal of the specific desires and values, the cultural differences, of "particular others." By contrast, an ethics of care is concerned with recognizing human interdependence and thereby caring for "particular others" to whom we have some connectedness and relation.

Nel Noddings

FEMINIST FEARS IN ETHICS

An ethic of care has received considerable attention in the past few years. Some see the ethic as an important "female ethic." But others argue that the emphasis on gender in the ethics of care may impede progress toward an adequate moral theory (Flanagan and Jackson, 1987; Okin 1989; Tronto 1987). This objection is more a political concern than a theoretical one, although one could, of course, argue that a genderized ethic is necessarily inadequate theoretically. However feminists have long argued that political and theoretical concerns cannot be easily separated. Therefore, the fears that some feminists have expressed about the relation of an ethic of caring to women's betterment are important to feminism as a political movement and also, from a feminist perspective, to the development of an adequate ethical theory. In this paper I will discuss several fears that feminists have raised about the ethics of care and attempt to respond to them.

1. THE DIFFERENCE DEBATE

The main fear of feminists is that any theoretical position that claims a difference between women and men will inevitably work to women's disadvantage. Several of the fears to be discussed in later sections—fears particular to features of the ethic of care—can be subsumed under this major concern. In a society characterized by large differences in power between men and women, it is unlikely that anything claimed as distinctively or chiefly feminine (or female, or belonging to women) will be highly valued. Therefore, the claim that an ethic of care is properly identified with women is self-defeating. Tronto makes this point explicit: "It is a strategically dangerous position for feminists because the simple assertion of gender difference in a social context that identifies the male as normal contains an implication of the inferiority of the distinctly female" (1987:646).

From *The Journal of Social Philosophy* (Fall/Winter 1990). Reprinted by permission.

On careful thought, it turns out that arguments for sameness do not work very well either. To argue that there is no difference—that women are the same as men—is to subject women to standards developed entirely from the needs and experience of men. As Catherine McKinnon has so forcefully pointed out, this approach (arguing for either sameness or difference) conceals "the substantive way in which man has become the measure of all things" (1987:34). MacKinnon advises concentration on the domination inherent in the cultural construction of gender and a vigorous campaign to redistribute power.

Although I agree with MacKinnon that we must find a way to eliminate domination, I think she is mistaken in supposing that this campaign can go on without a thorough examination of women's culture. By "women's culture" I mean the set of experiences more likely to be women's than men's and the meanings that women have attached to these experiences. Some political decisions can be made without such an examination. For example, any reasonable person ought to expect and demand equal pay for equal work. But other decisions require an analysis and reevaluation of women's traditional experience. For example, what value should be put on the following: teaching and caring for young children, caring directly for the elderly, nursing and teaching as professions, volunteer vs. paid work, raising one's own children, and revising the school curriculum to reflect values traditionally associated with women? To discuss these matters reasonably, a recognition of difference is at least implied.

But what is the locus of this difference? I would not want to give an essentialist argument; that is, I reject the hypothesis that women and men are essentially, innately, different in emotional, intellectual or moral makeup. However, it is obvious that women and men have had different kinds of experience and, further, our society's expectations and demands for their experience have differed. Thus, far more women than men have had actual experience in the areas listed above, and even when women have avoided such experience, they—and not men—have suffered consequences for that avoidance. For example, female academics early in this century were expected to resign their professional positions when they married, and they were considered "unnatural" if they were less than enthusiastic about resigning (Rossiter 1982). It was believed that married women (especially mothers) could not be adequate professionals, but if a woman tried to demonstrate or actually succeeded in demonstrating her professional adequacy, she was demeaned and found to be inadequate as a woman.

The experience just described is clearly an example of the power differences MacKinnon emphasizes. But raising children, caring for the elderly, maintaining a supportive home environment, nursing, and teaching are not only activities identified with oppression. They are activities in which women have exercised agency, from which a distinctive morality may indeed emerge, and in which, we might argue, all human beings should be prepared to engage (Martin 1984, 1985, 1987). They are activities in which all persons should be prepared to engage because they are the fundamental activities of human life.

I would not hesitate, then, to claim a substantial difference between men and women on the basis of experience and socialization, but here at least two problems arise—one seemingly easy to solve, the other enormously difficult. The first is one of language. In my own work, I have always intended to rely on women's experience, not women's nature, to build my arguments for an ethic of care. But I wasn't as careful earlier as I am now, and there are places where I've used the words "nature" and, more often, "naturally." I tried to explain this usage by referring to centuries of fairly stable experience that might indeed induce something like a "feminine nature." But now I think it may be best simply to avoid such language entirely.

A similar problem arises in the work of Carol Gilligan (1982) and Sara Ruddick (1980, 1989). Gilligan is often misunderstood as claiming that the "different voice" she identified in moral theory is women's voice—a voice different from men's. In fact, the voice is different from the one that speaks exclusively or emphatically in terms of rights and justice. But the different voice was discovered in conversations with women, and it probably is more often heard from women than from men. This predictable result can be traced to experience and socialization. Similarly, Ruddick has drawn fire for putting moral emphasis on maternal thinking, thereby—say her critics—excluding men. But Ruddick has said that men, too, are capable of maternal thinking. It is just that people not engaged in activities requiring attentive love to dependent beings are not likely to develop it; that is, maternal thought is unlikely to develop through meter intellectual processes. I said that this language problem is seemingly easy to solve, but in reality it is difficult, not only because avoiding misunderstanding requires constant vigilance but also because the favored privileged language is largely a product of masculine experience.

The second problem is one of analyzing experience and socialization. I make a distinction between the two as noted earlier. Even a woman who rejects traditional female experience has been subjected to a process of socialization that can make her uncomfortable with nontraditional choices. As traditional patterns of socialization change, young women may feel pressed to reject traditional experience. (This is already happening to a small but important group of educated women.) Without a thorough analysis of women's traditional experience, a sorting of cherished values from those to be abandoned, and a conscious celebration of the best in women's culture, that culture may be lost. And with it goes the foundation of fully human life.

It may be relatively easy to socialize young women to upgrade their education in, say, mathematics and science. They, as traditional underdogs, have much to gain by doing so. But it will be extremely difficult to socialize young men to upgrade their education so that they are prepared to care for young children, give direct care to the elderly, nurse the ill, be the full psychological parents of their own children. In addition to putting a social stamp of approval on these activities—real men do these things—we must also provide preparation through concrete experience in doing them.

Finally, traditional female experience has to be incorporated into the school curriculum. Socialization will operate in only one direction unless this happens, and the end result could be a world filled with females and males all thinking and behaving in traditional male ways. If anyone doubts that there is an enormous difference between male and female experience, let him or her take a close look at the school curriculum. The traditional interests of women, the undergirding of a whole human culture, are either absent entirely or relegated to classes for teenage mothers where they are often distorted by the alien structures of schooling.

We have to work with difference—not essential difference, but experiential difference. However, accepting and working with difference does not preclude push-ing for changes in power relations as MacKinnon has advised. In particular, analysis of experiential difference guides us to the situation where power differences are most frightening. We are directed to look at the educational deprivation of our young men and the one-sided nature of schooling. Stressing difference is risky, but denying it may cost more than we can afford to pay—the possibility of achieving a full human identity.

To conclude this section: What do we mean when we refer to caring as a female ethic? Certainly we do not mean that it is one applicable only in women's tradi-tional domains, nor do we mean that only women embrace it. We mean that it arises more reliably out of the logic of women's traditional experience than it does out of traditional male experience. If the ethic of care is valuable, that makes an ar-gument for changing the experience of men, not for rejecting the experience of women.

2.   PRINCIPLES

Among the greatest fears of feminists is that the de-emphasis of principles in an ethic of care will re-activate men's charge that women can't use principles. Feminist philosophers are aware of that charge made continually since the days of Aristotle. Even Kant said, "I hardly believe that the fair sex is capable of principles, . . ." Recognizing this assessment and confessing herself fearful of maintaining or re-awakening it, Jean Grimshaw writes:

> I think there are real dangers that a representation of women's moral reasoning based on such a sharp opposition will merely become a shadow of the belief that women per-ceive and act intuitively, situationally, pragmatically, "from the heart," and that their processes of reasoning, if they exist at all, are nebulous and unfathomable. (1986:211)

But we should not let fear drive ethical theory. To begin with, rationality and rea-soning involve more than the identification of principles and their deductive ap-plication. To evaluate the use of principles as minimally useful in ethics is very different from confessing oneself unable to use them. Such evaluation itself requires careful reasoning. Further, there is some empirical evidence to back up the claim that caring may motivate people to appropriate moral action more reliably than reflection on principles. In their impressive study of rescuers (non-Jews who, at con-siderable personal risk, saved Jews during the Holocaust), the Oliners [1988] found that only about 11 percent acted from principle. All the others responded either di-rectly out of compassion or from a sense of themselves as decent, caring people.

Is it possible, some theorists ask, that these people who report acting directly from compassion or sense of ethical self are really using implicit principles? I con-tend that there is a greater danger in arguing this way than in denying the use of principles. Grimshaw, in an otherwise rigorous and commendable analysis, suggests that women may in fact use principles implicitly. In support of her claim, she tells the story of her parents who both thought it was wrong for a man and woman to live together without being married. Her father backed up his rule against such behavior by deciding that he would not visit his daughter, for doing so would violate his principle against condoning morally wrong behavior. However, her mother continued to visit her daughter. Whereas I would say that her mother put persons over principles and employed caring as a mode of moral life, Grimshaw says that her mother held the same principle as her father but, in addition, used an implicit principle, "Consider whether your behavior will stand in the way of maintaining care and relationships" (209). This additional principle, Grimshaw suggests, overrode the first and allowed her mother to continue visiting her daughter while at the same time expressing her disapproval of the living arrangement.

Now it seems to me that, considering what a Kantian might say, this account is clearly more dangerous than mine. I argue that a moral agent can act—thoughtfully, reflectively—in direct response to human need and feeling. One need not always refer to principles, and it may be that actual moral agents in real world activity rarely use them. But Grimshaw allows the implicit use of principles. Surely Kant would say that such use proves his point about women. For Kant, use of principles must be explicit. One only gets moral credit for acts done out of commitment to principle. This means that one must have formulated a principle, reflected on it, and willed oneself to live by it. "Implicit" use, for Kant, is no use at all!

The problem here seems to be a conflation of scientific and ethical principles. We might indeed describe the behavior of Grimshaw's mother and many other moral agents as "principled' in the sense that we can observe certain commendable regularities in it. We can predict with some reliability how these people will behave. But this does not imply that their behavior is chosen in commitment to a principle. An ethical principle does not merely describe behavior.

But, others might argue, there does seem to be an ethical principle operating in the ethic of care. It looks like this: Always act so as to create, maintain, or enhance caring relations. Why isn't this a principle? I concede that one might cast things in this way, but why do it? If this is a principle, it certainly does not provide the sort of procedural guidance given by Kant's categorical imperative. I cannot, using it, lock myself in my study and decide logically what must be done. It is not a principle that depends strictly on logical inference, and I cannot deduce from it a subset of absolutes on stealing, killing, lying and the like. It can only remind me that I must stay in contact with those concerned about the problem at hand. I must remain receptive and responsive to needs and desires. What I might logically decide at the outset may be overturned as I listen to those I must care for. There is no recipe for caring and no algorithm for deciding.

Finally, there may be more danger than help in considering a "principle of care," for we are accustomed to think of principles as productive of decision-making procedures. This is exactly what an ethic of care rejects. There is no objection to the unproblematic, day-to-day use of principles as general guides to dependable behavior. Our object is to the underlying premise that one can deduce from them particular behaviors or patterns of behavior that can rule over all of moral life. The truth seems to be almost the reverse. Because certain regularities of moral life have been established and observed, we are able to state certain "principles," but these principles are minimally useful in new and genuinely puzzling situations. Here we do better to rely on a way of being, a basic condition of receptivity or empathy, that connects us to living others.

3. AUTONOMY AND RELATEDNESS

Philosophers have discussed at least four meanings of autonomy (Christman 1988; Hill 1987). The first, closely associated with impartiality in the Kantian tradition, will be discussed in the next section. A second is the notion of autonomy as a human right. An emphasis on relatedness arouses fears that women may sacrifice their right to autonomy by emphasizing connection, response, and relation in ethics. A third is the idea of autonomy as a moral ideal, and a fourth—similar to the third—is the notion of autonomy as an ego ideal. Acceptance or rejection of any of these interpretations raises special problems for feminists.

Consider autonomy as a human right. Here we suppose that every normal human adult has a right to make choices without coercion or undue interference. Certainly, this notion of autonomy enjoys widespread acceptance. But when we press the concept, difficulties arise. Exactly what is undue interference? When I make a choice that I suppose is truly my own, can I be sure that it is my own? Surely all of us are deeply influenced by individuals with whom we interact, and we are all—at least to some degree—unavoidably affected by socialization (Meyers 1987). Thus a question arises whether there is such a thing as true autonomy to which we have a right.

Still, because we all like to think of ourselves as people who can make independent choices, we want to protect ourselves from invasions of our "autonomy." For women, claiming autonomy in this sense is especially important, because it has so long been explicitly denied to us. Rousseau, for example, insisted that a woman's goodness depended on her reputation, not on her autonomy. "It follows," he wrote, "that the principle of her education must be in this respect contrary to that of ours [males]: opinion is the tomb of man's virtue and the throne of woman's" (quoted in Okin 1979, 162). The denial of a right to autonomy was grounded in a denial of women's capacity for it, and so when we reject the impartiality interpretation of autonomy (next section), we risk pulling the foundational carpet from under our feet as moral agents.

Here it is vital to understand that the Kantian description of autonomous capacity is not the only possible grounding for autonomy as a right. Indeed, many philosophers would grant all human beings the right to autonomy without demanding that they pass a strict Kantian test of rationality (see Hill 1987). An ethic of caring suggests that we consider the capacity of entities to respond rather than a narrow capacity of autonomy based on reason. Each capacity considered would have to be one of which we approve or with which we sympathize; we would not, for example, respect the capacity to inflict suffering and vow not to interfere with it. However, if an entity has the capacity to solve problems, we are obliged not to strip its environment of the possibility for problem solving. If it can suffer, we must not inflict suffering, and we must alleviate it if we are in a position to do so. If it shows affection for its young, we must not separate it from its young or block the expression of affection. If it can express preferences, we must attend to the expression and be cautious in denying a preference.

This last raises a question that is thorny in all ethical theories. When is it permissible to violate another's autonomy for his or her own good? The abandonment of a holistic notion of autonomy in favor of a wide range of respected capacities for response may give some guidance on this problem. Thomas Hill [1987] suggests that there may be occasional conflicts between autonomy and compassion; that is, we may sometimes have to violate another's autonomy out of a clear sense of what is best for the other. In our alternative framework, caring directs us to consider the full range of an entity's capacity. Thus we may occasionally have to interfere with the capacity of persons to make choices in order to preserve their lives, restore their capacities to reflect, or maintain their capacities to relate. But such acts are not wholesale affronts to "autonomy." On the contrary, they are properly done in order to preserve valued capacities, and they must be justified on such grounds.

Let us consider now the notion of autonomy as a moral ideal. Hill (1987) suggests that we concentrate here on the idea of autonomy as self-governance. Again, there is widespread intuitive understanding of what "self-governance" means. It is what every elementary school teacher hopes to instill in her pupils. When they can behave well while teacher is out of the room, they have achieved what their teacher thinks of as self-governance. But, of course, questions immediately arise whether such behavior is truly autonomous or just the product of thorough socialization.

In traditional ethics, the ideal of self-governance requires a carefully constructed and meticulously analyzed set of rules and principles to which an agent will turn for moral guidance. This set is built by (or discovered by) and built into the moral agent through strictly logical processes. An ideal agent can set aside the effects of socialization by examining each effect reflectively—accepting those that pass the hard tests of logical reason and rejecting those that fail. The result, ideally, is a universal or "true" ethical self that does not reflect the idiosyncracies of particular individuals.

Feminists who prefer an ethic of care or a "communicative ethic" (Benhabib 1987) accuse traditional ethics of building on an epistemological blindness to the needs of particular others. Benhabib says that such blindness is "an internal inconsistency in universalistic moral theories" (91): The methods required by universalizability ensure that a moral agent will not be able to take the standpoint of a particular other. All such an agent can take into account is the "generalized" other.

But, although advocates of caring or Benhabib's communicative ethics reject the notion of a generalized true self, they do not reject the idea that moral agents must have a way of monitoring and governing their own behavior. They reject, first, the notion of a universalistic true self and, second, the assumption that such governance must proceed by well defined rules. Diana Meyers [1987] suggests an alternative to impartial and universalistic reason in "responsibility reasoning." This form of reasoning is part of what Kari Waerness (1984) has called the "rationality of caring." It places the moral agent in a position of responsibility to assess needs, evaluate their legitimacy (from the explicit perspectives of all those involved), and respond in a way that creates, maintains, or enhances caring relations.

Meyers (1987) agrees that a person using responsibility reasoning needs a procedure to govern her or his moral decisions and behavior. She suggests "the person's sense of her own identity" (151) as a filter. I (Noddings 1984) have suggested the ethical ideal defined as reflectively constructed set of memories of caring and being cared for. It contains our best and worst moments, each carefully evaluated for its effects on others and on us as carers. When we are faced with responsibility for the needs of others, we either respond spontaneously with care and compassion (and this is a moral response) or, in times of conflict or indecision, we consult our ethical ideal. How would I behave now if I were guided by my best moments as a carer?

It can be argued, then, that an ethic of care incorporates a procedure for self-governance. Further, the ethical ideal as described in *Caring* is a product of each individual's quest to enter and remain in caring relations. The ideal itself is not universalistic. It varies properly from individual to individual. But it escapes radical relativism because it is constructed on a universal desire for connection.

Although the ethic of care (or communication or responsibility) can satisfy the traditional demand for a governance procedure, I would caution against describing this as an entirely self-governing or autonomous procedure. The ethical ideal is highly sensitive to the needs, values and suggestions of others. Indeed, an ethic of care is built on a relational ontology that stresses address and response. This ethic requires an ethical ideal that remains open and sensitive to possible instruction. In dialogue with others, we may put a new construal on old memories. The ideal provides guidance and stability, but it never closes off the self in a proud and lonely autonomy. Thus it is not clear that self-governance should be the moral idea. Rather, we seek something more like a well considered, shared, relational ideal of moral governance.

Finally, we must consider the sense of autonomy as ego ideal. An ethic of care induces fear in some feminists (e.g., Card 1990, Hoagland 1990, Houston 1990), because its relational emphasis seems to accept or even aggravate a lack of individuation. Women's ego boundaries have been described as permeable and fluid (Chodorow 1978) in contrast to those of males that are solid and clearly delineated. But, again, it is not clear that this is necessarily a weakness. A relational ego can be a disadvantage in an oppressive society and the fear of exploitation is justified, but, even in such a setting, consideration of relational strengths suggests optimal rather than absolute forms of individuation and an alternative to the form of ego development associated with individualism.

4. IMPARTIALITY

The association of impartiality with the moral point of view and, in particular, with the first meaning of autonomy noted in the prior section makes it difficult for feminists to reject it. By doing so, we risk denying the base on which autonomy as right and self-governance is built. But I have already suggested that it is a mistake to construe autonomy as one encompassing right and that some optimal form of relational or shared governance is not only closer to the reality of human interaction but, perhaps, more desirable morally than an absolute notion of self-governance.

Feminists are not alone in criticizing impartiality as the central tenet of ethics. For different reasons, both Bernard Williams (1981) and Alasdair MacIntyre (1981) criticize the impartiality criterion. Feminists who fear repercussions from the rejection of impartiality are rightly concerned about its association with biological women. Alison Jaggar (1989), for example, notes that I used the word "feminine" rather than "feminist" in writing about an ethic that rejects impartiality. She is right to object (and I wish I had never used the word), but the idea was to point to a difference in experience, not to a biological difference. If there is something vitally important in that experience, then it is as important to consider as Williams' projects or MacIntyre's communities.

This brings us back to the discussion with which we started. The forms of experience that give rise to caring as a moral orientation are today more available to women than to men. Hence the problematic association of women with ethics of care. But this is not, as we have already seen, a necessary association.

Does the rejection of impartiality contribute something positive to political philosophy and social thinking? This is too large a question to tackle here, but I can suggest a positive line of response. When we recognize that dealing with generalized others under a criterion of impartiality often leads to arrogant dismissal of their particular desires and values, to imposition of our own sense of the good on them, and to inadvertent maintenance of the structures of oppression, we have to ask how we can deal with concrete others at a distance. From the perspective of caring, we need to establish chains of concrete connection, to adopt a stance of receptivity, and to commit ourselves to "staying with" so that our attempts at caring can be completed. Here again it is necessary to recognize and celebrate difference—not to fear or ignore it. It is also necessary to recognize the limitations on individual attempts to care. We cannot, in any meaningful sense, care for every one. We can only be prepared to care, to recognize our interdependence in caring (sometimes all we can do is support others' efforts to care), and to behave politically in ways likely to establish structures that will support concrete caring relations.

5. CONCLUSIONS

I have described several feminist fears about ethics of caring and response, and I have argued that we should not let fear drive our attempts to construct an adequate moral theory. In particular, I have explored fears concerning gender difference, the use of principles, ambivalence about autonomy, and the rejection of impartiality. In every case, it seems to me that feminists have more to gain than to lose by pressing forward.

REFERENCES

Benhabib, Seyla. 1987. "The generalized and the concrete other." In *Feminism As Critique*, Seyla Benhabib and Drucilla Cornell, eds., 77–95. Minneapolis: University of Minnesota Press.

Card, Claudia. 1990. Caring and evil. *Hypatia* 5(1):101–108.

Chodorow, Nancy. 1978. *The Reproduction of Mothering*. Berkeley: University of California Press.

Christman, John. 1988. Constructing the inner citadel: Recent work on the concept of autonomy. *Ethics* 99(1):109–124.

Flanagan, Owen and Kathryn Jackson. 1987. Justice, care and gender: The Kohlberg-Gilligan debate revisited. *Ethics* 97(3):622–637.

Gilligan, Carol J. 1982. *In a Different Voice*. Cambridge: Harvard University Press.

Grimshaw, Jean. 1986. *Philosophy and Feminist Thinking*. Minneapolis: University of Minnesota Press.

Hill, Thomas E., Jr. 1987. "The importance of autonomy." In *Women and Moral Theory*, Eva Feder Kittay and Diana T. Meyers, eds., 129–138. Totowa, N.J.: Rowman & Littlefield.

Hoagland, Sarah Lucia. 1990. Some concerns about Nel Noddings' Caring. *Hypatia* 5(1):109–114.

Houston, Barbara. 1990. Caring and exploitation. *Hypatia* 5(1):115–119.

Jaggar, Alison M. 1989. Feminist ethics: Some issues for the nineties. *Journal of Social Philosophy* 20(1–2):91–107.

MacIntyre, Alasdair. 1981. *After Virtue*. Notre Dame: University of Notre Dame Press.

MacKinnon, Catherine A. 1987. *Feminism Unmodified*. Cambridge: Harvard University Press.

Martin, Jane Roland, 1984. Bringing women into educational thought. *Educational Theory* 34(4):341–354.

Martin, Jane Roland. 1985. *Reclaiming a Conversation*. New Haven, CT: Yale University Press.

Martin, Jane Roland, 1987. Transforming moral education. *Journal of Moral Education* 16(3):204–213.

Meyers, Diana T. 1987. "The socialized individual and individual autonomy: An intersection between philosophy and psychology." In *Women and Moral Theory*, Eva Feder Kittay and Meyers, eds., 139–153. Totowa, NJ: Rowman & Littlefield.

Noddings, Nel. 1984. *Caring: A Feminine Approach to Ethics and Moral Education*. Berkeley: University of California Press.

Okin, Susan Moller. 1979. *Women in Western Political Thought*. Princeton, NJ: Princeton University Press.

Okin, Susan Moller. 1989. Reason and feeling in thinking about justice. *Ethics* 99 (2):229–249.

Oliner, Samuel P., and Pearl M. 1988. *The Altruistic Personality: Rescuers of Jews in Nazi Europe*. New York: The Free Press.

Rossiter, Margaret W. 1982. *Women Scientists in America: Struggles and Strategies to 1940.* Baltimore and London: Johns Hopkins University Press.

Ruddick, Sara. 1980. Maternal thinking. *Feminist Studies* 6(2):342–367.

Ruddick, Sara, 1989. *Maternal Thinking: Towards a Politics of Peace.* Boston: Beacon Press.

Tronto, Joan. 1987. Beyond gender difference to a theory of care. *Signs* 12(4):644–663.

Waerness, Kari. 1984. The rationality of caring. *Economic and Industrial Democracy* 5(2):185–212.

Williams, Bernard. 1981. *Moral Luck.* Cambridge: Cambridge University Press.

■ ALISON JAGGAR (1942–): FEMINISM'S FUTURE

Alisan Jaggar addresses five pressing issues facing feminist ethics and their implications for the directions theoretical feminism is likely to take. First, Jaggar surveys the history of feminist theories concerning equality and differences between men and women, and among women. This research has led some feminists to distance themselves from the liberal view of equality as equal procedure or opportunity and to embrace a construal of equality as similarity of individual outcome or condition. Consequently, the liberal moralist's view that gender is a morally irrelevant difference, an assumption at the heart of Sommers' arguments, is considered to be deeply misguided, for men and women are rarely situated in similar circumstances.

The second issue, then, is how to construe impartiality. Linked conceptually with equality, rationality, and objectivity, liberal theorists (as we have seen) construe impartiality as the basic moral conception. But given deep gender differences in moral experience and conception, feminist and nonfeminist philosophers alike worry that impartiality can become a subterfuge for taking the male point of view as morally universal. Feminists thus need to evaluate the proper place of impartiality in ethics.

Third, feminists have criticized as ahistorical and essentialist the prevailing model of the moral self. The standard moral view conceives the self as disembodied, separate, autonomous, and rational, that is, as essentially similar to any other moral self. Feminist theorists are challenged accordingly to articulate ways of theorizing about moral subjects sensitive to their concreteness, particularity, and specificity. This necessitates conceiving moral subjects in terms both of their intrinsic and common value and of their membership in and relation to specific historical communities.

Central to this task, fourth, is to rethink the notion of autonomy, which traditionally presupposes isolation and separateness as the grounds of self-direction. Feminists are thus challenged to find ways of reconceiving moral agency, choice, and consent compatible with feminist theoretical commitments and critiques. This raises the fifth and final concern, namely, the traditional conception that morality consists in a set of universal moral rules. Feminists, like communitarians and others, have criticized this view as hiding bias and rationalizing dominance in the name of universality. But feminists worry that their critique of male dominance not be dismissed relativistically as just another point of view. Thus, Jaggar sees feminist ethics facing the crucial need to fashion a rigorous way of justifying feminist moral claims in the face of critical attack and dismissal.

Alison M. Jaggar

FEMINIST ETHICS: SOME ISSUES FOR THE NINETIES

Feminist approaches to ethics are distinguished by their explicit commitment to re-thinking ethics with a view to correcting whatever forms of male bias it may contain.[1] Feminist ethics, as these approaches are often called collectively, seeks to identify and challenge all those ways, overt but more often and more perniciously covert, in which western ethics has excluded women or rationalized their subordination. Its goal is to offer both practical guides to action and theoretical understandings of the nature of morality that do not, overtly or covertly, subordinate the interests of any woman or group of women to the interests of any other individual or group.

While those who practice feminist ethics are united by a shared project, they diverge widely in their views as to how this project may be accomplished. These divergences result from a variety of philosophical differences, including differing conceptions of feminism itself, a perennially contested concept. The inevitability of such disagreement means that feminist ethics cannot be identified in terms of a specific range of topics, methods or orthodoxies. For example, it is a mistake, though one to which even some feminists occasionally have succumbed, to identify feminist ethics with any of the following: putting women's interests first; focusing exclusively on so-called women's issues; accepting women (or feminists) as moral experts or authorities; substituting "female" (or "feminine") for "male" (or "masculine") values; or extrapolating directly from women's experience.

Even though my initial characterization of feminist ethics is quite loose, it does suggest certain minimum conditions of adequacy for any approach to ethics that purports to be feminist.

(1) Within the present social context, in which women remain systematically subordinated, a feminist approach to ethics must offer a guide to action that will tend to subvert rather than reinforce this subordination. Thus, such an approach

From *The Journal of Social Philosophy* (Fall/Winter 1990). Reprinted by permission of Alison Jaggar and *The Journal of Social Philosophy*.

must be practical, transitional and nonutopian, an extension of politics rather than a retreat from it. It must be sensitive, for instance, to the symbolic meanings as well as the practical consequences of any actions that we take as gendered subjects in a male dominated society, and it must also provide the conceptual resources for identifying and evaluating the varieties of resistance and struggle in which women, particularly, have tended to engage. It must recognize the often unnoticed ways in which women and other members of the underclass have refused co-operation and opposed domination, while acknowledging the inevitability of collusion and the impossibility of totally clean hands (Ringelheim 1985; King 1989).

(2) Since so much of women's struggle has been in the kitchen and the bedroom, as well as in the parliamentary chamber and on the factory floor, a second requirement for feminist ethics is that it should be equipped to handle moral issues in both the so-called public and private domains. It must be able to provide guidance on issues of intimate relations, such as affection and sexuality, which, until quite recently, were largely ignored by modern moral theory. In so doing, it cannot assume that moral concepts developed originally for application to the public realm, concepts such as impartiality or exploitation, are automatically applicable to the private realm. Similarly, an approach to ethics that is adequate for feminism must also provide appropriate guidance for activity in the public realm, for dealing with large numbers of people, including strangers.

(3) Finally, feminist ethics must take the moral experience of all women seriously, though not, of course, uncritically. Though what is *feminist* will often turn out to be very different from what is *feminine*, a basic respect for women's moral experience is necessary to acknowledging women's capacities as moralists and to countering traditional stereotypes of women as less than full moral agents, as childlike or "natural." Furthermore, as Okin (1987), among others, has argued, empirical claims about differences in the moral experiences of women and men make it impossible to assume that any approach to ethics will be unanimously accepted if it fails to consult the moral experience of women. Additionally, it seems plausible to suppose that women's distinctive social experience may make them especially perceptive regarding the implications of domination, especially gender domination, and especially well equipped to detect the male bias that has been shown to pervade so much of male-authored western moral theory.

On the surface, at least, these conditions of adequacy for feminist ethics are quite minimal—although I believe that fulfilling them would have radical consequences for ethics I think most feminist, and perhaps even many nonfeminist,[2] philosophers would be likely to find the general statement of these conditions relatively uncontroversial, but that inevitably there will be sharp disagreement over when the conditions have been met. Even feminists are likely to differ over, for instance, just what are women's interests and when they have been neglected, what is resistance to domination and which aspects of which women's moral experience are worth developing and in which directions.

I shall now go on to outline some of these differences as they have arisen in feminist discussions of five ethical and meta-ethical issues. These five certainly are not the only issues to confront feminist ethics; on the contrary, the domain of feminist ethics is identical with that of nonfeminist ethics—it is the whole domain of morality and moral theory. I have selected these five issues both because I believe they are especially pressing in the context of contemporary philosophical debate, and because I myself find them especially interesting. As will shortly become evident, the issues that I have selected are not independent of each other; they are unified at least by recurrent concern about questions of universality and particularity. Nevertheless, I shall separate the issues for the purposes of exposition.

1. EQUALITY AND DIFFERENCE

The central insight of contemporary feminism without doubt has been the recognition of gender as a sometimes contradictory but always pervasive system of social norms that regulates the activity of individuals according to their biological sex. Thus individuals whose sex is male are expected to conform to prevailing norms of masculinity, while female individuals are expected to conform to prevailing norms of femininity. In 1970, Shulamith Firestone began her classic *The Dialectic of Sex* with the words "Sex class is so deep as to be invisible" and, for the first decade of the contemporary women's movement, feminists devoted themselves to rendering "sex-class" or gender visible; to exploring (and denouncing) the depth and extent of gender regulation in the life of every individual. Norms of gender were shown to influence not only dress, occupation and sexuality, but also bodily comportment, patterns of speech, eating habits and intellectual, emotional, moral and even physical development—mostly in ways that, practically and/or symbolically, reinforced the domination of men over women.

The conceptual distinction between sex and gender enabled feminists to articulate a variety of important insights. These included recognizing that the superficially nondiscriminatory acceptance of exceptional, i.e., "masculine," women is not only compatible with but actually presupposes a devaluation of "the feminine." The sex/gender distinction also enabled feminists to separate critical reflection on cultural norms of masculinity from antagonism towards actual men (Plumwood 1989).

Useful as the concept of gender has been to feminism, however, more recent feminist reflection has shown that it is neither as simple nor as unproblematic as it seemed when feminists first articulated it. Some feminists have challenged the initially sharp distinction between sex and gender, noting that, just as sex differences have influenced (though not ineluctably determined) the development of gender norms, so gender arrangements may well have influenced the biological evolution of certain secondary sexual characteristics and even of that defining criterion of sex, procreation itself (Jaggar 1983). Other feminists have challenged the distinction between gender and other social categories such as race and class. Recognizing that feminist claims about "women" often had generalized illicitly from the experience of a relatively small group of middle-class white women, feminists in the last ten years have emphasized that gender is a variable rather than a constant, since norms of gender vary not only between but also within cultures, along dimensions such as class, race, age, marital status, sexual preference and so on. Moreover, since every woman is a woman of some determinate age, race, class and marital status, gender is not even an independent variable; there is no concept of pure or abstract gender that can be isolated theoretically and studied independently of class, race, age or marital status (Spelman, 1989). Neither, of course, can these other social categories be understood independently of gender.

Their increasingly sophisticated understandings of gender have complicated feminists' discussions of many moral and social issues. One of these is sexual equality. At the beginning of the contemporary women's movement, in the late 1960s, this seems to be a relatively straightforward issue. The nineteenth century feminist preference for "separate spheres" for men and women (Freedman 1979) had been replaced by demands for identity of legal rights for men and women or, as it came to be called, equality before the law. By the end of the 1960s, most feminists in the United States had come to believe that the legal system should be sex-blind, that it should not differentiate in any way between women and men. This belief was expressed in the struggle for an Equal Rights Amendment to the U.S. Constitution, an amendment that, had it passed, would have made any sex-specific law unconstitutional.

By the late 1970s and early 1980s, however, it was becoming apparent that the assimilationist goal of strict equality before the law does not always benefit women, at least in the short term. One notorious example was "no fault" divorce settlements that divided family property equally between husband and wife but invariably left wives in a far worse economic situation than they did husbands. In one study, for instance, ex-husbands' standard of living was found to have risen by 42% a year after divorce, whereas ex-wives' standard of living declined by 73% (Weitzman 1985). This huge discrepancy in the outcome of divorce resulted from a variety of factors, including the fact that women and men typically are differently situated in the job market, with women usually having much lower job qualifications and less work experience. In this sort of case, equality (construed as identity) in the treatment of the sexes appears to produce an outcome in which sexual inequality is increased.

The obvious alternative of seeking equality by providing women with special legal protection continues, however, to be as fraught with dangers for women as it was earlier in the century when the existence of protective legislation was used as an excuse for excluding women from many of the more prestigious and better paid occupations (Williams 1984–5). For instance, mandating special leaves for disability on account of pregnancy or childbirth promotes the perception that women are less reliable workers than men; recognizing "pre-menstrual syndrome" or post-partum depression as periodically disabling conditions encourages the perception that women are less responsible than men; while attempts to protect women's sexuality through legislation restricting pornography or excluding women from employment in male institutions such as prisons, perpetuate the dangerous stereotype that women are by nature the sexual prey of men. This cultural myth serves as an implicit legitimation for the prostitution, sexual harassment and rape of women, because it implies that such activities are in some sense natural. In all these cases, attempts to achieve equality between the sexes by responding to perceived differences between men and women seem likely to reinforce rather than reduce existing differences, even differences that are acknowledged to be social rather than biological in origin.

Furthermore, a "sex-responsive," as opposed to "sex-blind," conception of equality ignores differences *between* women, separating all women into a single homogenous category and possibly penalizing one group of women by forcing them to accept protection that another group genuinely may need.

Sooner or later, most feminist attempts to formulate an adequate conception of sexual equality run up against the recognition that the baseline for discussions of equality typically has been a male standard. In Catherine MacKinnon's inimitable words:

"Men's physiology defines most sports, their needs define auto and health insurance coverage, their socially designed biographies define workplace expectations and successful career patterns, their perspectives and concerns define quality in scholarship, their experiences and obsessions define merit, their objectification of life defines art, their military service defines citizenship, their presence defines family, their inability to get along with each other—their wars and rulerships—defines history, their image defines god, and their genitals define sex" (MacKinnon 1987:36).

Having once reached this recognition, some feminist theorists have turned away from debating the pros and cons of what MacKinnon calls the "single" versus the "double standard" and begun speculating about the kinds of far-reaching social transformation that would make sex differences "costless" (Littleton 1986). In discussions elaborating such notions as that of "equality as acceptance," feminists seem to be moving towards a radical construal of equality as similarity of individual outcome, equality of condition or effect, a conception quite at odds with traditional liberal understandings of equality as equality of procedure or opportunity.[3]

While some feminists struggle to formulate a conception of sexual equality that is adequate for feminism, others have suggested that the enterprise is hopeless. For them, equality is an integral part of an "ethic of justice" that is characteristically masculine insofar as it obscures human difference by abstracting from the particularity and uniqueness of concrete people in their specific situations and seeks to resolve conflicting interests by applying an abstract rule rather than by responding directly to needs that are immediately perceived. Such feminists suggest that a discourse of responsibility (Finley 1986) or care (Krieger 1987) may offer a more appropriate model for feminist ethics—even including feminist jurisprudence. Both of these suggestions remain to be worked out in detail.

The tangled debate over equality and difference provides an excellent illustration of one characteristic feature of contemporary feminist ethics, namely, its insistence that gender is often, if not invariably, a morally relevant difference between individuals. Given this insistence, the starting point of much feminist ethics may be different from that of modern moral theory: instead of assuming that all individuals should be treated alike until morally relevant ground for difference in treatment can be identified, feminist theorists may shift the traditional burden of moral proof by assuming, until shown otherwise, that contemporary men and women are rarely "similarly situated." This leads into a related and equally crucial question for feminist ethics in the nineties, namely, how to characterize and evaluate impartiality.

2. IMPARTIALITY

In the modern western tradition, impartiality typically has been recognized as a fundamental value, perhaps even a defining characteristic of morality, distinguishing true morality from tribalism (Baier 1958). Impartiality is said to require weighing the interests of each individual equally, permitting differentiation only on the basis of differences that can be shown to be morally relevant. Impartiality thus is linked conceptually with equality and also with rationality and objectivity, insofar as bias often has been defined as the absence of impartiality.

In the last few years, the preeminence traditionally ascribed to impartiality has been challenged both by feminist and nonfeminist philosophers. Nonfeminists have charged that an insistence on impartiality disregards our particular identities, constituted by reference to our particular projects and our unchosen relationships with others; and that it substitutes abstract "variables" for real human agents and patients. Williams (1973, 1981), for instance, has argued that the requirement of impartiality may undermine our personal integrity because it may require us to abandon projects that are central to our identity, and he also suggests that acting from duty may sometimes be less valuable than acting from an immediate emotional response to a particular other. MacIntyre (1981) and Sommers (1986) have argued that impartiality fails to respect tradition, customary expectations and unchosen encumbrances, and may require behavior that is morally repugnant.

While some of the moral intuitions that motivate the nonfeminist critics of impartiality certainly are shared by many feminists, other intuitions most likely are not. It is implausible to suppose, for instance, that most feminists would join Williams in applauding Gaugin's abandonment of his family in order to pursue his art, or that they would join Sommers in accepting without question the claims of customary morality on issues such as women's responsibilities. Instead, the feminist criticisms of impartiality tend to be both less individualistic and less conventionalist. They are quite varied in character.

Nel Noddings (1984) is one of the most extreme opponents of impartiality and her work has been influential with a number of feminists, even though the sub-title of her book makes it clear that she takes herself to be elaborating a feminine rather than a feminist approach to ethics. Noddings views the emotion of caring as the natural basis of morality, a view that would require impartiality to be expressed in universal caring. Noddings claims, however, that we are psychologically able to care only for particular others with whom we are in actual relationships, i.e., relationships that can be "completed" by the cared-for's acknowledgement of our caring. She concludes that pretensions to care for humanity at large are not only hypocritical but self defeating, undermining true caring for those with whom we are in actual relationship. Noddings' arguments, if valid, of course would apply indifferently to caring practiced either by men or by women, and so the distinctively feminist interest of Noddings' work might seem to reside solely in her obviously debatable claim that women are "better equipped for caring than men" (97) and therefore less likely to be impartial. As we have noted already, however, feminist ethics is not committed to reproducing the moral practice even of most women and so feminist (and nonfeminist) moral theorists need to evaluate critically all of Noddings' arguments against impartiality, independently of whether her claims about "feminine" morality can be empirically confirmed.

A different criticism of impartiality has been made by those feminist philosophers who assert that, while impartiality is associated historically with individualism, it paradoxically undermines respect for individuality because it treats individuals as morally interchangeable (Code 1988; Sherwin 1987). Many, though certainly not all, feminists claim that women are less likely than men to commit this alleged moral error because they are more likely to appreciate the special characteristics of particular individuals; again, however, feminist estimates of the soundness or otherwise of Code's and Sherwin's argument must be independent of this empirical claim.

Finally, at least one feminist has extended the claim that women need special protection in the law by recommending that feminist ethics should promote a double standard of morality, limiting moral communities on the basis of gender or perhaps gender solidarity. Susan Sherwin writes that feminists feel a special responsibility to reduce the suffering of women in particular; thus, "(b)y acknowledging the relevance of differences among people as a basis for a difference in sympathy and concern, feminism denies the legitimacy of a central premise of traditional moral theories, namely that all persons should be seen as morally equivalent by us" (Sherwin 1987:26. Cf. also Fisk 1980, Fraser 1986 and Hoagland 1989). However, since women and even feminists are not homogenous groups, as we have seen, this kind of reasoning seems to push the suggested double standard towards becoming a multiple moral standard—which Enlightenment theorists might well interpret as the total abandonment of impartiality and thus of morality itself.

A variety of responses seems to be available to the foregoing criticisms of impartiality. One alternative is to argue that the criticisms are unwarranted, depending on misrepresentation, misunderstanding and caricature of the impartialist position (Herman 1983; Adler 1990). If this response can be sustained, it may be possible to show that there is no real conflict between "masculine" impartialism and "feminine" particularism, "masculine" justice and "feminine" care. Another alternative is to bite the bullet of direct moral confrontation, providing arguments to challenge the intuitions of those who criticize impartiality as requiring courses of action that are morally repugnant or politically dangerous. Yet a third alternative may be to reconceive the concept of impartiality and the considerations appropriate for determining our responsibilities toward various individuals and groups. Feminist ethics must find a way of choosing between those or other options and evaluating the proper place of impartiality in ethics for the nineties.

3. MORAL SUBJECTIVITY

Related to the foregoing questions about impartiality are questions about how to conceptualize individuals, the subjects of moral theory. Feminists and nonfeminists alike have criticized the neo-Cartesian model of the moral self, a disembodied, separate, autonomous, unified, rational being, essentially similar to all other moral selves. Marx challenged the ahistoricism of this model; Freud challenged its claims to rationality; contemporary communitarians, such as Sandel and MacIntyre, challenge the assumption that individuals are "unencumbered," arguing instead that we are all members of communities from which we may be able to distance ourselves to some extent but which nevertheless are deeply constitutive of our identities; postmodernists have deconstructed the model to reveal fractured rather than unitary identities.

The gender bias alleged to contaminate each of the traditions mentioned above means that feminists cannot appropriate uncritically existing critiques of the neo-Cartesian moral self. Nevertheless, in developing their own challenges to this model of the self, feminist theorists often have paralleled and/or built on some non-feminist work. For instance, feminist investigations into the social imposition of gender have drawn on neo-Freudian object relations theory in demonstrating how this central feature of our identity is socially constructed rather than given (e.g., Chodorow 1978). Code's and Sherwin's previously mentioned accusations that modern moral theory recognizes individuals only as abstract variables, representatives of social types, is reminiscent of communitarian discussions of the encumbered self. And further connections with communitarianism, as well as phenomenology and Marxism, may be seen in the growing philosophical interest among feminists in embodiment and the ways in which it is constitutive of our identity (e.g., Spelman 1982; Young 1990). All these theorists offer distinctively feminist grounds for resisting the universalism, essentialism and ahistoricity of the Cartesian model and for refocusing on the need to recognize particularity and difference in conceptualizing the self.

Other feminist critiques of the neo-Cartesian subject concentrate on the common modern construal of rationality as egoism, which "overlooks the fact that millions of people (most of them women) have spent millions of hours for hundreds of years giving their utmost to millions of others" (Miller, 1976). Others have challenged the frequent modern assumption, (explicit, for instance, in utilitarian revealed preference theory), that expressed or even felt desires and needs can be taken at face value, as givens in moral theory, pointing to the need for feminist ethics to offer an account of the social construction of desire and to suggest a way of conceptualizing the distinction between what the Marxist tradition has called "true" and "false" needs (Jaggar 1983). Feminist explorations of the power of ideology over the unconscious and the revelation of conflicts within the self have challenged the Cartesian assumption of the unity of the self, as well as the assumption that the self is essentially rational (Grimshaw 1988). Finally, descriptions of women's supposed "morality of caring" (Gilligan 1982) have challenged the assumption of the ontological separateness of the self and reinforced the importance, perhaps even the moral or epistemological priority, of the self as part of a moral and epistemic community.

Given this burgeoning literature, it is evident that a central concern for feminist ethics in the nineties must be to develop ways of thinking about moral subjects that are sensitive both to their concreteness, inevitable particularity and unique specificity, expressed in part through their relations with specific historical communities, and to their intrinsic and common value, the ideal expressed in Enlightenment claims about common humanity, equality and impartiality (Benhabib, 1986).

4. AUTONOMY

One aspect of this task is the rethinking of autonomy which, like impartiality, (to which it is often conceptually connected), has been a continuing ideal of modern moral theory. (In addition, a closely related concept of autonomy has played a central role in the Cartesian epistemological tradition, which envisions the search for knowledge as a project of the solitary knower. The core intuition of autonomy is that of independence or self legislation, the self as the ultimate authority in matters of morality or truth. In the Kantian tradition, where the ideal of autonomy is particularly prominent, moral autonomy has been elaborated in terms of disinterest, detachment from particular attachments and interests, and freedom from prejudice and self-deception (Hill, 1987).

Contemporary feminists have had a mixed response to the modern ideal of moral autonomy. On the one hand, they have insisted that women are as autonomous in the moral and intellectual senses as men—as rational, as capable of a sense of justice, and so on: and they have also demanded political, social and economic autonomy for women through political representation, the abolition of sex discrimination and respect for women's choices on issues such as abortion. On the other hand, however, some feminists have questioned traditional interpretations of autonomy as masculine fantasies. For instance, they have explored some of the ways in which "choice" is socialized and "consent" manipulated (MacKinnon 1987; Meyers 1987). In addition, they have questioned the possibility of separating ourselves from particular attachments and still retaining our personal identity, and they have suggested that freeing ourselves from particular attachments might result in a cold, rigid, moralistic rather than a truly moral response (Noddings 1984). Rather than guaranteeing a response that is purely moral, freeing ourselves from particular attachments might instead make us incapable of morality if an ineliminable part of morality consists in responding emotionally to particular others.

Feminist ethics in the nineties must find ways of conceptualizing moral agency, choice and consent that are compatible with the feminist recognition of the gradual process of moral development, the gendered social construction of the psyche, and the historical constraints on our options. This is one area in which some promising work by feminists exists already (Holmstrom 1977; Gibson 1985: Meyers 1987).

5. MORAL EPISTEMOLOGY
AND ANTI-EPISTEMOLOGY

Enlightenment moral theory characteristically assumed that morality was universal—that, if moral claims held, they were valid at all times and in all places.
However, the modern abandonment of belief in a teleological and sacred universe
rendered the justification of such claims constantly problematic, and much moral
theory for the last three centuries has consisted in attempts to provide a rational
grounding for morality. At the present time, both the continental European tradition, especially but not only in the form of post-modernism, and the Anglo-
American tradition, especially but not only in the form of communitarianism, have
developed powerful challenges to the very possibility of the view that morality consists in universally valid rules grounded in universal reason. The inevitable result of
these skeptical challenges has been to reinforce normative and meta-ethical relativism.

Feminists are ambivalent about these challenges. On the one hand, many of
the feminist criticisms of modern moral theory parallel the criticisms made by communitarianism and post-modernism. On the other hand, however, feminists are un-
derstandably concerned that their critique of male dominance should not be
dismissed as just one point of view. It is therefore crucial for feminist ethics to develop some way of justifying feminist moral claims. However, moral epistemology is
an area in which feminists' critiques are better developed than their alternatives.

Feminist discussions of moral epistemology may be divided into two categories,
each distinguished by a somewhat different view of the nature of morality. Feminists
in the first category do not explicitly challenge the modern conception of morality as
consisting primarily in an impartial system of rationally justified rules or principles,
though few feminists would assert that it is possible to identify rules that are substantive, specific and hold in all circumstances. Those in the second category, by contrast,
deny that morality is reducible to rules and emphasize the impossibility of justifying
the claims of ethics by appeal to a universal, impartial reason. The contrast between
these two groups of feminists is not as sharp as this initial characterization might suggest: for instance, both share several criticisms of existing decision procedures in
ethics. But feminists in the former group are more hopeful of repairing those procedures, while feminists in the latter group seem ready to abandon them entirely.

Feminists in the latter group frequently claim to be reflecting on a moral experience that is distinctively feminine and for this reason they are often—in-
correctly—taken to represent a feminist orthodoxy. They include authors such as
Gilligan (1982), Noddings (1984), Baier (1987), Blum (1987), Ruddick (1989) and
Walker (1989). While there is considerable variation in the views of these authors,
they all reject the view attributed to modern moral theorists that the right course
of action can be discovered by consulting a list of moral rules, charging that undue emphasis on the epistemological importance of rules obscures the crucial role
of moral insight, virtue and character in determining what should be done. A feminist twist is given to this essentially Aristotelian criticism when claims are made
that excessive reliance on rules reflects a juridical-administrative interest that is

characteristic of modern masculinity (Blum 1982) while contemporary women, by contrast, are alleged to be more likely to disregard conventionally accepted moral rules because such rules are insensitive to the specificities of particular situations (Gilligan 1982; Noddings 1984). A morality of rule, therefore is alleged to devalue the moral wisdom of women, as well as to give insufficient weight to such supposedly feminine virtues as kindness, generosity, helpfulness and sympathy.

Some feminists have claimed that "feminine" approaches to morality contrast with supposedly masculine rule-governed approaches in that they characteristically consist in immediate responses to particular others, responses based on supposedly natural feelings of empathy, care and compassion (Gilligan 1982; Noddings 1984) or loving attention (Murdoch 1970; Ruddick 1989). However, apart from the difficulties of establishing that such a "particularist" approach to morality (Blum 1987) indeed is characteristically feminine, let alone feminist, attempts to develop a moral epistemology based on such responses face a variety of problems. First, they confront the familiar, though perhaps not insuperable, problems common to all moral epistemologies that take emotion as a guide to right action, namely, the frequent inconsistency, unavailability or plain inappropriateness of emotions (Lind 1989). In other words, they face the danger of degenerating into a "do what feels good" kind of subjective relativism. In addition, it is not clear that even our emotional responses to others are not responses to them under some universal description and so in this sense general rather than particular—or, if indeed particular and therefore nonconceptual, then perhaps closer to animal than to distinctively human responses. It is further uncertain how these sorts of particular responses can guide our actions towards large numbers of people, most of whom we shall never meet. Finally, the feminist emphasis on the need for "contextual" reasoning opens up the obvious dangers of ad hocism, special pleading and partiality.

Not all feminists, of course, are committed to a particularist moral epistemology. Even some of those who take emotions as a proper guide to morality emphasize the intentionality of emotions and discuss the need for their moral education. Additionally, while most feminists criticize certain aspects of the decision procedures developed by modern moral theory,[4] some believe it may be possible to revise and reappropriate some of these procedures. The main candidates for such revision are the methods developed by Rawls and Habermas, each of whom believes that an idealized situation of dialogue (which each describes differently) will both generate and justify morally valid principles.

Rawls's decision procedure has been the target of a number of feminist criticisms. Okin, for instance, as noted earlier, has argued that Rawls's procedure will not generate moral consensus unless the considered judgments of men and women coincide, a coincidence she believes quite unlikely in any society that continues to be structured by gender. She has also attacked Rawls's assumption that the parties in the original position will be heads of households, correctly noting that this precludes them from considering the justice of household arrangements (1987). Benhabib (1986) has argued that those who reason behind Rawls's veil of ignorance are so ignorant of their own circumstances that they have lost the specific identities characteristic of human agents. She takes this to mean that "there is no real *plurality* of perspectives in the Rawlsian original position, but only a *definitional identity*" (413, italics in original). Benhabib criticizes what she calls this "monological" model of moral reasoning on the grounds that, by restricting itself to "the standpoint of the generalized other" and ignoring the "standpoint of the concrete other," it deprives itself of much morally relevant information necessary to adequately utilize the Kantian moral tests of reversibility and universalizability. In spite of these criticisms, Okin (1989) believes that Rawls's hypothetical contract procedure can be revised in such a way as to incorporate feminist concerns about justice within the household, about empathy and care and about difference.

Benhabib (1986) suggests that a "communicative ethic of need interpretations," based on Habermas's account of an ideal dialogue, is capable of overcoming what she perceives as Rawlsian monologism. It does this by acknowledging the differences of concrete others in ways compatible with the contextualist concerns that Gilligan attributes to women who utilize the ethic of care. Other feminists, such as Fraser (1986) and Young (1986), also seem attracted to such a method, although Young criticizes Habermasian descriptions of ideal dialogue for failing to take account of the affective and bodily dimensions of meaning (395). In order to genuinely acknowledge the specific situations of concrete others, however, an actual rather than hypothetical dialogue seems to be required, albeit a dialogue under carefully specified conditions. But it is hard to imagine how actual dialogue could even approximate fairness in a world of unequal power, unequal access to the "sociocultural means of interpretation and communication" (Fraser 1986) and even unequal availability of time for moral reflection and debate.

One possible alternative both to an unwelcome relativism and to what many feminists see as the pretensions of moral rationalism may be the development of a moral standpoint that is distinctively feminist. Sara Ruddick claims that such a standpoint can be found in maternal thinking (1989) but her work has been criticized by some feminists as ethnocentric (Lugones 1988) and overvaluing motherhood (Hoagland 1989). Even if the feminist standpoint were differently identified, however, problems would remain. Standpoint epistemology derives from Marx and, at least in its Lukacsian version, it seems to require an objectivist distinction between appearance and reality that is quite alien to the social constructionist tendencies in much contemporary feminism.

The controversy in feminist moral epistemology currently is so sharp that Held (1984) has suggested abandoning the search for a "unified field theory" covering all domains of life activity. However, other authors have pointed to the danger that, if a supposedly feminine "ethic of care" were limited to the realm of personal life, as Kohlberg, for instance has suggested, it would be perceived as subordinate to the supposedly masculine "ethic of justice," just as, in contemporary society, the private is subordinate to the public.

CONCLUSION

Even such a limited survey as this should make it evident that feminist ethics, far from being a rigid orthodoxy, instead is a ferment of ideas and controversy, many of them echoing and deepening debates in nonfeminist ethics. The centrality of the issues and the liveliness of the on-going discussions suggest that the nineties will be a fruitful period for feminist ethics—and thus for ethics generally.

NOTES

1. Many of the ideas in this paper have been developed in the course of long-term discussions with Marcia Lind. This paper has benefitted tremendously from her insistent questioning and from her insightful responses to earlier drafts. Pamela Grath also made a number of helpful comments.

2. "Nonfeminists" here refers to philosophers who do not make their feminist concerns explicit in their philosophical work; it is not intended to imply that such philosophers do not demonstrate feminist concern in other ways.

3. Feminists moving in this direction seem to be paralleling Marx's move, in his *Critique of the Gotha Programme*, towards a society where an emphasis on equality of rights has been abandoned, since the differences between individuals result in its producing inequalities of outcome, and where the principle of social organization is: "From each according to his (sic) ability, to each according to his (sic) needs."

4. Most feminists, for instance, perceive traditional formulations of social contract theory to be male biased in various ways (Jaggar 1983; Held 1987; Pateman 1988).

REFERENCES

Adler, Jonathan, "Particularity, Gilligan and the Two-levels View: A Reply," *Ethics* 100:1 (October 1990).

Baier, Annette, "The Need for More than Justice," *Science, Morality and Feminist Theory*, ed. Marsha Hanen and Kai Nielsen, Calgary: University of Calgary Press, 1987.

Baier, Kurt, *The Moral Point of View: A Rational Basis of Ethics*, New York: Random House, 1958.

Benhabib, Seyla, "The Generalized and the Concrete Other: The Kohlberg-Gilligan Controversy and Feminist Theory," *Praxis International* 5:4 (January 1986).

Blum, Lawrence, "Kant's and Hegel's Moral Rationalism: A Feminist Perspective" *Canadian Journal of Philosophy* 12:2 (June 1982).

Blum, Lawrence, "Particularity and Responsiveness," *The Emergence of Morality in Young Children*, eds. Jerome Kagan and Sharon Lamb, Chicago: University of Chicago Press, 1987.

Chodorow, Nancy, *The Reproduction of Mothering: Psychoanalysis and the Sociology of Gender*, Berkeley: University of California Press, 1987.

Code, Lorraine, "Experience, Knowledge and Responsibility," *Feminist Perspectives in Philosophy*, edited by Morwenna Griffiths and Margaret Whitford, Bloomington & Indianapolis: Indiana University Press, 1988.

Finley, Lucinda M., "Transcending Equality Theory: A Way Out of the Maternity and the Workplace Debate," *Columbia Law Review* 86:6 (October, 1986).

Fisk, Milton, *Ethics and Society: A Marxist Interpretation of Value*, New York: New York University Press, 1980.

Fraser, Nancy, "Toward a Discourse Ethic of Solidarity," *Praxis International* 5:4 (January, 1986).

Freedman, Estelle, "Separatism as Strategy: Female Institution Building and American Feminism 1870-1930," *Feminist Studies* 5:3 (1979).

Gibson, Mary, "Consent and Autonomy," *To Breathe Freely: Risk, Consent and Air*, Totowa, NJ: Rowman & Allanheld, 1985.

Gilligan, Carol, *In a Different Voice: Psychological Theory and Women's Development*, Cambridge, MA: Harvard University Press, 1982.

Grimshaw, Jean, "Autonomy and Identity in Feminist Thinking," *Feminist Perspectives in Philosophy*, eds. Morwenna Griffiths and Margaret Whitford, Bloomington and Indianapolis: Indiana University Press, 1988.

Held, Virginia, *Rights and Goods*, New York: The Free Press, 1984.

Held, Virginia, "Non-Contractual Society," *Science, Morality and Feminist Theory*, eds. Marsha Hanen and Kai Nielsen, Calgary: University of Calgary Press, 1987.

Herman, Barbara, "Integrity and Impartiality," *The Monist* 66:2 (April 1983).

Hill, Thomas E., Jr., "The Importance of Autonomy," *Women and Moral Theory*, eds. Eva Feder Kittay and Diana T. Meyers, Totowa, NJ: Rowman and Littlefield, 1987.

Hoagland, Sarah Lucia, *Lesbian Ethics: Toward New Value*, Palo Alto, CA: Institute of Lesbian Studies, 1989.

Holmstrom, Nancy, "Firming Up Soft Determinism," *The Personalist* 58:1(1977).

Jaggar, Alison M., *Feminist Politics and Human Nature*, Totowa, NJ: Rowman and Allanheld, 1983.

King, Ynestra, "Afterword," *Rocking the Ship of State: Toward a Feminist Peace Politics*, ed. Adrienne Harris and Ynestra King, Boulder, CO: Westview Press, 1989.

Krieger, Linda J., "Through a Glass Darkly: Paradigms of Equality and the Search for a Woman's Jurisprudence," *Hypatia: A Journal of Feminist Philosophy* 2:1 (1987).

Lind, Marcia, "Hume and Feminist Moral Theory," paper read at conference on Explorations in Feminist Ethics: Theory and Practice, University of Minnesota-Duluth, October 7–8, 1988.

Lugones, Maria, "The Logic of Pluralism," paper read at the annual meeting of the American Philosophical Association (Eastern Division), Washington, D.C., December 1988.

MacIntyre, Alasdair, *After Virtue: A Study in Moral Theory*, London: Duckworth, 1981.

MacKinnon, Catharine A., *Feminism Unmodified: Discourses on Life and Law*, Cambridge, MA: Harvard University Press 1987.

Meyers, Diana T., "Personal Autonomy and the Paradox of Feminine Socialization," *Journal of Philosophy* LXXXIV:11 (November, 1987).

Meyers, Diana T., "The Socialized Individual and Individual Autonomy: An Intersection between Philosophy and Psychology," *Women and Moral Theory*, ed. Eva Feder Kittay and Diana T. Meyers, Totowa, NJ: Rowman & Allanheld, 1987.

Miller, Jean Baker, *Toward a New Psychology of Women*, Boston: Beacon, 1976.

Murdoch, Iris, *The Sovereignty of Good*, London: Routledge & Kegan Paul, 1970.

Noddings, Nel, *Caring: A Feminine Approach to Ethics and Moral Education*, Berkeley: University of California Press, 1984.

Okin, Susan Moller, "Justice and Gender," *Philosophy and Public Affairs*, 16:1, (Winter 1987).

Okin, Susan Moller, "Reason and Feeling in Thinking about Justice," *Ethics* 99:2 (January, 1989).

Plumwood, Val, "Do We Need a Sex/Gender Distinction?" *Radical Philosophy* 51 (Spring, 1989).

Ringelheim, Joan, "Women and the Holocaust: A Reconsideration in Research," *Signs* 10:4 (Summer 1985).

Ruddick, Sara, "Maternal Thinking," *Feminist Studies* 6:2 (Summer 1980).

Ruddick, Sara, "Preservative Love and Military Destruction: Some Reflections on Mothering and Peace," *Mothering: Essays in Feminist Theory*, ed. Joyce Trebilcot, Totowa, NJ: Rowman and Allanheld, 1984.

Ruddick, Sara, *Maternal Thinking: Toward a Politics of Peace*, Boston: Beacon Press, 1989.

Sherwin, Susan, "A Feminist Approach to Ethics," *Resources for Feminist Research* 16:3, 1987. (Special issue on Women and Philosophy)

Sommers, Christina Hoff, "Filial Morality," *The Journal of Philosophy* 83:8 (August 1986).

Spelman, Elizabeth V., Inessential Woman: Problems of Exclusion in Feminist Thought, Boston: Beacon, 1989.

Walker, Margaret, "Moral Understandings: Alternative 'Epistemology' for a Feminist Ethics," *Hypatia: A Journal of Feminist Philosophy* 4:2 (Summer 1989).

Weitzman, Lenore J., *The Divorce Revolution*, New York: The Free Press, 1985.

Williams, B., "A Critique of Utilitarianism," *Utilitarianism: For and Against*, Cambridge: Cambridge University Press, 1973.

Williams, B., "Morality and the Emotions," *Problems of the Self*, Cambridge: Cambridge University Press, 1973.

Williams, B., "Persons, Character, and Morality," "Moral Luck," and "Utilitarianism and Moral Self-indulgence," *Moral Luck*, Cambridge: Cambridge University Press, 1981.

Williams, Wendy W., "Equality's Riddle: Pregnancy and the Equal Treatment/Special Treatment Debate," *New York University Review of Law and Social Change* XIII:2 (1984–5).

Young, Iris Marion, "Impartiality and the Civic Public," *Praxis International* 5:4 (January 1986).

Young, Iris Marion, "Throwing Like a Girl: A Phenomenology of Feminine Body Comportment, Motility and Spatiality," "Pregnant Embodiment: Subjectivity and Alienation," "Breast as Experience: The Look and the Feeling," *Stretching Out: Essays in Feminist Social Theory and Female Body Experience*, Bloomington: Indiana University Press, 1990.

SUGGESTIONS FOR DISCUSSION

1. What are the characteristics of a specifically feminist moral theory? What are the differences between liberal feminism, gender feminism, radical feminism, and socialist feminism?
2. Is there a distinctively woman's voice regarding ethical matters? Would a woman's moral voice take issue with the principle of impartiality?
3. Would an ethics of care promote a different conception of citizenship than a Kantian, libertarian, or communitarian (see Chapter 8)? How might an ethics of care recommend we respond to the plight of a close friend or a distant co-worker we just learned is hospitalized with complications from AIDS (see Chapter 11)?

FOR FURTHER READING

Antony, L. M., and Witt, C., eds. *A Mind of One's Own: Feminist Essays on Reason and Objectivity.* Boulder: Westview Press, 1992.

Baier, A. "What Do Women Want in a Moral Theory." *Nous,* vol. 19 (March 1985): 53–63.

Card, C., ed. *Feminist Ethics.* Lawrence: University Press of Kansas, 1991.

Chodorow, N. *The Reproduction of Mothering: Psychoanalysis and the Sociology of Gender.* Berkeley: University of California Press, 1987.

Finley, L. M. "Transcending Equality Theory: A Way Out of the Maternity and the Workplace Debate." *Columbia Law Review* 86: 6 (October 1986: 1118–1183).

Fraser, N. *Unruly Practices.* Minneapolis: University of Minnesota Press, 1989.

Freedman, E., "Separatism as Strategy: Female Institution Building and American Feminism 1870–1930." *Feminist Studies* 5, 3 (1979) 512–29.

Gilligan, C. *In a Different Voice: Psychological Theory and Women's Development.* Cambridge: Harvard University Press, 1982.

Griffiths, M., and Whitford, M. *Feminist Perspectives in Philosophy.* Edited by Bloomington & Indianapolis: Indiana University Press, 1988.

Hanen, M., and Nielsen, K., eds. *Science, Morality and Feminist Theory.* Calgary: University of Calgary Press, 1987.

Held, V. *Rights and Goods,* New York: The Free Press, 1984.

Herman, B. "Integrity and Impartiality." *The Monist* 66, 2 (April 1983) 233–50.

Hoagland, S. L. *Lesbian Ethics: Toward New Value.* Palo Alto, Calif.: Institute of Lesbian Studies, 1989.

Jaggar, A. M. *Feminist Politics and Human Nature.* Totowa, N.J. Rowman and Allanheld, 1983.

King, Y. "Afterword." *Rocking the Ship of State: Toward a Feminist Peace Politics.* ed. A. Harris and Y. King, Boulder: Westview Press, 1989.

Kittay, E., and Meyers, D., eds. *Women and Moral Theory.* Totowa, N.J.: Rowman and Littlefield, 1987.

Krieger, L. J. "Through a Glass Darkly: Paradigms of Equality and the Search for a Woman's Jurisprudence." *Hypatia: A Journal of Feminist Philosophy* 2, 1 (1987) 45–61.

Larrabee, M. J., ed. *An Ethic of Care: Feminist and Interdisciplinary Perspectives.* New York: Routledge, 1993.

MacKinnon, C. A. *Feminism Unmodified: Discourses on Life and Law.* Cambridge: Harvard University Press, 1987.

Meyers, D. T. "Personal Autonomy and the Paradox of Feminine Socialization." *Journal of Philosophy* LXXXIV, 11 (November 1987) 619–29.

Noddings, N. *Caring: A Feminine Approach to Ethics and Moral Education.* Berkeley: University of California Press. 1984.

Okin, S. M. "Justice and Gender." *Philosophy and Public Affairs* 16, 1, (Winter 1987) 42–72.

————. "Reason and Feeling in Thinking about Justice." *Ethics* 99, 2 (January 1989) 229–49.

Ruddick, S. *Maternal Thinking: Toward a Politics of Peace.* Boston: Beacon Press, 1989.

Sherwin, S. "A Feminist Approach to Ethics." *Resources for Feminist Research* 16, 3 (1987) 25–8. (Special issue on Women and Philosophy).

Sommers, C. H. "Filial Morality." *The Journal of Philosophy* 83, 8 (August 1986) 439–56.

Spelman, E. V. *Inessential Woman: Problems of Exclusion in Feminist Thought.* Boston: Beacon, 1989.

Tong, R. *Feminine and Feminist Ethics.* Belmont: Wadsworth, 1993.

Trebilcot, Joyce, ed. *Mothering: Essays in Feminist Theory.* Totowa, N.J.: Rowman and Allanheld, 1984.

Walker, M. "Moral Understandings: Alternative 'Epistemology' for a Feminist Ethics." *Hypatia: A Journal of Feminist Philosophy* 4, 2 (Summer 1989) 15–28.

PART THREE

SOCIAL ISSUES:

CONTEMPORARY READINGS

INTRODUCTION

Moral Theory and Scientific Theory   The application of principles theoretically elaborated in Parts I and II to the pressing social issues of Part III will serve as a testing ground for moral theory. It may prove instructive to draw a parallel here between moral and scientific theory. Like scientific theories, moral theories must be assessed against empirical data. The data for morality are generally the set of common, firmly held, and reasoned convictions and principles concerning permissible social behavior and relationships. If a moral theory, directly or by implication, is inconsistent with some widely held, cherished, and reasoned conviction, such as the wrongness of taking innocent life, it may be sufficient grounds to reject the theory.

Moral theory can be likened to scientific theory in a further sense. An acceptable moral theory must not simply rationalize established or widely expressed beliefs and practices. A revolution in scientific theory will usually lead to new discoveries, to viewing the world in a new way, and to new knowledge. Similarly, a moral theory may lead us to acknowledge that some beliefs or social practices are morally unacceptable. We may discover something morally pertinent about ourselves, about our relations to others and to our world. If taken seriously, this discovery should lead us to change our social convictions and behavior in the relevant way.

A recent example of this is the widespread appeal to rights in social, political, and moral analysis. The concept of rights can be traced back in moral theory at least to Hobbes (Chapter 2). Nevertheless, the contemporary theoretical currency of rights analysis was prompted in large part by the civil rights and nationalist movements of the 1960s. The theoretical refinement of the concept that followed has established more clearly the kinds of social practices now—in this country at this time—generally deemed to be acceptable. Many of the arguments concerning the social issues discussed in Part III turn on basic appeals to rights. Application of this concept to actual social contexts and problems may lead in turn to further refinement or to acknowledging the limits of the concept's applicability.

Basic and Intermediate Principles   In applying moral theory to determine ethical practice, some ethicists have assumed the model of *deduction*. Moral policies or acts are supposed to be logically derivable directly from basic ethical principles and the relevant facts. Like the principles from which they are deduced, the policy or act conclusion is considered unchangeable, even if it is inconsistent with firmly held moral intuitions about the issue at hand. However, most agree that the application of theoretical ethics to genuine ethical problems requires sensitivity to a variety of issues. The choice of intermediate principles linking ethical theory to act or policy decisions for some concrete issue is crucially important. (Philosophers sometimes call these "bridging principles.") Choosing one intermediate or bridging principle rather than another as relevant to the case at hand is important, for it may critically alter how a proposed act or policy will be judged. For example, two people may agree on the basic importance of the Principle of Liberty (that is, that people should be free to do with their lives as they choose), yet disagree on which intermediate principles may limit liberty in some context. So one person may accept the Offense Principle as justifying a legitimate limitation of the liberty of sexist expression; while another may argue that only actual harm (the Harm Principle), and not mere subjective offense, supports morally acceptable restrictions on freedoms or rights (see Chapter 10). Moreover, different moral theories may weigh the same basic principle differently. Kantianism and utilitarianism may agree that respect for persons is an important value. Yet a Kantian must reject any attempt to qualify or override the Principle of Respect, while a utilitarian must be willing to sacrifice it if this would maximize utility.

In their concern to resolve a genuine moral dilemma posed by a specific social issue, many ethicists reject the constraints of deductive purism. Instead, they call to clarify the appropriate moral concepts and to present the moral facts accurately. The various basic and intermediate principles offered by each of the competing theories must be compared, their strengths assessed against the moral data and refined accordingly. For example, the morality of abortion will involve knowing the facts about fetal development and pertinent socioeconomic data, analyzing the concept of personhood, and weighing the relative importance of various basic principles (such as respect and autonomy) and intermediate principles (such as the right to life and the right to choose). In the final analysis, then, the moral decision must rest with informed and reasoned judgment.

Theory and Practice   Ethical theories, as Aristotle noted, are fundamentally theories of right action and virtuous character. One of the ultimate tests of a moral theory is whether it is capable of guiding action and public policy in a reasoned manner. Part III of this book provides contending philosophical analyses of important contemporary social and legal issues. These contending positions on such issues as the permissibility of euthanasia or capital punishment may be grounded in different, often competing ethical theories. Understanding the underlying theoretical terrain will clarify the respective arguments and reveal the seriousness of competing viewpoints. It will help to direct criticism where it is due and, most importantly, it should encourage tolerance for those whose reasoned views conflict with one's own. Attempting to resolve conflicts over social issues in this way will commit persons to use reasoned means when trying to convince those holding opposing views, for reasonable deliberation and critical exchange are surely preferable to the unpredictability of unreasonable aggression.

CHAPTER EIGHT

CITIZENSHIP

American citizenship is valued highly both by those who are U.S. citizens and by many who are not. Whether or not U.S. citizens honor the flag, sing the anthem, support particular military campaigns, or cheer for national teams, only revolution or emigration would amount to a wholesale rejection of citizen status. More generally, citizenship or belonging to some nation-state is virtually a practical necessity; the stateless condition is generally considered undesirable. Citizenship defines full membership in the modern nation state. Criteria of citizenship, then, define degrees of exclusion from such membership. The property, literacy, racial, and gender qualifications on citizenship in the eighteenth century have gradually given way, in theory and practice, to the insistence on equal treatment for all those meeting minimal formal criteria for membership. Traditionally, citizenship has turned on either *jus sanguinis* (the law of blood) or *jus naturalis* (the law of birth or naturalization). In the United States, unlike Germany, say, the latter has always been insisted upon and the former rejected. Citizens are those born in the United States or who meet broad formal criteria for naturalization, criteria that are expected to be applied equally and impartially to all applicants.

The fact that application has never been impartial or equal across groups (immigration law has long placed quotas in terms of national origins) raises central concerns about the justice of citizenship. Generally, are the criteria for membership in the society to be established on the basis of maximizing the interests of existing members? Liberal philosophers like Rousseau, Kant, and Rawls (see Chapter 3 and 5) might reject this basis because of its lack of impartiality (state membership may be considered a morally irrelevant category). By contrast, utilitarians might be committed to answering this question in the affirmative, which may justify at least property (or wealth) and skill qualifications for immigrants. If a distinction between treatment of members and nonmembers of the nation state can be sustained, we are left with the question concerning the nature of equal treatment of citizens. Minimally, membership would seem to entail equal treatment before the law and equal political rights, thereby denying hereditary privileges. The more controversial issues here concern, first, whether such rights imply any degree of social and economic equality and, second, what citizens obligations they presuppose or necessitate and what virtues define good citizenship.

It is in light of these questions, and various responses to them, that the following chapters are to be read. Thus, the later contributions in this book—those discussing affirmative action, censorship and bigoted speech, AIDS, discrimination, and the distribution of health care resources, and abortion, euthanasia, and capital punishment—may be interpreted as debates about the scope of rights and duties facing citizens in a liberal democratic polity and a capitalist economic order of the kind found in the United States or Canada.

■ **LAWRENCE MEAD: CITIZENSHIP AND ENTITLEMENTS**

Welfare programs in the United States are characterized usually as entitlements. Accordingly, those citizens who qualify for the programs can claim a right to their benefits. Since the 1930s, U.S. citizens have come to understand such entitlements as a mark or value of citizenship. Lawrence Mead argues that the problem with viewing welfare programs supporting the disadvantaged and unemployed as entitlements or rights-based is that they are too permissive. They extend benefits—or more rhetorically, handouts—while making no demands on the civic performance of recipients. Thus Mead attributes the central problem of welfare programs in the United States not to their size but to their failure to impose obligations on dependents. Equal citizenship here is taken to mean having the same rights and duties as others. Mead concludes that an authoritative social policy should require dependents to face the same sort of discipline and obligations regarding work and social relations as faced by those independent of direct government support. Noncompliance with these obligations would be rendered relatively intolerable by the sufferance of sanction. Mead's analysis rests on a Hobbesian conception of government: the purpose of the state is primarily to maintain order and security for its citizens rather than to promote freedom (on Hobbes, see Chapter 2). Social freedom is deemed possible only once the socioeconomic conditions for order have been substantially realized. Order presupposes self-discipline and a degree of worker competence on the part of all citizens, including welfare recipients, and *authoritative* rather than *permissive* social policies is thought to promote civic self-discipline.

Lawrence M. Mead

BEYOND ENTITLEMENT: THE SOCIAL OBLIGATIONS OF CITIZENSHIP

THE PROBLEM OF SOCIAL OBLIGATION IN SOCIAL POLICY

. . . My question is why federal programs since 1960 have coped so poorly with the various social problems that have come to afflict American society. These twenty-five years have seen a succession of new programs for the needy, disadvantaged, and unemployed pour forth from Washington. But during the same period welfare de-

From Lawrence M. Mead, *Beyond Entitlement: The Social Obligations of Citizenship* (New York: The Free Press, 1986). Reprinted by permission of the author and Macmillan.

pendency and unemployment have grown, standards have fallen in the schools, and rising crime has made some areas of American cities almost uninhabitable. In all these respects there has been a sharp decline in the habits of competence and restraint that are essential to a humane society. The public never wished for this state of affairs, but government has seemed powerless to affect it.

Part of the explanation, I propose, is that the federal programs that support the disadvantaged and unemployed have been permissive in character, not authoritative. That is, they have given benefits to their recipients but have set few requirements for how they ought to function in return. In particular, the programs have as yet no serious requirements that employable recipients work in return for support. There is good reason to think that recipients subject to such requirements would function better.

Policy is permissive, in turn, for reasons rooted in the libertarian nature of American politics, especially at the federal level. Because of the way social policy is approached in Washington, as well as for electoral and constitutional reasons, federal politicians tend to use social programs simply to give deserving people good things, seldom to set standards for how they ought to behave. Thus dependent groups are shielded from the pressures to function well that impinge on other Americans. A more authoritative social policy has begun to emerge, but it faces stiff resistance from the benefit-oriented habits of federal politics.[1]

The term "social policy" is less abstract than it sounds. Federal social policy is summed up in the specific programs Washington has developed over the years for meeting the needs of vulnerable Americans. They include programs like Social Security and Medicare that serve the general public without regard to need, but [here] the focus is mainly on programs for the needy and disadvantaged, particularly welfare and employment programs. In essence federal social policy amounts to the specific things these programs do for, and expect from, their recipients.

The "welfare state" is more than a metaphor. By what they do and do not expect, social programs directly govern their recipients. The fatal weakness of federal programs is that they award their benefits essentially as entitlements, expecting next to nothing from the beneficiaries in return. The world the recipients live in is economically depressed yet privileged in one sense, that it emphasizes their claims and needs almost to the exclusion of obligations.

The approach to social policy taken here emphasizes the balance of rights and duties that programs imply for recipients. Such an approach has not been usual. The programs have been planned and studied mainly by economists, who seldom address their legal and administrative aspects. Lawyers, who do, have usually been interested in defining the claims of the recipients against government even more clearly, not in strengthening government's claims on them. Political scientists tend to see programs as occasions for political dispute between the parties, politicians, Executive and Congress. Very little attention has been paid to the potential the programs have to set norms for the public functioning of citizens.

This history reflects the fact that American politics has largely been about the *extent* and not the *nature* of government. The main questions have been where to divide public authority from individual rights, and government regulation from the unfettered free market. Those are the issues that chiefly divide Republicans and Democrats, and have done so since the New Deal. Firmly in that tradition, most prescriptions for American social policy say that Washington is doing either *too much* or *too little* for the poor.

There is substantial agreement about the nature of the social problem. A class of Americans, heavily poor and nonwhite, exists apart from the social mainstream. That is, it has very little contact with other Americans in the public aspects of American life, especially in schools, the workplace, and politics. This *social* separation is more worrisome to most Americans than the material deprivations that go along with disadvantage. Secondarily, problems of nonwork and low productivity have recently surfaced even among better-integrated members of the workforce, helping to account for the country's declining economic competitiveness. While performance difficulties are greatest among the underclass, they are not at all confined to it. There is also substantial agreement that the solution for the disadvantaged must mean integration, that is, an end to the separation so that the disadvantaged can publicly interact with others and be accepted by them as equals. I shall use "social problem" to mean this separation and "integration" to mean overcoming it.

The disagreement is over the role of government in that solution, and specifically over the *scale* of government. Conservatives, for example George Gilder or Charles Murray, say that an overblown welfare state has undermined the vitality of the private economy and deterred the needy from getting ahead on their own.[2] Liberals say that the "war on poverty" achieved much, and would have achieved more if spending had not been cut by the Republican Administrations since 1969.[3] Those further left, for example Michael Harrington, deny that the "war" ever amounted to much at all.[4]

These criticisms have weight, but mainly in ways their makers do not intend. Washington does give too much to the poor—in the sense of benefits given as entitlements. It also gives too little—in the sense of meaningful obligations to go along with the benefits. What undermines the economy is not so much the burden on the private sector as the message government programs have given that hard work in available jobs is no longer required of Americans. The main problem with the welfare state is not its size but its permissiveness, a characteristic that *both* liberals and conservatives seem to take for granted. The challenge to welfare statesmanship is not so much to change the extent of benefits as to couple them with serious work and other obligations that would encourage functioning and thus promote the integration of recipients. The goal must be to create for recipients *inside* the welfare state the same balance of support and expectation that other Americans face *outside* it, as they work to support themselves and meet the other demands of society.

The liberal and conservative critiques both assume that greater freedom is what recipients need to progress in American society. Some impediment, it is said, must be holding them back. Liberals say it is the oppressive, unfair, sometimes racist demands of the private economy. Employers refuse to hire the poor or to pay them enough to escape poverty. Only government action can overcome these "barriers." Conservatives say the obstacle is government itself, whose programs keep recipients dependent and unable to get ahead on their own. The answer is to cut back the programs. For one persuasion freedom for the disadvantaged means to extend government's reach into society; for the other, to pull back.

Neither prescription, however, would fundamentally change the welfare state we have. Experience shows that big-government programs in the liberal or Harrington mode, which increase benefits without expecting any return, would not make the poor any less dependent. However, simply to cut back welfare as Gilder and Murray advise, while it would force independence on the recipients, lacks the political support to be carried very far, as the Reagan Administration has discovered. Most Americans, and their leaders want to continue a humanitarian social policy. Also, any dependent people could not immediately cope on their own. They need support and guidance, even if the goal is overcoming dependency.

Once we face these realities, the welfare problem emerges as one of authority rather than freedom. The best hope for solving it is, not mainly to shift the boundary between society and government, but to require recipients to function where they already are, as dependents. Even more than income and opportunity, they need to face the requirements, such as work, that true acceptance in American society requires. To create those obligations, they must be made *less* free in certain senses rather than more.

Even to speak of obligation as a goal of social policy, however, is novel in the American context. The idea that government might act to enforce social order may sound like a truism, but it has not been prominent in American politics. For most commentators and academics, American politics has been about freedom rather than order. Its essence is to be found in our freewheeling elections and in the jockeying for power among the various institutions and interests in Washington. It is a game played out among lobbies, parties, and politicians to decide, in Harold Lasswell's phrase, "who gets what, when, how."[5] The game is played by rules designed, by James Madison and the other Founders, to disperse and divide power rather than concentrate it. The political system offers access to all interests. Each meets limitation from the force of competing interests rather than government itself. There is no state separate from society, but only a political process through which social forces compete for power. Government does not make demands on the people; they make demands on it.

The Madisonian view of government, however, centers too much on the high politics of Washington. The average American actually has little interest in politics in this participatory sense. Public opinion studies show that his knowledge of government is usually quite limited, and his desire to participate in it even more so.[6] His concerns are usually closer at hand, rooted in his daily life of job, home, and family. He gets interested in government to the extent public policies make leading that life more or less difficult. His immediate attention is on law enforcement, the quality of the neighborhood schools and other public services, and employment prospects for himself, his family, and friends. In assuring these conditions the face of government as public authority, not as political arena, is almost salient. As Hobbes said, government's essential, if not only, purpose is to maintain public order.

"Order" here means more than just "law and order" in the narrow, police sense. It encompasses all of the social and economic conditions people depend on for satisfying lives, but which are government's responsibility rather than their own. It includes, in other words, all of the *public* conditions for the *private* assurance of what Jefferson called "life, liberty, and the pursuit of happiness." Which conditions are a public responsibility is, of course, for politics to decide. In modern conditions the public agenda is broad. Even conservatives believe that government must manage overall economic conditions and assure equal opportunity to all, alongside basic public services.

Even the most liberal government, however, could never assure the conditions for order by itself. Policymakers in Washington sometimes forget that order is not a service that they can provide just by spending money. It depends on the concurrence of people with government, and with each other. The frontispiece of Hobbes's *Leviathan* shows that the sovereign is literally made up of "his" citizens. Government is really a mechanism by which people force themselves to serve and obey *each other* in necessary ways.

"Compliance," further, is too passive a term for what order requires, particularly in complex modern societies. People must not only refrain from offenses against others but fulfill the expectations others have of them in public roles, as workers on the job, as neighbors, or simply as passers-by in the streets of our cities. Order requires not only self-discipline but *activity* and *competence*. It is achieved when a population displays those habits of mutual forbearance and reliability which we call civility.

American political culture gives pride of place to the value of freedom. But a "free" society is possible only when the conditions for order have substantially been realized. People are not interested in "freedom" from government if they are victimized by crime, cannot support themselves, or are in any fundamental way insecure. They will want more government rather than less. Nor are they likely to vote or otherwise participate politically unless they are employed and have their personal lives in order. A "free" political culture is the characteristic not of a society still close to the state of nature, as some American philosophers have imagined, but of one already far removed from it by dense, reliable networks of mutual expectations.

The conditions for order also extend across the border between the public and private sectors in the usual meanings of those words. Obligation usually connotes governmental duties such as paying taxes, obeying the law, or serving in the military (if there is a draft). But order also requires that people function well in areas of life that are not directly regulated. They must be educated in minimal ways, able to maintain themselves, able also to cooperate with others for common ends, whether political or economic—what Samuel Huntington has called the "art of associating together."[7] The capacities to learn, work, support one's family, and respect the rights of others amount to a set of *social* obligations alongside the political ones. A civic society might almost be defined as one in which people are competent in all these senses, as citizens and as workers. For people to fulfill these expectations or not is what I shall mean by their functioning or not functioning well.

Social policy should be seen as one of government's means of achieving order. Social programs define much of what society expects of people in the social realm, just as other laws and the Constitution do in the political realm. By the benefits they give to and withhold from different groups, the programs declare which needs government will help people manage, and which they must manage for themselves. The structure of benefits and requirements in the programs, then, constitutes an *operational definition of citizenship*. One of the things a government must do to improve social order is to use these programs to require better functioning of recipients who have difficulty coping. The tragedy of federal social programs is that they have only begun to do this. Federal political culture has such difficulty setting requirements for recipients that the programs have undermined social order rather than upheld it.

Functioning in American society has declined since 1960. . . . The rise in Aid to Families with Dependent Children (AFDC), the main federal welfare program, reflects the inability of increasing members of low-income families to stay together and support themselves, since eligibility is usually limited to one-parent families in need. Most recipient families are headed by mothers separated from their spouses. The rise in unemployment means that increasing proportions of the labor force are unable to find jobs—or to accept the jobs available to them. The rise in crime reflects mainly the explosion of violence against persons and property in the large cities. The steady decline in SAT scores indicates a fall in the academic skills of students seeking to go to college.

Each trend appears a little less worrisome on examination. Welfare has risen mainly because more broken families in need have decided to seek assistance, not because there are more such families, though both trends are involved. While joblessness is greater, especially among the unskilled, the proportion of the adult population working or seeking work has actually risen. Higher crime is partly due to the huge "baby boom" generation passing through its youth, since greater numbers of young people always produce more crime. Declining SAT scores partly reflect the fact that relatively more test-takers in recent years have been disadvantaged or nonwhite, groups that on average were less well prepared for college than the middle-class whites who dominated earlier cohorts.[8] Some of the rise in crime and dependency is due simply to population growth. The trends in crime and SAT scores had reversed by 1983, but dependency rebounded.

The magnitude of the changes, nevertheless, is so great that nothing can fully explain them away. Many Americans evidently are less able to take care of themselves and respect the rights of others than in earlier decades. The numbers give credibility to the concern over the decay of "traditional values" that has colored American politics since the late 1960s. The mystery is why the decline occurred in spite of sharp public disquiet.

Not all the causes are regrettable or governmental. A disproportionate number of criminals and welfare recipients are nonwhite, although all races are well represented. A rising willingness of black Americans to make demands on white society, though it inflated the welfare rolls, was also essential to the civil rights movement and to civil rights reforms needed to advance integration. Rising unemployment results, in part, from the fact that many people have become impatient with the demands of low-paid jobs because of rising affluence, in itself a good thing. The decline of social order, which most Americans regret, was also related in diffuse ways to political disillusionments, particularly over Vietnam and Watergate, which many would say were warranted.[9]

Is government also to blame? Liberal and conservative criticisms about the scale of government have already been mentioned. Some other critics disillusioned with American politics, whom I call radicals, believe that society unfairly burdens the poor, to the point where they are forced into dysfunction. Michael Harrington is one exemplar. That belief contributes an important idea—that one purpose of social policy can be to discipline the poor. But where radicals say that welfare programs regiment the dependent and should not, my conclusion is that they do not but might, in ways that would serve the poor themselves.

Federal benefit programs set the rules under which a good part of the population lives. People learn social mores initially from their families, but public institutions have a lot to do with whether they are taken seriously. There is little disagreement in American society that people should observe social obligations—work, support one's family, and obey the law, among other things. There is a good deal of disagreement, however, about how closely those norms must actually govern personal behavior. Whether the values are treated as obligatory ultimately depends for many—perhaps most—citizens on the presence of enforcement. Like duties to obey the law or pay taxes, obligations to function at school, at work, and in other social roles would wither to formalities unless noncompliance ultimately drew some kind of sanction.

But federal programs have special difficulties in setting standards for their recipients. They tend to shield their clients from the threats and rewards that stem from private society—particularly the marketplace—while providing few sanctions of their own. The recipients seldom have to work or otherwise function to earn whatever income, service, or benefit a program gives; meager though it may be, they receive it essentially as an entitlement. Their place in American society is defined by their need and weakness, not their competence. This lack of accountability is among the reasons why nonwork, crime, family breakup, and other problems are much commoner among recipients than Americans generally.

The authority of programs is decisive for a different reason too: It is in principle subject to public control. Americans cannot be said to have chosen the social and economic changes that have swept over them in recent decades, contributing to disorder. Politically, however, they have accepted a permissive welfare state, and they could demand a more exacting one. The search for social solutions, James Q. Wilson has said, must emphasize factors that are subject to public control, not those that are not.[10] Federal policymakers must start to ask how programs can affirm the norms for functioning on which social order depends. There are serious problems in doing so, but they are political problems subject, in principle, to public debate and resolution.

At first such an approach may seem nothing more than an elaborate way of "blaming the victim." Social policy is supposed to help the weak and vulnerable.

How could one justify burdening them with the responsibility for succeeding in school or at work when the conditions they face are difficult? The answer is simply that social programs have failed partly because they expect too little of their recipients, not too much, and there is evidence that clearer standards would improve functioning. A judgment against the poor could be accomplished simply by throwing them off programs to fend for themselves, the traditional conservative prescription. The idea of an authoritative policy, rather, is to *combine* requirements with support in a balance that approximates what the nondependent face outside government. This treats the dependent like other citizens in the ways essential to equality. Far from helping the poor, exaggerated fears of victim-blaming have themselves become a leading cause of dependency.

That fear expresses too crude a view of the role of authority in social order. As every political theorist—and policeman—knows, government can rarely control people if it merely blames or coerces them. Rather, citizens must *accept* its demands as legitimate, transmuting mere power into authority. Only then can compliance be widespread. Far from blaming people if they deviate, government must persuade them to *blame themselves*. This sense of responsibility, though it is individual, is not something individuals can produce alone. It rests ultimately on public norms and enforcement that are collective in character. It cannot last unless individuals finally get something out of compliance, unless they derive success and social acceptance from being "good citizens." That again only society can assure.

The idea of programs inculcating values may nevertheless seem foreign to American political mores. It conjures up a brutal, Hobbesian image of government deciding what is good for people and then imposing it on them by force. For policy to involve itself in the personal competencies of individuals is inherently sensitive, and whatever is required can seem invidious. It is important to emphasize that what standards to require is not for any one person to decide, and there is no one right answer to it. It is a political question, indeed the supreme question in social policy. Some social requirements, such as work, may reasonably be treated as enforceable, because there is good evidence that the public views them this way. However, the main point here is not to advocate a specific set of mores but rather to show that programs embody a decision about norms, not only for recipients, but for citizens in general. For that reason social policy should be made in a political way by politicians, not, as it often is in Washington, in an expert and technical way, clothed in the language of economics, that admits only liberal goals or suppresses value questions entirely.

Americans are easily tempted to seek technical, nonpolitical solutions to the social problem that avoid behavioral issues. Confronted by the problem of nonwork by the poor, many people respond that either the economy must be denying work to the poor, or they are disabled or otherwise unemployable and hence exempted from the normal work expectation. The question of employability is obviously crucial and prior to any talk of obligations, but it is also substantially a political question. Within very broad limits it cannot be settled on medical or economic grounds alone. There are a great many nonworking poor who may be termed employable or not depending on how demanding society wishes to be of its members. It is precisely the groups who do not work regularly yet are not clearly disabled—unskilled men and welfare mothers with children—who have been the crux of the social problem and will be the main focus here. Are they too burdened to work, or are they employable and hence "undeserving"? It is a political question, and welfare and employment policy increasingly revolves around the answer.

Even a very authoritative social policy would not involve imposing values on recipients that are foreign to American life. American politics is a good deal less demanding than American society. Benefit recipients live under a regime of political values that allows individuals to make demands on government rather than vice versa. But in private society pressures to perform are strong, and most people have to function reasonably well just to maintain their economic and social position, let alone improve it. The task in social policy is not to invent values supportive of order, but to elevate those that already exist from the social realm into the political. The problem is to overcome the political and ideological reflexes that drive social policymakers to emphasize only benefits for recipients, denying the more orderly values in which both they and the dependent also believe.

To speak of obligating the poor may sound like abandonment of the goal of equality in the sense of mainstream income and status for the poor, the traditional aim of social policy. In reality, the lack of standards in programs has probably increased inequality in this sense by undercutting the competencies the disadvantaged need to achieve status. But more important, equality to Americans tends not to mean middle-class income or status at all, but rather the enjoyment of equal citizenship, meaning the same rights and obligations as others. While we usually think of citizenship as something political, specifying rights like free speech and duties such as obedience to the law, it has a social dimension too. Benefit programs define a set of social rights for vulnerable groups, while Americans tend to regard minimal social competencies like work or getting through school as obligatory even if they are not legally enforced. These *social* obligations may not be governmental, but they are public in that they fall within the collective expectation that structures an orderly society. Both political and social duties are included in what I shall call the common obligations of citizenship.

The great merit of equal citizenship as a social goal is that it is much more widely achievable than status. It is not competitive. It does not require that the disadvantaged "succeed," something not everyone can do. It requires only that everyone discharge the common obligations, including social ones like work. At the same time no one is exempted on grounds of disadvantage. All competent adults are supposed to work or display English literacy, just as everyone is supposed to pay taxes or obey the law, without regard to income or social position.

Current programs infringe equality in this sense as much as they serve it. They raise the income of the needy, but they also exempt them from work and other requirements that are just as necessary for belonging. The novelty of an authoritative social policy would be to enforce social obligations, at least for the dependent, just as political obligations are enforced for the population in general. To obligate the dependent as others are obligated is essential to equality, not opposed to it. An effective welfare must include recipients in the common obligations of citizens rather than exclude them. . . .

NOTES

1. "Libertarian" and "permissive" will be used to connote the view that individuals should not be obligated to function well, whether by government or by private pressures like the marketplace. "Authoritative" connotes the view that they should. This distinction is different from that between "liberal" and "conservative," which connotes different views of the scale of government. See Lawrence M. Mead, *Beyond Entitlement: The Social Obligations of Citizenship* (New York: The Free Press, 1986), Chapter 11.

2. George Gilder, *Wealth and Poverty* (New York: Basic Books, 1981); Charles Murray, *Losing Ground: American Social Policy, 1950–1980* (New York: Basic Books, 1984).

3. Sar A. Levitan and Clifford M. Johnson, *Beyond the Safety Net: Reviving the Promise of Opportunity in America* (Cambridge, Mass.: Ballinger, 1984); John E. Schwarz, *America's Hidden Success: A Reassessment of Twenty Years of Public Policy* (New York: Norton, 1983).

4. Michael Harrington, *The New American Poverty* (New York: Holt, Rinehart & Winston, 1984).

5. Harold D. Lasswell, *Politics: Who Gets What, When, How* (New York: Meridian, 1958).

6. Angus Campbell et al., *The American Voter* (New York: Wiley, 1960), chs. 3–11, 20. There is some evidence that the public has become more ideological and issue-oriented due to the divisive controversies of the 1960s and 1970s—see e.g., Norman H. Nie et al., *The Changing American Voter*, Enlarged Ed. (Cambridge, Mass.: Harvard University Press, 1979)—but it has remained substantially ignorant of the details of government policy.

7. Samuel P. Huntington, *Political Order in Changing Societies* (New Haven: Yale University Press, 1968), p. 4. The phrase is from Tocqueville's *Democracy in America*. Huntington's thesis is that developing countries suffer mainly from insufficient government, not government that is insufficiently democratic, the usual subject of American rhetoric. My thesis here is similar: The main problem with the welfare state is that it lacks authority, not that it is too large or too small. Welfare institutions require further political development, even within otherwise highly developed Western polities.

8. Joseph E. Garvey, *Testing for College Admissions: Trends and Issues* (Arlington, Va.: Educational Research Service, 1981), pp. 25–28.

9. Alongside the decline in social functioning went changes in public attitudes that in some ways undercut political functioning. The public since the middle 1960s has grown more distrustful of government and parties, more supportive of groups making demands on government, and less likely to vote. See chapter 9, note 15.

10. James Q. Wilson, *Thinking About Crime* (New York: Vintage Books, 1977), ch. 3.

■ MICHAEL WALZER: CITIZENSHIP AND EXCLUSION

In contrast to Mead's call for the social imposition of obligation, Michael Walzer seeks to analyse the complex ways in which groups may be included in or excluded from political community. Walzer formulates an ideal critical standard of complex equality for community members: different goods in different social spheres would be distributed by and to different community members for different reasons. Consequently, no individual or group would be able to dominate or be excluded from all spheres. Walzer argues that there now nevertheless remain unjust systemic exclusions of groups. These exclusions fall outside the responsibility of the excluded for they are promoted by market and social arrangements over which group members have little or no control. Indeed, the exclusions are especially egregious for the groups are marked by discrimination, stereotyping, disregard, and disrespect; the exclusion of members is across almost all spheres of justice and is largely a matter of inheritance and systemic implication rather than autonomous, individual decision. What follows, Walzer thinks, is a primary social obligation to remedy these unjust exclusions rather than individual guilt or remorse. Justice requires a sustained public effort to enable re-inclusion in all public spheres; hence the need for enabling welfare and universal public education. Inclusion begins with citizenship and extends via voluntary civic associations and efforts throughout all spheres of justice. A democratic political community, concludes Walzer, recognizes that social marginalization and systemic exclusion of a class of citizens are always unjust and need to be abolished.

Michael Walzer

EXCLUSION, INJUSTICE, AND THE DEMOCRATIC STATE

Who is in and who is out?—these are the first questions that any political community must answer about itself. Particular communities are constituted by the answers

NOTE: This essay was written for a conference on "Social Justice and Inequality" sponsored by the French Commissariat General du Plan in Paris in November 1992. In it I respond to some questions prepared by the staff of the Commissariat, inviting me to reconsider aspects of my argument in *Spheres of Justice* (1983). Hence the self-referential style of the essay—not the way I usually write.—MW

From Michael Walzer, "Exclusion, Injustice, and the Democratic State," *Dissent* (Winter 1993): 55–64. Reprinted by permission of the author and *Dissent*.

they give or, better by the process through which it is decided whose answers count. This is true even if the decision isn't definitive, doesn't draw an absolute line between insiders and outsiders. In fact, absolutism is rarely possible here. Ancient Greeks and Israelites, for example, distinguished themselves from foreigners on relatively straightforward kinship lines. But their political communities included, alongside citizens and brethren, an intermediate group of resident aliens, *metics* or *ge'rim*—not kin, but not foreign either, sharing some but not all of the rights and duties of members. What may be more important, divisions of class and gender cut across all these categories, so that there were in both Greece and Israel powerless members and powerful strangers: the formal rules of inclusion and exclusion did not determine the actual process of political (or everyday social and economic) decision making. Nor would it have bothered Greek philosophers or Jewish sages that women, slaves, urban workers, and "people of the land" (*am ha-aretz*)—even if they were native born and genealogically correct—had little or no say in the government of their communities. The exclusion of such people was probably less problematic than that of resident aliens.

Among ourselves, with our huge populations of guest workers and illegal immigrants, we have reproduced the old intermediate class. We have our own resident aliens, in but not of the political community, their rights and obligations as disputed today as they were two thousand years ago. The other kind of exclusion, however, we at least pretend to have overcome. We have expanded the ancient understanding of citizenship and brotherhood, abolishing class and gender barriers, incorporating women, slaves, and workers, producing the modern, inclusive *demos*. All the people, every man and woman, are or are supposed to be equal participants in all the spheres of justice, sharing, as members, in the distribution of welfare, security, wealth, education, office, political power, and so on—and also joining in the debates about what that sharing involves and how it ought to be managed.

It was the argument of my book *Spheres of Justice* that this participation (with a little luck!) would give rise to a "complex equality" of members. Not that all goods would be distributed equally to all members: given the nature, that is, the social meaning and customary use, of the goods, equal distribution is neither desirable nor possible. Rather, different goods would be distributed for different reasons by different agents to different people—so that no single group of people would be dominant across the spheres; nor would the possession of one good, like wealth or power or familial reputation, bring all the others in train. People who fared badly in one distributive sphere would do better in another, and the result would be a horizontal and socially extended version of Aristotle's "ruling and being ruled in turn." No one would rule or be ruled all the time and everywhere. No one would be radically excluded.

But this is an ideal picture, a critical standard, describing how things would turn out if people actually joined in the distributive work and successfully defended the autonomy of the spheres. Defense is always necessary, since any socially significant good—money in a capitalist society is the obvious example—is likely to be convertible into all the other goods and so to serve as a medium of domination for those who possess it. Inequality is always worked through some such medium.

Land or money or political power or racial or religious identity (or some subset of these) become the means of access to the entire range of social goods. The agents of autonomous distributions are effectively disempowered. And then poor people, members of racial or religious minorities, heterodox men and women share only minimally in their country's good times, bear the brunt of economic decline, are shut out of the better schools and offices, carry everywhere the stigma of failure. We thus reproduce the internal exclusions of the ancient world: disenfranchised, powerless, unemployed, and marginalized members.

We don't quite know what to call these people—the dispossessed, the underclass, the truly disadvantaged, the socially isolated, the estranged poor—and this confusion about their classification reflects a deeper embarrassment about their existence. For the whole tendency of modern (welfarist or social) democracy, so we once thought, is to make the reproduction of marginality and exclusion increasingly difficult. Civil service exams and laws requiring "fair employment practices" open available careers to talented citizens, whoever they are—blocking the distribution of offices and jobs through a network of relatives, ethnic or religious kin, or "old boys." Public schools and meritocratic admissions policies guarantee the distribution of educational opportunities without regard to race or religion. Universal entitlement programs preclude the use of welfare as a form of political patronage. The public defender, the ban on bribery, and the new limits on campaign contributions protect the judicial system and the political process against the corruptions of wealth. Religious toleration and cultural pluralism allow individual men and women to worship and live independently, unconventionally, without fear of political or economic penalty. In all these, and many other, ways we defend the boundaries of the spheres of justice. Why, then, are we still so far from complex equality?

I want to make two arguments in response to this question: first, that the convertibility of social goods and the domination it makes possible take increasingly subtle and indirect forms in modern societies; they have hardly yet been subjected to democratic control. And second, that given the continued existence of excluded groups, the state must play a larger role in advancing the cause of complex equality than I envisaged for it when I wrote about these matters ten years ago. The first argument deals with an overestimation of the justice of contemporary distributions, the second with an underestimation of the state as an agent of distributive justice.

The old accounts of inequality and exclusion, focused on dominant goods and ruling classes, still carry a lot of weight, but they have tended in recent years to produce among excluded and marginal groups theories of systematic oppression, tales of conspiracy, that cannot sustain empirical analysis. In fact, active domination is less in evidence today; democratic membership brings with it significant protections that no one is prepared to challenge openly. Individual members of excluded groups, thus protected, make their way forward or upward, winning at least a small share of social goods. And so an insidious myth is born, a counter-myth to all the conspiracies, which holds that the remaining exclusions are no longer unjust, that they are indeed the unexpected product of justice itself. Excluded men and women get what they deserve, or what they have chosen, or they are the victims of bad luck; no one else is responsible for their fate. The assignment of responsibility is at stake here—with large consequences for social policy.

The myth of just or justified exclusion looks back, I think, to Michael Young's *Rise of the Meritocracy*, the classic dystopia of contemporary social science. What Young wrote was, in fact, a savage critique of meritocratic distributions in the absence of any sort of socialist solidarity. Equality of opportunity, he argued, would divide society into two classes—those who are capable and those who are incapable of seizing their opportunities. The second group would be a lower class without precedent in human history; not enslaved, not oppressed, not exploited; standing exactly where their own efforts (or lack thereof) had brought them; deprived even of a cause to rally around. Young's argument is repeated today without is critical thrust. Subordination and exclusion, it is said, are more the result of incapacity, apathy, or lack of interest than of domination. The excluded are simply the class of men and women deficient across the range of qualities, so that distributive processes working autonomously, exactly as they are supposed to work, bring them no goods or no goods that they can profitably use. Subtlety and indirection have nothing to do with their fate, for we have largely replaced the collective exclusion of women or workers or blacks or Jews with a new exclusion of individuals chosen, as it were, for the right reasons.

The triumph of equality, the democratic expansion of citizenship, turns out (on this view) to be a cruel hoax. It has simply made visible what was once concealed by the false abstractions of gender, race, and class: the presence of men and women who cannot (or will not) meet the standard, or even the pluralized standards, of citizenship. Those who can, do—barring bad luck, which is always someone's fate. Failure in all the spheres is no longer the result and therefore the visible sign of oppression and injustice. Hence the only motive we have for helping those who fail is sympathy or humane feeling. About this we must be careful, for it may well lead us to act unjustly, limiting the autonomous distribution of goods (as in cases of affirmative action or "reverse discrimination") and overbuilding the welfare system. All that humane feeling requires is humanitarian relief—a "safety net" so that those who are justly denied the most desirable social goods are not callously denied subsistence itself.

My own claim that exclusion is still unjust has to be defended against this neo-Youngian argument. Also, perhaps, against its libertarian variant, which holds that the last vestiges of domination won't be eliminated until we have curtailed the welfare system, deregulated the market, and given up affirmative action. Only when everyone is exposed to the harsh incentives as well as the golden opportunities of meritocracy and "free enterprise" will we know who the justly (or the not-unjustly) excluded really are. They will fall into two groups: those who work at low-paying jobs and survive on the social margins and those who can't or won't work and land in the safety net. A fixed determination not to accept any further responsibility for such people underlies, I think, the conservative social policies of the 1980s. We can find it articulated (though rarely as openly as in Young's satire) in recent academic literature dealing with intelligence, crime, poverty, and welfare. Also in a more popular style—in the columns of local newspapers, on radio talk shows, and in everyday conversation—often thought to express nothing but egotism and meanspiritedness: but behind this too there is a view of justice, according to which everything has been done for "those people" that ought to be done. This is the argument that I need to address, but first it will be useful to provide a model description of one of "those people" as seen from the neo-Youngian perspective.

Imagine, then, a man or woman who is a citizen, a full member as this is legally defined; who has been on the welfare rolls but was never enabled by the assistance he received to lead an independent life, a passive client of the state incapable of self-help or mutual aid, who is now pushed out of the system by (justified) budget cuts; who brings no skills or resources to the market, is only intermittently employed, displaying no entrepreneurial competence or energy; who has had a standard public education, up to the legally required minimum, which was largely ineffective, never engaging either his mental or material interests; who is therefore unqualified for the places on offer in the civil service or the professions or in the institutions that train their members; who is likely to do much more than a fair share of hard or dirty work; who has time to kill, being often out of work or (with good reason) in prison—but not much of the sort of time that we call "leisure"; who lives in a fragmented family or altogether without familial support, alone, sometimes literally homeless; who receives neither recognition nor respect from fellow citizens and suffers, as a result, from a loss of self-respect; who is politically powerless despite his suffrage, because he is numbered among those who need not be counted, a mass of unorganized, inarticulate, and therefore unrepresented men and women; and, finally, who is probably not even saved, though salvation is the social good most readily available to him, at the hands of itinerant (or radio and television) evangelists.

Has this person been treated unjustly? Isn't this simply a sad story of individual misfortune and failure, with all the distributive agencies doing the work they are supposed to do, as best they can, and always in accordance with the principles of justice? Social workers and teachers have tried to help; personnel managers have attended to her talents or lack of talent; democratic politicians have labored, unsuccessfully, to "build a base" among people like her; and so on. She has not been treated like a foreigner; not excluded without first being attended to. Given the attentiveness, what grounds of complaint can she possibly have for the exclusion? An individual in this situation can only complain, like Job, to God. This is a case, perhaps, of a good person suffering undeserved pain—but this is divine, not human, injustice.

I can imagine a social world in which such an account might have some plausibility, and I want to come back, later on, to the difficulties this might raise for the theory of justice. Can it be our aim to create a society where the poor and the powerless have no grounds of complaint? Is that the definition of a *just* society? In any case, we do not now live in a society like that. Among ourselves, excluded men and women are not a random series of failed individuals, rejected one by one, sphere by sphere.

Failure is not randomly distributed across the multicultural range of American society. Instead, the excluded mostly come in groups whose members share common experiences and, often enough, a family (racial, ethnic, gender) resemblance. Failure pursues them from sphere to sphere in the form of stereotyping, discrimination, and disregard, so that their condition is not in fact the product of a succession of autonomous decisions but rather of a single systematic decision or of an interconnected set. And for their children, exclusion is an inheritance; the qualities that supposedly produce it (and that might give it legitimacy) are now its products.

Groups like this take shape and reproduce themselves only under pressure. But the pressure, in order to be effective, need not take the form of organized and premeditated oppression—like the restraints that would be imposed on blacks today by white supremacists. Something less will do the job, as the black example suggests. The knowledge that white supremacists are still politically active has some effect, I suppose, on the everyday life of black Americans, but what is more important in explaining their (partial) exclusion from the American mainstream is the continuum of attitudes and practices that starts with racism at one end and has a long way to go before it reaches to a thoroughgoing egalitarian civility or friendship at the other. The greater number of people whose attitudes and practices are represented along this continuum would certainly repudiate racism if they were asked, but their own habits, expectations, and unspoken fears carry, as it were, the residues of racial prejudice and constitute a significant social force—even if this is a force whose consequences no one intends. Many of these people are agents of distribution, at work in welfare agencies or in school counseling offices or on admission and search committees or in political parties and movements. All of them are voters; all of them hold in their hands or, better, in their minds and eyes the power of recognition. When I suggested that the contemporary use of dominant goods across boundaries and the resulting forms of exclusion are subtle and indirect, I had in mind these people, myself, of course, among them. Because of what we do, even though there is no master plan directing what we do, and even though we do it in different ways and to different degrees—as we stand more to the right or more to the left on the continuum—the plight of an excluded man or woman is still today a social and not only a personal responsibility: ours, not only his or hers.

This argument is equally strong if exclusion is—as I suspect it most often is—as much a matter of class as of race (or ethnicity or religion). Describing domination in *Spheres of Justice*, I focused on how it worked for those individuals or groups who were able to wield the dominant good—to use their wealth, for example, to purchase goods that should never be up for sale. Consider now the people whose lack of wealth renders them liable to lose all those goods that are in fact being sold: market poor, they find themselves impoverished everywhere. In this case, too, their exclusion can take subtle and indirect forms. It does not depend upon the literal transfer for cash in hand of school places, or offices in the civil service, or political influence, or justice in the courts. The power of money is revealed in the way its owners are trained and tutored, the way they dress and talk, the generosity they are capable of, the services they can command, the attention they draw to themselves. And here again, all of us are complicit, to greater or lesser degree, in allowing these things to matter in our own and other people's distributive decisions.

No doubt, the exclusions of a class society, and even of a racist society, are structural in character and not merely attitudinal. But the impact of structures on what structuralists call "real life" is mediated by the ideas and actions of individuals, and that impact must vary significantly depending on the prevailing distribution of individuals along the attitudinal continuum from racism or snobbery to civic friendship. Established structures are more likely to be scrutinized and challenged by men and women inclined, as it were, to the left side of the continuum. But the greater number of individuals (at least in America today) are content with the established structures—precisely because the people they exclude or marginalize are "those people," black or poor or somehow stigmatized.

I don't make this argument in order to inspire guilt. The kinds of "doing" and "allowing" that I have attributed to large numbers of my fellows seem to me largely guilt-free. I doubt that many of us possess the capacity to purge ourselves of the residual prejudices of race or class. What follows from my argument is not private regret or remorse, but social obligation. Given the existence of excluded groups, justice requires a sustained public effort to enable their members to re-enter society and to function independently in all the distributive spheres. Indeed, this is the central purpose of two closely related social goods: welfare and education. Let me consider these two in turn, for they reveal the extent to which we are committed, despite our continued ineffectiveness and denial, to the creation of an inclusive society.

Welfare is sometimes understood as mere relief: the state as soup kitchen. This is the view of those contemporary writers and politicians who think that excluded men and women are responsible, insofar as anyone who is responsible, for their own fate. Expecting them to fail, we set a safety net in place—for their sakes or for ours, it doesn't matter. But I don't think that this has ever been the general understanding or the best reading of actual welfare practices (as distinct, say, from almsgiving). With regard to the able-bodied poor, from earliest times, the aim was never relief simply; state officials did what they could to coax or compel such people to re-enter the work force and make their own way. The chosen means were often punitive; I don't want to recommend them. But the project seems to fit well, without the punitiveness, into democratic conceptions of membership.

I have described in *Spheres of Justice* how the Jewish communities of medieval Europe designed a welfare system with this specific project in mind. The Jews were pioneers here, driven by their situation as a persecuted minority not to democracy but to a very strong version of mutuality. The resources of the communities were mobilized against exclusion, used, therefore, to provide schools, dowries, business loans and jobs, religious artifacts, as well as food and clothing—so that effective membership could be maintained. And while the explicit purpose of the mobilization was not to create a just society, the responsibility of each individual member was thought to be a matter of justice. It seems to me, however, that a society from which no one is excluded is more just than a society that includes, so to speak, excluded or marginalized men and women, nonparticipants in a world to which they willy-nilly belong. The contemporary critique of "welfare dependency," whatever its political motives, supports this view: the goal of public assistance is to produce active participants in the economy and the polity, not to maintain a permanent clientele.

But this last claim assumes that all the excluded are capable of participation; they have the appropriate ambitions and latent talents; they can take their turn, with only a little help, in at least some of the distributive spheres. This is also the underlying assumption of our own commitment to universal public education: that the children we force to attend school really can benefit from the experience and become active citizens and useful, self-reliant workers. We owe it to one another to reproduce these sorts of citizens and workers; the obligation follows from our agreement to sustain a society of people like ourselves, within which a secure and decent life is possible. But we also owe it to the children, because we, or some of us, have brought them into the world and because we will be responsible for the pain and unhappiness of their exclusion, insofar as we could have prevented it.

But maybe it can't be prevented. Maybe the only realizable purpose of public education is to sort out the children, distinguishing the included from the excluded in as fair a way as possible. Certainly many inner-city schools these days don't seem to be doing anything else, and without much concern for fairness: the children picked for exclusion come overwhelmingly from the same "families." But since these schools, like all schools in a democratic society, are educating *citizens*, even the strictest fairness in exclusion would represent a terrible defeat. Democratic education is a wager on universal or near-universal competence—or, better, democracy itself is the wager and education is the crucial means of winning. Of course, individuals are more or less competent: victories are always partial; and schools do a lot of sorting out in ways that verge on, though they need not establish or reinforce, the radical dichotomy of in and out. But teachers have to make the democratic wager; it is the moral prerequisite of their job.

It follows, then, that massive failure in the spheres of welfare and education or, more specifically, failure that massively affects particular groups, ought to suggest (if not a positive will to fail) a massive undercommitment of material and mental resources: not enough money, not enough people, not enough faith in the enterprise, not enough inventiveness and experiment. What constitutes a deficiency of resources changes over time. The more complicated modern political and economic life become, the greater the necessary commitment. Social reproduction and rescue today require large-scale resources—a requirement that has no precedent in the recent or distant past, when both these enterprises were sustained mostly by family members and communal volunteers, without professional training or much in the way of organizational support. I suspect that relatives and volunteers can still do a great deal of the necessary work, though they will work best within organizational frameworks: schools, hospitals, nursing homes, and so on. The frameworks themselves depend on the helping professions. Any modern society that devalues these professions (as most modern societies do, in part because so many citizens don't want to think about the social problems that make professional help necessary), and fails as a result to recruit talented men and women to teaching, nursing, counseling, and social work, is going to produce and reproduce exclusion. And it will be *unjust exclusion:* for then the excluded won't have received the attention that is due to every member of a democratic society.

I want to stress that though this is a matter of justice it isn't necessarily a matter for direct state action. The role of the state is very important, and I shall have no more to say about it later on; but many of the difficulties of excluded men and women are best handled within civil society, where the state can at most provide incentives and subsidies. Every voluntary association—church, union, co-op, neighborhood club, interest group, society for the preservation or prevention of this or that, philanthropic organization, and social movement—is an agency of inclusion. Alongside their stated purpose, whatever that is, the associations of civil society provide recognition, empowerment, training, and even employment. They serve to decentralize the spheres, multiplying settings and agents and guaranteeing greater diversity in the interpretation of distributive criteria. (Consider, for example, the different understandings of "merit" in churches, social movements, sports clubs, and the administrative apparatus of a modern state.) The officials and staff of all the associations taken together constitute an informal civil service, a social bureaucracy, and though it is in the nature of a democratic society that one can't assign tasks to these people, it is nonetheless important to acknowledge their centrality. The state can't direct their work, but it can, and therefore should, facilitate it. All the spheres of justice are implicated in the activity of voluntary associations; complex equality, under modern conditions, depends in large measure upon their success.

So we can re-describe excluded men or women, who lose out in every sphere, as victims. Anyone who claims this status makes a major political (and perhaps also a psychological) mistake, but the word is nonetheless accurate: these people have not received the attention or help that justice requires in the spheres of welfare and education, and the defeats there have carried over into market, polity, and family, producing the reiterated losses whose sum is exclusion itself. This is not to say that individuals bear no responsibility for their own situation, or that they have been treated unjustly everywhere, or that they are the literal prey of an oppressive or exploitative ruling class. They are not, as we might say of slaves or concentration-camp prisoners or stateless refugees, pure victims. Their situation is more complicated, and we can ask a great deal of them—so long as we recognize them as fellow members, who can ask a great deal of us.

But the question persists: what if we were to provide all that they can legitimately ask, and it still didn't help or didn't help enough? There are bound to be some people who can't be helped, who can't or won't help themselves. They don't study at school or their studying is without intellectual effect; they don't work hard or the work they do is badly done; they are clumsy or cruel in personal relationships; they avoid the political arena or act incoherently within it: they seek the available opportunities or the quick success of a criminal life; they choose marginality because it looks like freedom. At some point, we might want to turn away from these people, acknowledging only minimal obligations to them. I don't think it is crazy to imagine a just society as one in which turning away would not be unjust—so long as we kept the safety net in place. Only kindness or compassion would lead (some of) us to do more. But I cannot imagine a just society in which there were large numbers of people. Poverty and alienation are idiosyncratic, not popular, choices; and at least some of the incapacities of the poor and the alienated are remediable.

The myth of just or justified exclusion, transferred to some hypothetical future time, is still a myth. It derives from or depends upon a thin view of the individual person, according to which all his qualities are of a kind, flatly described. Either he is competent and willing across the board, though no doubt with strengths and weaknesses that get sorted out in the different spheres of justice, or he is incompetent and passive across the board, a failure everywhere. Complex equality merely reflects the sorting out: if distributive processes are working autonomously, competent men and women will be each other's equals in the way this ideal suggests. But the incompetent will be excluded from both complexity and equality; their lives will be simple and their social position uniformly subordinate. Justice is governed by this radical dichotomy between those who are eligible for complex equality and those who are not.

But this radical dichotomy is an ideological invention. Complex equality is matched (not only to a differentiation of goods but also) to a differentiation of persons and then of qualities, interests, and capacities within persons. There aren't only two sorts of persons; nor is any single person of one gross "sort." The range of qualities, interests, and capacities is very wide, and I don't know of any evidence—certainly my own experience provides no evidence—of any radical clustering of positive or negative versions of these in particular individuals. This brilliant mathematician is a political idiot. This talented musician doesn't have the faintest idea about how to deal with other people. This skillful and loving parent has no business sense. This adventurous and successful entrepreneur is a moral coward. This beggar on the street or criminal in prison is a competent craftsman, or a secret poet, or a superb orator. These easy contrasts are commonplace and obvious, but they hardly reach to the real complexity of individual men and women, for each of whom we could put together a long list not only of different but also of contradictory qualities, interests, and capacities. That is why the outcome of autonomous distributions is so utterly unpredictable, at least with regard to individuals. We can be sure, however, that these distributions won't divide any set of individuals into two radically distinct groups of "haves" and "have-nots"—unless autonomy itself has been corrupted in some major way.

If individual men and women were not complexly constituted, divided selves, then complex equality would be an example of bad utopianism—a false idea that served in fact to justify an unattractive reality. For it would then follow that the radical exclusion of flatly incompetent people was not unjust. They would have, as I have already suggested, nothing to complain about; it would be very difficult to organize a social movement on their behalf, for the organizers would not be able to appeal to the moral conscience of their fellow citizens. But there are no flatly incompetent people or, at least, no class of such people. The anxiety about just or justified exclusion is misplaced. The democratic wager is, in fact, a safe bet as bets go, though it is certainly not a bet that will be won, or even partly won, without a serious and sustained effort to win it. In any society where goods are differentiated and distributive processes putatively autonomous, across-the-board exclusion is and must be called unjust—a legitimate occasion, then, for political protest.

Political protest is aimed at the state; it is a call for state action (sometimes for an end to state action) of one sort or another. Public officials must do this or that (or stop doing this or that). In *Spheres of Justice*, the sorts of things that I imagined them doing were largely related to defending the boundaries of the spheres, as in the list that I have already provided: requiring meritocratic admission and appointment procedures, enforcing antidiscrimination laws, maintaining the integrity of the judicial system. The state also defends its own integrity, polices its own borders, by outlawing the sale of votes, for example, or by regulating campaign contributions or setting limits on the lobbying activities of former civil servants. Acting on its own behalf, it reveals the dual character of the political sphere. On the one hand, this is simply the bounded field or arena within which one highly valued social good—political power—is distributed. On the other hand, it is the base from which this power is deployed along all the social boundaries—and sometimes, of course, across them. When we protest against exclusion, we are working toward a redistribution and a redeployment of political power. The two go together in ways that I did not grasp in my earlier analysis, and this union of the two aspects of politics has far-reaching consequences.

Exclusion is a condition reiterated in each of the spheres, the sphere of politics one among the others. Hence the first goal of the protesters is to mobilize excluded men and women and bring them into the state. Because they are already citizens, this means to win for them a share of political power. And the first demand on the state is that it assist in this process—as the federal government did in the United States, for example, when it enforced voting rights on behalf of black Americans. We can understand this enforcement as a defense of political autonomy, in accordance with the principle, internal to democratic politics, that power is to be distributed with the consent of all the state's citizens and not by some racially marked subset of citizens. But the point of redistributing power to black Americans was not mere possession and enjoyment (though power is indeed enjoyable) but also use, a very specific use in this case: to open all the other spheres to these same hitherto excluded men and women. When citizens and officials act to reform the state, they are also acting to reform the larger society. They are advocates and agents of complex equality.

Once power has been redistributed, it will also be redeployed—and not just to defend the boundaries of the spheres. For the existence of an excluded group of men and women means that the boundaries have been violated to such a degree that they must now be redrawn before they can be defended. And they must be redrawn from within, with reference to the social meaning of the goods at stake. Arguments about affirmative action, for example, must deal with the idea of office-holding and the sorts of competence it has come to encompass. The result may be a call for changes in what it means to "qualify" for an office, but these can't be merely arbitrary changes, politically expedient for this or that party to the argument. Nonetheless, state agents—citizens and officials acting politically—will now play a part in interpreting the relevant meanings and in designing appropriate distributive arrangements. They will not play the only part, for they cannot usurp the authority of people more locally and directly involved: social workers, teachers, doctors and nurses, entrepreneurs, union members, parents, and so on. But citizens have an authority of their own, which derives from the fact that the boundaries of the spheres are not given but contested. Exclusion is a sign that the contests have gone badly—an invitation, therefore, to the state to set them right. Political protesters deliver the invitation.

Politics is implicated in all distributive disputes; the state cannot disregard what is going on in the different spheres of justice. . . . The state—or at least, the modern democratic state—must defend the values of complexity and equality on behalf of all its citizens. It can't, then be neutral or uncommitted with regard to the meaning of disputed social goods: decisions about the size of the bureaucracy depend upon a particular view of offices and their purposes; decisions about the scope of the market depend upon a view of commodities and entrepreneurial success; decisions about the number of school places depend upon a view of education. And all of these decisions are in something close to a foundational sense, warranted and (partly) determined by an understanding of citizenship.

Inclusion begins with citizenship, which then serves as a value reiterated through democratic political activity in all the spheres of justice. The reiteration is qualified by the nature of the goods at stake; participation in the different spheres takes different forms. But what marks a democratic political community is the recognition that all those social transactions that drive citizens toward the margins, that produce a class of excluded men and women—uneducated, unemployed, unrecognized, and powerless—are everywhere and always in the life of the community unjust.

■ BILL E. LAWSON: CITIZENSHIP AND SLAVERY

Bill E. Lawson addresses a concern about the citizenship status and marginalization of black persons in the United States. In this sense, he may be read as addressing the meaning and value of citizenship from the point of view of a group and its members so often denied the standing of citizens. Some theorists have advanced the argument that because voluntary consent on the part of autonomous agents is a basic precondition of citizenship, and because black persons were brought to the U.S. and eventually made citizens without their voluntary consent, African Americans are not citizens and are thus not bound by the ordinary obligations of citizens. Underlying this argument is the presupposition that citizen obligations are established by way of a Lockean social contract that elevates contracting parties out of the state of nature (on the state of nature and social contract theory, see Hobbes, Chapter 2). The implication of this argument is that many blacks remain in the state of nature.

Lawson responds by showing that historical evidence bears out the commitment of most blacks at the passage of the Thirteenth and Fourteenth Amendments to becoming U.S. citizens with all rights and responsibilities of citizenship. The problem was not black unwillingness but governmental inaction in satisfying the conditions of citizenship. The Equal Protection clause of the Fourteenth Amendment requires protection to be extended equally to all citizens. Failure to furnish such protection does not commit the unprotected to remaining in a Lockean state of nature; it does not end membership in the liberal democratic state by suspending citizenship rights and obligations. Indeed, the insistence that blacks remain in the state of nature is to deny their citizenship. Lawson concludes that the state has an obligation here to fulfill the rights of its black citizens.

Bill E. Lawson

CITIZENSHIP AND SLAVERY

One of the most important events of Reconstruction was the ratification of the Fourteenth Amendment to the United States Constitution.[1] Section One of the amendment states:

> all persons born or naturalized and subject to the jurisdiction thereof are citizens of the United States and of the state wherein they reside. No state shall make or enforce any laws which shall abridge the privileges or immunities of citizens of the United States: nor shall any state deprive any person of life, liberty, or property without due process of law; nor deny to any person within its jurisdiction the equal protection of the laws.[2]

The importance of this amendment for the political standing of blacks was cited by Senator Lot M. Morrill of Maine during debate in the Senate on the legislation:

> If there is anything with which the American people are troubled, and if there is anything with which the American statesman is perplexed and vexed, it is what to do with the negro, how to define him, what he is in American Law, and what rights he is entitled to. What shall we do with the everlasting, inevitable negro? is the question which puzzles all brains and vexes all statesmen. Now, as a definition, this amendment [to Section I which establishes the citizenship of the native of African descent] settles it. Hitherto we have said that he was nondescript in our statutes; he had no status; he was

From Bill E. Lawson, "Citizenship and Slavery," *Between Slavery and Freedom: Philosophy and American Slavery*, by Howard McGary and Bill E. Lawson (Bloomington, Ind.: Indiana University Press, 1993).

ubiquitous; he was both man and thing; he was three fifths of a person for representation and he was a thing for commerce and for use. In the highest sense, then . . . this
bill is important as a definition.[3]

While the adoption of the Fourteenth Amendment may have settled the question of citizenship for blacks in the minds of many legal theorists, there were some
black political theorists who still did not see themselves as Americans. They insisted that there is a fundamental incompatibility between what some whites
thought America stood for and what it means for blacks who find themselves physically within, but in all significant respects alien to, this polity.

Historically, there have always been people who denied that blacks belonged in
America.[4] Even some whites who fought against slavery thought that blacks could
not ever become full citizens.[5] In the 1850s a growing segment of Northern opinion
"opposed slavery but resisted the radical abolitionist demand that blacks be accepted after emancipation as a permanent and participating element in American
society."[6] There was a consensus among many whites that America had been
founded for the white man and that the two races were socially and politically incompatible. Blacks, it was argued, would never achieve equal citizenship status in
America.

Many black thinkers agreed that white Americans would never accept blacks as
equals. According to these thinkers, blacks could nourish only if they left the
United States and established their own country.[7] Prior to emancipation, the
United States Supreme Court, with the Dred Scott decision, did nothing to make
blacks think that their lowly status in America would change.

Much of the debate by blacks, from the beginning of their presence in America,
focused on what to do given the negative treatment of all blacks in America.
Proposals on how to respond generally took one of four routes: individual growth, or
improvement within the American system by moral suasion (integrationist); universal freedman betterment, or development of political power via separate social
institutions; resettlement, or development of separate communities in territories
not having slaves; and emigration/colonization, to Liberia, Haiti elsewhere in the
Caribbean, or West Africa.[8]

While these views merit philosophical analysis in their own right, I am concerned with an argument presented by Robert Brock, a political activist and president of the Self-Determination Committee of Los Angeles. His argument can be
stated as follows:

(1) blacks came to America by force;

(2) their presence here is not voluntary;

(3) their consent has never been sought;

(4) blacks were even made citizens without their consent;

(5) by not being allowed to choose, blacks were denied the basic rights that would
make them real citizens;

(6) failure to get their consent undermines any claim to citizenship; and

(7) therefore, blacks are not citizens.[9]

While this argument may appear valid, Harvey Natanson, a philosopher, realizes the importance of closely examining the soundness of such arguments. He argues that citizenship requires consent. He goes on to contend that a careful consideration of consent theory will show that some blacks in the United States were never in a position to consent to the state. These blacks, he concludes, were not legally obligated.[10]

Natanson's position draws on what he takes to be a Lockean model of the democratic state, relying heavily on John Locke's notion of government by consent. According to Locke, individuals incur political obligations by joining with other individuals in a social pact that gives rise to civil society. This pact is called a "social contract." An important aspect of the social contract is the belief that the individuals who form the pact are free, autonomous beings. Their consent to the contract must be freely given. The state should provide more protection than one would receive without a civil government. It almost goes without saying that Locke's political theory has had a powerful influence on American political thought.[11]

According to Natanson, given Locke's influence on American political thought, it is only natural to use Locke's theory of political consent to assess the political situation of blacks in America. He labels this Lockean position the "American-traditional" view of legal obligation.[12] Natanson believes that if we accept the Lockean account, some blacks, because of their unique history, remain in a Lockean "state of nature." The state of nature for Locke was a pre-civil society arrangement, where individuals had only themselves to depend on for the protection of their property. In this state there was no common law, no judge, and no agreed-upon person to punish violations of property rights.

This conclusion is worth examining for several reasons. First, the argument forces us to rethink our understanding of the nature of consent theory as a justification for state membership and political/legal obligation. Such an examination raises the following questions: what impact did being enslaved have on blacks giving political consent? Can we find a sign of black consent during Reconstruction?[13] Second, Natanson's argument is important for evaluating the present legal obligations of blacks.[14] Third, it may help us to better understand Locke's political theory. Fourth, while the Natanson article was written at the apex of the civil rights struggle, the argument that blacks did not consent to become United States citizens has a long history in the African-American community. In fact, it is still articulated by some members of the black community, as a call either for reparations or for the development of a black state.[15]

In what follows, I shall argue against both Natanson's conclusion about the citizenship status of blacks and his reading of Locke. I show that Locke's position, at least in *The Second Treatise*, supports the claim that all black Americans are citizens and, as such, have legal obligations as citizens. I shall also argue that there are no blacks in the United States who are in a Lockean state of nature. Natanson's argument is unsound because: he focuses on the wrong passages in Locke; he shows very little insight into the political history of black Americans; and he neglects the fact that citizenship through birthright is an important aspect of American law. Finally, Locke's work supports the position that the acts of civil disobedience in the 1960s were, in fact a justifiable and permissible response to the social and political injustices suffered by blacks.

THE SOCIAL CONTRACT AND BLACKS

An adequate defense of Natanson's position requires two arguments. First, that at the end of slavery some blacks remained in a state of nature, even after the passage of the Thirteenth and Fourteenth Amendments to the United States Constitution; and second, that there are some present-day blacks who are still in a state of nature. Let us now turn to the claim that some blacks after emancipation and the postwar amendments remained in a state of nature.

Natanson draws on two interrelated arguments from Locke to assess the political status of freed slaves at the end of the Civil War. He begins with the Lockean proviso that human beings have an inalienable right to life, liberty, and estate. This inalienable right existed in the state of nature and should be retained in civil society. Because civil society provides more security, people are quite willing to leave the state of nature and "join in society with others who are already united, or have a mind to unite for the mutual preservation of their lives, liberties and estates."[16]

Unfortunately, Natanson does not tell us what he means by "more security." The right to be protected is remarkably difficult to construe, but we do know that if a person is to be protected, presumably he or she must be protected from something. But what? We can, at least, agree to this: a liberal democratic state must provide protection from such abuses as lynching, assaults, and so forth. In addition, a liberal democratic state must ensure that a citizen be protected from political, legal, and public interferences in the exercise of his or her rights, provided that his or her actions do not violate the rights of others.[17]

Drawing on Locke, Natanson thinks that the state must provide the individual with more security than she or he would have had in the state of nature. Otherwise, there is no need to enter into the contract with other individuals. In the case of many blacks, it is clear that they were not accorded governmental protection as citizens while they were slaves. Blacks at the end of slavery, however, hoped that they would be accorded equal protection under the law. Unfortunately, their high hopes and government actions did not coincide.[18]

If, at emancipation, a pact was supposed to exist between blacks and the government, the government did not live up to its part of the contract. It is clear, according to Natanson, that some blacks never received the protection of their life, liberty, and property as would be mandated if they were citizens of the United States. Because governmental protection was never given, there was no social contract to accept. He thinks that it follows from this that the Negroes in question were not parties to the contract, for it is the acceptance of the governmental protective services which defines membership. According to Natanson, the government's failure to protect some blacks was not because these blacks did not want protection, but because it was never offered. As a consequence these blacks remained in the state of nature.[19]

CONSENT AND BLACKS

If the lack of protection were not enough, Natanson also thinks that Locke's position on consent, which forms the basis for his second argument, also supports the position that some blacks were still in a state of nature at the end of slavery.

Natanson realizes, however, that the political situation in America is very different from that Locke envisioned in *The Second Treatise*. He nevertheless thinks that historically the concept of consent (despite its weakness) has become important in the American political tradition as a justification for obedience to the law: the citizen ought to obey the law because he or she freely chose, by acceptance of government protection, to enter into a contract, one which provides him with a superior service that he or she cannot duplicate in a state of nature.

According to Natanson, when a native-born American joins those who accept the authority of the government, he or she does not indicate his consent either verbally or in writing, for there are no rites of entry into the social order. If explicit verbal or written consent is not given, is there some evidence that indicates that a native-born American acted by free choice and not coercion to become a willing party to the agreement? For Natanson, it is by acceptance of the most essential service the government can offer him, superior protection of his natural right to life, liberty, and estate (if we reason in line with the basic tenets of the natural-rights theory), that the individual expresses free consent to an agreement or contract with the government. Accepting government protection constitutes consent in its deepest meaning and at the same time is an establishment of contract.[20] In other words, to accept governmental protection willingly is to agree to government itself—in essence, it is an acceptance of genuine citizenship with all its benefits and responsibilities.

While noting that Locke thinks that only through explicit and expressed consent can a person become a true member of the state, Natanson contends that this is not completely applicable to the American political scene. In America, agreement to the social contract is made tacitly, by acceptance of government protection of one's natural rights. He admits that his version of tacit consent allows it to be as binding as Locke's expressed consent.

Using this modified version of Locke's position on consent, Natanson assesses the political status of freed slaves. His position here turns on whether or not, when American citizenship was conferred to blacks, they were in a position to give their consent. Natanson believes that politically unprotected blacks had not been in a position to dispose of their possessions and persons as they saw fit because slavery was a condition that severely restricted their personal autonomy. The inability of many blacks to have any control over their person caused many whites to conclude that slaves were children or childlike. Of course, one has to forget here that the behavior of blacks toward whites was impacted by the chattel slavery system.

Nevertheless, because blacks were seen as children or childlike, Natanson thinks that the government of the United States took a paternalistic position regarding citizenship and blacks. Blacks were denied the freedom to make any choice at all. The government thought that blacks were unable to choose and made them citizens without consent. "Thus, in their involuntary alienation from the American contract, these Negroes have been considered lacking in the potential for self-determination."[21]

If, however, blacks were capable of choosing United States citizenship and were not allowed to do so, they were denied a basic right: "Either way, these blacks were made citizens without their consent or input."[22] What, then, was the political status of those blacks who were made citizens? Natanson claims that they were nonpartici-pants in the contract, and, as such, not genuine citizens.

These blacks thus had a unique status. According to Natanson, because they were not allowed to freely choose, these blacks are still in a state of nature.[23]

The consideration of social contract thus leads Natanson to two conclusions: first, freed blacks are not genuine citizens; and second, they are still in a state of nature. According to Natanson, blacks must look to themselves for protection of their inalienable rights because the government cannot be counted upon to honor its part of the bargain. It follows, within the framework of the quid-pro-quo justice inherent in the American-traditional view of legal obligations, that "it cannot be held that these excluded Negroes [sic] ought to obey the law."[24]

THE STATE OF NATURE AND BLACKS

Let us assume that Natanson is correct about the following things: some blacks were not protected; there is no problem with his version of tacit consent; and his version of consent does bind an individual to the state. First, does it follow that those blacks were left in a state of nature? And second, does it also follow that some present-day blacks are still in a state of nature and not obligated to the government of America? The answer to both questions is no, but in order to see why, we need to assess Natanson's assumptions about the legal and moral status of blacks at the end of the Civil War.

Did slavery so undermine the autonomy of blacks that they were not in a position truly to consent to the state? Was slavery the ultimate destroyer of autonomy? Did slavery, as Stanley Elkins claims, render the slave incapable of making an informed decision?[25] Did the United States government fail to provide any assistance for newly freed slaves? What would show that former slaves had freely consented to the state?

It is possible to draw out one scenario to illustrate what needed to be done to ensure that blacks were informed about what it meant to be a citizen of the United States. Imari Obadele, founder and president of the Republic of New Africa, argues that blacks at the end of the Civil War should have been offered four options: become citizens of the United States; be allowed to leave the country; start their own country, either in the United States or some other country, or return to Africa.[26] It was the responsibility of the government to ensure that blacks were informed of their choices and then to provide the funding necessary for them to carry them out.

It must be assumed that, when Natanson claims that some blacks did not freely consent, he means either that at the enactment of the Fourteenth Amendment, some blacks were not in a position to understand what it meant to be citizens or that these blacks were not allowed to choose. Natanson, at times, seems to be making both claims. Either way, he believes, their acceptance of citizenship would not really be consent-based.

This position, however, is not supported by a careful reading of African-American history, in at least three important ways. First, the debate over the future of blacks in America was not limited to whites. Blacks had discussed the options open to them well before the Emancipation Proclamation. Paul Cuffe, a black businessman and merchant, as early as 1816 paid for the passage of free blacks to Freetown, Sierra Leone.[27]

But some people questioned the value of emigration as a way to solve the black problem. Frederick Douglass criticized all emigration schemes.[28] The general concerns of many blacks were stated in an open letter which Robert Purvis sent to the government emigration agent on August 28, 1862: "The children of the black man have enriched the soil by their tears, and sweat, and blood. Sir we were born here, and here we choose to remain."[29] Most blacks were committed to becoming United States citizens with all of the rights and responsibilities that come with citizenship.

Second, the view of blacks as hopeless victims has been challenged and shown to be false by W. E. B. DuBois, John Blassingame, Eric Foner and others. Their research also demonstrates that slavery was not as morally and intellectually damaging for blacks as had been suggested by Elkins.[30]

Freed slaves behaved responsibly. In South Carolina, for example, there was a generous appraisal of the personnel of a Negro delegation for the way they handled the responsibilities of government. Many of the state constitutions drawn up in 1867 and 1868, authored by blacks, were the most progressive the South had ever known.[31]

Furthermore, the federal government did try to help with the adjustment from slavery to freedom. When the Thirteenth Amendment was passed by Congress, Lincoln supported it; but it was his opinion that the transition from slavery to freedom should be a gradual procedure. After several plans to colonize freed slaves failed, he studied various means of making this transition. He favored a type of apprenticeship such as that tried by Great Britain, also later practiced in Maryland.[32]

In the end, the United States government established the Freedmen's Bureau as a government agency to oversee the social and political incorporation of blacks into the system. The bureau was established by an act of the United States Congress on March 3, 1965, to distribute clothing, food, and fuel to the destitute freedmen and oversee "all subjects" relating to their condition in the South. Despite its unprecedented responsibilities and powers, the bureau was clearly envisioned as a temporary expedient. Incredibly, no budget was appropriated—it would have to draw funds and staff from the War Department.[33]

The greatest impact of the Freedmen's Bureau was in the area of education. Education was not one of the original functions of the bureau but in 1866 became one of its authorized purposes:

> By 1869, there were 9,503 teachers in schools for freedmen, with about 5,000 of them from the Northern states. At the beginning, nearly all of the teachers were whites from

the North; but in 1870, the bureau reported that there were 1,324 Negro teachers out of a total of 3,300. By 1869, thirteen high schools or colleges had been established. In building the education system, the Freedmen's Bureau made major contributions, while the devoted and dedicated white teachers who came from Northern states were its agents in the schools. Their work was reflected in the noteworthy lives of many thousands of freedmen.[34]

The evidence is clear: the Freedmen's Bureau did have an important impact on the political and educational status of blacks after the Civil War.[35]

The government failed to protect the legal rights of many blacks, however, by withdrawing federal troops from Southern states, by failing to prevent the rise of the Ku Klux Klan, and by the enforcement of Jim Crow laws. Does this failure mean that blacks were no longer citizens? Before we address this question, we should note that blacks were cognizant of their choices; they chose to accept citizenship, and they attempted to make their citizenship real. It was not the willingness of blacks which caused the problems that developed around their citizenship, but governmental inaction.

To be specific, the governmental inaction was its failure to continue to ensure that the political power of blacks would not be usurped by the former slaveholders. The government pulled federal troops out of the south soon after the Civil War, which allowed the former slaveholders to regain political power. This action had the effect of denying to blacks the legal protections they were entitled to under the provisions of the Fourteenth Amendment. As citizens, they should have had governmental protection of their inalienable rights to life, liberty, and estate. It is clear that, at least in some Southern states, their political power had been usurped and, as a result, blacks were often tyrannized.[36] It is also clear that in many Southern states the governmental officials used race and racism as a basis for laws that restricted the political power of black citizens. One might think that all of this shows that blacks were not protected. But remember, Natanson's position is that being unprotected means that some blacks are not in a position to give consent. It is at this point that Locke's position . . . becomes crucial to the discussion.

LOCKE AND BLACK AMERICANS

. . . With emancipation, two amendments. the Fourteenth and Fifteenth, were written into the Constitution especially to protect the voting rights of the newly freed slaves. These amendments specifically directed states to guarantee voting rights to black citizens.

Three civil rights acts were enacted between 1866 and 1875 as a way of assuring equality of treatment (including the right to vote) to America's blacks. These acts—the Civil Rights Act of 1866, the Civil Rights Act of 1870, and the Civil Rights Act of 1875—along with the constitutional guarantee, permitted black people in the South to exercise the right to vote with relative ease during Reconstruction. After Reconstruction, however, several states adopted so-called grandfather clauses, which restricted registration and voting to persons who had voted prior to emancipation. This practice was finally declared unconstitutional by the

Supreme Court in 1915. With this defeat Southerners adopted the "white primary," through which the Democratic party prohibited blacks from participating in primary elections in nine states. When the white primary was outlawed, many Southern states resorted to gerrymandering as a way of disenfranchising blacks. In a long series of cases, the Supreme Court eventually curbed these practices, but blacks still lacked full participation in the political process.

The usurpation of political power was tyrannical in the sense that blacks were subject to laws they could not participate in making and, as free citizens, would not have given their consent to.[37] These blacks were denied both access to political information and the right to exercise their political rights. Many of the laws enacted without input from these blacks served to lower substantially the overall quality of their social and economic lives.[38] What did this tyrannical use of power do to the political status of blacks? Did this usurpation of political power force blacks back into a state of nature?

If we take seriously the notion that states can decide who is and who is not a citizen and if persons so described act as citizens—for example, pay taxes, defend the state, and demand that the state protect their political rights as citizens, then they are citizens. At the passage of the Fourteenth Amendment, blacks became citizens and their children and their children's children would be citizens. If we want to talk in Lockean terms, these citizens should have been protected.

For many blacks, both the federal and state governments failed to ensure blacks equal protection as prescribed by law. Locke thinks that when this happens the goal of citizens is to get the legislature to act according to the trust for which it was established: to protect property, broadly defined.[39] It is important to remember that for Locke, citizens have the right to judge whether or not the governmental trust has been broken. Unprotected black citizens are to be the judge of what actions to take against the government, but, of course, they should try to act within the established political framework to have their concerns addressed. Locke seems to think that representatives will be responsive and address the civil wrongs, once they are aware of them. But if the government is not responsive, civil disobedience can then be seen as a legitimate method both to make one's plight a matter of public concern and to force the government go uphold its part of the social contract.[40] The results of the civil rights movement seem to support Locke's contention.

At this point, the following claims can be made: first, many blacks wanted to be citizens, and when they gained American citizenship, they showed that they were capable of carrying out the responsibilities of citizenship; second, the federal government did make an attempt to help in the adjustment from slavery to freedom; and third, blacks were not in a state of nature.

BLACK AMERICANS AND THE STATE OF NATURE

How do these points affect the claim that present-day blacks are still in a state of nature? Obviously, they cannot still be in such a state if, . . . as my examination of black political history show[s], they were not in it to begin with.

Does it matter, as Natanson claims, that some blacks have never been in a position to exercise their political rights and have never enjoyed the protection of the government? There is no logical inconsistency between not being protected by the government in the American-traditional model and being a citizen. It is possible for citizens to have rights on the books but not be protected against the violation or infringement of these rights by others, even in a liberal democratic state. A political life in a liberal democratic state is compatible with the existence of laws that are not enforced. It does not follow that these politically unprotected individuals are not citizens. It does follow, however, that those citizens who are politically unprotected are justified in protesting the lack of protection of their rights, in the American-traditional model.[41]

CONSENT, CITIZENSHIP AND LEGAL STANDING

In the end, if we accept Natanson's position that some blacks are still in a state of nature, we encounter two more difficulties: first, if these individuals are not citizens of the state, their behavior cannot be seen as civil disobedience, but rather as an act of war against the state. It is a war they will lose. They can only claim rights as aliens, not as citizens. They must depend on the good will of those who are citizens (or perhaps some outside state) to try to convince the state to protect them and do whatever is necessary to make their citizenship real. It is unclear what legal claims they have against the state, however, since they are not citizens.

Second, to claim that some blacks are not genuine citizens is to deny the two conventional ways of assigning citizenship at birth. Legal scholars it has been noted:

> are generally content to distinguish between right of birth place (jus soli) and right of descent (jus sanguinis) as the two major alternative principles that states use in assigning citizenship at birth. They describe how different states use one or the other of these principles (or a combination of both) and discuss the problems posed for international order when the laws of different states conflict. They simply assume that people will normally acquire citizenship through birth and that there is nothing problematic about this. (States may permit citizenship to be to be acquired at a later stage but the very term used for this, "naturalization," suggests that birthright citizenship is the norm.)[42]

In the United States, being born in this country or to parents who are citizens makes one a citizen with all of the corresponding rights and responsibilities. To claim that some blacks are still in a state of nature is to claim that even though blacks are born in the United States, they are still not citizens.[43] The claim that some blacks, who have never relinquished their birthright citizenship, are in fact not citizens runs counter to our understanding of how an individual becomes a citizen of the United States.[44]

If Brock, Obadele, and Natanson are correct, what then is the status of those blacks who are not citizens? Aliens? Anyone who claims that blacks are not citizens of the United States has to explain why these blacks are not stateless beings—that is, citizens of no state.[45]

CONSENT, PROTECTION, AND CITIZENSHIP

Natanson's paper is important because he realizes that an argument like Brock's needs to be supported by a theory of what would count as legitimate consent. Since Natanson does allow for tacit consent, he has to show why consent theory in general is not undermined. We need to ask: if some present-day blacks have not consented, what counts as consent for present-day whites?

Natanson's use of Locke's theory of governmental protection to provide the other theoretical framework for understanding the legal status of some blacks[46] only pushes us back one step. Now we need a clear statement of Locke's theory of political protection. I have argued elsewhere that we can understand what it means to be unprotected within the Lockean state without returning to the state of nature.[47]

Natanson is correct that consent to political protection and the government's protection of members are important aspects of Locke's political theory, but his claim that some blacks are still in a state of nature is not supported by a careful reading of Locke. Locke seems only to claim that the state provides them with more benefits—protection, in this instance—than they would have in the state of nature.

Accepting minimal protection from the state does not entail that one is not entitled to greater protection from the state, owing to considerations of equality. Sometimes the claim "S accepts O" means that "S believes that S is entitled to no more than O." Sometimes, however, "S accepts O" means simply that S will start with O and go on from there. Natanson seems to have ignored the latter possibility.

Locke, and then later Rawls, realized that persons can be treated unjustly in a liberal democratic state, but neither thinks that these unjustly treated individuals lose their membership in the state nor their legal obligations.[48]

. . . It is tempting, in view of the racial oppression in America, to think that many blacks do not have political obligations to the state. The use of a Lockean argument is a doubled-edged sword: while the argument seems to show that blacks have no political obligations to the state, it also seems to show that the state has no political obligations to blacks.

But a careful reading of Locke's work and an insightful reading of black history support, as do our laws on citizenship, the conclusion that politically unprotected blacks in the United States are citizens and, as such, have legal obligations to the state. Just as important, the United States has obligations to its black citizens.

NOTES

1. See, for example, David Donald, *The Politics of Reconstruction* (Baton Rouge: Louisiana State University Press, 1965) and Horace E. Flack, *The Adoption of the Fourteenth Amendment* (Baltimore: Johns Hopkins University Press, 1988).

2. United States Constitution.

3. Quoted in Charles Fairman, *Reconstruction and Reunion 1864–1888: Part One* (New York: Macmillan, 1971), p. 1181.

4. Kwando M. Kinshasa, *Emigration vs. Assimilation* (Jefferson, N.C.: McFarland, 1988).

5. George M. Frederickson, *The Black Image in the White Mind: The Debate on Afro-American Character and Destiny, 1817–1914* (New York: Harper Torchbooks, 1972), pp. 130–64.

6. Frederickson, *Black Image*, p. 130.

7. Howard McGary, Jr., "Racial Integration and Racial Separatism: Conceptual Clarifications" in Leonard Harris, ed., *Philosophy Born of Struggle* (Dubuque, Ia.: Kendall/Hunt, 1983), pp. 199–211.

8. I follow here Kinshasa's summary of debates in the black press, in *Emigration vs. Assimilation*, pp. 110–20.

9. Robert Brock, "Morton Downey, Jr., Show," August 18, 1988. Brock also argues for reparations for blacks. The question of reparations has been discussed in the philosophical literature. See, for example, Bernard Boxill, "The Morality of Reparations," *Social Theory and Practice* 2: 1 (1972), 113–22; Howard McGary, "Justice and Reparations," *Philosophical Forum* 9: 2/3 (1977–78), 250–63 [See Chapter 10—ed.]; J. W. Nickle, "Should Reparations Be to Groups or Individuals?" *Analysis* 34: 5 (1973), 154–60.

10. Harvey Natanson, "Locke and Hume: Bearing on the Legal Obligation of the Negro," *Journal of Value Inquiry* 5: 1 (1970), 35–43. While blacks in the Northern part of the United States might have been denied some political protection, for many Southern blacks governmental protection was almost nil. It is these blacks that Natanson must believe are not members of the contract.

11. See, for example, Harry J. Carman and Harold C. Syrett, *A History of the American People* (New York: Alfred A. Knopf, 1975), pp 114ff.; J. W. Gough, *John Locke's Political Philosophy* (London: Oxford, 1950), p. 103, and Alfred H. Kelly; and Winfred A. Harbison, *The American Constitution* (New York: W. W. Norton, 1963), p. 90.

12. Natanson, "Locke and Hume," p. 35.

13. See, for example, Eric Foner, *Reconstruction: America's Unfinished Revolution 1863–1877* (New York: Harper & Row, 1988), pp. 163–65.

14. This does not mean that there has not been a change in their formal status, but that their real status has not changed. See, for example, Joe Feagin, "Slavery Unwilling to Die: The Background of Black Oppression in the 1980s," *Journal of Black Studies* 17: 2 (1986), 173–200.

15. See, for example, Imari Abubakari Obadele, *Free the Land!* (Washington D.C.: House of Songhay, 1984).

16. John Locke quoted in Natanson, "Locke and Hume," p. 36.

17. For a discussion of the issue of protection and political obligation, see Bill Lawson, "African-Americans, Crime Victimizations, and Political Obligations," in Diane Shank and David I. Caplan, eds., *To Be a Victim: Encounters with Crime and Injustice* (New York: Plenum, 1991), pp. 141–58.

18. "Reconstruction was a time of hope, the period when the Thirteenth, Fourteenth, and Fifteenth Amendments were adopted, giving Negroes the vote and the promise of equality.

"But campaigns of violence and intimidation accompanied these optimistic expressions of a new age, as the Ku Klux Klan and other secret organizations sought to suppress the emergence into society of the new Negro citizens. Major riots occurred in Memphis, Tennessee, where 46 Negroes were reported killed and 75 wounded, and in the Louisiana centers of Colfax and Coushatta where more than 100 Negro and white republicans were massacred."

Report of the National Advisory Commission on Civil Disorders (Washington, D.C.: U.S. Government Printing Office, 1968), p. 98.

19. Natanson, "Locke and Hume," p. 39.

20. Ibid., p. 37.

21. Ibid., p. 39.

22. Ibid.

23. Ibid.

24. Ibid.

25. Stanley M. Elkins, *Slavery: A Problem in American Institutional and Intellectual Life* (Chicago: University of Chicago Press, 1976), pp. 249–50.

26. I. A. Obadele, "The Struggle Is for Land," in Robert Chrisman and Nathan Hare, eds, *Pan-Africanism* (New York: Bobbs-Merrill, 1974), pp. 175–92.

27. Sheldon H. Harris, *Paul Cuffe: Black America and the African Return* (New York: Simon and Schuster, 1972), p. 69.

28. See, for example, Benjamin Quarles, *The Negro in the Civil War* (Boston: Little Brown, 1953), pp. 132–62.

29. Ibid., p. 157.

30. Elkins, *Slavery*; Foner, *Reconstruction*; John Blassingame, *The Slave Community* (New York: Oxford University Press, 1972); and W. E. B. DuBois, *Black Reconstruction* (1935; rpt. Millwood, N.Y.: Kraus-Thomas, 1963).

31. Franklin, *From Slavery to Freedom*, p. 317.

32. In 1833, the British Empire had attempted to solve its slave problem by the institution of a five-year period of transition called apprenticeship. This plan proved unsuccessful, however, and was terminated before the five years had ended. Complete and immediate emancipation was then adopted. Charles H. Wesley and Patricia W. Romero, *Negro Americans in the Civil War* (New York: Publishers Company, 1967), pp. 114–67.

33. Charles Sumner had proposed establishing the Freedmen's Bureau as a permanent agency with a secretary of cabinet rank—an institutionalization of the nation's responsibility to the freed slaves—but such an idea ran counter to the strong inhibitions against long-term guardianship. Indeed, at the last moment, Congress redefined the bureau's responsibilities so as to include Southern white refugees as well as freedmen, a vast expansion of its authority that aimed to counteract the impression of preferential treatment for blacks. Foner, *Reconstruction*, p. 69.

34. Wesley and Romero, *Negro Americans*, p. 134.

35. See for example, Horace Mann Bond, *The Education of the Negro in the American Social Order* (New York: Octagon Books, 1966); George R. Bentley,

A *History of the Freedmen's Bureau* (Philadelphia: University of Pennsylvania Press, 1955); Henderson H. Donald, *The Negro Freedman* (New York: Henry Schuman, 1952), W. E. B. DuBois, "The Freedmen's Bureau," *Atlantic Monthly* 87 (1901), pp. 354–65; Walter L. Fleming, *Civil War and Reconstruction in Alabama* (New York: Columbia University Press, 1905); Paul S. Pierce, *The Freedmen's Bureau: A Chapter in the History of Reconstruction* (Iowa City: Haskell House, 1904).

36. Milton D. Morris, *The Politics of Black America* (New York: Harper and Row, 1975), pp. 49–118; William A. Russ, "The Negro and White Disfranchisement during Radical Reconstruction," *Journal of Negro History* 19: 2 (1934), 171–92; C. Van Woodward, *Reunion and Reaction: The Compromise of 1877 and the End of Reconstruction* (Boston: Little, Brown, 1951).

37. Ibid., p. 111, sec. 198.

38. Sig Synnestvedt, *The White Response to Black Emancipation* (New York: Macmillan, 1972).

39. Locke, *Second Treatise*, p. 138, sec. 242.

40. Ibid., p. 130, sec. 233.

41. See John Rawls, *A Theory of Justice* (Cambridge, Mass.: Harvard University Press, 1971), pp. 46–70; and Larry Thomas, "To a Theory of Justice: An Epilogue," Philosophical Forum 6: 2–3 (1975), 244–53.

42. Joseph H. Carens, "Who Belongs? Theoretical and Legal Question about Birthright Citizenship in the United States," *University of Toronto Law Journal* 37: 4 (1987), 413–35.

43. The question of citizenship for blacks was thought to be resolved with the passage of the Fourteenth Amendment. The conferring of citizenship on blacks was first presented in the Civil Rights Act of 1866. Its most important part began: "all persons born in the United States are hereby declared to be citizens of the United States." See Terry Eastland and William J. Bennett, *Counting by Race: Equality from the Founding Fathers to Bakke and Weber* (New York: Basic Books, 1979), p. 61.

44. Carens notes that, for example, Britain and the United States took different views on the question of whether citizenship acquired at birth entailed perpetual allegiance or could be terminated by voluntary expatriation and subsequent naturalization in a new country. This was an important source of conflict between the two countries for much of the nineteenth century. The most common problems arise from the fact that differences in nationality laws leave some people stateless and others with dual citizenship (which sometimes entails conflicting sets of obligations). "Who Belongs?" p. 415.

45. See, for example, P. Weis, *Nationality and Statelessness in International Law* (Westport, Conn.: Hyperion Press, 1956), and Marc Vishniak, "The Legal Status of Stateless Persons," "Jews and the Postwar World" 6 (New York: American Jewish Committee, 1954).

46. Natanson, "Locke and Hume," p. 42.

47. See Bill Lawson, "Crime, Minorities and the Social Contract," *Criminal Justice Ethics* 9: 2 (1990), 16–24.

48. John Rawls, *A Theory of Justice*, pp. 363–94.

SUGGESTIONS FOR DISCUSSION

1. What rights and what duties does citizenship warrant? Do moral considerations license treating citizens differently from noncitizens in some respects?

2. Are there any justifiable grounds for restricting citizenship and thereby excluding some from the rights and responsibilities of citizenship?

3. Do historical considerations like slavery or denial of women's or blacks' rights to vote warrant special considerations today in combatting the legacy of sexist and racist exclusion? Or are demands of justice fulfilled by the social commitment to universal principles applicable to all irrespective of race and gender?

4. Is patriotism morally justifiable?

FOR FURTHER READING

Alejandro, R. *Hermeneutics, Citizenship, and the Public Sphere.* Albany, N.Y.: SUNY Press, 1993.

Aristotle. *The Politics.*

Baier, A. "Some Virtues of Resident Alienation." *Nomos* 34 (1992): 291–308.

Barber, B. *Strong Democracy: Participatory Politics for a New Age.* Berkeley: University of California Press, 1984.

Bookchin, M. *The Rise of Urbanization and the Decline of Citizenship.* San Francisco: Sierra Club Books, 1987.

Carens, J. H. "Who Belongs? Theoretical and Legal Questions about Birthright Citizenship in the United States." *University of Toronto Law Journal* 37, 4 (1987): 413–35.

Dietz, M. "Citizenship with a Feminist Face: The Problem with Maternal Thinking." *Political Theory* 13 (1985): 19–37.

Eastland, T., and Bennett, W. J. *Counting by Race: Equality from the Founding Fathers to Bakke and Weber.* New York: Basic Books, 1979.

Fogel, R. W. *Without Consent or Contract.* New York: W. W. Norton, 1989.

Goldwin, R. A., Kaufman, A., and Schambra, W. A., eds. *Forging Unity Out of Diversity: The Approach of Eight Nations.* Washington, D.C.: The American Enterprise Institute for Public Policy, 1989.

Hobbes, T. *De Cive, or the Citizen.*

Lawson, B. E. "Politically Oppressed Citizens." *Journal of Value Inquiry* 25, 4 (1991): 335–38.

Lively, D. *The Constitution and Race.* New York: Praeger, 1992.

Locke, J. *The Second Treatise of Government.*

McGary, H., and Lawson, B. E. *Between Slavery and Freedom: Philosophy and American Slavery.* Bloomington, In.: Indiana University Press, 1993.

Marshall, T. H. *Class, Citizenship and Social Development.* Garden City, N.Y.: Doubleday, 1964.

Nauta, L. "Changing Conceptions of Citizenship." *Praxis International* 12, 1 (April 1992): 20–34.

Oldfield, A. *Civic Republicanism and the Modern World.* New York: Routledge, 1990.

Pateman, C. *Participation and Democratic Theory.* Cambridge: Cambridge University Press, 1970.

Riesenberg, R. *Citizenship in the Western Tradition: Plato to Rousseau.* Chapel Hill, N.C.: University of North Carolina Press, 1992.

Ringer, B. *We the People and Others: Duality and America's Treatment of its Racial Minorities.* New York: Routledge, Chapman and Hall, 1985.

Shklar, J. *American Citizenship: The Quest for Inclusion.* Cambridge: Harvard University Press, 1991.

Skillen, T. "Active Citizenship as Political Obligation." *Radical Philosophy* (U.K.) 58 (Summer 1991): 10–13.

Takaki, R., ed. *From Different Shores: Perspectives on Race and Ethnicity in America.* New York: Oxford University Press, 1987.

Thompson, D. F. *The Democratic Citizen.* Cambridge: Cambridge University Press, 1970.

Walzer, M. *Spheres of Justice.* Princeton: Princeton University Press, 1983.

AFFIRMATIVE ACTION

Citizenship, it was argued in Chapter 8, defines full membership in the modern nation state. Membership has come to presuppose equal treatment for all who meet the criteria of citizenship, at least in formal terms of the law. Nevertheless, discrimination against members of racial groups defined as nonwhite has been a persistent feature of social history. It was widely held in the past that blacks were irrational or intellectually inferior and therefore incapable of performing intellectually demanding functions. These appeals served to legitimize or rationalize excluding blacks from the benefits of citizenship and often from rightful claims to membership.

Evidence that was cited to support such derogatory and injurious prejudice turned out to involve biased samples, the testing was inadequate and culturally skewed, and the test results were overgeneralized or manipulated to "substantiate" prejudiced hypotheses. Reasonable people generally now agree that it is wrong for both persons and social institutions to discriminate against others, citizens and noncitizens alike, on grounds of their race. An employer or educational institution, for example, should not exclude people because they are African American, or Jewish, or Latino. No natural or biological relation exists between racial membership, on one hand, and ability, task performance, or moral desert, on the other. Social institutions play a formative role in our lives, so institutional discrimination on the basis of race is especially unjust, because it excludes persons from social goods, services, and opportunities that ought to be available to all. In short, racial membership ought ideally to be irrelevant to just social distributions, and any form of racial discrimination violates the moral principle that people be treated equitably (see Chapters 5, 6, and 7).

Racially defined minorities, especially blacks, have suffered the injustices of being denied social goods readily available to others (notably white males). Racialized minorities have been handicapped in realizing available opportunities, and in many cases they have been completely excluded from the competition for social resources, as they also have been denied citizenship. A person whose grandparents or parents had been denied access to medical school, say, for no reason other than their racial constitution is unlikely now to enjoy the material and educational opportunities and resources available to one whose family members were not so denied. In turn, this inaccessibility to social goods militates against the self-respect of minority group members and undermines their sense of self-worth, often with devastating social implications.

Affirmative Remedies   Pressing questions arise concerning social justice. Given the long history and deep legacy of discrimination, would justice be best served simply by outlawing these unfair discriminatory practices, as some hold? If no affirmative programs are instituted to complement the declaration that such practices are illegal, would it not leave in place current control of social institutions and economic inequities that favor white males? Affirmative remedies may be introduced, accordingly, either to compensate for past wrongs and inequities or to institute a more just social arrangement.

Compensation and Equality   So, remedies for discrimination generally tend to be of two kinds. *Retrospective* remedies set out to rectify past harms by instituting compensatory programs. These remedies appeal to the principle of compensation, which claims that anyone harmed in violation of his or her rights should be (in legal language) "made whole again" by the injuring party; that is, they should be reinstated to the position they would have occupied had the harm not taken place. So these remedies are mainly *consequentialist* in aiming to remove the harms of extensive discrimination. By contrast, *prospective* remedies tend to be *deontological,* rejecting the appeal to consequences in favor of the principle of equality. The principle of equality maintains that the interests of each individual must carry the same weight as those of any other. Remedies appealing to the principle are concerned with the moral quality of future society and aim to bring about a representative racial blend in institutions, which is considered to be just independent of any good consequences that may follow from it. These retrospective-consequentialist and prospective-deontological patterns are trends, not hard and fast rules. Some have argued that a backward-looking duty of reparation is deontological; and some prospective arguments directed at achieving a good society are consequentialist.

Affirmative Action and Preferential Treatment   Affirmative action programs tend more to be prospective than retrospective. While they may aim at compensating for past wrongs, they tend mostly to establish equal opportunity (if not equal distributions) for those defined as protected groups. Accordingly, they can be viewed as modest redistributive mechanisms. Now the principle of equality might require much in this respect: that every effort be made to find candidates from protected groups in job hiring, promotions, and university and other admissions; that availability of positions be openly advertised and characterized in nondiscriminatory ways; and that hiring or admissions committees employ nondiscriminatory categories and criteria in their decisions. One prominent form that affirmative action programs have assumed is preferential treatment, that is, hiring or admitting members of protected population groups primarily because of their group membership. Some have objected that preferential treatment of groups whose members have been excluded from access to social resources amounts to unacceptable forms of reverse discrimination against those formerly favored (usually white males). Preferential treatment programs favoring minorities are taken to exclude or discriminate against others unfairly on the basis of their race. The moral question facing us here, then, is whether preferential treatment programs by nature discriminate in reverse against white men and so are morally impermissible, or whether to conceive of them in this way is to misunderstand their nature.

■ SUPREME COURT RULINGS: BAKKE AND CROSON

This issue can be illustrated in terms of recent Supreme Court decisions concerning remedies for racial discrimination. In *Brown v. Board of Education* (1954), the "separate but equal" principle was declared unconstitutional. This principle, articulated in *Plessy v. Ferguson* (1896), had afforded southern states convenient grounds for maintaining segregated schooling, despite the Fourteenth Amendment (1868). Over the ensuing two decades, the Court moved considerably beyond the race-neutral spirit of the Fourteenth Amendment and the Civil Rights Act (1964). Preferential treatment of minorities (and women) in job hiring and college admissions was considered permissible: minority (and women) candidates could be hired or admitted to positions reserved for them even when white or male candidates might be at least as well qualified. For institutions where the effects of racial discrimination were found to be deepseated, the Court permitted employment, promotion, or admissions quotas to be used. Quotas guarantee set proportions of available positions for candidates of protected groups. This progressive trend was restricted in a landmark ruling, *University of California v. Bakke* (1978). The University of California, Davis, Medical School had reserved 16 of 100 first-year slots for minority students (blacks, Hispanics, and Filipinos) whose entrance qualifications *might* be lower than those of white candidates. Alan Bakke, a white applicant, was twice rejected by Davis despite better test scores than those of some minority candidates who were accepted. The Court ruled that Bakke had been the victim of reverse racial discrimination. Use of racial quotas in hiring or admissions could not be justified simply on the basis of their beneficial social effects. The Court nevertheless upheld that colleges and universities may use "race" as one of their criteria for admission. Since Bakke, the Court has granted limited sanction to the temporary use of quotas. Quotas have been considered an exceptional institutional remedy for deep-seated intentional discrimination (as in the Alabama state police, which has continued to exclude blacks from promotions to senior positions). Use of quotas or goals becomes impermissible once it is evident that the discriminatory trend at issue has been reversed.

A recent case, *City of Richmond v. Croson* (1989), while continuing to acknowledge the constitutionality of preferential treatment programs, defined stricter standards for their acceptability. The City of Richmond, Virginia, had adopted an affirmative action plan setting aside 30 percent of the dollar amount of each construction contract to minority subcontractors as a condition of being awarded the contract. Previously, the Court had insisted for the program's constitutionality only that race not be the sole basis of selection and that government agencies or institutions meet a standard of intermediate scrutiny, a test showing reasonable cause for the program's effectiveness. In *Croson,* the Court significantly strengthened the standard for constitutionality of any preferential treatment program, demanding now that the City of Richmond show a compelling state interest or effectively prove that such a program was the only available means to address prior discrimination. This, in turn, would necessitate that the plan be narrowly tailored to remedy the effects strictly of demonstrable prior discrimination.

In his dissent, Justice Marshall argued that the majority's insistence on heightened scrutiny for the constitutionality of remedial programs indicates that the majority on the Court for the first time mistakenly consider racial discrimination to be a thing of the past. Marshall claimed that a city like Richmond nevertheless could offer two compelling interests in support of their minority set-aside programs. First, it could claim an interest in eradicating the continuing effects of past racist discrimination; second, it could commit itself to preventing its own spending decisions from reinforcing the continuing exclusionary effects of past discrimination.

Justice Lewis F. Powell, Jr.

MAJORITY OPINION IN UNIVERSITY OF CALIFORNIA v. BAKKE

I

Over the past 30 years, this Court has embarked upon the crucial mission of interpreting the Equal Protection Clause with the view of assuring to all persons "the protection of equal laws," in a Nation confronting a legacy of slavery and racial discrimination. Because the landmark decisions in this area arose in response to the continued exclusion of Negroes from the mainstream of American society, they could be characterized as involving discrimination by the "majority" white race against the Negro minority. But they need not be read as depending upon that characterization for their results. It suffices to say that "[o]ver the years, this Court has consistently repudiated '[d]istinctions between citizens solely because of their ancestry' as being 'odious to a free people whose institutions are founded upon the doctrine of equality.'"

Petitioner urges us to adopt for the first time a more restrictive view of the Equal Protection Clause and hold that discrimination against members of the white "majority" cannot be suspect if its purpose can be characterized as "benign." The clock of our liberties, however, cannot be turned back to 1868. It is far too late to argue that the guarantee of equal protection to all persons permits the recognition of special wards entitled to a degree of protection greater than that accorded others. "The Fourteenth Amendment is not directed solely against discrimination due to a 'two-class theory'—that is, based upon differences between 'white' and Negro." . . .

I I

We have held that in "order to justify the use of a suspect classification, a State must show that its purpose or interest is both constitutionally permissible and substantial, and that its use of the classification is 'necessary . . . to the accomplishment' of its purpose of the safeguarding of its interest." The special admissions program purports to serve the purposes of: (i) "reducing the historic deficit of traditionally disfavored minorities in medical schools and in the medical profession"; (ii) countering the effects of societal discrimination; (iii) increasing the number of physicians who will practice in communities currently underserved; and (iv) obtaining the educational benefits that flow from an ethnically diverse student body. It is necessary to decide

United States Supreme Court, 438 U.S. 265 (1978).

which, if any, of these purposes is substantial enough to support the use of a suspect classification. . . .

I I I

A

It may be assumed that the reservation of a specified number of seats in each class for individuals from the preferred ethnic groups would contribute to the attainment of considerable ethnic diversity in the student body. But petitioner's argument that this is the only effective means of serving the interest of diversity is seriously flawed. In a most fundamental sense the argument misconceives the nature of the state interest that would justify consideration of race or ethnic background. It is not an interest in simple ethnic diversity, in which a specified percentage of the student body is in effect guaranteed to be members of selected ethnic groups, with the remaining percentage an undifferentiated aggregation of students. The diversity that furthers a compelling state interest encompasses a far broader array of qualifications and characteristics of which racial or ethnic origin is but a single though important element. Petitioner's special admissions program, focused solely on ethnic diversity, would hinder rather than further attainment of genuine diversity.

Nor would the state interest in genuine diversity be served by expanding petitioner's two-track system into a multitrack program with a prescribed number of seats set aside for each identifiable category of applicants. Indeed, it is inconceivable that a university would thus pursue the logic of petitioner's two-track program to the illogical end of insulating each category of applicants with certain desired qualifications from competition with all other applicants. . . .

. . . [A]n admissions program which considers race only as one factor is simply a subtle and more sophisticated—but no less effective—means of according racial preference than the Davis program. A facial intent to discriminate, however, is evident in petitioner's preference program and not denied in this case. No such facial infirmity exists in an admissions program where race or ethnic background is simply one element—to be weighed fairly against other elements—in the selection process. "A boundary line," as Mr. Justice Frankfurther remarked in another connection, "is none the worse for being narrow." And a court would not assume that a university, professing to employ a facially nondiscriminatory admissions policy, would operate it as a cover for the functional equivalent of a quota system. In short, good faith would be presumed in the absence of a showing to the contrary in the manner permitted by our cases.

B

In summary, it is evident that the Davis special admissions program involves the use of an explicit racial classification never before countenanced by this Court. It tells applicants who are not Negro, Asian, or Chicano that they are totally excluded from a specific percentage of the seats in an entering class. No matter how strong their qualifications, quantitative and extracurricular, including their own potential for contribution to educational diversity, they are never afforded the chance to compete with applicants from the preferred groups for the special admissions seats. At the same time, the preferred applicants have the opportunity to compete for every seat in the class.

The fatal flaw in petitioner's preferential program is its disregard of individual rights as guaranteed by the Fourteenth Amendment. Such rights are not absolute. But when a State's distribution of benefits or imposition of burdens hinges on ancestry or the color of a person's skin or ancestry, that individual is entitled to a demonstration that the challenged classification is necessary to promote a substantial state interest. Petitioner has failed to carry this burden. For this reason, that portion of the California court's judgment holding petitioner's special admissions program invalid under the Fourteenth Amendment must be affirmed.

C

In enjoining petitioner from ever considering the race of any applicant, however, the courts below failed to recognize that the State has a substantial interest that legitimately may be served by a properly devised admissions program involving the competitive consideration of race and ethnic origin. For this reason, so much of the California court's judgment as enjoins petitioner from an consideration of the race of any applicant must be reversed.

Justice Sandra Day O'Connor

MAJORITY OPINION IN *CITY OF RICHMOND v. J. A. CROSON AND CO.*

Bidder brought suit challenging city's plan requiring prime contractors awarded city construction contracts to subcontract at least 30% of the dollar amount of each contract to one or more "Minority Business Enterprises." . . . The Supreme Court, Justice O'Connor, held that: (1) city failed to demonstrate compelling governmental interest justifying the plan, and (2) plan was not narrowly tailored to remedy effects of prior discrimination. . . .

In this case, we confront once again the tension between the Fourteenth Amendment's guarantee of equal treatment to all citizens, and the use of race-based measures to ameliorate the effects of past discrimination on the opportunities enjoyed by members of minority groups in our society. . . .

United States Supreme Court, 109 U.S. 706 (1989).

I

On April 11, 1983, the Richmond City Council adopted the Minority Business Utilization Plan (the Plan). The Plan required prime contractors to whom the city awarded construction contracts to subcontract at least 30% of the dollar amount of the contract to one or more Minority Business Enterprises (MBE's) . . . The 30% setaside did not apply to city contracts awarded to minority-owned prime contractors. . . .

[1] The Plan defined an MBE as "[a] business at least fifty-one (51) percent of which is owned and controlled . . . by minority group members." . . . "Minority group members" were defined as "[c]itizens of the United States who are Blacks, Spanishspeaking, Orientals, Indians, Eskimos, or Aleuts." . . .

I I I

A

[2] The Equal Protection Clause of the Fourteenth Amendment provides that "[n]o State shall . . . deny to *any person* within its jurisdiction the equal protection of the laws." (Emphasis added.) As this Court has noted in the past, the "rights created by the first section of the Fourteenth Amendment are, by its terms, guaranteed to the individual. The rights established are personal rights." . . . The Richmond Plan denies certain citizens the opportunity to compete for a fixed percentage of public contracts based solely upon their race. To whatever racial group these citizens belong, their "personal rights" to be treated with equal dignity and respect are implicated by a rigid rule erecting race as the sole criterion in an aspect of public decisionmaking.

Absent searching judicial inquiry into the justification for such race-based measure, there is simply no way of determining what classifications are "benign" or "remedial" and what classifications are in fact motivated by illegitimate notions of racial inferiority or simple racial politics. Indeed, the purpose of strict scrutiny is to "smoke out" illegitimate uses of race by assuring that the legislative body is pursuing a goal important enough to warrant use of a highly suspect tool. The test also ensures that the means chosen "fit" this compelling goal so closely that there is little or no possibility that the motive for the classification was illegitimate racial prejudice or stereotype.

[3] Classifications based on race carry a danger of stigmatic harm. Unless they are strictly reserved for remedial settings, they may in fact promote notions of racial inferiority and lead to a politics of racial hostility. . . .

"[B]ecause racial characteristics so seldom provide a relevant basis for disparate treatment, and because classifications based on race are potentially so harmful to the entire body politic, it is especially important that the reasons for any such classification be clearly identified and unquestionably legitimate." . . . The "evidence" relied upon by the dissent, the history of school desegregation in Richmond and numerous congressional reports, does little to define the scope of any injury to minority contractors in Richmond or the necessary remedy. The factors relied upon by the dissent could justify a preference of any size or duration. . . .

V

[9] Nothing we say today precludes a state or local entity from taking action to rectify the effects of identified discrimination within its jurisdiction. If the city of Richmond had evidence before it that non-minority contractors were systematically excluding minority businesses from subcontracting opportunities it could take action to end the discriminatory exclusion. Where there is a significant statistical disparity between the number of qualified minority contractors willing and able to perform a particular service and the number of such contractors actually engaged by the locality or the locality's prime contractors, an inference of discriminatory exclusion could arise. . . .

Justice Thurgood Marshall

DISSENTING OPINION IN *CITY OF RICHMOND v. J. A. CROSON AND CO.*

It is a welcome symbol of racial progress when the former capital of the Confederacy acts forthrightly to confront the effects of racial discrimination in its midst. In my view, nothing in the Constitution can be construed to prevent Richmond, Virginia, from allocating a portion of its contracting dollars for businesses owned or controlled by members of minority groups. Indeed, Richmond's set-aside program is indistinguishable in all meaningful respects from—and in fact was patterned upon—the federal set-aside plan which this Court upheld in *Fullilove v. Klutznick*, 448 U.S. 448, 100 S.Ct. 2758, 65 L.Ed.2d 902 (1980).

A majority of this Court holds today, however, that the Equal Protection Clause of the Fourteenth Amendment blocks Richmond's initiative. The essence of the majority's position is that Richmond has failed to catalog adequate findings to prove that past discrimination has impeded minorities from joining or participating fully in Richmond's construction contracting industry. I find deep irony in second-guessing Richmond's judgment on this point. As much as any municipality in the United States, Richmond knows what racial discrimination is; a century of decisions by this and other federal courts has richly documented the city's disgraceful history of public and private racial discrimination. In any event, the Richmond City Council *has* supported its determination that minorities have been wrongly excluded from local

United States Supreme Court, 109 U.S. 706 (1989).

construction contracting. Its proof includes statistics showing that minority-owned businesses have received virtually no city contracting dollars and rarely if ever belonged to area trade associations; testimony by municipal officials that discrimination has been widespread in the local construction industry; and the same exhaustive and widely publicized federal studies relied on in *Fullilove*, studies which showed that pervasive discrimination in the Nation's tight-knit construction industry had operated to exclude minorities from public contracting. These are precisely the types of statistical and testimonial evidence which, until today, this Court had credited in cases approving of race-conscious measure designed to remedy past discrimination. . . .

A

1

Richmond has two powerful interests in setting aside a portion of public contracting funds for minority-owned enterprises. The first is the city's interest in eradicating the effects of past racial discrimination. It is far too late in the day to doubt that remedying such discrimination is a compelling, let alone an important, interest. . . .

Richmond has a second compelling interest in setting aside, where possible, a portion of its contracting dollars. That interest is the prospective one of preventing the city's own spending decisions from reinforcing and perpetuating the exclusionary effects of past discrimination. . . .

The majority is wrong to trivialize the continuing impact of government acceptance or use of private institutions or structures once wrought by discrimination. When government channels all its contracting funds to a white-dominated community of established contractors whose racial homogeneity is the product of private discrimination, it does more than place its *imprimatur* on the practices which forged and which continued to define that community. It also provides a measurable boost to those economic entities that have thrived within it, while denying important economic benefits to those entities which, but for prior discrimination, might well be better qualified to receive valuable government contracts. In my view, the interest in ensuring that the government does not reflect and reinforce prior private discrimination in dispensing public contracts is every bit as strong as the interest in eliminating private discrimination—an interest which the court has repeatedly deemed compelling. . . . The more government bestows its rewards on those persons or businesses that were positioned to thrive during a period of private racial discrimination, the tighter the deadhand grip of prior discrimination becomes on the present and future. Cities like Richmond may not be constitutionally required to adopt set-aside plans. . . . But there can be no doubt that when Richmond acted affirmatively to stem the perpetuation of patterns of discrimination through its own decisionmaking, it served an interest of the highest order. . . .

2

Richmond's reliance on localized, industry-specific findings is a far cry from the reliance on generalized "societal discrimination" which the majority decries as a basis for remedial action. . . . But characterizing the plight of Richmond's minority contractors as mere "social discrimination" is not the only respect in which the majority's critique shows an unwillingness to come to grips with why construction-contracting in Richmond is essentially a whites-only enterprise. The majority also takes the disingenuous approach of disaggregating Richmond's local evidence, attacking it piecemeal, and thereby concluding that no *single* piece of evidence adduced by the city, "standing alone," . . . suffices to prove past discrimination. But items of evidence do not, of course, "stand[d] alone" or exist in alien juxtaposition; they necessarily work together, reinforcing or contradicting each other. . . .

I I I

A

Today, for the first time, a majority of this Court has adopted strict scrutiny as its standard of Equal Protection Clause review of race-conscious remedial measures. . . . This is an unwelcome development. A profound difference separates governmental actions that themselves are racist, and governmental actions that seek to remedy the effects of prior racism or to prevent neutral governmental activity from perpetuating the effects of such racism. . . .

Racial classifications "drawn on the presumption that once race is inferior to another or because they put the weight of government behind racial hatred and separatism" warrant the strictest judicial scrutiny because of the very irrelevance of these rationales. . . . By contrast, racial classifications drawn for the purpose of remedying the effects of discrimination that itself was race based have a highly pertinent basis: the tragic and indelible fact that discrimination against blacks and other racial minorities in this Nation has pervaded our Nation's history and continues to scar our society. . . .

In concluding that remedial classifications warrant no different standard of review under the Constitution than the most brutal and repugnant forms of state-sponsored racism, a majority of this Court signals that it regards racial discrimination as largely a phenomenon of the past, and that government bodies need no longer preoccupy themselves with rectifying racial injustice. I, however, do not believe this Nation is anywhere close to eradicating racial discrimination or its vestiges. In constitutionalizing its wishful thinking, the majority today does a grave disservice not only to those victims of past and present racial discrimination in this Nation whom government has sought to assist, but also to this Court's long tradition of approaching issues of race with the utmost sensitivity.

I V

The majority today sounds a full-scale retreat from the Court's longstanding solicitude to race-conscious remedial efforts "directed toward deliverance of the century-old promise of equality of economic opportunity." . . . The new and restrictive tests it applies scuttle one city's effort to surmount its discriminatory past, and imperil those of dozens more localities. I, however, profoundly disagree with the cramped vision of Equal Protection Clause which the majority offers today and with its application of that vision to Richmond, Virginia's, laudable set-aside plan. The battle against pernicious racial discrimination or its effects is nowhere near won. I must dissent.

■ **STEPHEN CARTER: BEST BLACK SYNDROME**

In his provocative analysis, Stephen Carter admits openly to being the beneficiary of special programs and preferences. But he adds that such programs carry with them a general social assumption that blacks, in particular, are unable to escape: no matter how well qualified, black people are considered incapable of competing intellectually with whites. Blacks, even if better than all others, are reduced stereotypically to competing only for special privileges with other blacks. Carter calls this phenomenon "The Best Black Syndrome." Thus blacks, no matter how good, are reduced to competing only with each other. In turn, this has a double effect: not only are mistakes by blacks amplified, but the best blacks stand out and are sought out too. Nevertheless, blacks have to work twice as hard to be considered half as good.

The best black syndrome, Carter argues, was not created by affirmative action but by the history of racist assumptions. However, affirmative action programs are thought to aggravate racist exclusions, for not only are they instituted in an insulting way, but they call into question the legitimate achievements of all highly qualified black professionals. Carter insists that setting aside racially defined positions inevitably leads to hiring less-qualified candidates. Thus Carter thinks that the only legitimate use of race in employment is to establish a pool of excellent candidates that is racially diverse. Race, he insists, should not be used to guarantee that racial quotas in hiring are met. Carter thinks that the use of race to establish a diverse competitive pool would suffice to ensure the competitiveness of those who, for reasons of race, were excluded in the past by removing artificial barriers to entering the labor market on fair and equal terms with all others.

Stephen L. Carter

THE BEST BLACK

Affirmative action has been with me always. I do not mean to suggest that I have always been the beneficiary of special programs and preferences. I mean, rather, that

From Stephen L. Carter, *Reflections of an Affirmative Action Baby* (New York: Basic Books, 1991).

no matter what my accomplishments, I have had trouble escaping an assumption that often seems to underlie the worst forms of affirmative action: that black people cannot compete intellectually with white people. Certainly I have not escaped it since my teen years, spent mostly in Ithaca, New York, where the presence of Cornell University lends an air of academic intensity to the public schools. At Ithaca High School in the days of my adolescence, we had far more than our share of National Merit Scholars, of students who scored exceptionally well on standardized tests, of students who earned advanced placement credits for college, and of every other commodity by which secondary schools compare their academic quality.

My father taught at Cornell, which made me a Cornell kid, a "fac-brat," and I hung out with a bunch of white Cornell kids in a private little world where we competed fiercely (but only with one another—no one else mattered!) for grades and test scores and solutions to brain teasers. We were the sort of kids other kids hated: the ones who would run around compiling lists of everyone else's test scores and would badger guidance counselors into admitting their errors in arithmetic (no computer then) in order to raise our class ranks a few notches. I held my own in this bunch, although I was forced by the norms of the fac-brat community to retake the Mathematics Level II achievement test to raise a humiliating score of 780 to an acceptable 800. (No one had yet told me that standardized tests were culturally biased against me.) Like the rest of the fac-brats, I yearned for the sobriquet "brilliant," and tried desperately to convince myself and everyone else who would listen that I had the grades and test scores to deserve it.

And yet there were unnerving indications that others did not see me as just another fac-brat, that they saw me instead as that black kid who hung out with the Cornell kids. There was, for example, the recruiter from Harvard College who asked to see those he considered the brightest kids in the school; I was included, so a guidance counselor said, because I was black. And when I decided that I wanted to attend Stanford University, I was told by a teacher that I would surely be admitted because I was black and I was smart. Not because I was smart and not even because I was smart and black, but because I was black and smart: the skin color always preceding any other observation.

All of this came to a head at National Merit Scholarship time. In those days (this was the early 1970s), the National Merit Scholarship qualifying Test was a separate examination, not combined with the Preliminary Scholastic Aptitude Test as it later would be. When the qualifying scores came in, I was in heaven. Mine was the third highest in the school. I saw my future then—best fac-brat!—and awaited my National Merit Scholarship. Instead, I won a National Achievement Scholarship, presented, in the awkward usage of the day, to "outstanding Negro students." Well, all right. If one wants more black students to go to college, one had better provide the necessary resources. College is expensive and money is money. Still, at first I was insulted; I saw my "best fac-brat" status slipping away, for what I craved was a National *Merit* Scholarship, the one not for the best black students, but for the *best* students. So I was turned down.

Here it is useful to add some perspective. All through my adolescence, when I failed at some intellectual task (always measuring failure by my distance from the top), I usually, and properly, blamed myself. At times, however, I attributed my inability to reach my goals as a kind of conspiracy to keep me, a black kid, from reaping the rewards I imagined my achievements deserved, and, at times, to keep me from even trying. And sometimes the conspiracy was real.

Particularly vivid is my memory of moving from a mostly black elementary school to a mostly white junior high school, where I was not allowed to enroll in even a basic Spanish class, despite three years' study of the language, because, my mother was told, the limited spaces were all allocated to graduates of a particular elementary school—which happened to be all white. I was assigned to vocational education instead. And when I moved on to high school, carrying with me an A average in mathematics and excellent test scores, not only was I prevented from enrolling in the highest math section—I was not even told that it existed!

Having faced these barriers before, I readily assumed that the National Achievement program was another. (In fact, for nearly twenty years, my memory of the incident was that I was forced to choose between accepting a National Achievement Scholarship and remaining eligible for a National Merit Scholarship.) But when the National Merit people reassured me that I could accept the one and remain eligible for the other, I accepted the offered scholarship, and even competed for the cherished National Merit Scholarship—which I didn't get. (That year, like most years, some students won both.) In time, I would come to support racially targeted scholarship programs, for reasons I explain in chapter 4. As a nervous 17-year-old, however, I worried that such programs were examples of the same old lesson: the smartest students of color were not considered as capable as the smartest white students, and therefore would not be allowed to compete with them, but only with one another.

I call it the "best black" syndrome, and all black people who have done well in school are familiar with it. We are measured by a different yardstick: *first black, only black; best black.* The best black syndrome is cut from the same cloth as the implicit and demeaning tokenism that often accompanies racial preferences: "Oh, we'll tolerate so-and-so at our hospital or in our firm or on our faculty, because she's the best black." Not because she's the best-qualified candidate, but because she's the best-qualified *black* candidate. She can fill the black slot. And then the rest of the slots can be filled in the usual way: with the best-*qualified* candidates.

This dichotomy between "best" and "best black" is not merely something manufactured by racists to denigrate the abilities of professionals who are not white. On the contrary, the durable and demeaning stereotype of black people as unable to compete with white ones is reinforced by advocates of certain forms of affirmative action. It is reinforced, for example, every time employers are urged to set aside test scores (even, in some cases, on tests that are good predictors of job performance) and to hire from separate lists, one of the best white scorers, the other of the best black ones. It is reinforced every time state pension plans are pressed to invest some of their funds with "minority-controlled" money management firms, even if it turns out that the competing "white" firms have superior track records.[1] It is reinforced every time students demand that universities commit to hiring some pre-set number of minority faculty members. What all of these people are really saying is, "There are black folks out there. Go and find the best of them." And the best black syndrome is further reinforced, almost unthinkingly, by politicians or bureaucrats or faculty members who see these demands as nothing more than claims for simple justice.

Successful black students and professionals have repeatedly disproved the proposition that the best black minds are not as good as the best white ones, but the stereotype lingers, even among the most ardent friends of civil rights. In my own area of endeavor, academia, I hear this all the time from people who should know better. It is not at all unusual for white professors, with no thought that they are indulging a demeaning stereotype, to argue for hiring the best available professors of color, whether or not the individuals on whom that double-edged mantle is bestowed meet the usual appointment standard. I put aside for the moment the question of the fairness of the standards, for the white people I am describing have few doubts about *that*; I have in mind white people who argue with straight face for the hiring of black people *they themselves* do not believe are good enough to be hired without extra points for race. For example, one prominent law professor, a strong and sincere proponent of racial diversity, sent me a list of scholars in his field who might be considered for appointment to the Yale faculty. The first part of list set out the names of the best people in the field; the second part, the names of people who were so-so; and the last part, the names of the leading "minorities and women" in the field, none of whom apparently qualified (in his judgment) for even the "so-so" category, let alone the best. I know that my colleague acted with the best of intentions, but the implicit invitation offered by this extraordinary document was to choose between diversity and quality. I suspect that to this day he is unaware of any insult and actually believes he was advancing the cause of racial justice.

"No responsible advocate of affirmative action," argues Ira Glasser, "opposes merit or argues . . . that standards should be reduced in order to meet affirmative action goals."[2] Perhaps not; but the language of standards and merit is slippery at best. I am reminded of a conversation I had some years ago with a veteran civil rights litigator who, concerned at charges that affirmative action sometimes results in hiring unqualified candidates, drew a sharp distinction between *unqualified* and *less qualified*. An employer, he mused, does not have to hire the *best* person for the job, as long as everyone hired is *good enough* to do the job. Consequently, he reasoned, it is perfectly fine to require employers to hire black applicants who are less qualified than some white applicants, as long as the black candidates are capable of doing the job. A tidy argument in its way but, of course, another example of an almost unconscious acceptance of a situation in which an employer is made to distinguish between the best black candidates and the best ones.

Even our sensible but sometimes overzealous insistence that the rest of the nation respect the achievements of black culture might reinforce the depressing dichotomy: if we insist, as often we must, that others appreciate "our" music and "our" literature, we should not be surprised if those others come to think of the best of our music and the best of our literature as distinct from the best music and the best literature. Indeed, this is the implication of Stanley Crouch's vigorous argument (on which I here express no view) that white critics accept a level of mediocrity from black artists, filmmakers, and writers that they would never tolerate from creative people who are white.[3]

The best black syndrome creates in those of us who have benefitted from racial preferences a peculiar contradiction. We are told over and over that we are among the best black people in our professions. And in part we are flattered, or should be, because, after all, those who call us the best black lawyers or doctors or investment bankers consider it a compliment. But to professionals who have worked hard to succeed, flattery of this kind carries an unsubtle insult, for we yearn to be called what our achievements often deserve: simply the best—no qualifiers needed! In *this* society, however, we sooner or later must accept that being viewed as the best blacks is part of what has led us to where we are; and we must further accept that to some of our colleagues, black as well as white, we will never be anything else.

I I

Despite these rather unsettling pitfalls, many of us resist the best black syndrome less than we should, and one of the reasons is surely that it can bestow considerable benefits. Racial preferences are perhaps the most obvious benefit, but there are others. In high school, for example, I quickly stood out, if only because I was the lone black student in any number of honors and advanced placement courses. Perhaps my intellect was not unusually keen; although I did as well as anyone, I have always thought that with proper training, scoring well on standardized tests is no great trick. Nevertheless, other students and, eventually, teachers as well concluded that I was particularly sharp. These perceptions naturally fed my ego, because all I really wanted from high school was to be considered one of the best and brightest.

What I could not see then, but see clearly now, two decades later, is that while the perceptions others had of my abilities were influenced in part by grades and test scores, they were further influenced by the fact that students and teachers (black and white alike) were unaccustomed to the idea that a black kid could sit among the white kids as an equal, doing as well, learning as much, speaking as ably, arguing with as much force. In their experience, I was so different that I had to be exceptional. But exceptional in a specific and limited sense: the best black.

College was not much different. My college grades were somewhat better than average, but at Stanford in the era of grade inflation, good grades were the norm. Nevertheless, I quickly discovered that black students with good grades stood out from the crowd. Other students and many of my professors treated me as a member of some odd and fascinating species. I sat among them as an equal in seminars, my papers were as good as anyone else's, so I had to be exceptionally bright. In their experience, it seemed, no merely ordinarily smart black person could possibly sit among them as an equal.

In law school, the trend continued. I was fortunate enough to come early to the attention of my professors, but all I was doing was playing by the rules: talking in class with reasonable intelligence, exhibiting genuine interest in questions at the podium later, and treating papers and examinations as matters of serious scholarship rather than obstacles to be overcome. Lots of students did the same—but, in the stereotyped visions of some of my professors, not lots of black students. Here was the best black syndrome at work once more: I was not just another bright student with an enthusiastic but untrained intellect; I was a bright *black* student, a fact that apparently made a special impression.

The stultifying mythology of racism holds that black people are intellectually inferior. Consistent survey data over the years indicate that this stereotype persists.[4] Such incidents as those I have described, however, make me somewhat skeptical of the familiar complaint that because of this mythology, black people of intellectual talent have a harder time than others in proving their worth. My own experience suggests quite the contrary, that like a flower blooming in winter, intellect is more readily noticed where it is not expected to be found. Or, as a black investment banker has put the point, "Our mistakes are amplified, but so are our successes."[5] And it is the amplification of success that makes the achieving black student or professional into the best black.

When people assign to a smart black person the status of best black, they do so with the purest of motives: the curing of bewilderment. There must be an explanation, the reasoning runs, and the explanation must be that this black person, in order to do as well as white people, is exceptionally bright. What I describe is not racism in the sense of a design to oppress, but it is in its racialist assumption of inferiority every bit as insulting and nearly as tragic. The awe and celebration with which our achievements are often greeted (by black and white people alike) suggest a widespread expectation that our achievements will be few. The surprise is greater, perhaps, when our achievements are intellectual, but other achievements, too, seem to astonish. The astonishment, moreover, takes a long time to fade: even, or perhaps especially, in the era of affirmative action, it seems, the need to prove one's professional worth over and over again has not receded.

I I I

Affirmative action, to be sure, did not create this particular box into which black people are routinely stuffed. Throughout the long tragic history of the interaction between white people and people of color in America (it is too often forgotten that there were people of color here before there were white people), the society has treated white as normal and color as an aberration that must be explained or justified or apologized for. Black people have always been the target of openly racist assumptions, perhaps the worst among these being that we are stupid, primitive people. Every intellectual attainment by black people in America has been greeted with widespread suspicion. When the American Missionary Association and other abolitionist groups established black colleges in the South after the Civil War and determined to offer to the freed slaves and their progeny classical educations (Eurocentric educations, I suppose they would be called on today's campuses), emulating those available at the best Northern schools, editorialists had a field day. By the turn of the century, a standing joke had it that when two black students met on the campus of one of these colleges, the first greeted the second with, "Is yo' done yo' Greek yet?" The joke has faded from national memory, but its import, I fear, remains part of the nation's swirling racial consciousness.

Small wonder, then, that every black professional, in our racially conscious times, is assumed to have earned his or her position not by being among the best available but by being among the best available blacks. Any delusions to the contrary I might have harbored about my own achievements were shattered a few months after I was voted tenure at the Yale Law School. Late one night, a reporter for the campus newspaper called my home to say that the paper was doing a story about my promotion. Why was that? I wanted to know. Lots of law professors earn tenure, I said. Oh, I know, said the reporter, unabashed. Still, wasn't it true that I was the first black one? But that was the luck of the draw, I protested. It could as easily have been someone else. And besides, I wanted to shout, but dared not; besides, that isn't why I was promoted! (I hope.)

My protests mattered not a jot, and the newspaper ran its story. A banner headline on the front page screamed that the law faculty had, for the first time, voted to promote a black professor to tenure. The tone of the article—years of lily-whiteness in the academy was its theme—suggested that my promotion was simple justice. But justice of a special sort: not the justice of earned reward for a job well done, but the justice due me as a professor who happens to be black. Whether I was a strong scholar or a weak one, a creative thinker or a derivative one, a diligent researcher or a lazy one, a good teacher or a bad one, mattered less to the newspaper than the fact that I was a black one. Evidently I had finally arrived, had I but the gumption to acknowledge it, as one of the best blacks.

I muted my protest, however. I did not complain, to the newspaper or to others, that I felt oppressed by this vision of tenure as an extension of affirmative action. Like many other black professionals, I simply wanted to be left alone to do my work. My hope, then as now, was that if I earned a place in the academic world, it would be for the seriousness of my research and the thoughtful contributions I hoped to make to legal knowledge—not for the color of my skin. Most of the scholarship I have committed has related to the separation of powers in the federal government, the regulation of intellectual property,* and the relationship of law and religion—to the lay person, perhaps not the most thrilling of topics, but, for me, intellectually engaging and lots of fun. I have always relished the look of surprise in the eyes of people who, having read my work in these areas, meet me for the first time. My favorite response (this really did happen) came at an academic conference at the University of Michigan Law School, where a dapper, buttoned-down young white man glanced at my name tag, evidently ignored the name but noted the school, and said, "If you're at Yale, you must know this Carter fellow who wrote that article about thus-and-so." Well, yes, I admitted. I did know that Carter fellow slightly. An awkward pause ensued. And then the young man, realizing his error, apologized with a smile warm enough to freeze butter. "Oh," he said, "*you're* Carter." (I have since wondered from time to time whether, had I been white and the error a less telling one, his voice would have been inflected differently: "You're *Carter*." Think

---

* Intellectual property is the field of law governing rights in intangible creation of the mind and includes such subjects as parents, copyrights, and trademarks.

about it.) Naturally, we then discussed the article, which happened to be about the separation of powers, and by way of showing the sincerity of his apology, he gushed about its quality in terms so adulatory that a casual observer might have been excused for thinking me the second coming of Oliver Wendell Homes or, more likely, for thinking my interlocutor an idiot. (That gushing is part of the peculiar relationship between black intellectuals and the white ones who seem loath to criticize us for fear of being branded racists—which is itself a mark of racism of a sort.) I suppose I should have been flattered, although, if the truth is told, I quickly gained the impression that he was excited more by the political uses to which my argument might be put than by the analysis in the article itself.

But there it was! The Best Black Syndrome! It had, as they say, stood up and bitten me! Since this young man liked the article, its author could not, in his initial evaluation, have been a person of color. He had not even conceived of that possibility, or he would have glanced twice at my name tag. No, if the work was of high quality, the author had to be white—there was no room for doubt! The best blacks don't do this stuff!

And if you're black, you can't escape it! It's everywhere, this awkward set of expectations. No matter what you might accomplish (or imagine yourself to have accomplished), the label follows you. A friend of mine who works in the financial services field—I'll call him X—tells the story of his arrival at a client's headquarters. The client had been told that a supervisor was on the way to straighten out a particularly knotty problem. When my friend arrived, alone, and gave his name, the client said, "But where is the supervisor? Where is Mr. X?" With my friend standing right in front of him, name already announced! My friend, being black, could not possibly be the problem solver who was awaited. He was only . . . THE BEST BLACK! The winner of the coveted prize!

And that's the way it works. This is the risk some critics see in setting up Afro-American Studies departments: Isn't there a good chance that the school will dismiss the professors in the department as simply the best blacks, saying, in effect, don't worry about the academic standards the rest of us have to meet, you've got your own department? The answer is yes, of course, the school might do that—but that isn't an argument against Afro-American studies as a discipline, any more than it's an argument against hiring black faculty at all. It's just an admission that this is the way many of the white people who provide affirmative action programs and other goodies tend to think about them: there's Category A for the smart folks, and Category B for the best blacks. It's also a reminder to all people of color that our parents' advise was true: we really do have to work twice as hard to be considered half as good.

This is an important point for those who are trapped by the best black syndrome. We cannot afford, ever, to let our standards slip. There are too many doubters waiting in the wings to pop out at the worst possible moment and cry, "See? Told you!" The only way to keep them off the stage is to make our own performances so good that there is no reasonable possibility of calling them into question. It isn't fair that so much should be demanded of us, but what has life to do with fairness? It was the artist Paul Klee, I believe, who said that one must adapt oneself to the contents of the paintbox. This is particularly true for upwardly mobile professionals who happen to be people of color, for people of color have had very little say about what those contents are.

So we have to adapt ourselves, a point I finally came to accept when I was in law school. In those days, the black students spent lots of time sitting around and discussing our obligations, if any, to the race. (I suppose black students still sit around and hold the same conversation.) In the course of one such conversation over a casual lunch, I blurted out to a classmate my driving ambition. It infuriated me, I said, that no matter what we might accomplish, none of us could aspire to anything more than the role of best black. What we should do for the race, I said, was achieve. Shatter stereotypes. Make white doubters think twice about our supposed intellectual inferiority.

A few years later, I foolishly imagined that I had attained my goal. It was the fall of 1981, and I was a young lawyer seeking a teaching position at a law school. I had, I was certain, played my cards right. In my law school years, I had managed to get to know a professor or two, and some of them liked me. I had compiled the right paper record before setting out to hunt for a job: my resume included practice with a well-regarded law firm, good law school grades, service on the Yale Law Journal, and a spate of other awards and honors, including a clerkship with a Justice of the Supreme Court of the United States. One might have thought, and I suppose I thought it myself, that someone with my credentials would have no trouble landing a teaching job. But what people told me was that any school would be happy to have a black professor with my credentials. (Did a white professor need more, or did white professors just make their schools unhappy?) In the end, I was fortunate enough to collect a flattering set of job offers, but the taste was soured for me, at least a little, by the knowledge that whatever my qualifications, they probably looked more impressive on the resume of someone black.

There is an important point here, one that is missed by the critics who point out (correctly, I think) that affirmative action programs tend to call into question the legitimate achievements of highly qualified black professionals. Yes, they do; but that is not the end of the story. A few years ago, in a panel discussion on racial preferences, the economist Glenn Loury noted that the Harvard Law School had on its faculty two black professors who are also former law clerks for Justices of the Supreme Court of the United States. (As I write, I believe that the number is three.) It isn't fair, he argued, that they should be dismissed as affirmative action appointments when they are obviously strongly qualified for the positions they hold. He is right that it isn't fair to dismiss them and he is right that they are obviously qualified, but it is also true that there are nowadays literally dozens of similarly qualified candidates for teaching positions every year. It is no diminution of the achievements of the professors Loury had in mind to point out that there is no real way to tell whether they would have risen to the top if not for the fact that faculties are on the lookout for highly qualified people of color. The same is surely true for many black people rising to the top of political, economic, and educational institutions.

There is a distinction here, however, that even the harshest critics of affirmative action should be willing to concede. Hiring to fill a slot that must be filled—the black slot, say—is not the same as using race to sort among a number of equally qualified candidates. Put otherwise, yes, it is true that the result of racial preferences is sometimes the hiring of black people not as well qualified as white people who are turned away, and preferences of that kind do much that is harmful and little that is good. But preferences can also be a means of selecting highly qualified black people from a pool of people who are all excellent. True, employers will almost always claim to be doing the second even when they are really doing the first; but that does not mean the second is impossible to do. And if an employer undertakes the second method, a sorting among the excellent, then although there might be legitimate grounds for concern, a criticism on the ground of lack of qualification of the person hired cannot be among them.

Ah, but are our analytical antennae sufficiently sensitive to detect the difference? I am not sure they are, and the sometimes tortured arguments advanced by the strongest advocates of affirmative action . . . occasionally leave me with a bleak and hopeless sense that all people of color who are hired for the tasks for which their intellects and professional training have prepared them will be dismissed, always, as nothing more than the best blacks. And I draw from all of this two convictions: first, that affirmative action will not alter this perception; and, second, that white Americans will not change it simply because it is unjust. Consequently change, if change there is to be, is in *our* hands—and the only change for which we can reasonably hope will come about because we commit ourselves to battle for excellence, to show ourselves able to meet any standard, to pass any test that looms before us, in short, to form ourselves into a vanguard of black professionals who are simply too good to ignore.

And that, I suppose, is why I relish the reactions of those who have liked my work without knowing I am black: in my mind I am proving them wrong, as I promised I would at that lunch so many years ago. No doubt my pleasure at the widened eyes is childish, but it is sometimes a relief to be sure for once that it is really the work they like, not the-unexpected-quality-of-the-work-given-the-naturally-inferior-intellects-of-those-with-darker-skins. It is a commonplace of social science, a matter of common sense as well, that an observer's evaluation of a piece of work is frequently influenced by awareness of the race of the author. Happily, I have found that people who like my work before they learn that I am black do not seem to like it less once they discover my color.*

And when those who read my work *do* know that I am black? Well, any prejudices that the readers might bring to bear are, at least, nothing new. John Hope Franklin, in his sparkling essay on "The Dilemma of the American Negro Scholar," details the struggles of black academics during the past century to have their work taken seriously by white scholars.[6] Although progress has obviously been made, the struggle Franklin describes is not yet ended, which means I have to face the likelihood that many white scholars who read my work will judge it by a different standard than the one they use to judge the work of white people. Perhaps the standard

---

* Often, however, they do suddenly assume that I must possess a special expertise in the most sophisticated quandaries and delicately nuanced esoterica of civil rights law, areas that take years of careful study to master, no matter the contrary impression given by the sometimes simpleminded reporting on civil rights law in the mass media.

will be higher, perhaps the standard will be lower, perhaps the standard will simply involve different criteria—but whatever the standard, all I can do is try to carry out the instruction that black parents have given their children for generations, and make the work not simply as good as the work of white scholars of similar background, but better. Sometimes I succeed, sometimes I fail; but to be a professional is always to strive. And while I am perfectly willing to concede the unfairness of a world that judges black people and white people by different standards, I do not lose large amounts of sleep over it. A journalist friend recently told my wife and me that he is tired of hearing black people complain about having to work twice as hard as white people to reach the same level of success. He says that if that's what we have to do, that's what we have to do, and it would not be a bad thing at all for us as a race to develop that habit as our defining characteristic: "Oh, you know those black people, they always work twice as hard as everybody else." If you can't escape it, then make the most of it: in my friend's racial utopia, it would no longer be taken as an insult to be called by a white colleague the best black.

I V

My desire to succeed in the professional world without the aid of preferential treatment is hardly a rejection of the unhappy truth that the most important factor retarding the progress of people of color historically has been society's racism. It is, rather, an insistence on the opportunity to do what the National Merit Scholarship people said I would not be allowed to, what I promised at that fateful lunch I would: to show the world that we who are black are not so marked by our history of racist oppression that we are incapable of intellectual achievement on the same terms as anybody else.

In a society less marked by racist history, the intellectual achievements of people of color might be accepted as a matter of course. In *this* society, however, they are either ignored or applauded, but never accepted as a matter of course. As I have said, however, the general astonishment when our achievements are intellectual carries with it certain benefits. Perhaps chief among these is the possibility of entree to what I call the "star system." The characteristics of the star system are familiar to anyone who has attended college or professional school or has struggled upward on the corporate ladder, and it has analogues in sports, the military, and other arenas. Early in their careers, a handful of individuals are marked by their teachers or supervisors as having the potential for special success, even greatness. Thereafter, the potential stars are closely watched. Not every person marked early as a possible star becomes one, but the vast majority of those who are never marked will never star. Even very talented individuals who lack entree to the star system may never gain attention in the places that matter: the hushed and private convergence rooms (I can testify to their existence, having sat in more than a few) where money is spent and hiring and promotion decisions are made.

Getting into the star system is not easy, and the fact that few people of color scramble to the top of it should scarcely be surprising. The reason is not any failing in our native abilities—although it is true that only in the past decade have we been present as students in numbers sufficient to make entry more plausible—but the social dynamics of the star system itself. Entree is not simply a matter of smarts, although that helps, or of working hard, although that helps, too. The star system rewards familiarity, comfort, and perseverance. It usually begins on campus, and so do its problems. One must get to know one's professors. Most college and professional school students are far too intimidated by their professors to feel comfortable getting to know them well, and for many students of color, already subject to a variety of discomforts, this barrier may seem especially high. When one feels uneasy about one's status in the classroom to begin with, the task of setting out to get to know the professor personally may seem close to insuperable. The fact that some students of color indeed reap the benefits of the star system does not alter the likelihood that many more would never dream of trying.

Exclusion from the star system is costly. Anyone left out will meet with difficulties in being taken seriously as a candidate for entry-level hiring at any of our most selective firms and institutions, which is why the failure of people of color to get into the star system makes a difference. Still, there is an opportunity here: because so little is expected of students of color, intellectual attainment is sometimes seen as a mark of genuine brilliance. (None of the merely ordinarily smart need apply!) So the best black syndrome can have a salutary side effect: it can help those trapped inside it get through the door of the star system. Certainly it worked that way for me. (Who *is* this character? my professors seemed to want to know.) The star system, in turn, got me in the door of the academy at the entry level. (From the doorway, I would like to think,I made the rest of the journey on my own; my achievements ought to speak for themselves. But in a world in which I have heard my colleagues use the very words *best black* in discussions of faculty hiring, I have no way to tell.) So, yes, I am a beneficiary of both the star system and the best black syndrome. Yet I hope it is clear that I am not a fan of either. The star system is exclusionary and incoherent; the best black syndrome is demeaning and oppressive. Both ought to be abandoned.

Consider the so-called glass ceiling, the asserted reluctance of corporations to promote people of color to top management positions. If indeed the glass ceiling exists, it is very likely a function of the star system. If people of color tend to have trouble getting in good, as the saying goes, with their professors, they are likely to have as much or more trouble getting in good with their employers. And if, once hired, people who are not white face difficulties in finding mentors, powerful institutional figures to smooth their paths, then they will naturally advance more slowly. Oh, there will always be some black participants in the star system, not as tokens but as people who have, as I said, taken to heart the adage that they must be twice as good. (One need but think of Colin Powell or William Coleman.) Still, plenty of people of color who are merely as good as or slightly better than white people who are inside the star system will find themselves outside. The social turns do not work for them, and their advancement on the corporate ladder will be slow or nonexistent.

To be sure, the star system cannot get all of the blame for the dearth of people who are not white in (and, especially, at the top of) the professions. That there is present-day racism, overt and covert, might almost go without saying, except that so many people keep insisting there isn't any. But one should not assume too readily that contemporary discrimination explains all of the observed difference. Groups are complex and no two groups are the same. With cultural and other differences, it would be surprising if all group outcomes were identical. When the nation's odious history of racial oppression is grafted onto any other differences that might exist, the numbers are less surprising still. What would be surprising would be if we as a people had so successfully shrugged off the shackles of that history as to have reached, at this relatively early stage in the nation's evolution, economic and educational parity.

But the star system is not exactly blameless, either. Any system that rewards friendship and comfort rather than merit will burden most heavily those least likely to find the right friends.[7] It is ironic, even awkward, to make this point in an era when the attack on meritocracy is so sharply focused, but the claims pressed by today's critics in that attack—bigotry, unconscious bias, corrupt and malleable standards, social and cultural exclusion—are among the reasons that led other ethnic groups in the past to insist on the establishment of measurable systems for rewarding merit. The star system is a corrupt and biased means for circumventing the meritocratic ideal, but its corruption should not be attributed to the ideal itself.

V

None of this means that affirmative action is the right answer to the difficulties the star system has spawned. Among the group of intellectuals known loosely (and, I believe, often inaccurately) as black conservatives, there is a widely shared view that the removal of artificial barriers to entry into a labor market is the proper goal to be pursued by those who want to increase minority representation. The economist Walter Williams often cities the examples of cities like New York that limit the number of individuals permitted to drive taxicabs. No wonder, he says, there are so few black cabdrivers: it's too difficult to get into the market. Consequently, says Williams, New York should abolish its limits and, subject only to some basic regulatory needs, open the field to anyone. This, he says, would automatically result in an increase in black drivers—assuming, that is, that there are black people who want to drive cabs.

Other strategies, too, are easy to defend. For example, it is difficult to quarrel with the idea that an employer concerned about diversity—whatever its needs and hiring standards—should be as certain as possible that any candidate search it conducts is designed to yield the names of people of color who fit the search profile. After centuries of exclusion by design, it would be a terrible tragedy were black and other minority professionals excluded through inadvertence. Mari Matsuda has argued that a serious intellectual ought to make an effort to read books by members of groups not a part of his or her familiar experience, and I think she is quite right.[8] It is in the process of that determined reading—that searching—that the people who have been overlooked will, if truly excellent, eventually come to light.

The example can be generalized. Searching is the only way to find outstanding people of color, which is why all professional employers should practice it. Although the cost of a search is not trivial, the potential return in diversity, without any con-comitant lowering of standards, is enormous—provided always that the employer is careful to use the search only to turn up candidates, not as a means of bringing racial preferences into the hiring process through the back door. For it is easy, but de-meaning, to conflate the goal of searching with the goal of hiring, and to imagine therefore that the reason for the search is to ensure that the optimal number of black people are hired. It isn't. The reason for the search isn't to find the blacks among the best, but the best among the blacks.

If this distinction is borne firmly in mind, then an obligation to search will of course provide no guarantee that the statistics will improve. But I am not sure that a guarantee is what we should be seeking. People of color do not need special treat-ment in order to advance in the professional world; we do not need to be considered the best blacks, competing only with one another for the black slots. On the con-trary, our goal ought to be to prove that we can compete with anybody, to demon-strate that the so-called pool problem, the alleged dearth of qualified entry-level candidates who are not white, is at least partly a myth. So if we can gain for our-selves a fair and equal chance to show what we can do—what the affirmative action literature likes to call a level playing field—then it is something of an insult to our intellectual capacities to insist on more.

And of course, although we do not like to discuss it, the insistence on more car-ries with it certain risks. After all, an employer can hire a candidate because the em-ployer thinks that person is the best one available or for some other reason: pleasing a powerful customer, rewarding an old friend, keeping peace in the family, keeping the work force all white, getting the best black. When the employer hires on one of these other grounds, it should come as no surprise if the employee does not perform as well as the best available candidate would have. There will be times when the performance will be every bit as good, but those will not be the norm unless the em-ployer is a poor judge of talent; and if the employer consistently judges talent poorly, a second, shrewder judge of talent will eventually put the first employer out of busi-ness.[9] That is not, I think, a web in which we as a people should want to be en-tangled.

Racial preferences, in sum, are not the most constructive method for overcom-ing the barriers that keep people of color out of high-prestige positions. They are often implemented in ways that are insulting, and besides, they can carry consider-able costs. Although there are fewer unfair and arbitrary barriers to the hiring and retention of black professionals than there once were, many barriers remain, and the star system, although some few of us benefit from it, is prominent among them. But if the barriers are the problem, then it is the barriers themselves that should be at-tacked. Should the star system be brushed aside, our opportunities would be con-siderably enhanced because many of the special advantages from which we are excluded would vanish.

Getting rid of the star system will not be easy. I have discovered through painful experience that many of its most earnest white defenders—as well as many of those who pay lip service to overturning it but meanwhile continue to exploit it—are also among the most ardent advocates of hiring black people who, if white, they would consider second-rate. They are saying, in effect, We have one corrupt system for helping out our friends, and we'll be happy to let you have one for getting the numbers right. Faced with such obduracy, small wonder that racial preferences seem an attractive alternative.

But people of color must resist the urge to join the race to the bottom. The stakes are too high. I am sensitive to Cornell University Professor Isaac Kramnick's comment that even if a school hires some black professors who are not first-rate, "it will take till eternity for the number of second-rate blacks in the university to match the number of second-rate whites."[10] Point taken: one can hardly claim that elite educational institutions have been perfect meritocracies. However, the claim that there are incompetent whites and therefore incompetent blacks should be given a chance is unlikely to resonate with many people's visions of justice. Because of the racial stereotyping that is rampant in our society, moreover, any inadequacies among second-rate white professionals are unlikely to be attributed by those with the power to do something about it to whites as a whole; with black professionals, matters are quite unfairly the other way around, which is why the hiring of second-rate black professionals in any field would be detrimental to the effort to break down barriers.

The corruption of the meritocratic ideal with bias and favoritism offers professionals who are not white an opportunity we should not ignore: the chance to teach the corrupters their own values by making our goal excellence rather than adequacy. Consider this perceptive advice to the black scholar from John Hope Franklin, one of the nation's preeminent historians: "He should know that by maintaining the highest standards of scholarship he not only becomes worthy but also sets an example that many of his contemporaries who claim to be the arbiters in the field to not themselves follow."[11] The need to beat down the star system should spur us not to demand more affirmative action but to exceed the achievements of those who manipulate the system to their advantage.

Besides, the star system does not taint every institution to an equal degree. Some hiring and promotion processes actually make sense. If we rush to graft systems of racial preference onto hiring processes rationally designed to produce the best doctors or lawyers or investment bankers or professors, we might all hope that the professionals hired because of the preferences turn out to be as good as those hired because they are expected to be the best, but no one should be surprised if this hope turns to ashes. Painful though this possibility may seem, it is consistent with a point that many supporters of affirmative action tend to miss, or at least to obscure: racial preferences that make no difference are unimportant.

Racial preferences are founded on the proposition that the achievements of their beneficiaries would be fewer if the preferences did not exist. Supporters of preferences cite a whole catalogue of explanations for the inability of people of color to get along without them: institutional racism, inferior education, overt prejudice, the lingering effects of slavery and oppression, cultural bias in the criteria for admission and employment. All of these arguments are most sincerely pressed, and some of them are true. But like the best black syndrome, they all entail the assumption that people of color cannot at present compete on the same playing field with people who are white. I don't believe this for an instant; and after all these years, I still wish the National Merit Scholarship people had given me the chance to prove it.

NOTES

1. See, for example, the account of the debate in *Maryland in Bond Buyer*, 31 July 1990, p. 32.

2. Ira Glasser, "Affirmative Action and the Legacy of Racial Injustice," in *Eliminating Racism: Profiles in Controversy*, ed. Phylis A. Katz and Dalmas A. Taylor (New York: Plenum Press, 1988), pp. 341–350.

3. Stanley Crouch, *Notes of a Hanging Judge* (New York: Oxford University Press, 1990).

4. The most recent General Social Survey, a regular report of the widely respected National Opinion Research Center, found that 53 percent of white respondents consider black people generally less intelligent than white people. ("Whites Retain Negative View of Minorities, a Survey Finds" *New York Times*, 10 January 1991, p. B10.) Prior surveys through the late 1960s had shown a decline in the percentage of white respondents who consider black people less intelligent. Historical polling results on the attitudes of white Americans about black Americans are collected in National Research Council, *A Common Destiny: Blacks and American Society* (Washington, D.C.: National Academy Press, 1989), pp. 120–23. For a more detailed discussion of data collected during the 1980s, see Lee Sigelman and Susan Welch, *Black Americans' Views of Racial Inequality* (Cambridge: Cambridge University Press, 1991), esp. pp. 85–100.

5. Quoted in Colin Leinster, "Black Executives: How They're Doing," *Fortune*, 18 January 1988, p. 109.

6. John Hope Franklin, "The Dilemma of the American Negro Scholar," in *Race and History Selected Essays 1938–1988* (Baton Rouge: Louisiana State University Press, 1989), p. 295. The essay was originally published in 1963.

7. My description of the star system might usefully be compared to the French sociologist Pierre Bourdieu's analysis of the role of "cultural capital" and "social capital" in the maintenance of the class structure: Pierre Bourdieu, "Cultural Reproduction and Social Reproduction," in *Power and Ideology in Education*, ed. J. Karabel and A. H. Halsey (New York: Oxford University Press, 1977), p. 487. I am less sure than Bourdieu is that the system works principally to the benefit of the children of those already part of it; my concern with the star system is that it is exclusionary and at the same time a distortion of the meritocratic ideal.

8. Mari Matsuda, "Affirmative Action and Legal Knowledge: Planting Seeds in Plowed-up Ground," *Harvard Women's Law Journal* 11 (Spring 1988): 5–6.

9. Although it is sometimes said that racial discrimination serves the interests of capitalism, the inefficiency of prejudice in the market is well understood in economics. The classic analysis of the market costs of discrimination on the basis of race is Gary S. Becker, *The Economics of Discrimination* (Chicago: University of Chicago Press, 1957). Much of the analysis in Becker's book is mathematical and may be inaccessible to the lay reader. A recent and more accessible treatment of the same issue is Thomas Sowell, *Preferential Policies: An International Perspective* (New York: William Morrow, 1990), esp. pp. 20–40. For a discussion of the way that racial discrimination following the Civil War retarded the growth of the Southern economy, see Roger L. Ransom and Richard Sutch, *One Kind of Freedom: The Economic Consequences of Emancipation* (Cambridge: Cambridge University Press, 1977).

10. Quoted in Adam Begley, "Black Studies' New Era: Henry Louis Gates, Jr.," *New York Times Magazine*, 1 April 1990, p. 24.

11. Franklin, "The Dilemma of the American Negro Scholar," p. 305.

■ GERTRUDE EZORSKY: AFFIRMATIVE ACTION AND MORALITY

In contrast to Carter, Gertrude Ezorsky supports preferential treatment programs as appropriate forms of compensation for black people, defending them against common criticisms. First, compensation for black people has been considered by many to be counterproductive. To this Ezorsky responds that if preferential treatment is counterproductive for black people, it must be considered so for beneficiaries of preferential programs generally, like veterans, Holocaust survivors, and those suffering industrial accidents. She concludes that compensation alone is not the cause of injury to recipients. Second, blacks have been thought not to deserve compensation. Here, Ezorsky argues that all blacks, including those who are better off, have suffered discriminatory injury. Just as there is no resistance to veterans receiving compensation for injuries acquired on duty even though they may be better off than some nonveterans, so there should be no resistance to better-off blacks receiving compensation. Third, even though it may be admitted that some blacks deserve compensation, it is sometimes held that black persons who are better off should not be compensated, especially if this is to the detriment of disadvantaged whites. Ezorsky responds that even employable blacks may be deserving of considerable compensation for the injuries suffered. In addition, preferential treatment for blacks helps to eradicate the evil of their occupational segregation. Fourth, preferential treatment programs are thought sometimes to deny employers their right to hire whomever they wish. Ezorsky argues that this claim rests on a deeply questionable analogy between hiring and marriage. Fifth, it is suggested by some that preferential treatment programs violate the principle of equal consideration, for whites are considered to be treated unfairly. Ezorsky admits that there may be some unfair costs whites have to bear as a consequence. She insists, nevertheless, that preferential treatment programs be instituted more equitably so that all whites bear their burden rather than that they be abandoned. This rests on the assumption, for which Ezorsky agues, that all whites deserve collectively to pay the costs of such programs for either they have been responsible for or they have benefitted from racism.

Ezorsky criticizes two additional arguments. Meritocrats argue that hiring should accord with the principle of highest quality, and that preferential treatment violates this principle. Ezorsky responds that merit selection is not the currently accepted rule. Finally, some claim that preferential treatment damages the self-respect of the very blacks whom such programs are designed to help. Ezorsky objects that this is either plainly false, or it follows unacceptably only from insisting that beneficiaries of preferences ought to feel a lack of self-respect, or that blacks fail to deserve such preference.

Gertrude Ezorsky

MORAL PERSPECTIVES ON AFFIRMATIVE ACTION

. . . Are affirmative action (AA) measures, such as preferential treatment in employment, an appropriate method of compensation for blacks? In fact, federal and state governments recognized the appropriateness of employment preference as an instrument of compensation to veterans long before the adoption of AA measures.[1] This court-sanctioned policy has affected the employment of millions of workers, and in some states where veteran preference is practiced, nonveterans have practically no chance to obtain the best positions.

What are the specific claims of those who find moral fault with such programs? First, concerning the compensatory rationale for AA, some analysts argue that compensation for blacks is counterproductive. Others claim that better-off blacks do not deserve the compensation of preferential treatment, especially where whites excluded by such preference are themselves disadvantaged. Second, AA trammels the rights of others—of employers who have a right to hire whomever they please, or of white candidates who are wrongfully excluded by preferential treatment. Finally, some critics suggest that blacks themselves may be morally injured by racial preference, which allegedly damages their self-respect.

COMPENSATION AS COUNTERPRODUCTIVE?

Shelby Steele, a professor of English, criticizes the compensatory claim for AA, according to which AA is "something 'owed,' as reparation": "Suffering can be endured and overcome, it cannot be repaid. To think otherwise is to prolong the suffering."[2] But if compensation should be withheld from blacks because suffering cannot be repaid, then for the same reason compensation should also be withheld from veterans, Holocaust survivors, and victims of industrial accidents. Members of these

From Gertrude Ezorsky, *Racism and Justice: The Case for Affirmative Action* (Ithaca, N.Y.: Cornell University Press, 1991). Reprinted by permission of the publisher.

groups do not complain that compensation prolongs their "suffering"; on the contrary, they have often insisted on their right to such benefits. I see no reason for assuming that compensation per se injures its recipients.

AFFLUENT BLACKS AS UNDESERVING

The philosopher William Blackstone criticizes the compensatory rationale for preferential treatment for affluent blacks . . .[3] Blackstone offers two arguments: (1) Black persons born into better-off black families have not suffered discrimination; hence, he suggests, they do not deserve compensation. (2) Preference that benefits these blacks at the expense of disadvantaged nonblacks is unjust.

First, it is false that blacks born into better-off families have not been injured by discrimination. Because racist treatment of blacks in business and professions reduced family income, it hurt their sons and daughters. Among the racist injuries these black parents suffered were the racially discriminatory policies of federal agencies in allocation of business loans, low-interest mortgages, agrarian price supports, and government contracts.[4] They also were victimized by racist exclusion from practice in white law firms and hospitals and by legally imposed or encouraged residential and school segregation that impaired their education and isolated them from white business contacts. Because of such invidious discrimination, black professionals and entrepreneurs could do far less for their children than their white counterparts. Moreover, the sons and daughters of black lawyers, doctors, and business persons have themselves suffered the experience of living in a segregated, pervasively racist society.

Laurence Thomas, a black university professor of philosophy, attests to the humiliating distrust that he and other well-placed black academics endure today in public places.[5] Fears that affect blacks of all classes are described by Don Jackson, a black police sergeant who, while investigating reports of police racism in 1989, was stopped by white police officers, one of whom shoved Jackson's head through a window during the arrest. . . .[6]

Even if one assumes that the economically better-off blacks are less deserving of compensation, it hardly follows that they do not deserve any compensation. As Bernard Boxill observes in *Blacks and Social Justice*: "Because I have lost only one leg, I may be less deserving of compensation than another who has lost two legs, but it does not follow that I deserve no compensation."[7]

It is true that where preference has been extended to blacks—as with craft workers, professionals, blue- and white-collar employees, teachers, police, and firefighters—some excluded whites may be financially less well off than the blacks who gained. This shift fails to show that these blacks were not victimized by invidious discrimination for which they should be compensated. Also, compensatory employment preference is sometimes given to veterans who are more affluent than the nonveterans who are thereby excluded from jobs. Indeed, some veterans gained, on the whole, from military life: placed in noncombat units, they often learned a valuable skill. Yet no one proposes that for this reason veteran preference be abandoned.

UNQUALIFIED BLACKS AS UNAFFECTED BY AA

Thomas Nagel, a philosopher who endorses preferential treatment, nevertheless faults the compensatory justification for such preference, claiming that blacks who benefit from it are probably not the ones who suffered most from discrimination; "those who don't have the qualifications even to be considered" do not gain from preferential policies.[8]

Of course, AA preference does not help blacks obtain very desirable employment if they lack the qualifications even to be considered for such positions. But preferential treatment in diverse areas of the public and private sector has benefitted not only highly skilled persons but also poorly educated workers. It is also true that blacks who lack the qualifications even to be considered for any employment will not gain from AA preference. As I indicated in my critique of William J. Wilson, AA cannot help those so destroyed as to be incapable of any work or on-the-job training, who require other compensatory race-specific rehabilitation programs. But AA employment programs should not perform the function of these programs. The claim that unemployable blacks are most deserving does not imply that employable blacks fail to deserve any—or even a great deal of—compensation.

Granted, we do not know whether the particular blacks who benefit from preference at each level in the hierarchy of employment are the very same individuals who, absent a racist past, would have qualified at that level by customary standards. Justified group compensation, however, does not require satisfaction of such rigid criteria. Veterans who enjoy hiring, promotion, and seniority preference are surely not the very same individuals who, absent their military service, would have qualified for the positions they gained by such preference.

Unlike job preference for veterans, AA racial preference in employment contributes to eradication of a future evil. It is an instrument for ending occupational segregation of blacks, a legacy of their enslavement.

THE RIGHTS OF EMPLOYERS

According to libertarian philosophers, laws that require any type of AA in the workplace—indeed, those merely requiring passive nondiscrimination—violate the rights of private employers. The philosopher Robert Nozick suggests that the right of employers to hire is relevantly similar to the right of individuals to marry.[9] Just as individuals should be free to marry whomever they please, so private entrepreneurs should be free to employ whomever they please, and government should not interfere with employers in their hiring decisions.

But surely the freedom to choose one's spouse and the freedom to select one's employees are relevantly different. Individuals denied such freedom of choice in marriage are forced to give their bodies to their spouses. They are subject to rape—a destructive, brutal, and degrading intrusion. Marital choices belong to the deeply personal sphere where indeed government should keep out. State intervention in employment is another matter. To require that an auto plant hire some black machinists falls outside the sphere of the deeply personal; it is not, like rape, a destructive, brutal, and degrading personal intrusion. I conclude that the analogy between freedom to marry and freedom to hire fails.

THE RIGHTS OF WHITE CANDIDATES

According to some philosophers, while the social goal of preferential treatment may be desirable, the moral cost is too high. The burden it imposes on adversely affected whites violates their right to equal treatment. They are unfairly singled out for sacrifice. Thomas Nagel states that "the most important argument against preferential treatment is that it subordinates the individual's right to equal treatment to broader social aims."[10]

Some proponents of preferential treatment reject the charge of unfairness because, as they see the matter, whites have either been responsible for immoral racist practices or have gained from them. According to this claim, all whites deserve to pay the cost of preferential treatment (hereafter, the desert claim).[11] I do not accept the desert claim; indeed, I suggest that the criticism of racial preference as unfair to adversely affected whites is not without merit. The relevant point is not that such preference be abandoned but rather that it be implemented differently.

According to the desert claim, whites either have been responsible for racism or have passively benefitted from it. Let us examine the responsibility claim first.

Certainly no one has demonstrated that all whites, or even a majority, are responsible for racism. How then shall the culpable whites be identified? Many employers and unions have certainly engaged in either overt racism or avoidable neutral practices that obviously excluded blacks. Perhaps they should pay the cost of discrimination remedies by, for example, continuing to pay blacks laid off by race-neutral seniority? But, on the other hand, some employers and union officials were not responsible for racist injury to blacks, and they do not deserve to pay the cost of a remedy for racism. Similar problems arise when we attempt to identify those who passively benefitted from racist practices. Let us assume that such beneficiaries do bear a measure of culpability for racism. How can we mark them out?

The salient fact is that white workers have both gained and lost from racism. On the one hand, the benefits to white workers from racism—overt and institutional—are undeniable. As a group, they have been first in line for hiring, training, promotion, and desirable job assignment, but last in line for seniority-based layoff. As white, they have also benefitted from housing discrimination in areas where jobs could be had and from the racist impact of selection based on personal connections, seniority, and qualifications. Indeed many white candidates fail to realize that their superior qualifications may be due to their having attended predominantly white schools.

On the other hand, white workers have also lost because of racism. As a divisive force, racism harms labor, both black and white. Since blacks have more reason to fear management reprisal, they are less unwilling to work under excessive strain or for lower wages. This attitude, although quite understandable, makes it more difficult for labor, white as well as black, to attain better working conditions. I give two illustrations:

In the early 1970s a speedup was established in an auto factory whereby jobs performed by a unit of whites were assigned to a smaller group of blacks. The heavier work load then became the norm for everyone. White workers who complained were told that if they couldn't do the job, there were people who would.[12]

In 1969, an AT&T vice president informed the assembled presidents of all Bell companies: "We must have access to an ample supply of people who will work at comparatively low rates of pay. . . . That means lots of black people." He explained that, of the persons available to work for "as little as four to five thousand a year," two-thirds were black.[13]

The willingness of blacks to accept lower wages and adverse working conditions reduces labor's bargaining power generally with management.

Racism also has inhibited the formation of trade unions. In the South, racism, because it impedes union organization, contributed to the low wage level of both white and black workers. Also some northern employers, attracted by cheaper labor costs, moved their plants—with their jobs—to the South. A labor historian summed up the divisive effect of racism: "Hiring black laborers . . . fit[s] conveniently into the anti-union efforts of many industrialists. . . . A labor force divided along ethnic and racial lines poses great difficulties for union organizers; by importing blacks, a cheap work force could be gained and unionization efforts weakened at the same time."[14]

On the whole, some white workers have lost and some have gained from racism. But to disentangle the two groups is a practical impossibility; the blameworthy cannot be marked off from the innocent.

COMPENSATING WHITES FOR BLACK PREFERENTIAL TREATMENT

In some situations compensation by innocent parties appears to be morally acceptable. For example, Germans born after World War II surely have no responsibility for the Holocaust, yet they pay taxes that fund reparations for Jewish victims. These Germans, however, pay a not exorbitant monetary assessment, but an individual white worker affected by preferential treatment loses a promotion or a job, surely a significant difference.

Someone must bear the cost of overcoming the evil of racism, but preferential treatment does seem to distribute that burden unfairly. Whites adversely affected by such treatment do appear singled out for sacrifice, while others—among whom are perpetrators of racism—pay nothing. The singling-out issue arises in two kinds of situations, in layoff and in hiring and advancement.

LAYOFF

If AA is to be effective, it must include measures that protect black employees from layoffs induced by poor business conditions. However, the sacrifice for white workers who are deprived of their jobs as a result of preferential retention of blacks is serious. Hence, wherever possible, alternatives to layoff which reduce the burden or spread it more equitably over the work force should be utilized. Among such alternatives are deferred salary arrangements (which in 1991 helped prevent teacher layoffs in New York City), payless holidays, early retirement incentives for older workers, and work-sharing. . . . Since the reduced work disbenefit is distributed equitably among all the employees of Smith and Co. through a reduced work week and partial unemployment insurance, neither blacks nor whites suffer disproportionate injury.

Where work-sharing or other measures that avoid or reduce layoffs is impossible, the adverse effect of seniority-based layoff on blacks can be decreased by a preferential treatment measure: At Smith and Co., 20 percent of the whites and 20 percent of the blacks would be laid off by seniority within their racial group; hence the layoff burden is shared equally by whites and blacks. Since blacks as a group are less senior than whites, however, some blacks who retain their jobs will be less senior than some whites who lose them.

The singling-out effect of such preferential treatment on white employees can be diminished by substantial monetary awards, funded by the federal government to supplement unemployment insurance. Such financial awards are important not only because many workers are far from affluent, but also because they would tend to minimize opposition to preferential retention.[15]

Compensation funded by a federal progressive tax would distribute the cost of a racially preferential remedy equitably throughout society. Taxes levied according to ability to pay best accord with the moral principle of fairness. Those whom payment hurts least, pay more. If payment for such measures (or, for that matter, for other social programs exemplifying fairness) were made by the wealthiest individuals, the unpopularity of further taxation would be greatly reduced. A federal progressive tax could also serve to spread the burden of payment for other AA measures, for example, to fund subsidies to employers for whom transporting minority workers from inner cities or the introduction of job-related testing is too costly.

HIRING AND PROMOTION

Preferential treatment in hiring is exemplified when a basically qualified black is selected over a more qualified white; preferential treatment in promotion occurs when a less qualified black is promoted or, where seniority determines promotion, when a black is advanced over a more senior employee. Although failure to gain a position or promotion is less serious than losing one's current job, the disbenefit of such singling out for affected whites is still significant. Monetary compensation to those whites, again funded by a progressive tax, appears to be a reasonable measure. Compensation, however, is a problem, because there is an important difference between seniority cases and qualifications cases—whether they involve promotion, hiring, or layoff. When preference is accorded to less senior blacks, the identity of the adversely affected, more senior whites is evident. Determining which white workers would be entitled to the financial awards I have proposed is an easy matter.

In qualifications cases, however, it is often not easy to determine which candidate, absent preferential treatment for blacks, would have been selected from among all the applicants. Does the past history of the firm or department show a clear commitment to the best-qualified candidate? Or were some candidates selected because they pandered to supervisors or knew how to use their influential contacts or because their ability posed no threat to mediocre incumbents?

Also, unless the qualifications criteria are themselves clear and objective, it would be very difficult to provide that one is the best qualified among all the candidates. Hence in qualification cases monetary awards to rejected whites are reasonable only if there is already in place a clear selection criterion, such as a test, a Ph.D., or a blind review of research that makes it evident who, absent racial preference, would have been selected from all the candidates.

Care should be taken, however, to prevent abuse of the right to such monetary compensation. For example, those who claim such payment should demonstrate that they unsuccessfully sought equivalent employment and that their application for this position is reasonable given their employment skills. Hence highly educated whites would not apply for unskilled positions in order to be eligible for such compensation. Also a once-in-a-lifetime limit on all compensatory financial awards appears reasonable.

MERITOCRATIC CRITICS

Some AA critics, whom I shall call meritocrats, believe that justice in the workplace is exemplified by selection according to merit standards. Hence they claim that racial preference violates the rights of more qualified white candidates. Note the difference between the meritocratic argument and the singling-out criticism I have just discussed. The meritocratic claim implies that the rights of rejected, more qualified whites are violated only because they are better qualified. Hence the meritocratic argument, unlike the singling-out criticism, has no bearing on racial preference in seniority-based selection.

. . . Whatever the effect of AA measures in their entirety, it is true that racial preference for a less qualified black can, in specific situations, reduce effective job performance. According to meritocrats, such selection violates the rights of adversely affected white candidates. . . .[16]

Let us assume that insofar as maximally qualified candidates have exerted effort to attain positions under an accepted and just rule, they have a prima facie right to such positions. But the fact is that, contrary to Goldman, hiring the most competent candidate is not the "currently accepted" rule in employment. Being the most qualified candidate is indeed one way to get the job, but employers' ignoring of merit standards and their explicit preference for specific groups are widespread. Merit criteria are either ignored or undermined in several ways.

In accordance with a traditional legal principle—employment "at will"—private U.S. employers have had the right to discharge their workers without a reasonable cause based on work performance. This principle gives employers the legal right to dismiss qualified employees merely for refusing to support political candidates of the employer's choice or for expressing unpopular views on the job or even in the privacy of their own homes. An employer right to arbitrary discharge without reasonable cause is hardly compatible with a merit system. Although the employer's right to discharge is now restricted by specific exceptions identified in union contracts and in federal and state laws (e.g., prohibiting race and sex discrimination), employment at will is still a significant legal principle in U.S. courts.[17]

Competent job performance has also been undermined by the widespread use of unvalidated employment tests and irrelevant subjective standards for hiring and promotion.

As I described earlier, federal and state governments have continuously given employment preference to veterans, thereby excluding large numbers of more qualified nonveterans.

Many employees obtain their vocational qualifications in colleges and professional schools. In some such institutions preference for admission has been extended to children of alumni. After Allan Bakke sued the University of California medical school, it was revealed that the dean had been permitted to select some admittees without reference to the usual screening process. As one writer noted, "The dean's 'special admissions program' was evidently devoted to the *realpolitik* of sustaining influential support for the school."[18]

Seniority-based selection for training, promotion, and retention in layoff is commonly practiced in both the private and public sector of the economy. Such selection is based on years of service, not evaluation of job performance. Adherence to meritocratic principles would in some situations require the abolition of seniority criteria for reward.

As emphasized earlier, reliance on personal connections is probably the most widely used recruitment method in American employment, a practice that often works against a merit system. An incumbent's graduate-school fiend, the boss's nephew, or a political-patronage appointee is frequently not the most qualified person available for the job.

Note too that gaining promotion through social networks within the firm may have a corrupting effect on job performance as well as on moral character. The employee may see pandering to the right people as the best route to success.

Because traditionally accepted preference is so widespread, some blacks selected by AA preference may in fact replace less qualified whites who would have been chosen by such traditional preference.

I conclude that merit selection is not . . . the currently accepted rule. . . .

A different version of the meritocratic claim might be that although hiring the best candidate is not the currently accepted rule and because (as Goldman says) merit selection has social utility, such selection ought to be the rule, and thus preferential treatment should not be extended to blacks. According to this meritocratic claim, all practices that often conflict with merit standards, such as selection by seniority ranking, veteran status, and powerful personal connections, should be eliminated. In that case, why not begin the struggle for merit in American employment by calling for an end to these practices? Why start by excluding members of a largely poor and powerless group, such as black people?

Let us focus on the consequences simply of denying preference to basically qualified blacks. Let us assume that this denial would produce some gain in social utility, that is, efficiency. That benefit would, I suggest, weigh very little in the moral balance against the double accomplishment of preferential treatment: compensation to blacks for past wrongs against them and achieving what this nation has never known—occupational integration, racial justice in the workplace.

PREFERENTIAL TREATMENT AND BLACK SELF-RESPECT

Some commentators suggest that preferential treatment may be morally injurious to black persons. Thus Midge Decter and the economist Thomas Sowell worry that preference damages the self-respect of blacks.[19]

Does preference really injure the self-respect of those it benefits? Traditional preference extended to personal connections has occasioned no such visible injury to self-respect. Career counselors who advise job seekers to develop influential contacts exhibit no fear that their clients will think less well of themselves; indeed, job candidates who secure powerful connections count themselves *fortunate*.

It might be objected that blacks (or any persons) who gain their positions through preferential treatment ought to respect themselves less. But this claim assumes that these blacks do not deserve such treatment. I believe that, because the overwhelming majority of blacks has been grievously wronged by racism, they deserve to be compensated for such injury and that black beneficiaries of employment preference—like veterans compensated by employment preference—have no good reason to feel unworthy.

Moreover, telling blacks—the descendants of slaves—that they ought to feel unworthy of their preferential positions can become self-fulfilling prophecy. Where are the black persons whose spirit and self-confidence have not already suffered because of the palpable barriers to attending white schools, living in white neighborhoods, and enjoying relations of friendship and intimacy with white people? Those blacks who, despite all the obstacles of overt and institutional racism, have become basically qualified for their positions should be respected for that achievement. Justice Marshall reminds us that the history of blacks differs from that of other ethnic groups. It includes not only slavery but also its aftermath, in which as a people they were marked inferior by our laws, a mark that has endured.[20] Opportunities created by preferential treatment should symbolize an acknowledgment of such injustice and a commitment to create a future free of racism.

NOTES

1. Robert Fullinwider, "The Equal Opportunity Myth," in *Report from the Center for Philosophy and Public Policy* (College Park: University of Maryland, Fall, 1981).

2. Shelby Steele, "A Negative Vote on Affirmative Action," *New York Times Magazine*, May 13, 1990.

3. William T. Blackstone, "Reverse Discrimination and Compensatory Justice," in *Social Justice and Preferential Treatment*, ed. William T. Blackstone and Robert T. Heslep (Athens: University of Georgia Press, 1977), p. 67.

4. Boris I. Bittker, *The Case for Black Reparations* (New York: Random House, 1973), pp. 16–17.

5. Laurence Thomas, *New York Times*, op-ed, August 13, 1990.

6. Don Jackson, *New York Times*, op-ed, January 23, 1989.

7. Bernard Boxill, *Blacks and Social Justice* (Totowa, NJ: Rowman and Alanheld, 1984), p. 148.

8. Thomas Nagel, "A Defense of Affirmative Action," in *Report from the Center for Philosophy and Public Policy*, p. 7.

9. Robert Nozick, *Anarchy, State, and Utopia* (New York: Basic Books, 1974), pp. 237–38.

10. Thomas Nagel, *Introduction to Equality and Preferential Treatment*, eds. Marshall Cohen, Thomas Nagel, and Thomas Scanlon (Princeton, N.J.: Princeton University Press, 1977), p. viii.

11. Steven S. Schwarzschild, American History, Marked by Racism," *New Politics* 1 (1987): 56–58.

12. Victor Perlo, *Economics of Racism U.S.A.* (New York: International Publishers, 1975), p. 172.

13. *"A Unique Competence"*: *A Study of Equal Employment Opportunity in the Bell System*, prepared by the Equal Employment Opportunity Commission, 1972.

14. Clement T. Imhoff, "The Recruiter," in *Working Lives*, ed. Marc S. Miller (New York: Pantheon, 1974), p. 56. For a comprehensive analysis of Marxian views of racial antagonisms within the working class, see Boxill, chap. 3.

15. For determining the specifics of awards to more senior white workers who lose their jobs because of racial preference during layoff, the Vulcan decision is instructive: "The court also concludes that those firefighters who have or will forfeit their seniority rights as a result of the affirmative action plan . . . ought to be compensated [by] . . . the federal government. . . . The amount of such compensation must, however, be 'just.' It is not intended to be a lifetime pension. Those senior firefighters who are laid off as a result of the affirmative action plan shall be under a duty to mitigate damages, by seeking to obtain other employment. Any claim for compensation shall be reduced by the amount of salaries or and benefits received as a result of such layoff. Moreover the period of compensation shall end upon the attainment of other employment but absent exceptional circumstances no later than one year from the date of layoff" (*Vulcan Pioneers v. New Jersey Department of Civil Service*, 34 Fair Empl. Prac. Cas. [BNA] 1247–48 [D.N.J. 1984]).

16. Alan Goldman, "Limits to the Justification of Reverse Discrimination," *Social Theory and Practice* 3 (1975): 289–91.

17. *Coppage v. Kansas*, 736 U.S. 441 (1914); Burton Hall, "Collective Bargaining and Workers' Liberty," in *Moral Rights in the Workplace*, ed. Gertrude Ezorsky (New York: State University of New York Press, 1987), pp. 161–65.

18. Allan P. Sindler, *Bakke, DeFunis, and Minority Admissions* (New York: Longman, 1978), p. 69n. This practice was ended in 1977.

19. Midge Decter, *New York Times*, op-ed, July 6, 1980; Thomas Sowell, "'Affirmative Action' Reconsidered," *Public Interest* no. 42 (1976): 64.

20. *Regents of University of California v. Bakke*, 438 U.S. 265 (1978) (Marshall, J., concurring in part and dissenting in part).

■ DAVID THEO GOLDBERG: REVERSING DISCRIMINATION

David Theo Goldberg constructs an argument to show that preferential treatment programs furnish a modest mechanism for hiring, promoting, or admitting blacks in the numbers and patterns that might be expected where there is no history and lingering legacy of racist practice. Accordingly, preferential programs are justifiable for they take nothing from nonblacks to which they have a rightful claim, and they give to blacks what they properly may claim. Thus preferential programs do not amount to reverse discrimination, for they do not exclude anybody from that to which they have a justifiable right; rather, they are mechanisms for reversing the legacy of discrimination.

David Theo Goldberg

REVERSE DISCRIMINATION OR REVERSING DISCRIMINATION?

Since the charge of reverse discrimination became closely associated with affirmative action programs in the wake of *Bakke v. Regents of the University of California* (1978), there has been an increasing tendency in the public mind as well as amongst policy and lawmakers to rationalize away racial exclusions as functions or outcomes of the cultural poverty of those excluded. In the past decade, for example, marginalized blacks in the United States have been castigated by some intellectuals and journalists, black and white alike, for failing to exert effort, for relying on

From David Theo Goldberg, "Reverse Discrimination or Reversing Discrimination?" *APA Newsletter on Philosophy and the Black Experience* 92,1 (Spring 1993) pp. 16–18.

government, politics, social engineering, and the language of affirmative action entitlements rather than on developing individual initiative, self-sufficiency, and the
competitive spirit of free and fair enterprise. The virtues of family are deemed to be
displaced by the vices of male irresponsibility, paternal commitments by the pleasure principle, the protestant work ethic by drug dealing and dreams of the easy life.
By waiting on redress for exclusions of past generations, blacks are thought to develop the 'help me and handout' mentality, low self-esteem, and bitterness. Moral
blackmail rather than merit is thought to be the proper mark of just advance. Thus,
ongoing contemporary racialized exclusions—exclusions from opportunities, powers, social goods and services, rights, and perhaps even from the possibility of fulfilling some responsibilities (jury service, for instance)—are explained away or
legitimated in terms of the black underclass's own misguided values and abrogation
of responsibility.[1] No matter that the standards of merit remain set in the terms of
race and class; that the relative material conditions of racialized class—the *de facto*
black bars of containment—are little different for many today than they were
twenty or forty years ago; that socioeconomic exclusions are in many instances as
racially entrenched; that the specificity and particularity of blacks is elided by an
image no less essentialized in the broad or in detail than that of the most extreme
white racists; or that legal entitlements constitutive of justice as fairness remain far
from secure or completely satisfied.[2]

It is against this background that affirmative action policies have come to be
the central object of contemporary concern in respect of matters racial. In undertaking to redress the wrongs of racism, policies of affirmative action are thought to
commit the kind of wrong they are supposed to be combatting, namely, privileging
some over others on the basis of racial membership. Stated in this way, the criticism
at the very least takes in too much. It fails to distinguish those features of affirmative
action that are morally uncontroversial from those about which questions might be
raised. Critics of affirmative action are invariably committed, at least in voice, to
the principle of equal opportunity for all. Affirmative admissions, appointments, or
promotions are considered to violate this principle. But there is much that the principle of equality might justifiably require: that every effort be made to find candidates for admissions, appointments, and promotions from those racialized groups
that remain relatively excluded; that availability of positions be openly advertized
and characterized in nondiscriminatory ways; and that admission, appointment, and
promotion categories and criteria be nondiscriminatory in both principle and application. Thus, what is at issue here is not affirmative action policies generically, but
the form of preferential treatment they are most often take to assume. The objection is usually that preferential treatment of racially defined groups whose members
have been excluded from access to social resources amounts to unacceptable forms
of reverse racial discrimination against those formerly favored (namely, white
males).[3]

I have supposed here that racism is to be most generally characterized in terms
of racially defined exclusions. Thus, I define racism (or more accurately racisms) as
any act, policy, or institutional arrangement that promotes exclusions or involves
actually excluding people in virtue of their being deemed members of different

racial groups, however racial groups are taken to be constituted. It follows that in some instances expressions may be racist on grounds of their effects. The mark of racism in these cases will be whether the discriminatory racial exclusion reflects a persistent pattern or could reasonably have been avoided.[4]

This raises a general consideration facing any characterization of racisms in terms of sets of exclusions. Are all racialized exclusions, and so seemingly preferential treatment programs, to be deemed objectionable because racist? Baier suggests one response to this problem. He insists that we distinguish between a 'morally neutral' and a 'morally committal' use of the term 'racism.' 'Compensatory racism,' like a program of preferential treatment, is a morally neutral usage: It takes further argument beyond mere use of the term to establish whether it is necessarily objectionable. Accordingly, some racialized exclusions—some racisms—are morally acceptable. They cannot be rationalized away as merely legitimate, but must be considered more strongly as justifiable.

There is another way of conceiving the issue, though. It may be denied that those cases where racism seems justifiable are properly cases of racist exclusion at all, even though there may be an appeal to the concept of race as a way of differentiating people. Baier rejects this option, without argument, as 'implausible'. It should be pointed out, however, that his definition of racism presupposes as a necessary condition appeal to the morally irrelevant category of "race."[5] Liberal moral theorists, largely following Rawls, have tended to dismiss the category of race as having no moral relevance in judgment of character because race represents biological characteristics, characteristics which could not be otherwise and so for which individuals are not personally responsible. Race is like height, something given rather than earned. Just as rewards or punishments predicated upon height distributions would be arbitrary and so unjustifiable, so too with race.[6] Notice, nevertheless, that critics of marginalized blacks in terms of their underclass position castigate the class on the basis not of biological but of *cultural* characteristics. If race is culturally conceived and one has some personal control over cultural commitments, then one is personally responsible for the cultural habits, the mores of one's race. Conceived thus, the question concerning justifiability of preferential treatment programs or policies becomes this: Can we differentiate racist exclusions from those cases that may look like them but are actually only racially describable?

To deem preferential treatment programs racist, on the view I have articulated, people would have to be excluded from institutional opportunities in virtue of their racial membership. Certainly, it is not the aim of preferential treatment programs to exclude anyone on racial grounds; the undertaking is to *include* those who would otherwise remain racially excluded. So the determination must rest on whether such programs have the patterned effect of excluding whites. Critics would argue that this is obviously so. Yet this charge necessarily presupposes that whites have a right to the positions in question, or at least to the opportunity to compete equally for the set asides. Competing on equal grounds is usually thought to involve being considered on individual merits. The criterion of merit, however, is similarly loaded. To serve as a principle of fairness, it must minimally presuppose that institutional access and opportunities, rights and liberties are equally open and available to all from the earliest moments of life, no matter racialized membership. Rhetoric aside, this is obviously not the world we have inherited and perpetuate. Thus, the actuality of 'equal opportunity' under present conditions involves perpetuation of privilege and discriminatory access. In light of this, it should be clear that preferential treatment programs do not exclude whites merely because of their whiteness. Rather, members of racialized groups who would likely continue to be excluded but for the program are given the possibility of access. The mark of inclusion is not the mere fact of racial belonging but what race stands for, namely, perpetuated discriminatory exclusion. Thus, Baier's 'compensatory racism' is not racism at all so long as there remain open to whites a range of opportunities that are not so readily available to members of those racialized groups whose opportunities continue to be curtailed.

A hypothetical example should serve to illustrate this point. Assume that the average white educated male may in principle compete, in the absence of preferential treatment programs, for approximately seventy-five jobs. From these, he may receive, say, three offers. A black person, equally qualified and without the benefit of preferential treatment programs, and in the sort of racially charged world we have been used to, may effectively compete, say, for twenty-five positions and be lucky to land one. (These ratios seem fair, given the recent findings in Washington D.C. and Chicago that black job-seekers will find it three times as difficult to get a job as a similarly qualified white person.) With preferential treatment programs in place, it seems reasonable to assume that the black candidate's competitive pool will be stretched by about half, and the white candidate's reduced by about the same amount the black person's is increased. The black candidate will now have a crack at something like forty positions, the white candidate close to sixty. Both can expect something like two offers. The difference between the number of positions each can expect to compete for is reflective of the fact that there will be more competitors in the non-preferential category, and so the greater number of competitive possibilities will more or less equalize the competitive chances of whites. The playing field has thus been relatively levelled, and the white candidate can hardly claim to be wronged. Of course, he no longer has the competitive edge he once enjoyed, but his original wealth of possibilities turned on the wrongful exclusion, the dearth of possibilities facing the black person. Accordingly, it can hardly claim justification. By contrast, where whites, individually or as a group, can show genuine exclusion in virtue of their racial characterization, this too would count as a case of racism.

This sort of analysis has a wide range of potential applications. It may be used to assess the justifiability not only of the sorts of admissions, hiring, and promotion programs or policies we have come most usually to associate with preferential treatment, but also of those undertakings neoconservative media critics like Dinesh D'Souza or George Will have found so abhorrent. Analyzed against the background of historical exclusion in this way, African American residence halls on college campuses or separate classes on contract or constitutional law for black students who feel (or, more strongly, are subtly or not so subtly made to feel) intimidated in "integrated" law school classes, for example, may be considered neither compensatory nor racist because exclusionary. Rather, they may be *contextually* necessary (and justifiable only where so necessary) to incorporate those who would otherwise continue to suffer the historical and contemporary legacy of racially defined exclusions, of a culture that remains deeply racist. Unlike integration, which presupposes the prevailing values of dominant culture, the standard of incorporation presupposes that prevailing cultural values themselves will give way, will transform in the cultural negotiation that necessarily takes place as the bars of discrimination are filed away from either side. That we approach this cultural negotiation with sensitivity not only to the cries of affirmative action and reverse discrimination babies but to the wide net of effects of past and present exclusions, a sensitivity altogether absent in the past decade, should help significantly in the ongoing struggle to reverse the historical tide of discrimination.

NOTES

1. For the most recent examples of this view, see Shelby Steele, *The Content of Our Character: A New Vision of Race in America* (New York: St. Martin's Press, 1990) and Jared Taylor, *Paved with Good Intentions: The Failure of Race Relations in Contemporary America* (New York: Carrol and Graf, 1992). Earlier versions of this view were articulated by economists Thomas Sowell, Walter Williams, and Glen Loury. It is interesting to note that Russell Lewis makes just this attack on blacks in Britain, and in doing so analogizes what he predicts to be the future of over-politicized black Britains with what he perceives to be the recent political experience of American Indians. Russell Lewis, *Anti-Racism: A Mania Exposed* (London: Quartet Books, 1988), esp. pp. 120 ff.

2. For a critique of this 'tradition' of rationalization, see Thomas Boston, *Race, Class, and Conservativism* (Boston: Unwin Hyman, 1988), and the provocative review of Shelby Steele's *The Content of Our Character* by Adolph Reed, "Steele Trap," *The Nation* (March 4, 1991, pp. 274–81). See also Adolph Reed, "Black Particularity Revisited," *Telos* (Spring 1979): 71–93.

3. See Lewis, op. cit., pp. 47ff; and Antony Flew, "The Race Relations Industry," *The Salisbury Review* (Winter 1984), pp. 24–27.

4. David Theo Goldberg, *Racist Culture: Philosophy and the Politics of Meaning* (Oxford: Basil Blackwell, 1993), Chapter 5, pp. 97–99.

5. Kurt Baier, "Merit and Race," *Philosophia* 8, 2–3 (1978), p. 127.

6. John Rawls, *A Theory of Justice* (Cambridge MA: Harvard University Press, 1971), p. 19; Joel Feinberg, *Social Philosophy* (Englewood Cliffs, NJ: Prentice Hall, 1973), p. 103.

SUGGESTIONS FOR DISCUSSION

1. Why are racial discrimination and gender discrimination respectively wrong? Are the wrongs involved merely offensive or harmful? Are racist wrongs analogous to sexist wrongs? In establishing discrimination, should one have to demonstrate intent on the part of the party accused of discrimination, or simply the discriminatory impact of action or institutional rules?

2. Does the severity of racial discrimination require preferential treatment programs as compensation or to institute equality, or is any form of preferential treatment tantamount to reverse discrimination? Would the same *kinds* of argument require or mitigate against preferential treatment in behalf of women?

3. Should hiring, promotions, and admissions be determined strictly on the basis of merit?

4. Is group representation in the population a fair goal for group distribution in employment?

FOR FURTHER READING

Bishop, S., and Weinzweig, M., eds. *Philosophy and Women.* Belmont, Calif.: Wadsworth, 1979.

Bittker, B. *The Case for Black Reparations.* New York: Random House, 1973.

Blackstone, W. T., and Heslep, R., eds. *Social Justice and Preferential Treatment.* Athens: University of Georgia Press, 1976.

Boxill, B. *Blacks and Social Justice.* Totowa, N.J.: Rowman and Littlefield, 1984.

Cohen, M., Nagel, T., and Scanlon, T., eds. *Equality and Preferential Treatment.* Princeton: Princeton University Press, 1977.

Eastland, T. and Bennett, W. *Counting by Race: Equality from the Founding Fathers to Bakke and Weber.* New York: Basic Books, 1979.

English, J., ed. *Sex Equality.* Englewood Cliffs, N.J.: Prentice-Hall, 1977.

Ezorsky, G. *Racism and Justice: The Case for Affirmative Action.* Ithaca: Cornell University Press, 1991.

Fuchs, L. H. *The American Kaleidoscope: Race, Ethnicity, and the American Culture.* Middletown, Conn.: Wesleyan University Press, 1991.

Fullinwider, R. *The Reverse Discrimination Controversy.* Totowa, N.J.: Rowman and Littlefield, 1980.

Glazer, N. *Affirmative Discrimination.* New York: Basic Books, 1975.

Goldberg, D. T. *Racist Culture: Philosophy and the Politics of Meaning.* Oxford: Basil Blackwell, 1993.

Goldberg, D. T., ed. *Anatomy of Racism.* Minneapolis: University of Minnesota Press, 1988.

Goldman, A. *Justice and Reverse Discrimination.* Princeton: Princeton University Press, 1979.

Gossett, T. *Race: The History of an Idea in America.* New York: Schocken Books, 1968.

Gould, S. J. *The Mismeasure of Man.* New York: W. W. Norton, 1981.

Gross, B., ed. *Reverse Discrimination.* Buffalo: Prometheus Books, 1976.

Hacker, A. *Two Nations: Black and White, Separate, Hostile, and Unequal.* New York: Scribner, 1991.

Jaynes, G. D., and Williams, R. M., Jr. *A Common Destiny: Blacks and American Society.* Washington, D.C.: National Academy Press, 1989.

Jencks, C. *Rethinking Social Policy.* Cambridge: Harvard University Press, 1992.

Jencks, C., et al. *Inequality.* New York: Basic Books, 1972.

Lawson, B. E. *The Underclass Question.* Philadelphia: Temple University Press, 1992.

Lynch, F. *Invisible Victims: White Males and the Crisis of Affirmative Action.* New York: Greenwood Press, 1989.

Roediger, D. *Wages of Whiteness: Race and the Making of the American Working Class.* London: Verso, 1991.

Sigelman, L., and Welch, S. *Black Americans' Views of Racial Inequality: The Dream Deferred.* Cambridge: Cambridge University Press, 1991.

Sowell, T. *Black Education: Myths and Tragedies.* New York: D. McKay, 1972.

Steele, S. *The Content of Our Character: A New Vision of Race in America.* New York: St. Martin's Press, 1990.

Taylor, B. R. *Affirmative Action at Work: Law, Politics, and Ethics.* Pittsburgh: University of Pittsburgh Press, 1991.

Vetterling-Braggin, M., Elliston, F., and English, J., eds. *Feminism and Philosophy.* Totowa, N.J.: Littlefield Adams, 1977.

Wartofsky, M., McDade, J., and Lesnor, C., eds. "Philosophy and the Black Experience." *The Philosophical* Forum IX, 2–3, 1977–78: 113–382.

Wasserstrom, R. *Philsophy and Social Issues: Five Studies.* Notre Dame: University of Notre Dame Press, 1980.

West, C. *Race Matters.* Boston: Beacon Press, 1993.

Young, I.M. *Justice and the Politics of Difference.* Princeton: Princeton University Press, 1990.

CHAPTER TEN

CENSORSHIP
AND HATE SPEECH

In the 1980s and 1990s, there was a resurgence of racist incidents and violence in cities and on campuses throughout the United States. Rodney King, a black man, was beaten by white policemen in Los Angeles. In the wake of the policemen's acquittal, Reginald Denny, a white truck driver, and others were beaten by a few black residents of South Central Los Angeles. Both beatings were videotaped and widely broadcast on television. Vincent Chin was beaten to death with a baseball bat in Detroit by disgruntled white auto workers who "mistook him for Japanese," and two young black men were killed at the hands of angry white mobs in Howard Beach and Bensonhurst, New York. A black resident of New York City, visiting Florida, was abducted by white men who then poured gasoline over him and set him alight just because he was black. In St. Paul, Minnesota, a white man burnt a cross on the front lawn of a black family, to encourage their departure from the neighborhood (see *R.A.V. v. City of St. Paul* in this chapter). African American and Korean residents have clashed bitterly in Los Angeles and New York City, as have white and Vietnamese fishermen in Texas. Public schools have become increasingly resegregated, not only from one school to another but also in classrooms within schools. Racist epithets have appeared in campus dormitories, malls, and unions throughout the country, and students have been subjected to racially motivated attacks.

At the same time, occurrence of rapes has increased, as has wife and partner abuse. Reports of date and acquaintance rape related to campus life have increased, and many women express fear in walking to their cars in campus and shopping mall parking lots. Entertainment arcades and video game malls off and on campus, mainly frequented by young men, offer virtually realistic possibilities for violence against women and a variety of racial "others." Recently, the public spotlight has focused on issues of sexual harassment in the workplace and learning environment. Colleges, universities, and employers generally have responded by introducing codes for dealing with racist and sexist expression and behavior.

Racism and Sexism Defined   There is considerable controversy over what particular acts, expressions, or events count as racist or sexist. Nevertheless, whatever counts as racist and sexist expressions, it is now generally acknowledged that they are wrong. The targets of such expressions are treated as objects, less than fully human. They are accorded less than the dignity and respect due full persons. The variety of wrongs we have come to understand as racist and sexist may be understood, then, as various forms and degrees of unjustifiable exclusion from the moral community.

Freedom We understand freedom to be a fundamental value; it is a general condition for developing the particular things each individual may value. Joel Feinberg suggests that there is a presumption always in freedom's favor. Should we face a choice between leaving people free to do something and coercing them to act in some way, *prima facie* we should favor leaving them free. As John Rawls argues (see Chapter 5), we ought to endorse the widest available liberties compatible with like liberties for all. These would include freedom of expression and—so it seems to follow—of racist or sexist expression.

The dilemma, then, is this: if we value freedom so highly, part of the price it seems we have to pay will be the license of those who choose to express themselves in a racist or sexist way. While we need not condone such expression, this basic commitment to freedom would seem to necessitate tolerance of what is regarded nevertheless as morally wrong. But tolerance does appear to imply social acceptance: the wrongs involved are regarded as insufficient to warrant restriction. By contrast, restricting such expression delimits—some would say undermines—the basic commitment to freedom.

Freedom, Offense, and Harm Underlying this dilemma is an understanding of racist and sexist expression as offensive. A moral offense involves behavior considered to go beyond the bounds of moral decency and propriety. It is unlike criminal acts such as murder, which are also morally unacceptable. Behavior or representations are offensive not because of serious harm they may cause, but because they tend largely to produce discomfort and ill-feeling. Recently some jurisdictions in the United States have introduced bias-enhancement statutes for what they define as hate crimes. These suggest that crimes motivated by bias toward their targets are somehow worse—more harmful or offensive—than the same crimes not so motivated. The general questions here are these: What (if any) are acceptable restrictions that may be imposed upon the freedom of expression, and on what grounds? Second, are racist or sexist expressions (including acts) morally repugnant only because they are offensive, or do they involve egregious harms for those targeted and for the body politic at large?

The basic dilemma may be stated more succinctly as follows: the First Amendment to the U.S. Constitution protects freedom of expression. Nevertheless, it seems unfair to guarantee to a small minority free expression of a racist and sexist sort at the expense of those targeted and objectified by the expressions. Free speech, it is argued, should not extend to morally offensive, and certainly not to harmful, expression; racism and sexism are not protected by the First Amendment. So, in light of the presumption favoring liberty, are there principles that may serve to justify limiting liberty? In particular, what grounds could there be for restricting freedom of expression?

Liberty-limiting Principles Joel Feinberg identifies six principles advanced as justifications for restricting liberty: Harm, Offense, Legal Paternalism, Legal Moralism, Extreme Paternalism, and Welfare. These principles provide reasons generally relevant, though perhaps not always conclusive, for coerced restriction of liberty. The most prominent is the Harm Principle, applied so eloquently by John Stuart Mill in "On Liberty" (see Chapter 4). This principle may be interpreted either "privately" or "publicly." The Private Harm Principle justifies limitations on liberty to prevent injury to individual persons. Those who claim a causal connection between racist or sexist expression and violent behavior against individuals advance the Private Harm Principle to support their proposed restrictions of free expression. The Public Harm Principle justifies restrictions on liberty to prevent impairment of institutional practices considered to be in the public interest. Pro-censorship arguments that criticize racist or sexist depictions because they fail to acknowledge diversity and so undermine communal cohesiveness appeal to the Public Harm Principle. (Mill is interpreted usually—and mistakenly—as defending only the Private Harm Principle.)

Second, the Offense Principle would limit liberty so as to prevent offense to others. Third, the principles of Legal Paternalism would justify legislation to prevent self-inflicted harms (for example, requiring seat belts in automobiles). Fourth, the principle of Legal Moralism undertakes to justify legal enforcement of morality for its own sake. Extreme Paternalism requires action to benefit the self, and the Welfare Principle to benefit others.

It is generally thought that racist or sexist expression may be delimited, if at all, to prevent harm or offense to others (Harm or Offense Principles) or to benefit others (Welfare Principle). Arguments for restriction that appeal to the Offense or Welfare Principles are considered to be weakest. In light of the strong commitment to freedom, in general, and the freedom of expression, in particular, many acknowledge only significant harm as warranting any restriction of racist or sexist expression.

■ SUPREME COURT RULING: R.A.V.

The city of St. Paul, Minnesota, introduced an ordinance for criminalizing those public expressions of hate or bias that are reasonably considered "to arouse anger, alarm or resentment . . . on the basis of race, color, creed, religion, or gender." In the cross-burning case, *R.A.V. v. City of St. Paul,* the Supreme Court unanimously ruled the ordinance unconstitutional on grounds of proscribing speech in virtue of the content or ideas it expresses. It thus violates the viewpoint neutrality requirement of First Amendment doctrine. The Court argued that combating messages of racial supremacy cannot take the form of selective limitations on speech based on the message or ideas conveyed by that speech. Even though there is a compelling state interest to combat racist discrimination, such interest can only override the viewpoint neutrality requirement if the state has no alternative content-neutral means for resisting racist discrimination. For instance, if the statute had undertaken to prohibit "fighting words" aimed at specific groups or persons, it could be considered facially valid in terms of the Equal Protection Clause of the Fourteenth Amendment. Thus, the Court held in the St. Paul case that content-based discrimination clearly is not the sole viable means at the state's disposal for resisting racist discrimination.

Justice Antonin Scalia

PLURALITY OPINION IN
R.A.V. v. CITY OF ST. PAUL, MINNESOTA

In the predawn hours of June 21, 1990, petitioner and several other teenagers allegedly assembled a crudely made cross by taping together broken chair legs. They then allegedly burned the cross inside the fenced yard of a black family that lived across the street from the house where petitioner was staying. Although this conduct could have been punished under any of a number of laws, one of the two provisions under which respondent city of St. Paul chose to charge petitioner (then a juvenile) was the St. Paul Bias-Motivated Crime Ordinance, . . . which provides:

> Whoever places on public or private property a symbol, object, appellation, characterization or graffiti, including but not limited to, a burning cross or Nazi swastika, which one knows or has reasonable grounds to know arouses anger, alarm or resentment in others on the basis of race, color, creed, religion or gender, commits disorderly conduct and shall be guilty of a misdemeanor.

Petitioner moved to dismiss this count on the ground that the St. Paul ordinance was substantially overbroad and impermissibly content-based and therefore facially invalid under the First Amendment. . . .

I

[1] . . . Assuming, *arguendo,* that all of the expression reached by the ordinance is proscribable under the "fighting words" doctrine, we nonetheless conclude that the ordinance is facially unconstitutional in that it prohibits otherwise permitted speech solely on the basis of the subjects the speech addresses.

[2,3] The First Amendment generally prevents government from proscribing speech, . . . because of disapproval of the ideas expressed. Content-based regulations are presumptively invalid. . . .

I I

[7,8] . . . What we have here, it must be emphasized, is not a prohibition of fighting words that are directed at certain persons or groups (which would be *facially* valid if it met the requirements of the Equal Protection Clause); but rather, a prohibition of fighting words that contain (as the Minnesota Supreme Court repeatedly emphasized) messages of "bias-motivated" hatred and in particular, as applied to this case,

United States Supreme Court, 112 U.S. 2538 (1992).

messages "based on virulent notions of racial supremacy." . . . One must wholeheart-edly agree with the Minnesota Supreme Court that "[i]t is the responsibility, even the obligation, of diverse communities to confront such notions in whatever form they appear," *ibid.*, but the manner of that confrontation cannot consist of selective limitations upon speech. St. Paul's brief asserts that a general "fighting words" law would not meet the city's needs because only a content-specific measure can com-municate to minority groups that the "group hatred" aspect of such speech "is not condoned by the majority." . . . The point of the First Amendment is that majority preferences must be expressed in some fashion other than silencing speech on the basis of its content. . . .

[9] Finally, St. Paul and its *amici* defend the conclusion of the Minnesota Su-preme Court that, even if the ordinance regulates expression based on hostility to-wards its protected ideological content, this discrimination is nonetheless justified because it is narrowly tailored to serve compelling state interests. Specifically, they assert that the ordinance helps to ensure the basic human rights of members of groups that have historically been subjected to discrimination, including the right of such group members to live in peace where they wish. We do not doubt that these interests are compelling, and that the ordinance can be said to promote them. But the "danger of censorship" presented by a facially content-based statute . . . requires that the weapon be employed only where it is "*necessary* to serve the asserted [com-pelling] interest," . . . The existence of adequate content-neutral alternatives thus "undercut[s] significantly" any defense of such a statute. . . . The dispositive question in this case, therefore, is whether content discrimination is reasonably necessary to achieve St. Paul's compelling interests; it plainly is not. An ordinance not limited to the favored topics, for example, would have precisely the same beneficial effect. In fact the only interest distinctively served by the content limitation is that of dis-playing the city council's special hostility towards the particular biases thus singled out. That is precisely what the First Amendment forbids. The politicians of St. Paul are entitled to express that hostility—but not through the means of imposing unique limitations upon speakers who (however benightedly) disagree.

* * *

Let there be no mistake about our belief that burning a cross in someone's front yard is reprehensible. But St. Paul has sufficient means at its disposal to prevent such behavior without adding the First Amendment to the fire. . . .

■ THOMAS C. GREY: STANFORD'S FUNDAMENTAL STANDARD

Stanford University was instrumental among institutions of higher learning in popularizing codes designed to counter discriminatory harassment. Stanford formulated a Fundamental Standard for behavior at the university: "Students should act with the respect for others' rights required of good citizens." Contemporary campus experience has suggested a tension between the right to be free of invidious discrimination and the right of free expression. Thomas Grey, a law professor who helped write Stanford's Fundamental Standard, offers an interpretation for applying it in cases of such tension. First, Grey claims, intimidation (in the form of violence or threat) is a violation of students' right to free expression even of those views others find abhorrent. Second, discriminatory harassment on the basis of race, sex, color, handicap, religion, sexual orientation, or national and ethnic origin violates students' right of equal access to education by creating a hostile environment. Third, expression (including speech) will be regarded as personally vilifying, and so harassment, if it meets three necessary conditions: it is intended to insult or stigmatize on the basis of stereotypical group characteristics; it is addressed directly to those it is intended to insult or stigmatize; and it uses insulting or "fighting" expression.

Thomas C. Grey

THE STANFORD DISCRIMINATORY HARASSMENT PROVISION

PREAMBLE

The Fundamental Standard requires that students act with "such respect for . . . the rights of others as is demanded of good citizens." Some incidents in recent years on campus have revealed doubt and disagreement about what this requirement means for students in the sensitive area where the right of free expression can conflict with the right to be free of invidious discrimination. The Student Conduct Legislative Council offers this interpretation to provide students and administrators with some guidance in this area.

FUNDAMENTAL STANDARD INTERPRETATION: FREE EXPRESSION AND DISCRIMINATORY HARASSMENT

1. Stanford is committed to the principles of free inquiry and free expression. Students have the right to hold and vigorously defend and promote their opinions, thus entering them into the life of the University, there to flourish or

Stanford University Student Conduct Policies. Office of the President. (Stanford: Stanford University, 1990), pp. 5–6.

wither according to their merits. Respect for this right requires that students tolerate even expression of opinions which they find abhorrent. Intimidation of students by other students in their exercise of this right, by violence or threat of violence, is therefore considered to be a violation of the Fundamental Standard.

2. Stanford is also committed to principles of equal opportunity and nondiscrimination. Each student has the right of equal access to a Stanford education, without discrimination on the basis of sex, race, color, handicap, religion, sexual orientation, or national and ethnic origin. Harassment of students on the basis of any of these characteristics contributes to a hostile environment that makes access to education for those subjected to it less than equal. Such discriminatory harassment is therefore considered to be a violation of the Fundamental Standard.

3. This interpretation of the Fundamental Standard is intended to clarify the point at which protected free expression ends and prohibited discriminatory harassment begins. Prohibited harassment includes discriminatory intimidation by threats of violence, and also includes personal vilification of students on the basis of their sex, race, color, handicap, religion, sexual orientation, or national and ethnic origin.

4. Speech or other expression constitutes harassment by personal vilification if it:

   a) is intended to insult or stigmatize an individual or a small number of individuals on the basis of their sex, race, color, handicap, religion, sexual orientation, or national and ethnic origin; and

   b) is addressed directly to the individual or individuals whom it insults or stigmatizes; and

   c) makes use of insulting or "fighting" words or non-verbal symbols.

In the context of discriminatory harassment, insulting or "fighting" words or non-verbal symbols are those "which by their very utterance inflict injury or tend to incite to an immediate breach of the peace," and which are commonly understood to convey direct and visceral hatred or contempt for human beings on the basis of their sex, race, color, handicap, sexual orientation, or national and ethnic origin.

■ NADINE STROSSEN: HATE SPEECH AND CIVIL RIGHTS

Nadine Strossen, currently President or the American Civil Liberties Union, develops a vigorous defense of the civil libertarian position on campus hate speech. Strossen is committed both to ending racial discrimination and promoting free speech, and thinks that educational institutions, in particular, should be home to equal opportunity and unrestricted exchange. To combat racism, however, she considers free speech basic, for free speech is deemed indispensable for promoting other rights and freedoms, including racial equality. Thus, regulating campus expression is seen as likely, though not necessarily, to undermine equality and free expression. Accordingly, while the presumption, she thinks, ought to be in favor of free expression, the First Amendment should not necessarily protect harassing speech targeted at specific individuals which creates a "demonstrably hindering" work or learning environment and thus violates the target's equal opportunity rights.

Strossen advances three conditions necessary for the justifiable regulation of speech: the utterance must likely cause immediate harm; the speech must be a necessary constituent of violent and unlawful behavior; and the speech must be addressed to a "captive audience" unable to avoid its harmful effects. To support the regulation of speech, Strossen insists that these criteria must be strictly construed and narrowly drawn. While she emphasizes that speech within the university setting especially should be protected, she argues that the permissibility of restricting hate speech will turn on the particular context within the university in which the speech occurs: the more captive the audience and the greater the power of the speaker over them (instructor speech in classrooms, for instance) or the less public the space (for instance, dormitory rooms), the more justifiable the hate speech restriction.

Strossen then examines three specific doctrines invoked to support campus hate speech regulations: the fighting words doctrine; the harm of intentionally inflicting emotional distress; and the harm of group defamation. She argues, on the basis of Supreme Court rulings, that these doctrines are incapable of sustaining any campus hate speech restrictions. Strossen then assesses the potential dangers of censoring racist speech: the regulation will more likely apply to the people it was designed to protect; its application will be arbitrary and so discriminatory; it will likely chill speech; it will apply only to a very small proportion of racist expression, and so at most is symbolic; the rules against racist speech may be employed to silence antiracist speech; the censorship may have the effect of making martyrs of those censored, and thus of glorifying racist expression as resistance to authority; campus speech codes perpetuate paternalistic stereotypes of helpless, vulnerable victims; and codes dampen vigorous intergroup discussion concerning racism and other biases. Finally, Strossen argues that means consistent with the First Amendment—especially more rather than less speech—better combats racist expression and promotes racial equality than censorship.

Nadine Strossen

BALANCING RIGHTS TO FREEDOM OF EXPRESSION AND EQUALITY: A CIVIL LIBERTIES APPROACH TO HATE SPEECH ON CAMPUS[1]

INTRODUCTION

Civil libertarians are committed to the eradication of racial discrimination and the promotion of free speech throughout society and have worked especially hard to combat both discrimination and free speech restrictions in educational institutions. Educational institutions should be bastions of equal opportunity and unrestricted exchange. Therefore, we find the upsurge of both campus racism and regulation of campus speech particularly disturbing, and we have undertaken efforts to counter both.

Because civil libertarians have learned that free speech is an indispensable instrument for the promotion of other rights and freedoms—including racial equality—we fear that regulating campus expression will undermine equality, as well as free speech. Combating racial discrimination and protecting free speech should be viewed as mutually reinforcing, rather than antagonistic, goals. A diminution in society's commitment to racial equality is neither a necessary nor an appropriate price for protecting free speech. Those who frame the debate in terms of this false dichotomy simply drive artificial wedges between would-be allies in what should be a common effort to promote civil rights and civil liberties.

SOME LIMITED FORMS OF CAMPUS HATE SPEECH MAY BE SUBJECT TO REGULATION UNDER CURRENT CONSTITUTIONAL DOCTRINE

GENERAL CONSTITUTIONAL PRINCIPLES APPLICABLE TO REGULATING CAMPUS HATE SPEECH

Professor Lawrence sets up a "straw civil libertarian" who purportedly would afford absolute protection to all racist speech—or at least "all racist speech that stops short of physical violence." In fact, as evidenced by American Civil Liberties Union (ACLU) policies, traditional civil libertarians do not take such an extreme position. Indeed, there is much overlap between Professor Lawrence's position and that of traditional civil libertarians. We all agree that some racist speech should be protected, and that some should not, although we draw the line between protected and unprotected racist speech at somewhat different points along the constitutional continuum.

At the end of the spectrum where speech is constitutionally protected, [some critics] agree with courts and traditional civil libertarians that the First Amendment should protect racist speech in a Skokie-type context.[2] The essentials of a Skokie-type setting are that the offensive speech occurs in a public place and the event is announced in advance. Hence, the offensive speech can be either avoided or countered by opposing speech. Traditional civil libertarians recognize that this speech causes psychic pain. We nonetheless agree with the judicial rulings in Skokie that this pain is a necessary price for a system of free expression, which ultimately redounds to the benefit of racial and other minorities.

At the other end of the spectrum, where expression may be prohibited, traditional civil libertarians agree with Professor Lawrence that the First Amendment should not necessarily protect targeted individual harassment just because it happens to use the vehicle speech. The ACLU maintains this non-absolutist position, for example, with regard to sexually harassing speech on campus or in the workplace. . . . These ACLU policies recognize that conduct that infringes on the right to equal educational (or employment) opportunities, regardless of gender (or other invidious classifications) should not be condoned simply because it includes expressive elements.

To be sure, there is no clear boundary between speech that "demonstrably hinders" a learning (or working) experience and speech that "creates an unpleasant learning" (or working) environment. Accordingly, even civil libertarians who agree that this is the appropriate line to draw between unprotected and protected speech in the harassment contest still would be expected to disagree about whether particular speech fell on one side of this boundary or the other.

Specifically in the context of racist speech, the ACLU has recognized that otherwise punishable conduct should not be shielded simply because it relies in part on words. Some examples were provided by former ACLU President Norman Dorsen:

> During the Skokie episode, the ACLU refused to defend a Nazi who was prosecuted for offering a cash bounty for killing a Jew. The reward linked the speech to action in an impermissible way. Nor would we defend a Nazi (or anyone else) whose speech interfered with a Jewish religious service, or who said, "There's a Jew; let's get him."[3]

The foregoing ACLU positions are informed by established principles that govern the predictability of speech. Under these principles, speech may be regulated if it is an essential element of violent or unlawful conduct,[4] if it is likely to cause an immediate injury by its very utterance,[5] and if it is addressed to a "captive audience" unable to avoid assaultive messages. It should be stressed that each of these criteria is ambiguous and difficult to apply in particular situations. Accordingly, the ACLU would insist that these exceptions to free speech be strictly construed and would probably find them to be satisfied only in rare factual circumstances. Nevertheless,

ACLU policies expressly recognize that if speech fits within these narrow parameters, then it could be regulable. . . .

The captive audience concept in particular is an elusive and challenging one to apply. Noting that we are "often 'captives' outside the sanctuary of the home and subject to objectionable speech," the Court has ruled that, in public places, we bear the burden of averting our attention from expression we find offensive.[6] Otherwise, the Court explained, a majority [could] silence dissidents simply as a matter of personal predilections."[7] The Court has been less reluctant to apply the captive audience concept to private homes. However, the Court has held that even in the home, free speech values may outweigh privacy concerns, requiring individuals to receive certain unwanted communications.

The Court's application of the captive audience doctrine illustrates the general notion that an important factor in determining the protection granted to speech is the place where it occurs. At one extreme, certain public places—such as public parks—have been deemed "public forums," where freedom of expression should be especially protected. At the other extreme, some private domains—such as residential buildings—have been deemed places where freedom of expression should be subject to restriction in order to guard the occupants' privacy and tranquility. In between these two poles, certain public areas might be held not to be public forums because the people who occupy them might be viewed as "captive."

The Supreme Court has declared that within the academic environment freedom of expression should receive heightened protection, and that "a university campus possesses many of the characteristics of a traditional public forum."[8] These conditions would suggest that hate speech should receive special protection within the university community. Conversely, Professor Mari Matsuda argues that equality guarantees and other principles that might weigh in favor of prohibiting racist speech also are particularly important in the academic context.[9]

The appropriate analysis is more complex than either set of generalizations assumes. In weighing the constitutional concerns of free speech, equality, and privacy that hate speech regulations implicate, decisionmakers must take into account the particular context within the university in which the speech occurs. For example, the Court's generalizations about the heightened protection due free speech in the academic world certainly are applicable to some campus areas, such as parks, malls, or other traditional gathering places. The generalizations, however, may not be applicable to other areas, such as students' dormitory rooms. These rooms constitute the students' homes. Accordingly, under established free speech tenets, students should have the right to avoid being exposed to others' expression by seeking a refuge in their rooms.

Some areas on campus present difficult problems concerning the appropriate level of speech protection because they share characteristics of both private homes and public forums. For example, one could argue that hallways, common rooms, and other common areas in dormitory buildings constitute extensions of the individual students' rooms. On the other hand, one could argue that these common areas constitute traditional gathering places and should be regarded as public forums, open to expressive activities at least by all dormitory residents if not by the broader community. Such an argument would derive general support from the Supreme Court decisions that uphold the free speech rights of demonstrators in residential neighborhoods on the theory that an individual resident's right of stopping "the flow of information into [his or her] household" does not allow him to impede the flow of this same information to his neighbors.[10] The Supreme Court, however, recently declined to resolve the specific issue of whether university dormitories constitute public forums for free speech purposes.[11]

Even in the areas of the university reserved for academic activities, such as classrooms, the calculus to determine the level of speech protection is complex. On the one hand, the classroom is the quintessential "marketplace of ideas,"[12] which should be open to the vigorous and robust exchange of even insulting or offensive words, on the theory that such an exchange ultimately will benefit not only the academic community, but also the larger community, in its pursuit of knowledge and understanding.

On the other hand, some minority students contend that in the long run, the academic dialogue might be stultified rather than stimulated by the inclusion of racist speech. They maintain that such speech not only interferes with equal educational opportunities, but also deters the exercise of other freedoms, including those secured by the First Amendment. Professor Lawrence argues that, as a consequence of hate speech, minority students are deprived of the opportunity to participate in the academic interchange, and that the exchange is impoverished by their exclusion. It must be emphasized, though, that expression subject to regulation on this rationale would have to be narrowly defined in order to protect the flow of ideas that is vital to the academic community. Thus, much expression would remain unregulated—expression which could be sufficiently upsetting to interfere with students' educational opportunities.

Another factor that might weigh in favor of imposing some regulations on speech in class is that students arguably constitute a captive audience. The characterization is especially apt when the course is required and class attendance is mandatory. Likewise, the case for regulation becomes more compelling the more power the racist speaker wields over the audience. For example, the law should afford students special protection from racist insults directed at them by their professors.

Even if various areas of a university are not classified as public forums, and even if occupants of such areas are designated captive audiences, any speech relations in these areas still would be invalid if they discriminated on the basis of a speaker's viewpoint. Viewpoint-based discrimination constitutes the most egregious form of censorship and almost always violates the First Amendment. Accordingly, viewpoint discrimination is proscribed even in regulations that govern non-public forum property and regulations that protect captive audiences.

Many proposed or adopted campus hate speech regulations constitute unconstitutional discrimination against particular views, either as they are written or as they are applied. Professor Lawrence, for example, endorsed a variation on the Stanford regulations that expressly would have excluded speech directed at "dominant majority groups."

As the foregoing discussion illustrates, the question whether any particular racist speech should be subject to regulation is a fact-specific inquiry. We cannot define particular words as inherently off limits, but rather we must examine every word in the overall context in which it is uttered.

PARTICULAR SPEECH-LIMITING DOCTRINES POTENTIALLY APPLICABLE TO CAMPUS HATE SPEECH

In addition to the foregoing general principles, . . . proponents of campus hate speech regulation invoke three specific doctrines in an attempt to justify such rules: the fighting words doctrine; the tort of intentional infliction of emotional distress; and the tort of group defamation. The Supreme Court has recognized that each of these doctrines may well be inconsistent with free speech principles. Therefore, these doctrines may not support any campus hate speech restrictions whatsoever. In any event, they at most would support only restrictions that are both narrowly drawn and narrowly applied.

Fighting Words   The fighting words doctrine is the principal model for the Stanford University code, which Professor Lawrence supports. However, this doctrine provides a constitutionally shaky foundation for several reasons: it has been substantially limited in scope and may no longer be good law; even if the Supreme Court narrowed its version of the doctrine, such an application would threaten free speech principles; and, as actually implemented, the fighting words doctrine suppresses protectible speech and entails the inherent danger of discriminatory application to speech by members of minority groups and dissidents.

Although the Court originally defined constitutionally regulable fighting words in fairly broad terms in *Chaplinsky v. New Hampshire*,[13] subsequent decisions have narrowed the definition to such a point that the doctrine probably would not apply to the campus racist speech that Professor Lawrence and others seek to regulate. As originally formulated in *Chaplinsky*, the fighting words doctrine excluded from First Amendment protection "insulting or 'fighting' words, those which by their very utterance inflict injury or tend to incite an immediate breach of the peace."[14]

In accordance with its narrow construction of constitutionally permissible prohibitions upon "fighting words," the Court has overturned every single fighting words conviction that it has reviewed since *Chaplinsky*. Accordingly, Supreme Court Justices and constitutional scholars persuasively maintain that *Chaplinsky's* fighting words doctrine is no longer good law.

More importantly, constitutional scholars have argued that this doctrine should no longer be good law, for reasons that are particularly weighty in the context of racial slurs. First, the asserted governmental interest in preventing a breach of the peace is not logically furthered by this doctrine:

> [I]t is fallacious to believe that personally abusive epithets, even if addressed face-to-face to the object of the speaker's criticism, are likely to arouse the ordinary law abiding person beyond mere anger to uncontrollable reflexive violence. . . .[15]

Second, just as the alleged peace-preserving purpose does not rationally justify the fighting words doctrine in general, that rationale also fails to justify the fighting words doctrine when applied to racial slurs in particular. Rather, the serious evil of racial slurs consists of the ugliness of the ideas they express and the psychic injury they cause to their addressees. Therefore, the fighting words doctrine does not address and will not prevent the injuries caused by campus racist speech.

Third, this doctrine "makes a man a criminal simply because his neighbors have no self-control and cannot refrain from violence."[16] In other contexts, the Court appropriately has refused to allow the addresses of speech to exercise such a "heckler's veto."[17]

The fighting words doctrine is constitutionally flawed for the additional reasons that it suppresses much protectible speech and that the protectible speech of minority group members is particularly vulnerable. Professor Gard concluded, based on a comprehensive survey of relevant court decisions, that, in the lower courts, the fighting words doctrine "is almost uniformly invoked in a selective and discriminatory manner by law enforcement officials to punish trivial violations of a constitutionally impermissible interest in preventing criticism of official conduct."[18] Even more disturbing is that the reported cases indicate that blacks are often prosecuted and convicted for the use of fighting words. . . . Thus, the record of the actual implementation of the fighting words doctrine demonstrates that—as in the case with all speech restrictions—it endangers principles of equality as well as free speech.

Intentional Infliction of Emotional Distress   A committee report submitted to the President of the University of Texas recommends the common law tort of intentional infliction of emotional distress as a basis for regulating campus hate speech.[19] This doctrinal approach has a logical appeal because it focuses on the type of harm potentially caused by racist speech that universities are most concerned with alleviating—namely, emotional or psychological harm that interferes with studies. In contrast, the harm at which the fighting words doctrine aims—potential violence by the addressee against the speaker—is of less concern to most universities.

Traditional civil libertarians caution that the intentional infliction of emotional distress theory should almost never apply to verbal harassment. A major problem with this approach is that

> the innate vagueness of the interest in preventing emotional injury to listeners suggests that any attempt at judicial enforcement will inevitably result in the imposition of judges' subjective linguistic preferences on society, discrimination against ethnic and racial minorities, and ultimately the misuse of the rationale to justify the censorship of the ideological content of the speaker's message.[20]

Again, as was true for the fighting words doctrine, there is a particular danger that this speech restrictive doctrine will also be enforced to the detriment of the very minority groups whom it is designed to protect. . . .

Group Defamation   The group defamation concept has been thoroughly discredited.

First, group defamation regulations are unconstitutional in terms of both Supreme Court doctrine and free speech principles. To be sure, the Supreme Court's only decision that expressly reviewed the issue, *Beauharnais v. Illinois*,[21] upheld a group libel statute against a First Amendment challenge. However, that 5-4 decision was issued almost forty years ago, at a relatively early point in the Court's developing free speech jurisprudence. *Beauharnais* is widely assumed no longer to be good law in light of the Court's subsequent speech-protective decisions on related issues, notably its holdings that strictly limit individual defamation actions so as not to chill free speech.

Statements that defame groups convey opinions or ideas on matters of public concern, and therefore should be protected even if those statements also injure reputations or feelings. The Supreme Court recently reaffirmed this principle in the context of an individual defamation action, in *Milkovich v. Lorain Journal Co.*[22]

In addition to flouting constitutional doctrine and free speech principles, rules sanctioning group defamation are ineffective in curbing the specific class of hate speech that Professor Lawrence advocates restraining. Even Justice Frankfurter's opinion for the narrow *Beauharnais* majority repeatedly expressed doubt about the wisdom or efficacy of group libel laws. Justice Frankfurter stressed that the Court upheld the Illinois law in question only because of judicial deference to the state legislature's judgment about the law's effectiveness.

The concept of defamation encompasses only false statements of fact that are made without a good faith belief in their truth. Therefore, any disparaging or insulting statement would be immune from this doctrine, unless it were factual in nature, demonstrably false in content, and made in bad faith. Members of minority groups that are disparaged by an allegedly libelous statement would hardly have their reputations or psyches enhanced by process in which the maker of the statement sought to prove his good faith belief in its truth, and they were required to demonstrate the absence thereof.

One additional problem with group defamation statutes as a model for rules sanctioning campus hate speech should be noted. As with the other speech-restrictive doctrines asserted to justify such rules, group defamation laws introduce the risk that rules will be enforced at the expense of the very minority groups sought to be protected. The Illinois statute upheld in *Beauharnais* is illustrative. According to a leading article on group libel laws, during the 1940s, the Illinois statute was "a weapon for harassment of the Jehovah's Witnesses," who were then "a minority . . . very much more in need of protection than most."[23]

EVEN A NARROW REGULATION COULD HAVE A NEGATIVE SYMBOLIC IMPACT ON CONSTITUTIONAL VALUES

Taking into account the constraints imposed by free speech principles upon doctrines potentially applicable to the regulations of campus hate speech, it might be possible—although difficult—to frame a rule that is sufficiently narrow to withstand a facial First Amendment challenge.

Even assuming that a regulation could be crafted with sufficient precision to survive a facial constitutional challenge, several further problems would remain, which should give any university pause in evaluating whether to adopt such a rule. First, because of the discretion entailed in enforcing any such rule, there is an inevitable danger of arbitrary or discriminatory enforcement. Therefore, the rule's implementation would have to be monitored to ensure that it did not exceed the bounds of the regulations' terms or threaten content—and viewpoint—neutrality principles.

Second, there is an inescapable risk that any hate speech regulation, no matter how narrowly drawn, will chill speech beyond its literal scope. Members of the university community may well err on the side of caution to avoid being charged with a violation.

A third problem inherent in any campus hate speech policy is that such rules constitute a precedent that can be used to restrict other types of speech. As the Supreme Court has recognized, the long-range precedential impact of any challenged governmental action should be a factor in evaluation of its lawfulness.

Further, in light of constitutional restraints, any campus hate speech policy inevitably would apply to only a tiny fraction of all racist expression, and accordingly it would have only a symbolic impact. Therefore, in deciding whether to adopt such a rule, universities must ask whether that symbolic impact is, on balance, positive or negative in terms of constitutional values. On the other hand, some advocates of hate speech regulations maintain that the regulations might play a valuable symbolic role in reaffirming our societal commitment to racial equality (although this is debatable). On the other hand, we must beware of even a symbolic or perceived diminution of our impartial commitment to free speech. Even a limitation that has a direct impact upon only a discrete category of speech may have a much more pervasive indirect impact—by undermining the First Amendment's moral legitimacy.

Recently, the Supreme Court ringingly affirmed the core principle that a neutral commitment to free speech should trump competing symbolic concerns. In *United States v. Eichman*, which invalidated the Flag Protection Act of 1989, the Court declared:

> Government may create national symbols, promote them and encourage their respectful treatment. But the Flag Protection Act goes well beyond this by criminally proscribing expressive conduct because of its likely communicative impact.

We are aware that desecration of the flag is deeply offensive to many. But the same might be said, for example, of virulent ethnic and religious epithets, vulgar repudiations of the draft, and scurrilous caricatures. "If there is a bedrock principle underlying the First Amendment, it is that the Government may not prohibit the expression of an idea simply because society finds the idea itself offensive or disagreeable." Punishing desecration of the flag dilutes the very freedom that makes this emblem so revered, and worth revering.[24]

PROHIBITING RACIST SPEECH WOULD NOT EFFECTIVELY COUNTER, AND COULD EVEN AGGRAVATE, THE UNDERLYING PROBLEM OF RACISM [25]

CIVIL LIBERTARIANS SHOULD CONTINUE TO MAKE COMBATTING RACISM A PRIORITY

I do not think it is worth spending a great deal of time debating the fine points of specific rules or their particular applications to achieve what necessarily will be only marginal differences in the amount of racist insults that can be sanctioned. The larger problems of racist attitudes and conduct—of which all these words are symptoms—would remain. Those who share the dual goals of promoting racial equality and protecting free speech must concentrate on countering racial discrimination, rather than on defining the particular narrow subset of racist slurs that constitutionally might be regulable.

Although ACLU cases involving the Ku Klux Klan and other racist speakers often generate a disproportionate amount of publicity, they constitute only a tiny fraction of the ACLU's caseload. In the recent past, the ACLU has handled about six cases a year advocating the free speech rights of white supremacists, out of a total of more than six thousand cases annually, and these white supremacist cases rarely consume significant resources. Moreover, the resources the ACLU does expend to protect hatemongers' First Amendment rights are well-invested. They ultimately preserve not only civil liberties, but also our democratic system, for the benefit of all.[26]

PUNISHING RACIST HATE SPEECH WOULD NOT EFFECTIVELY COUNTER RACISM

This Article has emphasized the principled reasons, arising from First Amendment theory, for concluding that racist speech should receive the same protection as other offensive speech. This conclusion also is supported by pragmatic or strategic considerations concerning the efficacious pursuit of equality goals. Not only would rules censoring racist speech fail to reduce racial bias, but they might even undermine that goal.

First, there is no persuasive psychological evidence that punishment for name-calling changes deeply held attitudes. To the contrary, psychological studies show that censored speech becomes more appealing and persuasive to many listeners merely by virtue of the censorship.[27]

Nor is there any empirical evidence, from the countries that do outlaw racist speech, that censorship is an effective means to counter racism. For example, Great Britain began to prohibit racist defamation in 1965. A quarter century later, this law has had no discernible adverse impact on the National Front and other neo-Nazi groups active in Britain. As discussed above, it is impossible to draw narrow regulations that precisely specify the particular words and contexts that should lead to sanctions. Fact-bound determinations are required. For this reason, authorities have great discretion in determining precisely which speakers and which words to punish. Consequently, even vicious racist epithets have gone unpunished under the British law. Moreover, even if actual or threatened enforcement of law has deterred some overt racist insults, that enforcement has had no effect on more subtle, but nevertheless clear, signals of racism. Some observers believe that racism is even more pervasive in Britain than in the United States.[28]

BANNING RACIST SPEECH COULD AGGRAVATE RACISM

For several reasons banning the symptom of racist speech may compound the underlying problem of racism. Professor Lawrence sets up a false dichotomy when he urges us to balance equality goals against free speech goals. Just as he observes that free speech concerns should be weighed on the pro-regulation, as well as the anti-regulation, side of the balance, he should recognize that equality concerns weigh on the anti-regulation, as well as the pro-regulation, side.

The first reason that laws censoring racist speech may undermine the goal of combating racism flows from the discretion such laws inevitably vest in prosecutors, judges and the other individuals who implement them. One ironic, even tragic, result of this discretion is that members of minority groups themselves—the very people whom the law is intended to protect—are likely targets of punishment. For example, among the first individuals prosecuted under the British Race Relations Act of 1965 were black power leaders. Their overtly racist messages undoubtedly expressed legitimate anger at real discrimination, yet the statute drew no such fine lines, nor could any similar statute possibly do so. Rather than curbing speech offensive to minorities, the British law instead has been regularly used to curb the speech of blacks, trade unionists, and anti-nuclear activities. In perhaps the ultimate irony, this statute, which was intended to restrain the neo-Nazi National Front, instead has barred expression by the Anti-Nazi League.

The general lesson that rules banning hate speech will be used to punish minority group members has proven true in the specific context of campus hate speech regulations. In 1974, in a move aimed at the National Front, the British National Union of Students (NUS) adopted a resolution that representatives of "openly racist and fascist organizations" were to be prevented from speaking on college campuses "by whatever means necessary (including disruption of the meeting)."[29] A substantial motivation for the rule had been to stem an increase in campus anti-Semitism. Ironically, however, following the United Nations' cue, some British students deemed Zionism a form of racism beyond the bounds of permitted discussion. Accordingly, in 1975, British students invoked the NUS resolution to disrupt speeches by Israelis and Zionists, including the Israeli ambassador to England. The intended target of the NUS resolution, the National Front, applauded this result. However, the NUS itself became disenchanted by this and other unintended consequences of its resolution and repealed it in 1977.

The British experience under its campus anti-hate speech rule parallels the experience in the United States under the one such rule that has led to a judicial decision. During the approximately one year that the University of Michigan rule was in effect, there were more than twenty cases of whites charging blacks with racist speech. More importantly, the only two instances in which the rule was invoked to sanction racist speech (as opposed to sexist and other forms of hate speech) involved the punishment of speech by or on behalf of black students. Additionally, the only student who was subjected to a full-fledged disciplinary hearing under the Michigan rule was a black student accused of homophobic and sexist expression. In seeking clemency from the sanctions imposed following this hearing, the student asserted he had been singled out because of his race and his political views. Others who were punished for hate speech under the Michigan rule included several Jewish students accused of making an anti-black comment. Likewise, the student who recently brought a lawsuit challenging the University of Connecticut's hate speech policy, under which she had been penalized for an allegedly homophobic remark, was Asian-American. She claimed that, among the other students who had engaged in similar expression, she had been singled out for punishment because of her ethnic background.

A second reason why censorship of racist speech actually may subvert, rather than promote, the goal of eradicating racism is that such censorship measures often have the effect of glorifying racist speakers. Efforts at suppression result in racist speakers receiving attention and publicity which they otherwise would not have garnered. As previously noted, psychological studies reveal that whenever the government attempts to censor speech, the censored speech—for that very reason—becomes more appealing to many people. Still worse, when pitted against the government, racist speakers may appear as martyrs or even heroes.

Advocates of hate speech regulations do not seem to realize that their own attempts to suppress speech increase public interest in the ideas they are trying to stamp out. Thus, Professor Lawrence wrongly suggests that the ACLU's defense of hatemongers' free speech rights "makes heroes out of bigots"; in actuality, experience demonstrates that it is the attempt to suppress racist speech that has this effect, not the attempt to protect such speech.[30]

There is a third reason why laws that proscribe racist speech could well undermine goals of reducing bigotry. As Professor Lawrence recognizes, given the overriding importance of free speech in our society, any speech regulation must be narrowly drafted. Therefore, it can affect only the most blatant, crudest forms of racism. The more subtle, and hence potentially more invidious, racist expressions will survive. Virtually all would agree that no law could possibly eliminate all racist speech, let alone racism itself. If the marketplace of ideas cannot be trusted to winnow out the hateful, then there is no reason to believe that censorship will do so. The most it could possibly achieve would be to drive some racist thought and expression underground, where it would be more difficult to respond to such speech and the underlying attitudes it expresses. The British experience confirms this prediction.

The positive effect of racist speech—in terms of making society aware of and mobilizing its opposition to the evils of racism—is illustrated by the wave of campus racist incidents now under discussion. Ugly and abominable as these expressions are, they undoubtedly have had the beneficial result of raising public consciousness about the underlying societal problem of racism. If these expressions had been chilled by virtue of university sanctions, then it is doubtful that there would be such widespread discussion on campuses, let alone more generally, about the real problem of racism. Consequently, society would be less mobilized to attack this problem. Past experience confirms that the public airing of racist and other forms of hate speech catalyzes communal efforts to redress the bigotry that underlies such expression and to stave off any discriminatory conduct that might follow from it.

Banning racist speech could undermine the goals of combating racism for additional reasons. Some black scholars and activists maintain that an anti-racist speech policy may perpetuate a paternalistic view of minority groups, suggesting that they are incapable of defending themselves against biased expressions. Additionally, an anti-hate speech policy stultifies the candid intergroup dialogue concerning racism and other forms of bias that constitutes an essential precondition for reducing discrimination. In a related vein, education, free discussion, and the airing of misunderstandings and failures of sensitivity are more likely to promote positive intergroup relations than are legal battles. The rules barring hate speech will continue to generate litigation and other forms of controversy that will exacerbate intergroup tensions. Finally, the censorship approach is diversionary. It makes it easier for communities to avoid coming to grips with less convenient and more expensive, but ultimately more meaningful, approaches for combating racial discrimination.

MEANS CONSISTENT WITH THE FIRST AMENDMENT CAN PROMOTE RACIAL EQUALITY MORE EFFECTIVELY THAN CAN CENSORSHIP

The Supreme Court recently reaffirmed the time-honored principle that the appropriate response to speech conveying ideas that we reject or find offensive is not to censor such speech, but rather to exercise our own speech rights. In *Texas v. Johnson*, the Court urged this counter-speech strategy upon the many Americans who are deeply offended by the burning of their country's flag: "The way to preserve the flag's special role is not to punish those who feel differently about these matters. It is to persuade them that they are wrong."[31] In addition to persuasion, the types of private expressive conduct that could be invoked in response to racist speech include censure and boycotts.

In the context of countering racism on campus, the strategy of increasing speech, rather than decreasing it, not only would be consistent with First Amendment principles, but also would be more effective in advancing equality goals. All government agencies and officers, including state university officials, should condemn slavery, *de jure* segregation, and other racist institutions that the government formerly supported. State university and other government officials also should affirmatively endorse equality principles. Furthermore, these government representatives should condemn racist ideas expressed by private speakers. In the same vein, private individuals and groups should exercise their First Amendment rights by speaking out against racism. Traditional civil libertarians have exercised their own free speech in this fashion and also have defended the First Amendment freedoms of others who have done so.

In addition to the preceding measures, which could be implemented on a society-wide basis, other measures would be especially suited to the academic setting. First, regardless of the legal limitations on rules barring hate speech, universities should encourage members of their communities voluntarily to restrain the form of their expression in light of the feelings and concerns of various minority groups. Universities could facilitate voluntary self-restraint by providing training in communication, information about diverse cultural perspectives, and other education designed to promote intergroup understanding. Members of both minority and majority groups should be encouraged to be mutually respectful. Individuals who violate these norms of civility should not be subject to any disciplinary action, but instead should be counselled. These educational efforts should be extended to members of the faculty and administration, as well as students. Of course, universities must vigilantly ensure that even voluntary limits on the manner of academic discourse do not chill its content.

In addition to the foregoing measures, universities also should create forums in which controversial race-related issues and ideas could be discussed in a candid but constructive way. Another possibility would be for universities to encourage students to receive education in the history of racism and the civil rights movement in the United States and an exposure to the culture and traditions of racial and ethnic groups other than their own. Consistent with free speech tenets, these courses must allow all faculty and students to express their own views and must not degenerate into "reeducation camps."

The proposed measures for eliminating racism on campus are consistent not only with American constitutional norms of free speech and equality, but also with internationally recognized human rights. For example, article 26(2) of the Universal Declaration of Human Rights provides that individuals have a right to receive, and states have an obligation to provide, education which "promote[s] understanding, tolerance and friendship among all nations, racial or religious groups."

If universities adopt narrowly framed rules that regulate racist expression, then these rules should constitute one element of a broader program that includes the more positive, direct strategies outlined above. Many universities appear to be responding constructively to the recent upsurge in campus hate speech incidents by adopting some of the measures suggested here. This development demonstrates the positive impact of racist speech, in terms of galvanizing community efforts to counter the underlying attitudes it expresses.

It is particularly important to devise anti-racism strategies consistent with the First Amendment because racial and other minority groups ultimately have far more to lose than to gain through the weakened free speech guarantee. History has demonstrated that minorities have been among the chief beneficiaries of a vigorous free speech safeguard.

Professor Lawrence offers two rebuttals to the proposition that blacks are (on balance) benefitted rather than hurt by a strong free speech guarantee. First, he notes that "[t]he First Amendment coexisted with slavery." It is undeniable that, until the Union won the Civil War, not only the First Amendment, but also all of the Constitution's provisions guaranteeing liberty, coexisted with the total negation of liberty through the institution of slavery. It also is true, however, that the free speech guarantees of the federal Constitution and some state constitutions allowed abolitionists to advocate the end of slavery. Further, although the First Amendment from its adoption provided theoretical protection against actions by the national government, it did not provide any protection whatsoever against speech restrictions enacted by state and local governments until the 1930s, and in practice it was not enforced judicially until the latter half of the 20th century. Not until 1965 did the Supreme Court initially exercise its power to invalidate unconstitutional congressional statutes in the First Amendment context.

In short, although slavery coexisted with the theoretical guarantees enunciated in the First Amendment, slavery did not coexist with the judicially enforceable version of those guarantees that emerged fully only in the mid-1960s. We never can know how much more quickly and peacefully the anti-slavery forces might have prevailed if free speech and press, as well as other rights, had been judicially protected against violations by all level of government earlier in our history. That robust freedoms of speech and press ultimately might have threatened slavery is suggested by southern states' passage of laws limiting these freedoms, in an effort to undermine the abolitionist cause.

The second basis for Professor Lawrence's lack of "faith in free speech as the most important vehicle for liberation" is the notion that "equality [is] a precondition to free speech." Professor Lawrence maintains that racism devalues the ideas of non-whites and of anti-racism in the marketplace of ideas. Like the economic market, the ideological market sometimes works to improve society, but not always. Odious ideas, such as the idea of black inferiority, will not necessarily be driven from the marketplace. Therefore, the marketplace rationale alone might not justify free speech for racist thoughts. But that rationale does not stand alone.

The civil libertarian and judicial defense of racist speech also is based on the knowledge that censors have stifled the voices of oppressed persons and groups far more often than those of their oppressors. Censorship traditionally has been the tool of people who seek to subordinate minorities, not those who seek to liberate them. [T]he civil rights movement of the 1960s depended upon free speech principles. These principles allowed protestors to carry their messages to audiences who found such messages highly offensive and threatening to their most deeply cherished views of themselves and their way of life. Equating civil rights activists with Communists, subversives, and criminals, government officials mounted inquisitions against the NAACP, seeking compulsory disclosure of its membership lists and endangering the members' jobs and lives. Only strong principles of free speech and association could—and did—protect the drive for desegregation. Martin Luther King, Jr. wrote his historic letter from a Birmingham jail but the Birmingham parade ordinance that King and other demonstrators had violated eventually was declared an unconstitutional invasion of their free speech rights. Moreover, the Civil Rights Act of 1964, which these demonstrators championed, did become law.

The more disruptive forms of protest, which Professor Lawrence credits with having been more effective—such as marches, sit-ins, and kneel-ins—were especially dependent on generous judicial constructions of the free speech guarantee.

Notably, many of these protective interpretations initially had been formulated in cases brought on behalf of anti-civil rights demonstrators. Similarly, the insulting and often racist language that more militant black activists hurled at police officers and other government officials also was protected under the same principles and precedents.[32]

The foregoing history does not prove conclusively that free speech is an essential precondition for equality, as some respected political philosophers have argued. But it does belie Professor Lawrence's theory that equality is an essential precondition for free speech. Moreover, this history demonstrates the symbiotic interrelationship between free speech and equality, which parallels the relationship between civil liberties and civil rights more generally. Both sets of aims must be pursued simultaneously because the pursuit of each aids the realization of the other.

CONCLUSION

Some traditional civil libertarians may agree with Professor Lawrence that a university rule banning a narrowly defined class of assaultive, harassing racist expression might comport with First Amendment principles and make a symbolic contribution to the racial equality mandated by the Fourteenth Amendment. However, Professor Lawrence and other members of the academic community who advocate such steps must recognize that educators have a special responsibility to avoid the danger posed by focusing on symbols that obscure the real underlying issues. The recent exploitation of the American flag as a symbol of patriotism, to distort the true nature of that concept, serves as a sobering reminder of this risk.

An exaggerated concern with racist speech creates a risk of elevating symbols over substance in two problematic respects. First, it may divert our attention from the causes of racism to its symptoms. Second, a focus on the hateful message conveyed by particular speech may distort our view of fundamental neutral principles applicable to our system of free expression generally. We should not let the racist veneer in which expression is cloaked obscure our recognition of how important free expression is and of how effectively it has advanced racial equality.

NOTES

1. Ed. note: This is an abridged version of the article, "Balancing the Rights to Freedom of Expression and Equality: A Civil Liberties Approach to Speech on Campus," in *Striking a Balance: Hate Speech, Freedom of Expression, and Non-Discrimination,"* ed. Sandra Godiver (International Center Against Censorship). Both are versions of a longer article, "Regulating Racist Speech on Campus: A Modest Proposal," *Duke Law Journal* 1990: 484–568. Printed by permission of author. The essay addresses the various issues raised by hate speech in general, and responds to specific points made by Charles Lawrence, professor of law at Stanford University in "If He Hollers Let Him Go: Regulating Racist Speech on Campus," 1990 *Duke Law Journal* 431.

2. The reference is to an American neo-Nazi group's efforts, in 1977–78, to gain permission to demonstrate in Skokie, Illinois, a community with a large Jewish population, including many Holocaust survivors. . . .

3. N. Dorsen, "Is There a Right to Stop Offensive Speech? The Case of Nazis in Skokie," in L. Gostin, ed., *Civil Liberties In Conflict* (London and New York: Routledge, 1988), 133–34.

4. Crimes and torts that may consist primarily of words include bribery, fraud and libel. Sex-designated advertisements for jobs or housing are also unprotected, as integral elements of proscribed discriminatory conduct.

5. This category is illustrated by Oliver Wendell Holmes' proverbial example of "falsely shouting fire in a theater and causing a panic." *Schenck v. United States,* 249 U.S. 47, 52 (1919). This theory also is invoked to justify regulating "fighting words" and group defamation. Although the ACLU has no policy expressly addressing the fighting words doctrine, it explicitly rejects group defamation laws as inconsistent with the First Amendment. See ACLU Policy Guide, at Policy No. 6(c).

6. *Rowan v. United States Post Office Dep't,* 397 U.S. 728, 738 (1970).

7. *Cohen v. California,* 402 U.S. 15, 21 (1971).

8. *Cornelius v. NAACP Legal Defense and Educ. Fund,* 473 U.S. 788, 803 (1985); see also *Sweeney v. New Hampshire,* 354 U.S. 234, 250 (1957).

9. Matsuda, "Public Response to Racist Speech; Considering the Victim's Story," 87 *Michigan Law Review* 2320, 2370 (1989).

10. *Organization for a Better Austin v. Keefe,* 402 U.S. 415, 420 (1971).

11. See *Board of Trustees v. Fox,* 492 U.S. 469, 473 n.2 (1989).

12. *Keyishian v. Board of Regents,* 385 U.S. 589, 603 (1967).

13. 315 U.S. 568 (1942).

14. Id. at 572.

15. Gard, "Fighting Words as Free Speech," 58 *Washington U. Law Quarterly* 531, 580 (1980).

16. Z. Chafee, *Free Speech in the United States* (1941), 151.

17. See, e.g., *Gregory v. City of Chicago,* 394 U.S. 111 (1969).

18. Gard, supra note 19, at 580.

19. See Report of President's Ad Hoc Committee on Racial Harassment, University of Texas (Nov. 27, 1989) (defining prohibited "racial harassment" as "extreme or outrageous acts or communications that are intended to harass, intimidate, or humiliate a student or students on account of race, color, or national origin and that reasonably cause them to suffer severe emotional distress").

21. 343 U.S. 250 (1952).

22. 497 U.S., 110 S. Ct. 2695 (1990).

23. J. Tannenhaus, "Group Libel," 35 *Cornell Law Quarterly* 261, 279–80 (1950).

24. *United Sates v. Eichman,* 496 U.S. 310, 110 S. Ct. 2404, 2409-10 (1990).

25. Some specific points made in this section and the following one were previously included in Gale and Strossen, "The Real ACLU," 2 *Yale J.L. and Feminism* 161 (1990).

26. Aryeh Neier persuasively drew this conclusion with respect to the ACLU's defense of the American Nazi Party's right to demonstrate in Skokie:

> [W]hen it was all over no one had been persuaded to join [the Nazis]. They had disseminated their message and it had been rejected. Why did the Nazi message fall on such deaf ears? Revolutionaries and advocates of destruction attract followers readily when the society they wish to overturn loses legitimacy. Understanding this process, revolutionaries try to provoke the government into using repressive measures. They rejoice, as the American Nazis did, when their rights are denied to them; they count on repression to win them sympathizers.

In confronting the Nazis, however, American democracy did not lose, but preserved its legitimacy. . . . The judges who devoted so much attention to the Nazis, the police departments that paid so much overtime, and the American Civil Liberties Union, which lost half a million dollars in membership income as a consequence of this defense, used their time and money well. They defeated the Nazis by preserving the legitimacy of American democracy. . . .

27. See Brock, "Erotic Materials: A Commodity Theory Analysis of Availability and Desirability," in *Technical Report of the U.S. Comm'n on Obscenity and Pornography* 131, 132 (1971); Worchel & Arnold, "The Effects of Censorship and Attractiveness of the Censor on Attitudinal Change," 9 *Journal of Experimental Social Psychology* 365 (1973).

28. For example, speaking in 1988 about incidents of violence against blacks and Asians in London, Paul Boateng, one of the four minority members then in the 650-member House of Commons, stated: "[This] violence is linked to the deeper patterns of prejudice in a society in which racist behavior is more socially acceptable than in the United States. . . . The basic difference between the United States and Britain is that no one in America questions the concept of the black American. In Britain, we still have not won the argument of whether it is possible to be black and British." Raines, "London Police Faulted as Racial Attacks Soar," *New York Times,* 24 March 1988, at A1, col. 1.

29. A. Neier, supra note 1, at 155–56.

30. For example, when the American Nazi Party finally was allowed to march in Illinois in 1978, following the government's and Anti-Defamation League's attempts to prevent this demonstration, 2000 onlookers watched the 20 Nazis demonstrate. Throughout the protracted litigation that the Nazis predictably won, the case received extensive media attention all over the country. The event probably would have received little if any attention had the Village of Skokie simply allowed the Nazis to demonstrate in the first place.

31. 491 U.S. 397 (1989), at 419.

32. See, e.g., *Brow v. Oklahoma,* 408 U.S. 914 (1972) (the Supreme court reversed the conviction of a Black Panther who had referred, during a political meeting, to specific policemen as "mother-fucking fascist pig cops").

■ ANDREW ALTMAN: LIBERALISM AND HATE SPEECH

Andrew Altman fashions an argument between those liberals who insist that hate speech codes necessarily violate the viewpoint neutrality requirement of the First Amendment and those liberals who claim regulation to be a justifiable means for combating discrimination and subordination (on liberalism generally, see Chapter 5). Altman admits that rules against hate speech are not viewpoint neutral, for they rest on the assumption that racism, sexism, and homophobia are morally wrong. Because liberals are open to a variety of possibly conflicting views about what people consider good or bad, viewpoint neutrality resists regulation of speech on the basis of value laden moral grounds. Altman admits that hate speech can cause serious psychological harm to members of target groups. He argues nevertheless that appeals to such harm cannot justify regulation, for they sweep too broadly against speech for a liberal to accept them as ground for regulation. However, some forms of hate speech commit a characteristic harm in virtue of the kind of speech acts that they are, namely, the wrong of treating someone as morally subordinate and their interests as intrinsically less important, their lives inherently less valuable, than those of the reference group. Altman concludes that only regulations narrowly targeted to restrict hate speech acts for this wrong, which they necessarily commit, will be justifiable. It follows that any speech act not targeting a specific person for subordination would escape regulation. So regulation is not being promoted on the viewpoint neutral basis of the ideas the speech is expressing. Altman suggests that the Stanford code represents quite well the sorts of preconditions that on his view will turn out to be justifiable for regulating campus hate speech.

Andrew Altman

LIBERALISM AND CAMPUS HATE SPEECH: A PHILOSOPHICAL EXAMINATION

INTRODUCTION

In recent years a vigorous public debate has developed over freedom of speech within the academic community. The immediate stimulus for the debate has been the enactment by a number of colleges and universities of rules against hate speech. While some have defended these rules as essential for protecting the equal dignity of all members of the academic community others have condemned them as intolerable efforts to impose ideological conformity on the academy.

From *Ethics* 103 (January 1993): 302–17. Reprinted by permission of author and University of Chicago Press.

Liberals can be found on both sides of this debate. Many see campus hate-speech regulation as a form of illegitimate control by the community over individual liberty of expression. They argue that hate-speech rules violate the important liberal principle that any regulation of speech be viewpoint-neutral. But other liberals see hate-speech regulation as a justifiable part of the effort to help rid society of discrimination and subordination based on such characteristics as race, religion, ethnicity, gender, and sexual preference.

In this article, I develop a liberal argument in favor of certain narrowly drawn rules prohibiting hate speech. The argument steers a middle course between those who reject all forms of campus hate-speech regulation and those who favor relatively sweeping forms of regulation. Like those who reject all regulation, I argue that rules against hate speech are not viewpoint-neutral. Like those who favor sweeping regulation I accept the claim that hate speech can cause serious psychological harm to those at whom it is directed. However, I do not believe that such harm can justify regulation, sweeping or otherwise. Instead, I argue that some forms of hate speech inflict on their victims a certain kind of wrong, and it is on the basis of this wrong that regulation can be justified. The kind of wrong in question is one that is inflicted in virtue of the performance of a certain kind of speech-act characteristic of some forms of hate speech, and I argue that rules targeting this speech-act wrong will be relatively narrow in scope.[1]

HATE SPEECH, HARASSMENT, AND NEUTRALITY

Hate-speech regulations typically provide for disciplinary action against students for making racist, sexist, or homophobic utterances or for engaging in behavior that expresses the same kinds of discriminatory attitudes. The stimulus for the regulations has been an apparent upsurge in racist, sexist, and homophobic incidents on college campuses over the past decade. The regulations that have actually been proposed or enacted vary widely in the scope of what they prohibit.

The rules at Stanford University are narrow in scope. They require that speech meet three conditions before it falls into the proscribed zone: the speaker must intend to insult or stigmatize another on the basis of certain characteristics such as race, gender, or sexual orientation; the speech must be addressed directly to those whom it is intended to stigmatize; and the speech must employ epithets or terms that similarly convey "visceral hate or contempt" for the people at whom it is directed.[2]

On the other hand, the rules of the University of Connecticut, in their original form, were relatively sweeping in scope. According to these rules, "Every member of the University is obligated to refrain from actions that intimidate, humiliate or demean persons or groups or that undermine their security or self-esteem." Explicitly mentioned as examples of proscribed speech were "making inconsiderate jokes . . . stereotyping the experiences, background, and skills of individuals, . . . imitating stereotypes in speech or mannerisms [and] attributing objections to any of the above actions to 'hypersensitivity' of the targeted individual or group."[3]

Even the narrower forms of hate-speech regulation, such as we find at Stanford, must be distinguished from a simple prohibition of verbal harassment. As commonly understood, harassment involves a pattern of conduct that is intended to annoy a person so much as to disrupt substantially her activities.[4] No one questions the authority of universities to enact regulations that prohibit such conduct, whether the conduct be verbal or not. There are three principal differences between hate-speech rules and rules against harassment. First, hate-speech rules do not require a pattern of conduct: a single incident is sufficient to incur liability. Second, hate-speech rules describe the offending conduct in ways that refer to the moral and political viewpoint it expresses. The conduct is not simply annoying or disturbing; it is racist, sexist, or homophobic.

The third difference is tied closely to the second and is the most important one: rules against hate speech are not viewpoint-neutral. Such rules rest on the view that racism, sexism, and homophobia are morally wrong. The liberal principle of viewpoint-neutrality holds that those in authority should not be permitted to limit speech on the ground that it expresses a viewpoint that is wrong, evil, or otherwise deficient. Yet, hate-speech rules rest on precisely such a basis. Rules against harassment, on the other hand, are not viewpoint-based. Anyone in our society could accept the prohibition of harassment because it would not violate their normative political or moral beliefs to do so.[5] The same cannot be said for hate-speech rules because they embody a view of race, gender, and homosexuality contrary to the normative viewpoints held by some people.[6]

If I am correct in claiming that hate-speech regulations are not viewpoint-neutral, this will raise a strong prima facie case against them from a liberal perspective. Contrary to my claim, however, Thomas Grey, author of Stanford's hate-speech policy, argues that his regulations are viewpoint-neutral. He claims that the policy "preserves practical neutrality—that is, it does not differentially deprive any significant element in American political life of its rhetorical capital. . . . The Right has no special stake in the free face-to-face use of epithets that perform no other function except to portray whole classes of Americans as subhuman and unworthy of full citizenship."[7]

I cannot agree with Grey's contentions on this score. The implicit identification of groups such as the neo-Nazis and the KKK as insignificant presupposes a value judgment that is not viewpoint-neutral, namely, that the views of such groups have no significant merit. If Grey claims that he is simply making the factual judgment that the influence of these groups on the political process is nil, it is not clear why that is relevant (even assuming its truth—which is debatable). Certainly, such groups aim to become significant influences on the process, and their use of language that would violate Stanford's rules is a significant part of their rhetoric. In fact, I will argue later that the use of such language is tied in an especially close way to their substantive moral and political views.

Grey might be suggesting that our public political discourse does not tolerate the sorts of slurs and epithets his rules proscribe: public debate proceeds with an unwritten prohibition on that kind of language. Such a suggestion is certainly correct, as can be seen by the fact that racists who enter the public arena must rely on "code words" to get their message across. But from the racists' point of view, this is just further evidence of how our public political discourse has been captured by "liberals" and is biased against their view.

Viewpoint-neutrality is not simply a matter of the effects of speech regulation on the liberty of various groups to express their views in the language they prefer. It is also concerned with the kinds of justification that must be offered for speech regulation. The fact is that any plausible justification of hate-speech regulation hinges on the premise that racism, sexism, and homophobia are wrong. Without that premise there would be no basis for arguing that the viewpoint-neutral proscription of verbal harassment is insufficient to protect the rights of minorities and women. The liberal who favors hate-speech regulations, no matter how narrowly drawn, must therefore be prepared to carve out an exception to the principle of viewpoint-neutrality.

THE HARMS OF HATE SPEECH

Many of the proponents of campus hate-speech regulation defend their position by arguing that hate speech causes serious harm to those who are the targets of such speech. Among the most basic of these harms are psychological ones. Even when it involves no direct threat of violence, hate speech can cause abiding feelings of fear, anxiety, and insecurity in those at whom it is targeted. As Mari Matsuda has argued, this is in part because many forms of such speech tacitly draw on a history of violence against certain groups.[8] The symbols and language of hate speech call up historical memories of violent persecution and may encourage fears of current violence. Moreover, hate speech can cause a variety of other harms, from feelings of isolation, to a loss of self-confidence, to physical problems associated with serious psychological disturbance.[9]

The question is whether or not the potential for inflicting these harms is sufficient ground for some sort of hate-speech regulation. As powerful as these appeals to the harms of hate speech are, there is a fundamental sticking point in accepting them as justification for regulation, from a liberal point of view. The basic problem is that the proposed justification sweeps too broadly for a liberal to countenance it. Forms of racist, sexist, or homophobic speech that the liberal is committed to protecting may cause precisely the kinds of harm that the proposed justification invokes.

The liberal will not accept the regulation of racist, sexist, or homophobic speech couched in a scientific, religious, philosophical, or political mode of discourse. The regulation of such speech would not merely carve out a minor exception to the principle of viewpoint-neutrality but would, rather, eviscerate it in a way unacceptable to any liberal. Yet, those forms of hate speech can surely cause in minorities the harms that are invoked to justify regulation: insecurity, anxiety, isolation, loss of self-confidence, and so on. Thus, the liberal must invoke something beyond these kinds of harm in order to justify any hate-speech regulation.

Liberals who favor regulation typically add to their argument the contention that the value to society of the hate speech they would proscribe is virtually nil, while scientific, religious, philosophical, and political forms of hate speech have at least some significant value. Thus, Mary Ellen Gale says that the forms she would prohibit "neither advance knowledge, seek truth, expose government abuses, initiate dialogue, encourage participation, further tolerance of divergent views, nor enhance the victim's individual dignity or self respect."[10] As an example of such worthless hate speech Gale cites an incident of white students writing a message on the mirror in the dorm room of blacks: "African monkeys, why don't you go back to the jungle."[11] But she would protect a great deal of racist or sexist speech, such as a meeting of neo-Nazi students at which swastikas are publicly displayed and speeches made that condemn the presence of Jews and blacks on campus.[12]

Although Gale ends up defending relatively narrow regulations, I believe liberals should be very hesitant to accept her argument for distinguishing regulable from nonregulable hate speech. One problem is that she omits from her list of the values that valuable speech serves one which liberals have long considered important, especially for speech that upsets and disturbs others. Such speech, it is argued, enables the speaker to "blow off steam" in a relatively nondestructive and nonviolent way. Calling particular blacks "African monkeys" might serve as a psychological substitute for harming them in a much more serious way, for example, by lynchings or beatings.

Gale would respond that slurring blacks might just as well serve as an encouragement and prelude to the more serious harms. But the same can be said of forms of hate speech that Gale would protect from regulation, for example the speech at the neo-Nazi student meeting. Moreover, liberals should argue that it is the job of legal rules against assault, battery, conspiracy, rape, and so on to protect people from violence. It is, at best, highly speculative that hate speech on campus contributes to violence against minorities or women. And while the claim about blowing off steam is also a highly speculative one, the liberal tradition clearly puts a substantial burden of proof on those who would silence speech. . . .

SUBORDINATION AND SPEECH ACTS

Some proponents of regulation claim that there is an especially close connection between hate speech and the subordination of minorities. Thus, Charles Lawrence contends, "all racist speech constructs the social reality that constrains the liberty of non-whites because of their race."[13] Along the same lines, Mari Matsuda claims, "racist speech is particularly harmful because it is a mechanism of subordination."[14]

The position of Lawrence and Matsuda can be clarified and elaborated using J. L. Austin's distinction between perlocutionary effects and illocutionary force.[15] The perlocutionary effects of an utterance consist of its causal effects on the hearer: infuriating her, persuading her, frightening her, and so on. The illocutionary force of an utterance consists of the kind of speech act one is performing in making the utterance: advising, warning, stating, claiming, arguing, and so on. Lawrence and Matsuda are not simply suggesting that the direct perlocutionary effects of racist speech constitute harm. Nor are they simply suggesting that hate speech can persuade listeners to accept beliefs that then motivate them to commit acts of harm against racial minorities. That again is a matter of the perlocutionary effects of hate speech. Rather, I believe that they are suggesting that hate speech can inflict a wrong in virtue of its illocutionary acts, the very speech acts performed in the utterances of such speech.[16]

What exactly does this speech-act wrong amount to? My suggestion is that it is the wrong of treating a person as having inferior moral standing. In other words, hate speech involves the performance of a certain kind of illocutionary act, namely, the act of treating someone as a moral subordinate.

Treating persons as moral subordinates means treating them in a way that takes their interests to be intrinsically less important, and their lives inherently less valuable, than the interests and lives of those who belong to some reference group. There are many ways of treating people as moral subordinates that are natural as opposed to conventional: the status of these acts as acts of subordination depend solely on universal principles of morality and not on the conventions of a given society. Slavery and genocide, for example, treat people as having inferior moral standing simply in virtue of the affront of such practices to universal moral principles.

Other ways of treating people as moral subordinates have both natural and conventional elements. The practice of racial segregation is an example. It is subordinating because the conditions imposed on blacks by such treatment violate moral principles but also because the act of separation is a convention for putting the minority group in its (supposedly) proper, subordinate place.

I believe that the language of racist, sexist, and homophobic slurs and epithets provides wholly conventional ways of treating people as moral subordinates. Terms such as "kike," "faggot," "spic," and "nigger" are verbal instruments of subordination. They are used not only to express hatred or contempt for people but also to "put them in their place," that is, to treat them as having inferior moral standing.

It is commonly recognized that through language we can "put people down," to use the vernacular expression. There are many different modes of putting people down: putting them down as less intelligent or less clever or less articulate or less skillful. Putting people down in these ways is not identical to treating them as moral subordinates, and the ordinary put-down does not involve regarding someone as having inferior moral standing. The put-downs that are accomplished with the slurs and epithets of hate speech are different from the ordinary verbal put-down in that respect, even though both sorts of put-downs are done through language.

I have contended that the primary verbal instruments for treating people as moral subordinates are the slurs and epithets of hate speech. In order to see this more clearly, consider the difference between derisively calling someone a "faggot" and saying to that person, with equal derision, "You are contemptible for being homosexual." Both utterances can treat the homosexual as a moral subordinate, but the former accomplishes it much more powerfully than the latter. This is, I believe, because the conventional rules of language make the epithet "faggot" a term whose principal purpose is precisely to treat homosexuals as having inferior moral standing.

I do not believe that a clean and neat line can be drawn around those forms of hate speech that treat their targets as moral subordinates. Slurs and epithets are certainly used that way often, but not always, as is evidenced by the fact that sometimes victimized groups seize on the slurs that historically have subordinated them and seek to "transvalue" the terms. For example, homosexuals have done this with the term "queer," seeking to turn it into a term of pride rather then one of subordination.

Hate speech in modes such as the scientific or philosophical typically would not involve illocutionary acts of moral subordination. This is because speech in those modes usually involves essentially different kinds of speech acts: describing, asserting, stating, arguing, and so forth. To assert or argue that blacks are genetically inferior to whites is not to perform a speech act that itself consists of treating blacks as inferior. Yet, language is often ambiguous and used for multiple purposes, and I would not rule out a priori that in certain contexts even scientific or philosophical hate speech is used in part to subordinate.

The absence of a neat and clean line around those forms of hate speech that subordinate through speech acts does not entail that it is futile to attempt to formulate regulations that target such hate speech. Rules and regulations rarely have an exact fit with what they aim to prevent: over- and underinclusiveness are pervasive in any system of rules that seeks to regulate conduct. The problem is to develop rules that have a reasonably good fit. Later I argue that there are hate-speech regulations that target subordinating hate speech reasonably well. But first I must argue that such speech commits a wrong that may be legitimately targeted by regulation.

SPEECH-ACT WRONG

I have argued that some forms of hate speech treat their targets as moral subordinates on account of race, gender, or sexual preference. Such treatment runs counter to the central liberal idea of persons as free and equal. To that extent, it constitutes a wrong, a speech-act wrong inflicted on those whom it addresses. However, it does not follow that it is a wrong that may be legitimately targeted by regulation. A liberal republic is not a republic of virtue in which the authorities prohibit every conceivable wrong. The liberal republic protects a substantial zone of liberty around the individual in which she is free from authoritative intrusion even to do some things that are wrong.

Yet, the wrongs of subordination based on such characteristics as race, gender, and sexual preference are not just any old wrongs. Historically, they are among the principal wrongs that have prevented—and continue to prevent—Western liberal democracies from living up to their ideals and principles. As such, these wrongs are especially appropriate targets of regulation in our liberal republic. Liberals recognize the special importance of combating such wrongs in their strong support for laws prohibiting discrimination in employment, housing, and public accommodations. And even if the regulation of speech-act subordination on campus is not regarded as mandatory for universities, it does seem that the choice of an institution to regulate that type of subordination on campus is at least justifiable within a liberal framework.

In opposition, it may be argued that subordination is a serious wrong that should be targeted but that the line should be drawn when it comes to subordination through speech. There, viewpoint-neutrality must govern. But I believe that the principle of viewpoint-neutrality must be understood as resting on deeper liberal concerns. Other things being equal, a departure from viewpoint-neutrality will be justified if it can accommodate these deeper concerns while at the same time serving the liberal principle of the equality of persons.

The concerns fall into three basic categories. First is the Millian idea that speech can promote individual development and contribute to the public political dialogue, even when it is wrong, misguided, or otherwise deficient.[17] Second is the Madisonian reason that the authorities cannot be trusted with formulating and enforcing rules that silence certain views: they will be too tempted to abuse such rules in order to promote their own advantage or their own sectarian viewpoint.[18] Third is the idea that any departures from viewpoint-neutrality might serve as precedents that could be seized upon by would-be censors with antiliberal agendas to further their broad efforts to silence speech and expression.[19]

These concerns that underlie viewpoint-neutrality must be accommodated for hate-speech regulation to be justifiable from a liberal perspective. But that cannot be done in the abstract. It needs to be done in the context of a particular set of regulations. In the next section, I argue that there are regulations that target reasonably well those forms of hate speech that subordinate, and in the following section I argue that such regulations accommodate the concerns that underlie the liberal endorsement of the viewpoint-neutrality principle.

TARGETING
SPEECH-ACT WRONG

If I am right in thinking that the slurs and epithets of hate speech are the principal instruments of the speech-act wrong of treating someone as a moral subordinate and that such a wrong is a legitimate target of regulation, then it will not be difficult to formulate rules that have a reasonably good fit with the wrong they legitimately seek to regulate. In general, what are needed are rules that prohibit speech that (a) employs slurs and epithets conventionally used to subordinate persons on account of their race, gender, religion, ethnicity, or sexual preference, (b) is addressed to particular persons, and (c) is expressed with the intention of degrading such persons on account of their race, gender, religion, ethnicity, or sexual preference. With some modification, this is essentially what one finds in the regulations drafted by Grey for Stanford.[20]

Restricting the prohibition to slurs and epithets addressed to specific persons will capture many speech-act wrongs of subordination. But it will not capture them all. Slurs and epithets are not necessary for such speech acts, as I conceded earlier. In addition, it may be possible to treat someone as a moral subordinate through a speech act, even though the utterance is not addressing that person. However, prohibiting more than slurs and epithets would run a high risk of serious overinclusiveness, capturing much speech that performs legitimate speech acts such as stating and arguing. And prohibiting all use of slurs and epithets, whatever the context, would mandate a degree of intrusiveness into the private lives of students that would be difficult for liberals to license.

The regulations should identify examples of the kinds of terms that count as epithets or slurs conventionally used to perform speech acts of subordination. This is required in order to give people sufficient fair warning. But because the terms of natural languages are not precise, univocal, and unchanging, it is not possible to give an exhaustive list, nor is it mandatory to try. Individuals who innocently use an epithet that conventionally subordinates can plead lack of the requisite intent.

The intent requirement is needed to accommodate cases in which an epithet or slur is not used with any intent to treat the addressee as a moral subordinate. These cases cover a wide range including the efforts of some minorities to capture and transvalue terms historically used to subordinate them. There are several different ways in which the required intent could be described: the intent to stigmatize or to demean or to insult or to degrade and so on. I think that "degrade" does the best job of capturing the idea of treating someone as a moral subordinate in language the average person will find familiar and understandable. "Insult" does the poorest job and should be avoided. Insulting someone typically does not involve treating the person as a moral subordinate. Rather, it involves putting someone down in other ways: as less skillful, less intelligent, less clever, and the like.

The regulations at some universities extend beyond what I have defended and prohibit speech that demeans on the basis of physical appearance. I do not believe that such regulations can be justified within the liberal framework I have developed here. Speech can certainly be used to demean people based on physical appearance. "Slob," "dog," "beast," "pig": these are some examples of terms that are used in such verbal put-downs.[21] But I do not believe that they are used to treat people as moral subordinates, and thus the terms do not inflict the kind of speech-act wrong that justifies the regulation of racist, sexist, or homophobic slurs and epithets.

It should not be surprising that terms which demean on the basis of appearance do not morally subordinate, since the belief that full human moral standing depends on good looks is one that few people, if any, hold.[22] The terms that put people down for their appearance are thus fundamentally different from racist, sexist, or homophobic slurs and epithets. The latter terms do reflect beliefs that are held by many about the lower moral standing of certain groups.

ACCOMMODATING LIBERAL CONCERNS

I have argued that regulations should target those forms of hate speech that inflict the speech-act wrong of subordination on their victims. This wrong is distinct from the psychological harm that hate speech causes. In targeting speech-act subordination, the aim of regulation is not to prohibit speech that has undesirable psychological effects on individuals but rather, to prohibit speech that treats people as moral subordinates. To target speech that has undesirable psychological effects is invariably to target certain ideas, since it is through the communication of ideas that the psychological harm occurs. In contrast, targeting speech-act subordination does not target ideas. Any idea would be free from regulation as long as it was expressed through a speech act other than one which subordinates: stating, arguing, claiming, defending, and so on would all be free of regulation.[23]

Because of these differences, regulations that target speech-act subordination can accommodate the liberal concerns underlying viewpoint-neutrality, while regulations that sweep more broadly cannot. Consider the important Millian idea that individual development requires that people be left free to say things that are wrong and to learn from their mistakes. Under the sort of regulation I endorse, people would be perfectly free to make racist, sexist, and homophobic assertions and arguments and to learn of the deficiencies of their views from the counterassertions and counterarguments of others. And the equally important Millian point that public dialogue gains even through the expression of false ideas is accommodated in a similar way. Whatever contribution a racist viewpoint can bring to public discussion can be made under regulations that only target speech-act subordination.

The liberal fear of trusting the authorities is somewhat more worrisome. Some liberals have argued that the authorities cannot be trusted with impartial enforcement of hate-speech regulations. Nadine Strossen, for example, claims that the hate-speech regulations at the University of Michigan have been applied in a biased manner, punishing the racist and homophobic speech of blacks but not of whites.[24] Still, it is not at all clear that the biased application of rules is any more of a problem with rules that are not viewpoint-neutral than with those that are. A neutral rule against harassment can also be enforced in a racially discriminatory manner. There is no reason to think a priori that narrowly drawn hate-speech rules would be any more liable to such abuse. Of course, if it did turn out that there was a pervasive problem with the biased enforcement of hate-speech rules, any sensible liberal would advocate rescinding them. But absent a good reason for thinking that this is likely to happen—not just that it could conceivably happen—the potential for abusive enforcement is no basis for rejecting the kind of regulation I have defended.

Still remaining is the problem of precedent: even narrowly drawn regulations targeting only speech-act subordination could be cited as precedent for more sweeping, antiliberal restrictions by those at other universities or in the community at large who are not committed to liberal values.[25] In response to this concern, it should be argued that narrowly drawn rules will not serve well as precedents for would-be censors with antiliberal agendas. Those who wish to silence socialists, for example, on the ground that socialism is as discredited as racism will find scant precedential support from regulations that allow the expression of racist opinions as long as they are not couched in slurs and epithets directed at specific individuals.

There may be some precedent-setting risk in such narrow regulations. Those who wish to censor the arts, for example, might draw an analogy between the epithets that narrow hate-speech regulations proscribe and the "trash" they would proscribe: both forms of expression are indecent, ugly, and repulsive to the average American, or so the argument might go.

Yet, would-be art censors already have precedents at their disposal providing much closer analogies in antiobscenity laws. Hate-speech regulations are not likely to give would-be censors of the arts any additional ammunition. To this, a liberal opponent of any hate-speech regulation might reply that there is no reason to take the risk. But the response will be that there is a good reason, namely, to prevent the wrong of speech-act subordination that is inflicted by certain forms of hate speech.

CONCLUSION

There is a defensible liberal middle ground between those who oppose all campus hate-speech regulation and those who favor the sweeping regulation of such speech. But the best defense of this middle ground requires the recognition that speech acts of subordination are at the heart of the hate-speech issue. Some forms of hate speech do wrong to people by treating them as moral subordinates. This is the wrong that can and should be the target of campus hate speech regulations.

NOTES

1. In this discussion of the strictly legal issues surrounding the regulation of campus hate speech, the distinction between private and public universities would be an important one. The philosophical considerations on which this article focuses, however, apply both to public and private institutions.

2. The full text of the Stanford regulations is in Thomas Grey, "Civil Rights v. Civil Liberties: The Case of Discriminatory Verbal Harassment," *Social Philosophy and Policy* 8 (1991): 106–7. [Editor's note: See the extract earlier in this chapter.]

3. The University of Connecticut's original regulations are found in the pamphlet "Protect Campus Pluralism," published under the auspices of the Department of Student Affairs, the Dean of Students Office, and the Division of Student Affairs and Services. The regulations have since been rescinded in response to a legal challenge and replaced by ones similar to those in effect at Stanford. See *University of Connecticut Student Handbook* (Storrs: University of Connecticut, 1990–91), p. 62.

4. Kingsley Browne points out that the legal understanding of harassment as conceived under current interpretations of Title VII of the Civil Rights Act of 1964 departs from the ordinary understanding in important ways. See Kingsley Browne, "Title VII as Censorship: Hostile Environment Harassment and the First Amendment," *Ohio State Law Journal* 52 (1991): 486.

5. Laws against the defamation of individuals are essentially viewpoint-neutral for the same reasons: anyone in society can accept them, regardless of their moral or political viewpoint.

6. Compare Kent Greenawalt, "Insults and Epithets," *Rutgers Law Review* 24 (1990): 3006–7.

7. Grey, pp. 103–4.

8. Mari Matsuda, "Legal Storytelling: Public Response to Racist Speech: Considering the Victim's Story," *Michigan Law Review* 87 (1989): 2329–34, 2352.

9. See Richard Delgado, "Words that Wound: A Tort Action for Racial Insults, Epithets and Name-Calling," *Harvard Civil Rights—Civil Liberties Law Review* 17 (1982): 137, 146.

10. Mary Ellen Gale, "Reimagining the First Amendment: Racist Speech and Equal Liberty," *St. John's Law Review* 65 (1991): 179–80.

11. Ibid., p. 176.

12. Ibid.

13. Charles Lawrence, "If He Hollers Let Him Go: Regulating Racist Speech on Campus," *Duke Law Journal* (1990), p. 444.

14. Matsuda, p. 2357.

15. J. L. Austin, *How to Do Things with Words* (New York: Oxford University Press, 1962), pp. 98 ff. The concept of an illocutionary act has been refined and elaborated by John Searle in a series of works starting with "Austin on Locutionary and Illocutionary Acts," *Philosophical Review* 77 (1968): 420–21. Also see his *Speech Acts* (New York: Cambridge University Press, 1969), p. 31, and *Expression and Meaning* (New York: Cambridge University Press, 1979); and John Searle and D. Vanderveken, *Foundations of Illocutionary Logic* (New York: Cambridge University Press, 1985).

16. Both Lawrence and Matsuda describe racist speech as a unique form of speech in its internal relation to subordination. See Lawrence, p. 440, n. 42; and Matsuda, p. 2356. I do not think that their view is correct. Homophobic and sexist speech, e.g., can also be subordinating. In fact, Lawrence and Matsuda are applying to racist speech essentially the same idea that several feminist writers have applied to pornography. These feminists argue that pornography does not simply depict the subordination of women; it actually subordinates them. See Melinda Vadas, "A First Look at the Pornography/Civil Rights Ordinance: Could Pornography Be the Subordination of Women?" *Journal of Philosophy* 84 (1987): 487–511.

17. See Robert Post, "Racist Speech, Democracy, and the First Amendment," *William and Mary Law Review* 32 (1991): 290–91.

18. See Frederick Schauer, "The Second-Best First Amendment," *William and Mary Law Review* 31 (1989): 1–2.

19. Peter Linzer, "White Liberal Looks at Racist Speech," *St. John's Law Review* 65 (1991): 219.

20. Stanford describes the intent that is needed for a hate speaker to be liable as the intent to insult or stigmatize. My reservations about formulating the requisite intent in terms of "insult" are given below.

21. Most such terms are conventionally understood as applying to women and not to men, a clear reflection of our culture's way of perceiving men and women.

22. Some people believe that being overweight is the result of a failure of self-control and thus a kind of moral failing. But that is quite different from thinking that the rights and interests of overweight people are morally less important than those of people who are not overweight. See n. 23 above.

23. A similar argument was made by some supporters of a legal ban on desecrating the American flag through such acts as burning it: to the extent that the ban would prohibit some people from expressing their political viewpoints, it was only a minor departure from viewpoint-neutrality, since those people had an array of other ways to express their views. But the critical difference between the flag-burning case and the hate-speech case is that flag burning is not an act that treats anyone as a moral subordinate.

24. Nadine Strossen, "Regulating Racist Speech on Campus: A Modest Proposal?" *Duke Law Journal* (1990), pp. 557–58. Eric Barendt argues that the British criminal law against racist speech "has often been used to convict militant black spokesmen" (Eric Barendt, Freedom of Speech [Oxford: Clarendon, 1985], p. 163).

25. This concern should be distinguished from the idea that any hate-speech regulation is a step down the slippery slope to the totalitarian control of ideas. That idea is difficult to take seriously. Even for nations that have gone much farther in regulating hate speech than anything envisioned by liberal proponents of regulation in the United States, countries such as England, France, and Germany, the idea that they are on the road to totalitarianism is preposterous. A summary of the laws against racist speech in Britain, France, and Germany can be found in Barendt, pp. 161–66.

■ STANLEY FISH: THE POLITICS OF SPEECH

Stanley Fish offers a more general set of arguments for regulating speech, in keeping with postmodern critiques of universal moral principles like free speech (see, for example, Rorty, Chapter 5). For Fish, there is quite literally no free speech. Speech is considered always an instrument of political purpose, the use and meaning of which is to advance partisan political ends. Restriction of speech accordingly is not exceptional but constitutive of the very possibility of being able to make meaning, to say anything, at all. Being able to say something meaningful requires silencing what is considered meaningless. It follows that speech in general, and free speech in particular, is not a value overriding all others; it can be trumped, and so silenced, if its exercise conflicts with the values on which the society or institution rests. A university, for example, exists for the purpose of education. Speech that undermines that purpose is proscribable. The scope of speech, how far it is deemed free, is considered thus to turn not on principle or constitutional doctrine but on politics. Fish thinks that it will turn on the power of some person to rewrite principle or doctrine in ways promoting protection of speech they would prefer heard and restriction of the speech they would silence. Fish concludes that First Amendment protections constitute a victory not for free speech but for politics. Racist speech is expressed characteristically for nefarious political purposes. Given the lack of principled objection to regulating speech, Fish adds that it would be better, then, and for political reasons, to restrict racist expression than it would to be license it.

Stanley Fish

THERE'S NO SUCH THING AS FREE SPEECH, AND IT'S A GOOD THING TOO

Nowadays the First Amendment is the First Refuge of Scoundrels.
—S. Johnson and S. Fish

Lately many on the liberal and progressive left have been disconcerted to find that words, phrases and concepts thought to be their property and generative of their politics have been appropriated by the forces of neoconservatism. This is particularly true of the concept of free speech, for in recent years First Amendment rhetoric has been used to justify policies and actions the left finds problematical if not abhorrent: pornography, sexist language, campus hate-speech. How has this happened? The answer I shall give in this essay is that abstract concepts like free speech do not have any "natural" content but are filled with whatever content and direction one can manage to put into them. "Free speech" is just the name we give to verbal behavior that serves the substantive agendas we wish to advance; and we give our preferred verbal behaviors *that* name when we can, when we have the power to do so, because in the rhetoric of American life, the label "free speech" is the one you want your favorites to wear. Free speech, in short, is not an independent value, but a political prize, and if that prize has been captured by a politics opposed to yours, it can no longer be invoked in ways that further your purposes, for it is now an obstacle to those purposes. This is something that the liberal left has yet to understand, and what follows is an attempt to pry its members loose from a vocabulary that may now be a disservice to them.

Not far from the end of his *Aereopagitica,* and after having celebrated the virtues of toleration and unregulated publication in passages that find their way into every discussion of free speech and the First Amendment, John Milton catches himself up short and says, of course I didn't mean Catholics, them we exterminate:

> I mean not tolerated popery, and open superstition, which as it extirpates all religions and civil supremacies, so itself should be extirpate . . . that also which is impious or evil absolutely against faith or manners no law can possibly permit that intends not to unlaw itself.

Notice that Milton is not simply stipulating a single exception to a rule generally in place; the kinds of utterance that might be regulated and even prohibited on pain of trial and punishment constitute an open set; popery is named only as a particularly perspicuous instance of the advocacy that cannot be tolerated. No doubt there are other forms of speech and action that might be categorized as "open superstitions" or as subversive of piety, faith, and manners, and presumably these too would be candidates for "extirpation." Nor would Milton think himself culpable for having failed to provide a list of unprotected utterances. The list will fill itself out as utterances are put to the test implied by his formulation: would this form of speech or advocacy, if permitted to flourish, tend to undermine the very purposes for which our society is constituted? One cannot answer this question with respect to a particular utterance in advance of its emergence on the world's stage; rather one must wait and ask the question in the full context of its production and (possible) dissemination. It might appear that the result would be ad hoc and unprincipled, but for Milton the principle inheres in the core values in whose name individuals of like mind came together in the first place. Those values, which include the search for truth and the promotion of virtue, are capacious enough to accommodate a diversity of views. But at some point—again impossible of advance specification—capaciousness will threaten to become shapelessness, and at that point fidelity to the original values will demand acts of extirpation.

I want to say that all affirmations of freedom of expression are like Milton's, dependent for their force on an exception that literally carves out the space in which expression can then emerge. I do not mean that expression (saying something) is a realm whose integrity is sometimes compromised by certain restrictions, but that restriction, in the form of an underlying articulation of the world that necessarily (if silently) negate alternatively possible articulations, is constitutive of expression. Without restriction, without an inbuilt sense of what it would be meaningless to say or wrong to say, there could be no assertion and no reason for asserting it. The exception to unregulated expression is not a negative restriction, but a positive hollowing out of value—we are for *this*, which means we are against *that*—in relation to which meaningful assertion can then occur. It is in reference to that value—constituted as all values are by an act of exclusion—that some forms of speech will be heard as (quite literally) intolerable. Speech, in short, is never a value in and of itself, but is always produced within the precincts of some assumed conception of the good to which it must yield in the event of conflict. When the pinch comes (and sooner or later it will always come) and the institution (be it church, state, or university) is confronted by behavior subversive of its core rationale, it will respond by declaring "of course we mean not tolerated——, that we extirpate," not because an exception to a general freedom has suddenly and contradictorily been announced, but because the freedom has never been general and has always been understood against the background of an originary exclusion that gives it meaning.

This is a large thesis, but before tackling it directly I want to buttress my case with another example, taken not from the seventeenth century but from the Charter and case law of Canada. Canadian thinking about freedom of expression departs from the line usually taken in the United States in ways that bring that country very close to the *Aereopagitica* as I have expounded it. The differences are fully on display in a recent landmark case, *R v. Keegstra*. James Keegstra was a high school teacher in Alberta who, it was established by evidence, "systematically denigrated Jews and Judaism in his classes." He described Jews as treacherous, subversive, sadistic, money-loving, power hungry, and child-killers. He declared them "responsible for depressions, anarchy, chaos, wars, and revolution," and required his students "to regurgitate these notions in essays and examinations." Keegstra was indicted under section 319(2) of the Criminal Code and convicted. The Court of Appeal reversed and the Crown appealed to the Supreme Court, which reinstated the lower court's verdict.

Section 319(2) reads in part, "Everyone who, by communicating statements other than in private conversation, willfully promotes hatred against any identifiable group is guilty of . . . an indictable offense and is liable to imprisonment for a term not exceeding two years." In the United States, this provision of the code would almost certainly be struck down because, under the First Amendment, restrictions on speech are apparently prohibited without qualification. To be sure, the Canadian Charter has its own version of the First Amendment, in section 2(b): "Everyone has the following fundamental freedoms . . . (b) freedom of thought, belief, opinion, and expression, including freedom of the press and other media of communication." But section 2(b), like every other section of the Charter, is qualified by section 1: "The Canadian Charter of Rights and Freedoms guarantees the rights and freedoms set out in it subject only to such reasonable limits prescribed by law as can be demonstrably justified in a free and democratic society." Or in other words, every right and freedom herein granted can be trumped if its exercise is found to be in conflict with the principles that underwrite the society.

This is what happens in *Keegstra* as the majority finds that section 319(2) of the Criminal Code does in fact violate the right of freedom of expression guaranteed by the Charter, but is nevertheless a *permissible* restriction because it accords with the principles proclaimed in section 1. There is, of course, a dissent that reaches the conclusion that would have been reached by most, if not all, U.S. courts; but even in dissent the minority is faithful to Canadian ways of reasoning. "The question," it declares, "is always one of balance," and thus even when a particular infringement of Charter section 2(b) has been declared unconstitutional, as it would have been by the minority, the question remains open with respect to the next case. In the United States the question is presumed closed and can only be pried open by special tools. In our legal culture as it is now constituted, if one yells "free speech" in a crowded courtroom and makes it stick, the case is over.

Of course, it is not that simple. Despite the apparent absoluteness of the First Amendment, there are any number of ways of getting around it, ways that are known to every student of the law. In general, the preferred strategy is to manipulate the distinction, essential to First Amendment jurisprudence, between speech and action. The distinction is essential because no one would think to frame a First Amendment that began "Congress shall make no law abridging freedom of action;" for that would amount to saying "Congress shall make no law," which would amount to saying "There shall be no law," only actions uninhibited and unregulated. If the First Amendment is to make any sense, have any bite, speech must be declared not to be a species of action, or to be a special form of action lacking the aspects of action that cause it to be the object of regulation. The latter strategy is the favored one and usually involves the separation of speech from consequences. This is what Archibald Cox does when he assigns to the First Amendment the job of protecting "expressions separable from conduct harmful to other individuals and the community." The difficulty of managing this segregation is well known: speech always seems to be crossing the line into action where it becomes, at least potentially, consequential. In the face of this categorical instability, First Amendment theorists and jurists fashion a distinction within the speech/action distinction: some forms of speech are not really speech because their purpose is to incite violence or because they are, as the court declares in *Chaplinsky v. New Hampshire* (1942), "fighting words," words "likely to provoke the average person to retaliation, and thereby cause a breach of the peace."

The trouble with this definition is that it distinguishes not between fighting words and words that remain safely and merely expressive, but between words that are provocative to one group (the group that falls under the rubric "average person") and words that might be provocative to other groups, groups of persons not now considered average. And if you ask what words are likely to be provocative to those non-average groups, what are likely to be *their* fighting words, the answer is anything and everything, for as Justice Holmes said long ago (in *Gitlow v. New York*), every idea is an incitement to somebody, and since ideas come packaged in sentences, in words, every sentence is potentially, in some situation that might occur tomorrow, a fighting word and therefore a candidate for regulation.

This insight cuts two ways. One could conclude from it that the fighting words exception is a bad idea because there is no way to prevent clever and unscrupulous advocates from shoveling so many forms of speech into the accepted category that the zone of constitutionally protected speech shrinks to nothing and is finally without inhabitants. Or, alternatively, one could conclude that there was never anything in the zone in the first place and that the difficulty of limiting the fighting words exception is merely a particular instance of the general difficulty of separating speech from action. And if one opts for this second conclusion, as I do, then a further conclusion is inescapable: insofar as the point of the First Amendment is to identify speech separable from conduct and from the consequences that come in conduct's wake, there is no such speech and therefore nothing for the First Amendment to protect. Or, to make the point from the other direction, when a court invalidates legislation because it infringes on protected speech, it is not because the speech in question is without consequences but because the consequences have been discounted in relation to a good that is judged to outweigh them. Despite what they say, courts are never in the business of protecting speech per se, "mere" speech (a nonexistent animal); rather, they are in the business of classifying speech (as protected or regulatable) in relation to a value—the health of the republic, the vigor of the economy, the maintenance of the status quo, the undoing of the status—that is the true, if unacknowledged, object of their protection.

But if this is the case, a First Amendment purist might reply, why not drop the charade along with the malleable distinctions that make it possible, and declare up front that total freedom of speech is our primary value and trumps anything else, no matter what? The answer is that freedom of expression would only be a primary value if it didn't matter what was said, didn't matter in the sense that no one gave a damn but just liked to hear talk. There are contexts like that, a Hyde Park corner or a call-in talk show where people get to sound off for the sheer fun of it. These, however, are special contexts, artificially bounded spaces designed to assure that talking is not taken seriously. In ordinary contexts, talk is produced with the goal of trying to move the world in one direction rather than another. In these contexts—the contexts of everyday life—you go to the trouble of asserting that X is Y only because you suspect that some people are wrongly asserting that X is Z or that X doesn't exist. You assert, in short, because you give a damn, not about assertion—as if it were a value in and of itself—but about what your assertion is about. It may seem paradoxical, but free expression could only be a primary value if what you are valuing is the right to make noise; but if you are engaged in some purposive activity in the course of which speech happens to be produced, sooner or later you will come to a point when you decide that some forms of speech do not further but endanger that purpose.

Take the case of universities and colleges. Could it be the purpose of such places to encourage free expression? If the answer were "yes" it would be hard to say why there would be any need for classes, or examinations, or departments, or disciplines, or libraries, since freedom of expression requires nothing but a soapbox or an open telephone line. The very fact of the university's machinery—of the events, rituals, and procedures that fill its calendar—argues for some other, more substantive, purpose. In relation to that purpose (which will be realized differently in different kinds of institutions), the flourishing of free expression will in almost all circumstances be an obvious good; but in some circumstances, freedom of expression may pose a threat to that purpose, and at that point, it may be necessary to discipline or regulate speech, lest, to paraphrase Milton, the institution sacrifice itself to one of its *accidental* features.

Interestingly enough, the same conclusion is reached (inadvertently) by Congressman Henry Hyde, who is addressing these very issues in a recently offered amendment to Title VI of the Civil Rights Act. The first section of the amendment states its purpose, to protect "the free speech rights of college students" by prohibiting private as well as public educational institutions from "subjecting any student to disciplinary sanctions solely on the basis of conduct that is speech." The second section enumerates the remedies available to students whose speech rights may have been abridged; and the third, which is to my mind the nub of the matter, declares as an exception to the amendment's jurisdiction any "educational institution that is controlled by a religious organization," on the reasoning that the application of the amendment to such institutions "would not be consistent with the religious tenets of such organizations." In effect, what Congressman Hyde is saying is that at the heart of these colleges and universities is a set of beliefs, and it would be wrong to require them to tolerate behavior, including speech behavior, inimical to those beliefs. But insofar as the logic is persuasive, it applies across the board; for all educational institutions rest on some set of beliefs—no institution is "just there" independent of any purpose—and it is hard to see why the rights of an institution to protect and preserve its basic "tenets" should be restricted only to those that are religiously controlled. Read strongly, the third section of the amendment undoes sections one and two—the exception becomes, as it always was, the rule—and points us to a balancing test very much like that employed in Canadian law: given that any college or university is informed by a core rationale, an administrator faced with complaints about offensive speech should ask whether damage to the core would be greater if the speech were tolerated or regulated.

The objection to this line of reasoning is well known and has recently been re-formulated by Benno Schmidt, former president of Yale University. According to Schmidt, speech-codes on campuses constitute "well-intentioned but misguided efforts to give values of community and harmony a higher place than freedom" (*Wall Street Journal*, May 6, 1991). "When the goals of harmony collide with freedom of expression," he continues, "freedom must be the paramount obligation of an academic community." The flaw in this logic is on display in the phrase "academic community"; for the phrase recognizes what Schmidt would deny, that expression only occurs in communities; if not in an academic community, then in a shopping mall community or a dinner-party community or an airplane-ride community or an office community. In these communities and in any others that could be imagined (with the possible exception of a community of major league baseball fans), limitations on speech in relation to a defining and deeply assumed purpose are inseparable from community membership.

Indeed, "limitations" is the wrong word because it suggests that expression, as an activity and a value, has a pure form that is always in danger of being compromised by the urgings of special interest communities; but independently of a community context informed by interest (that is, purpose), expression would be at once inconceivable and unintelligible. Rather than being a value that is threatened by limitations and constraints, expression, in any form worth worrying about, is a *product* of limitations and constraints, of the already-in-place presuppositions that give assertions their very particular point. Indeed, the very act of thinking of something to say (whether or not it is subsequently regulated) is already constrained—rendered impure, and because impure, communicable—by the background context within which the thought takes its shape. (The analysis holds too for "freedom," which in Schmidt's vision is an entirely empty concept referring to an urge without direction. But like expression, freedom is a coherent notion only in relation to a goal or good that limits and, by limiting, shapes its exercise.)

Arguments like Schmidt's only get their purchase by first imagining speech as occurring in no context whatsoever, and then stripping particular speech acts of the properties conferred on them by contexts. The trick is nicely illustrated when Schmidt urges protection for speech "no matter how obnoxious in content." "Obnoxious" at once acknowledges the reality of speech-related harms and trivializes them by suggesting that they are *surface* injuries that any large-minded ("liberated and humane") person should be able to bear. The possibility that speech-related injuries may be grievous and *deeply* wounding is carefully kept out of sight, and because it is kept out of sight, the fiction of a world of weightless verbal exchange can be maintained, at least within the confines of Schmidt's carefully denatured discourse.

To this Schmidt would no doubt reply, as he does in his essay, that harmful speech should be answered not by regulation but by more speech; but that would make sense only if the effects of speech could be canceled out by additional speech, only if the pain and humiliation caused by racial or religious epithets could be ameliorated by saying something like "So's your old man." What Schmidt fails to realize at every level of his argument is that expression is more than a matter of proffering and receiving propositions, that words do work in the world of a kind that cannot be confined to a purely cognitive realm of "mere" ideas.

It could be said, however, that I myself mistake the nature of the work done by freely tolerated speech because I am too focused on short-run outcomes and fail to understand that the good effects of speech will be realized, not in the present, but in a future whose emergence regulation could only inhibit. This line of reasoning would also weaken one of my key points, that speech in and of itself cannot be a value and is only worth worrying about if it is in the service of something with which it cannot be identical. My mistake, one could argue, is to equate the something in whose service speech is with some locally espoused value (e.g., the end of racism, the empowerment of disadvantaged minorities), whereas in fact we should think of that something as a now-inchoate shape that will be given firm lines only by time's pencil. That is why the shape now receives such indeterminate characterizations (e.g., true self-fulfillment, a more perfect polity, a more capable citizenry, a less partial truth); we cannot now know it, and therefore we must not prematurely fix it in ways that will bind successive generations to error.

This forward-looking view of what the First Amendment protects has a great appeal, in part because it continues in a secular form the Puritan celebration of millenarian hopes, but it imposes a requirement so severe that one would expect more justification for it than is usually provided. The requirement is that we endure whatever pain racist and hate speech inflicts for the sake of a future whose emergence we can only take on faith. In a specifically religious vision like Milton's this makes perfect sense (it is indeed the whole of Christianity), but in the context of a politics that puts its trust in the world and not in the Holy Spirit, it raises more questions than it answers and could be seen as the second of two strategies designed to delegitimize the complaints of victimized groups. The first strategy, as I have noted, is to define speech in such a way as to render it inconsequential (on the model of "sticks and stones will break my bones, but . . . ."); the second strategy is to acknowledge the (often grievous) consequences of speech, but declare that we must suffer them in the name of something that cannot be named. The two strategies are denials from slightly different directions of the *present* effects of racist speech; one confines those effects to a closed and safe realm of pure mental activity; the other imagines the effects of speech spilling over into the world, but only in an ever-receding future for whose sake we must forever defer taking action.

I find both strategies unpersuasive, but my own skepticism concerning them is less important than the fact that in general they seem to have worked; in the parlance of the market-place (a parlance First Amendment commentators love), many in the society seemed to have bought them. Why? The answer, I think, is that people cling to First Amendment pieties because they do not wish to face what they correctly take to be the alternative. That alternative is *politics*, the realization (at which I have already hinted) that decisions about what is and is not protected in the realm of expression will rest not on principle or firm doctrine, but on the ability of some persons to interpret—recharacterize or rewrite—principle and doctrine in ways that lead to the protection of speech they want heard and the regulation of speech they want silenced. (That is how George Bush can argue *for* flag-burning statutes and *against* campus hate-speech codes.) When the First Amendment is successfully invoked the result is not a victory for free speech in the face of a challenge from politics, but a *political victory* won by the party that has managed to wrap its agenda in the mantle of free speech.

It is from just such a conclusion—a conclusion that would put politics *inside* the First Amendment—that commentators recoil, saying things like "This could render the First Amendment a dead letter," or "This would leave us with no normative guidance in determining when and what speech to protect," or "This effaces the distinction between speech and action," or "This is incompatible with any viable notion of freedom of expression." To these statements (culled more or less at random from recent law review pieces) I would reply that the First Amendment has always been a dead letter if one understood its "liveness" to depend on the identification and protection of a realm of "mere" expression distinct from the realm of regulatable conduct; the distinction between speech and action has always been effaced in principle, although in practice it can take whatever form the prevailing political conditions mandate; we have never had any normative guidance for marking off protected from unprotected speech; rather, the guidance we have has been fashioned (and refashioned) in the very political struggles, over which it then (for a time) presides. In short, the name of the game has always been politics, even when (indeed, especially when) it is played by stigmatizing politics as the area to be avoided.

In saying this, I would not be heard as arguing either for or against regulation and speech codes as a matter of general principle. Instead my argument turns away from general principle to the pragmatic (anti)principle of considering each situation as it emerges. The question of whether or not to regulate will always be a local one, and we cannot rely on abstractions that are either empty of content or filled with the content of some partisan agenda to generate a "principled" answer. Instead we must consider in every case what is at stake and what are the risks and gains of alternative courses of action. In the course of this consideration many things will be of help, but among them will not be phrases like "freedom of speech" or "the right of individual expression," because as they are used now, these phrases tend to obscure rather than clarify our dilemmas. Once they are deprived of their talismanic force, once it is no longer strategically effective simply to invoke them in the act of walking away from a problem, the conversation could continue in directions that are now blocked by a First Amendment absolutism that has only been honored in the breach anyway. To the student reporter who complains that in the wake of the promulgation of a speech code at the University of Wisconsin there is now something in the back of his mind as he writes, one could reply, "There was always something in the back of your mind and perhaps it might be better to have this code in the back of your mind than whatever was in there before." And when someone warns about the slippery slope and predicts mournfully that if you restrict one form of speech, you never know what will be restricted next, one could reply, "Some form of speech is always being restricted; else there could be no meaningful assertion; we have always and already slid down the slippery slope; someone is always going to be restricted next, and it is your job to make sure that the someone is not you." And when someone observes, as someone surely will, that anti-harassment codes chill speech, one could reply that since speech only becomes intelligible against the background of what isn't being said, the background of what has already been silenced, the only question is the political one of which speech is going to be chilled, and, all things considered, it seems a good thing to chill speech like "nigger," "cunt," "kike," and "faggot." And if someone then says, "But what happened to free speech principles?" one could say what I have now said a dozen times, free speech principles don't exist except as a component in a bad argument in which such principles are invoked to mask motives that would not withstand close scrutiny.

An example of a wolf wrapped in First Amendment clothing is an advertisement that ran recently in the Duke University student newspaper, The Chronicle. Signed by Bradley R. Smith, well known as a purveyor of anti-Semitic neo-Nazi propaganda, the ad is packaged as a scholarly treatise: four densely packed columns complete with "learned" references, undocumented statistics, and an array of so-called authorities. The message of the ad is that the Holocaust never occurred and that the German state never "had a policy to exterminate the Jewish people (or anyone else) by putting them to death in gas chambers." In a spectacular instance of the increasingly popular "blame the victim" strategy, the Holocaust "story" or "myth" is said to have been fabricated in order "to drum up world sympathy for Jewish causes." The "evidence" supporting these assertions is a slick blend of supposedly probative facts—"not a single autopsied body has been shown to be gassed"—and sly insinuations of a kind familiar to readers of Mein Kampf and The Protocols of the Elders of Zion. The slickest thing of all, however, is the presentation of the argument as an exercise in free speech—the ad is subtitled "The Case for Open Debate"—that could be objected to only by "thought police" and censors. This strategy bore immediate fruit in the decision of the newspaper staff to accept the ad despite a long-standing (and historically honored) policy of refusing materials that contain ethnic and racial slurs or are otherwise offensive. The reasoning of the staff (explained by the editor in a special column) was that under the First Amendment advertisers have the "right" to be published. "American newspapers are built on the principles of free speech and free press, so how can a newspaper deny these rights to anyone?" The answer to this question is that an advertiser is not denied his rights simply because a single media organ declines his copy, so long as other avenues of publication are available and there has been no state suppression of his views. This is not to say that there could not be a case for printing the ad; only that the case cannot rest on a supposed First Amendment obligation. One might argue, for example, that printing the ad would foster healthy debate, or that lies are more likely to be shown up for what they are if they are brought to the light of day, but these are precisely the arguments the editor disclaims in her eagerness to take a "principled" free speech stand.

What I find most distressing about this incident is not that the ad was printed but that it was printed by persons who believed it to be a lie and a distortion. If the editor and her staff were in agreement with Smith's views or harbored serious doubts about the reality of the Holocaust, I would still have a quarrel with them, but it would be a different quarrel; it would be a quarrel about evidence, credibility, documentation. But since on these matters the editors and I are in agreement, my quarrel is with the reasoning that led them to act in opposition to what they believed to be true. That reasoning, as I understand it, goes as follows: although we ourselves are certain that the Holocaust was a fact, facts are notoriously interpretable and disputable; therefore nothing is ever really settled, and we have no right to reject something just because we regard it as pernicious and false. But the fact—if I can use that word—that settled truths can always be upset, at least theoretically, does not mean that we cannot affirm and rely on truths that according to our present lights seem indisputable; rather, it means exactly the opposite: in the absence of absolute certainty of the kind that can only be provided by revelation (something I do not rule out but have not yet experienced), we must act on the basis of the certainty we have so far achieved. Truth may, as Milton said, always be in the course of emerging, and we must always be on guard against being so beguiled by its present shape that we ignore contrary evidence; but, by the same token, when it happens that the present shape of truth is compelling beyond a reasonable doubt, it is our moral obligation to act on it and not defer action in the name of an interpretative future that may never arrive. By running the First Amendment up the nearest flagpole and rushing to salute it, the student editors defaulted on that obligation and gave over their responsibility to a so-called principle that was not even to the point.

Let me be clear. I am not saying that First Amendment principles are inherently bad (they are *inherently* nothing), only that they are not always the appropriate reference point for situations involving the production of speech, and that even when they are the appropriate reference point, they do not constitute a politics-free perspective because the shape in which they are invoked will always be political, will always, that is, be the result of having drawn the relevant line (between speech and action, or between high-value and low-value speech, or between words essential to the expression of ideas and fighting words) in a way that is favorable to some interests and indifferent or hostile to others. This having been said, the moral is not that First Amendment talk should be abandoned, for even if the standard First Amendment formulas do not and could not perform the function expected of them (the elimination of political considerations in decisions about speech), they still serve a function that is not at all negligible: they slow down outcomes in an area in which the fear of overhasty outcomes is justified by a long record of abuses of power. It is often said that history shows (itself a formula) that even a minimal restriction on the right of expression too easily leads to ever-larger restrictions; and to the extent that this is an empirical fact (and it is a question one could debate), there is some comfort and protection to be found in a procedure that requires you to jump through hoops—do a lot of argumentative work—before a speech regulation will be allowed to stand.

I would not be misunderstood as offering the notion of "jumping through hoops" as a new version of the First Amendment claim to neutrality. A hoop must have a shape—in this case the shape of whatever binary distinction is representing First Amendment "interests"—and the shape of the hoop one is asked to jump through will in part determine what kinds of jumps can be regularly made. Even if they are only mechanisms for slowing down outcomes, First Amendment formulas by virtue of their substantive content (and it is impossible that they be without content) will slow down some outcomes more easily than others, and that means that the form they happen to have at the present moment will favor some interests more than others. Therefore, even with a reduced sense of the effectivity of First Amendment rhetoric (it can not assure any particular result), the counsel with which I began remains relevant: so long as so-called free-speech principles have been fashioned by your enemy (so long as it is *his* hoops you have to jump through), contest their relevance to the issue at hand; but if you manage to refashion them in line with your purposes, urge them with a vengeance.

It is a counsel that follows from the thesis that there is no such thing as free speech, which is not, after all, a thesis as startling or corrosive as may first have seemed. It merely says that there is no class of utterances separable from the world of conduct, and that therefore the identifications of some utterances as members of that non-existent class will always be evidence that a political line has been drawn rather than a line that denies politics entry into the forum of public discourse. It is the job of the First Amendment to mark out an area in which competing views can be considered without state interference; but if the very marking out of that area is itself an interference (as it always will be), First Amendment jurisprudence is inevitably self-defeating and subversive of its own aspirations. That's the bad news. The good news is that precisely *because* speech is never "free" in the two senses required—free of consequences and free from state pressure—speech always matters, is always doing work; because everything we say impinges on the world in ways indistinguishable from the effects of physical action, we must take responsibility for our verbal performances—*all* of them—and not assume that they are being taken care of by a clause in the Constitution. Of course, with responsibility come risks, but they have always been our risks and no doctrine of free speech has ever insulated us from them. They are the risks, respectively, of permitting speech that does obvious harm and of shutting off speech in ways that might deny us the benefit of Joyce's *Ulysses* or Lawrence's *Lady Chatterly's Lover* or Titian's paintings. Nothing, I repeat, can insulate us from those risks. (If there is no normative guidance in determining when and what speech to protect, there is no normative guidance in determining what is art—like free speech a category that includes everything and nothing—and what is obscenity.) Moreover, nothing can provide us with a principle for deciding which risk in the long run is the best to take. I am persuaded that at the present moment, right now, the risk of not attending to hate speech is greater than the risk that by regulating it we will deprive ourselves of valuable voices and insights or slide down the slippery slope toward tyranny. This is a judgment for which I can offer reasons but no guarantees. All I am saying is that the judgments of those who would come down on the other side carry no guarantees either. They urge us to put our faith in apolitical abstractions, but the abstractions they invoke—the marketplace of ideas, speech alone, speech itself—only come in political guises, and therefore in trusting to them we fall (unwittingly) under the sway of the very forces we wish to keep at bay. It is not that there are no choices to make or means of making them; it is just that the choices as well as the means are inextricable from the din and confusion of partisan struggle. There is no safe place.

SUGGESTIONS FOR DISCUSSION

1. Why does liberalism place such emphasis on freedom of speech? What is characteristically wrong about "hate speech"? Are these wrongs sufficient to warrant social protection of that speech in a society like the United States, or are there grounds for censoring such speech in spite of the commitment to liberty?

2. Is speech necessarily political? If so, does it follow that any speech is open potentially to justifiable proscription? What philosophical principles underlie the view that speech is inherently political?

3. You are the collective members of your student newspaper editorial board. A well-known racist applies to place an advertisement in your newspaper denying the occurrence of the Holocaust and arguing for the necessity of racial purity. Debate whether to run the advertisement, and then vote.

4. You are the collective members of the Student Representative Council on campus. Student members of a group historically discriminated against apply to your council for funds to pay for a public lecture on campus by a speaker known for his derogatory remarks against other social groups. How should you respond to the request for funds?

5. On what grounds, if any, are campus speech and behavioral codes justifiable? Why do you think they have become controversial only in the last decade or so? Are they effective measures in reducing discrimination, or are they merely symbolic?

FOR FURTHER READING

Barnes, R. "Standing Guard for the P.C. Militia, or, Fighting Hatred and Indifference: Some Thoughts on Expressive Hate-Conduct And Political Correctness," *University of Illinois Law Review* 1992, 4979–95.

Bell, D. *Race, Racism and American Law,* 3rd ed. Boston: Little Brown, 1992.

Berger, F. *Freedom of Expression.* Belmont, Calif.: Wadsworth 1980.

Calleros, C. "Reconciliation of Civil Rights and Civil Liberties After *R.A.V. v. City of St. Paul:* Free Speech, Antiharassment Policies, Multicultural Education, and Political Correctness." *Utah Law Review* 1992: 1205–1333.

Carter, S. "Does the First Amendment Protect More than Free Speech?" *William and Mary Law Review* 33 (1992): 871–94.

Cohen, J. "Freedom of Expression." *Philosophy and Public Affairs* 22, 3 (Summer 1993): 206–63.

Delagado, R. "Campus Antiracism Rules: Constitutional Narratives in Collision." *Northwestern University Law Review* 85 (1992): 343–87.

Feinberg, J. *Social Philosophy.* Englewood Cliffs, N.J.: Prentice-Hall, 1973.

———— *Harm to Others.* Oxford: Oxford University Press, 1984.

———— . *Offense to Others.* Oxford: Oxford University Press, 1988.

Fish, S. *There's No Such Thing as Free Speech and It's a Good Thing Too.* New York: Oxford University Press, 1993.

Goldberg, D. T. "Hate, or Power?" *American Philosophical Association Newsletter* 93, 1 (Spring 1992): 16–18.

Greenawalt, K. *Speech, Crime and the Uses of Language.* Oxford: Oxford University Press, 1989.

Grey, T. "Civil Rights vs. Civil Liberties: The Case of Discriminatory Verbal Harassment." *Social Philosophy and Policy* 8 (1991), no. 2: 81–107.

Hart, H. H., ed. *Censorship: For and Against.* New York: Hart Publishing, 1971.

Kretzmer, L. "Freedom of Speech and Racism." *Cardozo Law Review* 8, 3 (1987): 445–513.

Lawrence, C. "If He Hollers Let Him Go: Regulating Racist Speech on Campus." *Duke Law Journal* 431 (1990): 431–83.

MacKinnon, C. *Only Words.* Cambridge: Harvard University Press, 1993.

Matsuda et al. *Words That Wound: Critical Race Theory, Assaultive Speech, and the First Amendment.* Denver: Westview Press, 1993.

Moore, T. H. "R.A.V. v. City of St Paul: A Curious Way to Protect Speech." *North Carolina Law Review* 71 (1993): 1252–81.

Post, R. "Racist Speech, Democracy, and the First Amendment." *William and Mary Law Review* 32 (1991): 267–327.

Schwartz, D. R. "A First Amendment Justification for Regulating Racist Speech on Campus." *Case Western Reserve Law Review* 40, 3 (1989–1990): 733–79.

Shapiro, J. T. "The Call for Campus Conduct Policies: Censorship or Constitutionally Permissible Limitations on Speech." *Minnesota Law Review* 75 (1990): 201–38.

Siegel, E. G. S. "Closing the Campus Gates to Free Expression: The Regulation of Offensive Speech at Colleges and Universities." *Emory Law Journal* 39 (1990): 1351–1400.

Sunstein, C. *Democracy and the Problem of Free Speech.* New York: The Free Press, 1993.

Weinstein, J. "A Constitutional Roadmap to the Regulation of Campus Hate Speech." *Wayne Law Review* 38, 1 (Fall 1991): 247.

Williams, P. *"Metro Broadcasting, Inc. v. FCC:* Regrouping in Singular Times." *Harvard Law Review* 104 (1990): 525–546.

Wisconsin v. Mitchell 113 U.S. S. Ct. 2194 (1993).

CHAPTER ELEVEN

AIDS

Over the past decade, HIV (the Human Immunodeficiency Virus) has emerged as the fastest growing mortal disease afflicting human beings, both in the United States and worldwide. Directly or indirectly, almost nobody in the United States is unaffected. Known popularly as AIDS (Acquired Immuno-Deficiency Syndrome), the human drama associated with the virus recently has become the stuff of television and movies, rock concerts and media award shows, gay activism and political debates about research, treatment funding, educational programs and advertisements, international medical conferences and the closely watched race for a vaccine or cure. This rush of activity around AIDS is relatively recent. While the first HIV cases were identified early in the 1980s, the virus's manner of transmission came to be associated in the public imagination first with homosexuality and then with intravenous drug use. Because of the social stigmas attached to both, public concern over AIDS was reduced largely to marginalizing its effects. Those with AIDS were rendered invisible. Then actor Brad Davis left a scathing note at his death that said he had been shunned in Hollywood as a result of knowledge about his condition. In the wake of his coming out, Rock Hudson suffered the last few months of his life before the public glare. As a result of becoming seropositive, the ever popular Magic Johnson was forced into early retirement from professional basketball. And during the final months of Arthur Ashe's remarkable life, the painful public and personal conditions surrounding AIDS were dramatized before a nation that had shunned the disease and its victims for nearly ten years. In the United States, at least, we can all now say we know *of* someone by name who has died from complications related to HIV.

HIV and AIDS   Technically, AIDS is the final stage of the syndrome caused by HIV. HIV attacks the human immune system by targeting T-cells in the blood, undermining the body's capacity to resist *opportunistic infections* that the immune systems of uninfected persons are able to fight off with ease. Within a fortnight or so of HIV exposure, many will experience a flu-like condition that passes after a few weeks. In the following six months most will test seropositive on an HIV antibody test and will remain seropositive for the duration of their lives, which might last as long as a dozen years. While infectious throughout this period, those who are HIV positive may suffer little if any of the opportunistic infections, malignancies, or neurological afflictions that mark the final stages of the disease. Illness and ultimately death inevitably follow from the body's inability to limit or stave off the course of such infections.

Despite substantial medical knowledge regarding HIV transmission, general public ignorance has caused widespread panic, often prompting violations of the infected person's rights. HIV is considered a "fragile" virus, for it is readily destroyed and transmitted only when concentrations of the virus are significant. The known modes of transmission are limited to the mixing of body fluids—blood, semen, vaginal/cervical fluids, and perhaps breast milk—of someone infected with those of another not yet infected. Activities known to promote high risk of infection include unprotected sexual intercourse, particularly but not only anal intercourse, blood transfusions, transplantation of an infected organ, intravenous drug use when contaminated needles are shared, and the prenatal nurturance of a fetus by its mother or perhaps postnatal breastfeeding. The virus has been discovered in saliva and tears, but in concentrations so low that transmission is highly improbable. Casual contact, including hugging, handshakes, or sharing utensils or toothbrushes, involve no risk of transmission. Though AIDS strikes people across race, class, and gender, the overwhelming majority of reported AIDS cases in the United States concern homosexual men and intravenous drug users, while those classified as "Black" or "Hispanic" are infected disproportionately to their percentage of the general population. More than fifty percent of gay men in San Francisco, for example, are HIV positive. In parts of Central Africa, AIDS is decimating the population, wiping out entire villages in some cases, and infection is beginning to spread rapidly in parts of Asia.

Public Health and Individual Rights   The dramatic spread of HIV infection and AIDS and the severity of the set of associated medical conditions pose deep ethical dilemmas. These conflicts surrounding the epidemic manifest in everyday social experiences, in medical research and treatment, in social science research concerning the social implications of AIDS, and in legal considerations. In the most general terms, the dilemma concerns the conflict between individual rights and public health, that is, between the commitment to respect the rights of individuals infected by AIDS, on one hand, and the right of society and the obligation of the government to protect its members from serious, life threatening harms, on the other. The basic ethical concern, then, is the balance between rights and duties across a range of important social issues. Individual *rights* to autonomy, respect, and privacy must be balanced with the public health *duty* to protect and promote social welfare, even if coercion is needed to do so.

This conflict between a state's duty to protect the public health and individual rights not to be discriminated against will be especially deep where the public health mandate is defended on utilitarian grounds, while the commitment to individual rights is defended on deontological, rights-based, or contractarian grounds (for more on utilitarianism, see Chapter 4; on deontology, see Kant, Chapter 3; on rights-based theories, see Mackie and Nozick respectively, Chapter 5; and on social contract theory, see Rawls, Chapter 15). It may be that the public health can be protected against further HIV infection in some cases only by discriminating against those already infected. Alternatively, moral equality may be maintained only by risking additional infections. Such cases raise both normative and empirical questions. Normatively, the Harm Principle reveals that it is wrong to spread HIV knowingly, intentionally, recklessly, or negligently, or to allow it to be spread when it could be controlled (for a discussion of the Harm Principle, see John Stuart Mill, Chapter 4, and Chapter 10). In terms of the public health mandate, those who are infected by HIV have a responsibility to proceed carefully in situations where risk of infecting others is involved. If those infected generally and obviously fail to act responsibly, society may mandate effective measures to restrict their possibility of promoting further harms of the same kind.

This raises empirical issues: measures adopted in the name of the public health must be those that in fact diminish the possibility of harm while *least* violating the rights of those so restricted. Suggestions made in the past included universal, involuntary testing for HIV antibodies; mandatory quarantining or employment restriction of those who test seropositive; registering homosexuals, prostitutes, and other high-risk groups; excluding students from school if they are HIV infected; and prohibiting gay men from traveling to and from San Francisco. All these measures are empirically and morally dubious for promoting the public health; it is not clear that any will have much effect on reducing HIV transmission, and they discriminate unfairly against those infected and at risk. In effect, they serve to punish the stigmatized rather than to address real concerns of public health.

Closing the Bathhouses   Consider for example the controversial case of closing gay bathhouses in San Francisco or New York. Three lines of argument were offered by public health officials in the mid-1980s to support such closings: The Paternalistic Argument—that the bathhouses enable people seriously to harm themselves; the Moral Offense Argument—that the bathhouses promote activities inimical to moral sentiment; and the Harms to Others Argument—that the bathhouses threaten human well-being. First, paternalism requires strong reasons for restricting people from engaging in freely chosen activities. If the risk of known HIV infection suffices, then so perhaps must the more direct risks of death and injury from physical contact sports like boxing and football or of long-term health problems from use of tobacco and alcohol products. If there are ways of diminishing risks of HIV infection without invading people's rights to choose freely and knowingly the practices they consider best to promote their own well-being, then it seems morally reasonable to insist they be chosen over more invasive measures. Second, legal moralism seeks to enforce a particular moral view as universal. It thus imposes upon people a conception of morality, or of the good life, that they may reject. (If a society moves to restrict lifestyles on the basis of offense, what is to prevent it restricting yours?) In a society committed to diversity of lifestyles and values, moral offense must be regarded as especially incapable of furnishing grounds for restricting the activities of its members. Third, harm to others is the strongest reason for restricting a practice. Gay bathhouses, however, seem not to threaten the health of those who choose not to frequent them, or more particularly of those who do not voluntarily seek out multiple sexual encounters upon visiting them. In any case, there seem to be more direct and less discriminatory means of addressing the question of HIV transmission such as, in the case of gay sexual practices, explicit education about safe sex practices.

This raises more general questions concerning the ethical permissibility of a range of possible responses to AIDS: of voluntary, nonvoluntary, or involuntary testing; of providing clean syringes and needles to drug addicts; of sex education concerning HIV transmission at public schools; of handing out free condoms to sexually active teenagers; of a publicly funded safe sex advertizing campaign; and of notifying the partner of a person testing seropositive, with or without the latter's permission. Again, the moral permissibility of the practices involved in each case will turn on balancing normative and empirical considerations in the potential conflicts between the public health mandate and the social commitment to equal individual rights, and between concerns of care and responsibility (for more on care and responsibility, see Chapter 7).

■ **STATE SUPREME COURT RULING: ST. MARK'S BATHS**

In 1986, the New York State Supreme Court considered arguments concerning the closing of bathhouses in New York's Greenwich Village. The public health authorities of New York City, acting on a newly passed city ordinance, had moved to close gay bathhouses in the city as a precaution against the spread of AIDS. The proprietors of the St. Mark's Baths, joined by some of its individual patrons, sought to restrict this action. City health authorities submitted documentation of repeated high-risk sexual activity at the particular bathhouse. Justice Wallach argued for the Court that this evidence, along with the conditions then known to facilitate transmission of HIV, amounted to the city demonstrating a compelling state interest to protect the health of its citizens (even though he admitted some merit to the counterpoint that an alternative like the required use of prophylactic sheaths might just as well reduce the spread of HIV). Justice Wallach further argued that patrons' individual privacy and associational rights would not be violated as these constitutional protections apply only to activities engaged in the privacy of a home and do not extend to commercial ventures.

Justice Richard W. Wallach

THE CITY OF NEW YORK, ET AL., PLAINTIFFS, v. THE NEW ST. MARK'S BATHS, ET AL., DEFENDANTS

THE AIDS HEALTH EMERGENCY

. . . This action by the health authorities of the City of New York is taken against defendant The New St. Mark's Baths ("St. Mark's") as a step to limit the spread of the disease known as AIDS (Acquired Immune Deficiency Syndrome). The parties are in agreement with respect to the deadly character of this disease and the dire threat that its spread, now in epidemic proportions, pose to the health and well-being of the community. . . . [E]ffective treatment is wholly lacking, and approximately 50% of all persons diagnosed with AIDS have died. The death rate for this disease increases to nearly 85% two years after diagnosis. The same percentage of AIDS patients suffer from special forms of pneumonia or cancer which are untreatable, and about 30% of these patients show symptoms of brain disease or severe damage to the spinal cord.

Immediately relevant to this litigation are the scientific facts with respect to AIDS risk groups. During the five years in which the disease has been identified and studied 73% of AIDS victims have consisted of sexually active homosexual and

New York State Supreme Court, Special Term, Part I, January 6, 1986.

bi-sexual men with multiple partners. AIDS is not easily transmittable through air, water or food. Direct blood-to-blood or semen-to-blood contact is necessary to transmit the virus. Cases of AIDS among homosexuals and bi-sexual males are associated with promiscuous sexual contact, anal intercourse and other sexual practices which may result in semen-to-blood or blood-to-blood contact.

According to medical evidence submitted by defendants . . . : "The riskiest conduct is thought to be that which allows the introduction of semen into the bloodstream. Because anal intercourse may result in a tearing of internal tissues, that activity is considered high-risk for transmission." Fellatio is also a high-risk activity. . . .

PRIOR PROCEEDINGS

On October 25, 1985, the State Public Health Council, with the approval of the intervening New York State Commissioner of Health, adopted an emergency resolution adding a new regulation to the State Sanitary Code. . . .

> Prohibited Facilities: No establishment shall make facilities available for the purpose of sexual activities in which facilities high-risk sexual activity takes place. Such facilities shall constitute a public nuisance dangerous to the public health. . . .
> a. "Establishment" shall mean any place in which entry, membership, goods or services are purchased.
> b. "High Risk Sexual Activity" shall mean anal intercourse and fellatio.

The Public Health Council based this regulation on the Commissioner's "findings" that:

> Establishments including certain bars, clubs and bathhouses which are used as places for engaging in high risk sexual activities contribute to the propagation and spread of such AIDS-associated retro-viruses;

* * *

> Appropriate public health intervention to discontinue such exposure at such establishments is essential to interrupting the epidemic among the people of the State of New York.

Thereafter, on or about December 9, 1985, the City commenced this action by order to show cause for an injunction closing the New St. Mark's Baths (St. Mark's) as a public nuisance citing the health risks at St. Mark's as defined in the state regulation. . . .

CONSTITUTIONAL CONSIDERATIONS

The City has submitted ample supporting proof that high risk sexual activity has been taking place at St. Mark's on a continuous and regular basis. Following numerous on site visits by City inspectors, over 14 separate days, these investigators have submitted affidavits describing 49 acts of high risk sexual activity (consisting of 41 acts of fellatio involving 70 persons and 8 acts of anal intercourse involving 16 persons). This evidence of high risk sexual activity, all occurring either in public areas of St. Mark's or in enclosed cubicles left visible to the observer without intrusion therein, demonstrates the inadequacy of self-regulatory procedures by the St. Mark's attendant staff, and the futility of any less intrusive solution to the problem other than closure.

[1] With a demonstrated death rate from AIDS during the first six months of 1985 of 1,248 . . . , plaintiffs and the intervening State officers have demonstrated a compelling state interest in acting to preserve the health of the population. . . . Where such a compelling state interest is demonstrated even the constitutional rights of privacy and free association must give way provided, as here, it is also shown that the remedy adopted is the least intrusive reasonably available.

[2] Furthermore, it is by no means clear that defendants' rights will, in actuality, be adversely affected in a constitutionally recognized sense of closure of St. Mark's. The privacy protection of sexual activity conducted in a private home . . . does not extend to commercial establishments simply because they provide an opportunity for intimate behavior or sexual release. . . . ". . . [P]rivacy and freedom of association . . . rights do not extend to commercial ventures." . . .

[3] . . . To be sure, defendants and the intervening patrons challenge the soundness of the scientific judgments upon which the Health Council regulations is based, citing *inter alia* the observation of the City's former Commissioner of Health in a memorandum dated October 22, 1985 that "closure of bathhouses will contribute little if anything to the control of AIDS." . . . Defendants particularly assail the regulation's inclusion of fellatio as a high risk sexual activity, and argue that enforced use of prophylactic sheaths would be a more appropriate regulatory response. They go further and argue that facilities such as St. Mark's, which attempts to educate its patrons with written materials, signed pledges, and posted notices as to the advisability of safe sexual practices, provide a positive force in combatting AIDS, and a valuable communication link between public health authorities and the homosexual community. While these arguments and proposals may have varying degrees of merit, they overlook a fundamental principle of applicable law: "It is not for the courts to determine which scientific view is correct in ruling upon whether the police power has been properly exercised. 'The judicial function is exhausted with the discovery that the relation between means and end is not wholly vain and fanciful, an illusory pretense . . .' Justification for plaintiffs' application here more than meets that test. . . .

[4] . . . Accordingly defendants' motion to dismiss the complaint is in all respects denied. . . ."

■ U.S. BISHOPS: COMPASSION AND RESPONSIBILITY

In their second major statement on the HIV/AIDS crisis, "A Call to Compassion and Responsibility," the U.S. Catholic Conference of Bishops issues a call in response to those suffering from HIV/AIDS to compassion, integrity, responsibility, and to social justice. Compassion they define in terms of the experience of intimate involvement and participation in another person's life. It accordingly involves working to alleviate the misery and suffering of others even at considerable cost to oneself. Those with AIDS, urge the bishops, should be embraced as members and extended the virtues and benefits of community. This presupposes recognizing the integrity and inherent dignity in each human being, and it entails that we respect our own bodies and those of others. This respect, it is argued, is best lived out in terms of chastity, for in this way the lust to possess and dominate the bodies of others, and the attendant alienation and personal and social disintegration, are purportedly best avoided. Chastity, in short, is taken to represent the life of sexual responsibility. For those for whom the vows of chastity are too onerous, sexual intercourse should be encouraged—the bishops emphasize—only in the mature and exclusive relation of a committed heterosexual marriage. Thus, one of the responses the bishops suggest to the crisis of AIDS is a transformation in contemporary sexual culture, re-emphasizing monogamous relations and sexual intercourse only within the content of long-term, loving marriages.

On the question of homosexuality, the bishops reiterate the Catholic Church's condemnation of homosexual activity as intrinsically wrong. While "homosexual inclination" (as opposed to activity) is considered not to be inherently sinful, "heterosexual orientation," because mandated by the *Natural Law* ordained by God, is deemed normative. Nevertheless, while urging them to foster "chaste, stable relationships" the bishops reaffirm the humanity of homosexual persons, extending homosexuals the dignity and protection from violence and suffering properly accorded all human beings. While stressing the need to educate the general public regarding HIV transmission, the bishops are critical of any "safe sex" educational programs. They argue that such programs promote promiscuity, and that—given the failure rate of prophylaxis—they offer a false sense of security from HIV. Similarly, the bishops urge care and compassion for drug addicts, advocating education and treatment programs over needle distribution.

Thus, as a matter of social justice and consistent with their stress on the inherent dignity of human beings, the Bishops urge a range of social, institutional, and personal responses to the crisis concerning HIV/AIDS: continued care and research for a vaccine and cure; vigorous educational programs coupled with *voluntary* testing; promoting the civil rights—including privacy and qualified confidentiality rights—of those infected with HIV, extending AIDS patients entitlements due handicapped persons, and resisting the social discrimination those with AIDS continue to suffer; and continued support for those furnishing care, professionally and personally, to persons with HIV.

U.S. Catholic Conference of Bishops

CALLED TO COMPASSION AND RESPONSIBILITY: A RESPONSE TO THE HIV/AIDS CRISIS

THE INTENT OF THIS DOCUMENT

. . . In . . . this document we issue [the following] calls: to compassion, to integrity, to responsibility, to social justice. . . .

I. A CALL TO COMPASSION

1. COMPASSION AND HUMAN DIGNITY

Compassion is much more than sympathy. It involves an experience of intimacy by which one participates in another's life. The Latin word *misericordia* expresses the basic idea: for those in misery. This is not simply the desire to be kind. The truly compassionate individual works at his or her own cost for the others' real good, helping to rescue them from danger as well as alleviate their suffering.

2. THE MINISTRY OF JESUS

We learn compassion's meaning from the model of Jesus. His ministry contains many examples. He gives sight to the blind . . . and makes the crippled walk . . . ; he touches and heals lepers . . . ; he shares a meal with people considered legally impure . . . ; he shames the judges of the adulterous woman and forgives her sin. . . . With compassion, Jesus breaks through the barriers of sickness and sinfulness in order to encounter and heal the afflicted. . . .

3. THE GOOD SAMARITAN

The story of the good Samaritan presents the call to compassion in concrete terms (Lk. 10:30–37). Pope John Paul graphically demonstrated its meaning when in 1987 he embraced a young boy with AIDS at Mission Dolores Basilica in San Francisco. This was a way of saying that in each case AIDS has a human face, a unique personal history. The Holy Father verbalized that message on Christmas Day 1988, in his *Urbi et Orbi* blessing. "I think of them all, and to all of them I say, 'Do not lose hope.'" And he added that those with AIDS are "called to face the challenge not only of their sickness, but also the mistrust of a fearful society that instinctively turns away from them." On May 4, 1989, he returned to this subject, declaring in a homily in Lusaka that the church "proclaims a message of hope to those of you who suffer . . . to the sick and dying, especially those with AIDS and those who lack medical care."

In his apostolic letter on "The Christian Meaning of Human Suffering" (1984), Pope John Paul calls each of us to imitate the good Samaritan: "Man owes to suffering that unselfish love which stirs in his heart and actions. The person who is a 'neighbor' cannot indifferently pass by the suffering of another." . . .

Persons with AIDS are not distant, unfamiliar people, the objects of our mingled pity and aversion. We must keep them present to our consciousness as individuals and a community, and embrace them with unconditional love. The Gospel demands reverence for life in all circumstances. Compassion—love—toward persons infected with HIV is the only authentic Gospel response.

II. A CALL TO INTEGRITY

1. THE DIGNITY OF THE HUMAN PERSON

In his 1980 encyclical "Rich in Mercy," Pope John Paul says that compassion and mercy are rooted in the recognition of human dignity and integrity. Authentic compassion and mercy calls us to "a whole lifestyle (which) consists in the constant discovery and persevering practice of love as a unifying and also elevating power despite all difficulties of a psychological or social nature" . . .

All human beings are created in God's image and are called to the same end, namely, eternal life in communion with God and one another. For this reason, the greatest commandment is to love the Lord with all one's heart and soul and mind; and the second is like the first: to love one's neighbor as oneself. For people growing daily more mutually dependent and a world in which interdependence is increasing, this is a truth of paramount importance since it provides a transcendent rationale for the pursuit of good human relationships.

2. HUMAN INTEGRITY

God is love. . . . This means that the inner reality of God is a mystery of relationship. But God has created humankind to share in his divine life. . . . The basic goodness of humanity is confirmed in Genesis 1:31: "God looked at everything he had made, and he found it very good."

Pope Paul VI in his encyclical *Humanae Vitae* (1968) underscored the importance of the "total vision of man" (No. 7). Yet today this "total vision" is often dismissed or ignored in favor of particular elements or aspects of personhood and limited ideas of human fulfillment.

Fundamentally, we are called to realize the basic goodness of our personhood as God has created it. This is not a prerogative or an obligation only for Christians. Everyone, whether believer or non-believer, is obliged to honor the integrity of the human person by respecting himself or herself along with all other persons.

The meaning of sexuality and personhood can only be fully discerned within this framework of human integrity. In God's plan as it existed at the beginning (Gn. 1:1, 17) we find the true meaning of our bodies: We see that in the mystery of creation man and woman are made to be a gift to each other and for each other. By their very existence as male and female, by the complementarity of their sexuality and by the responsible exercise of their freedom, man and woman mirror the divine image implanted in them by God.

The church makes an invaluable contribution to society by pointing out that the full meaning of human integrity is found within the context of redemption and its call in Christ to "live in newness of life" (Rom. 6:4). St. Paul reminds us that redemption means, among other things, that we must "respect" our own bodies and the bodies of others, and must live always "in holiness and honor." By self-respect and mutual respect we observe God's original plan.

Originally, God endowed our bodies with a harmony which St. Paul speaks of as "mutual care of the members for one another." It corresponds to that authentic "purity of heart" by which man and woman "in the beginning" were able to unite as a community of persons. Now, by redeeming us, Jesus graces us with a new dignity: the Holy Spirit dwelling within us. We are called to live as temples of the Spirit.

All this requires that we understand ourselves and live not just naturalistically, as it were—as bundles of bodily drives and instincts—but in a manner which respects the integrity of our personhood, including its spiritual dimension. Through the grace of the Spirit, that can be done.

3. THE CHALLENGE OF CHASTITY

Human integrity requires the practice of authentic chastity. Chastity is understood as the virtue by which one integrates one's sexuality according to the moral demands of one's state in life. It presupposes both self-control and openness to life and interpersonal love which goes beyond the mere desire for physical pleasure. In particular, desire for union with another must not degenerate into a craving to possess and dominate. Chastity calls us to affirm and respect the value of the person in every situation.

While chastity has special meaning for Christians, it is not a value only for them. All men and women are meant to live authentically integral human lives. Chastity is an expression of this moral goodness in the sexual sphere. It is also a source of that spiritual energy by which, overcoming selfishness and aggressiveness, we are able to act lovingly under the pressure of sexual emotion. Chastity makes a basic contribution to an authentic appreciation of human dignity.

4. OBSTACLES TO INTEGRITY AND CHASTITY

Many factors militate against the practice of chastity today. Our culture tends to tolerate and even foster the exploitation of the human person. People are pressured to seek power and domination, especially over other persons, or else to escape into self-gratification. Television, movies and popular music spread the message that "everybody's doing it."

One can scarcely exaggerate the impact this has. Casual sexual encounters and temporary relationships are treated on a par with permanent commitment in marriage. It is taken for granted that fidelity and permanence are not to be expected and may even be undesirable. Sin is made easy because the reality of sinfulness is denied.

What is sin? It is an act motivated by the deliberate refusal to live according to God's plan. It is a disruption, more or less serious, of the order which should prevail in our relationships with God and with one another. It is the root cause of alienation and disintegration in individual and social life. It is a practical denial of God's presence in oneself and one's neighbor.

5. THE CHALLENGE AND CALL TO YOUTH

A. Hope of the Future   The obstacles to human integrity of which we speak are especially daunting today for young people. Yet the church sees in the young the hope of the future. . . .

That underlies how necessary it is that the rest of us help young people live chaste and responsible lives. Youth should be a time of idealism. And most young people do wish to do what is right. They want to be responsible, and they are capable of understanding that authentic integrity, while demanding much of them, offers them rich rewards in individual and communal fulfillment. Adults for their part must actively support young people, not stand by idly while media and other social influences inundate them with amoral and immoral messages.

Integrity and chastity are virtues which with God's grace can be realized by all people of good will, by people of any religion and indeed of no religion. But their realization not only presupposes a creation that is good—it presupposes a willingness on society's part to create and sustain a social environment in which individuals truly can know and choose what is right.

Perhaps the most important thing which adults can do in this regard is themselves to be models of upright living. Young people are bewildered by the contradiction between adult preachments about the dangers of drugs and alcohol and adult reliance on the same substances; by adult messages on the theme of sexual responsibility and adult models of extreme irresponsibility in the sexual sphere. This sort of double standard has a debilitating impact on the young.

B. Youth, Sexuality and Marriage   The sexual dimension of a person is ordered to establishing and maintaining honest, committed personal relationships. The Holy See's "Declaration on Certain Questions Concerning Sexual Ethics" affirms that sexuality is not only "one of the principal formative elements in the life of a man or woman" but "the source of the biological, psychological and spiritual characteristics which . . . considerably influence each individual's progress toward maturity and membership in society" (No. 1).

Sexual intercourse is an expression of maturity achieved within the committed relationship of marriage. Adolescents who engage in sexual intercourse are sometimes misled into believing that they have already arrived at maturity; indeed, many are pressured to have sexual intercourse precisely as a sign that they have reached adulthood. Not only is this a great temptation for them, it fails the test of human integrity.

Sexual intercourse is meant to be both exclusive and committed, and it has these characteristics only in marriage. It should never be regarded as a form of conquest or as a means of paying for attentions. One of the great evils of casual sexual intercourse is that, more often than not, the relationship is exploitative for one or both of the parties.

Nor does sex before marriage really shed light on whether a potential partner is, for example, trustworthy, even-tempered, capable of loving and being loved, caring, affectionate, industrious, considerate, faithful, sensitive, stable, disciplined. It takes time and a variety of different friendships to find a suitable marriage partner. During adolescence, young people should be developing attachments and testing them through companionship. In this process, sexual intercourse is not a research tool for ascertaining compatibility. Rather, it is meant for marriage, to express and complete a compatibility whose existence has already been established by more reliable means.

Sexual intimacy is thus a sign of a special kind of relationship which has two inseparable aspects: It is unitive (the persons give themselves unreservedly to each other, take permanent and public responsibility for each other, accept the risk of a shared life); and it is procreative (that is, fundamentally related to begetting, bearing and raising children).

Sexual intercourse is the expression of this special marital relationship. Only in the context of this relationship do genital sex acts have full human meaning. It is marriage which gives intercourse its true meaning.

Once a man and woman are married, they begin a journey which is uniquely theirs. Sexual intercourse forms part of the background against which they grow in love and knowledge of each other. The words of Pope John Paul in *Familiaris Consortio* are of great importance: "To bear witness to the inestimable value of the indissolubility and fidelity of marriage is one of the most precious and most urgent tasks of Christian couples in our time" (No. 20). Important too is what he said to young people in 1987 at the Louisiana Superdome:

"Jesus and his church hold up . . . God's plan for human love, telling you that sex is a great gift of God that is reserved for marriage. At this point, the voices of the world will try to deceive you with powerful slogans, claiming that you are 'unrealistic,' 'out of it,' 'backward,' even 'reactionary.' But the message of Jesus is clear. 'Purity means true love and it is the total opposite of selfishness and escape.'"

C. Youth and HIV National studies on contraception and teen-age pregnancy suggest that young people are not particularly knowledgeable or skillful in dealing with their sexual lives. Moreover, teen-age pregnancy is very often related to socio-economic problems. The experience of poverty is frequently accompanied by fatalism, deprivation and boredom, while pregnancy holds out the promise of status and a sense of self-worth. These circumstances have at least two implications for the transmission of HIV. First, there is a large group of heterosexually active but relatively immature young people; second, there is little understanding of how to encourage change in their behavior patterns once these are already well established.

This, however, is scarcely a problem only for the poor. Today sexual intercourse seems to be an element in the experience of a majority of young people in our country. For some, apparently, it is no longer linked to marriage or even to permanent relationships. Yet at the same time many young men and women feel profound anxiety in their struggles to establish sexual identity and fit sexuality into their lives. This underscores how critically important it is that the moral and religious values we have sketched in speaking of integrity and sexuality be properly taught to the young.

Education in human sexuality which tells young people in effect that abstinence and "safe sex" are equally acceptable options sends a contradictory, confusing message. Nor should education in sexuality be reduced to mere biological facts and processes, unrelated to their ethical significance.

We repeat: Young people need to know the human and religious meanings of personal integrity and chastity. Chastity requires treating the gift of human sexuality with reverence. Chastity is both a human attitude and a spiritual gift which helps overcome selfishness and aggressiveness. It empowers people to act lovingly while avoiding destructive relationships which are superficial and trivializing.

. . . In the name of self-giving love, we too must accept the discipline of sacrifice so to achieve true happiness and fulfillment for ourselves and others. Casual and permissive sex does not prepare people for faithfulness in marriage or help them appreciate the sanctity and dignity of the human person.

III. A CALL TO RESPONSIBILITY

1. AIDS AND HOMOSEXUALITY

It is a matter of grave concern that, while many homosexual persons may be making changes in specific sexual practices in response to HIV/AIDS, fewer may be choosing to live chaste lives. This further underlines the critical importance of the church's teaching on homosexuality.

In 1975 the Congregation for the Doctrine of the Faith presented this teaching in its "Declaration on Certain Questions Concerning Sexual Ethics." The document reiterates the church's constant teaching regarding the intrinsic immorality of homosexual activity, while recognizing that not every homosexual is "personally responsible" for his or her homosexual orientation.

The teaching was further clarified in 1986 in the congregation's "Letter to the Bishops of the Catholic Church on the Pastoral Care of Homosexual Persons." It affirms the church's view that heterosexuality is normative. While homosexual inclination in itself is not a sin, neither is homosexual activity "a morally acceptable option." This conclusion rests on the vision in Genesis of the God-given complementarity of male and female and the responsibility for the transmission of human life.

HIV and AIDS have had a terrible impact on the homosexual community. The report of the presidential commission says, for example, that "violence against those perceived to carry HIV . . . is a serious problem. The commission has heard reports in which homosexual men in particular have been victims of random violent acts that are indicative of some persons in society who are not reacting rationally to the epidemic. This type of violence is unacceptable and should be condemned by all Americans" (9–103). We emphatically condemn such violence. It is entirely contrary to Gospel values.

The church holds that all people, regardless of their sexual orientation, are created in God's image and possess a human dignity which must be respected and protected. Thus we affirmed in "To Live in Christ Jesus" (1976): "The Christian community should provide them (homosexual persons) with a special degree of pastoral understanding and care" (No. 9). Specific guidelines regarding such pastoral support are found in our 1973 document "Principles to Guide Confessors in Questions of Homosexuality." It envisages a pastoral approach which urges homosexual persons to form chaste, stable relationships.

2. AIDS AND SUBSTANCE ABUSE

. . . [H]owever, HIV/AIDS is by no means exclusively a homosexual problem. Intravenous drug use also plays a large role in the spread of HIV. Nearly 70 percent of the reported cases of heterosexually acquired AIDS in the United States have been associated with IV drug use; almost 75 percent of pediatric AIDS cases have been diagnosed in cities with high seroprevalence rates among IV drug users. These data, combined with the potential for the rapid spread of HIV infection among IV drug users through needle sharing, define a problem whose solution requires both immediate action and long-term research.

Drugs and HIV are linked in several ways.

1. Direct transmission of HIV occurs through the sharing of hypodermic needles, syringes and paraphernalia used in "shooting up" drugs.
2. Sexual transmission occurs from infected IV drug users to their sexual partners.
3. Perinatal transmission occurs when women are IV drug users or the sexual partners of drug users become infected and transmit the virus to their infants during pregnancy, delivery or breast-feeding.

One must also recognize the fact of increased sexual risk and needle-using behavior on the part of persons under the influence of drugs or alcohol. Even with good intentions, abusers may not live up to promises they have made to themselves and others. Those at risk because of their use of alcohol and drugs are called to change their behavior. They merit our special attention and need to be embraced in light of their double burden of illness and addiction.

In evaluating the moral issue here, it is important to see substance abuse as an actual or potential disease for some persons—a disease, however, for which there are treatment and hope. It should not be supposed that a confirmed substance abuser can simply stop, and this assumption—that the addict would stop if he or she really wanted to—can easily become a rationale for not aggressively encouraging treatment. Often drug or alcohol abuse points to an underlying emotional illness of which it is a symptom rather than the cause. We believe those who suffer from substance abuse should be referred to appropriate treatment programs and should also receive necessary mental health counseling.

While drug abuse is a chronic, progressive, life-threatening disease, addicts can be freed from this form of enslavement. Participation in a treatment program is an interim step which allows substance abusers to receive comprehensive psychological help and counseling on how to avoid HIV.

As that suggests, drug dependency treatment should always be accompanied by education and counseling about the risk of infection and how to avoid it. Education for intravenous drug users who reject treatment should focus on the risk of repeated exposure to HIV and on the availability of help in conquering their addiction.

In this whole area, education and treatment are of paramount importance. Specific programs suited to particular groups are needed. Persons who have not begun intravenous drug use but are at risk of doing so may be reached through programs in elementary and high schools; those who do not attend school may be reached through health clinics and clinics for sexually transmitted disease, neighborhood and religious groups, day-care centers, employers, job-training programs and street outreach projects; in areas with high rates of drug use, health departments can open storefront AIDS education centers and use mobile vans, with staffing by professionals and "street-smart" personnel.

Education and treatment aimed at changing behavior are the best way to control the spread of HIV among intravenous drug users and to prevent passage of the virus to their sexual partners and to children in the womb. Although some argue that distribution of sterile needles should be promoted, we question this approach for both moral and practical reasons:

— More drug use might result while fewer intravenous drug users might seek treatment.

— Poor monitoring could lead to the increased spread HIV infection through the use of contaminated needles.

— Distribution of sterile needles and syringes would send the message that intravenous drug use can be made safe. But IV drug users mutilate and destroy their veins, introduce infection through contaminated skin, inject substances which often contain lethal impurities and risk death from overdoses.

A better approach to the drug epidemic would be increased government support for outreach and drug treatment programs.

3. AIDS AND THE USE OF PROPHYLACTICS

The "safe-sex" approach to preventing HIV/AIDS, though frequently advocated, compromises human sexuality and can lead to promiscuous sexual behavior. We regard this as one of those "quick-fixes" which the report of the presidential commission says foster "a false sense of security and actually lead to a greater spread of the disease."

Sexual intercourse is appropriate and morally good only when, in the context of heterosexual marriage, it is a celebration of faithful love and is open to new life. The use of prophylactics to prevent the spread of HIV is technically unreliable. Moreover, advocating this approach means in effect promoting behavior which is morally unacceptable. Campaigns advocating "safe/safer" sex rest on false assumptions about sexuality and intercourse. Plainly they do nothing to correct the mistaken notion that non-marital sexual intercourse has the same value and validity as sexual intercourse within marriage.

We fault these programs for another reason as well. Recognizing that casual sex is a threat to health, they consistently advise the use of condoms in order to reduce the danger. This is poor and inadequate advice, given the failure rate of prophylactics and the high risk that an infected person who relies on them will eventually transmit the infection in this way. It is not condom use which is the solution to this health problem, but appropriate attitudes and corresponding behavior regarding human sexuality, integrity and dignity.

By contrast, there is an urgent need for education campaigns in the media, in schools and in the home which foster a variety of human sexuality that is sound from every point of view. At the same time we are conscious of the powerful relationship between economics—the profit motive—and the promotion of contraceptives, pornography and the marketing of sex in entertainment. This fact should be taken into account in our education efforts.

IV. A CALL TO SOCIAL JUSTICE

1. CONTINUED RESEARCH AND CARE

We urge continued scientific and medical research aimed at finding a cure for HIV as well as treating persons with AIDS. Government agencies should draw up clear educational guidelines on the use and effectiveness of new and emerging drugs (e.g., AZT, azidathymidine). Similarly government and private agencies should provide the public with information about new methods and drugs.

Social justice also requires that public and private agencies seek creative ways to meet the health and human service needs of those who are HIV positive. To date, acute general hospitals have borne the primary burden of caring for this population. It is imperative that a continuum of care be developed which allows for the integration of all necessary services within a given community: nutritional services, home health care, ambulatory care, transportation, hospital services, extended and/or skilled nursing care and hospice services.

Such a system of care will assure the appropriate placement within the continuum of care persons who are HIV positive or who have AIDS and will avoid placing an unnecessary and inappropriate burden on any given sector of the provider community. All health and human services for persons who are HIV positive or who have AIDS should be delivered in a sensitive and nondiscriminatory manner. At the same time, we also recognize the right of surgeons and other medical personnel to adequate protection against HIV.

The health and human services described should be available to all who suffer from the disease, including those without the resources to pay.

2. ROUTINE VOLUNTARY
TESTING AND EDUCATIONAL PROGRAMS

Broadly based, routine voluntary testing and educational programs are needed as a matter of public policy. These voluntary programs should always guarantee anonymity and should be preceded and followed by necessary counseling for individuals diagnosed as HIV positive or negative. Counseling should supply information about the disease, the moral aspects involved, immediate emotional support and information about resources for continuing emotional and spiritual support. It should also underscore, sensitively but forthrightly, the grave moral responsibility of individuals with HIV to inform others who are at risk because of their condition.

3. IMMIGRANTS AND REFUGEES

There are special programs associated with HIV testing for immigrants and refugees: For example, false positive test results from other countries may have the effect of excluding people from the United States. In addition, permanent resident aliens may be unjustly deported before their circumstances can be adequately examined. A more flexible and humane government policy seems necessary.

4. THE PERSON WITH AIDS
AS A HANDICAPPED OR DISABLED PERSON

A growing body of legislation considers the individual with HIV a handicapped or disabled person. In 1978, in a statement on the handicapped, we said: "Defense of the right to life . . . implies the defense of other rights which enable the handicapped individual to achieve the fullest measure of personal development of which he or she is capable" (Pastoral Statement of the U.S. Catholic Bishops on Handicapped People, Nov. 15, 1978, No. 10).

Pope John Paul has recently spoken to this same point, defending the inalienable dignity of all human persons and the need especially to protect those "who are vulnerable and most helpless: This is the task which the Catholic Church, in the name of Christ, cannot and will not forsake."

Discrimination against those suffering from HIV or AIDS is a deprivation of their civil liberties. The church must be an advocate in this area, while also promulgating its own nondiscrimination policies in employment, housing, delivery of medical and dental care, access to public accommodations, schools, nursing homes and emergency services.

5. THOSE WHO CARE FOR PERSONS WITH HIV

The provision of HIV/AIDS services involves some unusual problems. One of these is stress on staff. Many feel a growing and eventually intolerable sense of helplessness as they watch patients, mostly young people, die. In providing services, it is important to take into account how long a particular individual can remain on the front line, as it were, and to provide support systems which help these dedicated people deal with their own grief and anger. We also urge all health facilities to develop practical guidelines to protect physicians, nurses, paramedics and all other healthcare workers against contracting HIV, and to provide adequate training and supplies for infection control.

Similar guidelines should be developed for the protection of law-enforcement and corrections personnel and others in public service who may be at risk.

Dioceses should also develop guidelines not only for preventing infection, but also for respite and counseling of health-care professionals, volunteers and pastoral workers and for family and loved ones who care for HIV-infected persons.

While some have allowed their disapproval of the actions of certain persons with AIDS to interfere with the provision of care to these persons, the report of the presidential commission points out that this is a "minority view" (Section VII). Generally speaking, health-care workers tirelessly provide quality care to HIV sufferers with compassion and sensitivity. We applaud and thank them, and we encourage all health professionals to rise to the same high level of care and beneficence.

6. FAMILIES OF PERSONS WITH AIDS

The consequences of whether a person with HIV/AIDS lives hopefully or dies in despair are borne not only by that individual, but by his or her entire family. An HIV or AIDS diagnosis may mark the first time the family has had to confront a loved one's drug problem or homosexuality. This sharp encounter with a difficult reality can lead to anger, guilt, sorrow and even rejection on the part of family members; it can even drive a family into a kind of collective isolation. Families should recognize that Jesus has set for all of us an example of loving kindness to all persons and that he now calls us to reconciliation with those from whom we have been estranged.

Catholic communities, especially parishes, should reach out to these families with understanding and practical help—for example, by providing respite time from caring for their sick members. Acceptance and emotional and spiritual support are crucial needs.

Families of HIV patients badly need to talk about what they are experiencing. Although family members usually are ambivalent about disclosing the nature of their relative's disease to outsiders, it is important for them to communicate. The Catholic community should create networks of people prepared to assist such families in this way.

7. THE PUBLIC GOOD AND CONFIDENTIALITY

A. Non-Discrimination and Individual Privacy   Our understanding of the common good expresses our vision as a people of the kind of society we want this to be. The common good is, therefore, central to the evaluation of legislative and public policy proposals. Two objectives are fundamental to any adequate understanding of the common good: first, preserving and protecting human dignity while guaranteeing the rights of all; second, caring for all who need help and cannot help themselves.

The appropriate goals of AIDS-related legislation include helping to prevent the transmission of HIV, providing adequate medical care and protecting civil rights, that is, non-discrimination in employment, schooling, entertainment, business opportunities, housing and medical care, along with the protection of privacy.

Dioceses and church-related institutions should also pursue these objectives in appropriate ways through their own policies and practices. Their hiring decisions, for example, should not be based on the fact that particular job applicants are HIV-infected, but on other factors such as qualifications, ability to do the work and moral character.

Individual privacy and liberty are highly valued in our society. Liberty, however, carries with it the obligation not to harm or interfere with others. If HIV-infected persons have rights which others must respect, they also must fulfill their fundamental ethical responsibility to avoid doing harm to others. As the report of the presidential commission says, this is "an affirmation of the rights of others" (9–99).

B. Rights of the Human Person   Framing and implementing public policy frequently requires the balancing of individual and community rights and interests. With respect to HIV/AIDS, it is important to infringe as little as possible, in light of community needs, on individual liberty, privacy and confidentiality. Other quite specific conditions must also be met. For example, respect for persons requires informing people that they are being tested when donating blood; they also have a right to be informed of test results; and both pre- and post-testing counseling should be available.

Although specific exceptions might be made, universal mandatory testing does not seem justified at this time.

C. Disclosure and Confidentiality: General Guidelines   While the presumption should always favor confidentiality, there may be circumstances that warrant disclosure. In deciding for disclosure or confidentiality in a particular case, the following points are relevant.

1. The two main factors in favor of disclosure are (a) the need to prevent the infection of others and (b) the need to provide medical care to the person who is HIV positive or has AIDS. If disclosure in a particular case will reduce the danger of infection to others or increase the ability to treat the individual effectively, it may be the right course of action if no other effective action is possible.

2. Of primary importance in weighing the individual's interest in and right to confidentiality are (a) the ability to confine the disclosure to those who have the right to know, (b) the likelihood that recipients of the information will use it for proper purposes, and (c) the obligation to maintain patient confidentiality. . . .

■ PATRICIA ILLINGWORTH: AIDS AND SOCIAL RESPONSIBILITY

Patricia Illingworth examines the tensions between understanding AIDS as a harm that is self-inflicted and one that is not self-inflicted because those primarily afflicted—gay men and IV drug users—do not act autonomously. If, in engaging in gay sexual practices or shooting up, persons are not acting autonomously, their actions are not free, and they cannot be held (fully) responsible for the outcomes. To assess whether the threat of AIDS justifies the state in interfering with individual liberty to engage in gay sexual practices or intravenous drug abuse, Illingworth distinguishes between the "strong" and "weak" versions of the Harm Principle (for other discussions of the Harm Principle, see Mill, Chapter 4, and Censorship and Hate Speech, Chapter 10). The Strong Harm Principle claims that the rightness or wrongness of interfering in a person's freely chosen actions depends on whether an act harms others. The Weak Harm Principle claims that the rightness or wrongness of interfering in a person's freely chosen actions depends on whether an act harms oneself. The latter would justify paternalistic intervention in ways the former would not. In particular, if the harm to self follows from non-autonomous actions or determinations, the Weak Harm Principle would justify state interference to reinstate autonomy. Illingworth criticizes the Weak Harm Principle for too readily justifying paternalistic intervention. She argues that autonomy develops and is cultivated not only through autonomous choices, but through contrasting these with the experience of nonautonomous experiences. In this sense, people cannot be forced to be autonomous, but need to be given the chance of developing and refining their own authentic autonomy through experience and experiment.

Illingworth further argues that in the cultures of gay sex and IV drug use, those activities most readily related to the causal production of HIV are not performed autonomously. This fact does not license intervention on either of the Harm Principles, for the autonomy of gay men and IV drug users is diminished by social factors. They have had options open to them narrowed by their social circumstances. The stigma generally attached to their social circumstances often provokes a loss of self-esteem, which is essential for successfully pursuing one's life plan. It follows that gay men and IV drug users do not enjoy equal opportunity to cultivate their conceptions of the good life. Where society is instrumental in blocking such cultivation—via discriminatory laws, regulations, and intolerance, it wrongs the victims. In turn, the negative attitudes held by society toward homosexuals and IV drug users are transferred to those with AIDS. A social policy responding to the plight of those with AIDS should not further harm the harmed. Thus, in order properly to promote the autonomous decision making of those especially at risk for AIDS, social conditions should be changed rather than individual liberty curtailed. In the case of AIDS, Illingworth concludes, this means that social programs should not aim simply at stopping the spread of HIV. Policies should intend also, via compensatory programs, to rectify some of the harms inflicted unjustifiably by social conditions on gay men and IV drug users.

Patricia Illingworth

SOCIAL RESPONSIBILITY

Two questions needed to be answered before the moral worthiness of AIDS policies, which would interfere with people's liberty, could be assessed. Those questions were: 1) Are the actions through which HIV/AIDS is transmitted primarily self-regarding or other-regarding? and 2) If the virus is transmitted primarily through self-regarding actions, are those actions performed autonomously?

. . . [T]ransmission of HIV/AIDS within the two highest risk groups is primarily a case of self-harm and not harm to others. This is an important point because in the good society caution needs to be exercised before interfering with actions that do not have harmful consequences for others. . . . [T]he risky behavior of IV drug-users and gay men was seen to be less than fully autonomous. The high-risk choices made by people in these communities were a function *not* of their autonomous desires, but of the reduced options with which they were presented and the psychological mayhem which this reduction in options may have wrought.

The unwary reader may be confused at this point. On the one hand I assert that HIV/AIDS is a self-inflicted harm. Yet, on the other hand, I claim that gay men and IV drug-users do not act autonomously. These two claims are not incompatible. What I have shown is that according to one criterion, HIV/AIDS is a self-inflicted harm, but that according to another crucial criterion for assessing whether or not an action is performed *freely,* it is not a self-inflicted disease. Against the background of this analysis, the more practical matter of AIDS social policy can be addressed.[1]

To justify liberty-limiting social policy in the *good society* either the weak or the strong version of the *harm principle* can be adopted. By showing that transmission of HIV/AIDS within the two highest risk groups is primarily a case of harm to self, I also show that according to the *strong harm principle*, liberty-limiting policies are not justified. Does the *weak harm principle* speak for or against liberty-limiting social policy? In this chapter, I will argue that even on the basis of this stronger criterion for interfering with individual liberty, liberty-limiting policies are not justified. Having established that the high-risk actions of gay men and IV drug-users are not performed autonomously for reasons which have to do with external conditions, namely, social conditions, it is open to advocates of the *weak harm principle* to recommend liberty-limiting social policy. Now the question is, should they avail themselves of this option? The answer to this question is no.

Because those who support the *weak harm principle* are interested in maintaining the autonomy of individuals, they are committed to interfering with liberty *only* when absolutely necessary. I show that according to the long-term goal of this version of the principle, preserving autonomy, it is important to look not just at the fact

From Patricia Illingworth, *AIDS and the Good Society* (London: Routledge), 1990.

that some decisions are not autonomous, but also at the specific obstacles to autonomy. In the case at hand, the obstacles to autonomous decision-making are the socially induced desires of gay men and IV drug-users. Given this, and the interest in maintaining autonomy, it would be wrong to adopt AIDS policies which would further interfere with the autonomy of gay men and IV drug-users.

I buttress this position by showing that it is especially important not to saddle those who have already had their autonomy diminished with further diminishments when the original diminishment of autonomy has 1) harmed the individual and 2) been achieved by means which are morally wrong. . . .

AUTONOMY, SELF-ESTEEM AND EQUAL OPPORTUNITY IN THE GOOD SOCIETY

According to the *weak harm principle*, our duty not to interfere with self-regarding behavior holds only with respect to fully autonomous actions. That is, actions which are not autonomous can be interfered with. For example, it might be argued by those who endorse the *weak harm principle* that bathhouses ought to be closed given that attendance at them is not autonomous. In the following, I will argue that although there is good reason to think that the high-risk behavior of gay men and IV-users is not performed autonomously, even from the point of view of the *weak harm principle*, interference with it is not justified.

THE WEAK HARM PRINCIPLE AND INDIVIDUAL AUTONOMY

Those who subscribe to the weak harm principle want to be sure that decisions and actions are performed autonomously. If a certain action does not meet this condition then interference is justified just so that autonomy is reinstated. There are problems with this position.

For one thing, individuals can benefit in important ways from their non-autonomous choices. The capacity to be autonomous is a skill that can be honed only with practice and experience. A policy which forces people to be autonomous by respecting only their autonomous desires denies them crucial opportunities to refine their autonomy skills through the experience of coming to be autonomous on their own.[2] The *weak harm principle*, by respecting only autonomous decisions, does not give people the opportunity to cultivate their capacity to be autonomous. Taken to an extreme it may destroy the conditions necessary to attain the goal it is designed to realize.

This point needs to be underscored. Imagine that it were possible to accurately determine whether or not a decision is autonomous and that only autonomous decisions were respected. In other words, people would only be allowed to act in ways which were harmful to themselves if they autonomously chose to do so. It goes without saying that people would be prevented from doing a wide variety of things which they now do. For example, Bob would not be allowed to smoke; Joan would not be permitted to eat that extra piece of chocolate mousse cake; and Mrs. Robinson could not have that affair with Benjamin. The list goes on. There are many reasons why such a scenario is disturbing which I shall not discuss. From the point of view of autonomy, it is especially problematic. If people are denied opportunities to act in non-autonomous ways they are, to all intents and purposes, denied an opportunity to be autonomous. Without opportunities to experiment with different options (smoking, overeating, infidelity) they cannot come to know what options are suited to them. Sometimes, personal experience is the best way to discover whether or not one endorses a particular desire.

Second, respect for persons requires that the whole person be respected and not just that part of the person which is autonomous; it requires that a person be given the freedom to make choices which he might later disavow and also to develop his own autonomy in a way which is authentic to him.

The main problem with this version of the *harm principle* is that by respecting only autonomous desires, it denies important aspects of the person. By taking as crucial whether or not a desire is autonomous, it undermines the very capacity that allows people to come to have autonomous desires. If the *weak harm principle* were the rule rather than the exception, there would be few autonomous desires to respect because the capacity to be autonomous would not develop to an extent sufficient to allow individuals to cultivate these desires.

But even if one endorses the *weak harm principle* it does not follow that interference with the liberty of gay men and IV-users is justified. This point needs to be highlighted. Although the relevant behavior is primarily self-regarding (no one is harmed unless he chooses to be harmed) and the behavior which is causally linked to the harm (HIV/AIDS) is not performed autonomously, it does not follow that the liberty of gay men and IV-users ought to be interfered with. Those who support the *weak harm principle* argue that in the *good society* there is a duty to respect only the autonomous (and self-regarding) choices that people make because they are interested in maintaining and enhancing the individual autonomy.[3] The conclusion that AIDS liberty-limiting policies are justified according to the *weak harm principle* fails to take into account one very important consideration. Namely, that the autonomy of gay men and IV drug-users has been diminished by factors which have much more to do with social conditions than with individual gay men and IV drug-users. If I am right about this, then autonomous decision-making can be reinstated by changing the relevant social conditions. If this option is available, then according to the value the *weak harm principle* itself places on autonomy, it would be morally wrong not to take it. Hence, even from the point of view of this version of the *harm principle* it is wrong to interfere with liberty when autonomy can be reinstated through means which do not interfere with it.

SOCIALLY INDUCED DESIRES AND SOCIAL RESPONSIBILITY

There are other reasons why it would be wrong to interfere with the liberty of gay men and IV drug-users with AIDS liberty-limiting policy. First, members of these two communities have already endured more than enough harm because of social conditions. Second, even if it is granted that some harm to individuals is inevitable in the *good society*, that harm should not occur through mechanisms which are morally reprehensible.

The harm to gay men and IV drug-users has come about through adaptive preferences. By narrowing the options open to gay men and IV drug-users society has induced certain desires in them. Obviously this kind of thing happens all the time. Many of the consumer desires that people have are a function of prevailing social conditions. For example, a yuppie's desire for a BMW is probably due, in large part, to how society is arranged. But no one concludes that society has wronged the yuppie or that it has a moral duty to extend special consideration to the yuppie's plight. Why should the socially induced desires of gay men and IV drug-users be treated any differently than the socially induced desires of the yuppie?

The yuppie's BMW-desire and the gay man's desire for a freewheeling sexual life are alike in that both are fostered by social conditions and unalike in that our intuitions about what society owes to each differ. It is at least plausible in the case of gay men and IV drug-users that society is morally culpable for the diminishment of autonomy whereas it is counter-intuitive to think that this is so in the case of the yuppie-desire. By comparing these two cases, we can see what, specifically, it is about the socially induced desires of gay men and IV drug-users that indicate that society is morally responsible for the creation of their desires.[4]

HARM AND SOCIALLY INDUCED DESIRES

The most obvious difference between the socially induced desire for a freewheeling sexual life and the socially induced desire for a BMW is that the former, unlike the latter, is extremely harmful to the person who has it. A worst case scenario for the yuppie is that he or she suffer from the extreme stress associated with doing what has to be done in order to be in the financial position to buy the BMW. In some rare instances, this might mean enduring a heart attack. The consequences for a gay man of his socially induced desire for the *fast track* have included HIV infection and AIDS. This means that for all too many gay men a consequence of their socially induced desire for a certain kind of sexual lifestyle is death. Certainly, one of the reasons for thinking that society is culpable for its role in creating the desire for a freewheeling sexual lifestyle is the severity of the harm to gay men of that desire.

A similar line of reasoning holds for IV drug-users. Not only is there a correlation between narcotic use and minority status, but in addition, a correlation between prohibiting narcotics, sharing needles and coming into contact with HIV/AIDS. This suggests that social conditions are responsible for the desire to take drugs as well as the desire to share needles. Moreover, the harm to IV drug-users is compounded by the prohibitions on narcotic use mainly because drug laws make it impossible to exercise any quality control on illegal substances.

Consumers of heroin and the various synthetic substances sold on the street face . . . severe consequences, including fatal overdoses and poisonings from unexpectedly potent or impure drug supplies. More often than not, the quality of a drug addict's life depends greatly upon his or her access to reliable supplies. Drug-enforcement operations that succeed in temporarily disrupting supply networks are thus a double-edged sword: they encourage some addicts to seek admission into drug-treatment programs, but they oblige others to seek out new and hence less reliable suppliers; the result is that more, not fewer, drug-related emergencies and deaths occur.[5]

Thus drug-addicts experience a twofold harm. Social conditions contribute to the formation of the desire to take drugs. Then laws which prohibit narcotic use make the practice of taking illicit drugs extremely hazardous because of needle-sharing and the absence of quality control.

The crux of the harm argument has little to do with the fact that the harmed groups are also highly stigmatized. Our moral intuitions would be the same if it were the case that as a result of a socially induced desire yuppies suffered severe harm. Imagine the following. Suppose that the socially induced desire to drive a BMW turned out to be extremely risky. Imagine that 1 out of every 100 times a yuppie slipped the key into the ignition, the beautiful BMW, including the yuppie, blew up. Would we not, given this scenario, hold the source of this desire morally responsible for cultivating it?

This comparison shows that, of the desires that are socially induced, there is an inclination to hold society morally responsible for those that saddle individuals with harm. When there is no severe harm to the individual as a result of holding the desire, there is no compelling reason to hold society responsible. In the case of the high-risk choices made by gay men and IV-users the harm is serious enough to commend social culpability.

Not only are gay men and IV drug-users harmed by their *adaptive desires*, but they have very little to gain from having these desires. This too distinguishes them from the yuppie. Consider the benefits of having the desires for those who are saddled with them. In some cases society confers sufficient benefits on those who assume the desires to justify the risks associated with them. This is probably the case with the yuppie's desire for a BMW. Although there are the harms associated with yuppie-stress, which come about from having the desire, there are also social rewards to be held. In return for the yuppie's cultivation of the BMW-desire, he gains social acceptance, respect and high self-esteem (not to mention a shiny, new BMW). The same is not true for the gay man who cultivates the socially induced desire for the *fast track* or ghetto Blacks who come to desire narcotics. Not only are they not showered with respect and admiration for cultivating the desires and requisite behavior, but they are often blamed for having them. Princess Anne, proponent of the blame the victim position, bears witness to this in her comments about AIDS. The following is a precis of Princess Anne's view.

> [W]hy on earth should homosexuals (the main carriers, whose sexual practices and promiscuity are tailor-made for transmitting the disease) regard themselves, or be regarded by others, as victims? We do not talk of syphilis *victims* or *herpes victims*, or *gonorrhoea victims*. We regard the majority of those who contract the diseases as suffering the consequences of their own voluntary acts. It is surely the same with AIDS.[6]

Princess Anne is not unique in believing that gay men are to be blamed for their promiscuous lifestyle and, in turn, for AIDS. She ignores the role that society has played in creating the crucial desires. Unlike the yuppie, the gay man is condemned by society for the very desires which society has fostered. Unlike the yuppie, he is not rewarded for his cooperation, but punished. Finally, unlike the yuppie, he has very little to gain from society for coming to have the socially induced desire. . . .

EQUAL OPPORTUNITY

Discriminatory laws, regulations and intolerance toward homosexuals deny them an equal opportunity to express their sexuality and intimacy preferences. Monogamous relationships, either long-term or sequential, are not as viable an option for gay men as they are for heterosexuals. This is so, in part, because society does not encourage and promote (let alone tolerate) romantic liaisons among homosexuals in the same way as it does heterosexuals. Same sex relationships are not sanctioned by society through tax benefits, joint health insurance policies or other state plans which reward heterosexuals. In some places sodomy continues to be against the law. Effectively, what society has done is to put severe obstacles in the way of gay men choosing a life-plan that suits them.

Promoting some conceptions of the *good life* over others has the consequence of favoring some life-plans over others. To the extent that some life-plans are given a preferred status over others, those that are not preferred lose their status as real alternatives. This, in turn, discourages people from making decisions for conceptions which are not favored. Discrimination against same sex predispositions is a good example of this.

The only *real* sexual lifestyle option open to gay men is the one many of them have chosen, multiple anonymous sexual encounters. This is not to say that it is impossible for a gay man to choose an alternative sexual lifestyle, but to say that it is more difficult for him to do so. Nor does the position I support condemn frequent anonymous sex as an option. My view is not that no one ought to choose multiple anonymous sex as a way of conducting their sexual lives, but that no one ought to be forced to choose it, for lack of other viable options. As things stand now, gay men have very few sexual lifestyle options from which to choose. This makes remote the possibility of choosing autonomously the *fast track* or any other sexual lifestyle; the circumstances are ripe for adaptive preference formation.

That people are given equal opportunities to develop their particular conceptions of the *good life* is important for a number of reasons. In the *good society*, the state is designed to foster social conditions which will allow individuals to pursue their own life-plans and conceptions of the *good life*.[7] Fairness considerations require that all life-plans have an equal standing with respect to the state (that is, that the state not favor some over others) at least in so far as they do not harm others. Doing otherwise violates the basic tenet of neutrality among conceptions of the good, and in turn, denies everyone within a particular society the benefits of pluralism.

PATERNALISTIC LEGISLATION

Laws which prohibit the private use of narcotics are paternalistic. In a society committed to respecting individual autonomy they constitute a harm on this ground alone because violations to autonomy are in and of themselves harms. In view of much of the crime and corruption alleged to be associated with narcotics, the idea that drug-use is a self-regarding action may strike some as surprising. How can anything which appears to have such obviously harmful consequences for society be construed as a self-regarding activity?

It is important to distinguish the harms connected with drug-use from those connected with prohibitions on it. In the U.S., laws which prohibit the private consumption of narcotics are costly and, as Ethan Nadelmann has argued, counterproductive.[8] The crime and corruption associated with drugs are more a function of the laws against drugs than of the drugs themselves. Consider the following. If drug laws were repealed, the producing, selling, buying and consuming of narcotics would no longer be criminal activities. Similarly, the crimes drug-users commit in order to obtain the money to purchase expensive illicit drugs would decrease dramatically. If drugs were legal substances, as alcohol is, they would become much less expensive and the crimes which are now executed in order to purchase them would become unnecessary.[9]

Drug-related violence in the form of violent crimes committed by people under the influence of narcotics is another kind of criminal activity associated with drugs. Some drugs may have the effect of increasing violent behavior. But Nadelmann points out that it is just not clear yet whether or not drugs such as *crack* contribute to an increase in violent behavior. He also very astutely points out that "no illicit drug is as widely associated with violent behavior as alcohol."[10] It may also be the case that the violent behavior which is thought to be fostered by drugs would diminish with the decriminalization and regulation of drugs. If drugs were regulated in the same way that alcohol is, some quality control could be exercised. The violence associated with drugs might diminish as the quality was enhanced.

Many of the harmful consequences which illicit drug-use is thought to be responsible for would more accurately be attributed to drug laws and the *war* on drugs. If this is so, then drug-use should remain in the self-regarding camp and laws which prohibit it should be rightly described as paternalistic interferences. According to the *strong harm principle* such interference is wrong because it fails to respect the individual claims of people to do what they want in areas which concern only themselves.

Laws prohibiting narcotic use do not fare much better with the *weak harm principle*. Although the primarily self-regarding activity of taking illicit drugs may not be performed autonomously, this diminishment in autonomy can in many cases accurately be ascribed to external social conditions such as poverty, racism and a lack of opportunities for social mobility. So even on the *weak harm principle* paternalistic laws which prohibit drug-use constitute wrongful interference in people's lives. . . .

SELF-ESTEEM, GAY MEN AND IV DRUG-USERS

Society has made it perfectly clear that from its point of view homosexuality is not to be tolerated and is certainly not something about which to be proud. It has succeeded in conveying the message that homosexuality is something about which one ought to be ashamed. Given social attitudes towards homosexuality one certain way to maintain whatever self-esteem that one has is to prevent information about one's sexual tastes from becoming public. For gay men public knowledge about their sexual preferences often entails more than public contempt; it also entails self-contempt. IV drug-users are viewed with similar disdain; they are often thought to be worthless people who are only a burden on society. . . .

If homosexuality and IV drug-use carry with them a loss of self-esteem, and self-esteem is essential for successfully pursuing one's life-plan, then it is also the case that gay men and IV drug-users do not have an equal opportunity to cultivate their conceptions of the *good life*. If the *good society* has a mandate to be neutral with respect to life plans, then by denying gay men and IV drug-users access to self-esteem, they have thereby wronged them. Gay men have not had an equal opportunity to cultivate and develop different kinds of relationships, nor, in turn, the capacities that they would need in order successfully to negotiate such relationships. Because their sexuality is viewed with contempt and disdain, they have often not had an opportunity to develop the self-esteem needed to pursue and enjoy different kinds of personal relationships were they to become available.

The self-esteem of IV drug-users is often similarly diminished. In some cases this is because narcotic users, as such, are seen as worthless; in other cases it is because they are often drawn from minority communities that are thought to be worthless; and in still other cases it is simply because IV drug-users are often from working class and poor environments which are viewed as worthless. . . .

. . . Discrimination against homosexuals continues to be widespread.[11] Even if this discrimination had ended prior to the advent of AIDS it would not have ended soon enough to have diminished its harmful effects on gay men. . . . [T]he high-risk lifestyle embraced by many gay men was a reaction to an extremely oppressive society; it was a movement of liberation. If I am right about this, then even if discrimination had ended altogether prior to AIDS, its detrimental effects were still being experienced by gay men.

AIDS will only make the problem of discrimination against homosexuals worse. . . . The negative attitude held by the general public towards homosexuals and IV drug-users is transferred to persons with AIDS. It would not be at all surprising if in addition to this, the fear and panic associated with AIDS fuels further hostility towards members of both communities.

It would be a mistake to conclude from this that negative attitudes towards persons with AIDS are restricted to the general public or to those who are uneducated about the disease. In this case prejudice is not just a matter of ignorance. A recent study looked at the attitudes of medical students to homosexuals and persons with AIDS.[12] The students were presented with one of four patient scenarios which differed only in how the patient was identified. In two of the scenarios the patient was identified as having either AIDS or leukaemia and in the other two as either homosexual or heterosexual.

The students were then asked to answer a survey which was designed to assess their attitudes to the patients described in the scenario. Students were asked questions of the following sort. 1) Would they be willing to attend a party where the patient prepared the food? 2) Would they be willing to work in the same office as the patient? 3) Would they be willing to have a conversation with the patient? 4) Would they be willing to allow one of their children to visit the patient? The following results were reported. The students were asked to rate their willingness on a scale of 1 to 6 with 1 representing the least favorable and 6 the most. In response to 1) when the patient was identified as an AIDS carrier the mean score among respondents was 4.84, contrasted with a score of 5.55 when the patient was described as having leukaemia. Similarly, when the patient was described as a homosexual leukaemia patient the respondent mean score was 4.88 compared to 5.51 when the patient was described as heterosexual. A similar trend was witnessed with question number 3); respondents tended to have less favorable attitudes to the persons with AIDS and the homosexuals. An even stronger bias against these two groups was witnessed in response to questions 2) and 4). With respect to the former, scores of 4.88/6.00 were reported for the AIDS/leukaemia patients and 5.06 and 5.81 for the homosexual/heterosexual leukaemia patient. And with the latter, respondents scored a 3.31/5.53 for the AIDS/leukaemia patients and a 3.83 and a 5.00 for the homosexual/heterosexual patients.[13] The authors have the following to say about the results of the survey:

> [O]n seven of the 12 prejudice items, the AIDS patients were evaluated much more harshly than the leukemia victims. A similar pattern emerged with respect to sexual preference. Regardless of which disease was involved, the homosexual patients were viewed as being more responsible for their illness . . . more dangerous to others . . . and suffering less pain than the heterosexual patients. . . .[14]

What this study shows is that discriminatory attitudes against gays and persons with AIDS are not restricted to the ignorant, but extend also to health professionals, those who are will informed about the disease.

The point that I have been making in this chapter and in the last is that a serious wrong has been committed against both gay and IV drug-users and that as a consequence of this they have suffered. Not only have they endured a serious loss of self-esteem, dignity and liberty, but more recently many of them have developed either a positive HIV status or full-blown AIDS. Many have died from the disease and many more will in the future. This, of course, is terrible for any individual to have to endure. But in the particular case of AIDS the people who have been most affected by the disease are gay men and IV drug-users, individuals who have already suffered enormously and who have been stigmatized by society. For the most part, society has responded to the AIDS crisis and to those who have been struck by it with fear, hatred and hostility. This may explain the reluctance of many governments to fund AIDS research and care for AIDS patients.

The one point that should emerge from the arguments that I have presented is that in view of the harm that society has already inflicted on gay men and IV drug-users further harms are absolutely unjustified from the point of view of the *good society*. Policies, such as contact-tracing mandatory testing and isolation, infringe on liberty and hence on autonomy. They constitute harms for this reason alone. In the *good society* an individual whose autonomy is not respected is harmed.

The considerations that I have outlined suggest that not only should any social policy which is adopted not further harm gay men and IV drug-users, but should to some extent alleviate some of the harm that they have already experienced. AIDS social policy provides society with a good opportunity to mend some of the suffering that past policies have caused both gay men and IV drug-users. AIDS social policy should not just stop the spread of the virus, but also right some of the wrongs which have been inflicted on gay men and IV drug-users. At the very least what I have shown is that on the two versions of the *harm principle*, such policies are not justified.

NOTES

1. I wish to thank Jim Hankinson for suggesting that I clarify this point.

2. See Gerald Dworkin, 'Autonomy and Behavior Control', *Hastings Center Report*, (1976), vol. 6, no. 1, pp. 23–8.

3. See Harry Frankfurt, 'Freedom of Will and Concept of a Person', *Journal of Philosophy*, (1971), vol. 68, pp. 5–20.

4. I wish to thank Michael Hancock for bringing this example to my attention and for extensive discussion of it.

5. Ethan A. Nadelmann, 'The Case for Legalization', *The Public Interest*, (Summer 1988), vol. 92, p. 21.

6. 'Anne Shows Ministers the Way', *Daily Express*, (January (28) 1988).

7. For a classic discussion of this conception of the state, see John Stuart Mill, 'On Liberty', in *John Stuart Mill: On Liberty*, Hackett Publishing Co., Indianapolis, (1978); and R. Dworkin, 'Liberalism', in *Public and Private Morality*, Stuart Hampshire (ed.), Cambridge University Press, Cambridge, (1978), pp. 113–43.

8. Nadelmann, 'The Case for Legalization', pp. 3–31.

9. Ibid., p. 17.

10. Ibid., p. 18.

11. It might be thought that this recent legislation is prompted strictly by AIDS and that prior to AIDS there was no discrimination against homosexuals. It is more likely that discrimination against homosexuals has been widespread and continuous. AIDS has certainly made matters worse, but more importantly it has made discrimination against homosexuals acceptable once again. It is naive to assume that the only time discrimination exists is when it is seen by mainstream society as acceptable behavior.

12. Jeffrey A. Kelly, J. S. St. Lawrence, S. Smith, H. V. Hood and D. J. Cook, 'Medical Students' Attitudes Towards AIDS and Homosexual Patients', *Journal of Medical Education*, (July 1987), vol. 62, no. 7, pp. 549–56.

13. Ibid., p. 553.

14. Ibid.

■ RICHARD MOHR: AIDS AND HOMOSEXUALITY

Richard Mohr extends the line of argument opened by Illingworth. Mohr argues that government should fund both preventive medicine (the search for a vaccine) and patient care (especially hospice care) as a matter of compensatory justice to gay men. The fact that AIDS is not a general contagion and that the causes and routes of HIV transmission are now well known entails that any state policy suspending civil rights in order to protect society from indiscriminate harm (for example, by quarantining AIDS-exposed persons) is unwarranted. Similarly, since paternalistic state intervention comes at the expense of violating individual rights, the state would require strong justification to prevent someone paternalistically from harming himself (by risking his health, say) through autonomously chosen associates. State coercion may be warranted temporarily to inform persons of the risks attendant to their choices. But because sex is one of the central values of human life, it must be weighed up by autonomous individuals against other central values like independence. The relative importance of the value, and so the sacrifices that will be made in its behalf, will differ for different persons. Thus, concludes Mohr, the balance between the values of sex and health are like those between religious conviction and health. In a society for which freedom is a primary good (for a discussion of primary goods, see Rawls, Chapter 5), this balance cannot be determined by state coercion for the individual's good.

Moreover, Mohr argues that gay men should be considered morally innocent regarding the spread of AIDS. This moral innocence follows from a set of social factors he identifies: the initial absence of knowledge about conditions in which the disease could spread, the general lack of social response in terms of educational materials, the centrality of sex drives to ordinary human satisfaction, the unsatisfactory nature of safe sex, and the social self-despising promoted in a gay male culture, which society has largely reduced to a sexual delivery service. Mohr argues that it does not follow that government has a license to intervene paternalistically in gay lifestyles; rather, it follows that gay patients suffering from advanced manifestation of HIV-related illness are owed long-term hospice and nursing care by the state as a form of compensatory justice. It is now the obligation of the patient's family to arrange and pay for long-term health care for those dying from AIDS-related causes. Society and state have prohibited the creation of gay families. Mohr identifies self-internalized hatred of gays—a condition exacerbated by the AIDS crisis—as the leading cause of the failure of stable gay relations to materialize and mature. Thus, Mohr concludes, society owes those gay people dying from AIDS-related conditions the care they would have received from the nuclear families they would have created had society and the state not blocked them from doing so.

Richard Mohr

WHAT TO DO AND NOT TO DO ABOUT AIDS

In February 1993—a dozen years into the AIDS crisis—the research wing of the National Academy of Sciences released a study on the social impact of AIDS on America. It found that the disease had not fundamentally changed any basic social institution. However, the report ominously suggested that because the disease, both as scientifically appraised and as socially perceived, has remained largely confined to certain disfavored groups, society's response was shifting from generally liberal public health measures to punitive approaches, which increasingly involve state coercion. Almost as a confirmation of the study's predictions, Congress in May 1993 reinstated a statutory ban on immigration by people with the virus which causes AIDS. Congress had originally imposed such a ban in 1987, but rescinded it in 1990. Further, if the report is right, the country's overall concern for the disease may well fade, and so too will diminish political pressures for government funding of AIDS research and patient care. Indeed, it appears that through the 1980s AIDS funding rose significantly only as AIDS came to be perceived as a threat to the dominant, nongay culture. It is time to revisit arguments for and against government coercion and funding in the AIDS crisis.

In Cuba, the government has forced every citizen to be tested for the AIDS virus and then quarantined those testing positive in internment camps, which the government euphemistically terms "a sanitorium system"—where, in the absence of a cure, the infected are locked up forever. The United States has not generally followed the Cuban model, though quarantines for people with the AIDS virus have been set up in parts of the armed forces, in some prisons, and at refugee detention centers. Hysterical calls early in the crisis for quarantines went largely unheeded, as indeed they should have been, for reasons which show more generally that any specifically AIDS-directed coercive responses by the government are unwarranted.

The hysteria, when not simply an expression of old anti-gay prejudices, was based on the presumption that the disease is spread indiscriminately. This misconception and fear of general contagion was fixed in the public mind by *Life* magazine. In three-inch letters, its July 1985 cover screamed to the nation "NOW NO ONE IS SAFE FROM AIDS." The magazine used as its allegedly compelling example a seemingly typical Pennsylvania family all but one of whose members has the disease. But the ways they became infected were all clear and discrete. The father was a hemophiliac infected before blood supplies were screened for the virus; his wife was infected through sex with him; and she conveyed the virus to a child in the process of giving birth. No one got the disease either mysteriously or through casual contact. The family example in fact was evidence against the article's generic contagion thesis. But into the 1990s, even some medically trained minds, like New York City Commissioner of Health Stephen C. Joseph, have tried to justify quarantines of people with the AIDS virus, by miscomparing AIDS to such air- and water-borne diseases as typhus, influenza, contagious tuberculosis, and, for that matter, the common cold, all of which can be contracted simply from sharing public spaces with strangers.

For public policy purposes the most important fact about AIDS is not that it is deadly but that it, like hepatitis B, is caused by a blood-transmitted virus. AIDS is infectious, but not casually contagious. For the disease to spread, bodily fluids of someone with the virus must directly enter the bloodstream of another. And among bodily fluids, only blood, semen, vaginal fluids and (possibly) breast milk have been implicated in the virus's transmission.

That the virus is blood transmitted means first and foremost that, with very rare exceptions, you get the virus from the actions you perform in conjunction with someone who already has the virus. Now that blood supplies are screened with a test for antibodies to the AIDS virus, the exceptions consist pretty much just of infants who are infected in being born. And no one has seriously suggested exerting the coercive power of government against mothers who infect their infants in this way, even when the mothers could be considered morally culpable.

The disease's mode of infection means that those infected are those whose actions directly contribute to their risk of infection—chiefly through sexual contact and shared hypodermic needles. The case for general, casual contagion cannot be made. In consequence, coercive government policy which is based on that fear is unwarranted. The extraordinary measures—including the suspension of civil liberties—which government might justifiably take, as in war, to prevent wholesale slaughter simply do not apply here. In particular, quarantining people with the AIDS virus in order to protect society at large from indiscriminate harm is unwarranted, as is the screening and exclusion of foreigners with the virus.

In addition, the mode of AIDS's transmission means that other recent and increasingly prevalent attempts to institute mandatory testing and even to invoke criminal law to prevent the spread of AIDS are seriously misguided. Calls for various forms of mandatory testing have swept the nation in waves.

In 1987, a scattered rash of states passed laws making AIDS testing a requirement for getting a marriage license. Within two years, these laws had all been revoked. Couples in droves were simply driving to neighboring states to get married. When Illinois revoked its law, it also dropped all mandatory premarital testing for other venereal diseases. But reason was restored to AIDS policy only briefly.

The early 1990s saw a tidal wave of calls, including eighty-one votes in the U.S. Senate, for mandatory testing of all medical personnel who perform invasive procedures—mainly doctors and dentists. The calls were prompted by a Florida dentist who, apparently by failing to use even minimal sanitary procedures, infected six of his patients. In over a decade of medical invasions by infected personnel, these cases are the only such infections to come to light. Here testing, with its enormous costs to the medical industry in terms of dollars and lost personnel, would prevent at best only the oddest of cases. Such mandatory testing is as rational as requiring people to stay indoors in order to reduce their risk of being hit by stray meteors. A far more rational approach, given the disease's mode of transmission, would be to promote and enforce medical hygiene, which would protect patients against a vast array of infection, not just AIDS.

Coercive sexual contact tracing is required in a few jurisdictions and permitted in many more. Where it is permitted but not required, public health agencies in fact do not do it. For they recognize that the labor-intensive practice is an inefficient means of stopping the disease, especially since it is one for which there is no current cure. And such tracing violates to boot the privacy rights which cover both sexual behavior and doctor-patient confidentiality. Public health agencies generally agree that safe-sex education is a more efficient use of scarce public health resources.

The latest trend to deploy the coercive, even punitive, power of government is to classify the knowing exposure of someone to the virus (say, through sexual behavior) as attempted murder or manslaughter. Half of the states have already adopted such laws. These laws argue that someone who exposes another to the virus is like a drunk driver or like someone shooting randomly in a theater. But the element of self-exposure in infection with the virus makes its mode of transmission relevantly dissimilar to both of these fatal behaviors. Acts of will on the part of a bystander hit by a drunkenly driven car or the theater goer struck by a bullet are not directed toward, do not actively participate in, nor contribute to the course of events that harms these people. Their presence by the road or in the theater is merely a necessary condition for the harm—as are millions of other states of affairs, such as their being born in the first place. One would not say that it was in virtue of their actions that they were harmed. But one would say this of the person who gets AIDS through sexual contacts or shared needles knowing that the virus can be transmitted this way. He actively participated in the very action that harms him. His deeds are not merely necessary conditions for harm but contribute to the causal chain by which he is harmed. It was in virtue of his actions that harm came to him. He is not a victim. His sex partner is not a murderer. People, like valuable antiques, come as is. We would not want it any other way.

The coercive power of the state has also been used in many jurisdictions to close gay bathhouses. Most frequently the argument for these closures is a misguided analogy holding that the closures are no different than quarantining Typhoid Mary and removing the handle from her water pump, which if used will indiscriminately kill people since typhus is a water-borne disease. This argument fails for the same reason that calls for quarantines fail. More subtle arguments are paternalistic: closing bathhouses takes care of those who fail to take care of themselves, just as a parent coercively prevents a child from putting himself in harm's way. But these arguments too must fail. For if independence—the permission to guide one's life by one's own lights to an extent compatible with a like ability on the part of others—is, as it is, a major value, one cannot respect that value while preventing people from putting themselves at risk through voluntary associations. Voluntary associations are necessarily examples of people acting in accordance with the principle of independence, for mutual consent guarantees that the "compatible extent" proviso of the independence principle is fulfilled. But the state and even the courts have not been very sensitive to the distinction between one harming oneself and one harming another—nor has the medical establishment. It appears to all of them that a harm is a harm, a disease a disease, however caused or described. The moral difference, however, is enormous. Preventing a person from harming another is required by the principle of independence, but preventing someone from harming himself is incompatible with it. While no further justification is needed for the state to protect a person from others, a rather powerful justification is needed if the state is to be warranted in protecting a person from himself.

Occasionally, to be sure, the case for paternalism can be made to work. One legitimate way to justify paternalistic coercion is to claim as warrant for it a lack of rationality on the part of an agent (say, an insane person). By "rationality" here I mean having relevant information and certain mental capacities, including the ability to reason from ends to means, but I do not presume that making the best possible assessment of means to an end is a requirement for rationality—error is compatible with rationality.

A presumption of an agent's rationality is a necessary condition for the very respect which is owed to her making her own decisions and guiding her life by them. Thus, paternalistic interference is warranted when a person is operating at risks which she is unable to assess due to diminished mental skills or lack of information. But education, not coercion, is the solution which is tailored to, and so appropriate for, such incapacities.

Far from justifying major paternalistic coercion of gay institutions, say, closing gay bathhouses, the argument from rationality here indeed suggests that paternalistic arguments surrounding AIDS are not even being advanced in good faith. For though education is one of government's highest spending priorities, governments have made no serious attempt to educate people about medically informed risks of AIDS and of safe alternatives to high-risk sexual practices. For example, school superintendents who have tried to introduce safe-sex education into curriculums have found themselves fired by their school boards, who agree with James Mason, who, as the director of the Center for Disease Control, claimed: "We don't think that citizens care to be funding material that encourages gay sex lifestyles." Thus any argument for governmental coercion of gay institutions on paternalistic grounds is probably disingenuous. At most the argument from rationality warrants placing warning labels on bathhouses as they are placed on cigarettes, the use of which also threatens death.

The other legitimate argument for paternalistic coercion is that one should be protected from ceding away the very conditions that enable one to be an independent agent. Thus one cannot legitimately contract to become a slave or to sign away rights to the equitable administration of justice. Is exposing oneself to AIDS relevantly like contracting into slavery?

No, first, slavery *by definition* is a condition of lost independence. However, as with other venereal diseases, not every sexual encounter—even a maximally "unsafe" one—with an infected partner causes a person to become infected. Studies of couples with one infected partner have shown that susceptibility varies widely both from person to person and from partner to partner. And it is known from hepatitis B studies that even when no precautions are taken against the transmission of blood-borne diseases, they only ever partially saturate a population which exposes itself to them—that is, the percent of infected members among those potentially infected reaches a certain point and goes no higher. With the hepatitis B virus, the plateau is about sixty-six percent; with the much harder to contract AIDS virus, the percent is lower. Because the risks are high but the results not invariably catastrophic, putting oneself at risk for AIDS becomes less like contracting into slavery and more like being a race-car driver, mountain climber, logger, or astronaut. In the absence of in-evitability, the assessment of risk should be left to the individual, and indeed, as the examples of space flight, mountaineering, logging, and race-car driving show, this is the considered standard of society.

Second, sex is one of the central values of human life. Individuals, not govern-ment, must make the difficult choices where values centrally affecting the self come in conflict. That such choice falls to the individual is generally recognized where religious commitment and health come in conflict. The state cannot legitimately make the trade-offs that an informed adult will make between religious values and health by, say, coercing an adult—for the sake of preserving his own indepen-dence—to have a blood transfusion against his belief that a transfusion, even a co-erced one, will damn him for all eternity. So, sexual attitudes and acts in accord with them are not fit subjects of state coercion for the individual's own good, even when the good is the continued ability to make choices.

The centrality of sex to individual lives, however, provides a justification for state funding for preventing AIDS research. People ought not to be in the position where they have to make trade-offs between the components of a complete life. Ending the conflict of central personal values will be especially attractive when the means to it places no nearly comparable burden on others. The case at hand requires tax dollars for basic immunological research and applied viral research. Yet, given the ends likely to be achieved and assuming an equitable tax system, taxation places no comparable burden on those taxed.

A second argument for preventive AIDS funding is that no one should have to live in a condition of terror. Imagine a prisoner who is never actually tortured but who daily witnesses the torture of others. His witnessings are not merely one more unpleasant component of prison life, on a par, say, with tasteless food. Rather, both the torture victims and the observer have experienced cruel and unusual punish-ment. Constantly expected but uncertain pain and destruction seizes up the mind, destroying the equanimity necessary for thinking, deciding, and acting, and grotesquely turns the mind against itself, punishing itself as a way to avoid uncer-tainty and to produce the appearance of order and progression. Human dignity on pretty much any account is here destroyed.

Gay men now live in such a condition of generalized terror. When there were few cases of AIDS and its horrors seemed personally remote, gay men understand-ably dealt with it as the mind can do with forebodings on the horizon—they avoided it through denial, a typical coping mechanism of the already beleaguered. But as the number of AIDS cases rose exponentially, spreading from cities to towns and leaving nearly everyone with the memory of lost acquaintances, the terror of constantly expected but uncertain destruction and its attendant contortions have become quite general. It turns out, for instance, that gay doctors, who cannot easily sustain the denial stage, experience more anxiety and mental disturbances over AIDS than people who actually have the disease. Everyone exposed to terror has a positive claim that it be ended.

Though AIDS is a disease caught in a condition where one has put oneself at risk, nevertheless gay men in general ought in consequence of certain natural and cultural forces to be viewed as morally innocent in its contagion and spread. The disease should not be viewed as a matter of paying the piper, as suffering from a mountain climbing accident might be, where the costs of the effects of one's negligence are to be borne by oneself. And so even in the absence of justification for perfectly general government health-care plans, funding should nevertheless be provided for the care of those whose life chances in civil society have been permanently destroyed by natural catastrophes that elude the protections of civil defense—so that their dying might at least avoid unnecessary suffering and the indignity to which this disease in particular tends to expose patients.

The general case for innocence is one to be made from an accumulation of factors. Consider, first, that the incubation period for the disease is indeterminately long. This means that there are people who even under maximal conditions of risk avoidance—totally swearing off sex on first hearing in 1981 of the disease as potentially contagious—are still even now coming down with the disease. Social policy has no way of telling who these innocent people are. Second, educational material that would make people aware of their risks has not been made available, indeed in many cases had been blocked, by governments. And the mass media continue to be more than a little reluctant to provide details of safe-sex practices. No television network will air ads for condoms. Public service announcements on AIDS tell the audience to be concerned about AIDS, but give no safe-sex information. So many people even now are taking risks in situations of constrained information. These people too should be viewed as innocent.

Yet, even in conditions of complete information, most individuals are not very good at risk management. So even with a knowledge of the likelihood of contagion per sexual contact, many people would still make mistakes. Such errors, however, are not the product of negligence: it's just that most human beings have very poor intuitions about statistics and probabilities. That such intuitions are so poor makes a big difference in assigning fault to individuals. Successful choice and guilt do not jointly exhaust the moral field. The high value society places on choice despite a significant propensity of people to make poor choices creates a zone of the failed innocent.

Further, there are a number of reasons why the gay sexual agent, even with complete knowledge and clear capacities, might be led to take risks which many would think extraordinary. First, sex drive is not something over which one has an unrestrained control. The Centers for Disease Control now recommend that gay men simply be celibate—unless they have lived in completely monogamous, long-term relationships. This advice seems remote from reality and quite oblivious to the cussedness of sex and culture. On the one hand, the recurring and intrusive nature of sexual desire guarantees that in general gay men, like others, will not be celibate. On the other, long-term gay relations, if not as rare as adamant, are at least as rare as rubies. And fear is a particularly poor forge for working the most delicate of human bonds with a view to future domestic continence.

Worse still for the likely escape from risk is the layering over of sexual drive with certain cultural forces. Even now most men who have gay sex are not gay self-identified and, in order to keep jobs, preserve marriages, and otherwise accommodate the dominant culture as a condition for social life, they necessarily have sex on the run. Many of these men consciously do not have safe-sex, lest that, paired with the dominant culture's virtual identification of AIDS and "queers," force them to a recognition that they themselves are after all "queer."

Society, in focusing its concerns exclusively on the single characteristic by which an individual deviates from the norm, makes that one characteristic into the whole person: the homosexual, the faggot. Forthright gays in the process of reappropriating for themselves that very characteristic by which the dominant culture transfixes them, indeed reinforce (reasonably enough) its very centrality to themselves. As a result, something more than just pleasure and the fulfillment of need is wrapped up in sex for gays. With some slight exceptions like the gay choral movement and (sure enough) AIDS support groups, sex is the only mode in which gays in current culture are allowed to identify themselves to themselves. Self-respect, such as it is, for gay men in our culture is often the product of a robust sex life.

Even so, it is likely that the core of that respect is poisoned. One cannot completely withdraw oneself from one's culture, in this case a culture that takes gays to be worth less than nongays and very likely to be entirely worthless. In this circumstance, one is likely to make unwise decisions about one's sex life. Self-hatred and sexual desire tend to become fused. Just as violence—even against oneself (as in the "rough trade" phenomenon)—can be an especially effective object of sexual arousal, so can death—even one's own. AIDS is such a situation into which many gay men are drifting in part as the fulfillment of the dominant culture's appraisal of them, in part as a spin-off from the search for self-respect in a society that thwarts it. This is not idle speculation: it turns out that the same gay doctors who have extreme anxieties over the AIDS crisis have proven to be particularly unable to live by the safe-sex guidelines they prescribe to others. And in a similar pattern, one reminiscent of other survivor syndromes, it also turns out that partners who suffer through the AIDS death of their lovers frequently themselves then go on binges of unsafe sex.

Doctors cure, but there is no cure. Rather, care for AIDS patients chiefly requires routine nursing and hospice care. The disease is typically characterized by a progressive loss of energy and bodily control, punctuated by opportunistic infections which bring with them debilitating pain, disorientation, incontinence and an inability to perform even basic functions without assistance. Historically, routine nursing and hospice functions have been performed by family members, and long-term terminal illnesses were thus not major public policy concerns.

Compensatory justice requires that hospice and nursing care is owed to gay patients by the state in consequence of society's and government's prohibition against the creation of gay families. If society barred a motorcyclist from wearing a helmet which he would have worn, he would certainly be owed compensation from society for any injury which a helmet could have prevented. So too, in forbidding gay families, society owes gays the protections and comforts which it prevents them from acquiring on their own. It perhaps goes without saying that attempts of gays to create blood relations and extended families of their own have been blocked by both society and the state. At every turn, gays are effectively denied the possibility of creating their own nurturing families.

Compassion would suggest, and compensatory justice should require, that the day-to-day care of the final-stage AIDS patient be provided in lieu of the care he would have likely had but for society's blocking his creation of his own family.

SUGGESTIONS FOR DISCUSSION

1. Should religious belief, inform, determine, or dictate public policy? Should moral belief? What, if any, are the relevant differences between setting policy based on religious belief and doing so based on moral belief?

2. Are promiscuity and drug consumption inherently disrespectful of persons or inherently immoral in some other sense? In the face of the AIDS crisis, is there a moral duty to promote abstinence from sex or drugs? Is promotion of abstinence a viable public policy response to the AIDS crisis?

3. Identify the relevant individual rights and the relevant public health concerns at issue with respect to AIDS. In what ways do or could they clash? Can you think of principles that may apply generally for resolving such clashes?

4. Divide the class into equal groups. Assign each group an ethical theory (for example, utilitarianism, Kantianism, contractarianism, or feminism) or a moral principle (autonomy, public welfare, respect for the individual, self-interest, or responsibility). Decide and defend what would be morally required in the following cases:

   a. As the board of directors of an insurance company, decide whether to insure patients who are HIV positive.

   b. As members of your local school board, determine policy concerning the continued attendance of children who are infected with HIV.

   c. Develop a policy statement on HIV/AIDS for your university or college.

5. Do homosexual men have special duties with respect to AIDS?

FOR FURTHER READING

AIDS. Special Supplement, Hastings Center Report, December 1986.

AIDS. Special Supplement, Hastings Center Report, April/May 1988.

AIDS and Public Policy Journal. Includes a range of articles on medical, public policy, and ethical considerations pertaining to AIDS.

Almond, B. "AIDS and International Ethics." *Ethics and International Affairs* 2 (1988): 139–54.

Bayer, R. *Private Acts, Social Consequences: AIDS and the Politics of Public Health.* New York: The Free Press, 1989.

Conway, D. A. "AIDS and Legal Paternalism." *Social Theory and Practice* 13 (1987): 287–302.

Crisp, R. "Autonomy, Welfare, and the Treatment of AIDS." *Journal of Medical Ethics* 15 (1989): 68–73.

Feinberg, J. *Social Philosophy.* Englewood Cliffs, N.J.: Prentice-Hall, 1973.

——— . *Harm to Others.* Oxford: Oxford University Press, 1984.

——— . *Harm to Self.* Oxford: Oxford University Press, 1987.

——— . *Harmless Wrongdoings.* Oxford: Oxford University Press, 1988.

——— . *Offense to Others.* Oxford: Oxford University Press, 1988.

Freud, S. *Three Essays on the Theory of Sexuality.* New York: Basic Books, 1962.

Gillick, V. "Confidentiality and Young People." *Ethics and Medicine* 4 (1988): 21–23.

Gillett, "AIDS and Confidentiality." *Journal of Applied Philosophy* 4 (1987): 15–20.

Hayry, H., and Hayry, M. "AIDS Now." *Bioethics* 1 (1987): 339–56.

Homosexuality and the Law. Special double issue. *Journal of Homosexuality* 5 (1979–80): 1–160.

Illingworth, P. *AIDS and the Good Society: From Philosophy to Social Policy.* London: Routledge, 1989.

Leiser, B. *Liberty, Justice and Morals.* 3rd ed. New York: Macmillan, 1986.

Lloyd, A., ed. *Proceedings of the Conference AIDS: Social Policy, Ethics, and the Law.* Monash: Centre of Human Bioethics, 1986.

Manuel, F. et al. "The Ethical Approach to AIDS: A Bibliographical Review." *Journal of Medical Ethics* 16 (1990): 14–27.

Matthews, E. "AIDS and Sexual Morality." *Bioethics* 2 (1988): 118–28.

Mohr, R. *Gays/Justice: A Study of Ethics, Society, and Law.* New York: Columbia University Press, 1988.

Nagel, T. "Sexual Perversion." *Journal of Philosophy* 66 (1969): 5–17.

O'Brien, M. "Mandatory HIV Antibody Testing Policies: An Ethical Analysis." *Bioethics* 3, 4 (1989): 273–300.

Pargetter, R., and Prior, E. "Discrimination and AIDS." *Social Theory and Practice* 13, 2 (Summer 1987): 129–53.

Pierce, C., and VanDeVeer, D., eds. *AIDS: Ethics and Public Policy.* Belmont, Calif.: Wadsworth, 1987.

Sontag, S. *AIDS and its Metaphors.* New York: Farrar, Strauss and Giroux, 1988.

Tinker, J., ed. *Blaming Others: Prejudice, Race, and Worldwide AIDS.* London: The Panos Institute, 1988.

Watney, S. *Policing Desire: Pornography, AIDS and the Media.* Minneapolis: University of Minnesota Press, 1987.

Winston, M. "AIDS, Confidentiality and then Right to Know." *Public Affairs Quarterly* 2 (1991): 91–104.

CHAPTER TWELVE

ABORTION

Almost more than any other issue in the United States, abortion raises passion. Images of antiabortion protestors screaming at pro-choice supporters on the streets of cities have become commonplace. Abortion clinics have been fire-bombed, and doctors who are committed to the practice targeted for sometimes violent abuse. A doctor in Florida was shot dead by an anti-abortionist, another in Wichita, Kansas, was wounded. Politicians, particularly at the state level, have introduced legislation restricting the right to abortion, while federal legislation has been proposed protecting that right. Both sides have taken to the courts to determine the constitutionality and scope of the claimed right.

All this is not altogether new. As sexual attitudes and behavior in the second half of this century have become increasingly liberalized, views concerning abortion have also been debated more openly and heatedly. Although philosophers and theologians have addressed the moral issues of abortion for many centuries, increasing sexual tolerance and a reawakening of a religious fundamentalism have focused general social attention upon the pressing moral and legal questions that abortion raises.

Viability   Abortion may be defined as the termination of pregnancy either spontaneously or by artificial induction. Viability is the point at which the fetus is capable of development independent of its mother. Removal of the fetus from the woman's body prior to viability involves its inevitable destruction. At present, the earliest viable point occurs at approximately twenty weeks. It is possible, nevertheless, that technological advance could reduce the time it takes for the fetus to become viable, though at this point reduction to much before sixteen or eighteen weeks is virtually inconceivable.

The point at which the fetus becomes viable is considered irrelevant to the morality of abortion by those holding either that abortion is always wrong or that it is generally permissible. The point of viability tends to make a difference only for those who hold that abortion will be permissible up to some point in fetal development and impermissible after that point. Underlying these differences in moral attitude to abortion are different views about the fetus's moral status. The basic question here has been the moral one of whether the fetus is a person.

Personhood and Rights   Intentional killing of an innocent person is *prima facie* wrong. If a fetus is an innocent person, abortion must be (*prima facie*) wrong also. Antiabortionists usually argue that conception is the only nonarbitrary point during pregnancy at which personhood can be established (see the discussion by John T. Noonan later in this chapter). Accordingly, moral and legal protection from abortion must be provided for the full term of the fetus. This argument is often cast in terms of rights. (For more on right-based moral theories, see Mackie, Chapter 5.) If the fetus is a person, it has the full rights a person enjoys, and hence the right to life. Yet the appeal to rights suggests a qualification of the extreme antiabortion position. Some have argued that where a woman's life is endangered by pregnancy, her right to life would override the fetus's, for autonomous life is considered more worthy than dependent life. An abortion may be performed in such circumstances. (Note that this qualification does not represent the formal Roman Catholic position, which allows only "indirect" abortion resulting from necessary treatment that the fetus is highly unlikely to survive, but where there is no intention to terminate fetal life. An example is the removal of a cancerous uterus.)

A common objection to this line of analysis in terms of personhood is that the fetus clearly fails to possess characteristics definitive of a person (see the discussion by Mary Anne Warren later in this chapter). Antiabortionists usually respond by emphasizing the potentiality of the fetus to acquire personhood rather than its possessing the actual characteristics of full personhood. Potentiality is thought to be a sufficient condition for possessing full human rights.

By contrast, the proabortion argument tends to deny that the fetus has personhood and hence that it has the human right to life. Personhood is taken usually to arise at birth rather than at conception. Proabortionists may admit that the fetus is human in the biological or genetic sense, yet insist that this differs from the morally relevant sense of being a person with human rights. The proabortionist can even admit that the fetus has some rights, while insisting that these rights are not (fully) human and hence that they can be easily overridden. While the antiabortionist holds that the fetus has the rights of a person, the proabortionist usually insists that the fetus has no (full) human rights. Fetal potentiality for personhood is taken by the proabortionist to be neither a necessary nor a sufficient condition for having rights. Accordingly, abortion is not murder, for no human is killed. The woman's right to choose what befalls her body is taken to be the only or at least the crucial right that counts here.

Many have tried to fashion a path between the antiabortion and pro-choice views. Intermediate positions are united in holding that abortion is permissible under some conditions and impermissible under others (see the discussion by R. M. Hare later in this chapter). Some (though not Hare) argue that the fetus has no rights at conception. It acquires rights later in its development—at viability, say, or at quickening (the point at which the woman begins to feel fetal movement, generally between the twelfth and sixteenth weeks). Accordingly, abortion may be performed until that point, but not after. One justification commonly cited for permitting abortion before but not after viability is that the likelihood of a woman's death in an abortion prior to viability is less than in childbirth, while it is greater after the fetus becomes viable. It follows that if technological developments make possible an earlier point of viability, the fetus on this view must acquire its rights at the earlier point. Moreover, potential conflicts between the woman's and the fetus's rights would be commonplace. Some mechanism must be provided for their resolution.

■ SUPREME COURT RULINGS: ROE AND PLANNED PARENTHOOD

Prior to the 1970s, most states in the Union criminalized abortions. In 1973, a pregnant woman (under the pseudonym of Jane Roe) challenged the Texas statute in the courts. In a landmark decision, *Roe v. Wade,* the Supreme Court ruled that the Constitution nowhere recognizes the unborn as legal persons and that state criminalization of abortion in the first trimester (or three months) of pregnancy violates women's rights to privacy. The Court concluded that the decision to abort during this period must be left to the woman and her physician. Nevertheless, the right to privacy, though a fundamental right, was found not to be absolute, for it could be overridden by "compelling" interests with which it competes at later stages of pregnancy. States were considered to have legitimate interests in protecting and preserving the health and life of pregnant women. These interests were thought to become compelling or binding in the second trimester and to justify state regulation of abortion from that point. Regulation could range from administering abortion procedures to prohibiting abortion unless necessary to save the woman's life. It was ruled, finally, that states have an interest in protecting the potential human life of the fetus. This interest begins to become compelling from the point of viability. It could justify legal prohibition of abortion from this point, save when it is necessary to preserve the woman's life or health.

The Court reaffirmed *Roe*'s finding in numerous cases, most notably a decade later, in *Akron v. Akron Center for Reproductive Health* (1983). However, in the dissenting opinion to *Akron,* newly appointed Justice Sandra Day O'Connor criticized the ruling in *Roe.* O'Connor agreed that states have a legitimate interest from the second trimester in ensuring maternal safety, but she argued that this does not entail that there is no legitimate state interest in the first trimester. O'Connor admitted similarly that states have legitimate interests in protecting potential human life. She contended here also that state interests are compelling throughout pregnancy, and not only from the point of viability. O'Connor concluded that the Court's findings in both *Roe* and *Akron* should have been to prohibit abortion. On the strength of these arguments and three further appointments of justices during the Reagan and Bush administrations, antiabortionists were encouraged to challenge again the constitutionality of abortion. The State of Pennsylvania, led by its antiabortion governor Robert Casey, passed legislation sharply delimiting the ability to acquire an abortion in the state. The law attempted to restrict a woman's choice to abort save in rare circumstances where pregnancy endangers her life or results from incest or rape. The law also required counseling for those seeking abortion, a twenty-four hour waiting period, and parental consent for minors. The law amounted to a challenge to the Supreme Court to revisit its decision in *Roe v. Wade.* Planned Parenthood, the family planning clinic committed to providing abortion on demand, sued.

The majority decision in *Planned Parenthood of Pennsylvania v. Casey* (1992) was cowritten by two recent appointees, Justices David Souter and Anthony Kennedy, together with Sandra Day O'Connor. The majority reaffirmed the Court's commitment to protecting liberty and rejected moral offense, however deep, as grounds for restricting liberty. They noted that the Court had protected from governmental intrusion those choices central to personal dignity and autonomy. These include choices pertaining to marriage, contraception, family relationships, child rearing, and education, and they involve the most personal and intimate concerns a person can have. To these choices the majority added abortion. Acknowledging the consequences for others of a woman's decision to abort, the majority nevertheless argued that the experience of pregnancy and childbirth are so intimate and intense that they preclude the state from mandating choice. Thus, the force of *stare decisis* (the Court's prior decisions) coupled with the importance of individual liberty led the majority to reaffirm the central holding of *Roe v. Wade*.

However, the majority admitted that some limits justifiably could be placed on women's liberty to choose abortion. The state has an interest in protecting the life of the unborn, an interest that increases in later stages of pregnancy. Criticizing the trimester model articulated in *Roe* as not necessary to secure a woman's liberty in choosing to abort, the majority replaced it with a dual model. Prior to the point of viability a woman's choice to abort was deemed paramount; after viability a state may promote its profound interest in protecting life by insisting that the woman's choice is informed. Thus, after viability a state may try to persuade women to choose childbirth over abortion by placing before them information concerning alternatives, as well as regulating and possibly even proscribing abortion except where medically necessary to preserve the life or health of pregnant women. State intervention, however, cannot amount to placing an *undue burden* upon women's choice.

Accordingly, *Planned Parenthood v. Casey* altered the standard applicable in assessing the constitutionality of abortion legislation from *strict scrutiny* to *undue burden*. Under *Roe*, the standard of strict scrutiny required a state to show a compelling interest in limiting a woman's right to choose abortion. It was commonly assumed that no limitations on women's right to abort in the first two trimesters would be tolerated. The undue burden standard articulated in *Planned Parenthood* would allow state limitations on choice after viability as long as they did not place an undue burden on women's choice. In other words, the means chosen by the state to further its interest in potential life must be designed to further women's choice, not hinder it.

Justice Harry A. Blackmun

MAJORITY OPINION IN *ROE v. WADE*

This right of privacy, whether it be founded in the Fourteenth Amendment's concept of personal liberty and restrictions upon state action, as we feel it is, or, as the District Court determined, in the Ninth Amendment's reservation of rights to the people, is broad enough to encompass a woman's decision whether or not to terminate her pregnancy. . . .

. . . [A]ppellants and some amici argue that the woman's right is absolute and that she is entitled to terminate her pregnancy at whatever time, in whatever way,

United States Supreme Court, 410 U.S. 113 (1973).

and so for whatever reason she alone chooses. With this we do not agree. Appellants' arguments that Texas either has no valid interest at all in regulating the abortion decision, or no interest strong enough to support any limitation upon the woman's sole determination, is unpersuasive. The Court's decisions recognizing a right of privacy also acknowledge that some state regulation in areas protected by that right is appropriate. As noted above, a state may properly assert important interests in safe-guarding health, in maintaining medical standards, and in protecting potential life. At some point in pregnancy, these respective interests become sufficiently compelling to sustain regulation of the factors that govern the abortion decision. The privacy right involved, therefore, cannot be said to be absolute.

We therefore conclude that the right of personal privacy includes the abortion decision, but that this right is not unqualified and must be considered against important state interests in regulation. . . .

With respect to the State's important and legitimate interest in the health of the mother, the "compelling" point, in the light of present medical knowledge, is at approximately the end of the first trimester. This is so because of the now established medical fact . . . that until the end of the first trimester mortality in abortion is less than mortality in normal childbirth. It follows that, from and after this point, a State may regulate the abortion procedure to the extent that the regulation reasonably relates to the preservation and protection of maternal health. Examples of permissible state regulation in this area are requirements as to the qualifications of the person who is to perform the abortion; as to the licensure of that person; as to the facility in which the procedure is to be performed, that is, whether it must be a hospital or may be a clinic or some other place of less-than-hospital status; as to the licensing of the facility; and the like.

. . . The decision leaves the State free to place increasing restrictions on abortion as the period of pregnancy lengthens, so long as those restrictions are tailored to the recognized state interests. The decision vindicates the right of the physician to administer medical treatment according to his professional judgment up to the points where important state interests provide compelling justifications for intervention. Up to those points the abortion decision in all its aspects is inherently, and primarily, a medical decision, and basic responsibility for it must rest with the physician. If an individual practitioner abuses the privilege of exercising proper medical judgment, the usual remedies, judicial and intraprofessional, are available. . . .

Justices David Souter, Sandra Day O'Connor, and Anthony Kennedy

MAJORITY OPINION IN
PLANNED PARENTHOOD v. CASEY

I I   [6]

. . . Men and women of good conscience can disagree, and we suppose some always shall disagree, about the profound moral and spiritual implications of terminating a pregnancy, even in its earliest stage. Some of us as individuals find abortion offensive to our most basic principles of morality, but that cannot control our decision. Our obligation is to define the liberty of all, not to mandate our own moral code. The underlying constitutional issue is whether the State can resolve these philosophic questions in such a definitive way that a woman lacks all choice in the matter, except perhaps in those rare circumstances in which the pregnancy is itself a danger to her own life or health, or is the result of rape or incest. . . .

Our law affords constitutional protection to personal decisions relating to marriage, procreation, contraception, family relationships, child rearing, and education . . . Our cases recognize "the right of the *individual,* married or single, to be free from unwarranted governmental intrusion into matters so fundamentally affecting a person as the decision whether to bear or beget a child."

. . . Our precedents "have respected the private realm of family life which the state cannot enter." . . . These matters, involving the most intimate and personal choices a person may make in a lifetime, choices central to personal dignity and autonomy, are central to the liberty protected by the Fourteenth Amendment. At the heart of liberty is the right to define one's own concept of existence, of meaning, of the universe, and of the mystery of human life. Beliefs about these matters could not define the attributes of personhood were they formed under compulsion of the State.

These considerations begin our analysis of the woman's interest in terminating her pregnancy but cannot end it, for this reason: though the abortion decision may originate within the zone of conscience and belief, it is more than a philosophic exercise. Abortion is a unique act. It is an act fraught with consequences for others: for the woman who must live with the implications of her decision; for the persons who perform and assist in he procedure; for the spouse, family, and society which must confront the knowledge that these procedures exist, procedures some deem nothing short of an act of violence against innocent human life; and, depending on one's beliefs, for the life or potential that is aborted. Though abortion is conduct, it does not follow that the State is entitled to proscribe it in all instances. That is because the liberty of the woman is at stake in a sense unique to the human condition and so

United States Supreme Court, 112 U.S. 2791 (1992).

unique to the law. The mother who carries a child to full term is subject to anxieties, to physical constraints, to pain that only she must bear. That these sacrifices have from the beginning of the human race been endured by woman with a pride that ennobles her in the eyes of others and gives to the infant a bond of love cannot alone be grounds for the State to insist she make the sacrifice. Her suffering is too intimate and personal for the State to insist, without more, upon its own vision of the woman's role, however dominant that vision has been in the course of our history and our culture. The destiny of the woman must be shaped to a large extent on her own conception of her spiritual imperatives and her place in society.

It should be recognized, moreover, that in some critical respects the abortion decision is of the same character as the decision to use contraception, to which *Griswold v. Connecticut, Eisenstadt v. Baird*, and *Carey v. Population Services International* afford constitutional protection. We have no doubt as to the correctness of those decisions. They support the reasoning in *Roe* relating to the woman's liberty because they involve personal decisions concerning not only the meaning of procreation but also human responsibility and respect for it. As with abortion, reasonable people will have differences of opinion about these matters. One view is based on such reverence for the wonder of creation that any pregnancy ought to be welcomed and carried to full term no matter how difficult it will be to provide the child and ensure its well-being. Another is that the inability to provide for the nurture and care of the infant is a cruelty to the child and an anguish to the parent. These are intimate views with infinite variations, and their deep, personal character underlay our decisions in *Griswold, Eisenstadt*, and *Carey*. The same concerns are present when the woman confronts the reality that, perhaps despite her attempts to avoid it, she has become pregnant.

It was this dimension of personal liberty that *Roe* sought to protect, and its holding invoked the reasoning and the tradition of the precedents we have discussed, granting protection to substantive liberties of the person. *Roe* was, of course, an extension of those cases and, as the decision itself indicated, the separate States could act in some degree to further their own legitimate interests in protecting prenatal life. The extent to which the legislatures of the States might act to outweigh the interests of the woman in choosing to terminate her pregnancy was a subject of debate both in Roe and in decisions following it.

While we appreciate the weight of the arguments made on behalf of the State in the case before us, arguments which in their ultimate formulation conclude that Roe should be overruled, the reservations any of us may have in reaffirming the central holding of *Roe* are outweighed by the explication of individual liberty we have given combined with the force of *stare decisis*. . . .

I V   [1 5]

. . . [I]t is a constitutional liberty of the woman to have some freedom to terminate her pregnancy. We conclude that the basic decision in *Roe* was based on a constitutional analysis which we cannot now repudiate. The woman's liberty is not so unlimited, however, that from the outset the State cannot show its concern for the life of the unborn, and at a later point in the fetal development the State's interest in life has sufficient force so that the right of the woman to terminate the pregnancy can be restricted.

That brings us, of course, to the point where much criticism has been directed at *Roe*, a criticism that always inheres when the Court draws a specific rule from what in the Constitution is but a general standard. We conclude, however, that the urgent claims of the woman to retain the ultimate control over her destiny and her body, claims implicit in the meaning of liberty, require us to perform that function. Liberty must not be extinguished for want of a line that is clear. And it falls to us to give some real substance to the woman's liberty to determine whether to carry her pregnancy to full term.

[1 6]

We conclude the line should be drawn at viability, so that before that time the woman has a right to choose to terminate her pregnancy. We adhere to this principle for two reasons. First, as we have said, is the doctrine of *stare decisis*. Any judicial act of line-drawing may seem somewhat arbitrary, but *Roe* was a reasoned statement, elaborated with great care. We have twice reaffirmed it in the face of great opposition. . . .

The second reason is that the concept of viability, as we noted in *Roe*, is the time at which there is a realistic possibility of maintaining and nourishing a life outside the womb, so that the independent existence of the second life can in reason and all fairness be the object of the state protection that now overrides the rights of the woman. . . . Consistent with other constitutional norms, legislatures may draw lines appear arbitrary without the necessity of offering a justification. But courts may not. We must justify the lines we draw. And there is no line other than viability which is more workable. To be sure, as we have said, there may be some medical developments that affect the precise point of viability, see *supra*, at——, but this is an imprecision within tolerable limits given that the medical community and all those who must apply its discoveries will continue to explore the matter. The viability line also has, as a practical matter, an element of fairness. In some broad sense it might be said that a woman who fails to act before viability has consented to the State's intervention on behalf of the developing child.

The woman's right to terminate her pregnancy before viability is the most central principle of *Roe v. Wade*. It is a rule of law and component of liberty we cannot renounce.

On the other side of the equation is the interest of the state in the protection of potential life. The Roe Court recognized the State's "important and legitimate interest in protecting the potentiality of human life." . . . And we have concluded that the essential holding of *Roe* should be reaffirmed.

Yet it must be remembered that *Roe v. Wade* speaks with clarity in establishing not only the woman's liberty but also the State's "important and legitimate interest in potential life." . . . That portion of the decision in *Roe* has been given too little acknowledgement and implementation by the Court in its subsequent cases. Those cases decided that any regulation touching upon the abortion decision must survive strict scrutiny, to be sustained only if drawn in narrow terms to further a compelling state interest. . . .

[1 7]

Roe established a trimester framework to govern abortion regulations. Under this elaborate but rigid construct, almost no regulation at all is permitted during the first trimester of pregnancy; regulations designed to protect the woman's health, but not to further the State's interest in potential life, are permitted during the second trimester; and during the third trimester, when the fetus is viable, prohibitions are permitted provided the life or health of the mother is not at stake. . . .

The trimester framework no doubt was erected to ensure that the woman's right to choose not become so subordinate to the State's interest in promoting fetal life that her choice exists in theory but not in fact. We do not agree, however, that the trimester approach is necessary to accomplish this objective. A framework of this rigidity was unnecessary and in its later interpretation sometimes contradicted the State's permissible exercise of its powers.

Though the woman has a right to choose to terminate or continue her pregnancy before viability, it does not at all follow that the State is prohibited from taking steps to ensure that this choice is thoughtful and informed. Even in the earliest stages of pregnancy, the State may enact rules and regulations designed to encourage her to know that there are philosophic and social arguments of great weight that can be brought to bear in favor of continuing the pregnancy to full term and that there are procedures and institutions to allow adoption of unwanted children as well as a certain degree of state assistance if the mother chooses to raise the child herself . . . It follows that States are free to enact laws to provide a reasonable framework for a woman to make a decision that has such profound and lasting meaning. This, too, we find consistent with *Roe*'s central premises, and indeed the inevitable consequence of our holding that the State has an interest in protecting the life of the unborn.

We reject the trimester framework, which we do not consider to be part of the essential holding of *Roe*. . . . Measures aimed at ensuring that a woman's choice contemplates the consequences for the fetus do not necessarily interfere with the right recognized in *Roe*, although those measures have been found to be inconsistent with the rigid trimester framework announced in that case. A logical reading of the central holding in *Roe* itself, and a necessary reconciliation of the liberty of the woman and the interest of the State in promoting prenatal life, require, in our view, that we abandon the trimester framework as a rigid prohibition on all previability regulation aimed at the protection of fetal life. The trimester framework suffers from these basic flaws: in its formulation it misconceives the nature of the pregnant woman's interest; and in practice it undervalues the State's interest in potential life, as recognized in *Roe*.

[2 0]

The very notion that the State has a substantial interest in potential life leads to the conclusion that not all regulations must be deemed unwarranted. Not all burdens on the right to decide whether to terminate a pregnancy will be undue. In our view, the undue burden standard is the appropriate means of reconciling the State's interest with the woman's constitutionally protected liberty. . . .

[2 1]

A finding of an undue burden is a shorthand for the conclusion that a state regulation has the purpose or effect of placing a substantial obstacle in the path of a woman seeking an abortion of a nonviable fetus. A statute with this purpose is invalid because the means chosen by the State to further the interest in potential life must be calculated to inform the woman's free choice, not hinder it. And a statute which, while furthering the interest in potential life or some other valid state interest, has the effect of placing a substantial obstacle in the path of a woman's choice cannot be considered a permissible means of serving its legitimate ends. To the extent that the opinions of the Court or of individual Justices use the undue burden standard in a manner that is inconsistent with this analysis, we set out what in our view should be the controlling standard. . . .

[2 4 – 2 7]

. . . We give this summary: [of the undue burden standard]

(a) To protect the central right recognized by *Roe v. Wade* while at the same time accommodating the State's profound interest in potential life, we will employ the undue burden analysis as explained in this opinion. An undue burden exists, and therefore a provision of law is invalid, if its purpose or effect is to place a substantial obstacle in the path of a woman seeking an abortion before the fetus attains viability.

(b) We reject the rigid trimester framework of *Roe v. Wade*. To promote the State's profound interest in potential life, throughout pregnancy the State may take measures to ensure that the woman's choice is informed, and measures designed to advance this interest will not be invalidated as long as their purpose is to persuade the woman to choose childbirth over abortion. These measures must not be an undue burden on the right.

(c) As with any medical procedure, the State may enact regulations to further the health or safety of a woman seeking an abortion. Unnecessary health regulations that have the purpose or effect of presenting a substantial obstacle to a woman seeking an abortion impose an undue burden on the right.

(d) Our adoption of the undue burden analysis does not disturb the central holding of Roe v. Wade, and we affirm that holding. Regardless of whether exceptions are made for particular circumstances, a State may not prohibit any woman from making the ultimate decision to terminate her pregnancy before viability.

(e) We also reaffirm *Roe*'s holding that "subsequent to viability, the State in promoting its interest in the potentiality of human life may, if it chooses, regulate, and even proscribe, abortion except where it is necessary, in appropriate medical judgment, for the preservation of the life or health of the mother." . . .

■ **JOHN T. NOONAN, JR.: ABORTION AND GENETIC PERSONHOOD**

Representing the Natural Law tradition, Roman Catholic scholar and judge John T. Noonan critically rejects all attempts to establish the point at which humanity is acquired any later than at conception. He defines a human being as a being conceived by human parents, having a human genetic code, and so possessing at least the potentiality of "becoming a man." Noonan claims to derive the equal right to life of the fetus from the humanity of the fetus and the principle of "equality of human lives." This view leads to the obligation "not to injure another without reason." Noonan contends that abortions violate both the principle of equality and the obligation not to harm. He concludes that the life of a fetus may not be taken except, in rare cases, to save the woman's life.

John T. Noonan, Jr.

AN ALMOST ABSOLUTE VALUE IN HISTORY

The most fundamental question involved in the long history of thought on abortion is: How do you determine the humanity of a being? To phrase the question that way is to put in comprehensive humanistic terms what the theologians either dealt with as an explicitly theological question under the heading of "ensoulment" or dealt with implicitly in their treatment of abortion. The Christian position as it originated

From *The Morality of Abortion*, edited by John T. Noonan, Jr. (Cambridge, Mass.: Harvard University Press, 1970). Reprinted by permission of the author and publisher. Copyright © 1970 by The President and Fellows of Harvard College.

did not depend on a narrow theological or philosophical concept. It had no relation to the theories of infant baptism. It appealed to no special theory of instantaneous ensoulment. It took the world's view on ensoulment as that view changed from Aristotle to Zacchia. There was, indeed, theological influence affecting the theory of ensoulment finally adopted, and, of course, ensoulment itself was a theological concept, so that the position was always explained in theological terms. But the theological notion of ensoulment could easily be translated into humanistic language by substituting "human" for "rational soul"; the problem of knowing when a man is a man is common to theology and humanism.

If one steps outside the specific categories used by the theologians, the answer they gave can be analyzed as a refusal to discriminate among human beings on the basis of their varying potentialities. Once conceived, the being was recognized as man because he had man's potential. The criterion for humanity, thus, was simple and all-embracing: if you are conceived by human parents, you are human.

The strength of this position may be tested by a review of some of the other distinctions offered in the contemporary controversy over legalizing abortion. Perhaps the most popular distinction is in terms of viability. Before an age of so many months, the fetus is not viable, that is, it cannot be removed from the mother's womb and live apart from her. To that extent, the life of the fetus is absolutely dependent on the life of the mother. This dependence is made the basis of denying recognition to its humanity.

There are difficulties with this distinction. One is that the perfection of artificial incubation may make the fetus viable at any time: it may be removed and artificially sustained. Experiments with animals already show that such a procedure is possible. This hypothetical extreme case relates to an actual difficulty: there is considerable elasticity to the idea of viability. Mere length of life is not an exact measure. The viability of the fetus depends on the extent of its anatomical and functional development. The weight and length of the fetus are better guides to the state of its development than age, but weight and length vary. If viability is the norm, the standard would vary with . . . many individual circumstances.

The most important objection to this approach is that dependence is not ended by viability. The fetus is still absolutely dependent on someone's care in order to continue existence; indeed a child of one or three or even five years of age is absolutely dependent on another's care for existence; uncared for, the older fetus or the younger child will die as surely as the early fetus detached from the mother. The unsubstantiated lessening in dependence at viability does not seem to signify any special acquisition of humanity.

A second distinction has been attempted in terms of experience. A being who has had experience, has lived and suffered, who possesses memories, is more human than one who has not. Humanity depends on formation by experience. The fetus is thus "unformed" in the most basic human sense.

This distinction is not serviceable for the embryo which is already experiencing and reacting. The embryo is responsive to touch after eight weeks and at least at that point is experiencing. At an earlier stage the zygote is certainly alive and responding to its environment. The distinction may also be challenged by the rare case where aphasia has erased adult memory: has it erased humanity? More fundamentally, this distinction leaves even the older fetus or the younger child to be treated as an unformed inhuman thing. Finally, it is not clear why experience as such confers humanity. It could be argued that certain central experiences such as loving or learning are necessary to make a man human. But then human beings who have failed to love or to learn might be excluded from the class called man.

A third distinction is made by appeal to the sentiments of adults. If a fetus dies, the grief of the parents is not the grief they would have for a living child. The fetus is an unnamed "it" till birth, and is not perceived as personality until at least the fourth month of existence when movements in the womb manifest a vigorous presence demanding joyful recognition by the parents.

Yet feeling is notoriously an unsure guide to the humanity of others. Many groups of humans have had difficulty in feeling that persons of another tongue, color, religion, sex, are as human as they. Apart from reactions to alien groups, we mourn the loss of a ten-year-old boy more than the loss of his one-day-old brother or his 90-year-old grandfather. The difference felt and the grief expressed vary with the potentialities extinguished, or the experience wiped out; they do not seem to point to any substantial difference in the humanity of baby, boy, or grandfather.

Distinctions are also made in terms of sensation by the parents. The embryo is felt within the womb only after about the fourth month. The embryo is seen only at birth. What can be neither seen nor felt is different from what is tangible. If the fetus cannot be seen or touched at all, it cannot be perceived as man.

Yet experience shows that sight is even more untrustworthy than feeling in determining humanity. By sight, color became an appropriate index for saying who was a man, and the evil of racial discrimination was given foundations. Nor can touch provide the test; a being confined by sickness, "out of touch" with others, does not thereby seem to lose his humanity. To the extent that touch still has appeal as a criterion, it appears to be a survival of the old English idea of "quickening"—a possible mistranslation of the Latin *animatus* used in the canon law. To that extent touch as a criterion seems to be dependent on the Aristotelian notion of ensoulment, and to fall when this notion is discarded.

Finally, a distinction is sought in social visibility. The fetus is not socially perceived as human. It cannot communicate with others. Thus, both subjectively and objectively, it is not a member of society. As moral rules are rules for the behavior of members of society to each other, they cannot be made for behavior toward what is not yet a member. Excluded from the society of men, the fetus is excluded from the humanity of men.

By force of the argument from the consequences, this distinction is to be rejected. It is more subtle than that founded on an appeal to physical sensation, but it is equally dangerous in its implications. If humanity depends on social recognition, individuals or whole groups may be dehumanized by being denied any status in their society. Such a fate is fictionally portrayed in *1984* and has actually been the lot of many men in many societies. In the Roman empire, for example, condemnation to slavery meant the practical denial of most human rights; in the Chinese Communist world, landlords have been classified as enemies of the people and so treated as nonpersons by the state. Humanity does not depend on social recognition, though often the failure of society to recognize the prisoner, the alien, the heterodox as human has led to the destruction of human beings. Anyone conceived by a man and a woman is human. Recognition of this condition by society follows a real event in the objective order, however imperfect and halting the recognition. Any attempt to limit humanity to exclude some group runs the risk of furnishing authority and precedent for excluding other groups in the name of the consciousness or perception of the controlling group in the society.

A philosopher may reject the appeal to the humanity of the fetus because he views "humanity" as a secular view of the soul and because he doubts the existence of anything real and objective which can be identified as humanity. One answer to such a philosopher is to ask how he reasons about moral questions without supposing that there is a sense in which he and the others of whom he speaks are human. Whatever group is taken as the society which determines who may be killed is thereby taken as human. A second answer is to ask if he does not believe that there is a right and wrong way of deciding moral questions. If there is such a difference, experience may be appealed to: to decide who is human on the basis of the sentiment of a given society has led to consequences which rational men would characterize as monstrous.

The rejection of the attempted distinction based on viability and visibility, experience and feeling, may be buttressed by the following considerations: Moral judgments often rest on distinction, but if the distinctions are not to appear arbitrary fiat, they should relate to some real difference in probabilities. There is a kind of continuity in all life, but the earlier stages of the elements of human life possess tiny probabilities of development. Consider, for example, the spermatozoa in any normal ejaculate: There are about 200,000,000 in any single ejaculate, of which one has a chance of developing into a zygote. Consider the oocytes which may become ova: there are 100,000 to 1,000,000 oocytes in a female infant, of which a maximum of 390 are ovulated. But once spermatozoon and ovum meet and the conceptus is formed, such studies as have been made show that roughly in only 20 percent of the cases will spontaneous abortion occur. In other words, the chances are about 4 out of 5 that this new being will develop. At this stage in the life of the being there is a sharp shift in probabilities, an immense jump in potentialities. To make a distinction between the rights of spermatozoa and the rights of the fertilized ovum is to respond to an enormous shift in possibilities. For about twenty days after conception the egg may split to form twins or combine with another egg to form a chimera but the probability of either even happening is very small.

It may be asked, What does a change in biological probabilities have to do with establishing humanity? The argument from probabilities is not aimed at establishing humanity but at establishing an objective discontinuity which may be taken into account in moral discourse. As life itself is a matter of probabilities, as most moral reasoning is an estimate of probabilities, so it seems in accord with the structure of reality and the nature of moral thought to found a moral judgment on the change in probabilities at conception. The appeal to probabilities is the most commonsensical of arguments, to a greater or smaller degree all of us base our actions on probabilities, and in morals, as in law, prudence and negligence are often measured by the account one has taken of the probabilities. If the chance is 200,000,000 to 1 that the movement in the bushes into which you shoot is a man's, I doubt if many persons would hold you careless in shooting; but if the chances are 4 out of 5 that the movement is a human being's, few would acquit you of blame. Would the argument be different if only one out of ten children conceived came to term? Of course this argument would be different. This argument is an appeal to probabilities that actually exist, not to any and all states of affairs which may be imagined.

The probabilities as they do exist do not show the humanity of the embryo in the sense of a demonstration in logic any more than the probabilities of the movement in the bush being a man demonstrate beyond all doubt that the being is a man. The appeal is a "buttressing" consideration, showing the plausibility of the standard adopted. The argument focuses on the decisional factor in any moral judgment and assumes that part of the business of a moralist is drawing lines. One evidence of the nonarbitrary character of the line drawn is the difference of probabilities on either side of it. If a spermatozoon is destroyed, one destroys a being which had a chance of far less than 1 in 200 million of developing into a reasoning being, possessed of the genetic code, a heart and other organs, and capable of pain. If a fetus is destroyed, one destroys a being already possessed of the genetic code, organs, and sensitivity to pain, and one which had an 80 percent chance of developing further into a baby outside the womb who, in time, would reason.

The positive argument for conception as the decisive moment of humanization is that at conception the new being receives the genetic code. It is this genetic information which determines his characteristics, which is the biological carrier of the possibility of human wisdom, which makes him a self-evolving being. A being with a human genetic code is man.

This review of current controversy over the humanity of the fetus emphasizes what a fundamental question the theologians resolved in asserting the inviolability of the fetus. To regard the fetus as possessed of equal rights with other humans was not, however, to decide every case where abortion might be employed. It did decide in the case where the argument was that the fetus should be aborted for its own good. To say a being was human was to say it had a destiny to decide for itself which could not be taken from it by another man's decision. But human beings with equal rights often come in conflict with each other, and some decision must be made as whose claims are to prevail. Cases of conflict involving the fetus are different only in two respects: the total inability of the fetus to speak for itself and the fact that the right of the fetus regularly at stake is the right to life itself.

The approach taken by the theologians to these conflicts was articulated in terms of "direct" and "indirect." Again, to look at what they were doing from outside their categories, they may be said to have been drawing lines or "balancing values." "Direct" and "indirect" are spatial metaphors; "line-drawing" is another. "To weigh" or "to balance" values is a metaphor of a more complicated mathematical sort hinting at the process which goes on in moral judgments. All the metaphors suggest that, in the moral values made, comparisons were necessary, that no value completely controlled. The principle of double effect was no doctrine fallen from heaven, but a method of analysis appropriate where two relative values were being compared. In Catholic moral theology, as it developed, life even of the innocent was not taken as an absolute. Judgments on acts affecting life issued from a process of weighing. In the weighing, the fetus was always given a value greater than zero, always a value separate and independent from its parents. This valuation was crucial and fundamental in all Christian thought on the subject and marked it off from any approach which considered that only the parents' interests needed to be considered.

Even with the fetus weighed as human, one interest could be weighed as equal or superior: that of the mother in her own life. The casuists between 1450 and 1895 were willing to weigh this interest as superior. Since 1895, that interest was given decisive weight only in the two special cases of the cancerous uterus and the ectopic pregnancy. In both of these cases the fetus itself had little chance of survival even if the abortion were not performed. As the balance was once struck in favor of the mother whenever her life was endangered, it could be so struck again. The balance reached between 1895 and 1930 attempted prudentially and pastorally to forestall a multitude of exceptions for interests less than life.

The perception of the humanity of the fetus and the weighing of fetal rights against other human rights constituted the work of the moral analysts. But what spirit animated their abstract judgments? For the Christian community it was the injunction of Scripture to love your neighbor as yourself. The fetus as human was a neighbor, his life had parity with one's own. The commandment gave life to what otherwise would have been only rational calculation.

The commandment could be put in humanistic as well as theological terms: Do not injure your fellow man without reason. In these terms, once the humanity of the fetus is perceived, abortion is never right except in self-defense. When life must be taken to save life, reason alone cannot say that a mother must prefer a child's life to her own. With this exception, now of great rarity, abortion violates the rational humanist tenet of the equality of human lives.

For Christians the commandment to love had received a special imprint in that the exemplar proposed of love was the love of the Lord for his disciples. In the light given by this example, self-sacrifice carried to the point of death seemed in the extreme situations not without meaning. In the less extreme cases, preference for one's own interests to the life of another seemed to express cruelty or selfishness irreconcilable with the demands of love.

■ R. M. HARE: ABORTION, KANTIANISM, AND UTILITARIANISM

R. M. Hare rejects as leading to a dead end the common appeals in the abortion debate to the personhood of the fetus or to the rights of the fetus or the woman. The important question here, Hare thinks, is whether there is anything about the fetus that constitutes a reason we ought not to kill it. At earlier stages of fetal life its central nervous system is insufficiently developed for it to experience pain. So fetal suffering, at least prior to viability, cannot be such a reason. Hare argues that fetal potentiality, or the properties it does not now have but will have later if it survives, provides one reason. Pregnancies should not be terminated because they will likely result in people being born who will be glad later to have been born. He offers two related arguments in support of this claim, the first Kantian and the second utilitarian. First, abortion is not generally a universalizable choice (see Kant, Chapter 3). On pain of contradiction, nobody rationally can will their mothers to have had an abortion for accordingly they would not be present now to will this. But underlying this is the fact, second, that we value our existence not for its own sake but for the sake of the good things that happen to us that would not happen if we did not exist (for more on utilitarianism, see Chapter 4). Hare concludes that, *prima facie,* pregnancies should not be terminated because they will likely result in people who through their lives will be glad to have been born.

    While this constitutes one reason against the permissibility of abortion, Hare admits that there may be competing reasons sometimes for its permissibility. Hare reiterates the Kantian principle to treat people as ends in themselves, with the respect due them as human. From this follows the utilitarian consideration that if there are interests affected by a decision concerning abortion, those interests should be protected impartially. Hare thinks that the demands of impartiality will be satisfied most likely if those with interests in the decision have a say in it (or at least are represented). The greater the interests, the greater the say should be. Those with interests in an abortion decision include the mother and father, the person into whom the fetus would turn if not aborted, but also the (potential) children who might be born if this fetus is aborted (discounted by probabilities), the medical personnel who would be involved in the abortion procedure, and so on. While Hare acknowledges the mother's interest to be preponderant, it is not the only one. A woman's obligation to abort or not will be determined on Hare's view by a utilitarian calculus, weighing up the probability of a future fetus developing into a person living a happy as opposed to a harmful life against the probability of same for the present fetus. Hare concludes that the *prima facie* wrongness of abortion consists in preventing a person coming into existence, not in any wrong done to the fetus as such. Yet this general wrongness of abortion may be overridden quite easily in given cases, if the satisfaction of interests that follows from terminating a pregnancy outweighs the sacrifice of other interests.

R. M. Hare

A KANTIAN APPROACH TO ABORTION

The position of somebody wondering whether to have an abortion is usually too wretched for it to be decent for a philosopher to try to make her decision depend on

From *Social Theory and Practice* 15, 1 (Spring 1989): 1–14. Copyright © R. M. Hare. Reprinted by permission of author.

the definitions of words that could in principle have several different definitions.[1] So let us start by putting to rest the question "Is the foetus a person?," which has occupied so many pages in discussion of this problem. It leads straight to a dead end, and we would best avoid it. We know what a foetus is, in the sense that if anybody were to ask whether an object before us or even inside us was a human foetus, there would be no difficulty in principle in determining whether it was. For the same sort of reason, we know how to determine some of the properties the foetus has. We know, for example, that it has the potentiality of becoming a human adult—that is, that if the pregnancy comes to term, it will have turned into a baby, and if the baby survives it will turn into an adult more or less like us.

There are some things of the same ordinary sort about which we cannot be so certain, but which do not present great problems. For example, we do not know for certain whether foetuses, at any rate at a late stage of pregnancy, may not have some rudimentary conscious experiences, including experiences of suffering. It is fairly certain that at earlier stages, before their nervous systems have become at all developed, they do not have such experiences. So let us avoid this question by supposing, either that the abortion in question would be at such an early stage of pregnancy, or, if later, that it could be done without causing pain to the foetus (for example, by anaesthesia).

As I said, there seems to be no difficulty in principle in deciding these facts about the foetus. They are facts which may be, and I think are, morally relevant when we are deciding what it is all right to do to the foetus. But what about the question whether the foetus is a person? How would we answer that? We have to see that it is not the same kind of question at all as the question "Will the foetus, if the pregnancy continues and the child survives, turn into a human adult like us, or into, say, a horse?" The reason is that it is uncertain what we mean by "person," whereas it is not uncertain what we mean by "horse," or "human adult." We all know how to tell whether something is a horse or a human adult. But we do not know how to tell whether the foetus is a person. To that extent the term "person" is unclear.

The main trouble is that "person," and other words like "human being" which have been used in this dispute, all have several different meanings. There is a clear sense in which a foetus is not a person. It is altogether too different from the things which we instantly recognize as people. If the notice in the elevator says it may not carry more than six persons, a pregnant woman is still allowed to have five adult companions in the elevator.

At the opposite extreme, there is a sense in which it is a necessary condition for something's being called a person that it has the rights which persons have, or that the duties are owed to it which we owe to persons. Obviously, if the foetus were a person in that sense, it would have the rights that other persons have, and to kill it would be murder. But for that very reason, if having the rights is a qualification for being called a person, then we cannot know whether the foetus is a person without first deciding whether the foetus has the rights. But that was the question we started with. So it is obviously no use trying to settle that question by asking whether the foetus is a person; we shan't know whether it is, in the required sense, until we have already decided the question about its rights.

There are going to be a lot of senses of "person" besides these, or in between these, and there will not be room even to list them all. It should be clear already that most of the disputes about this allegedly crucial question of whether the foetus is a person are going to be a waste of time and can never get anywhere.

How do people get into this impasse? The cause is this: they have some excellent firm principles about murder and about liberty, and in this difficult case of abortion it looks as if the principles conflict. If one forbids the abortion, one infringes the liberty of the mother; if one allows it, one is allowing murder. So people take sides for one principle or the other, call themselves "pro-life" or "pro-choice," and stop thinking. They even start bombing one another.

We start with these good firm simple principles about life and liberty (though we do not know how to formulate them clearly and explicitly), and then they come into conflict. If we terminate a pregnancy, we are offending against the principle requiring us to preserve life. If we stop women terminating their pregnancies, we are offending against the other principle requiring us to preserve liberty or choice. The right thing to do in this predicament is to think some more and try to formulate the principles exactly and apply them to this case, and see whether we can find forms of them that do not conflict with each other. That indeed is what people are trying to do when they argue about whether the foetus is a person. For if there were a sense in which the foetus is not a person, the conflict might be resolved; in killing the foetus, one would not be committing the murder, because killing is not murder unless it is the killing of people. And so we could observe the principle about liberty by letting the foetus be killed, without breaking the principle about murder.

As we saw, this manoeuvre does not do any good, because the word "person" is indeterminate; taken one way, we can say that it is all right to kill the foetus because it is not a person (in the sense of occupying one person's place in the elevator); but the side that does not think the foetus ought to be killed was not using the word in that sense. It was using it in the sense in which to be a person is to be a possessor of the rights that ordinary persons have. And we are not in a position to say whether the foetus is a person in that sense. This is a moral, not a factual question, and we cannot answer it until we have settled the prior question of whether we have the duties to the foetus that we have to ordinary adults, that is, whether the foetus has the same rights as adults have.

So what ought we to do, instead of disputing endlessly about whether the foetus is a person? My advice is that we forget about the word "person," and ask instead about the properties of the foetus that might be reasons why we ought not to kill it—properties in the ordinary factual sense in which we can determine whether or not it has them. It may be that the word "person" stands for some combination of these properties, or ambiguously for more than one possible set of them. In that case, if we can isolate a set of ordinary properties of the foetus which together constitute a reason why we ought not to let it be killed, we might sum up this set of properties by saying that the foetus is a person. But, for the reasons I have given, we should be able to do this only after first answering the moral question. The word "person" would not have helped in the argument; it would at most be a convenient way of summarizing its conclusion. The real work would have been done in identifying the ordinary properties of the foetus that made us want to say (if that was what we did want to say) that it ought not to be killed. The hard part of the moral thinking is that involved in this identification of the ordinary properties which are the reasons for or against killing the foetus.

What then are these ordinary properties? One is that, if the foetus suffered while being killed, then that would be a reason for not inflicting this suffering on it, though there could be reasons on the other side. But we can ignore this property if we confine ourselves, as I have proposed, to cases where we can all be sure it will not suffer.

What other properties of the foetus, besides its capacity for suffering which we have now discounted, could give us reasons for not killing it? I cannot think of any besides the foetus's potentiality, already mentioned, of turning into someone like us. Here is an example that will illustrate why I cannot think of any. Suppose that in the case of a given pregnancy we can be absolutely certain that for reasons beyond anybody's control the foetus will not survive. It has, say, some recognizable disease from which foetuses never recover. Let us suppose additionally that, if we did kill the foetus, we could do so painlessly, say by using an anaesthetic. In such a case is there any reason for not killing the foetus if there are other grounds for killing it (say the health of the mother)? This case illustrates rather well what is wrong with what I shall call the absolutist pro-life position. It also illustrates the difference between foetuses and ordinary human persons. In the case of an ordinary person who you were certain would die in a month, there would be reasons for not killing that person. It would disappoint hopes of what he (or she) might have done in the remaining month; the process of killing might cause fear; it might cause sorrow to others; the terminally ill patient might be deprived of the chance of ordering his financial affairs for the benefit of his family, or even reconciling himself and them to his impending death. There could be reasons, all the same, on the other side, such as the suffering he would undergo if his life were prolonged. None of these reasons applies to the foetus. The foetus does not have now, at the present moment, properties which are reasons for not killing it, given that it will die in any case before it acquires those properties which ordinary human adults and even children have, and which are our reasons for not killing them. A foetus before it has achieved sentience does not currently possess any properties that could be morally relevant to its treatment and which are not possessed equally by oysters and earthworms.

If we are to find reasons for not killing the foetus, we must look for some properties which it does not have now, but which it will have later if it survives. Philosophers call these potential properties, and argue about whether the potentiality that the foetus has of turning into someone like us is morally relevant to what we may or may not do to the foetus now. The case that I have just described shows that defenders of the foetus, if they are going to make good their defence, have nothing else that they can rely on except the foetus's potentiality. But I shall be arguing in a moment, against the views of many philosophers like Michael Tooley,[2] that potentiality does provide a powerful weapon with which to defend the foetus in normal cases.

In order to set up this argument I shall have to do a little ethical theory, though I will try to make as light work of it as I can. The ethical theory I am going to use is of a more or less Kantian sort.[3] I am also going, for reasons which I hope will become clear in a moment, to make a time-switch into the past. Suppose that it is not this woman now who is deciding whether or not to have an abortion, but some other woman in the past. Suppose, for example, it was my own mother deciding whether or not to terminate the pregnancy which actually resulted in me. In that case, am I going to say that it is morally quite all right for her to have an abortion?

Please note that the question is not "What would I say if I were speaking to her at that time?" Nor is it "What would I say now if I did not exist?" I have deliberately formulated the question in such a way as to avoid the difficulties with those other questions. The question is, "What do I (presently existing person) now say about this past situation?"

I will draw attention to an obvious reason why I might not like to say that it was all right for her to have an abortion. It is a reason which might be outweighed by other reasons, but it is at least a reason. The reason is that if she had had an abortion, I would not now have existed. Let us suppose that I am able to reach back in time and give instructions to my mother as to what she should do. Suppose, even, that she is able to ask me questions about what she ought to do. In order to get into a position in which I can communicate with her at that time, I shall have to penetrate some noumenal world outside time (this is really getting very Kantian) and have access to her in that past time. This of course raises deep philosophical problems, into which I am not going to go. But just suppose I can do it. What shall I say to her?

I am sure I shall not say "Carry on, have the abortion; it's all the same to me." Because my existence now is valuable to me, I shall not, other things being equal, will (to use another Kantian term) that she should have the abortion, thereby depriving me of the possibility of existence. I value my existence, not for its own sake, but for the sake of the nice things that happen to me, which couldn't happen if I did not exist. There is a sentence in the Anglican Prayer Book in which we thank God for our creation, preservation, and all the blessings of this life.[4] If there were no blessings but only curses, then we could not thank him for our creation either, but he has been good enough to arrange things otherwise for most of us. That we can thank him for our creation does not show that mere existence in itself is a good; but it does show that it is a good at least as a means to the other good things that those who exist can have. Therefore, faced with the possibility of either existing now or not existing now, the normally happy person will tell his mother not to have the abortion. And therefore, all things being equal (if, for example, she is not going to die if the pregnancy is not terminated), he will say that she ought not to have it.

I put the whole dialogue in the past, because of an argument which is sometimes used by philosophers who write about this question. They say that potential people or merely possible people do not have any rights, and we cannot have any duties to them. But in the case I describe we were talking about an actual person, namely myself. I am asking myself, as an actual person, to prescribe what ought to have been done at a time in the past when my mother was contemplating having an abortion. Potential people do not come into this argument.

It is a part of ethical theory that is accepted by almost all moral philosophers, however, that if one makes a moral judgement about any case or situation, one must, to be consistent, make the same moral judgement about any other case which resembles it in all its non-moral particulars. For example, if it is all right for one person to do something (call him A), it must be all right for anybody else to do the same thing in exactly the same situation. By "the same situation," I mean the same in all respects, and these include the properties of the people in it. So I am not saying that if it is all right for A to tickle B when B likes being tickled, it must be all right for B to tickle A who hates being tickled. What I am saying is that if the circumstances and all the properties, including the wishes, of the people are the same, the moral judgement has to be the same.

In applying this theoretical doctrine, which, as I said, is accepted by nearly all moral philosophers, at least all who understand what the doctrine is (some have denied it through not understanding it), we have to apply it to hypothetical cases as well as to actual ones. If it was wrong for my mother to have an abortion, then it would be wrong for any other mother to have an abortion in exactly the same circumstances, and therefore would now be wrong for the woman we started with to have an abortion, if the circumstances were the same. And this, in general, is the prima facie case for being against abortion, as most of us are in general. By that I mean that most of us, if asked whether it just does not matter in the least whether people have abortions or not, would say that we think that in most cases it does matter; most pregnancies ought to be allowed to continue; those who want to legalize abortion want to do so because that will leave the decision to the individuals concerned in special cases where there are strong grounds for termination. Nobody thinks that no abortions matter, except those who do not care whether the human race survives or not, or who even want it not to survive.

The reason why most of us think that all things being equal pregnancies should not be terminated, is that we think that on the whole they are likely to result in people being born who will in the course of their lives be glad to have been born. There is of course a problem about having too many people: if there were so many people, and the results of over-population made them so unhappy, that they wished they had not been born, that would be different; but I am assuming that this is not the case yet. I shall be returning to this point.

Reverting for a moment, however, to the dialogue between myself in the present and my mother in the past, there is one other thing that I might think I could say. We have considered two things I might say, namely "Do not have the abortion" and "You ought to have the abortion." What I said was that I would not say "You ought to have the abortion," because this would be a prescription to her to have the abortion, and I do not want that. So, if those were the only two things I could say, I would choose the first, "Do not have the abortion," and rule out the second "You ought to have the abortion." But a third thing I might say is "I do not say you ought to have an abortion; but I do not claim, either, that you ought not to have it; of course I want you not to have it, because otherwise I shall not exist; so I still go on saying, so far as I am concerned 'Do not have it.' But if you ask me whether it is the case, morally speaking, that you ought not to have it, I would not go so far as that. You will not be doing wrong if you have it, but please do not."

This possibility, though important, raises difficulties which are really too great for me to deal with here. If I am trying to give my mother positive moral guidance, I shall be confined to the two answers, "You ought" and "You ought not"; and, if this is so then, because I prefer to be existing now, I shall not say "You ought," and shall therefore have to say "You ought not."[5]

There is, then, a reason for accepting the general principle which forbids abortions in ordinary cases. The question is, then, whether we ought to allow any exceptions to this principle, and whether they ought to extend further than the exceptions that can be made to the principle that we should not kill adults. Let us ask what are the reasons for having the latter principle. We have looked at some of them already. Nearly all of us want not to be killed, and want not to live in fear of being killed. So, when faced with a choice between a universal prohibition on killing people and a universal license to kill them, we would choose the former. But most of us do not want to have to choose between these stark alternatives; we want to make some exceptions to the principle forbidding killing people, of which killing in self-defence is an obvious one, and killing in war or as a penalty for murder are more controversial. If we are speaking, as we are, of a general principle to be inculcated in children when we bring them up, and protected by the law, the principle has to be fairly simple and cannot contain too many complicated exceptions. So we allow killing in self-defence and perhaps in these other cases, but try to keep the prohibition as simple as we can. This is in the interests of workability.

It is sometimes said that if one allows exceptions to such simple principles one will be inserting the thin end of a wedge, or starting down a slippery slope. This is indeed sometimes the case; but sometimes it is not. Whether it is will depend on whether there is a clear stopping-place on the slope where we can dig in our heels— and sometimes there is. When it was decided in the United States to allow cars to turn right at a red light after stopping, did anybody say "You are starting down a slippery slope: if you let people turn right on a red light, then you will have breached the absolute ban on crossing a red light, and people will soon begin crossing it when they want to go straight ahead or turn left"? People realized that it was quite easy to distinguish the cases in which it was now to be legal to cross the red light from those in which it was still to be forbidden. So the slope was not slippery.

Similarly, nobody says that we ought to forbid killing even in self-defence because if you allow that, people will start killing for other reasons too. In this case, there is a real difficulty in deciding what counts as self-defence, and no doubt there are volumes of cases in the criminal law in which this has had to be sorted out. But even so (even though, that is, the slope is a little bit slippery) we do allow killing in self-defence, and the slope has not in practice proved too slippery.

In principle, we could do the same for abortion. The argument is sometimes used that if we allow the killing of foetuses, people will soon be killing adults ad lib. I cannot see much force in this argument. In many countries the killing of foetuses has been legalized under certain conditions, and in others it has never been illegal. I know of no evidence that this has led to a greater incidence of ordinary murder.

Although the slope from killing foetuses to killing adults is not slippery, there is a slippery slope from killing foetuses under certain conditions to killing them under other conditions. This is because it is rather difficult to delimit precisely in law the conditions under which abortion is allowable. Expressions like "congenital defect" and "the health of the mother" are capable of being stretched. Whether we think it is dangerous that this slope is slippery, however, will depend on what view we take about the general question of what abortions should be allowed, and who should make the decision. For example, if we took the view that abortion should be allowed freely and the mother should decide, we should not mind the law being stretched in this way. I do not myself take so extreme a view; but I do not think it bad that the law has been stretched a bit, as it has been in different ways in different countries.

But at any rate the slope from killing foetuses to killing adults is not slippery. So we can reasonably ask whether it would be all right to allow an exception, in the case of foetuses, to the general ban on killing. How would we decide such a question? The general ban on killing has a point, as we saw earlier, namely that people want not to be killed. But does this point extend to foetuses? They do not want not to be killed.

I have argued that most people prefer not to have been killed when they were foetuses; and that this gives us a general reason for having a principle that we ought not to kill foetuses. But here we have to be rather careful. The general preference for existence over non-existence does not justify the principle that we ought to bring into existence all the people we could bring into existence. If we tried to do that, there would obviously be too many people, and perhaps a majority of those people would wish that we had not brought them into existence, thus destroying the premiss of our argument. So evidently any principle that we are likely to accept is going to allow some limitation of the population, if only by the use of the methods approved by the Pope.

However we limit the population, it is going to result in some people not being born who could have been born. We have to ask next, "Is there any reason for giving precedence to some of these people over others?" Notice that the argument used earlier in defence of the foetus does not provide any such reason. Suppose that if this woman does not have a baby now she will have one in a year's time, but that she will not have that other baby if she has one now. Each of these people, if born, will, we hope, have reason to be thankful that he or she was born; but, other things being equal, neither will have any more reason for being thankful than the other has. So, given that we are going to limit the population, does it make any difference which of the possible people is born, and which gets excluded? The argument used so far does not provide any reason for saying that it makes a difference.

There are certainly factors which could make a difference. If, for example, the mother is not at present married but hopes to be soon, this might mean that the present foetus, if born, will not have such a good start in life as the other would. Or, to take a case which points in the opposite direction: if the mother is thirty-five years old, there is a reason for having a child in the next five years. The reason is that if she postpones having it until she is forty, the chance of the child being born with Down's syndrome is greater. So there can be reasons for choosing to have a child later rather than now, or the reverse. But we have so far not been able to discover any general reason for giving precedence to the child that this foetus would turn into over other possible future children, given that one or another of them is going to be born.

Are there any strong reasons for preferring the child that this foetus would turn into? The feeling many people have that it should have precedence may be due to a false analogy between foetuses and adults. Certainly it would be wrong to kill an adult in order to replace him or her with some other person who might be born. This is because the existing adult has desires (above all the desire to live) which will be frustrated if he is killed. That is the reason why we have the general ban on killing adults. And this applies even to young children. Whether it applies to neonates, who do not have the desire to live, is a controversial question which there is no room to discuss here. It certainly applies to children from a very early age. But it does not apply to foetuses; so at any rate that reason for saying that foetuses ought not to be killed lacks force.

At this point it will be claimed that the argument so far provides no reason for forbidding abortions that does not apply equally to contraception or even to abstinence. I think that this is right. So far we have no such reason. Perhaps reasons can be found, but they are relatively weak ones. Abortion is a more tricky procedure medically than contraception. But there are contraceptive methods which are really abortifacients, because, when used before or during copulation, they kill the zygote (perhaps by preventing implantation) after it has been formed. There is no clear reason for distinguishing such methods from the kind which prevents the formation of zygotes. Again, the feeling that there is a difference is due to a false analogy.

There is also the consideration that normally the foetus attracts feelings of affection on the part of the mother and perhaps others—feelings which do not yet attach to a possible future child that she might have. To kill the foetus, even if the mother herself desires this all things considered, is bound to wound those feelings. She might feel that it would have been better to have used contraception.

There is also what might be called the "bird in the hand" argument. The foetus is there, and will turn into an adult if it survives; future conceptions and births are more problematical. Given, however, that there is likely to be a child that will be born, if not to this family, then to some other family, and so occupy the place in the demography that this child would occupy, that does not seem a very strong argument.

If, as already argued, abortions are in general wrong, but allowable in particular cases, what such exceptions ought the law to allow, and who should have the task of deciding when to perform an abortion? The general principle is that, if there are interests affected by a decision, then, since we have to treat people as ends, those interests should be protected impartially; and this is most likely to happen if those who have the interests have a say in the decision, or, if they are not in a position to have a say, are in some way represented, and if the greater interests have the greater say. This is likely to result in the maximal and impartial protection of the interests. Those who like to speak about rights (and I see no harm in that) can speak equally well of the protection of their rights. But interests will do for the present argument.

Obviously the mother has a very great interest in the outcome. That is the justification for the claim that the mother ought to have the only say; and this would indeed be so if there were no other interests affected. But there are other interests, and we must consider them. The father has an interest—certainly a smaller one than the mother, but not negligible. The person into whom the foetus would turn if not aborted has an interest—a very great one. But this interest may be counterbalanced by those of other children who might be born thereafter, if the family is in any case to be limited. Certainly, if it is known that this foetus is seriously defective (the mother, say, had rubella) but she could have a normal child later, the interest of that normal child is much greater than that of the defective child who would be born from this pregnancy.

There is also the interest of doctors, surgeons, and nurses who may be called upon to perform the abortion. If ever we have an abortifacient pill that can be bought at pharmacies and used at any stage in early pregnancy, that would cut out the doctors; but I think it unlikely that such a pill will be developed soon which could safely be sold without prescription, although an abortion pill is now available on prescription in France. So for the moment we have to consider the interest of the doctor who is being asked to act against his conscience—and this is an interest, even if the conscience is misguided.

The question of who should decide whether to allow an abortion is the question of how best to be fair to all these interests. The mother's interest is preponderant but not the sole one. What the best procedure is depends on a lot of factors which I am not able to assess with confidence. But I am inclined to think that there are procedures now followed in some countries which have worked well in practice and have done reasonable justice between the interests affected. In any case, that is what we should be aiming at.[6]

N O T E S

1. I have tried in this paper to improve the argument in my "Abortion and the Golden Rule," *Philosophy and Public Affairs* 4 (1975): 20–22; German translation in A. Leist, ed., *Um Leben und Tod*, forthcoming. There are, however, some important points in that earlier paper which are not here repeated.

2. M. Tooley, "Abortion and Infanticide," *Philosophy and Public Affairs* 2 (1972): 37–65, revised in Joel Feinberg, ed., *The Problem of Abortion* (Belmont, Calif.: Wadsworth, 1973).

3. The theory can also be put into a utilitarian form, and I have often so put it. The idea that Kantianism and utilitarianism are irreconcilable is the result of attempts by modern deontologists to borrow Kant's authority for their own intuitionist positions; but they seldom document their claims about Kant, and it could in fact be shown that a properly formulated utilitarianism and a properly formulated Kantianism need not conflict. For hints, see references to Kant in index to my *Moral Thinking* (Oxford: Oxford University Press, 1981), and my "Punishment and Retributive Justice," *Philosophical Topics* 14 (1986): 219; reprinted in my *Essays on Political Morality* (Oxford University Press, 1989) pp. 211–15.

4. *Book of Common Prayer* (old and new versions), the General Thanksgiving.

5. I deal at length with this problem in my *Moral Thinking*, pp. 182 ff.

6. This is a revised version of a paper presented at a colloquium with R. B. Brandt at Florida State University on March 11, 1988. This paper also appears in *Right Conduct: Theories and Applications*, 2nd ed., ed. by Michael D. Bayles and Kenneth Henley (New York: Random House, 1989).

■ MARY ANNE WARREN: ABORTION, WOMEN'S RIGHTS, AND FETAL RIGHTS

Mary Anne Warren examines three lines of pro-choice argument: those concerning consequences, rights, and the moral status of the fetus. First, involuntary childbearing and life threatening back-alley abortions are the costly consequences women have suffered as a result of the prohibition on abortion. Moreover, contraception and celibacy are not always viable alternatives, for the former may be unaffordable or unavailable for many women and women may be raped even if celibate. So the costs of abortion are far outweighed by the benefits from its availability, and the costs of its denial outweigh the accrual of any benefits from its prohibition.

Second, basic moral rights, those all persons have as persons, include the rights to life, liberty, self-determination, and freedom from harm. Warren argues that prohibition of abortion appears to infringe upon all of these basic rights. Denial of safe and legal abortions increases the likelihood of death and denies freedom to choose. Women accordingly are forced to suffer not just the inconvenience but the traumas and dangers of unwanted pregnancies and their unhappy outcomes. Warren points out, moreover, that in no other case does the law require anyone not convicted of a crime to sacrifice liberty, self-determination, and bodily integrity to preserve the lives of others.

Third, the question of the moral status of the fetus turns on the more general question concerning what qualifies as having moral status. The most commonly cited criteria include life, sentience (the capacity to have experiences, including ones of pain), genetic humanity (biological identity as a member of the species *Homo sapiens*), and personhood. On balance, we respect biological life not just for the good consequences that follow for humanity but because the unspoiled natural world is worth valuing for its own sake. It follows from this view that one should never kill a living thing without good reason, though killing is sometimes unavoidable. Warren argues that the wrongness of abortion does not necessarily follow from this perspective, for some abortions at least may be defended as necessary killings.

A being is human in the genetic sense simply if it is a member of the species Homo sapiens; a being is human in the moral sense if it is a fully developed member of the moral community, with complete moral rights. John Noonan, for example, defines humanity only in the genetic sense. If he is to show that it is almost always impermissible to abort, he must demonstrate that the genetic and moral senses of humanity are equivalent. Warren contends that this cannot be demonstrated, for the moral community consists of persons and not simply of biological entities. Persons are defined by characteristics a fetus fails to possess, including consciousness, reasoning, communicability, self-motivation, and self-awareness. Warren concludes that a fetus, even at late stages of development, is not personlike and so may be aborted. Nevertheless, the fact that fetuses in later stages of development are increasingly sentient and so capable of experiencing pain means that aborting them will be more difficult, though not necessarily impossible, to justify. The principle of respect for sentient beings does not entail that all beings have an equal right to life. Warren argues that most people tolerate the killing of sentient (nonhuman) life on utilitarian grounds if its death will increase the good overall. That this is thought not to extend to human beings has to do with the fact that the moral status of human beings is not based on sentience alone but is tied up with the complex notion of personhood. Persons are to be treated as moral equals simply in virtue of their personhood. Personhood then is an "inclusion criterion" for moral equality.

Because of the special relation of pregnant women to the fetus, Warren argues that it is impossible to grant equal moral rights to fetuses without denying them to women. If sentience were the sole criterion of personhood, then abortions could only be justified in the first trimester. Yet women face circumstances beyond this point in pregnancy that may lead them to choose abortion. Denying women that right effaces their equal moral status. Warren thus stresses birth as the initiating point of moral equality. Birth initiates the possibility of extending personhood and equal moral rights without violating the basic rights of anyone else. From this line of analysis Warren draws three conclusions: First, we should respect women's over fetal rights in cases of conflict. Second, though personhood serves as an inclusion criterion for moral equality, it cannot serve as an exclusion criterion, for upon birth infants and the mentally handicapped assume the equal rights any other person ought to be accorded. Third, potential personhood cannot sustain the extension of equal rights to the fetus, for in no other case is potential for achieving status grounds for extending status rights.

Mary Anne Warren

ABORTION

INTRODUCTION

Do women have the right to abort unwanted pregnancies? Or is the state entitled (or perhaps ethically required) to prohibit deliberate abortion? Should some abortions be permitted and others not? Does the proper legal status of abortion follow directly from its moral status? Or should abortion be legal, even if it is sometimes or always morally wrong?

Such questions have aroused intense debate during the past two decades. Interestingly enough, in most of the industrialized world abortion was not a criminal of-

From A *Companion to Ethics*, ed. Peter Singer (Oxford: Basil Blackwell, 1991), pp. 303–14.
Reprinted by permission of the publisher.

fence until a series of anti-abortion laws were passed during the second half of the nineteenth century. At that time, proponents of the prohibition of abortion generally stressed the medical dangers of abortion. It was also sometimes argued that fetuses are human beings from conception onward, and that deliberate abortion is therefore a form of homicide. Now that improved techniques have made properly performed abortions much safer than childbirth, the medical argument has lost whatever force it may once have had. Consequently, the focus of anti-abortion arguments has shifted from the physical safety of women to the moral value of fetal life.

Advocates of women's right to choose abortion have responded to the anti-abortion argument in several ways. I shall examine three lines of argument for the pro-choice view: (1) that abortion should be permitted, because the prohibition of abortion leads to highly undesirable consequences; (2) that women have a moral right to choose abortion; and (3) that fetuses are not yet persons and thus do not yet have a substantial right to life.

CONSEQUENTIALIST ARGUMENTS FOR ABORTION

If actions are to be morally evaluated by their consequences, then a strong case can be made that the prohibition of abortion is wrong. Throughout history women have paid a terrible price for the absence of safe and legal contraception and abortion. Forced to bear many children, at excessively short intervals, they were often physically debilitated and died young—a common fate in most pre-twentieth-century societies and much of the Third World today. Involuntary childbearing aggravates poverty, increases infant and child death rates, and places severe strains upon the resources of families and states.

Improved methods of contraception have somewhat alleviated these problems. Yet no form of contraception is 100 percent effective. Moreover, many women lack access to contraception, e.g., because they cannot afford it, or it is unavailable where they live, or unavailable to minors without parental permission. In most of the world paid work has become an economic necessity for many women, married or single. Women who must earn have an acute need to control their fertility. Without that control, they often find it impossible to obtain the education necessary for any but the most marginal employment, or impossible to combine the responsibilities of childbearing and paid labour. This is as true in socialist as in capitalist economies, since in both economic systems women must contend with the double responsibility of paid and domestic work.

Contraception and abortion do not guarantee reproductive autonomy, because many people cannot afford to have (and properly raise) any children, or as many children as they would like; and others are involuntarily infertile. However, both contraception and abortion are essential if women are to have the modest degree of reproductive autonomy which is possible in the world as it is presently constructed.

In the long run, access to abortion is essential for the health and survival not just of individual women and families, but also that of the larger social and biological systems on which all our lives depend. Given the inadequacy of present methods of contraception and the lack of universal access to contraception, the avoidance of rapid population growth generally requires some use of abortion. Unless population growth rates are reduced in those impoverished societies where they remain high, malnutrition and starvation will become even more widespread than at the present. There might still be enough food to feed all the people of the world, if only it were more equitably distributed. However, this cannot remain true indefinitely. Soil erosion and climatic changes brought about by the destruction of forests and the burning of fossil fuels threaten to reduce the earth's capacity for food production—perhaps drastically—within the next generation.

Yet opponents of abortion deny that abortion is necessary for the avoidance of such undesirable consequences. Some pregnancies are the result of rape or involuntary incest, but most result from apparently voluntary sexual behaviour. Thus, anti-abortionists often claim that women who seek abortions are "refusing to take responsibility for their own actions." In their view, women ought to avoid heterosexual intercourse unless they are prepared to complete any resulting pregnancy. But is this demand a reasonable one?

Heterosexual intercourse is not *biologically* necessary for women's—or men's—individual survival or physical health. On the contrary, women who are celibate or homosexual are less vulnerable to cervical cancer, AIDS, and other sexually transmitted diseases. Nor is it obvious that sex is necessary for the psychological health of either women or men, although the contrary belief is widespread. It is, however, something that many women find intensely pleasurable—a fact which is morally significant on most consequentialist theories. Furthermore, it is part of the form of life which the majority of women everywhere appear to prefer. In some places, lesbian women are creating alternative forms of life which may better serve their needs. But for most heterosexual women, the choice of permanent celibacy is very difficult. In much of the world, it is very difficult for single women to support themselves (let alone support a family); and sexual intercourse is usually one of the 'duties' of married women.

In short, permanent celibacy is not a reasonable option to impose upon most women. And since all women are potentially vulnerable to rape, even those who are homosexual or celibate may face unwanted pregnancies. Hence, until there is a fully reliable and safe form of contraception, available to all women, the consequentialist arguments for abortion will remain strong. But these arguments will not persuade those who reject consequentialist moral theories. If abortion is inherently wrong, as many believe, then it cannot be justified as a means of avoiding undesirable consequences. Thus, we must also consider whether women have a moral right to seek abortion.

ABORTION AND WOMEN'S RIGHTS

Not all moral philosophers believe that there are such things as moral rights. Thus, it is important to say a bit here about what moral rights are; in the section [on personhood and moral rights below] I will say more about why they are important [see also Mackie, Chapter 6, Ed.]. Rights are not mysterious entities that we discover in nature; they are not, in fact, entities at all. To say that people have a right to life is to say, roughly, that they should never deliberately be killed or deprived of the necessities of life, unless the only alternative is some much greater evil. Rights are not absolute, but neither are they to be overridden for just any apparently greater good. For instance, one may kill in self-defence when there is no other way to protect oneself from death or serious harm unjustly inflicted; but one may not kill another person merely because others may gain a great deal from the victim's death.

Basic moral rights are those which all persons have, in contrast to those rights which depend upon particular circumstances, e.g., promises or legal contracts. The basic moral rights of persons are usually held to include the rights to life, liberty, self-determination, and freedom from the infliction of bodily harm. The prohibition of abortion appears to infringe upon all of these basic rights. Women's lives are endangered in at least two ways. Where abortion is illegal, women often seek unsafe illegal abortions; the World Health Organization estimates that over 200,000 women die from this cause each year. Many others die from involuntary childbirth, when abortion is unavailable, or when they are pressured not to use it. Of course, voluntary childbirth also involves some risk of death: but in the absence of coercion, there is no violation of the woman's right to life.

The denial of abortion also infringes upon women's rights to liberty, self-determination, and physical integrity. To be forced to bear a child is not just an 'inconvenience', as opponents of abortion often claim. To carry a pregnancy to term is an arduous and risky undertaking, even when voluntary. To be sure, many women enjoy (much of) their pregnancies; but for those who remain pregnant against their will the experience is apt to be thoroughly miserable. And involuntary pregnancy and childbirth are only the beginning of the hardships caused by the denial of abortion. The woman must either keep the child or surrender it for adoption. To keep the child may make it impossible to continue her chosen life work, or to meet her other family obligations. To surrender the child means that she must live with the unhappy knowledge that she has a daughter or son for whom she cannot care, often cannot even know to be alive and well. Studies of women who have surrendered infants for adoption show that, for most, the separation from their child is a great and lasting grief.

Even if we accept the view that fetuses have a right to life, it is difficult to justify the imposition of such hardships upon unwilling individuals for the sake of fetal lives. As Judith Thomson pointed out in her much-discussed 1971 article, "A defense of abortion," there is no other case in which the law requires individuals (who have been convicted of no crime) to sacrifice liberty, self-determination, and bodily integrity in order to preserve the lives of others. Perhaps one analogy to involuntary childbirth is military conscription. However, that comparison can lend only moderate support to the anti-abortion position, since the justifiability of compulsory military service is itself debatable.

In popular rhetoric, especially in the United States, the abortion issue is often seen as purely and simply one of "women's right to control their bodies." If women have the moral right to abort unwanted pregnancies, then the law should not prohibit abortion. But the arguments for this right do not entirely solve the moral issue of abortion. For it is one thing to have a right, and another to be morally justified in exercising that right in a particular case. If fetuses have a full and equal right to life, then perhaps women's right to abort should be exercised only in extreme circumstances. And perhaps we should question further whether fertile human beings—of either sex—are entitled to engage in heterosexual intercourse when they are not willing to have a child and assume the responsibility for it. If popular heterosexual activities are costing the lives of millions of innocent 'persons' (i.e., aborted fetuses), then should we not at least try to give up these activities? On the other hand, if fetuses do not yet have a substantial right to life, then abortion is not nearly so difficult to justify.

QUESTIONS ABOUT THE MORAL STATUS OF FETUSES

When in the development of a human individual does she or he begin to have a full and equal right to life? Most contemporary legal systems treat birth as the point at which a new legal person comes into existence. Thus, infanticide is generally classified as a form of homicide, whereas abortion—even where prohibited—generally is not. But, at first glance, birth seems to be an entirely arbitrary criterion of moral status. Why should human beings attain full and equal basic moral rights at birth, rather than at some earlier or later point?

Many theorists have sought to establish some universal criterion of moral status, by which to distinguish between those entities that have full moral rights and those that have no moral rights may feel the need for a universally applicable criterion of moral status. For instance, utilitarians need to know which entities have interests that must be considered in calculations of moral utility, while Kantian deontologists need to know which things are to be treated as ends in themselves, and not merely means to the ends of others. Many criteria of moral status have been proposed. The most common include life, sentience (the capacity to have experiences, including that of pain), genetic humanity (biological identification as belonging to the species *Homo sapiens*), and personhood (which will be defined later).

How are we to choose among these conflicting criteria of moral status? Two things are clear. First, we may not treat the selection of a criterion of moral status as a mere matter of personal preference. Racists, for instance, are not entitled to recognize the moral rights only of members of their own racial group, since they have never been able to prove that members of 'inferior' races lack any property that can reasonably be held to be relevant to moral status. Second, a theory of moral status must provide a plausible account of the moral status not only of human beings, but also of non-human animals, plants, computers, possible extra-terrestrial life forms, and anything else that might come along. I will argue that life, sentience and personhood are all relevant to moral status, though not in the same ways. Let us consider these criteria in turn, beginning with the most basic, i.e., biological life.

THE ETHIC OF "REVERENCE FOR LIFE"

Albert Schweitzer argued for an ethic of reverence for all living things. He held that all organisms, from microbes to human beings, have a "will to live." Thus, he says, anyone who has "an unblunted moral sensibility will find it natural to share concern with the fate of all living creatures." Schweitzer may have been wrong to claim that all living things have a *will* to live. Will is most naturally construed as a faculty which requires at least some capacity for thought, and is thus unlikely to be found in simple organisms that lack central nervous systems. Perhaps the claim that all living things share a will to live is a metaphorical statement of the fact that organisms are teleologically organized, such that they generally function in ways that promote their own survival or that of their species. But why should this fact lead us to feel a reverence for all life?

I suggest that the ethic of reverence for life draws strength from ecological and aesthetic concerns. The destruction of living things often damages what Aldo Leopold has called the "integrity, stability and beauty of the biotic community." Protecting the biotic community from needless damage is a moral imperative, not just for the good of humanity, but because the unspoiled natural world is worth valuing for its own sake.

Reverence for life suggests that, other things being equal, it is always better to avoid killing a living thing. But Schweitzer was aware that not all killing can be avoided. His view was that one should never kill without good reason, and certainly not for sport or amusement. Thus, it does not follow from an ethic of reverence for all life that abortion is morally wrong. Human fetuses are living things, as are unfertilized ova and spermatozoa. However, many abortions may be defended as killing "under the compulsion of necessity."

GENETIC HUMANITY

Opponents of abortion will reply that abortion is wrong, not simply because human fetuses are alive, but because they are *human*. But why should we believe that the destruction of a living human organism is always morally worse than the destruction of an organism of some other species? Membership in a particular biological species does not appear to be, in itself, any more relevant to moral status than membership in a particular race or sex.

It is an accident of evolution and history that everyone whom we currently recognize as having full and equal basic moral rights belongs to a single biological species. The "people" of the earth might just as well have belonged to many different species—and indeed perhaps they do. It is quite possible that some non-human animals, such as dolphins and whales and the great apes, have enough so-called "human" capacities to be properly regarded as persons—i.e., beings capable of reason, self-awareness, social involvement, and moral reciprocity. Some contemporary philosophers have argued that (some) non-human animals have essentially the same basic moral rights as human persons. Whether or not they are right, it is certainly true that any superior moral status accorded to members of our own species must be justified in terms of morally significant differences between humans and other living things. To hold that species alone provides a basis for superior moral status is arbitrary and unhelpful.

THE SENTIENCE CRITERION

Some philosophers hold that sentience is the primary criterion of moral status. Sentience is the capacity to have experiences—for instance, visual, auditory, olfactory, or other perceptual experiences. However, the capacity to have pleasurable and painful experiences seems particularly relevant to moral status. It is a plausible postulate of utilitarian ethics that pleasure is an intrinsic good and pain an intrinsic evil. True, the capacity to feel pain is often valuable to an organism, enabling it to avoid harm or destruction. Conversely, some pleasures can be harmful to the organism's long-term well-being. Nevertheless, sentient beings may be said to have a basic interest in pleasure and the avoidance of pain. Respect for this basic interest is central to utilitarian ethics.

The sentience criterion suggest that, other things being equal, it is morally worse to kill a sentient than a non-sentient organism. The death of a sentient being, even when painless, deprives it of whatever pleasurable experiences it might have enjoyed in the future. Thus, death is apt to be a misfortune for that being, in a way that the death of a non-sentient organism is not.

But how can we know which living organisms are sentient? For that matter, how can we know that non-living things, such as rocks and rivers, are not sentient? If knowledge requires the absolute impossibility of error, then we probably cannot know this. But what we do know strongly suggests that sentience requires a functioning central nervous system—which is absent in rocks, plants, and simple microorganisms. It is also absent in the early human fetus. Many neurophysiologists believe that normal human fetuses begin to have some rudimentary capacity for sentience at some stage in the second trimester of pregnancy. Prior to that stage, their brains and sensory organs are too undeveloped to permit the occurrence of sensations. The behavioural evidence points in the same direction. By the end of the first trimester, a fetus may have some unconscious reflexes, but it does not yet respond to its environment in a way suggestive of sentience. By the third trimester, however, some parts of the fetal brain are functional, and the fetus may respond to noise, light, pressure, motion, and other sensory stimuli.

The sentience criterion lends support to the common belief that late abortion is more difficult to justify than early abortion. Unlike the presentient fetus, a third-trimester fetus is already *a being*—already, that is, a centre of experience. If killed, it may experience pain. Moreover, its death (like that of any sentient being) will mean the termination of a stream of experiences, some of which may have been pleasurable. Indeed, the use of this criterion suggests that early abortion poses no very serious moral issue, at least with respect to the impact upon the fetus. As a living but non-sentient organism, the first-trimester fetus is not yet a being with an interest in continued life. Like the unfertilized ovum, it may have the potential to *become* a sentient being. But this means only that it has the potential to become a being with an interest in continued life, not that it already has such an interest.

While the sentience criterion implies that late abortion is more difficult to justify than early abortion, it does not imply that late abortion is as difficult to justify as homicide. The principle of respect for the interests of sentient beings does not imply that all sentient beings have an equal right to life. To see why this is so, we need to give further thought to the scope of that principle.

Most normal mature vertebrate animals (mammals, birds, reptiles, amphibians and fish) are obviously sentient. It is also quite likely that many invertebrate animals, such as anthropods (e.g., insects, spiders, and crabs), are sentient. For they too have sense organs and nervous systems, and often behave as if they could see, hear, and feel quite well. If sentience is the criterion of moral status then not even a fly should be killed without some good reason.

But what counts as a good enough reason for the destruction of a living thing whose primary claim to moral status is its probable sentience? Utilitarians generally hold that acts are morally wrong if they increase the total amount of pain or suffering in the world (without some compensatory increase in the total amount of pleasure or happiness), or vice versa. But the killing of a sentient being does not always have such adverse consequences. There is room in any environment for only a finite number of organisms of any given species. When a rabbit is killed (in some more or less painless fashion), another rabbit is likely to take its place, so that the total amount of rabbit-happiness is not decreased. Moreover, rabbits, like many other rapidly reproducing species, must be preyed upon by some other species if the health of the larger biological system is to be maintained.

Thus, the killing of sentient beings is not always an evil in utilitarian terms. However, it would be morally offensive to suggest that people can be killed just because they are too numerous, and are upsetting the natural ecology. If killing people is harder to justify than killing rabbits—as even most animal liberationists believe— it must be because people have some moral status that is not based upon sentience alone. In the next section, we consider some possible arguments for this view.

PERSONHOOD AND MORAL RIGHTS

Once they are past infancy, human beings typically possess not only a capacity for sentience, but also such 'higher' mental capacities as self-awareness and rationality. They are also highly social beings, capable—except in pathological cases—of love, nurturance, co-operation, and moral responsibility (which involves the capacity to guide their actions through moral principles and ideals). Perhaps these mental and social capacities can provide sound reasons for ascribing a stronger right to life to persons than to other sentient beings.

One argument for that conclusion is that the distinctive capacities persons have enable them to value their own lives and those of other members of their communities more than other animals do. People are the only beings who can plan years into the future, and who are often haunted by the fear of premature death. Perhaps this means that the lives of persons are worth more to their possessors than those of sentient non-persons. If so, then killing a person is a grater moral wrong than killing a sentient being which is not a person. But it is also possible that the absence of fear for the future tends to make the lives of sentient non-persons more pleasant, and more valuable to them, than ours are to us. Thus, we need to look elsewhere for a rationale for the superior moral status than most (human) persons accord to one another.

Moral rights are a way of talking about how we should behave. That it is evidently only persons who understand the idea of a moral right does not make us "better" than other sentient beings. However, it does give us compelling reasons for treating one another as moral equals, with basic rights that cannot be overridden for narrowly utilitarian reasons. If we could never trust other persons not to kill us whenever they judged that some net good might result, social relationships would become immeasurably more difficult, and the lives of all but the most powerful persons would be greatly impoverished.

A morally sensitive person will respect all life-forms, and will be careful to avoid needlessly inflicting pain or death upon sentient beings. However, she will respect the basic moral rights of other persons *as equal to her own,* not just because they are alive and sentient, but also because she can reasonably hope and demand that they will show her the same respect. Mice and mosquitoes are not capable of this kind of moral reciprocity—at least not in their interactions with human beings. When their interests come into conflict with ours, we cannot hope to use moral argument to persuade them to accept some reasonable compromise. Thus, it is often impossible to accord them fully equal moral status. Even the Jain religion of India, which regards the killing of any being as an obstacle to spiritual enlightenment, does not require the total avoidance of such killing, except in the case of those who have taken special religious vows. . . .

If the capacity for moral reciprocity is essential to personhood, and if personhood is the criterion for moral equality, then human fetuses do not satisfy that criterion. Sentient fetuses are closer to being persons than are fertilized ova or early fetuses, and may gain some moral status on that account. However, they are not yet reasoning, self-aware beings, capable of love, nurturance, and moral reciprocity. These facts lend support to the view that even late abortion is not quite the equivalent of homicide. On this basis, we may reasonably conclude that the abortion of sentient fetuses can sometimes be justified for reasons that could not justify the killing of a person. For instance, late abortion may sometimes be justified because the fetus has been found to be severely abnormal, or because the continuation of the pregnancy threatens the woman's health, or creates other personal hardships.

Unfortunately, the discussion cannot end at this point. Personhood is important as an *inclusion* criterion for moral equality: any theory which denies equal moral status to certain persons must be rejected. But personhood seems somewhat less plausible as an *exclusion* criterion, since it appears to exclude infants and mentally handicapped individuals who may lack the mental and social capacities typical of persons. Furthermore—as opponents of abortion point out—history proves that it is all too easy for dominant groups to rationalize oppression by claiming, in effect, that the oppressed persons are not really persons at all, because of some alleged mental or moral deficiency.

In view of these points it may seem wise to adopt the theory that all *sentient* human beings have full and equal basic moral rights. (To avoid 'speciesism', we could grant the same moral status to sentient members of any other species whose normal, mature members we believe to be persons.) On this theory, so long as an individual is both human and capable of sentience, his or her moral equality cannot be questioned. But there is an objection to the extension of equal moral status even to sentient fetuses; it is impossible in practice to grant equal moral rights to fetuses without denying those same rights to women.

WHY BIRTH MATTERS MORALLY

There are many instances in which the moral rights of different human individuals come into apparent conflict. Such conflicts cannot, as a rule, be solved justly by denying equal moral status to one of the parties. But pregnancy is a special case. Because of the unique biological relationship between the woman and the fetus, the extension of equal moral and legal status to fetuses has ominous consequences for women's basic rights.

One consequence is that abortion "on request" would not be permitted. If sentience is the criterion, then abortion might be permitted only in the first trimester. Some argue that this is a reasonable compromise, since it would allow most women time enough to discover that they are pregnant, and decide whether or not to abort. But problems involving fetal abnormality, the woman's health or personal or economic situation, sometimes arise or become severe only at a later stage. If fetuses are presumed to have the same moral rights as already-born human beings, then women will often be compelled to remain pregnant at great risk to their own lives, health, or personal well-being. They may also be compelled to submit, against their will, to dangerous and invasive medical procedures such as Caesarean section, when others judge that this would be beneficial to the fetus. (A number of such cases have already occurred in the United States.) Thus, the extension of full and equal basic moral rights to fetuses endangers the basic rights of women.

But, given these apparent conflicts between fetal rights and women's rights, one may still wonder why it is women's rights that should prevail. Why not favour fetuses instead, e.g., because they are more helpless, or have a longer life expectancy? Or why not seek a compromise between fetal and maternal rights, with equal concessions on each side? If fetuses were already persons, in the sense I have described, then it would be arbitrary to favour the rights of woman over theirs. But it is difficult to argue that either fetuses or newborn infants are persons in this sense, since the capacities for reason, self-awareness, and social and moral reciprocity seem to develop only after birth.

Why, then, should we treat birth, rather than some later point, as the threshold of moral equality? A major reason is that birth makes it possible for the infant to be granted equal basic rights without violating anyone else's basic rights. It is possible in many countries to find good homes for most infants whose biological parents are unable or unwilling to raise them. Since most of us strongly desire to protect infants, and since we can now do so without imposing excessive hardships upon women and families, there is no evident reason why we should not. But fetuses are different: their equality would mean women's inequality. Other things being equal, it is worse to deny the basic moral rights to beings that are clearly not yet full persons. Since women are persons and fetuses are not, we should come down on the side of respecting women's rights in case of apparent conflict.

POTENTIAL PERSONHOOD

Some philosophers argue that, although fetuses may not be persons, their potential to become persons gives them the same basic moral rights. This argument is implausible, since in no other case do we treat the potential to achieve some status entailing certain rights as itself entailing those same rights. For instance, every child born in the United States is a potential voter, but no-one under the age of 18 has the right to vote in that country. Besides, the argument from potential proves too much. If a fetus is a potential person, then so is an unfertilized human ovum, together with enough viable spermatozoa to achieve fertilization; yet few would seriously suggest that *these* living human entities should have full and equal moral status.

Yet the argument from fetal potential refuses to go away. Perhaps this is because the potential which fetuses have is often a sound reason for valuing and protecting them. Once a pregnant woman has committed herself to the continued nurturance of the fetus, she and those close to her are likely to think of it as an "unborn baby," and to value it for its potential. The fetus's potential lies not just in its DNA, but in that maternal (and paternal) commitment. Once the woman has committed herself to the pregnancy, it is appropriate for her to value the fetus and protect its potential—as most women do, without any legal coercion. But it is wrong to demand that a woman complete a pregnancy when she is unable or unwilling to undertake that enormous commitment.

SUMMARY AND CONCLUSION

Abortion is often approached as if it were only an issue of fetal rights; and often as if it were only an issue of women's rights. The denial of safe and legal abortion infringes upon women's rights to life, liberty, and physical integrity. Yet if the fetus had the same right to life as a person, abortion would still be a tragic event, and difficult to justify except in the most extreme cases. Thus, even those who argue for women's rights must be concerned with the moral status of fetuses.

Even an ethic of reverence for all life does not, however, preclude all intentional killing. All killing requires justification, and it is somewhat more difficult to justify the deliberate destruction of a sentient being than of a living thing which is not (yet) a centre of experience; but sentient beings do not all have equal rights. The extension of equal moral status to fetuses threatens women's most basic rights.

Unlike fetuses, women are already persons. They should not be treated as something less when they happen to be pregnant. That is why abortion should not be prohibited, and why birth rather than some earlier point, marks the beginning of full moral status.

REFERENCES

Jaini, P.: *The Jaina Path of Purification* (Berkeley: University of California Press, 1979).

Leopold, A.: *A Sand County Almanac* (New York: Ballantine Books, 1970).

Schweitzer, A.: *The Teaching of Reverence for Life*, trans. R. and C. Winston (New York: Holt, Rinehart, and Winston, 1965).

Thomson, J. J.: "A defense of abortion," *Philosophy and Public Affairs* I:I (Fall 1971), 47–66.

SUGGESTIONS FOR DISCUSSION

1. How might Noonan defend his view against the criticism that his appeal to statistics commits the fallacy of deriving an "ought" from an "is" (see Hume, Chapter 2)?
2. What is the basis of Hare's criticisms of antiabortion appeals to the "personhood" of the fetus? Why are the reasons Hare himself offers against abortion Kantian and utilitarian, respectively? How does Hare's appeal to the principle of the (potential) value of his own life differ from Noonan's principle "not to injure another without reason?"
3. What does privacy mean? Why are (some) feminists critical of the right to privacy? On what grounds might feminists defend abortion without appealing to the right to privacy?
4. Does the point at which humanity is supposed to begin make a difference to the justifiability of abortion? If so, in what ways? If not, why not?
5. If abortion is justifiable, are there any grounds on the basis of which the practice of abortion might be regulated or restricted? Are regulations of a woman's pregnancy, related, say, to diet, substance consumption, or workplace hazards, justifiable?
6. If abortion is murder, is contraception also murder? If abortion is murder, does this preclude abortion in the case of pregnancies developing from rape or incest?

FOR FURTHER READING

Barry, R. L. *Medical Ethics: Essays on Abortion and Euthanasia.* New York: Lang, 1989.

Brody, B. *Abortion and the Sanctity of Human Life.* Cambridge, Mass.: MIT Press, 1975.

Callahan, D. *Abortion. Law, Choice and Morality.* New York: Macmillan, 1970.

Cohen, M., Nagel, T., and Scanlon, T., eds. *Rights and Wrongs of Abortion.* Princeton: Princeton University Press, 1974.

Dworkin, R. *Life's Dominion: An Argument About Abortion, Euthanasia, and Individual Freedom.* New York: Knopf, 1993.

Feinberg, J., ed. *The Problem of Abortion.* 2nd ed. Belmont, Calif.: Wadsworth, 1984.

Fischer, J. M. "Abortion and Self-Determination." *Journal of Social Philosophy* 22, 2 (Fall 1991): 5–13.

Gomberg, P. "Abortion and the Morality of Nurturance." *Canadian Journal of Philosophy* 21, 4 (December 1991).

Grisez, G. *Abortion. The Myths, the Realities and the Arguments.* New York: Corpus Books, 1970.

Kaveny, M. C. "Toward a Thomistic Perspective on Abortion and the Law in Contemporary America." *Thomist* 55, 3 (July 1991): 343–395.

Marquis, D. "Why Abortion Is Immoral." *Journal of Philosophy* 86 (1989): 183–202.

Noonan, J. T., Jr. *The Morality of Abortion.* Cambridge, Mass.: Harvard University Press, 1970.

———. *How to Argue About Abortion.* New York: The Free Press, 1979.

Perkins, R. L., ed. *Abortion.* Cambridge: Shenkman, 1975.

Quinn, W. "Abortion: Identity and Loss." *Philosophy and Public Affairs* 13, 1 (Winter 1984): 24–54.

Rorty, A., ed. *The Identity of Person.* Berkeley: University of California Press, 1976.

Sumner, L. W. *Abortion and Moral Theory.* Princeton: Princeton University Press, 1981.

Thomson, J. J. "A Defense of Abortion." *Philosophy and Public Affairs* 1 (Fall 1971): 47–66.

Tooley, M. *Abortion and Infanticide.* New York: Oxford University Press, 1983.

Tribe, L. H. *Abortion: The Clash of Absolutes.* New York: Norton, 1992.

CHAPTER THIRTEEN

EUTHANASIA

Murder, or the intentional killing of an innocent person, is wrong and so it is morally impermissible. Nevertheless, we make exceptions for some sorts of killing: taking another's life in legitimate self-defense, for example, is permissible, for the victim here is not really innocent. The sophistication of medical technology has made it possible to extend human life; yet, the quality of life is not necessarily sustained when it is extended in this way. *Euthanasia* involves terminating the life of an ailing person in order to prevent his or her further suffering. Thus the question of whether euthanasia is in any form morally permissible has become especially acute.

Reasons for Euthanasia   Since euthanasia is clearly the intentional taking of life, the person who dies is in the relevant sense innocent. So, if any act of euthanasia is to be morally permissible, a candidate must be subject at least to the following conditions: the suffering must be present, persistent, and severe, and death must appear reasonably imminent. The sole reason for terminating the person's life must be to end her or his suffering. (Thus the horrors of the Nazi euthanasia program are patently unjustifiable.) The clearest candidates for justifiable euthanasia involve a person's uncoerced request to die, either in person and repeatedly or by way of a living will. A *living will* is a testament drawn up privately, upon cool and quiet deliberation, prior to the onset of terminal illness or incompetence. It expresses one's desired treatment in the case of incompetence and may include a request for terminating life in case of severely debilitating or painful terminal illness. Standard cases where euthanasia may be an option include when a person is suffering excruciating pain that can no longer be lessened by drugs (as in advanced forms of bone cancer, say, or where a person has third-degree burns over extensive areas of the body), when a patient is in an irreversible coma, or when a patient is suffering advanced forms of senility. In these cases, prospects for any future well-being and enjoyment are minimal.

Classifications: Kinds of Euthanasia   Conscious and clear requests for euthanasia are called voluntary. Voluntary euthanasia is distinguished from both involuntary euthanasia and nonvoluntary euthanasia. *Involuntary euthanasia* occurs where a person, despite severe suffering and faced with the prospect of a painful end, expresses the desire *not* to die but is killed or allowed to die anyway; many people would rightfully take this to be murder. The most complicated cases for the morality of euthanasia are those that are *nonvoluntary*. Here patients are incapable of requesting or indicating a desire for death or of forming judgments in the matter. Standard cases involve comatose or senile patients incapable of rational thought and leaving no living will; or defective newborns like those with Down's syndrome or with extreme brain incapacity. (For theoretical elaboration of the distinction between voluntary and involuntary action, see Aristotle, Chapter 1.)

Many have considered the distinction between *killing* and *letting die* to be crucial in analyzing the moral status of euthanasia, Thus *active euthanasia* involves killing a patient; that is, causing death by administering some lethal (though humane) treatment such as a drug overdose. *Passive euthanasia* involves letting the patient die by withholding or withdrawing all extraordinary treatment that may prolong life. The cause of death would be whatever ailment naturally afflicts the patient, not any artificially administered treatment. *Extraordinary*—as opposed to *ordinary*—means of prolonging life are those that impose an undue burden both on those providing care and on those suffering from the illness. Extraordinary means include a respirator, iron lung, or radiation treatment; ordinary means include food or common antibiotics.

Accordingly, six types of euthanasia may be distinguished: voluntary active and voluntary passive, nonvoluntary active and nonvoluntary passive, and involuntary active and involuntary passive. Because involuntary active and involuntary passive forms of euthanasia are extreme and are imposed coercively, against a person's expressed will, they are generally impermissible.

Permissibility of Euthanasia   The moral question of euthanasia may be posed this way: Is it ever permissible to kill persons or let them die voluntarily or nonvoluntarily for and only for their own benefit? It is usually agreed that if any form is permissible, then only *voluntary passive euthanasia* will be. (The American Medical Association permits discontinuing or withholding only "extraordinary" treatment and only where there is undeniable evidence that the patient is about to die. Any act of killing a patient, no matter what the reason, is considered by the AMA to be unjustifiable.) Further, permissibility will be limited to cases where extraordinary life-prolonging treatment can be withheld or withdrawn. Active euthanasia or failure to administer ordinary treatment is generally considered unacceptable. Dr. Jack Kervorkian's persistence in assisting suicides of the terminally ill, and the state of Oregon's recent vote to permit doctor-assisted suicides, places in sharp relief the tension between two competing principles: the commitment, especially incumbent upon the medical profession, to promote and prolong life, and the value of enabling people to limit their suffering by choosing to end their lives with dignity. Nevertheless, a case like that of Nancy Cruzan better exemplifies the problematic issues involved.

■ SUPREME COURT RULING: CRUZAN

In *Cruzan v. Director, Missouri Dept. of Health,* Chief Justice William Rehnquist, writing for the majority, reaffirmed the individual's constitutionally protected right of self-determination. This would seem to entail a personal right to decide when to die. Nevertheless, Rehnquist argues that a state need not facilitate this choice. A state has a compelling interest to protect human life, as exemplified in universal laws against murder and the fact that most states in the union criminalize *assistance* to suicide. (Michigan introduced such legislation in the wake of Dr. Jack Kervorkian's repeated involvement in suicides by the terminally ill.) Accordingly, a state may express an unqualified interest in preserving human life and so refuse to judge the quality of life of a person sustained by life-support technology.

As the choice between life and death is an extremely personal one, a state may seek to protect the personal nature of this choice. Before permitting termination of life-sustaining technology, a state could thus insist that the patient clearly indicate that death in specific circumstances would be the voluntary choice made (the heightened evidentiary requirement). A state may permit the substitute judgment of family or guardian if no explicit wish of the patient is in evidence or available. Nevertheless, this does not entail that such a surrogate decision is constitutionally mandated. Rehnquist principally argues that if a decision not to terminate a patient's life is counter to his or her will, nothing is lost; by contrast, an erroneous decision to terminate is irreversible.

In his dissent from Rehnquist's opinion in *Cruzan,* Justice William Brennan affirms the individual's fundamental right to be free of unwanted artificial nutrition and hydration. This right is an instance of the general and basic individual right to self-determination (see Kant, Chapter 3). As fundamental, this right cannot be overridden by any state interest. Thus a state's heightened evidentiary requirement for invoking this fundamental individual right constitutes an impermissible burden on its satisfaction. This is especially the case, argues Brennan, since no good follows from requiring a person in Nancy Cruzan's situation to be sustained by life-support technology.

Chief Justice William Rehnquist

MAJORITY OPINION IN *CRUZAN* v. *DIRECTOR, MISSOURI DEPT. OF HEALTH*

Petitioner Nancy Beth Cruzan was rendered incompetent as a result of severe injuries sustained during an automobile accident. Co-petitioners Lester and Joyce Cruzan, Nancy's parents and co-guardians, sought a court order directing the withdrawal of their daughter's artificial feeding and hydration equipment after it became apparent that she had virtually no chance of recovering her cognitive faculties. The Supreme Court of Missouri held that because there was no clear and convincing evidence of Nancy's desire to have life-sustaining treatment withdrawn under such circumstances, her parents lacked authority to effectuate such a request. . . .

United States Supreme Court 110 U.S. 2841 (1990).

[3] Whether or not Missouri's clear and convincing evidence requirement comports with the United States Constitution depends in part on what interests the State may properly seek to protect in this situation. Missouri relies on its interest in the protection and preservation of human life, and there can be no gainsaying this interest. As a general matter, the States—indeed, all civilized nations—demonstrate their commitment to like by treating homicide as serious crime. Moreover, the majority of States in this country have laws imposing criminal penalties on one who assists another to commit suicide. We do not think a State is required to remain neutral in the face of an informed and voluntary decision by a physically able adult to starve to death. . . .

[4] But in the context presented here, a State has more particular interests at stake. The choice between life and death is a deeply personal decision of obvious and overwhelming finality. We believe Missouri may legitimately seek to safeguard the personal element of this choice through the imposition of heightened evidentiary requirements. It cannot be disputed that the Due Process Clause protects an interest in life as well as an interest in refusing life-sustaining medical treatment. Not all incompetent patients will have loved ones available to serve as surrogate decision-makers. And even where family members are present, "[t]here will, of course, be some unfortunate situations in which family members will not act to protect a patient." . . . A State is entitled to consider that a judicial proceeding to make a determination regarding an incompetent's wishes may very well not be an adversarial one, with the added guarantee of accurate fact finding that the adversary process brings with it . . . Finally, we think a State may properly decline to make judgments about the "quality" of life that a particular individual may enjoy, and simply assert an unqualified interest in the preservation of human life to be weighed against the constitutionally protected interest of the individual. . . .

[5] In our view, Missouri has permissibly sought to advance these interests through the adoption of a "clear and convincing" standard of proof to govern such proceedings. . . .

. . . An erroneous decision not to terminate results in a maintenance of the status quo; the possibility of subsequent developments such as advancements in medical science, the discovery of new evidence regarding the patient's intent, changes in the law, or simply the unexpected death of the patient despite the administration of life-sustaining treatment, at least create the potential that a wrong decision will eventually be corrected or it impact mitigated. An erroneous decision to withdraw life-sustaining treatment, however, is not susceptible of correction. In *Santosky*, one of the factors which led the Court to require proof by clear and convincing evidence in a proceeding to terminate parental rights was that a decision in such a case was final and irrevocable. . . . The same must surely be said of the decision to discontinue hydration and nutrition of a patient such as Nancy Cruzan, which all agree will result in her death. . . .

[6] In sum, we conclude that a State may apply a clear and convincing evidence standard in proceedings where a guardian seeks to discontinue nutrition and hydration of a person diagnosed to be in the persistent vegetative state. We note that many courts which have adopted some sort of substituted judgment procedure in situations like this, whether they limit consideration of evidence to the prior ex-

pressed wishes of the incompetent individual, or whether they allow more general proof of what the individual's decision would have been, require a clear and convincing standard of proof for such evidence. . . .

In *Michael H.*, we *upheld* the constitutionality of California's favored treatment of traditional family relationships; such a holding may not be turned around into a constitutional requirement that a State *must* recognize the primacy of those relationships in a situation like this. And in *Parham*, where the patient was a minor, we also *upheld* the constitutionality of a state scheme in which parents made certain decisions for mentally ill minors. Here again petitioners would seek to turn a decision which allowed a State to rely on family decisionmaking into a constitutional requirement that the State recognize such decisionmaking. But constitutional law does not work that way.

No doubt is engendered by anything in this record but that Nancy Cruzan's mother and father are loving and caring parents. If the State were required by the United States Constitution to repose a right of "substituted judgment" with anyone, the Cruzans would surely qualify. But we do not think the Due Process Clause requires the State to repose judgment on these matters with anyone but the patient herself. Close family members may have a strong feeling—a feeling not at all ignoble or unworthy, but not entirely disinterested, either—that they do not wish to witness the continuation of the life of a loved one which they regard as hopeless, meaningless, and even degrading. But there is no automatic assurance that the view of close family members will necessarily be the same as the patient's would have been had she been confronted with the prospect of her situation while competent. All of the reasons previously discussed for allowing Missouri to require clear and convincing evidence of the patient's wishes lead us to conclude that the State may choose to defer only to those wishes, rather than confide the decision to close family members. . . .

Justice William Brennan

DISSENTING OPINION IN *CRUZAN v. DIRECTOR, MISSOURI DEPT. OF HEALTH*

"Medical technology has effectively created a twilight zone of suspended animation where death commences while life, in some form, continues. Some patients, however, want no part of a life sustained only by medical technology. Instead, they

United States Supreme Court 110 U.S. 2841 (1990).

prefer a plan of medical treatment that allows nature to take its course and permits them to die with dignity." [*Rasmussen v. Fleming,* 1987]

Nancy Cruzan has dwelt in that twilight zone for six years. She is oblivious to her surroundings and will remain so. . . .

"Nancy will never interact meaningfully with her environment again. She will remain in a persistent vegetative state until her death." . . . Because she cannot swallow, her nutrition and hydration are delivered through a tube surgically implanted in her stomach.

A grown woman at the time of the accident, Nancy had previously expressed her wish to forgo continuing medical care under circumstances such as these. Her family and friends are convinced that this is what she would want. . . . A guardian *ad litem* appointed by the trial court is also convinced that this is what Nancy would want. . . . Yet the Missouri Supreme Court, alone among state courts deciding such a question, has determined that an irreversibly vegetative patient will remain a passive prisoner of medical technology—for Nancy, perhaps for the next 30 years. . . .

Today the Court while tentatively accepting that there is some degree of constitutionally protected liberty interest in avoiding unwanted medical treatment, including life-sustaining medical treatment such as artificial nutrition and hydration, affirms the decision of the Missouri Supreme Court. The majority opinion, as I read it, would affirm that decision on the ground that a State may require "clear and convincing" evidence of Nancy Cruzan's prior decision to forgo life-sustaining treatment under circumstances such as hers in order to ensure that her actual wishes are honored. . . . Because I believe that Nancy Cruzan has a fundamental right to be free of unwanted artificial nutrition and hydration, which right is not outweighed by any interests of the State, and because I find that the improperly biased procedural obstacles imposed by the Missouri Supreme Court impermissibly burden that right, I respectfully dissent. Nancy Cruzan is entitled to choose to die with dignity. . . .

I I

B

Although the right to be free of unwanted medical intervention, like other constitutionally protected interests, may not be absolute, no State interest could outweigh the rights of an individual in Nancy Cruzan's position. Whatever a State's possible interests in mandating life-support treatment under other circumstances, there is no good to be obtained here by Missouri's insistence that Nancy Cruzan remain on life-support systems if it is indeed her wish not to do so. Missouri does not claim, nor could it, that society as a whole will be benefitted by Nancy's receiving the medical treatment. No third party'[s] situation will be improved and no harm to others will be averted. . . .

The only state interest asserted here is a general interest in the preservation of life. But the State has no legitimate general interest in someone's life, completely abstracted from the interest of the person living that life, that could outweigh the person's choice to avoid medical treatment. "[T]he regulation of constitutionally protected decisions . . . must be predicted on legitimate state concerns *other than* disagreement with the choice the individual has made. . . . Otherwise, the interest in liberty protected by the Due Process Clause would be a nullity." . . . Thus, the State's general interest in life must accede to Nancy Cruzan's particularized and intense interest in self-determination in her choice of medical treatment. There is simply nothing legitimately within the State's purview to be gained by superseding her decision.

I I I

This is not to say that the State has no legitimate interests to assert here. As the majority recognizes, . . . Missouri has a *parens patriae* interest in providing Nancy Cruzan, now incompetent, with as accurate as possible a determination of how she would exercise her rights under these circumstances. Second, if and when it is determined that Nancy Cruzan would want to continue treatment, the State may legitimately assert an interest in providing that treatment. But *until* Nancy's wishes have been determined, the only state interest that may be asserted is an interest in safe-guarding the accuracy of the determination. . . .

Accuracy, therefore, must be our touchstone. Missouri may constitutionally impose only those procedural requirements that serve to enhance the accuracy of a determination of Nancy Cruzan's wishes or are at least consistent with an accurate determination. The Missouri "safeguard" that the Court upholds today does not meet that standard. The determination needed in this context is whether the incompetent person would choose to live in a persistent vegetative state on life-support or to avoid this medical treatment. Missouri's rule of decision imposes a markedly asymmetrical evidentiary burden. Only evidence of specific statements of treatment choice made by the patient when competent is admissible to support a finding that the patient, now in a persistent vegetative state, would wish to avoid further medical treatment. Moreover, this evidence must be clear and convincing. No proof is required to support a finding that the incompetent person would wish to continue treatment.

■ J. GAY-WILLIAMS: AGAINST EUTHANASIA

J. Gay-Williams offers one Natural Law argument and two consequentialist arguments against the permissibility of euthanasia (on Natural Law, see Aquinas, Chapter 1; on consequentialism, see Chapter 4). The Natural Law argument presumes that euthanasia necessarily undermines human dignity. Dignity is achieved by seeking human goals, and a basic natural goal is human survival. Thus euthanasia is contrary to human nature and so inherently wrong

Gay-Williams appeals to consequences in two ways. First, he argues that even the best medical practitioners sometimes make mistakes and that the possibility of euthanasia causes patients to give up too readily. He concludes that undertaking euthanasia or "mercy-killing" is contrary to self-interest. Second, Gay-Williams contends that euthanasia as a social policy could lead to callousness in the medical profession and to the widespread social abuse of involuntary euthanasia. He suggests that these possible social effects are too dangerous and undesirable to warrant any euthanasia at all.

J. Gay-Williams

THE WRONGFULNESS OF EUTHANASIA

My impression is that euthanasia—the idea, if not the practice—is slowly gaining acceptance within our society. Cynics might attribute this to an increasing tendency to devalue human life, but I do not believe this is the major factor. The acceptance is much more likely to be the result of unthinking sympathy and benevolence. Well-publicized, tragic stories like that of Karen Quinlan elicit from us deep feelings of compassion. We think to ourselves, "She and her family would be better off if she were dead." It is an easy step from this very human response to the view that if someone (and others) would be better off dead then it must be all right to kill that person.[1] Although I respect the compassion that leads to this conclusion, I believe the conclusion is wrong. I want to show that euthanasia is wrong. It is inherently wrong, but it is also wrong judged from the standpoints of self-interest and of practical effects.

Before presenting my arguments to support this claim, it would be well to define "euthanasia." An essential aspect of euthanasia is that it involves taking a human life, either one's own or that of another. Also, the person whose life is taken must be someone who is believed to be suffering from some disease or injury from which recovery cannot reasonably be expected. Finally, the action must be deliberate and intentional. Thus, euthanasia is intentionally taking the life of a presumably hopeless person. Whether the life is one's own or that of another, the taking of it is still euthanasia.

From *Intervention and Reflection: Basic Issues in Medical Ethics*, edited by Ronald Munson (Belmont, Calif.: Wadsworth Publishing, 1979). Copyright © 1992 by Ronald Munson. First published in Ronald Munson, *Intervention and Reflection: Basic Issues in Medical Ethics*, 4th ed., Wadsworth Publishing Co: Belmont, Calif. Reprinted by permission.

It is important to be clear about the deliberate and intentional aspect of the killing. If a hopeless person is given an injection of the wrong drug by mistake and this causes his death, this is wrongful killing but not euthanasia. The killing cannot be the result of accident. Furthermore, if the person is given an injection of a drug that is believed to be necessary to treat his disease or better his condition and the person dies as a result, then this is neither wrongful killing nor euthanasia. The intention was to make the patient well, not kill him. Similarly, when a patient's condition is such that it is not reasonable to hope that any medical procedures or treatments will save his life, a failure to implement the procedures or treatments is not euthanasia. If the person dies, this will be as a result of his injuries or disease and not because of his failure to receive treatment.

The failure to continue treatment after it has been realized that the patient has little chance of benefitting from it has been characterized by some as "passive euthanasia." This phrase if misleading and mistaken.[2] In such cases, the person involved is not killed (the first essential aspect of euthanasia), nor is the death of the person intended by the withholding of additional treatment (the third essential aspect of euthanasia). The aim may be to spare the person additional and unjustifiable pain, to save him from the indignities of hopeless manipulations, and to avoid increasing the financial and emotional burden on his family. When I buy a pencil it is so that I can use it to write, not to contribute to an increase in the gross national product. This may be the unintended consequence of my action, but it is not the aim of my action. So it is with failing to continue the treatment of a dying person. I intend his death no more than I intend to reduce the GNP by not using medical supplies. His is an unintended dying, and so-called "passive euthanasia" is not euthanasia at all.

1. THE ARGUMENT FROM NATURE

Every human being has a natural inclination to continue living. Our reflexes and responses fit us to fight attackers, flee wild animals, and dodge out of the way of trucks. In our daily lives we exercise the caution and care necessary to protect ourselves. Our bodies are similarly structured for survival right down to the molecular level. When we are cut, our capillaries seal shut, our blood clots, and fibrogen is produced to start the process of healing the wound. When we are invaded by bacteria, antibodies are produced to fight against the alien organisms, and their remains are swept out of the body by special cells designed for clean-up work.

Euthanasia does violence to this natural goal of survival. It is literally acting against nature because all the processes of nature are bent towards the end of bodily survival. Euthanasia defeats these subtle mechanisms in a way that, in a particular case, disease and injury might not.

It is possible, but not necessary, to make an appeal to revealed religion in this connection.[3] Man as trustee of his body acts against God, its rightful possessor, when he takes his own life. He also violates the commandment to hold life sacred and never to take it without just and compelling cause. But since this appeal will persuade only those who are prepared to accept that religion has access to revealed truths, I shall not employ this line of argument.

It is enough, I believe, to recognize that the organization of the human body and our patterns of behavioral responses make the continuation of life a natural goal. By reason alone, then, we can recognize that euthanasia sets us against our own nature.[4] Furthermore, in doing so, euthanasia does violence to our dignity. Our dignity comes from seeking our ends. When one of our goals is survival, and actions are taken that eliminate that goal, then our natural dignity suffers. Unlike animals, we are conscious through reason of our nature and our ends. Euthanasia involves acting as if this dual nature—inclination towards survival and awareness of this as an end—did not exist. Thus, euthanasia denies our basic human character and requires that we regard ourselves or others as something less than fully human.

2. THE ARGUMENT FROM SELF-INTEREST

The above arguments are, I believe, sufficient to show that euthanasia is inherently wrong. But there are reasons for considering it wrong when judged by standards other than reason. Because death is final and irreversible, euthanasia contains within it the possibility that we will work against our own interest if we practice it or allow it to be practiced on us.

Contemporary medicine has high standards of excellence and a proven record of accomplishment, but it does not possess perfect and complete knowledge. A mistaken diagnosis is possible, and so is a mistaken prognosis. Consequently, we may believe that we are dying of a disease when, as a matter of fact, we may not be. We may think that we have no hope of recovery when, as a matter of fact, our chances are quite good. In such circumstances, if euthanasia were permitted, we would die needlessly. Death is final and the chance of error too great to approve the practice of euthanasia.

Also, there is always the possibility that an experimental procedure or a hitherto untried technique will pull us through. We should at least keep this option open, but euthanasia closes it off. Furthermore, spontaneous remission does occur in many cases. For no apparent reason, a patient simply recovers when those all around him, including his physicians, expected him to die. Euthanasia would just guarantee their expectations and leave no room for the "miraculous" recoveries that frequently occur.

Finally, knowing that we can take our life at any time (or ask another to take it) might well incline us to give up too easily. The will to live is strong in all of us, but it can be weakened by pain and suffering and feelings of hopelessness. If during a bad time we allow ourselves to be killed, we never have a chance to reconsider. Recovery from a serious illness requires that we fight for it, and anything that weakens our determination by suggesting that there is an easy way out is ultimately against our own interest. Also, we may be inclined towards euthanasia because of our concern for others. If we see our sickness and suffering as an emotional and financial burden on our family, we may feel that to leave our life is to make their lives easier.[5] The very presence of the possibility of euthanasia may keep us from surviving when we might.

3. THE ARGUMENT FROM PRACTICAL EFFECTS

Doctors and nurses are, for the most part, totally committed to saving lives. A life lost is, for them, almost a personal failure, an insult to their skills and knowledge. Euthanasia as a practice might well alter this. It could have a corrupting influence so that in any case that is severe doctors and nurses might not try hard enough to save the patient. They might decide that the patient would simply be "better off dead" and take the steps necessary to make that come about. This attitude could then carry over to their dealings with patients less seriously ill. The result would be an overall decline in the quality of medical care.

Finally, euthanasia as a policy is a slippery slope. A person apparently hopelessly ill may be allowed to take his own life. Then he may be permitted to deputize others to do it for him should he no longer be able to act. The judgment of others then becomes the ruling factor. Already at this point euthanasia is not personal and voluntary, for others are acting "on behalf of" the patient as they see fit. This may well incline them to act on behalf of other patients who have not authorized them to exercise their judgment. It is only a short step, then, from voluntary euthanasia (self-inflicted or authorized), to directed euthanasia administered to a patient who has given no authorization, to involuntary euthanasia conducted as part of a social policy.[6] Recently many psychiatrists and sociologists have argued that we define as "mental illness" those forms of behavior that we disapprove of.[7] This gives us license then to lock up those who display the behavior. The category of the "hopelessly ill" provides the possibility of even worse abuse. Embedded in a social policy, it would give society or its representatives the authority to eliminate all those who might be considered too "ill" to function normally any longer. The dangers of euthanasia are too great to all to run the risk of approving it in any form. The first slippery step may well lead to a serious and harmful fall.

I hope that I have succeeded in showing why the benevolence that inclines us to give approval of euthanasia is misplaced. Euthanasia is inherently wrong because it violates the nature and dignity of human beings. But even those who are not convinced by this must be persuaded that the potential personal and social dangers inherent in euthanasia are sufficient to forbid our approving it either as a personal practice or as a public policy.

Suffering is surely a terrible thing, and we have a clear duty to comfort those in need and to ease their suffering when we can. But suffering is also a natural part of life with values for the individual and for others that we should not overlook. We may legitimately seek for others and for ourselves an easeful death, as Arthur Dyck has pointed out.[8] Euthanasia, however, is not just an easeful death. It is a wrongful death. Euthanasia is not just dying. It is killing.

NOTES

1. For a sophisticated defense of this position see Philippa Foot, "Euthanasia," *Philosophy and Public Affairs* 6 (1977): 85–112.[Editor's note: Foot's essay is reprinted in the following section.] Foot does not endorse the radical conclusion that euthanasia, voluntary and involuntary, is always right.

2. James Rachels rejects the distinction between active and passive euthanasia as morally irrelevant in his "Active and Passive Euthanasia," *New England Journal of Medicine* 292: 78–80. [Editor's note: Rachels' essay is reprinted later in this chapter.] But see the criticism by Foot, 100–3.

3. For a defense of this view see J. V. Sullivan, "The Immorality of Euthanasia," in *Beneficent Euthanasia*, ed. Marvin Kohl (Buffalo: Prometheus Books, 1975), 34–44.

4. This point is made by Ray V. McIntyre in "Voluntary Euthanasia: The Ultimate Perversion," *Medical Counterpoint* 2: 26–29.

5. See McIntyre, 28.

6. See Sullivan, "Immorality of Euthanasia," 34–44, for a fuller argument in support of this view.

7. See, for example, Thomas S. Szasz, *The Myth of Mental Illness*, rev. ed. (New York: Harper & Row, 1974).

8. Arthur Dyck, "Beneficent Euthanasia and Benemortasia," Kohl, op. cit., 117–29.

■ JAMES RACHELS: ACTIVE AND PASSIVE EUTHANASIA

James Rachels advances four arguments against the standard view that active euthanasia is impermissible while passive euthanasia is sometimes permissible. Rachels argues, first, that if euthanasia is permissible at all, then active killing will be more humane than passive letting die: suffering is relieved more quickly by killing. However, as Foot points out in criticism of an argument like this, a humane act may be unjust or morally objectionable because it infringes upon a person's rights. Rachels argues, second, that the distinction between active and passive euthanasia rests on the basis of *chance* whether a person may live or die. Chance has no moral relevance, and so the distinction based upon it must be irrelevant from the moral point of view, too. Rachels adds, third, that this distinction between active and passive euthanasia presupposes the distinction between killing and letting die. If the latter distinction is to be morally pertinent in any case, it would have to be so in every appropriate case. Rachels shows that it is not. Rachels's fourth argument turns on the claim that to call euthanasia *passive* is misleading, for there is an act here also—that is, one of *letting die*. He concludes that, if there is any difference between active and passive euthanasia, it lies in their respective consequences, and that here the balance favors active euthanasia. Finally, Rachels illustrates the application of two moral theories to the issue of euthanasia. He shows, first, the utilitarian form an argument for justified mercy-killing would have to assume; and second, how the Golden Rule or Kantian categorical imperative justifies active euthanasia in some cases (for more on utilitarianism, see Chapter 4; for more on Kant's categorical imperative, see Chapter 3).

James Rachels

ACTIVE AND PASSIVE EUTHANASIA

The distinction between active and passive euthanasia is thought to be crucial for medical ethics. The idea is that it is permissible, at least in some cases, to withhold treatment and allow a patient to die, but it is never permissible to take any direct action designed to kill the patient. This doctrine seems to be accepted by most doctors, and it is endorsed in a statement adopted by the House of Delegates of the American Medical Association on December 4, 1973:

> The intentional termination of the life of one human being by another—mercy killing—is contrary to that for which the medical profession stands and is contrary to the policy of the American Medical Association.
>
> The cessation of the employment of extraordinary means to prolong the life of the body when there is irrefutable evidence that biological death is imminent is the decision of the patient and/or his immediate family. The advice and judgment of the physician should be freely available to the patient and/or his immediate family.

However, a strong case can be made against this doctrine. In what follows I will set out some of the relevant arguments, and urge doctors to reconsider their views on this matter.

To begin with a familiar type of situation, a patient who is dying of incurable cancer of the throat is in terrible pain, which can no longer be satisfactorily alleviated. He is certain to die within a few days, even if present treatment is continued, but he does not want to go on living for those days since the pain is unbearable. So he asks the doctor for an end to it, and his family joins in the request.

Suppose the doctor agrees to withhold treatment, as the conventional doctrine says he may. The justification for his doing so is that the patient is in terrible agony, and since he is going to die anyway, it would be wrong to prolong his suffering needlessly. But now notice this. If one simply withholds treatment, it may take the

From *The New England Journal of Medicine* 292 (1975). Reprinted by permission of The New England Journal of Medicine and the author. Copyright 1975 Massachusetts Medical Society.

patient longer to die, and so he may suffer more than he would if more direct action were taken and a lethal injection given. This fact provides strong reason for thinking that, once the initial decision not to prolong his agony has been made, active euthanasia is actually preferable to passive euthanasia, rather than the reverse. To say otherwise is to endorse the option that leads to more suffering rather than less, and is contrary to the humanitarian impulse that prompts the decision not to prolong his life in the first place.

Part of my point is that the process of being "allowed to die" can be relatively slow and painful, whereas being given a lethal injection is relatively quick and painless. Let me give a different sort of example. In the United States about one in 600 babies is born with Down's syndrome. Most of these babies are otherwise healthy— that is, with only the usual pediatric care, they will proceed to an otherwise normal infancy. Some, however, are born with congenital defects such as intestinal obstructions that require operations if they are to live. Sometimes, the parents and doctor will decide not to operate, and let the infant die. Anthony Shaw describes what happens then:

> . . . When surgery is denied [the doctor] must try to keep the infant from suffering while natural forces sap the baby's life away. As a surgeon whose natural inclinations is to use the scalpel to fight off death, standing by and watching a salvageable baby die is the most emotionally exhausting experience I know. It is easy at a conference, in a theoretical discussion, to decide that such infants should be allowed to die. It is altogether different to stand by in the nursery and watch as dehydration and infection wither a tiny being over hours and days. This is a terrible ordeal for me and the hospital staff—much more so than for the parents who never set foot in the nursery.[1]

I can understand why some people are opposed to all euthanasia, and insist that such infants must be allowed to live. I think I can also understand why other people favor destroying these babies quickly and painlessly. But why should anyone favor letting "dehydration and infection wither a tiny being over hours and days?" The doctrine that says that a baby may be allowed to dehydrate and wither, but may not be given an injection that would end its life without suffering, seems so patently cruel as to require no further refutation. The strong language is not intended to offend, but only to put the point in the clearest possible way.

My second argument is that the conventional doctrine leads to decisions concerning life and death made on irrelevant grounds.

Consider again the case of the infants with Down's syndrome who need operations for congenital defects unrelated to the syndrome to live. Sometimes, there is no operation, and the baby dies, but when there is no such defect, the baby lives on. Now, an operation such as that to remove an intestinal obstruction is not prohibitively difficult. The reason why such operations are not performed in these cases is, clearly, that the child has Down's syndrome and the parents and the doctor judge that because of that fact it is better for the child to die.

---

[1] A. Shaw, "Doctor, Do We Have a Choice?" *New York Times Magazine*, Jan. 30, 1972, p. 59.

But notice that this situation is absurd, no matter what view one takes of the lives and potentials of such babies. If the life of such an infant is worth preserving, what does it matter if it needs a simple operation? Or, if one thinks it better that such a baby should not live on, what difference does it make that it happens to have an obstructed intestinal tract? In either case, the matter of life and death is being decided on irrelevant grounds. It is the Down's syndrome, and not the intestines, that is the issue. The matter should be decided, if at all, on that basis, and not be allowed to depend on the essentially irrelevant question of whether the intestinal tract is blocked.

What makes this situation possible, of course, is the idea that when there is an intestinal blockage, one can "let the baby die," but when there is no such defect there is nothing that can be done, for one must not "kill" it. The fact that this idea leads to such results as deciding life or death on irrelevant grounds is another good reason why the doctrine should be rejected.

One reason why so many people think that there is an important moral difference between active and passive euthanasia is that they think killing someone is morally worse than letting someone die. But is it? Is killing, in itself, worse than letting die? To investigate this issue, two cases may be considered that are exactly alike except that one involves killing whereas the other involves letting someone die. Then, it can be asked whether this difference makes any difference to the moral assessments. It is important that the cases be exactly alike, except for this one difference, since otherwise one cannot be confident that it is this difference and not some other that accounts for any variation in the assessment of the two cases. So, let us consider this pair of cases.

In the first, Smith stands to gain a large inheritance if anything should happen to his six-year-old cousin. One evening while the child is taking his bath, Smith sneaks into the bathroom and drowns the child, and then arranges things so that it will look like an accident.

In the second, Jones also stands to gain if anything should happen to his six-year-old cousin. Like Smith, Jones sneaks in planning to drown the child in his bath. However, just as he enters the bathroom Jones sees the child slip and hit his head, and fall face down in the water. Jones is delighted; he stands by, ready to push the child's head back under if it is necessary, but it is not necessary. With only a little thrashing about, the child drowns all by himself, "accidentally," as Jones watches and does nothing.

Now Smith killed the child, whereas Jones "merely" let the child die. That is the only difference between them. Did either man behave better, from a moral point of view? If the difference between killing and letting die were in itself a morally important matter, one should say that Jones's behavior was less reprehensible than Smith's. But does one really want to say that? I think not. In the first place, both men acted from the same motive, personal gain, and both had exactly the same end in view when they acted. It may be inferred from Smith's conduct that he is a bad man, although that judgment may be withdrawn or modified if certain further facts are learned about him—for example, that he is mentally deranged. But would not the very same thing be inferred about Jones from his conduct? And would not the same further considerations also be relevant to any modification of this judgment? Moreover, suppose Jones pleaded, in his own defense, "After all, I didn't do anything except just stand there and watch the child drown. I didn't kill him; I only let him die." Again, if letting die were in itself less bad than killing, this defense should have at least some weight. But it does not. Such a "defense" can only be regarded as a grotesque perversion of moral reasoning. Morally speaking, it is no defense at all.

Now, it may be pointed out, quite properly, that the cases of euthanasia with which doctors are concerned are not like this at all. They do not involve personal gain or the destruction of normal healthy children. Doctors are concerned only with cases in which the patient's life is of no further use to him, or in which the patient's life has become or will soon become a terrible burden. However, the point is the same in these cases: the bare difference between killing and letting die does not, in itself, make a moral difference. If a doctor lets a patient die, for humane reasons, he is in the same moral position as if he had given the patient a lethal injection for humane reasons. If his decision was wrong—if, for example, the patient's illness was in fact curable—the decision would be equally regrettable no matter which method was used to carry it out. And if the doctor's decision was the right one, the method used is not in itself important.

The AMA policy statement isolates the crucial issue very well: the crucial issue is "the intentional termination of the life of one human being by another." But after identifying this issue, and forbidding "mercy-killing," the statement goes on to deny that the cessation of treatment is the intentional termination of a life. This is where the mistake comes in, for what is the cessation of treatment, in these circumstances, if it is not "the intentional termination of the life on one human being by another?" Of course it is exactly that, and if it were not, there would be no point to it.

Many people will find this judgment hard to accept. One reason, I think, is that it is very easy to conflate the question of whether killing is, in itself, worse than letting die, and with the very different question of whether most actual cases of killing are more reprehensible than most actual cases of letting die. Most actual cases of killing are clearly terrible (think, for example, of all the murders reported in the newspapers), and one hears of such cases every day. On the other hand, one hardly ever hears of a case of letting die, except for the action of doctors who are motivated by humanitarian reasons. So one learns to think of killing in a much worse light than of letting die. But this does not mean that there is something about killing that makes it in itself worse then letting die, for it is not the bare difference between killing and letting die that makes the difference in these cases. Rather, the other factors—the murderer's motive of personal gain, for example, contrasted with the doctor's humanitarian motivation—account for different reactions to the different cases.

I have argued that killing is not in itself any worse than letting die; if my contention is right, it follows that active euthanasia is not any worse than passive euthanasia. What arguments can be given on the other side? The most common, I believe, is the following:

"The important difference between active and passive euthanasia is that, in passive euthanasia, the doctor does not do anything to bring about the patient's death. The doctor does nothing, and the patient dies of whatever ills already afflict him. In active euthanasia, however, the doctor does something to being about the patient's death: he kills him. The doctor who gives the patient with cancer a lethal injection has himself caused his patient's death; whereas if he merely ceases treatment, the cancer is the cause of the death."

A number of points need to be made here. The first is that it is not exactly correct to say that in passive euthanasia the doctor does nothing, or he does do one thing that is very important: he lets the patient die. "Letting someone die" is certainly different, in some respects, from other types of action—mainly in that it is a kind of action that one may perform by way of not performing certain other actions. For example, one may let a patient die by way of not giving medication, just as one may insult someone by way of not shaking his hand. But for any purpose of moral assessment, it is a type of action nonetheless. The decision to let a patient die is subject to moral appraisal in the same way that a decision to kill him would be subject to moral appraisal: it may be assessed as wise or unwise, compassionate or sadistic, right or wrong. If a doctor deliberately let a patient die who was suffering from a routinely curable illness, the doctor would certainly be to blame for what he had done, just as he would be to blame if he had needlessly killed the patient. Charges against him would then be appropriate. It would be no defense at all for him to insist that he didn't "do anything." He would have done something very serious, indeed, for he let his patient die.

Fixing the cause of death may be very important from a legal point of view, for it may determine whether criminal changes are brought against the doctor. But I do not think that this notion can be used to show a moral difference between active and passive euthanasia. The reason why it is considered bad to be the cause of someone's death is that death is regarded as a great evil—and so it is. However, if it has been decided that euthanasia—even passive euthanasia—is desirable in a given case, it has also been decided that in this instance death is no greater an evil than the patient's continued existence. And if this is true, the usual reason for not wanting to be the cause of someone's death simply does not apply.

Finally, doctors may think that all of this is only academic interest—the sort of thing that philosophers may worry about but that has no practical bearing on their own work. After all, doctors must be concerned about the legal consequences of what they do, and active euthanasia is clearly forbidden by the law. But even so doctors should also be concerned with the fact that the law is forcing upon them a moral doctrine that may well be indefensible, and has a considerable effect on their practices. Of course, most doctors are not now in the position of being coerced in this matter, for they do not regard themselves as merely going along with what the law requires. Rather, in statements such as the AMA policy statement that I have quoted, they are endorsing this doctrine as a central point of medical ethics. In that statement, active euthanasia is condemned not merely as illegal but as "contrary to that for which the medical profession stands," whereas passive euthanasia is approved. However, the preceding considerations suggest that there is really no moral difference between the two, considered in themselves (there may be important moral differences in some cases in their consequences but, as I pointed out, these differences may make active euthanasia, and not passive euthanasia, the morally preferable option). So, whereas doctors may have to discriminate between active and passive euthanasia to satisfy the law, they should not do any more than that. In particular, they should not give the distinction any added authority and weight by writing it into official statements of medical ethics.

THE ARGUMENT FROM MERCY

THE UTILITARIAN VERSION OF THE ARGUMENT

. . . The utilitarian argument may be elaborated as follows:

1. Any action or social policy is morally right if it serves to increase the amount of happiness in the world or to decrease the amount of misery. Conversely, an action or social policy is morally wrong if it serves to decrease happiness or to increase misery.
2. The policy of killing, at their own request, hopelessly ill patients who are suffering great pain, would decrease the amount of misery in the world. . . .
3. Therefore, such a policy would be morally right.

The first premise of this argument, (1), states the Principle of Utility, which is the basic utilitarian assumption. Today most philosophers think that this principle is wrong, because they think that the promotion of happiness and the avoidance of misery are not the *only* morally important things. Happiness, they say, is only one among many values that should be promoted: freedom, justice, and a respect for people's rights are also important. To take one example: People *might* be happier if there were no freedom of religion; for, if everyone adhered to the same religious beliefs, there would be greater harmony among people. There would be no unhappiness caused within families by Jewish girls marrying Catholic boys, and so forth. Moreover, if people were brainwashed well enough, no one would mind not having freedom of choice. Thus happiness would be increased. But, the argument continues, even if happiness *could* be increased this way, it would not be right to deny people freedom of religion, because people have a right to make their own choices. Therefore, the first premise of the utilitarian argument is unacceptable.

From *Matters of Life and Death: New Introductory Essays in Moral Philosophy*, edited by Tom Regan (New York: Random House, 1980). Reprinted by permission of Random House and the author.

There is a related difficulty for utilitarianism, which connects more directly with the topic of euthanasia. Suppose a person is leading a miserable life—full of more unhappiness than happiness—but does *not* want to die. This person thinks that a miserable life is better than none at all. Now I assume that we would all agree that the person should not be killed; that would be plain, unjustifiable murder. Yet it *would* decrease the amount of misery in the world if we killed this person—it would lead to an increase in the balance of happiness over unhappiness—and so it is hard to see how, on strictly utilitarian grounds, it could be wrong. Again, the Principle of Utility seems to be an inadequate guide for determining right and wrong. So we are on shaky ground if we rely on *this* version of the argument from mercy for a defense of euthanasia.

DOING WHAT IS IN EVERYONE'S BEST INTERESTS

Although the foregoing utilitarian argument is faulty, it is nevertheless based on a sound idea. For even if the promotion of happiness and avoidance of misery are not the *only* morally important things, they are still very important. So, when an action or a social policy would decrease misery, that is *a* very strong reason in its favor. In the cases of voluntary euthanasia we are now considering, great suffering is eliminated, and since the patient requests it, there is no question of violating individual rights. That is why, regardless of the difficulties of the Principle of Utility, the utilitarian version of the argument still retains considerable force.

I want now to present a somewhat different version of the argument from mercy, which is inspired by utilitarianism but which avoids the difficulties of the foregoing version by not making the Principle of Utility a premise of the argument. I believe that the following argument is sound and proves that active euthanasia can be justified:

1. If an action promotes the best interests of *everyone* concerned, and violates *no one's* rights, then that action is morally acceptable.
2. In at least some cases, active euthanasia promotes the best interests of everyone concerned and violates no one's rights.
3. Therefore, in at least some cases active euthanasia is morally acceptable.

THE ARGUMENT FROM THE GOLDEN RULE

"Do unto others as you would have them do unto you" is one of the oldest and most familiar moral maxims. Stated in just that way, it is not a very good maxim: Suppose a sexual pervert started treating others as he would like to be treated himself; we might not be happy with the results. Nevertheless, the basic idea behind the Golden

Rule is a good one. The basic idea is that moral rules apply impartially to everyone alike; therefore, you cannot say that you are justified in treating someone else in a certain way unless you are willing to admit that that person would also be justified in treating you in that way if your positions were reversed.

KANT AND THE GOLDEN RULE

The great German philosopher Immanuel Kant (1724–1804) incorporated the basic idea of the Golden Rule into his System of ethics. Kant argued that we should act only on rules that we are willing to have applied universally; that is, we should behave as we would be willing to have everyone behave. He held that there is one supreme principle of morality, which he called "the Categorical Imperative." The Categorical Imperative says:

> Act only according to that maxim by which you can at the same time will that it should become a universal law.[1]

Let us discuss what this means. When we are trying to decide whether we ought to do a certain action, we must first ask what general rule or principle we would be following if we did it. Then, we ask whether we would be willing for everyone to follow that rule, in similar circumstances. (This determines whether "the maxim of the act"—the rule we would be following—can be "willed" to be "a universal law.") If we would not be willing for the rule to be followed universally, then we should not follow it ourselves. Thus, if we are not willing for others to apply the rule to us, we ought not apply it to *them*.

In the eighteenth chapter of St. Matthew's gospel there is a story that perfectly illustrates this point. A man is owed money by another, who cannot pay, and so he had the debtor thrown into prison. But he himself owes money to the king and begs that his *debt* be forgiven. At first the king forgives the debt. However, when the king hears how this man has treated the one who owed him, he changes his mind and "delivers him unto the tormentors" until he can pay. The moral is clear: If you do not think that others should apply the rule "Don't forgive debts!" to *you*, then you should not apply it to others.

The application of all this to the question of euthanasia is fairly obvious. Each of us is going to die someday, although most of us do not know when or how. But suppose you were told you would die in one of two ways, and you were asked to choose between them. First, you could die quietly, and without pain, from a fatal injection. Or second, you could choose to die of an affliction so painful that for several days before death you would be reduced to howling like a dog, with your family standing by helplessly, trying to comfort you, but going through its own psychological hell. It is hard to believe that any sane person, when confronted by these possibilities, would choose to have a rule applied that would force upon him or her the second option. And if we would not want such a rule, which excludes euthanasia, applied to us, then we should not apply such a rule to others.

---

[1] *Foundations of the Metaphysics of Morals*, 422. [Editorial note: See Chapter 3.]

IMPLICATIONS FOR CHRISTIANS

There is considerable irony here. Kant, as we have already noted, was personally opposed to active euthanasia, yet his own Categorical Imperative seems to sanction it. The larger irony, however, is for those in the Christian Church who have for centuries opposed active euthanasia. According to the New Testament accounts, Jesus himself promulgated the Golden Rule as the supreme moral principle—"This is the Law and the Prophets," he said. But if this is the supreme principle of morality, then how can active euthanasia be always wrong? If I would have it done to me, how can it be wrong for me to do likewise to others?

R. M. Hare has made this point with great force. A Christian as well as a leading contemporary moral philosopher, Hare has long argued that "universalizability" is one of the central characteristics of moral judgment. ("Universalizability" is the name he gives to the basic idea embodied in both the Golden Rule and the Categorical Imperative. It means that a moral judgment must conform to universal principles, which apply to everyone alike, if it is to be acceptable.) In an article called "Euthanasia: A Christian View," Hare argues that Christians, if they took Christ's teaching about the Golden Rule seriously, would not think that euthanasia is always wrong. He gives this (true) example:

> The driver of a petrol lorry [i.e., a gasoline truck] was in an accident in which his tanker overturned and immediately caught fire. He himself was trapped in the cab and could not be freed. He therefore besought the bystanders to kill him by hitting him on the head, so that he would not roast to death. I think that somebody did this, but I do not know what happened in court afterwards.
>
> Now will you please all ask yourselves, as I have many times asked myself, what you wish that men should do to you if you were in a situation of that driver. I cannot believe that anybody who considered the matter seriously, as if he himself were going to be in that situation and had now to give instructions as to what rule the bystanders should follow, would say that the rule should be one ruling out euthanasia absolutely.[2]

We might note that *active* euthanasia is the only option here; the concept of passive euthanasia, in these circumstances, has no application.

SUGGESTIONS FOR DISCUSSION

1. Why is Gay-Williams's appeal to "human dignity" in attacking euthanasia deontological in nature? What consequentialist arguments does he develop against euthanasia? How do the deontological and consequentialist arguments for euthanasia outlined by Rachels differ from the arguments against euthanasia formulated by Gay-Williams?
2. Is there a right to privacy? If there is, is it sufficiently strong to ground the permissibility of euthanasia, active or passive?

---

[2] *Philosophic Exchange* (Brockport, N.Y.) II:1 (Summer 1975): 45.

FOR FURTHER READING

Baird, R. M., and Rosebaum, E., ed. *Euthanasia and the Moral Choices*. Buffalo: Prometheus, 1989.

Barry, R. L., *Medical Ethics: Essays on Abortion and Euthanasia*. New York: Lang, 1989.

Bayles, M., and High, D., eds. *Medical Treatment of the Dying: Moral Issues*. Boston: G. K. Hall and Schenkman, 1978.

Beauchamp, T., and Perlin, S., eds. *Ethical Issues in Death and Dying*. Englewood Cliffs, N. J.: Prentice-Hall, 1978.

Behnke, J., and Bok, S., eds. *The Dilemmas of Euthanasia*. Garden City, N. Y.: Anchor Books, 1975.

Berger, J., and Berger, A. S., eds. *To Die or Not to Die?* New York: Praeger, 1990.

Bopp, James, Jr. "Choosing Death for Nancy Cruzan." *Hastings Center Report* (January–February 1990): 42–44.

Brody, D., ed., *Suicide and Euthanasia*. Norwell, Mass.: Kluwer, 1989.

Callahan, D. *Setting Limits: Medical Goals in an Ageing Society*. New York: Simon and Schuster, 1988.

Crigger, B-J., ed. *Cases in Bioethics: Selections from the Hastings Center Report*. New York: St. Martin's Press, 1993.

Downing, A., ed. *Euthanasia and the Right to Death: The Case for Voluntary Euthanasia*. New York: Humanities Press, 1979.

Dworkin, R., *Life's Dominion: An Argument About Abortion, Euthanasia, and Individual Freedom*. New York: Knopf, 1993.

Feinberg, J. "Voluntary Euthanasia and the Inalienable Right to Life." *Philosophy and Public Affairs, 7,2* (1978): 93-123.

Feldman, F. *Confrontations with the Reaper*. Oxford: Oxford University Press, 1991.

Fischer, J. M., ed. *The Metaphysics of Death*. Stanford: Stanford University Press, 1993.

Gervais, K. G. *Redefining Death*. New Haven: Yale University Press, 1986.

Glover, J. *Causing Death and Saving Lives*. New York: Penguin, 1977.

Gorowitz, S., *Drawing the Line: Life and Death Choices in an American Hospital*. Oxford: Oxford University Press, 1991.

Grisez, G., and Boyle, J. *Life and Death with Liberty and Justice*. Notre Dame: Notre Dame University Press, 1979.

Kohl, M., ed. *Beneficent Euthanasia*. Buffalo: Prometheus Books, 1975.

Ladd, J., ed. *Ethical Issues Relating to Life and Death*. New York: Oxford University Press, 1979.

Lamb, D. "Diagnosing Death." *Philosophy and Public Affairs* 7, 2 (1978): 144–53.

McCarrick, P. M. "Active Euthanasia and Assisted Suicide," *Kennedy Institute of Ethics Journal* 2, 1 (1992): 79–100.

Mappes, T., and Zembaty, J., eds. *Biomedical Ethics*. 2nd ed. New York: McGraw-Hill, 1986.

Sherwin, B. L. *In Partnership with God: Contemporary Jewish Law and Ethics*. Syracuse: Syracuse University Press, 1990.

Smith, G. P. *Final Choices: Autonomy in Health Care Decisions*. Springfield: Thomas, 1989.

Steinbock, B., ed. *Killing and Letting Die*. Englewood Cliffs, N. J.: Prentice-Hall, 1980.

Thomasma, D. C. *Euthanasia: Toward an Ethical Social Policy.* New York: Continuum, 1990.

Veatch, R. *Death, Dying and the Biological Revolution.* New Haven: Yale University Press, 1976.

Wikler, Daniel. "Not Dead, Not Dying? Ethical Categories and Persistent Vegetative State." *Hastings Center Report* (February–March 1988): 41–47

Wolf, Susan M., "Nancy Beth Cruzan: In No Voice at All," *Hastings Center Report* (January–February 1990): 38–41.

CHAPTER FOURTEEN

PUNISHMENT AND THE DEATH PENALTY

The basic legal structure of any society undertakes to establish and maintain organization and order. If members of society naturally ordered their social relations and actions to accord with the principles of perfect justice, laws would be unnecessary. For societies less than perfectly just in this way, it is not enough that a basic legal structure merely exist; its laws must be enforced. If a person breaks a law, some effective action must be taken to reimpose order. Failing this, laws would have little effect, and anarchy would reign. Now it is generally agreed that punishment is the appropriate response to law breaking. We deem liberty a basic value, and punishment deprives persons of liberty in some way or it imposes a hardship. What, then, is the general justification for punishment? What justifies punishment as the appropriate response to violations of law? In particular, what forms of punishment are most appropriate to violations of the law? Types of punishment most commonly include public censure, fines, community service, physical suffering, or imprisonment. Thus it is important to inquire whether there are moral or social limits to the forms and severity of punishment that the law may impose.

It is within this context of the theory of punishment that the issue of capital punishment or the death penalty must be addressed. On one hand, the death penalty is one punishment among others, and so it is subject to the same form of justification as punishment in general. On the other hand, it is the most extreme form punishment can assume. It especially raises the question of whether the institution of capital punishment would exceed the bounds of morality. Thus if it is to be morally permissible in some cases, capital punishment seems to require special justification.

Theories of justification for punishment generally assume one of two contending forms: *retributivist* or *utilitarian*. The differences between the two theories of punishment reflect differences between deontological and consequentialist moral theories; that is, between those theories that reject and those that appeal to consequences as the basis for determining what is just and what is not (see, respectively, Kant, Chapter 3; and Chapter 4).

Justifications for Punishment For the *retributivist,* guilt is a necessary and sufficient condition for punishment. Crimes are to be punished; the nature, motive, and degree of the crime determine the appropriate punishment. Punishment is justified insofar as it "fits the crime" or "redresses the moral balance," and it must be "of equal magnitude" to the crime committed. Thus retributivism is backward-looking in its concern to reinstate justice as it existed before the crime took place. It is deontological in ignoring any social utility that punishment may afford. In this view, punishment is considered good in itself, demanded by the dictates of justice despite any valuable consequences it may bring about and though there may be none. This is considered one of the main failings of retributivism. Where no social usefulness would flow from it "punishment for punishment's sake" seems excessively moralistic. Another criticism is that punishment is not always the appropriate response to a violation of the law. Failure to convict a "mercy-killer" or someone like Dr. Kervorkian who aids in suicides by the terminally ill may be a case in point (for more on euthanasia, see Chapter 13). It follows that, though the guilt of an agent is a necessary condition for his or her punishment, it is not sufficient.

Utilitarian theories of punishment attempt to avoid retributivism's difficulties. Here punishment is justified according to the good consequences or social utility it would produce. Utilitarian forms of punishment are prospective: if punishment would not produce future social value in some case, it would not be required. Utilitarian justifications of punishment are usually of two kinds: reform or deterrence. On the *reformative* view, punishment is to provide a criminal with a socially desirable set of skills and attitudes. In this sense, punishment is to have the end of education, moral and otherwise. Yet it is often countered that, though it is important, reform fails to exhaust the various complex ways the criminal law is intended to affect society. The *deterrent* consideration assumes primacy here. The prospect of punishment is designed to deter potential violators of the law. Potential criminals are supposed to factor in their possible punishment when calculating the projected consequences of their criminal acts. This raises a question of fact as to whether punishment deters in this way. Should some kinds of punishment prove upon examination not to deter as such, they would be unjustified on the deterrence view. The major shortcoming of deterrence theories is that they may justify punishment of innocent persons if this served to deter others from committing crimes. Guilt is not a necessary condition for punishment; nor in fact is it sufficient. This is unfair and contrary to the dictates of justice.

The Permissibility of Capital Punishment   Justifications for the death penalty have assumed both retributivist and utilitarian forms. In the case of retribution, it has been suggested that no punishment so fits the crime of murder as death. In utilitarian terms, it is often argued that the prospect of death is the sole sufficient deterrent of vicious crimes. Again there is a factual question here that is to be resolved by the appropriate empirical studies: Is it true that the prospect of death deters potential murderers? Some have argued that death is warranted for criminals who prove to be beyond reform. These considerations raise two questions. First, are some transgressions of the law so extreme and some criminals so dangerous that no punishment is too severe? Second, and by contrast, are some punishments too unjust—too "cruel and unusual"—to be warranted no matter their social utility?

■ **SUPREME COURT RULINGS: GREGG AND MCCLESKEY**

The Eighth Amendment (1791) prohibits any punishment that is "cruel and unusual." This clause was drafted primarily to outlaw such inhumane punishments as torture, the rack, the wheel, burning at the stake, and so forth. It is to this clause, and to the "due process" clause of the Fourteenth Amendment (1868), that legal opposition to capital punishment has usually appealed. A narrow majority of the Supreme Court ruled in 1972 that the death penalty as instituted by numerous states at the time was unconstitutional (*Furman v. Georgia*). Two of the five justices making up the majority considered capital punishment to be inherently cruel and excessive. The remaining three ruled that it was unconstitutional only as the states at the time instituted it. State courts were found to apply the death penalty in an arbitrary way, establishing no standards to determine when a jury may choose capital punishment and when not. One result, the Court concluded, is the disproportionate and discriminatory sentencing to death of black criminals, in violation of the Fourteenth Amendment.

In *Gregg v. Georgia* (1976), the Supreme Court ruled that the death penalty is not unconstitutional and that it is acceptably administered in the state of Georgia. The Court held that capital punishment is endorsed by a majority in contemporary American society and that it is consistent with the concept of human dignity, which is basic to the Eighth Amendment. Though it was admitted that the death penalty is an extreme sanction, it was held to be appropriate in the case of extreme crimes, and so not to be disproportionate punishment. It was also found to serve both retributive and deterrent social purposes. Moreover, in *Furman* the Court had decided that the Georgia statute allowed the death penalty to be arbitrarily applied. Since then, the Georgia legislature had ruled that a jury must find a crime to be characterized by at least one from a list of aggravating factors before the death penalty could be imposed. Consequently, the Court acknowledged in *Gregg* that the death penalty is no longer arbitrarily applied in Georgia.

In a dissenting opinion, Justice Thurgood Marshall contended that if the American public were fully informed, they would find capital punishment unacceptable. Marshall argued that the death penalty is in any case unconstitutional, because it is excessive punishment. It is not necessary as a deterrent, for the alternative of life imprisonment serves equally well; and it is inconsistent with any retributive standard, for it denies the wrongdoer's dignity and worth.

The central issue in a more recent case, *McCleskey v. Kemp* (1986), was whether a broad ranging statistical study is sufficient to establish discrimination by the State of Georgia in sentencing persons convicted of a capital crime. The Baldus study dramatically illustrated that the death penalty was differentially imposed in Georgia in the 1970s in terms of the race both of the murder victim and of the defendant. In light of these findings, McCleskey argued that the Georgia capital punishment statute violates the Fourteenth Amendment's Equal Protection Clause. It seemed to suggest that the lives of white persons are considered more valuable in Georgia than those of blacks. In his majority opinion, Justice Powell argued that McCleskey was effectively charging every actor in the Georgia capital sentencing process—from prosecutor and judge to Georgia legislators—with discrimination. If so, such a charge needs to demonstrate that the actors in the case purposefully discriminated against McCleskey personally. Justice Powell contended that McCleskey offered no evidence to this effect, relying solely on Baldus's statistical study. The Baldus study only indicates a discrepancy in sentencing that correlates with race, not necessarily one based on race. Thus, concluded Justice Powell, the study does not show that the Georgia capital sentencing process significantly risks constitutionally unacceptable discrimination.

In his dissenting opinion, Justice Brennan insisted that the Baldus study demonstrates that the race of convicted defendants in Georgia capital cases prominently affects the chances of their being sentenced to death. Justice Brennan argued that because death is ir-revocable, it requires heightened scrutiny as punishment. Thus, McCleskey should not have to show purposeful discrimination against him in his sentencing decision by some state agent. The constitution requires only that he demonstrate a significant *risk* of being subjected to an arbitrary sentence. McCleskey was the first to demonstrate empirically how the capital sentencing system works in a discriminatory fashion. Justice Brennan concluded that a system of capital sentencing in which there is a significant risk that race plays a role does not meet the heightened scrutiny test.

Justices Potter Stewart, Lewis F. Powell, Jr. and John Paul Stevens

MAJORITY OPINION IN *GREGG v. GEORGIA*

The petitioner, Troy Gregg, was charged with committing armed robbery and mur-der. In accordance with Georgia procedure in capital cases, the trial was in two stages, a guilt stage and a sentencing stage. . . .

. . . The jury found the petitioner guilty on two counts of armed robbery and two counts of murder.

At the penalty stage, which took place before the same jury, . . . the trial judge instructed the jury that it could recommend either a death sentence or a life prison sentence on each count. . . . The jury returned verdicts of death on each count.

The Supreme Court of Georgia affirmed the convictions and the imposition of the death sentences for murder. . . . The death sentences imposed for armed robbery, however, were vacated on the grounds that the death penalty had rarely been im-posed in Georgia for that offense. . . .

We address initially the basic contention that the punishment of death for the crime of murder is, under all circumstances, "cruel and unusual" in violation of the Eighth and Fourteenth Amendments of the Constitution. . . .

The court on a number of occasions has both assumed and asserted the consti-tutionality of capital punishment. In several cases that assumption provided a nec-essary foundation for the decision, as the Court was asked to decide whether a particular method of carrying out a capital sentence would be allowed to stand under the Eighth Amendment. But until *Furman v. Georgia* (1972), the Court never confronted squarely the fundamental claim that the punishment of death always, re-gardless of the enormity of the offense or the procedure followed in imposing the

United States Supreme Court, 428 U.S. 153 (1976).

sentence, is cruel and unusual punishment in violation of the Constitution. Although this issue was presented and addressed in Furman it was not resolved by the court. . . . We now hold that the punishment of death does not invariably violate the Constitution. . . .

The death penalty is said to serve two principal social purposes: retribution and deterrence of capital crimes by prospective offenders.[1]

In part, capital punishment is an expression of society's moral outrage at particularly offensive conduct. This function may be unappealing to many, but it is essential in an ordered society that asks its citizens to rely on legal processes rather than self-help to vindicate their wrongs.

> The instinct of retribution is part of the nature of man, and channeling that instinct in the administration of criminal justice serves an important purpose in promoting the stability of a society governed by law. When people begin to believe that organized society is unwilling or unable to impose upon criminal offenders the punishment they "deserve," then there are sown the seeds of anarchy—of self-help, vigilante justice and lynch law. *Furman v. Georgia* (Stewart, J., concurring).

"Retribution is no longer the dominant objective of the criminal law," but neither is it a forbidden objective nor one inconsistent with our respect for the dignity of men. Indeed, the decision that capital punishment may be the appropriate sanction in extreme cases is an expression of the community's belief that certain crimes are themselves so grievous an affront to humanity that the only adequate response may be the penalty of death.

Statistical attempts to evaluate the worth of the death penalty as a deterrent to crimes by potential offenders have occasioned a great deal of debate. The results simply have been inconclusive. . . .

Although some of the studies suggest that the death penalty may not function as a significantly greater deterrent than lesser penalties, there is no convincing empirical evidence either supporting or refuting this view. We may nevertheless assume safely that there are murderers, such as those who act in passion, for whom the threat of death has little or no deterrent effect. But for many others, the death penalty undoubtedly is a significant deterrent. There are carefully contemplated murders, such as murder for hire, where the possible penalty of death may well enter into the cold calculus that precedes the decision to act. And there are some categories of murder, such as murder by a life prisoner, where other sanctions may not be adequate.

The value of capital punishment as a deterrent of crime is a complex factual issue the resolution of which properly rests with the legislatures, which can evaluate the results of statistical studies in terms of their own local conditions and with a flexibility of approach that is not available to the courts. Indeed, many of the post-*Furman* statutes reflect just such a responsible effort to define those crimes and those criminals for which capital punishment is most probably an effective deterrent.

In sum, we cannot say that the judgment of the Georgia Legislature that capital punishment may be necessary in some cases is clearly wrong. Considerations of federalism, as well as respect for the ability of a legislature to evaluate, in terms of its particular State, the moral consensus concerning the death penalty and its social utility as a sanction, requires us to conclude, in the absence of more convincing evidence, that the infliction of death as a punishment for murder is not without justification and thus is not unconstitutionally severe.

Finally, we must consider whether the punishment of death is disproportionate in relation to the crime for which it is imposed. There is no question that death as a punishment is unique in its severity and irrevocability. When a defendant's life is at stake, the Court has been particularly sensitive to insure that every safeguard is observed. But we are concerned here only with the imposition of capital punishment for the crime of murder, and when a life has been taken deliberately by the offender,[2] we cannot say that the punishment is invariably disproportionate to the crime. It is an extreme sanction, suitable to the most extreme crimes.

We hold that the death penalty is not a form of punishment that may never be imposed, regardless of the circumstances of the offense, regardless of the character of the offender, and regardless of the procedure followed in reaching the decision to impose it.

N O T E S

1. Another purpose that has been discussed is the incapacitation of dangerous criminals and the consequent prevention of crimes that they may otherwise commit in the future.

2. We do not address here the question whether the taking of the criminal's life is a proportionate sanction where no victim has been deprived of life—for example, when capital punishment is imposed for rape, kidnapping, or armed robbery that does not result in the death of any human being.

Justice Thurgood Marshall

DISSENTING OPINION IN *GREGG v. GEORGIA*

In *Furman v. Georgia* (1972) (concurring opinion), I set forth at some length my views on the basic issue presented to the Court in [this case]. The death penalty, I

United States Supreme Court, 428 U.S. 153 (1976).

concluded, is a cruel and unusual punishment prohibited by the Eighth and Fourteenth Amendments. That continues to be my view. . . .

In *Furman* I concluded that the death penalty is constitutionally invalid for two reasons. First, the death penalty is excessive. And second, the American people, fully informed as to the purposes of the death penalty and its liabilities, would in my view reject it as morally unacceptable. . . .

Even assuming, however, that the post-*Furman* enactment of statutes authorizing the death penalty renders the prediction of the views of an informed citizenry an uncertain basis for a constitutional decision, the enactment of those statutes has no bearing whatsoever on the conclusion that the death penalty is unconstitutional because it is excessive. An excessive penalty is invalid under the Cruel and Unusual Punishments Clause "even though popular sentiment may favor" it. The inquiry here, then, is simply whether the death penalty is necessary to accomplish the legitimate legislative purposes in punishment, or whether a less severe penalty—life imprisonment—would do as well.

The two purposes that sustain the death penalty as nonexcessive in the Court's view are general deterrence and retribution. . . .The available evidence, I concluded in *Furman* was convincing that "capital punishment is not necessary as a deterrent to crime in our society." . . .

. . . The evidence I reviewed in *Furman* remains convincing, in my view, that "capital punishment is not necessary as a deterrent to crime in our society." The justification for the death penalty must be found elsewhere.

The other principal purpose said to be served by the death penalty is retribution. The notion that retribution can serve as a moral justification for the sanction of death finds credence in the opinion of my Brothers Stewart, Powell, and Stevens.

. . . It is this notion that I find to be the most disturbing aspect of today's unfortunate [decision].

The concept of retribution is a multifaceted one, and any discussion of its role in the criminal law must be undertaken with caution . . . .

The . . . contentions—that society's expression of moral outrage through the imposition of the death penalty pre-empts the citizenry from taking the law into its own hands and reinforces moral values—are not retributive in the purest sense. They are essentially utilitarian in that they portray the death penalty as valuable because of its beneficial results. These justifications for the death penalty are inadequate because the penalty is, quite clearly, I think, not necessary to the accomplishment of those results.

There remains for consideration, however, what might be termed the purely retributive justification for the death penalty—that the death penalty is appropriate, not because of its beneficial effect on society, but because the taking of the murderer's life is itself morally good. . . .

. . . The mere fact that the community demands the murderer's life in return for the evil he has done cannot sustain the death penalty, for as Justices Stewart, Powell and Stevens remind us, "the Eighth Amendment demands more than that a challenged punishment be acceptable to contemporary society." To be sustained under the Eighth Amendment, the death penalty must "compor[t] with the basic concept of human dignity of [other] men." Under these standards, the taking of life "because the wrongdoer deserves it" surely must fail, for such a punishment has as its very basis the total denial of the wrongdoer's dignity and worth.

The death penalty, unnecessary to promote the goal of deterrence or to further any legitimate notion of retribution, is an excessive penalty forbidden by the Eighth and Fourteenth Amendments. I respectfully dissent from the Court's judgment upholding the [sentence] of death imposed upon the [petitioner in this case].

Justice Lewis F. Powell, Jr.

MAJORITY OPINION IN *MCCLESKEY v. KEMP*

[McCleskey's] petition included a claim that the Georgia capital sentencing process was administered in a racially discriminatory manner in violation of the Eighth and Fourteenth Amendments. In support of the claim, petitioner proffered a statistical study (the Baldus study) that purports to show a disparity in the imposition of the death sentence in Georgia based on the murder victim's race and, to a lesser extent, the defendant's race. The study is based on over 2,000 murder cases that occurred in Georgia during the 1970s, and involves data relating to the victim's race, the defendant's race, and the various combinations of such persons' races. The study indicates that black defendants who killed white victims have the greatest likelihood of receiving the death penalty. Rejecting petitioner's constitutional claims, the court denied his petition insofar as it was based on the Baldus study. . . .

I I

1   McCleskey's first claim is that the Georgia capital punishment statute violates the Equal Protection Clause of the Fourteenth Amendment. He argues that race has infected the administration of Georgia's statute in two ways: persons who murder whites are more likely to be sentenced to death than persons who murder blacks, and black murderers are more likely to be sentenced to death than white murderers. As a black defendant who killed a white victim, McCleskey claims that the Baldus study demonstrates that he was discriminated against because of his race and

United States Supreme Court 481 U.S. 282 (1986).

because of the race of his victim. In its broadest form, McCleskey's claim of discrimination extends to every actor in the Georgia capital sentencing process, from the prosecutor who sought the death penalty and the jury that imposed the sentence, to the State itself that enacted the capital punishment statute and allows it to remain in effect despite its allegedly discriminatory applications. We agree with the Court of Appeals, and every other court that has considered such a challenge, that this claim must fail. . . .

A

Our analysis begins with the basic principle that a defendant who alleges an equal [2, 3] protection violation has the burden of proving "the existence of purposeful discrimination." . . . A corollary to this principle is that a criminal defendant must prove that the purposeful discrimination "had a discriminatory effect" on him. . . . Thus, to prevail under the Equal Protection Clause, McCleskey must prove that the decision-makers in *his* case acted with discriminatory purpose. He offers no evidence specific to his own case that would support an inference that racial considerations played a part in his sentence. Instead, he relies solely on the Baldus study. McCleskey argues that the Baldus study compels an inference that his sentence rests on purposeful discrimination. McCleskey's claim that these statistics are sufficient proof of discrimination, without regard to the facts of a particular case, would extend to all capital cases in Georgia, at least where the victim was white and the defendant is black. . . .

The Court has accepted statistics as proof of intent to discriminate in certain limited contexts. First, this Court has accepted statistical disparities as proof of an equal protection violation in the selection of the jury venire in a particular district. Although statistical proof normally must present a "stark" pattern to be accepted as the sole proof of discriminatory intent under the constitution, . . . "[b]ecause of the nature of the jury-selection task, . . . we have permitted a finding of constitutional violation even when the statistical pattern does not approach [such] extremes." . . . Second, this Court has accepted statistics in the form of multiple-regression analysis to prove statutory violations under Title VII of the Civil Rights Act of 1964. . . .

But the nature of the capital sentencing decision, and the relationship of the statistics to that decision, are fundamentally different from the corresponding elements in the venire-selection of the Title VII cases. . . .

In those cases, the statistics relate to fewer entities, and fewer variables are relevant to the challenged decisions. . . .

Finally, McCleskey's statistical proffer must be viewed in the context of his [4, 5] challenge. McCleskey challenges decisions at the heart of the State's criminal justice system. "[O]ne of society's most basic tasks is that of protecting the lives of its citizens and one of the most basic ways in which it achieves the task is through criminal laws against murder." *Gregg v. Georgia* . . . Implementation of these laws necessarily requires discretionary judgments. Because discretion is essential to the criminal justice process, we would demand exceptionally clear proof before we would infer that the discretion has been abused. The unique nature of the decisions at issue in this case also counsels against adopting such an inference from the disparities indicated by the Baldus study. Accordingly, we hold that the Baldus study is clearly insufficient to support an inference that any of the decisionmakers in McCleskey's case acted with discriminatory purpose.

B

6, 7　McCleskey also suggests that the Baldus study proves that the State as a whole has acted with a discriminatory purpose. He appears to argue that the State has violated the Equal Protection Clause by adopting the capital punishment statute and allowing it to remain in force despite its allegedly discriminatory application. But "'[d]iscriminatory purpose' . . . implies more than intent as volition or intent as awareness of consequences. It implies that the decisionmaker, in this case a state legislature, selected or reaffirmed a particular course of action at least in part 'because of,' not merely 'in spite of,' its adverse effects upon an identifiable group." . . . For this claim to prevail, McCleskey would have to prove that the Georgia Legislature enacted or maintained the death penalty statute *because of* an anticipated racially discriminatory effect. In *Gregg v. Georgia, supra,* this Court found that the Georgia capital sentencing system could operate in a fair and neutral manner. There was no evidence then, and there is none now, that the Georgia Legislature enacted the capital punishment statute to further a racially discriminatory purpose.

8　　Nor has McCleskey demonstrated that the legislature maintains the capital punishment statute because of the racially disproportionate impact suggested by the Baldus study. As legislatures necessarily have wide discretion in the choice of criminal laws and penalties, and as there were legitimate reasons for the Georgia Legislature to adopt and maintain capital punishment, see *Gregg v. Georgia,* we will not infer a discriminatory purpose on the part of the State of Georgia. . . .

　　Accordingly, we reject McCleskey's equal protection claims.

I V

C

23, 25　At most, the Baldus study indicates a discrepancy that appears to correlate with race. Apparent disparities in sentencing are an inevitable part of our criminal justice system. The discrepancy indicated by the Baldus study is "a far cry from the major systemic defects identified in *Furman*. . . . As this Court has recognized, any mode for determining guilt or punishment "has its weaknesses and the potential for misuse." . . .

　　Specifically, "there can be 'no perfect procedure for deciding in which cases governmental authority should be used to impose death.'" . . . Despite these imperfections, our consistent rule has been that constitutional guarantees are met when "the mode [for determining guilt or punishment] itself has been surrounded with safeguards to make it as fair as possible." . . . Where the discretion that is fundamental to our criminal process is involved, we decline to assume that what is unexplained is invidious. In light of the safeguards designed to minimize racial bias in the process, the fundamental value of jury trial in our criminal justice system, and the benefits that discretion provides to criminal defendants, we hold that the Baldus study does not demonstrate a constitutionally significant risk of racial bias affecting the Georgia capital sentencing process.

Justice William Brennan

DISSENTING OPINION IN *MCCLESKEY v. KEMP*

I I

At some point in this case, Warren McCleskey doubtless asked his lawyer whether a jury was likely to sentence him to die. A candid reply to this question would have been disturbing. First, counsel would have to tell McCleskey that few of the details of the crime or of McCleskey's past criminal conduct were more important than the fact that his victim was white. . . . Furthermore, counsel would feel bound to tell McCleskey that defendants charged with killing white victims in Georgia are 4.3 times as likely to be sentenced to death as defendants charged with killing blacks. In addition, frankness would compel the disclosure that it was more likely than not that the race of McCleskey's victim would determine whether he received a death sentence: 6 of every 11 defendants convicted of killing a white person would not have received the death penalty if their victims had been black, . . . while, among defendants with aggravating and mitigating factors comparable to McCleskey's, 20 of every 34 would not have been sentenced to die if their victims had been black. . . . Finally, the assessment would not be complete without the information that cases involving black defendants and white victims are more likely to result in a death sentence than cases featuring any other racial combination of defendant and victim. . . . The story could be told in a variety of ways, but McCleskey could not fail to grasp its essential narrative line: there was a significant chance that race would place a prominent role in determining if he lived or died.

The Court today holds that Warren McCleskey's sentence was constitutionally imposed. It finds no fault in a system in which lawyers must tell their clients that race casts a large shadow on the capital sentencing process. . . .

United States Supreme Court 481 U.S. 282 (1986).

I I I

A

It is important to emphasize at the outset that the Court's observation that McCleskey cannot prove the influence of race on any particular sentencing decision is irrelevant in evaluating his Eighth Amendment claim. Since *Furman v. Georgia*, . . . (1972), the Court has been concerned with the *risk* of the imposition of an arbitrary sentence, rather than the proven fact of one. . . .

Defendants challenging their death sentences thus never have had to prove that impermissible considerations have actually infected sentencing decisions. We have required instead that they establish that the system under which they were sentenced posed a significant risk of such an occurrence. McCleskey's claim does differ, however, in one respect from these earlier cases: it is the first to base a challenge not on speculation about how a system *might* operate, but on empirical documentation of how it *does* operate.

C

The majority thus misreads our Eighth Amendment jurisprudence in concluding that McCleskey has not demonstrated a degree of risk sufficient to raise constitutional concern. The determination of the significance of his evidence is at its core an exercise in human moral judgment, not a mechanical statistical analysis. It must first and foremost be informed by awareness of the fact that death is irrevocable, and that as a result "the qualitative difference of death from all other punishments requires a greater degree of scrutiny of the capital sentencing determination." . . . For this reason, we have demanded a uniquely high degree of rationality in imposing the death penalty. A capital sentencing system in which race more likely than not plays a role does not meet this standard. It is true that every nuance of decision cannot be statistically captured, nor can any individual judgment be plumbed with absolute certainty. Yet the fact that we must always act without the illumination of complete knowledge cannot induce paralysis when we confront what is literally an issue of life and death. Sentencing data, history, and experience all counsel that Georgia has provided insufficient assurance of the heightened rationality we have required in order to take a human life. . . .

It is tempting to pretend that minorities on death row share a fate in no way connected to our own, that our treatment of them sounds no echoes beyond the chambers in which they die. Such an illusion is ultimately corrosive, for the reverberations of injustice are not so easily confined. "The destinies of the two races in this country are indissolubly linked together," . . . and the way in which we choose those who will die reveals the depth of moral commitment among the living.

The Court's decision today will not change what attorneys in George tell other Warren McCleskeys about their chances of execution. Nothing will soften the harsh messages they must convey, nor alter the prospect that race undoubtedly will continue to be a topic of discussion. McCleskey's evidence will not have obtained judicial acceptance, but that will not affect what is said on death row. However many criticisms of today's decision may be rendered, these painful conversations will serve as the most eloquent dissents of all.

■ **ERNEST VAN DEN HAAG: THE DEATH PENALTY AND DETERRENCE**
Ernest van den Haag admits that whether the death penalty deters crime is an unresolved factual issue. However, he suggests that the principle of inherent dignity of human life implies the following rule: if human life is to be risked, it is preferable to risk the life of the guilty than that of the innocent. For it is more important to protect prospective victims than to spare murderers. So if imposing the death penalty could conceivably save the lives of future murder victims, there is a moral obligation to impose it. (Note that this argument may presuppose hypothetical guilt for a potential crime before the crime is actually committed.)

Ernest van den Haag

ON DETERRENCE AND THE DEATH PENALTY

. . . If we do not know whether the death penalty will deter others [in a uniquely effective way], we are confronted with two uncertainties. If we impose the death penalty, and achieve no deterrent effect thereby, the life of a convicted murderer has been expended in vain (from a deterrent viewpoint). There is a net loss. If we impose the death sentence and thereby deter some future murderers, we spared the lives of some future victims (the prospective murderers gain too; they are spared punishment because they were deterred). In this case, the death penalty has led to a net gain, unless the life of a convicted murderer is valued more highly than that of the unknown victim, or victims (and the non-imprisonment of the deterred non-murderer).

The calculation can be turned around, of course. The absence of the death penalty may harm no one and therefore produce a gain—the life of the convicted and thus produce a loss—their life.

To be sure, we must risk something certain—the death (or life) of the convicted man, for something uncertain—the death (or life) of the victims of murder-

From the *Journal of Criminal Law, Criminology, and Police Science* 60, 2 (1969: 146–47. Reprinted by special permission of Northwestern University School of Law.

ers who may be deterred. This is in the nature of uncertainty—when we invest, or gamble, we risk the money we have for an uncertain gain. Many human actions, most commitments—including marriage and crime—share this characteristic with the deterrent purpose of any penalization, and with its rehabilitative purpose (and even with the protective).

More proof is demanded for the deterrent effect of the death penalty than is demanded for the deterrent effect of other penalties. This is not justified by the absence of other utilitarian purposes such as protection and rehabilitation; they involve no less uncertainty than deterrence.[1]

Irrevocability may support a demand for some reason to expect more deterrence than revocable penalties might produce, but not a demand for more proof of deterrence, as has been pointed out above. The reason for expecting more deterrence lies in the greater sovereignty, the terrifying effect inherent in finality. Since it seems more important to spare victims than to spare murderers, the burden of proving the greater severity inherent in irrevocability adds nothing to deterrence lies on those who oppose capital punishment. Proponents of the death penalty need show only that there is no more uncertainty about it than about greater severity in general.

The demand that the death penalty be proved more deterrent than alternatives cannot be satisfied any more than the demand that six years in prison be proved to be more deterrent than three. But the uncertainty which confronts us favors the death penalty as long as by imposing it we might save future victims of murder. This effect is as plausible as the general idea that penalties have deterrent effects which increase with their severity. Though we have no proof of the positive deterrence of the penalty, we also have no proof of zero, or negative effectiveness. I believe we have no right to risk additional future victims of murder for the sake of sparing convicted murderers; on the contrary, our moral obligation is to risk the possible ineffectiveness of executions. However rationalized, the opposite view appears to be motivated by the simple fact that executions are more subjected to social control than murder. However, this applies to all penalties and does not argue for the abolition of any.

THOMAS HURKA: RIGHTS AND THE DEATH PENALTY

In contrast to both retributivist and utilitarian accounts, Thomas Hurka develops a right-based theory of punishment (for more on rights-based moral theories, see Nozick, and Mackie,

---

[1] Rehabilitation or protection are of minor importance in our actual penal system (though not in our theory). We confine many people who do not need rehabilitation and against whom we do not need protection (e.g., the exasperated husband who killed his wife); we release many unrehabilitated offenders against whom protection is needed. Certainly rehabilitation and protection are not, and deterrence is, the main actual function of legal punishment if we disregard nonutilitarian purposes.

Chapter 5). Hurka contends that his rights-based theory incorporates the appealing aspects of both retributivist and utilitarian theories, while avoiding their deficiencies. Hurka characterizes persons in terms of natural rights. Each has a right to the most extensive liberty compatible with the like liberty for all. This right entails an enforcement right to use coercion, including some threats and the *minimum* harms necessary, in legitimate self-defense of one's rights. Hurka derives the right to punish from this right to make threats: punishment is justified as the right to inflict harms on others for rights violated. Harms inflicted in punishment cannot exceed the degree of importance of the rights violated. So death cannot be mandated for relatively minor criminal violations of others' rights. For deterrence theories, successful criminal deterrence is both a necessary and sufficient condition for imposing capital punishment. For retributivist theories, necessary and sufficient conditions for the death penalty are that the person is guilty and that the punishment "fit" the class of crime. On Hurka's rights theory, by contrast, the deterrence effect (if factually established) *and* the actual guilt of a criminal in violating the right to life of an innocent person are each individually necessary conditions for instituting the death penalty. In other words, capital punishment is not justifiable without both of these conditions. Yet they would be sufficient to justify capital punishment if and only if they hold conjointly.

Thomas Hurka

RIGHTS AND CAPITAL PUNISHMENT

Discussions of the morality of capital punishment, and indeed discussions of the morality of punishment in general, usually assume that there are two possible justifications of punishment, a deterrence justification associated with utilitarianism and other consequentialist moral theories, and a retributive justification associated with deontological moral theories. But now that rights-based theories are attracting the increasing attention of moral philosophers it is worth asking whether these theories may not employ a different justification of punishment, and that this justification combines many of the attractive features of the deterrence and retributive justifications while avoiding their unattractive features. In particular, I will argue that the rights-based justification has more attractive consequences for the morality of capital punishment than either the deterrence or retributive justifications.[1]

Rights-based moral theories hold that persons have certain natural rights, and the fact that these rights are natural is often expressed by saying that persons would

From *Dialogue* XXI, 4 (December 1982). Reprinted by permission of *Dialogue* and the author.

possess them "in the state of nature." Among the rights which persons are usually said to possess in the state of nature is the right to punish those who violate the rights of others. In section 7 of the *Second Treatise*, Locke says that the state of nature has a Law of Nature to govern it, and that "everyone has a right to punish the transgressors of the Law to such a Degree, as may hinder its Violation."[2] Nozick too includes a right to punish among those he grants in *Anarchy, State and Utopia*, quoting Locke's description of this right with approval, and devoting an entire section to a discussion of "the right of all to punish."[3] If persons have a right to punish in the state of nature, then they are permitted to punish the violators of rights if they want to, but they are also permitted to refrain from punishing them if they do not want to. . . .

The right to punish which persons have in the state of nature is not a primitive right, but derives from another more general right which they possess. Whenever persons in the state of nature have a natural right they also have the right to enforce that right, that is, the right to use coercion against other persons to prevent them from violating it.[4] The most familiar form of coercion is the use of force, and persons in the state of nature therefore have the right to use force to defend themselves against would-be violators of their rights, and also to defend third parties. But this right of self- (and other-) defense is not the only enforcement right which they possess. The making of threats is also a form of coercion, and persons in the state of nature therefore also have the right to threaten others with certain harms if they succeed in violating their rights, or succeed in violating the rights of third parties. It is from this second enforcement-right that the right to punish derives. If persons in the state of nature have the right to threaten others with harms if they succeed in violating rights, then they surely also have the right to inflict these harms on them once the relevant rights have been violated. But this is just what the right to punish is: a right to inflict harms on persons who have successfully violated the rights of others.[5]

Although Locke and Nozick include a right to punish among those possessed in the state of nature they do not provide any justification of this right. They do not show *why* rights theories should contain a right to punish, or even why they should contain enforcement rights in general, but simply include these rights on a list of those possessed in the state of nature. There is one kind of rights theory, however, which in a somewhat stricter usage of the term than is usual I will call a "libertarian" rights theory, which can provide such a justification. A libertarian rights theory holds that there is really only one natural right, namely the equal right of all persons to the *most extensive* liberty compatible with a like liberty for other persons, and that all other natural rights are species or instances of the right to liberty. They are all rights to exercise liberty in certain specified areas, and impose on other persons the duty not to interfere with liberty in those areas.[6] Because these rights are instances of a right to the most extensive liberty we are to identify them by identifying the most extensive right to liberty possible. Comparing the extent of different liberties in the way this requires involves some obvious difficulties, but the following should be uncontroversial. If one liberty contains another as a proper part, so that exercising the second liberty always involves exercising the first, but exercising the first liberty does not always involve exercising the second, then the first liberty is more extensive than the second (some examples: the liberty to buy property in Canada is more extensive than the liberty to buy property in Alberta, for it contains it as a proper part; the liberty to move either of one's arms freely is more extensive than the liberty to move one's left arm freely, for it contains it as a proper part, and so on). But this is all we need to show why a libertarian rights theory has to contain enforcement rights. Let us imagine that we have discovered that L is the most extensive liberty not containing the liberty to do any enforcing such that every person can have an equal right to exercise all the liberties in L, and no one person's right conflicts with that of any other. Then in deciding whether to grant enforcement rights we are deciding whether to add to L the liberty of removing from other persons the liberty of removing liberties in L from other persons. We have every reason to do this and no reason not to. If we add this liberty—and it is once again best described as the liberty to remove from other persons the liberty of removing liberties in L from other persons—we will be creating a new liberty L^1, which contains L as a proper part, and is therefore more extensive than it. But at the same time we will not be subtracting liberties from any other person's liberty L. Although the liberty we are adding conflicts with some liberties of other persons all these are liberties which have already been excluded from L and have therefore already been excluded from the protection of their natural right to liberty. Allowing enforcement rights enables us to extend the scope of everyone's right to liberty—which is just what a libertarian rights theory requires us to do—without detracting in any way from the right to liberty of others. And if this is the case, then a libertarian rights theory can give exactly the same justification for these rights as for any other rights it grants.

This justification of enforcement rights, which I have presented so far in a fairly abstract way, applies most directly to the right of self- (or other-) defense. If we give persons the right to use force to prevent rights violations then we are obviously extending the scope of their right to liberty without limiting the right to liberty of anyone else, for no one has the right to violate rights. But it also applies to the right to make and carry out threats which lies behind the right to punish. When we threaten a person with harms if he successfully violates rights we do not remove from him the liberty of violating rights as such. But we do remove from him the more complex liberty of violating rights and not having those harms inflicted on him afterwards. If he does not have the right to exercise the simple liberty he does not have the right to exercise the more complex one either, and in giving other persons the right to remove the more complex liberty from him a libertarian rights theory is once again extending the scope of their right to liberty without in any way detracting from his.

Because it derives the right to punish from a right to make certain threats, the rights-based justification has two attractive consequences which also follow from the retributive justification. The first is that it is never permissible to punish persons who have not violated, or who have not been found by reliable proceedings to have violated, the rights of other persons. Guilt, in other words, is a necessary condition of the permissibility of punishment on the rights-based view. The reasoning leading up to this consequence should be fairly evident. The right to use coercion to prevent others from violating rights only entitles us to make a very specific threat, namely the threat to inflict certain harms on them if they actually succeed in violating rights, and we could not claim to be carrying out this threat if we inflicted harms on someone whom we did not have reliable reasons to think had violated rights. The first consequence also follows from the retributive justification, but it is a well-known objection to the deterrence justification that no such consequence follows from it. Critics of the deterrence justification often point out that it could license the framing and "punishment" of an innocent man if this would be sufficiently effective in deterring future crimes. The rights-based justification is not open to this objection for it holds, along with the retributive justification, that guilt is always a necessary condition of the permissibility of punishment. The second consequence is that it is never permissible to punish persons for rights violations unless our intention to punish persons for those violations has been publicly announced in the past. The reasoning leading up to this consequence should also be evident. If punishment is only permissible because it is the carrying out of a permissible threat, then it is only permissible when that threat has actually been made. Punishments for the violation of secret laws, or for the violation of retroactive laws, are never permissible on the rights-based view, though we can easily imagine circumstances in which they would be permissible and even required on the deterrence view, and perhaps even on some retributive views as well.

The rights-based justification, then, has some attractive consequences in common with the retributive justification for the question when punishment is permissible. But when it turns to the question of how much punishment is permissible, or how severe a punishment is permissible, it has some consequences in common with the retributive justification and some in common with the deterrence justification. The important thing to realize here is that the enforcement rights which persons have in the state of nature are not unqualified. They are subject to at least two qualifications, and these qualifications place limits on the severity of the punishments which they may inflict in the state of nature, and which their governments may inflict in civil society. To set out these qualifications I will begin by examining some particular cases involving self-defense where I think their intuitive attractiveness is especially evident, and then give them a theoretical justification. I will conclude by showing what the implications of these qualifications are for questions about the morality of punishment, and in particular for questions about the morality of capital punishment.

Let us begin by imagining the following case. One person X is trying to violate a fairly unimportant right of another person Y, say, the right not to be tickled, and Y is considering how to prevent this. Y is not nearly as strong as X, so he cannot hope to stop X just by resisting him physically. Nor will any threat of Y's deter X. But Y does have in his hands a pistol with which he can kill X. If killing X is the only way Y can prevent X from violating his right not to be tickled, is it permissible for Y to use his pistol? . . . We would insist that there is an upper limit on the amount of coercion persons can use to enforce their rights, and that this limit is lower the less important the rights are which they are enforcing. For Y to kill X just to prevent him from tickling him is for Y quite clearly to overstep a limit which is, in the case of a very unimportant right like the right not to be tickled, very low indeed.

Reflection on this case suggests what I will call an *upper limit* qualification on persons' enforcement rights. The most natural way for a rights theory to express this qualification is as follows. Although Y's right to enforce his right to Φ entitles him to act in ways which would otherwise involve violating some rights of X's, it does not entitle him to act in ways which would otherwise involve violating any rights of X's which are more important than his own right to Φ. In the course of enforcing his right to Φ Y can act in ways which would otherwise involve violating X's right to Φ, or any rights of X's which are less important than his right to Φ. So if X is trying to kill him Y can kill X in self-defense, or assault him or tie him up. But he cannot act in ways which would otherwise involve violating any rights of X's which are more important than his right to Φ. . . .

Now let us imagine another case. X is attacking Y with the intention of killing him, and Y is considering how to prevent this. He has in one hand a pistol, with which he can kill X, and in the other hand a tranquilizer gun, with which he can sedate X long enough to make his escape but with which he will not do X any permanent damage. The two weapons will be equally effective in repelling X's attack and Y knows this. Is it permissible for Y to use his pistol and kill X? Although Y's killing X would not violate the upper limit qualification I think most of us would agree that it is not permissible. We would insist that there is another limitation on the amount of coercion Y can use to enforce his rights, one which requires him never to use more than the minimum amount of coercion necessary to prevent the violation of his rights. In this case Y's killing X would involve more than the minimum amount of coercion, for he can also use the tranquilizer gun on X, and killing him is therefore impermissible.

This second case suggests another qualification on persons' enforcement rights, one which I will call a *minimum necessary* qualification, and which is most natural for a rights theory to express as follows. Although Y's right to enforce his right to Φ sometimes entitles him to act in ways which would otherwise involve violating X's right to Ψ, it only does so when it is not possible for Y to prevent the violation of his right to Φ just as effectively by acting in ways which would otherwise involve violating only rights of X's which are less important than his right to Ψ. (If it is possible for Y to prevent the violation of his right to Φ by acting in ways which would not otherwise involve violating any of X's rights, e.g., by running away, this qualification requires him to run away.). . .

In discussing the upper limit and minimum necessary qualifications I have made extensive use of the notion of the *importance* of a natural right, and there will no doubt be questions about exactly what this notion involves. In speaking of the importance of a right I have intended in the first place to speak of something intuitive. We all have, I trust, an intuitive sense that the right to life is more important than the right not to be physically assaulted, which in turn is more important than the right not to be tickled. But the notion can also be given a formal representation in a libertarian rights theory of the kind we have been discussing. If every right is an instance of the right to liberty, then it seems natural to say that one right is more important than another whenever it is a right to a more extensive liberty than the other. And although comparing the extent of some liberties raises obvious difficulties the following should once again be uncontroversial. If one liberty contains another as a proper part, so that exercising the second liberty always involves exercising the first, but exercising the first liberty does not always involve exercising the second, then the first liberty is more extensive than the second. The ranking procedure which these two suggestions yield is perhaps most usefully put as follows: one right is more important than another whenever violating the first always involves violating the second, but violating the second right does not always involve violating the first (an example: the right to buy property in Canada is more important than the right to buy property in Alberta because preventing a person from buying property in Canada always involves preventing him from buying it in Alberta, but preventing him from buying it in Alberta does not always involve preventing him from buying it in Canada.) This ranking procedure does not generate anything like a complete ordering over rights. It only generates a partial ordering, but the ordering is not so partial as to be useless. It has, for instance, some clear results about a number of rights that are important for questions about self-defense. It holds that the right not to be both tied up and beaten is more important than the right simply not to be tied up, that the right not to have both arms broken is more important than the right not to have one's left arm broken, and that the right not to have property valued at $100 destroyed is more important than the right not to have property valued at $1 destroyed. It also has some clear results about a number of rights that are important for questions about punishment. It holds that the right not to be imprisoned for ten years is more important than the right not to be imprisoned for five years, and that the right not to be fined $100 is more important than the right not to be fined $1. Most importantly for our concerns, however, it has clear results about the right which is most centrally involved in questions about capital punishment, namely the right to life. On a libertarian view the right to life is the right to exercise the liberty of choosing life over death, and imposes on others the duty not to remove that liberty, as they would do if they forcibly chose death for us. But this means that the right to life has to be the most important natural right there is. Choosing life is choosing to exercise all the liberties we do exercise when we are alive, while choosing death is choosing to exercise no further liberties at all. A person who removes the liberty of choosing life from us is therefore removing all our other liberties from us. In violating our right to life he is violating all our other rights as well, for he is leaving us in a position where we can never exercise those rights again. Although the proper part ranking procedure has clear results in these areas it does not have clear results in certain others. It does not say anything determinate about the relative importance of property rights and rights not to be physically assaulted, for instance, or of property rights and rights not to be imprisoned. These gaps in the ordering it generates weaken but they do not prevent the operation of the upper limit and minimum necessary qualifications. If property rights and rights not to be physically assaulted are unranked with respect to each other then neither is more important than the other, and persons may if necessary use force against others to prevent them from destroying their property, and destroy others' property to prevent them from assaulting them. Far from being an unwanted result this is one which I think we ought to welcome, for our intuitions seem to support the view that in most cases these two forms of self-defense are, if necessary, permissible. . . .

Having discussed the upper limit and minimum necessary qualifications in a general way let us now see what their implications are for questions about punishment. The qualifications place limits on the severity of the punishments which persons are permitted to inflict in the state of nature, and which their governments are permitted to inflict in civil society. It follows from the upper limit qualification that they are never permitted to inflict punishments which infringe rights that are more important than the ones which the offender has violated, and which they are therefore enforcing. And it follows from the minimum necessary qualification that they are never permitted to inflict punishments which infringe rights that are more important than is necessary to prevent further violations of the right which they are enforcing. If two punishments will be equally effective in deterring violations of this right, they have a duty to impose the less severe punishment; and if no punishments will be effective in deterring violations, they have a duty to impose no punishment at all. . . .

Of these two consequences the one which follows from the upper limit—qualification also follows from many versions of the retributive justification. Many retributive theorists also hold that there is an upper limit on the severity of the punishments we can inflict for certain crimes, and that we do wrong if we exceed this limit. But no such consequence follows from the deterrence justification. The deterrence justification permits and even requires as severe a punishment as will best promote the overall good of society, and this punishment can sometimes be very severe indeed. It might well be the case that capital punishment would be an effective deterrent to the crime of shoplifting, and that the benefits to society as a whole of the huge reduction in shoplifting resulting from its imposition would far outweigh the harms to the one or two individuals foolish enough to be caught and executed for shoplifting. Most of us do not think, however, that it could ever be permissible to impose capital punishment for the crime of shoplifting, and take it to be a serious objection to the deterrence justification that it could sometimes require it. The consequence which follows from the minimum necessary qualification also follows from the deterrence justification, but it does not follow from the retributive justification. The retributive justification can require us to impose severe punishments when no further rights violations will be prevented by them, and indeed when no further social good will result from them at all. Some retributive theorists like Kant have of course revelled in this fact, but I think most of us find it repugnant. We think that punishment is only permissible when it does something to promote social good, and take it to be a serious objection to the retributive justification that it requires it even when it does nothing to promote social good.

What are the consequences of the rights-based justification for the special case of capital punishment? Capital punishment infringes the right to life of a criminal, and the right to life is the most important right there is. This means that, given the upper limit qualification, the rights-based justification will only allow capital punishment to be imposed on persons who have violated the right to life of another, that is, it will only allow capital punishment to be imposed for the crime of murder. At the same time, however, given the minimum necessary qualification, the rights-based justification will only allow capital punishment to be imposed for the crime of murder if there is no other less severe punishment which is equally effective at deterring murder. Extensive criminological studies have failed to produce any evidence that capital punishment is a more effective deterrent to murder than life imprisonment, and the rights-based justification will therefore hold that, until such evidence is produced the imposition of capital punishment for any crime at all is impermissible.[7] This is in my view an attractive consequence, and it is one which also follows from the deterrence justification. But it is not bought at the cost of the many unattractive consequences of the deterrence justification. Many of us believe that if capital punishment is not an effective deterrent to murder then it ought not to be imposed. But we would not want this view to commit us to the simple deterrence justification, with all the unattractive consequences which that justification has. We would not want it to commit us to the view that capital punishment could be permissible or even a required punishment for shoplifting, and we would not want it to commit us to the view that it could be permissible or even required to frame and "punish" an innocent man. The rights-based justification allows us to give some weight to the question of deterrence in assessing the morality of capital punishment, without giving it the overwhelming weight which it has in the deterrence justification.

Perhaps the distinctive consequences of the rights-based justification for the morality of capital punishment can best be summarized as follows. Assuming that a retributive calculus will find capital punishment a "fitting" punishment for the crime of murder, the retributive justification holds that it is a necessary and sufficient condition for the permissibility (and even requiredness) of imposing capital punishment on a person that he be guilty of murder. The rights-based justification agrees that this is a necessary condition but denies that it is sufficient; for a punishment to be permissible, it maintains, it must have some independent deterrent effect. The deterrence justification, by contrast, holds that it is a necessary and sufficient condition for the permissibility (and even requiredness) of imposing capital punishment on a person that this punishment have some independent deterrent effect. The rights-based justification once again agrees that this is a necessary condition but denies that it is sufficient; for a punishment to be permissible the person who undergoes it must be guilty of a crime, and guilty of a crime which violated rights at least as important as those which his punishment will infringe. In the rights-based justification conditions which are individually both necessary and sufficient in the deterrence and retributive justifications are made individually necessary but only jointly sufficient, and for this reason the rights-based justification can be said to combine the attractive features of the other two justifications while avoiding their unattractive features. The view that the conditions focused on by the deterrence and retributive justifications are individually necessary but only jointly sufficient for the permissibility of punishment has of course been defended by a number of philosophers. But I think it is only in the context of a rights-based moral theory that this view can be given a theoretical justification, and the attractive features of the deterrence and retributive justifications combined in a manner that is principled rather than *ad hoc*.

NOTES

1. Some philosophers have argued that we should apply the deterrence justification to the institution of punishment and the retributive justification to particular acts within this institution; for classic statements of this "mixed" view see John Rawls, "Two Concepts of Rules," *Philosophical Review* 64 (1955): 3–32, and H. L. A. Hart, "Prolegomenon to the Principles of Punishment," in his *Punishment and Responsibility* (Oxford, 1968), 1–13. But these arguments seem to me to rely on a dubious distinction between an institution and the acts of which it is composed. The rights-based justification I will defend has many of the same attractive consequences as this mixed view without relying on its dubious assumptions about institutions.

2. John Locke, *Two Treatises of Government*. 2d ed., ed. Peter Laslett (New York, 1967).

3. Robert Nozick, *Anarchy, State and Utopia* (New York, 1974), 10, 137–42.

4. On this see H. L. A. Hart, "Are There Any Natural Rights?" *Philosophical Review* 64 (1955): 175–91.

5. Enforcement rights are often said to include not only a right of self- (and other-) defense and a right to punish but also a right to exact compensation, where this right to exact compensation is sometimes exercised alongside the right to punish and sometimes exercised when it would be wrong to punish. The right to exact compensation, however, need not be regarded as a separate enforcement right. If we say that alongside their ordinary rights persons have more complex rights not to be harmed without compensation being paid them afterwards, we can say that exacting compensation prevents the violation of these rights in exactly the same way that self-defense prevents the violation of simpler rights. . . .

6. A libertarian rights theory of this kind is presented in Immanuel Kant, The *Metaphysical Elements of Justice: Part I of the Metaphysics of Morals*, John Ladd, trans. (Indianapolis, 1965), and discussed by Hart in "Are There Any Natural Rights?"

7. As is often pointed out, the studies have not produced evidence that capital punishment is not a deterrent to murder either. But the onus of proof in this question is surely on the defenders of capital punishment to show that it is.

■ HUGO ADAM BEDAU: FOR AND AGAINST CAPITAL PUNISHMENT

Hugo Adam Bedau criticizes both deterrence and retributivist arguments as inadequate to justify capital punishment. He rejects the claim that the death penalty deters capital offenses:

very few nonexecuted murderers repeat their crimes, whether or not the death penalty is in effect. Moreover, the death penalty has no noticeably greater deterrent effect than long-term imprisonment. If the same effect is to be achieved by one punishment as by some other one, but at the expense of less human suffering, then the less extreme punishment is preferable. This renders the death penalty obsolete. Bedau supports this criticism by noting the many hidden costs, both individual and social, that the death penalty carries. The retributivist argument for capital punishment rests upon the principle of retaliation or *lex talionis* (literally, a "life for a life"). This presupposes the principle of just distribution: that severity of punishment is determined by gravity of offense. Bedau argues that only a literal interpretation of the principle of just distribution could support the institution of capital punishment. He contends that no literal-minded interpretation of the principle will be defensible. He concludes that capital punishment cannot be supported by claiming that it institutes just retribution. Bedau insists that we can accept the principle of just retribution to support a schedule of strict and severe punishments, while rejecting *lex talionis* and capital punishment. Finally, he lays out a practical argument against the death penalty in showing that it is applied unequally and arbitrarily to the poor and unprivileged in violation of the Fourteenth Amendment: In the words of a popular slogan, "Those without the capital get the punishment."

Bedau issues a humanistic plea for long-term imprisonment rather than capital punishment. Long-term imprisonment is retributive, socially protective, and a deterrent. In addition, it has a symbolic benefit: There is no need to employ the inhumane means in punishment that were employed in the crime.

Hugo Adam Bedau

CAPITAL PUNISHMENT

CAPITAL PUNISHMENT AND SOCIAL DEFENSE

DETERRENCE, INCAPACITATION, AND CRIME PREVENTION

The analogy with self-defense leads naturally to the empirical and the conceptual questions surrounding the death penalty as a method of crime prevention. Notice

From *Matters of Life and Death: New Introductory Essays in Moral Philosophy*, 3rd ed., edited by Tom Regan (New York: McGraw Hill, 1993). Copyright © 1993. Reprinted by permission of the author and publisher.

first that crimes can be prevented without recourse to punishment; we do that when we take weapons from offenders, protect targets by bolts and alarms, and educate the public to be less vulnerable to victimization. As for punishment, it prevents crimes by *incapacitation* and by *deterrence*. The two are theoretically independent because they achieve prevention very differently. Executing a murderer prevents crimes by means of *incapacitation* to the extent that the murderer would have committed further crimes if not executed. Incapacitating a murderer will not have any preventive benefits, however, unless the murderer would otherwise have committed some further crimes. (In fact relatively few murderers turn out to be homicidal recidivists). Nor is killing persons the only way to incapacitate them; isolation and restraints will suffice. Executing a murderer prevents crimes by means of *deterrence* to the extent that others are frightened into not committing any capital crimes by the knowledge that convicted offenders are executed. Thus, successful deterrence is prevention by a psychologically effective threat; incapacitation, if it prevents crimes at all, does so by physically disabling the offender.

THE DEATH PENALTY AND INCAPACITATION

Capital punishment is unusual among penalties because its incapacitative effects limit its deterrent effects. The death penalty can never deter an executed person from further crimes. At most, it incapacitates the executed person from committing them. (Popular discussions of the death penalty are frequently confused because they so often assume that the death penalty is a perfect and infallible deterrent so far as the executed criminal is concerned.) Even more important, it is also wrong to think that in every execution the death penalty has proved to be an infallible crime preventive. True, once an offender has been executed, it is physically impossible for that person to commit any further crimes, since the punishment is totally incapacitative. But incapacitation is not identical with prevention. Prevention by means of incapacitation occurs only if the executed criminal would have committed other crimes if he or she had not been executed and had been punished only in some less incapacitative way (e.g., by imprisonment).

What evidence is there that the incapacitative results of the death penalty are an effective crime preventive? From the study of imprisonment, parole, and release records, this much is clear: If the murderers and other criminals who have been executed are like the murderers who were convicted but not executed, then (1) executing all convicted murderers would have prevented many crimes, including some murders; and (2) convicted murderers, whether inside prison or outside after release, have as good a record of no further criminal activity as any other class of convicted felon. . . .

THE DEATH PENALTY AND DETERRENCE

Determining whether the death penalty is an effective deterrent is even more difficult than determining its effectiveness as a crime preventive. In general, our knowledge about how penalties deter crimes and whether in fact they do—whom they deter, from which crimes, and under what conditions—is distressingly inexact. Most people nevertheless are convinced that punishments do deter, and that the more severe a punishment is the better it will deter. For half a century, social scientists have studied the questions whether the death penalty is a deterrent and whether it is a better deterrent than the alternative of imprisonment. Their verdict, while not unanimous, is nearly so. Whatever may be true about the deterrence of lesser crimes by other penalties, the deterrence achieved by the death penalty for murder is not measurably any greater than the deterrence achieved by long-term imprisonment. In the nature of the case, the evidence is quite indirect. No one can identify for certain any crimes that did not occur because the would-be offender was deterred by the threat of the death penalty and could not have been deterred by a less severe threat. Likewise, no one can identify any crimes that did occur because the offender was not deterred by the threat of prison even though he or she would have been deterred by the threat of death. Nevertheless, such evidence as we have fails to show that the more severe penalty (death) is really a better deterrent than the less severe penalty (imprisonment) for such crimes as murder.

If the death penalty and long-term imprisonment are equally effective (or ineffective) as deterrents to murder, then the argument for the death penalty on grounds of deterrence is seriously weakened. One of the moral principles identified earlier now comes into play: Unless there is a good reason for choosing a more rather than a less severe punishment for a crime, the less severe penalty is to be preferred. This principle obviously commends itself to anyone who values human life and who concedes that, all other things being equal, less pain and suffering is always better than more. Human life is valued in part to the degree that it is free of pain, suffering, misery, and frustration, and in particular to the extent that it is free of such experiences when they serve no purpose. If the death penalty is not a more effective deterrent than imprisonment, then its greater severity amounts to nothing less than gratuitous suffering and deprivation. Accordingly, we must reject it in favor of some less severe alternative, unless we can identify some more weighty moral principle that the death penalty serves better and that any less severe mode of punishment ignores. Whether there is any such principle is unclear.

A COST/BENEFIT ANALYSIS OF THE DEATH PENALTY

A full study of the costs and benefits involved in the practice of capital punishment would not be confined solely to the question of whether it is a better deterrent or preventive of murder than imprisonment. Any thoroughgoing utilitarian approach to the death-penalty controversy would need to examine carefully other costs and benefits as well, because maximizing the balance of all the social benefits over all the social costs is the sole criterion of right and wrong according to utilitarianism. . . . Let us consider, therefore, some of the other costs and benefits to be calculated. Clinical psychologists have presented evidence to suggest that the death penalty actually incites some persons of unstable mind to murder others, either because they are afraid to take their own lives and hope that society will punish them for murder by putting them to death, or because they fancy that they, too, are killing with justification analogously to the lawful and presumably justified killing involved in capital punishment. If such evidence is sound, capital punishment can serve as a counterpreventive or even an incitement to murder; such incited murders become part of its social cost. Imprisonment, however, has not been known to incite any murders or other crimes of violence in a comparable fashion. (A possible exception might be found in the imprisonment of terrorists, which has inspired other terrorists to take hostages as part of a scheme to force the authorities to release their imprisoned comrades.) The risks of executing the innocent are also part of the social cost. The historical record is replete with innocent persons arrested, indicted, convicted, sentenced, and occasionally legally executed for crimes they did not commit. This is quite apart from the guilty persons unfairly convicted, sentenced to death, and executed on the strength of perjured testimony, fraudulent evidence, subornation of jurors, and other violations of the civil rights and liberties of the accused. Nor is this all. The high costs of a capital trial and of the inevitable appeals, the costly methods of custody most prisons adopt for convicts on "death row," are among the straight-forward economic costs that the death penalty incurs. Conducting a valid cost/benefit analysis of capital punishment would be extremely difficult; nevertheless, on the basis of the evidence we have, it is quite possible that such a study would show that abolition of all death penalties is much less costly than their retention.

WHAT IF EXECUTIONS DID DETER?

From the moral point of view, it is quite important to determine what one should think about capital punishment if the evidence were clearly to show that the death penalty is a distinctly superior method of social defense by comparison with less severe alternatives. Kantian moralists . . . would have no use for such knowledge, because their entire case for the morality of the death penalty rests on the way it is thought to provide a just retribution, not on the way it is thought to provide superior social defense. For a utilitarian, however, such knowledge would be conclusive. Those who follow Lock's reasoning would also be gratified, because they defend the morality of the death penalty both on the ground that it is retributively just and on the ground that it provides needed social defense.

What about the opponents of the death penalty, however? To oppose the death penalty in the face of incontestable evidence that it is an effective method of social defense violates the moral principle that where grave risks are to be run, it is better that they be run by the guilty than by the innocent. . . . If opposition to the death penalty is to be morally responsible, then it must be conceded that there are conditions (however unlikely) under which that opposition should cease.

But even if the death penalty were known to be a uniquely effective social defense, we could still imagine conditions under which it would be reasonable to oppose it. Suppose that in addition to being a slightly better preventive and deterrent than imprisonment, executions also have a slight incitive effect (so that for every ten murders an execution prevented or deterred, another murder was incited). Suppose also that the administration of criminal justice in capital cases was inefficient, unequal, and tended to secure convictions and death sentences only for murderers who least "deserve" to be sentenced to death (including some death sentences and a few executions of the innocent). Under such conditions, it would be reasonable to oppose the death penalty, because on the facts supposed more (or not fewer) innocent lives would be threatened and lost by using the death penalty than would be risked by abolishing it. It is important to remember throughout our evaluation of the deterrence controversy that we cannot ever apply the principle . . . that advises us to risk the lives of the guilty to save the lives of the innocent. Instead, we must rely on a weaker principle: Weigh the risk for the general public against the execution of those who are found guilty by an imperfect system of criminal justice. These hypothetical factual assumptions illustrate the contingencies upon which the morality of opposition to the death penalty rests. And not only the morality of opposition; the morality of any defense of the death penalty rests on the same contingencies. This should help us understand why, in resolving the morality of capital punishment one way or the other, it is so important to know, as well as we can, whether the death penalty really does prevent or incite crime, whether the innocent really are ever executed, and how likely is the occurrence of these things in the future.

HOW MANY GUILTY LIVES
IS ONE INNOCENT LIFE WORTH?

The great unanswered question that utilitarians must face concerns the level of social defense that executions should be expected to achieve before it is justifiable to carry them out. Consider three possible situations: (1) At the level of a hundred executions per year, each additional execution of a convicted murderer reduces the number of murder victims by ten. (2) Executing every convicted murderer reduces the number of murders to 5,000 victims annually, whereas executing only one out of ten reduces the number to 5,001. (3) Executing every convicted murderer reduces the murder rate no more than does executing one in a hundred and no more than does a random pattern of executions. . . .

Since no adequate cost/benefit analysis of the death penalty exists, there is no way to resolve these questions from that standpoint at this time. Moreover, it can be argued that we cannot have such an analysis without already establishing in some way or other the relative value of innocent lives versus guilty lives. Far from being a product of cost/benefit analysis, a comparative evaluation of lives would have to be available to us before we undertook any such analysis. Without it, no cost/benefit analysis of this problem can get off the ground. Finally, it must be noted that our knowledge at present does not indicate that we are in anything like the situation described above in (1). On the contrary, from the evidence we do have it seems we achieve about the same deterrent and preventive effects whether we punish murder by death or by imprisonment. . . . Something like the situation in (2) or in (3) may therefore be correct. If so, this shows that the choice between the two policies of capital punishment and life imprisonment for murder will probably have to be made on some basis other than social defense; on that basis alone, the two policies are equivalent and therefore equally acceptable.

CAPITAL PUNISHMENT
AND RETRIBUTIVE JUSTICE

No discussion of the morality of punishment would be complete without taking into account the two leading principles of retributive justice relevant to the capital punishment controversy. One is the principle that crimes ought to be punished. The other is the principle that the severity of a punishment ought to be proportional to the gravity of the offense. These are moral principles of recognized weight. Leaving aside all questions of social defense, how strong a case for capital punishment can be made on their basis? How reliable and persuasive are these principles themselves?

CRIME MUST BE PUNISHED

Given the general rationale for punishment sketched earlier . . . there cannot be any dispute over the principle that crime ought to be punished. In embracing it, of course, we are not automatically making a fetish of "law and order," in the sense that we would be if we thought that the most important single thing to do with social resources is to punish crimes. Fortunately, this principle need not be in dispute between proponents and opponents of the death penalty. Even defenders of the death penalty must admit that putting a convicted murderer in prison for years is a punishment of that criminal. The principle that crime must be punished is neutral to our controversy, because both sides acknowledge it.

The other principle of retributive justice is the one that seems to be a decisive. Under *lex talionis*, it must always have seemed that murderers ought to be put to death. Proponents of the death penalty, with rare exceptions, have insisted on this point, and even opponents of the death penalty must give grudging assent to the seeming fittingness of demanding capital punishment for murder. The strategy for opponents of the death penalty is to argue either that (1) this principle is not really a principle of justice after all, or that (2) to the extent it is, it does not require death for murderers, or that (3) in any case it is not the only principle of punitive justice. As we shall see, all these objections have merit.

IS MURDER ALONE TO BE PUNISHED BY DEATH?

Let is recall, first, that not even the biblical world limited the death penalty to the punishment of murder. Many other nonhomicidal crimes also carried this penalty (e.g., kidnapping, witchcraft, cursing one's parents). In our own nation's recent history, persons have been executed for aggravated assault, rape, kidnapping, armed robbery, sabotage, and espionage. It is not possible to defend any of these executions (not to mention some of the more bizarre capital statutes, like the one in Georgia that used to provide an optional death penalty for desecration of a grave) on grounds of just retribution. Either such executions are not justified or are they justified on some ground other than retribution. In actual practice, few if any defenders of the death penalty have ever been willing to rest their case entirely on the moral principle of just retribution as formulated in terms of "a life for a life." (Kant was a conspicuous exception.) Most defenders of the death penalty have implied by their willingness to use executions to defend not only life but limb and property as well, that they did not place much value on the lives of criminals when compared with the value of both lives and things belonging to innocent citizens.

ARE ALL MURDERS TO BE PUNISHED BY DEATH?

. . . The abstract principle that the punishment of death best fits the crime of murder turns out to be extremely difficult to interpret and apply.

If we look at the matter from the standpoint of the actual practice of criminal justice, we can only conclude that "a life for a life" plays little or no role whatever. Plea bargaining (in which a person charged with a crime pleads guilty in exchange for a less severe sentence than he might have received if his case went to trial and he was found guilty), even where murder is concerned, is widespread. Studies of criminal justice reveal that what the courts (trial or appellate) in a given jurisdiction decide on a given day is first-degree murder suitably punished by death could just as well have been decided in a neighboring jurisdiction on another day either as second-degree murder or as first-degree murder but without the death penalty. The factors that influence prosecutors in determining the charge under which they will prosecute go far beyond the simple principle of "a life for a life." Cynics, of course will say that these facts show that our society does not care about justice. To put it succinctly, one might also reply that either justice in punishment does not consist of retribution, because there are other principles of justice; or there are other moral considerations besides justice that must be honored; or retributive justice is not adequately expressed in the idea of "a life for a life"; or justice in the criminal justice system is beyond our reach.

IS DEATH SUFFICIENTLY RETRIBUTIVE?

Those who advocate capital punishment for murder on retributive grounds must face the objection that, on their own principles, the death penalty in some cases is morally inadequate. How could death in the electric chair or the gas chamber or before a firing squad or by lethal injection suffice as just retribution, given the savage, brutal, wanton character of so many murders? How can retributive justice be served by anything less than equally savage methods of execution? From a retributive point of view, the oft-heard exclamation, "Death is too good for him!" has a certain truth. Are defenders of the death penalty willing to embrace this consequence of their own doctrine?

If they were they would be stooping to the methods and thus to the squalor of the murderer. Where the quality of the crime sets the limits of just methods of punishment, as it will if we attempt to give exact and literal implementation to lex talionis, society will find itself descending to the cruelties and savagery that criminals employ. What is worse, society would be deliberately authorizing such acts, in the cool light of reason, and not (as is usually true of vicious criminals) impulsively or in hatred and anger or with an insane or unbalanced mind. Moral constraints, in short, prohibit us from trying to make executions perfectly retributive. Once we grant that such constraints are proper, it is unreasonable to insist that the principle of "a life for a life" nevertheless by itself justifies the execution of murderers. . . .

DIFFERENTIAL SEVERITY
DOES NOT REQUIRE EXECUTIONS

What, then, emerges from our examination of retributive justice and the death penalty? If retributive justice is thought to consist in lex talionis, all one can say is that this principle has never exercised more than a crude and indirect effect on the actual punishments meted out by society. Other moral principles interfere with a literal and single-minded application of this one. Some homicides seem improperly punished by death at all; others would require methods of execution too horrible to inflict. In any case, proponents of the death penalty rarely confine themselves to reliance on nothing but this principle of just retribution, since they rarely confine themselves to supporting the death penalty only for murder.

But retributive justice need not be identified with *lex talionis*. One may reject that principle as too crude and still embrace the retributive principle that the severity of punishments should be graded according to the gravity of the offense. Even though one need not claim that life imprisonment (or any kind of punishment other than death) "fits" the crime of murder, one can claim that this punishment is the proper one for murder. To do this, the schedule of punishments accepted by society must be arranged so that this mode of imprisonment is the most severe penalty used. Opponents of the death penalty can embrace this principle of retributive justice, even though they must reject a literal *lex talionis*.

EQUAL JUSTICE AND CAPITAL PUNISHMENT

During the past generation, the strongest practical objection to the death penalty has been the inequity with which it has been applied. As the late Supreme Court Justice William O. Douglas once observed, "One searches our chronicles in vain for the execution of any member of the affluent strata of this society." One does not search our chronicles in vain for the crime of murder committed by the affluent. All the sociological evidence points to the conclusion that the death penalty is the poor man's justice; hence the slogan, "Those without the capital get the punishment." The death penalty is also racially sensitive. Every study of the death penalty for rape (unconstitutional only since 1977) has confirmed that black rapists (especially where the victim is white) are far more likely to be sentenced to death and executed than white rapists. Convicted black murderers are more likely to be sentenced to death than are the killers of nonwhites.

Let us suppose that the factual basis for such a criticism is sound. What follows for the morality of capital punishment? Many defenders of the death penalty have been quick to point out that since there is nothing intrinsic about the crime of murder or rape dictating that only the poor or only racial minority males will commit it, and since there is nothing overtly racist about the statutes that authorize the death penalty for murder or rape, capital punishment itself is hardly at fault if in practice it falls with unfair impact on the poor and the black. There is, in short, nothing in the death penalty that requires it to be applied unfairly and with arbitrary or discriminatory results. At worst such results stem from defects in the system of administering criminal justice. (Some, who dispute the facts cited above, would deny even this.) There is an adequate remedy—execute more whites, women, and affluent murderers.

Presumably, both proponents and opponents of capital punishment would concede that it is a fundamental dictate of justice that a punishment should not be unfairly—inequitably or unevenly—enforced and applied. They should also be able to agree that when the punishment in question is the extremely severe one of death, then the requirement to be fair in using such a punishment becomes even more stringent. There should be no dispute in the death penalty controversy over these principles of justice. The dispute should begin only when one attempts to connect the principles with the actual use of this punishment.

In this country, many critics of the death penalty have argued, we would long ago have got rid of it entirely if equal and fair application had been a condition of its use. In the words of the attorneys who argued against the death penalty in the Supreme Court during 1972, "It is a freakish aberration, a random extreme act of violence, visibly arbitrary and discriminatory—a penalty reserved for unusual application because, if it were usually used, it would affront universally shared standards of public decency." It is difficult to dispute this judgment, when one considers that there have been in the United States during the past fifty years about a half a million criminal homicides, about a third of a million persons arrested for these crimes, but fewer than four thousand executions (all but three dozen of which were of men).

We can look at these statistics in another way to illustrate the same point. If we could be assured that the nearly 4,000 persons executed were the worst of the bad, repeated offenders impossible to incarcerate safely (much less rehabilitate), the most dangerous murderers in captivity—the ones who had killed more than once and were likely to kill again, and the least likely to be confined in prison without chronic danger to other inmates and the staff—then one might accept half a million murders and a few thousand executions with a sense that rough justice had been done. But the truth is otherwise. Persons are sentenced to death and executed not because they have been found uncontrollably violent or hopelessly poor risks for safe confinement and release. Instead, they are executed because at trial they had a poor defense (inexperienced or overworked counsel); they had no funds to bring sympathetic witnesses to court; they are transients or strangers in the community where they are tried; the prosecuting attorney wanted the publicity that goes with "sending a killer to the chair," there were no funds for an appeal or for a transcript of the trial record; they are members of a despised racial or political minority. In short, the actual study of why particular persons have been sentenced to death and executed does not show any careful winnowing of the worst from the bad. It shows that those executed were usually the unlucky victims of prejudice and discrimination, the losers in an arbitrary lottery that could just as well have spared them, the victims of the disadvantages that almost always go with poverty. A system like this does not enhance human life; it cheapens and degrades it. However heinous murder and other crimes are, the system of capital punishment does not compensate for or erase those crimes. It only tends to add new injuries of its own to the catalogue of human brutality.

CONCLUSION

Our discussion of the death penalty from the moral point of view shows that there is no one moral principle that has paramount validity that decisively favors one side of the controversy. Rather, we have seen how it is possible to argue either for or against the death penalty, and in each case to be appealing to moral principles that derive from the worth, value, or dignity of human life. We have also seen how it is impossible to connect any of these abstract principles with the actual practice of capital punishment without a close study of sociological, psychological, and economic factors. By themselves, the moral principles that are relevant are too abstract and uncertain in application to be of much help. Without the guidance of such principles, of course, the facts (who gets executed, and why) are of little consequence, either.

My own view of the controversy is that, given the moral principles identified in the course of our discussion (including the overriding value of human life), and given all the facts about capital punishment, the balance of reasons favors abolition of the death penalty. The alternative to capital punishment that I favor, as things currently stand, is long-term imprisonment. Such a punishment is retributive and can be made more or less severe to reflect the gravity of the crime. It gives adequate (though hardly perfect) protection to the public. It is free of the worst defect to which the death penalty is liable: execution of the innocent. It tacitly acknowledges that there is no way for a criminal, alive or dead, to make complete amends for murder or other grave crimes against the person. Last but not least, long-term imprisonment has symbolic significance. The death penalty, more than any other kind of killing, is done by officials in the name of society and on its behalf. Each of us, therefore, has a hand in such killings. Unless they are absolutely necessary they cannot be justified. Thus, abolishing the death penalty represents extending the hand of life even to those who by their crimes have "forfeited" any right to live. A penal policy limiting the severity of punishment to long-term incarceration acknowledges that we must abandon the folly and pretense of attempting to secure perfect justice in an imperfect world.

Searching for an epigram suitable for our times, in which governments have waged war and suppressed internal dissent by methods that can be described only as savage and criminal, Camus was prompted to admonish "Let us be neither victims nor executioners." Perhaps better than any other, this exhortation points the way between unacceptable extremes if we are to respect the humanity in each of us.

SUGGESTIONS FOR DISCUSSION

1. Construct a utilitarian argument (see Chapter 4) for capital punishment. How would this argument differ from a Kantian justification of the death penalty (see Chapter 3)? Is either argument convincing?
2. Are all rights-based arguments (see Mackie, Chapter 5) for capital punishment necessarily inconsistent and therefore self-defeating?
3. How would Hobbes justify punishment (see Chapter 2)? Would the same kind of argument also justify capital punishment?

FOR FURTHER READING

Acton, H. B., ed. *The Philosophy of Punishment.* London: MacMillan, 1969.

Bayles, M. "A Note on the Death Penalty as the Best Bet." *Criminal Justice Ethics* 10 (1), Winter-Spring, 1991: 7–10.

Bedau, H. A., ed. *The Death Penalty in America.* 3rd ed. New York Oxford University Press, 1982.

Berns, W. *For Capital Punishment.* New York: Basic Books, 1979.

Black, C. L. *Capital Punishment: The Inevitability of Caprice and Mistake.* New York: W. W. Norton, 1974.

Calvert, B. "Retribution, Arbitrariness, and the Death Penalty." *Journal of Social Philosophy* 23, 3 (Winter 1992): 140–65.

Christie, N. *Crime Control as Industry: Towards GULAGS, Western Style?* New York: Routledge, 1993.

Dolinko, D. "Some Thoughts About Retributivism." *Ethics* 101, 3 (April 1991): 537–39.

Ellis, R. D., and Ellis, C. S. *Theories of Criminal Justice: A Critical Reappraisal.* Wolfboro, Mass.: Longwood, 1989.

Ezorsky, G., ed. *Philosophical Perspectives on Punishment.* Albany: SUNY Press, 1972.

Feinberg, J., and Gross, H., eds. *Punishment: Selected Readings.* Belmont, Calif.: Dickinson, 1975.

Goldinger, M., ed. *Punishment and Human Rights.* Cambridge, Mass.: Schenkman, 1974.

Hampton, J., and Murphy, J. *Forgiveness and Mercy.* Cambridge: Cambridge University Press, 1988.

Hart, H. L. A. *Punishment and Responsibility,* New York: Oxford University Press, 1968.

Honderich, T. *Punishment. The Supposed Justifications.* Baltimore: Penguin Books, 1968.

Lyons, D. *Ethics and the Rule of Law.* New York: Cambridge University Press, 1984.

McCafferty, J., ed. *Capital Punishment.* New York: Lieber-Atherton, 1972.

Meyers, C. "Racial Bias, the Death Penalty, and Desert." *The Philosophical Forum* 22 (2) Winter 1990–1991: 139-48.

Morris, N. and Tonry, M. *Between Prison and Probation: Intermediate Punishments in a Rational Sentencing System.* Oxford: Oxford University Press, 1993.

Murphie, J. G. *Retribution. Justice and Therapy.* Dordrecht: D. Reidel, 1979.

Natanson, S. "Does It Matter If the Death Penalty Is Arbitrarily Administered?" *Philosophy and Public Affairs* 14, 2 (1985): 149–64.

Reimen, J. "Justice, Civilization, and the Death Penalty." *Philosophy and Public Affairs* 14, 2 (1985): 115–48.

Richards, D. A. J. *The Moral Criticism of Law.* Encino, Calif.: Dickenson, 1977.

Van den Haag, E., and Conrad, J. P. *The Death Penalty: A Debate.* New York: Plenum, 1983.

NOTE: The glossary consists of brief definitions and explanations of key terms appearing either in the introductions or readings. *Italicized* words are cross-referenced in the glossary.

Abortion   The termination of a pregnancy prior to birth, resulting in the death of the fetus. A miscarriage is a spontaneous abortion that is not caused by the pregnant woman or anyone else. An induced abortion is caused by someone other than the pregnant woman, usually at her request, while a self-induced abortion is caused by the pregnant woman on her own.

Absolutism   The theory that there are invariant and objective moral truths or rules. Absolutists may nevertheless hold that there are sometimes exceptions to the absolute moral rules or principles. This theory is contrasted with *relativism*.

Affirmative action   Any policy or program the aim of which is to institute greater social equality, especially of opportunity, for racially defined minorities and women. Affirmative action programs include widening the applicant pool for jobs, promotions, and college admissions; advertising widely and in nondiscriminatory ways; using nondiscriminatory categories and criteria in hiring, promotions, and admissions; and preferential treatment.

Agent   Any person who acts, has acted, or is contemplating action. A moral agent is one bearing moral qualities of responsibility and who may be judged accordingly as good or bad, virtuous or vicious, just or unjust.

AIDS   The Acquired Immuno-Deficiency Syndrome is the final stage of the syndrome caused by HIV (the Human Immunodeficiency Virus). HIV attacks the human immune system by targeting T-cells in the blood, undermining the body's capacity to resist opportunistic infections that the immune systems of uninfected persons are able to fight off with ease. Technically, persons now are defined as having AIDS when their T-cell count is lower than 200.

Altruism   Any action that aims at producing good for another for the other person's sake. It is usually contrasted with *egoism*.

A posteriori   *Judgments* or *principles* the *justification* for which is *empirical* or factual, and which are said to be acquired by the sense-impressions.

A priori   *Judgments* or *principles* the validity of which is independent of any sense-impressions or *empirical justification*. The term is used more generally to designate anything knowable by reason alone, or anything that is nonempirical.

Autonomy   The capacity of the *will* to command a (moral) law for itself, and to follow it. For Kant, moral action is always autonomous or self-imposed. Autonomy is the precondition for moral responsibility. (See *Heteronomy*.)

Capital punishment   Punishment by death for having committed crimes of the worst order ("capital crimes").

Care (Ethics of)   An ethics of care contrasts itself to *liberalism*'s autonomous moral agent who on the basis of abstract and formal reason establishes and applies a set of universal moral principles. An ethics of care and responsibility is a feminist theory of morality principally concerned with responsiveness to others and committed primarily to providing care, preventing harm, and maintaining relationships.

Categorical imperative   For Kant, this is the basic *principle* of morality. It is the supreme law of self-legislating, rational beings. It commands unconditional obedience to the practical moral law formulated by reason. It obliges or binds any rational agent to act as the moral law commands and only for the sake of the moral law. Kant contrasts this with the *hypothetical imperative*.

Communitarianism   This is the view of morality that is defined largely in terms of criticisms it fashions against *liberalism*. Communitarianism rejects liberalism's assumption of the individual as isolated, rational, and self-interested. Rather, communitarians consider persons to be situated in specific social contexts, sharing moral values, a common conception of the good, and mutual goals acquired in and through community membership. Individuals' necessary socialization in a community fashion their views of the good, of what ought to be pursued as a matter of morality.

Consequentialism   The class of ethical theories that determines the morality or immorality of any act, policy, principle, or institution on the basis solely of its consequences or outcomes. (See *Utilitarianism*.)

Contractarianism (contractualism)   The theory that moral rules are established and justified by a hypothetical (or implicit) agreement or contract between *agents* upon whom the rules would then be binding. (See *Social contract*.)

Cultural relativism   The theory that moral values or standards are thought to be conditioned by (or relative to) the particular culture in which they arise, and so hold only for that culture. According to this view, there are no absolute or universal moral standards. (See *Absolutism; Relativism*.)

Deontology   The set of theories that rejects the claim that moral values like rightness or wrongness are to be defined in terms of the production of goodness or badness. Most commonly attributed to Kant, it is the study of *duty* as the basic moral concept and of the moral concepts derivative from duty.

Descriptive ethics   A description of the ethical values, practices, and customs of a particular society at a particular time. (See *Metaethics; Normative ethics*.)

Duty   An act that an *agent* is morally obliged or bound or ought to do, in contrast with what one may find pleasing or have an inclination to do. (See *Prima facie duty*.)

Egalitarianism   The view that all humans are equal and therefore should be treated equally in terms of *liberties* or *rights* or *respect* or opportunities or distributions.

Egoism

    Ethical egoism   The theory that persons ought to act only from self-interest.

    Psychological egoism   A view about the actual psychological motivations of humans. It claims that the effective, though possibly hidden, motive of all voluntary acts is a desire for one's own welfare. So one can be a psychological egoist without being an ethical egoist.

Empirical   Of or pertaining to experience of actual facts.

Ethical relativism   The view that an act, rule, or practice which is right for one society, culture, or individual actually may be wrong for another.

Ethical theory (normative) A set of principles or rules more or less systematically related that provides criteria for determining what one ought to do and for evaluating actions.

Eudaimonia For Aristotle, this is the highest good in life, or happiness or well-being. It is not pleasure.

Euthanasia Literal Greek meaning: a good death. It is commonly used as a synonym for "mercy killing" or, less often and in a more restricted sense, for "letting someone die."

Felicific Making happy; giving rise to happiness or pleasure. In Bentham, the felicific calculus is used interchangeably with the hedonic calculus. (See *Hedonism.*)

Feminism A wide variety of views committed to analysing critically and challenging the ways ethics in the western philosophical tradition has excluded women, licensed their oppression, and rationalized their subordination.

Golden Rule Do unto others as you would want others to do unto you; or Do not unto others what you would not want done to you.

Hate speech Includes any speech or expression directed at a person that is prompted by animus or undertaken to promote his or her degradation or exclusion on the basis of that person's race, ethnicity, national origin, religion, or sexual orientation.

Hedonism The theory that the only *intrinsic good* or value in human life is pleasure or happiness. On the hedonic or *felicific* calculus, the value of all things is to be measured in terms of the pleasure or happiness they promote. An action is considered moral if it generates the greatest happiness or pleasure, or the least amount of pain, among the conceivable alternatives.

Heteronomy The character of a *will* that is determined to act by motivations external to itself, like desires or inclinations. For Kant, heteronomous acts have no moral worth, and in that sense they are sharply contrasted with *autonomous* acts.

Hypothetical imperative For Kant, any command to action for an *agent* that is conditional or dependent upon the goals aimed at. In general, it commands one to act on the basis of self-interest or prudence (for the sake of fulfilling happiness). It is contrasted with the unconditional or morally obligatory command of the *categorical imperative*.

Innate properties Properties or characteristics of humans that are claimed to be given at birth; properties that all human beings are supposed to possess by nature and universally.

Intrinsic good The goodness of something in itself, the goodness of which is not conditional upon any property external to the thing.

Judgment A decision or conclusion about an action, belief, *rule*, or *principle*.

Justification Providing convincing and independent reasons in support of a *judgment*.

Liberalism This is the set of philosophical and social theories that, despite their differences, are committed to a common set of presuppositions and *principles*. Liberalism is committed, first, to individualism, for the moral, political, and legal claims of the individual are considered to have priority in contest with the claims of the collective. Second, liberalism seeks foundations in universal principles applicable to all human beings or rational *agents* in virtue of their humanity or rationality. Liberalism thus seeks to transcend particular historical, social, and cultural differences. The philosophical basis of this common human nature is presumed to lie in a rational core common to each individual, and so in the (potential) capacity to be moved by reason. Third, liberalism presupposes that all social arrangements may be ameliorated by rational reform. Fourth, liberalism is committed to the equality of individuals. Liberalism recognizes all human beings to enjoy a common moral standing, no matter individual differences. This commitment is open to a wide range of interpretations the particular nature of which distinguishes one liberalism from another.

Libertarianism   The theory that endorses exercise of the greatest possible unrestrained social, political, and economic *liberty.*

Liberty   The unrestricted *right* to choose between alternative actions, aims, or ends; the right not to be restricted in pursuing the objects of one's desires; the freedom from external constraint ("negative liberty"); the freedom to act on one's choices ("positive liberty").

Maxim   For Kant, a general principle of action upon which the agent actually acts or is considering acting, which specifies the action to be performed. The maxim is stated in general terms as though it were the agent's policy to act this way whenever appropriate circumstances arise.

Metaethics   The analysis of the concepts, methods, and logical structure of ethical reasoning, of moral *judgments* and their *justification,* and of the meanings of moral terms. (See *Descriptive ethics; Normative ethics.*)

Moral sense   For Hume, the special moral feeling or emotion that causes agents to approve of some actions or circumstances and to disapprove of others.

Naturalistic fallacy   The view, claimed by G. E. Moore to be a fallacy or mistake in reasoning, of defining moral concepts in terms of nonmoral ones or of deducing moral conclusions from nonmoral premises.

Natural law   A moral *principle* or standard established by the nature of things or by God, to which human actions and law ought to conform. For Hobbes, by contrast, it is that general rule discovered by reason which forbids human beings doing anything that would threaten their own lives.

Necessary condition   Y is a necessary condition for X if and only if X cannot pertain unless Y pertains. (See *Sufficient condition.*)

Normative ethics   The inquiry into the norms or standards of moral behavior, and their *justification.* Normative ethics sets out to establish how human *agents* ought morally to conduct their lives and to evaluate how they in fact do. (See *Metaethics; Descriptive ethics.*)

Objective right/good   The right or good established independent of what any *agent* subjectively considers it right or good to do; it is what would be right or good for any agent in the circumstances to do.

Obligation   The necessity or requirement an agent has to do some specified act. Moral obligation or *duty* is considered by some to be conditional upon desiring an end like happiness; by others, such as Kant, it is considered to be *categorical* or unconditional. Unconditional moral obligations impose duties upon agents independent of any consideration external to the nature of the act contemplated, such as the happiness or benefits it may cause.

Offense Principle The *principle* that restriction of a person's *liberty* can be justified to prevent offense to others.

Passion For Hume, a feeling or emotion.

Postmodernism The set of theories that refuse any appeal in *justification* or explanation of states of affairs or social conditions to universal and absolute principles beyond those of specific historical communities.

Preferential treatment The policy of hiring, promoting, or admitting those defined as racial minorities and of women primarily because of their group membership. The aims of any such policy are to eliminate discriminatory employment, seniority, or admissions patterns and to effect greater social justice.

Prima facie duty This is a duty that tends to make a claim on a person in virtue of some relation she may have; it is, in that respect, a conditional duty or *obligation* and not an actual one. In a specific act-situation, a person may have various relations and so tend to be bound by conflicting *prima facie* duties, only one of which she will actually be able to fulfill. (See Duty.)

Principle A general statement that serves as the basis for justifying, evaluating, or guiding beliefs, acts, or moral rules.

Relativism The view that moral values are conditional upon or relative to individuals or to groups or to cultures (societies). Values are taken to be conditional upon the particular social formation in which they arise. (See *Cultural relativism*; *Ethical relativism*; *Absolutism*.)

Respect for Persons (Principle of) The *principle* that persons are owed respect as autonomous *agents*. (See also *Autonomy*.)

Reverse discrimination The claim that policies of *preferential treatment*, in which women and those defined as racial minorities are hired, promoted, or admitted to colleges primarily on the basis of their race or sex, discriminate in reverse against those who thus purportedly are denied equal opportunity (namely, white males). (See also *Preferential treatment*; *Affirmative action*.)

Rhetoric The art and power of persuasion. Techniques of rhetoric were of particular concern to Plato's antagonists, the Sophists of Greece, and later to the Romans.

Right That which is valuable or proper. A right is that for which one has a justifiable claim or demand, often a *liberty* or power, which is authorized by those in a position to do so. Human or civil rights are those claims to which individuals are entitled in virtue of being human or citizens.

Rule General guidelines governing what ought or ought not to be done for a class of cases. (See *Principle*.)

Social contract The original implicit agreement by which, according to some modern philosophers, individuals are united in forming the state. Civil society and its power are justified, and political, legal, and moral values are binding, insofar as they are implicitly or hypothetically agreed to by the parties to the contract. (See *State of nature*; *Contractarianism*.)

State of nature For Hobbes and Rousseau, a hypothetical situation in which people live without government or positive law. The concept is used as a premise in the argument to justify fundamental principles of morality, law, and political structure. (See *Social contract*; *Contractarianism*.)

Stoicism   The theory, important in antiquity, that every person must follow the rational will of the universe and act consistent with the divine laws of nature; and that all persons must accept and act in keeping with their proper place in the scheme of the universe.

Sufficient condition X is a sufficient condition for Y if, whenever X occurs, Y will also occur. Nevertheless, Y can occur without X occurring. (See also *Necessary condition*.)

Teleological ethics   The set of theories holding that the moral worth of an act is determined by whether the act achieves its proper end, aim, or goal.

Utilitarianism   The theory that holds that the measure of moral rightness or wrongness is whether an act, rule, or policy maximizes utility. In the work of Bentham and Mill utility is interpreted as happiness or pleasure; more recently, it has been interpreted as preferences, interests, welfare, or benefits. (See *Hedonism*; *Felicific*.)

   Act-utilitarianism   The theory that one ought morally to undertake only those acts that maximize utility.

   Ideal utilitarianism   The theory that the moral rightness or wrongness of an act is determined by whether or not it adds to the greatest total amount of good, where good is not limited to pleasure but includes other *intrinsic goods*.

   Rule-utilitarianism   The theory that moral *rules* are to be chosen that maximize utility, and that to act morally one must follow the rules.

Virtue(s)   For Aristotle, excellent states of character established by the rational faculty and by which human conduct is habitually to be directed if it is to be moral.

Will, general   For Rousseau, the faculty of willing ascribed to the general (political) collective (that is, the state). The general will is usually opposed to the wills of isolated individuals, or to the wills of a group of individuals not bound by a coherent principle.

Will, good   For Kant, the self-conscious resolve to act in a way that is morally right and to do so only because it is morally right. A will is not good because of any beneficial consequences it may have; it has *intrinsic* moral worth. The good will is the only thing that is good without qualification; it is necessary for the production of any other good, including happiness.